Courting the Yankees

Courting the Yankees

Legal Essays on the Bronx Bombers

Edited by
Ettie Ward

CAROLINA ACADEMIC PRESS
Durham, North Carolina

ISBN: 0-89089-204-0
LCCN: 2003113002

Carolina Academic Press
700 Kent Street
Durham, North Carolina 27701
Telephone (919) 489-7486
Fax (919) 493-5668
www.cap-press.com

Printed in the United States of America

Contents

II. Notable Incidents

III. Scandalous Behavior

Chapter 10 Crimes and Misdemeanors
by Phyllis Coleman

Chapter 11 Affairs of the Heart
by Michael T. Flannery   183

IV. Yankee Stadium

Chapter 15 Up from Baltimore
by Maura Flood

Chapter 16 The House That Ruth Built
by Gregory M. Stein

Chapter 17 Greener Pastures
by Rebecca M. Bratspies

Foreword

In early 1995, the Dean of my law school approached me about teaching Sports Law. I'm not sure that the Dean knew exactly what Sports Law was, but he knew that there was a great student demand for the course. When I said yes, I'm not sure I knew what Sports Law was, but I was a big sports fan and thought it might be nice to combine a personal interest with a professional one.

Seventeen years later, I'm still not sure I could come up with a precise or universally accepted definition of what Sports Law is or what it encompasses. However, I am convinced that it is a course worth including in the law school curriculum because it provides a great vehicle for educating law students. I am also convinced that it provides an equally good vehicle for educating the lay public about law.

For Supreme Court Justice Oliver Wendell Holmes was right. The law is a "brooding omnipresence." There is no area of human endeavor and (*Flood v. Kuhn* notwithstanding) there is no industry that is totally immune from the law. So if one wants to teach students a little labor law, contract law or even a little antitrust law, the world of sports provides a sugar-coated context in which students can learn law and see how an industry's needs shape the law or its application. Similarly, because the world of sports is subject to the commands and workings of our legal system, the sports fan who goes beyond the box scores invariably learns a little law.

This collection of essays bridges both worlds. Although the cases and topics discussed here might not be taught in the average Sports Law course, they do provide discussions about the law in the context of the sports world. Similarly, they are organized and focused in a way that invites the sports fan (even those of us who are not Yankees' fans) to read about sports and learn about the law.

Part I of the book focuses on some of the most famous Yankees. In James Devine's "Joe DiMaggio(And His Lawyer)," we hear about the Yankee Clipper's various legal problems, including his contract squabbles with the Yankees, his divorces and his sponsorship dealings with Mr. Coffee and the Bowery Savings Bank. In Joel Goldstein's "The Law and Yogi," we learn how Yogi Berra's sayings have crept into the law and how their use has made legal concepts more accessible. In Timothy Hall's "Mickey Mantle," we confront some of the legal and ethical issues involved in organ transplants, including the question of whether a long-term alcoholic should be entitled to a liver transplant and the role that his celebrity status might have played in his obtaining that transplant. In Robert Strassfeld's "George Steinbrenner," we learn about Steinbrenner's role as owner of a ship called the "Kinsman Transit" which, as Torts students know, caused great damage in the Buffalo area.

Part II focuses on notable incidents. It starts with Thomas Galligan's chapter, "A Most Dangerous Ball," about a variety of on and off the field injuries resulting from hit baseballs. Mitchell Nathanson's "The Tell-All Hurler" discusses the impact of Jim Bouton's bestseller ("Ball Four") on the sports industry. My chapter, "An Inquiring Woman," explores the problems raised when a female reporter sought equal access to the Yankees' locker room. In "The Catcher Who Fell to Earth," Ettie Ward discusses the litigation that arose after Thurman Munson's tragic death in a Cessna airplane crash. Paul McGreal's chapter, "The Pine Tar Incident," examines what happened after the Yankees invoked a technical rule to nullify a George Brett homerun.

Part III focuses on some notorious instances of scandalous behavior. In "Crimes and Misdemeanors," Phyllis Coleman discusses various crimes committed by Yankees and their fans, from streaking to murder. In "Affairs of the Heart," Michael Flannery discusses a variety of family issues (including sex scandals and drug use) involving former Yankees. In "Unlucky Numbers," Ron Rychlak discusses some run-ins that Yankees (including George Steinbrenner and Mickey Mantle) had with the Commissioner's office as a result of gambling. In "Foul Language," Mark Kende deals with speech-related legal problems. Finally, in "The Czar's Court," Charles Palmer discusses the interactions between the Baseball Commissioner and the Yankees over the years. Once again, the story is not limited to the players; George Steinbrenner is also a featured participant

Part IV deals with issues related to Yankee Stadium. In "Up From Baltimore," Maura Flood tells the story of how the Yankees evolved from the demise of the original Baltimore Orioles. Gregory Stein tells the story of Yankee Stadium in "The House That Ruth Built." Last, in "Greener Pastures," Rebecca Bratspies deals with what is, today, a common problem in sports: a team's demand (here, the Yankees) for a new or improved stadium.

Finally, in Part V, the book deals with more global issues. In "Cornering the Market," Edmund Edmunds discusses *Toolson v. The New York Yankees* and the interplay of sports and antitrust law. The issue of sports and race relations is discussed by Tim Davis in "Breaking the Color Barrier." In "The Tax Man Cometh," Jack Williams takes on a variation of the adage that there are few things in life that are certain except death and taxes. Finally, in "A Global Enterprise," Alex Glashausser discusses international issues raised by the recruitment of foreign players and the baseball teams' trips abroad.

Regardless of whether you think baseball or litigation is the true national pastime, this book should provide interesting reading for baseball fans, lawyers, and those in both categories.

Jan Stiglitz
San Diego, October 2002

I. Famous Yankees

DiMaggio and Monroe have just been married in a judge's chambers; nine months later they will again be before a judge, this time to get a divorce. Photo © Bettmann/COR-BIS.

Joe DiMaggio (and His Lawyer)

by James R. Devine*

In February, 1999, during NBC's "Dateline," a crawler running at the bottom of the television screen announced that baseball legend Joe DiMaggio, recently released from a Florida hospital, had suddenly died. Soon afterwards, NBC retracted its announcement, however, because ESPN reported that DiMaggio had called that network to say that he was still very much alive. DiMaggio's attorney, Morris Engleberg, reported to the New York news media that DiMaggio was "'furious'" at the untimely announcement of his demise.[1]

Despite this characterization, however, Joe DiMaggio was, and had been for some time, a very sick man. In fact, within two weeks of Joe DiMaggio Day at Yankee stadium, the last weekend in September, 1998, DiMaggio underwent surgery to remove a cancerous tumor from one lung. He later developed an infection and pneumonia in the other lung. He was able to breathe only with the aid of a respirator and had a feeding tube. He could not talk and he did not recognize others in his hospital room. Although he was released from the hospital on January 18, 1999, DiMaggio spent most of the rest of his days under the care of a critical care nurse and a respiratory technician. He took only a few steps and was able to breathe on his own for only about ten minutes. He was also fed intravenous nutrients on a virtually constant basis.[2] Even New York Yankee owner, George Steinbrenner, was denied access to DiMaggio fearing that Steinbrenner would not be recognized. Considering DiMaggio's actual condition, then, it is a little difficult to determine how "furious" he could have been.

As it now appears, many of attorney Morris Engleberg's reports concerning Joe DiMaggio's health, during the fall and winter preceding his death were, at best, questionably accurate and, at worst, totally false. During the World Series in October, 1998, DiMaggio was hospitalized and unable to throw out the first ball as scheduled.[3] Engleberg reportedly said Joe had "'walking pneumonia.'" DiMaggio was said, however, to be "'eating like a horse.'" In an apparent effort to give these reports credibility, Engleberg was seen "bearing doughnuts and blueberry muffins when he paid a morning visit" to his client.[4] During the World Series, Engleberg reportedly told the media that DiMaggio ordered pizza and was sitting up, watching the World Series on television, and that he hoped to be home for his 84th birthday, November 25, 1998. As his 84th birthday approached, Joe DiMaggio was reported to have lung cancer. Mr. Engleberg sent faxes to the media reporting only that DiMaggio was improving and was "'doing well.'"[5] Mr. Engleberg indicated that DiMaggio's family was "'very upset'" by media reports that the star was gravely ill, reportedly calling those reports "'totally false.'"[6] He indicated that DiMaggio would leave the hospital.

When his reports about DiMaggio's health were questioned, Morris Engleberg initially reported that he was being "'misquoted'" by the press. The hospital where DiMaggio was confined, however, was not allowed to provide his medical information. According to one hospital spokesperson, all inquiries about DiMaggio were to be directed to Mr. Engleberg. Later, following DiMaggio's death, Mr. Engleberg admitted that much of the information he provided was false. DiMaggio, known to zealously guard his privacy, reportedly wanted the press "sealed off" from his illness, and Morris Engleberg was willing to oblige. "'I was his liar,'" Engleberg reportedly told *Vanity Fair*.[7]

And therein lies a problem.

As a lawyer representing Joe DiMaggio, Mr. Engleberg was forbidden from making "a false statement of material fact" to third parties.[8] The reason for this is simple: a lawyer's professional standards are higher than those of the average business person. "Lawyers are more than fiduciaries;" they are representatives of our judicial system. As a result, lawyers are held to a trust that is "built on centuries of honesty and faithfulness."[9] Those centuries of trust require the lawyer to deal honestly with third parties. In dealing with the events surrounding Joe DiMaggio's death, it appears that Morris Engleberg was not.

In a modern baseball world, with an average of 118 runs batted in a year and a lifetime .325 batting average, Joe DiMaggio would be able to approach New York Yankee owner George Steinbrenner with the greeting, "'Hello partner.'"[10] But in his baseball career, and after, DiMaggio's interactions with the law and legal matters were anything but successful. At least until he teamed with Morris Engleberg.

To understand this relationship between Joe DiMaggio and Morris Engleberg, the focus of this chapter, and a relationship that encompassed the final sixteen years of DiMaggio's life,[11] requires a complete review of Joe DiMaggio and his relationship to the law, both inside and outside baseball, as well as an understanding of how DiMaggio developed a basic distrust of others. From that basic understanding comes a realization of the role Mr. Engleberg played in DiMaggio's final years. At that point, a study of the relationship between Joe DiMaggio as client/principal and Morris Engleberg as attorney/agent is actually a case study in the duties of lawyer to client, which, when coupled with DiMaggio's prior dealings with the law and distrust of people, also becomes a case study in how that relationship can turn sour.

I. Joe D. and Baseball — Beginning a Career of Contract Disputes

A. Pre-Contract Years

One of baseball's founding fathers, Albert Spalding, saw baseball owners as having "absolute control and direction of the" game of baseball, while baseball players engaged only in the work of producing the game on the field.[12] To no one in the history of the game does this apply more than to Joe DiMaggio.

Joe DiMaggio's father, Giuseppe, emigrated to the United States in 1898 from his family home on an island northwest of Palermo, Sicily. When he arrived in the United States, Giuseppe bypassed the migrant-laden city of New York, and continued west to join others from Palermo, many of whom, like him, made their living at fishing. They settled in Collinsville, California. He worked at fishing and for the Union Pacific Railroad, saving enough money to send, in 1902, for his wife Rosalie and his first child, Nellie, who had been born shortly after Giuseppe left Sicily. The family moved to Martinez, California where Giuseppe devoted full-time to fishing, and by 1912, the DiMaggio family had added six more children, three boys and three girls in addition to Nellie. Joseph Paul DiMaggio was born on November 25, 1914, the eighth child. He shared the American-ization of both his father's first name and the middle name of Giuseppe's favorite saint. Indeed, all of the male DiMaggio children received the middle name Paul. The family moved to San Francisco's North Beach where a ninth child, and fifth son, Dominic Paul, was born in 1917. It was in this home, near the fishing pier where Giuseppe's boat, the *Rosalie*, served as the family business, that Joe DiMaggio was raised.[13] Though not a gifted baseball player to start, DiMaggio "drifted to playing baseball…when I should have been helping my father" with either the fishing itself or cleaning the fishing boat. For the young Joe, baseball became merely an excuse for avoiding household chores.[14]

Neither was DiMaggio a student. A childhood friend remembers Joe cutting class "'all the time'" to play "'baseball on an empty lot.'"[15] Joe himself acknowledged a lack of happiness with high school. Two years after his brother Vince quit high school, Joe followed suit believing that if his brother could make money playing baseball, he could do the same.

B. Joe Signs with the Pacific Coast League

After playing for several sandlot baseball teams, Joe DiMaggio, at age seventeen, was of-fered the opportunity to play with the San Francisco Missions in the Pacific Coast League. Their manager, and former New York Yankee Fred Hoffman, offered DiMaggio $150 a month, an amount about $25 a month more than the average salary offered to new players. Before he signed a contract with the Missions, however, DiMaggio was offered an opportu-nity to work out with, and subsequently try out for, the San Francisco Seals, his brother's team.[16] Following a rookie season with the Seals in which DiMaggio hit in 61 straight games,[17] DiMaggio's contract value increased to the point were he was earning a reported $4,500 in his final year with the Seals.[18] Unfortunately, following a game during his 1934 season, DiMaggio took a "jitney cab home." Evidently, his foot fell asleep in the crowded cab and as he got out he placed all his weight on one foot. He heard four sharp cracks. "Down I went, as though I had been shot," DiMaggio recalls.[19] His resulting cartilage in-jury discouraged fifteen of sixteen major league teams. Only the New York Yankees were actively interested in the young player, and they only conditionally purchased his contract from the Seals.[20] The Yankees wanted DiMaggio to play for the Seals in 1935 and prove his knee was recovered. DiMaggio proved himself ready for the majors by batting .398 with thirty-four home runs in 172 games with the PCL pennant-winning Seals, becoming the league's MVP. And that's when DiMaggio's baseball contract problems really began.

II. Yankee Contract Disputes and Holdouts

Baseball tradition at the time required a major league team to offer a former minor lea-guer a 25% increase from the player's last minor league contract when the player signed with a major league team. The Yankees did that, offering DiMaggio $5,625 for his rookie 1936 season. Before ever playing a major league game, and despite baseball's Reserve Rule making DiMaggio the property of the Yankees with no option to play for any other team, DiMaggio held out, demanding in excess of $8,000 for his rookie season.

Thereafter, DiMaggio repeatedly held out, refusing to sign the Yankee's proffered contract in 1937 (holding out for $17,500); 1938 (holding out for $40,000); 1940 (again holding out for $40,000); 1941 (holding out for an undisclosed amount); and 1942 (holding out for an amount estimated to be approximately $80,000).

Two of these salary disputes—those preceding the 1938 and 1942 seasons—are instructive in showing the way the Yankees controlled DiMaggio and the contract process. They also demonstrate that despite his immense baseball power, Joe DiMaggio possessed little contract power.

A. Joe's 1938 Salary Holdout

In each of his first two seasons with the Yankees, 1936 and 1937, Joe DiMaggio started in the All-Star Game. Although enlarged tonsils caused DiMaggio arm trouble at the outset of the 1937 season, he still led the American League in home runs with 46 and in slugging percentage at .673. In a poll of 247 sportswriters at the end of the '37 season, DiMaggio received 245 all-star votes, "more than any other player." He was also voted "Player of the Year" by New York sportswriters.

As was their custom,[21] the Yankees offered Joe DiMaggio a 1938 salary equal to his 1937 salary of $15,000. DiMaggio, however, demanded $40,000. When he attempted to meet with owner Jacob Ruppert, he was kept waiting 45 minutes but eventually left with the club's final offer of $25,000. "'The Yankees can get along without DiMaggio,'" Yankee manager Joe McCarthy apparently indicated. His comments were reportedly seconded by owner Ruppert: "'If DiMaggio isn't out there, we have Myril Hoag for center field.'" In the press, DiMaggio was pilloried. "He was portrayed as a greedy, self-centered prima donna."[22] When he finally agreed to the Yankees' offer on April 20,[23] Ruppert released DiMaggio's terse telegram, "[y]our terms accepted," to show Joe's total capitulation.

Even capitulation, however, was not enough. Joe DiMaggio had to be totally humiliated. While Yankee owner Jacob Ruppert usually celebrated Yankee signings, he did something different for this one. Ruppert held a press conference and paraded DiMaggio, virtually prisoner-of-war like, before reporters:

"'Here's your contract, Joe DiMaggio,' said Col. Ruppert icily, 'Now go ahead and sign it.'"

"Giuseppe signed without a word, and handed the papers back to the Colonel."

"'Now go ahead and play ball, Joe DiMaggio' ordered the Colonel like a stern country judge. 'Do your best. I hope you have a great year.'"

"'Thanks,' said Joe. 'I'll do my best.'"

"Someone asked if Joe was getting a bonus for signing."

"'Joe DiMaggio,' barked the Colonel, 'are you getting any bonus for this?'"

"'No bonus,' gulped Joe."

"'That's right,' continued the Colonel. 'And furthermore Joe DiMaggio will not get a cent of pay until he starts to play ball.'"[24]

Further, according to the Yankee owner, DiMaggio could not start to actually play "'[u]ntil he is in condition. If he wants to travel with the Yankees, he'll have to pay his own way.'"[25] DiMaggio did not play until April 30, "missing 12 days and $1,944 of my pay." DiMaggio most remembered that he returned to boos, both on the road and at home.[26] Despite sportswriters' view that DiMaggio was the best player in baseball, DiMaggio was required to suffer because of his 1938 contract dispute. And the same would happen again, four seasons later.

B. Joe's 1942 Salary Holdout

According to one author, no athlete held America's daily or weekly attention the way Joe DiMaggio did during the summer of 1941. "All across America, the question each morning was simple: 'Did he get a hit yesterday?'"[27] "The Streak" started on May 15, 1941 with an RBI single scoring Phil Rizzuto, and ended after fifty-six games, on July 17, in a game against the Cleveland Indians. "DiMaggio batted .408 during this period, with 16 doubles, 4 triples and 15 home runs among the 91 hits he amassed in 223 at bats." The Yankees were in 4th place, five and one-half games out of first place when DiMaggio's streak started. When it ended, the Yankees were in first place by six games.[28]

During the same 1941 season, Ted Williams, of the Boston Red Sox, amassed a batting average of .406, the last time this magic number was reached. Joe Louis, boxing's 1941 heavyweight champion, successfully defended his heavyweight title seven times during that year. It was, however, Joe DiMaggio's hitting streak that is still termed the record that "may never be broken."[29] DiMaggio was again selected to the All-America baseball team. It was DiMaggio, not Williams, who was selected as the American League's Most Valuable Player. It was DiMaggio, not Williams nor Louis, who was selected as outstanding male athlete of the year. The vote was not even close: DiMaggio, 157, Williams, 74, Louis, 64. "In an era of big stars, [DiMaggio] was the biggest."[30] He had gone from being just a star to being a god.[31]

The following winter, however, the Yankees deviated from their normal practice by not sending Joe DiMaggio a contract for 1942 that matched his 1941 contract of $37,500. Instead, the Yankees sent DiMaggio a contract with a $5,000 *reduction*.[32] Between the end of the 1941 season and the mailing of DiMaggio's 1942 contract, the Japanese attack on Pearl Harbor and World War II intervened. Then Yankees president, Ed Barrow,[33] issued a press release in which DiMaggio was portrayed as un-American. He expressed "disdain that [the Yankees] number one player wanted 'a big raise while American soldiers are making $21 a month.'" In fact, DiMaggio's status under baseball's reserve clause in 1942 forced DiMaggio to accept a contract with a mere $5,000 raise following one of the best seasons in baseball history.[34]

C. Non-Legal Help with Baseball Contracts Provides Only Marginal Success

Despite the general view that baseball players' contracts were negotiated without outside advisors or agents, Joe DiMaggio was rarely alone in his negotiations, although none of those helping him were lawyers.

One of his earliest advisors was DiMaggio's oldest brother Tom. In fact, DiMaggio would not sign his first contract with the San Francisco Missions without having it reviewed by Tom, then the senior American DiMaggio family advisor. When Joe was offered a position with the Seals, Tom DiMaggio helped his brother negotiate a 1933 rookie contract for $225 a month, more than double the amount normally paid to Pacific Coast League rookies. Later, when Joe became a PCL star, it was Tom DiMaggio who understood the major league value of his brother. He tried to convince Seals' management to sell Joe to a major league team for $75,000 and to give the DiMaggio family a healthy $6,500 from that sale, an idea unheard of at the time.[35] Even following Joe's injury, Tom DiMaggio continued to push this plan, reportedly telling the Seals' owner that Joe would simply pull out of baseball and take up fishing if the family did not get a cut of the Seals' sale of the young star.[36] This ploy was unsuccessful.

DiMaggio had other contract assistance. While Tom DiMaggio is normally credited with assisting the $8,500 negotiation with the Yankees,[37] at least one report has DiMaggio being assisted by another famous baseball hold-out. According to that report, the Yankees originally offered DiMaggio only $5,000, an amount considered "paltry," "even by 1930's standards."[38] Legendary baseball player, and perennial hold-out, Ty Cobb, was a regular in the DiMaggio family restaurant on Fisherman's Wharf in San Francisco.[39] Cobb was apparently outraged at the amount the Yankees offered DiMaggio,[40] and wrote a strongly-worded letter to the Yankees, which DiMaggio then copied into his own hand and sent. The Yankees increased their offer by $500. Cobb then wrote another letter, which DiMaggio copied, and the Yankees increased their offer another $500. This continued for seven letters until the offer reached the $8,500 figure that became DiMaggio's rookie salary.[41] Yankee president, Ed Barrow, apparently ended the exchange: " 'Tell Cobb to stop writing letters.' "[42]

Finally, DiMaggio was often advised by Joe Gould,[43] manager for heavyweight boxing champion Jim Braddock.[44] Gould advised DiMaggio on his contracts and on endorsements. In fact, it has been alleged that it was Gould who acted as a go-between with the Yankees in DiMaggio's 1938 holdout. The Yankees were so angered by the possibility that DiMaggio was using an "agent" that they reportedly complained to baseball commissioner Kenesaw Mountain Landis, who first indicated that DiMaggio "could be thrown out of baseball" for such a practice[45] and then held a hearing and "hassled" DiMaggio "for an hour" before finding no substance to the claim.[46]

DiMaggio's statements about these advisors reflects his view of his normally unsuccessful role in baseball contract disputes. He reportedly told sports writer Roger Kahn: " 'All I was trying to do was make as much money as I could.' " He also reportedly told sports writer Bob Considine much the same: " 'I talk to anybody I think can help me get paid what I deserve. This isn't Germany. It's America, a free country.' "[47]

III. Joe Dimaggio and the Law Outside Baseball

Outside of baseball, Joe DiMaggio had several experiences with the law and lawyers that helped shape his view of both. Two of these experiences involved family matters. Others involved non-baseball business negotiations.

A. Joe and Dorothy — Joe and Marilyn — Joe and Family Court

The two family law matters involved the two principal women in Joe DiMaggio's adult life. "Biographers agree that [DiMaggio] was a better suitor and ex-husband than a husband."[48] It was this shortcoming that introduced him to the family court system.

1. Joe and Dorothy

Manhattan Merry-Go-Round was a 1937 movie "about a sentimental racketeer who acquires a record company" and was based on a then-hit radio program. It starred Phil Regan and Ann Dvorak and also featured Gene Autry and several bands including that of Cab Calloway.[49] In August, 1937, Joe DiMaggio was asked to play a role in the movie and reported for duty "to the Biograph Studios on 175th Street in the Bronx." While completing the twelve takes it took to record his three lines, he met a number of women in the movie's chorus, some of whom thought of DiMaggio as "'colossal.'"[50] Among those was a blond actress from Minnesota with a bit part. Dorothy Arnold said of her encounter on the set with DiMaggio: "'I fell in love with him before I even knew who he was.'" DiMaggio and Arnold made a date for that night, and a relationship developed over the next two years. Joe and Dorothy became fixtures in the Italian social scene of nearby Newark, New Jersey. On April 25, 1939, Dorothy announced the couple's engagement. The next day Joe denied it, but later recanted, apparently acknowledging that he and Dorothy would wed. He assured the sports world, however, that a wedding would not interrupt his baseball season. Joe and Dorothy were married the following November, in San Francisco, where they were celebrities. Approximately 30,000 fans filled the streets around the cathedral. There were so many people that Joe and his brothers, Vince and Dom, needed a police escort to get to the church.

Following the marriage, in New York, the DiMaggios were often socially coupled with Yankee pitcher, and DiMaggio's road roommate, Lefty Gomez and his wife, actress June O'Dea. "They made a stylish quartet around town, two of the headline heroes of the Yankees and the actresses they had married."

The marriage between Joe DiMaggio and Dorothy Arnold produced DiMaggio's only child, Joseph Paul DiMaggio, Jr., who was born in 1941. Although stories were written about the happiness between Joe and Dorothy, the marriage lasted only three years. The couple then separated with Dorothy and Joe, Jr. moving out of the DiMaggio's apartment in New York to Reno, Nevada. During this separation, there were attempts at reconciliation. DiMaggio, for example, flew to Reno to beg Dorothy to return. There was even a time of reconciliation after Joe enlisted during World War II. In 1943, however, after hiring a lawyer, Dorothy filed for divorce. By that time, DiMaggio was in the military, and while he did not have a lawyer, he requested one postponement of the divorce date claiming he wanted to attend. He did not, and the divorce went through uncontested. In California, at the time, however, the initial divorce decree was interlocutory only, so the divorce was not final for another year. Again, Joe DiMaggio thought there might be a reconciliation during this interlocutory period, but again, he was wrong. Even after the war, with the divorce final, a further reconciliation was tried. Joe, Dorothy and Joe, Jr. lived together while Joe was working on his autobiography, *Lucky to be a Yankee*. Ultimately, however, Dorothy remarried, and Joe then realized the impossibility of permanent reconciliation.

2. Joe and Marilyn

In 1952, Joe DiMaggio saw a photograph of Philadelphia A's Gus Zernial showing a posing Marilyn Monroe how to bat. DiMaggio was reportedly upset that Zernial, a "'busher,'" in DiMaggio's words, got to meet such a beautiful woman. DiMaggio found out the name of Monroe's business manager from Zernial, had a friend call the business manager and set up a date between DiMaggio and the 25 year old starlet. Monroe was apparently unimpressed and, indeed, a bit distracted on that date, until actor Mickey Rooney came by "and started fawning over DiMaggio." Thus started the chronologically second, but decidedly paramount love affair of Joe's life.[51]

Joe and Marilyn "had a courtship that lasted two years and a marriage that lasted" less than half that time. On their blind date, Marilyn announced at 11:00 that she had to leave, but agreed to drop DiMaggio off at his hotel. He tried to call her several times thereafter, until she finally called him. As the relationship progressed, it was DiMaggio's role to rescue Marilyn, usually from film studios or others who demanded too much of her. They were married by a Municipal Court judge on January 14, 1954. The unlikelihood of the marriage's survival was summed up by Marilyn when asked if she was going to be an actress or a housewife: " 'I'm going to continue my career, but I'm looking forward to being a housewife too.' " What Marilyn perhaps meant was that she wanted to act, and Joe wanted her to be a housewife, a situation that ultimately doomed the marriage. There were allegations of fights between them; and there were stories of how incompatible they were, but in the end, they simply divorced as Joe and Dorothy had done. On October 27 following their January marriage, Marilyn and her lawyer appeared in divorce court. Marilyn indicated that Joe was cold and indifferent; Joe said nothing. As was the case with Dorothy, Marilyn was granted an essentially uncontested divorce.

That was not, however, the end. Even after their divorce, Joe continued to be Marilyn's protector. In 1961, for example, Marilyn checked herself into a mental hospital in New York. Believing it was a mistake, she then tried to leave but could not. She called Joe, claiming the hospital was doing her more harm than good. DiMaggio flew in from San Francisco and made two points with the hospital: First, he was Joe DiMaggio and would personally look out for Marilyn Monroe. Second, he was Joe DiMaggio and if the hospital did not release Marilyn, "he would tear down the hospital brick by brick." The hospital conceded that it would not be good public relations to be on DiMaggio's bad side.

A year later Marilyn died, and her sister called DiMaggio to again take care of her— this time by arranging her funeral. He did so, excluding most of Marilyn's Hollywood friends from the service. In DiMaggio's view, it was they who had killed Marilyn. As with Dorothy, DiMaggio continued to believe that he and Marilyn would reconcile. Even after her death, he told friends that if she had lived, they would likely have remarried.[52]

The bottom line, of course, was that Joe DiMaggio's two attempts at marriage contracts had been as unsuccessful as most of his baseball negotiations.

B. Joe's Post-Baseball Business Contracts

In 1972, ten years after Marilyn's funeral, Joe DiMaggio stepped back into the public eye, although in quite a different way. He was still hitting line drives from home plate at Yankee Stadium, but as a 57 year old, he was no longer knocking in runs; he was instead attracting depositors to New York's Bowery Savings Bank. He talked about how, when you got older, you had to take better care of money. The bank surrounded DiMaggio with children and the public loved it. Deposits at the Bowery soared. DiMaggio was paid $60,000 the first year and $65,000 the second, for filming three commercials each year for the bank. The bank renewed his contract for two more years. When bank directors were told that the bank was paying DiMaggio $70,000 during the extension, the directors "were aghast.... They thought it was too little." Somebody would pay him more; the Directors made the bank pay Joe $100,000. Thus, even in a contract in which Joe DiMaggio was the acknowledged star, he was not a very successful negotiator and Joe was still not being paid the market value of his services.

Approximately two years after he became the voice of the Bowery Savings Bank, DiMaggio's friend, Vince Merada, asked Joe to do some advertising spots for Mr. Coffee, which Merada owned. The Bowery did not object to DiMaggio's work for Mr. Coffee. In fact, many Bowery customers thought Joe, having a cup of coffee on screen, was doing it for the bank. DiMaggio negotiated his own contract to sell Mr. Coffee because he trusted the friend who asked him to do the advertising. Later, however, when Joe actually read the written contract, he found changes in the deal that he did not approve. He tore up the contract, broke off his friendship, and ended his appearances for Mr. Coffee.[53] Again, Joe DiMaggio stood foiled in a contract transaction.

IV. Joe Dimaggio as the "Toast of the Town"

Regardless of Joe DiMaggio's lack of success in all matter of contract transactions, his public persona was consistently that of the "Toast of the Town."[54]

Even while playing baseball, DiMaggio was the subject of numerous items of popular culture. During his 1941 hitting streak, Les Paul and his Band of Renown, with Betty Bonney on vocals, recorded "Joltin' Joe DiMaggio;" the song reached number one on the Hit Parade. It struck a theme for the popular view of Joe: "Joe, Joe DiMaggio! We want you on our side."[55] In the dark days as the world wound its way into World War II, Joe DiMaggio on "our side" was an obvious reference to Joe's internal strength and pride. This theme continued in song long after Joe's playing career. In the aftermath of the turbulent 1960's and early 1970's, Joe DiMaggio was again looked upon as the personification of strength and American honesty. Paul Simon, in his theme for the movie "The Graduate," wrote in "Mrs. Robinson:" "Where have you gone Joe DiMaggio, A nation turns its lonely eyes to you. What's that you say Mrs. Robinson, Joltin' Joe has left and gone away."[56] If baseball was a metaphor for life in America, then it was Joe DiMaggio who best exhibited the grace, the excellence, the power and majesty of the game.[57]

Joe DiMaggio was likewise immortalized in print. In Ernest Hemingway's classic "The Old Man and the Sea," the protagonist listened to baseball on the radio and talked to himself while fishing. After hooking the giant Marlin and having it drag him through the ocean, the Old Man asked himself if "the great DiMaggio would stay with" the giant fish "as long as I will?" He then decided that DiMaggio had the requisite courage and character. "I'm sure he would and more."[58] DiMaggio was viewed as the perfect Hemingway character because of how he consistently exhibited "'grace under pressure.'"[59]

Even in the final decade of his life, and after his passing, the name Joe DiMaggio remained synonymous with grace, courage and dignity.

In the October 30, 2001 episode of NBC's *Frasier*, star character Dr. Frasier Crane held a Halloween Party in which his guests were to come dressed as their "hero." Frasier's father, Martin Crane, dressed as Joe DiMaggio. When Frasier's party started to go badly, it was Martin, as Joe DiMaggio, who wanted it to continue. "Joltin' Joe wouldn't quit, and neither will I," he told the others.[60]

And, in a 1991 episode of *Seinfeld*, Jerry Seinfeld's friend, Kramer, believed he saw DiMaggio dunking a donut at "Dinky Donuts," a local eatery frequented by Kramer. Jerry responded: "I can't see Joe DiMaggio sitting at the counter in…Dinky Donuts." Kramer, of course, wanted to know why Joe DiMaggio "can't have a donut like everyone else," to which Jerry responded, indicating DiMaggio's class: "He can have a donut, but not at Dinky," and "if Joe DiMaggio wants a donut he goes to a fancy restaurant or a hotel."[61] Joe DiMaggio was seen by the *Seinfeld* cast as simply having too much class for Dinky Donuts.

V. Joe Dimaggio's View of "Self" in His Twilight Years

In the twilight of his years, then, how did the public image of Hemingway's "Great DiMaggio" contrast with Joe's image of himself and his success? He was spokesperson for a bank; he was, after 1968, "baseball's greatest living player;"[62] he was a public icon in print, in song, and on television. As a public figure, Joe DiMaggio remained the epitome of all that is good in the American male superstar.

But all was still not right in Joe's world. While he had more worldly possessions than his brother Vince, who led the National League in strikeouts six times, he did not have Vince's "'long, happy marriage.'" And, while he was more popular than his younger brother Dom, who displayed very little baseball power during his years with the Boston Red Sox, Dom married a wealthy woman and became a millionaire as president of a fiber cushions manufacturing firm.[63] Thus, while it was Joe among the DiMaggio boys who was the nationwide household name, he had neither the stable home life of his older brother, nor the financial success of his younger one. He had neither wealth nor family stability in part because of his lack of success in contract matters.

He also had something else. Given the way others dealt with him, Joe DiMaggio had a way of dealing with people: "'I don't trust anyone. No exceptions.'"[64] Several DiMaggio anecdotes show this distrust.

VI. The Famous Dimaggio Distrust

A. Joe and Eddie

Eddie Liberatore was a former Dodger scout who had his own family. But, for the better part of thirty years, when Joe DiMaggio called, Liberatore moved out of his house to move in with Joe in whatever hotel he was staying. As someone said, "Liberatore had blisters on his lips from kissing the ground Joe walked on."

Liberatore worked out a business deal with some Philadelphia friends. Joe DiMaggio would sign two thousand large photographs of himself for $50 each, a $100,000 payday for DiMaggio. These photographs would then be sold by the Philadelphia friends of Liberatore for $350 each. Because of this public sales price, DiMaggio wanted a higher percentage of the deal. Cash flow, however, was apparently a problem. The deal was re-worked to allow DiMaggio to receive an additional $100 for each photograph after it was sold, another $200,000, provided the photos all sold. But the photographs did not sell, and the company went bankrupt. Joe, therefore, did not get any of the back-end money. As for the photographs, themselves, however, another dealer bought half of the fourteen hundred left-over photographs for a "distressed" price and immediately resold them to Hammacher Schlemmer who then offered the same photographs in their up-scale catalogue for $500 each. The photos immediately sold, and Hammacher Schlemmer bought out the balance and sold them as well. Everybody made money, except DiMaggio, who only got $50 for each photograph. And as far as Joe was concerned, the entire incident was Liberatore's fault. Liberatore received no more phone calls from Joe DiMaggio, in part, because Joe trusted no one—no exceptions.

B. Joe and Barry

For Joe DiMaggio, the memorabilia business was all about him. "Why should [others] make a buck off my life?" And it was worse if those others were friends: only dis-loyal friends wanted to make money from Joe DiMaggio's life.

One such former friend was famed memorabilia buff Barry Halper, a minority shareholder in DiMaggio's old New York Yankees. Halper, who has a gallery at Base-ball's Hall of Fame named after him,[65] met DiMaggio at a Yankee Old Timer Day in the 1970s. DiMaggio evidently knew something of Halper's background and interest in the Yankees and asked Halper for a ride that began their association. From that point forward, Halper shepherded DiMaggio, from flying to Florida so he could drive DiMaggio to and from the Yankee spring training camp, to hosting him at Yankee Sta-dium or at his New Jersey home while Halper's wife was assigned the duty of prepar-ing DiMaggio's favorite meals. Halper's wife, in fact, went to cooking school in Italy to learn more about cooking for DiMaggio. Halper took DiMaggio along so Joe could have a European vacation. Halper, in short, was in the business of "caring for DiMag-gio." One item in Halper's collection was DiMaggio's 1951 Yankee World Series ring, something Joe had traded away. Halper offered the ring to Joe, but DiMaggio de-clined.

When Halper purchased part-ownership of a baseball card company, it seemed per-fectly natural for that company to pay Joe DiMaggio $100,000 to sign baseball cards that were randomly inserted into packs. The deal worked so well that other baseball card companies sought Joe's services, and Halper's company had to pay DiMaggio $250,000 to renew the transaction. At $250,000, only DiMaggio was making money, so Halper and his associates sold their interests to a rival company that was forced to honor the DiMaggio contract. At the end of the contract, Joe DiMaggio still owed the company a small amount of time, and the company decided to sponsor a contest with toy store Toys-R-Us to have DiMaggio take five winners on a tour of Barry Halper's famous memorabilia collection. Unfortunately, Toys-R-Us invited a photographer from a sports collectors' weekly newspaper. DiMaggio's contract called for no press coverage. Joe was done with the tour, and Barry Halper was out of the DiMaggio entourage. So far from grace did he fall that Halper would later be accused of stealing the 1951 World Series ring that he offered to return to DiMaggio. Joe trusted no one—no exceptions.

C. Joe and Dom

Offered as final proof that, without exception, DiMaggio trusted no one is the fact that Joe even fell out with his brother Dom over the use of Joe's likeness. Dominic wrote a book about his experiences with the Boston Red Sox during that famous 1941 season, when Ted Williams hit .406 and Joe DiMaggio batted in fifty-six consecutive games. When the book was published, a picture of Joe was on the cover, and Dom was accused of "capitalizing on the Yankee Clipper mystique for his own commercial interest."

As these anecdotes demonstrate, Joe DiMaggio was spoiled by his friends. "Even the high and mighty...gave advice, logistical support, and personal favors." DiMaggio wanted advice, but he also wanted complete loyalty and ultimate control of the advice. He was willing to cut off in an instant anyone, like Liberatore and Halper, who was perceived as disloyal.

VII. Joe Dimaggio and Morris Engleberg

Into DiMaggio's world of unsuccessful negotiations and distrust entered Morris Engleberg, who unabashedly considered Joe his hero.[66] Actually, it was when DiMaggio needed to renegotiate his Bowery Savings Bank appearance contract that he first called Engleberg to assist. Despite the bank's acknowledged need to increase payment to DiMaggio, Joe was afraid the bank was going to cut his salary. He was so impressed that Engleberg obtained a raise for him that he attempted to pay Engleberg $20,000 which Engleberg refused.

As a result of representing DiMaggio in negotiations with the Bowery Savings Bank, the attorney-client relationship was formed that would last until DiMaggio's death, and beyond. Engleberg turned the office building complex, in which his law firm was housed, into the Yankee Clipper Center. Among the lined parking spaces in the lot, the first space was always "Reserved for the Yankee Clipper, No. 5." On the other side of this primary spot was another, "Reserved for "Morris Engleberg." Engleberg was often referred to as DiMaggio's " 'close friend and personal attorney,' " or as DiMaggio's "friend [or sometimes longtime friend] and lawyer,"[67] In fact, by the end of DiMaggio's life, it was Engleberg who admitted he was running DiMaggio's life.

And it is at this point, with knowledge of Joe DiMaggio's needs as a client, that the case study of the client-attorney relationship begins in earnest.

A. Attorney's Basic Duty

From the beginning of any attorney-client relationship, the attorney owes to the client a duty of competence, an obligation to do that which other similarly situated lawyers would do under similar circumstances.[68] The central component of competence is loyalty to the interests of the client, a duty that stems from the attorney's position as an agent of the client principal.[69] In those duties, Morris Engleberg initially performed admirably helping to make Joe DiMaggio a very wealthy man.

When the pair first met, DiMaggio was making approximately $10,000 for a three-hour autograph session at a memorabilia show. Engleberg helped negotiate increased fees for DiMaggio's presence, raising Joe's fee to $75,000 for the same session, and eventually having DiMaggio paid on a piece-by-piece basis with a minimum guarantee of $150,000 for an autograph session. He also created demand for DiMaggio memorabilia by limiting access to DiMaggio. Despite intense fan interest in DiMaggio's autograph, Engleberg allowed Joe to do only five shows per year. Engleberg accompanied DiMaggio to these shows, evidently to assure the transactions went according to his standards.

Engleberg appeared on the national scene as Joe DiMaggio's attorney in 1991 when he announced jointly with Score Board, Inc. a two-year exclusive deal for Joe DiMaggio to sign baseballs and flat items. It was a deal that Score Board expected would generate $10 million for the company.[70] The deal also benefitted Yankee Clipper Enterprises, the company Engleberg created for Joe's memorabilia interests. Under the Score Board deal, DiMaggio signed approximately one thousand baseballs and a like number of photographs each month and was paid somewhere between $7 and $9 million.

In addition, DiMaggio, with Engleberg's assistance, entered into an arrangement with Score, Barry Halper's baseball card manufacturer, to autograph a limited number of baseball cards, at a profit to DiMaggio of approximately $3 million. A further deal with Pro Sports Services whereby DiMaggio signed a limited number of baseball bats produced an additional return in excess of $3 million.

Engleberg's assistance to DiMaggio was not limited to the memorabilia business. Engleberg was also able to move DiMaggio from California to Florida, successfully resolving outstanding tax issues in Joe's favor. When DiMaggio tired of living in an apartment near the Fontainebleau Hotel where Joe and Marilyn Monroe had once stayed, DiMaggio, evidently with Engleberg's assistance, worked out an apartment living arrangement whereby DiMaggio received a free apartment, furnishings worth approximately $200,000 and an annual income of about $100,000 in exchange for being a spokesperson for a residential community and playing golf three times each month. When DiMaggio grew lonely in this apartment, Engleberg moved him across the street in the residential community where Engleberg lived, again for free, in exchange for DiMaggio being a spokesperson for this community. Engleberg had a golf cart purchased for DiMaggio, and then had it painted in Yankee blue with hubcaps in Yankee pinstripes. Engleberg rearranged his own schedule so he could care for DiMaggio virtually full time. In 1998, it was Engleberg who insisted that the Yankees hold Joe DiMaggio Day at Yankee Stadium and replace eight World Series rings that had been stolen from DiMaggio's hotel room. Engleberg did grocery shopping for DiMaggio, he ate breakfast and lunch with him, and he "'gave up his normal life to be with his man.'"

And for all of these legal and additional services, Morris Engleberg "never charged [Joe DiMaggio] a cent."

B. Problems Arise in the Dimaggio-Engleberg Relationship

Obviously, there is nothing wrong with a lawyer working for free for a client; history is replete with lawyers who have devoted countless unbilled hours to protect the interests of some person or entity. By the same token, however, lawyers earn their living by practicing law.[71] While Morris Engleberg clearly made a great deal of money in representing clients before Joe DiMaggio, mostly in estate and business matters, lawyers cannot exist without some *quid pro quo* for their services. It is the nature of that recompense for Morris Engleberg's services that caused some to wonder if Engleberg was "trying to profit from his relationship with DiMaggio."

There were additional issues in this lawyer-client relationship besides those of control and access. It was alleged Morris Engleberg ran DiMaggio's life, even attempting to keep others out, in a relationship that DiMaggio might have ended had he been well enough to do so. In his book, Richard Ben Cramer wrote that he contacted Morris Engleberg and indicated the book would contain "serious allegations" concerning Engleberg's conduct. A review of some of those allegations reveals several problems with the DiMaggio-Engleberg attorney-client relationship.

1. *Problems with Gifts*

Following DiMaggio's death, Engleberg turned up with "dozens of signed" DiMaggio items, most of which Engleberg apparently claimed were gifts from his grateful client. Engleberg attempted to sell these items on his own behalf at auction. Some of these were one of a kind DiMaggio items, including several very personal items, as well as a Yankee uniform shirt. There was also an allegation that even before Joe's death, Engleberg made arrangements to sell DiMaggio autographed baseballs for his benefit. Engleberg had accumulated these baseballs in his closet and reportedly told a colleague that he had so many DiMaggio autographed baseballs he could no longer hang up his clothes.

Then, there was Joe's ring. In one report, members of the hospital nursing staff began to prepare Joe's body just after his death. At that time, Morris Engleberg noticed, on Joe's finger, the 1936 World Series ring from DiMaggio's rookie year with the Yankees. Engleberg reportedly told the nurse that the 1936 ring had to come off. After some struggle, the ring came free, and Engleberg left the room with it. At DiMaggio's funeral, however, Engleberg sported the ring on his own finger, reportedly telling others that DiMaggio gave him the ring "on his deathbed—before Joe died in his arms."

In the attorney-client relationship, it is important to understand this: There is absolutely nothing wrong with a lawyer receiving gifts from a client. Standing alone, the fact that Joe DiMaggio's lawyer, Morris Engleberg, owned autographed Joe DiMaggio baseballs and other memorabilia, including DiMaggio's rookie-year World Series ring, is not a problem of legal ethics. In response to Cramer's letter, Mr. Engleberg's partner indicated that Engleberg and DiMaggio maintained "an extremely close personal and business relationship."[72] It is difficult to imagine that is not the case. As a result, suppose someone believes the autographed baseballs and other memorabilia possessed by Engleberg following DiMaggio's death were indeed gifts from a grateful client to an underpaid lawyer?

Isn't the problem the fact that we won't know if this is true?

While the attorney-client relationship is one in which the client is the master or principal and the lawyer is the servant or agent, the relationship is inherently unequal. Contrary to logic, it is not unequal with the client-principal having the upper hand. It is, instead, an unequal relationship "in which it is [the lawyer] who is in control."[73] Indeed, Morris Engleberg acknowledges this dichotomy in his relationship with DiMaggio. On one hand, Engleberg said that DiMaggio "'owned me'" and that he was DiMaggio's "'slave.'" On the other hand, however, Engleberg notes: "'People thought I was running his life, which I did,'" and that DiMaggio "'couldn't live without me. If he hated me, he'd have to stay with me.'"

Because it is the lawyer in the attorney-client relationship who holds the balance of power, the attorney is a fiduciary to the client and, as a result, is prohibited from using the client's trust in a way that either benefits the lawyer or disadvantages the client.[74] Undertaking that relationship, the attorney must not engage in conduct that even appears untoward.[75] And that is exactly what happens when a lawyer, claiming the items as "gifts" winds up with thousands of dollars of client assets upon the client's demise. It simply looks like the lawyer has taken advantage of the inequality of the relationship.

This is a particular problem for the DiMaggio/Engleberg relationship because of DiMaggio's prior dealings with people. If Engleberg had demanded payment from DiMaggio, it is likely DiMaggio would discharge him because anybody who knew DiMaggio knew that he did not pay for anything. This, notwithstanding the fact that Engleberg claims DiMaggio offered to pay for Engleberg's negotiations with Bowery Bank at the outset of their relationship. Further, if Engleberg had tried to sell DiMaggio memorabilia for his own profit while DiMaggio was alive, DiMaggio would have cut him off, as he did with his brother Dom and friends Liberatore and Halper. And Engleberg knew it.

Consider the "gifts" issue again in conjunction with the two stories surrounding DiMaggio's 1936 rookie-year World Series ring. In one rendition of the story, Engleberg had a nurse pull the ring from a recently deceased Joe DiMaggio's swollen finger. In the other rendition, DiMaggio gives the ring to his grateful lawyer immediately prior to dying in Engleberg's arms. Engleberg then proudly wears the ring to the funeral of his deceased client. It is because DiMaggio is deceased, and because Engleberg, as his attorney, had such easy access to Joe at the end of his life that we likely will never know the truth between the two stories. And it is because we won't know the truth, and because of the lawyer's inherently unequal bargaining power, that the lawyer's conduct is inherently suspect.

2. Engleberg's Book Deal and Confidentiality

In addition to receiving gifts from DiMaggio, Morris Engleberg indicated that he was going to write a book about his relationship with DiMaggio. Engleberg reportedly was going to detail how he spent his life away from the active practice of law, devoted to DiMaggio. He apparently expected to offer it to publishers for over a million dollars. Joe's heirs have apparently expressed concern about this book, "given [DiMaggio's] own desire for privacy."

As was the case with gifts, the fact that a lawyer writes a book about the law, or even a book about the attorney-client relationship, is not a problem of professional responsibility. Further, the fact that DiMaggio's family and friends might not like this endeavor because of Joe's long-stated and publicly known desire to maintain his privacy is not a legal issue. Instead, for Engleberg, or any other attorney, the issue of writing a book about a particular client relationship is an issue of confidentiality.

In the attorney-client relationship, a lawyer's primary duty is to maintain as confidential any information that relates to the attorney-client relationship. This duty is so important that it survives even after the attorney-client relationship has terminated. As a result, the lawyer cannot use any information that relates to the representation in a way that would harm the interests of the client, even when the client is deceased.[76] Because DiMaggio was such a private person, and had specifically instructed Engleberg to keep information relating to his illness, and presumably other matters, out of the public domain, the release of any such information would be adverse to DiMaggio's desire for privacy, and presumably, would not be permissible.

There is, however, an exception to this general rule. It arises in the Joe DiMaggio-Morris Engleberg relationship, in part, because of the book published about this relationship by author Richard Ben Cramer. When the conduct of the lawyer in representing a client is called into question, the lawyer is permitted to reveal confidential information about the relationship. This right to reveal rests with the lawyer and is not subject to veto by the client or their heirs or family. Thus, for example, when DiMaggio's possible gifts to Engleberg were raised as potential misconduct, Engleberg was entitled to reveal information about his relationship with DiMaggio that sheds light on how Engleberg acquired the items.

In addition to a specific response to allegations about gifts, when Engleberg knew that Cramer was about to publish a book containing "serious allegations" against Engleberg, Engleberg was entitled to respond generally to those allegations. As a result, statements by Engleberg, in a *Vanity Fair* magazine article "in response to" the allegations in Cramer's book, were entirely appropriate. Engleberg is not required to maintain the traditional lawyer's silence in the face of allegations against him arising from his relationship with DiMaggio.

But a lawyer can reveal too much information. Generally, in responding to charges relating to the representation of a client, a lawyer's response must be proportionate to the amount of information revealed about the relationship and restrained so that the lawyer's duty of loyalty still exists toward preserving as much client confidential information as possible.[77] Thus, when Engleberg apparently claims that DiMaggio "divulged stories and facts relating to his life that this 'private man' never told anyone before," and hints at using this information in a book, he likely goes beyond permissible bounds. Further, when he indicates that if any of DiMaggio's family criticizes him for writing a book about his representation, he will " 'give them a chunk of money. They'll stop resenting me,' " Engleberg only demonstrates that he has missed the professional point entirely.

3. Conflict of Interest Problems

Morris Engleberg may also miss the point in dealing with conflict of interest. As an attorney, Engleberg must remain loyal to his client's interests. In doing that, it is not permissible for Engleberg to allow other interests, including his own, to interfere with his obligation to act "solely for the benefit" of Joe DiMaggio.[78]

In September, 1998, when the Yankees held Joe DiMaggio Day, Engleberg reportedly arranged for production of a Joe DiMaggio commemorative baseball. Some fifteen thousand of these commemorative baseballs were to be autographed by DiMaggio, thereby producing significant income for the Yankee Clipper. Production of this baseball is not a problem. A problem arises, however when it was reported that Engleberg kept some two thousand special DiMaggio Day baseballs for himself, and was planning on having DiMaggio sign them for sale, and profit, by Engleberg and his colleagues. Those two thousand baseballs were scheduled for sale at $200 each. Further, Engleberg lined up a promoter for the other autographed DiMaggio baseballs that Engleberg claimed crowded his closet and that he referred to as gifts from DiMaggio. Sales of these baseballs would also benefit Engleberg personally.

On the surface, these transactions seem like a win-win situation. If all the Joe DiMaggio Day baseballs were autographed and sold for $200 each, DiMaggio would make some $3 million, his lawyer $400,000. Unfortunately, however, Engleberg was not DiMaggio's partner. He was his lawyer. As his lawyer and agent, he owed DiMaggio a duty to act solely for DiMaggio's interests. Translated strictly into a duty of attorney to client, Engleberg was not permitted to continue to represent DiMaggio's interests if his representation of those interests would be "materially limited...by the lawyer's own interests," unless DiMaggio permitted the representation to continue.[79] Further, Engleberg could not become a partner with DiMaggio unless DiMaggio understood all of the ramifications of that partnership, including Engleberg's participation, and agreed to it.[80] And there is the rub. Engleberg knew that DiMaggio would not consent. In fact, he specifically asked his business associates to keep his personal transactions from DiMaggio. Engleberg also knew DiMaggio's negative reaction to others making money from Joe's name.

But, again, if they both made money, how could there be "material" differences between Engleberg's personal interests and those of DiMaggio? And again, Engleberg already knew the problem. That's why he permitted DiMaggio to appear at only five autograph shows per year. Too many autographed items would produce market saturation, and saturation would drive down the price of DiMaggio autographed merchandise. If, because Engleberg's personal autographed baseballs were in the marketplace, the price of autographed baseballs belonging to DiMaggio went down, there is certainly material adversity between Engleberg's personal interests and those of DiMaggio.

Further problems arose in late 1998. During Joe's hospitalization late in the year, Engleberg admittedly lied to the general public about DiMaggio's condition. He knew that DiMaggio did not want his real condition subject to public knowledge, particularly if the news was not good news. Engleberg used ruses, such as carrying a pizza box—albeit empty—into the hospital in an attempt to make observers think DiMaggio was eating, and therefore, on the mend. He attempted to withhold information from DiMaggio's brother Dom claiming any information was protected by attorney-client privilege.

Then, suddenly, in December, Engleberg's strategy of secrecy apparently changed. On December 9, 1998, Engleberg was quoted as thinking that DiMaggio "'was near death,'" and that the situation was "'day-to-day.'" He reportedly made it clear that even if he should survive the present, "'he won't be the same.'"[81] Why the sudden candor by the same lawyer who did not care about his reputation when earlier lying for DiMaggio? December, of course, was the height of the Christmas rush. Could it be that news of DiMaggio's real condition was good for holiday memorabilia sales?[82] And if in increasing those sales, some of which went for his personal benefit, Engleberg abused confidential information that DiMaggio did not wish disclosed, there are certainly materially differing interests.[83]

Similar problems arose following DiMaggio's death when Engleberg became "Personal Representative and Trustee" under DiMaggio's Will. While the Will permits no fee for Engleberg's personal representation, he is entitled to a fee as Trustee of the Trusts created in the Will.[84] As representative of the estate, Engleberg sold some 10,000 items of DiMaggio memorabilia to North Carolina businessman Ralph Perillo for an estimated $33.5 million.[85] Among the items were autographed baseballs, authenticated by Engleberg that were far from DiMaggio's normal, "meticulously crafted" signature. These baseballs, instead, contained a reportedly "'scrawled, weak signature.'"[86]

In making that sale, Engleberg fulfilled his duty as fiduciary for the beneficiaries of the DiMaggio estate. Even when he sold some 10,000 pieces to one buyer, pieces that would no doubt bring more if sold individually, Engleberg cannot be significantly faulted for not wasting estate monies on the administrative costs of conducting such sales.[87] That the signatures on these baseballs did not appear as fastidious as the traditional Joe DiMaggio autographed baseball is simply not a representation problem.

The problem is not this sale, but another one, conducted primarily for the benefit of "'employees of the law firm'" of Mr. Engleberg. At that second auction, the following items, among others were offered: The golf cart DiMaggio had been given and that Engleberg outfitted in Yankee blue; DiMaggio's Florida "DiMag5" License Plate; DiMaggio's Master Card; DiMaggio's driver's license; DiMaggio's insurance cards from the Screen Actor's Guild and the American Federation of Television and Radio Actors; and a Yankee uniform shirt.

Besides the problems associated with receiving these items as gifts from DiMaggio, their sale again raises the question of market saturation. If sale of his personal items would diminish the value of the collective items Engleberg sought to sell to the North Carolina promoter, there are materially differing interests between Engleberg's personal interests and those of the estate.

In addition to being Personal Representative and Trustee of the trusts set up under DiMaggio's Will, Engleberg was named as attorney for the estate. His professional obligation, then, was to the estate, not to himself. In attempting to sell or promote his own personal memorabilia holdings, Engleberg was required to sacrifice his personal interests to those of the estate. If he did not, Engleberg has a conflict with his duty as attorney to the estate to generate the maximum income possible.[88] And it is not enough that, in reality, the DiMaggio estate was not harmed, or that the heirs of DiMaggio thought that Engleberg was acting appropriately. We expect more out of our attorneys.

4. If There Is No Real Harm, Is There Really a Foul?

When initially read, the story of how Morris Engleberg fit into Joe DiMaggio's life sounds like the pair were made for each other. Engleberg, searching for a father figure, was willing to virtually exchange his family to have Hemingway's "'great DiMaggio'" take him "into his life." DiMaggio, publicly idolized, but privately the victim of questionable business deals and distrusting of everyone, got a lawyer he could trust. For his services, it seems inherently fair that Morris Engleberg be entitled to something for the care he provided DiMaggio. In the overall scheme of DiMaggio's estate, an estate built largely because of Engleberg's effort, minor self-dealing seems relatively harmless.

In reality, however, what Engleberg did for DiMaggio is what lawyers are supposed to do for their clients. Particularly dealing with famous or public clients, it goes with the representation to be asked, like Mr. Engleberg, to be available for on-call travel, to attend galas with the client, to care for household needs of the client and to arrange for meals and other creature comforts.[89] When doing so, if any significant part of the duties involved the practice of law, the attorney for famous clients is considered to be acting as a lawyer, regardless of whether they call themselves friend, confidant, advisor, agent or something else. As an attorney, Engleberg was subject to the rules of the legal profession for his conduct.[90] He could not sidestep those roles either because DiMaggio was a friend or because Engleberg was not being paid.

VIII. Conclusion

Joe DiMaggio, so successful on the baseball diamond, so idolized by the public, but rarely so successful in contractual endeavors, needed a lawyer like Morris Engleberg. Weathered in tax and estate law, Engleberg had already successfully represented rich and very public clients before DiMaggio. For DiMaggio, who had previously negotiated almost all of his own contracts, even his own divorces, Engleberg was a jewel that Joltin' Joe, who normally paid for nothing, was even willing to pay. And Engleberg, who told his elementary school classmates in the 1940's that DiMaggio was his father, would not take money from his idol.[91] Instead, Engleberg made DiMaggio the kind of wealth that someone in DiMaggio's very public social station deserved.

Then two things happened.

First, Joe DiMaggio got older, and later more ill. With his history of less than successful contract ventures, the normally distrustful DiMaggio became even more dependent on Engleberg. He developed what some of Joe's associates said was "Stockholm syndrome," an emotional attachment between the captor that friends said Engleberg became, and the hostage that was the dependent DiMaggio.[92] Morris Engleberg, as DiMaggio's attorney, was obligated to recognize that a lawyer is not a consigliere.[93] Instead of misusing DiMaggio's natural distrust, Engleberg was obligated to provide independent professional advice, even if Joe did not want to hear it. Instead of being Joe's liar, Engleberg again was required to exercise independent professional judgment and to do what was right for DiMaggio under the rules of professional conduct for lawyers. Those rules require lawyers to be truthful to third parties when acting on behalf of a client.

Second, Morris Engleberg himself became a "player," known as DiMaggio's confident, friend and lawyer; the person who personally authenticated baseballs autographed by Joe DiMaggio on his deathbed.[94] As a player, there is a natural temptation for Engleberg to strike out on his own, to sell autographed baseballs and other merchandise and keep the profits for himself or for the benefit of colleagues. And that presents conflict of interest problems. Morris Engleberg may have been representing a famous client, but he was only DiMaggio's lawyer. As a result, his obligation was exclusively to the interests of Joe DiMaggio; he could not allow his own interests to conflict with his duties to his client.

Trust and loyalty; these are two of the essential characteristics of lawyers. It is not enough that Morris Engleberg made millions for Joe DiMaggio. Without trust and loyalty, a lawyer is no more than a friend giving advice. Joe DiMaggio had plenty of friends who gave him advice. Much of that advice, however, was only what Joe wanted to hear. What he needed in the waning days of his life, and thereafter, was a lawyer, acting like the conflict-free independent advisor lawyers are professionally required to be.

Yogi Berra, baseball pundit and author of several books on his life and sayings, doing some light reading. Photo © Bettmann/CORBIS.

The Law and Yogi

by Joel K. Goldstein[*]

Few Americans have been quoted to explain American legal doctrine as often as Lawrence "Yogi" Berra. It may seem surprising that the words and wisdom of a former baseball player with an eighth grade education could affect the evolution of American law. Yet especially during the last two decades, Berra's words have appeared with increasing frequency in legal literature. Since 1984 at least 74 cases and more than 150 law review articles have cited Berra's teachings. To be sure, some citations to Berra are superfluous, used to produce a comic effect or to demonstrate that the writer is a regular person. Yet judicial opinions and legal scholarship also cite Berra's sayings to explain difficult concepts, fortify arguments, and defend results.

In the recent past, lawyers have borrowed the analytical beacons of other disciplines to cast new light on the law. These appropriations have given rise to a variety of "law and" movements: law and economics, law and history, law and philosophy, and so forth. Berra's influence on law does not rival those movements. Yet it is not entirely facetious to suggest we may be witnessing something of a law and Berra movement. Many Berraisms convey legal concepts in relatively simple and engaging fashion, thereby making law accessible to a wider audience. In embracing Yogi, the law adopts an appealing voice which represents many of its best characteristics and aspirations. This chapter documents Berra's influence on the law, explains it, and identifies other opportunities to use Berra's words to convey legal concepts.

I. Berra, the Ballplayer

Lawrence Peter "Yogi" Berra was born in St. Louis, Missouri on May 12, 1925. He grew up in the Italian neighborhood known as "The Hill." Joe Garagiola, a future major leaguer and broadcaster, lived across Elizabeth Avenue and was a close childhood friend. Although Berra left school after eighth grade to help support his family, he continued to play ball. Garagiola was deemed the better prospect of the two. Legendary Cardinal General Manager Branch Rickey, himself a lawyer, thought Berra would rise no higher than Triple A minor league ball. The hometown Cardinals signed Garagiola for a $500 bonus but offered Berra only $250. Offended, Berra, while still a teenager, signed with the Yankees, who matched the sum Garagiola was paid. His minor league career was interrupted when he joined the Navy at 18; he participated in the D-Day invasion at Omaha Beach and served in North Africa and Italy.

Berra homered in his major league debut on September 22, 1946. He spent his entire playing career, through 1963, with the Yankees except for four games and nine at bats for the Mets in 1965. During his first two years, Berra split time between catcher and outfield.

His work behind the plate was not initially impressive. The Yankees imported Hall of Famer Bill Dickey to tutor Berra on the fine arts of the trade. "He's learning me all his experience," said Berra.[1] Through hard work, Berra emerged as the Yankees' catcher in 1949. Not coincidentally, the Yankees won their first of five consecutive World Championships that year. During the 17 full seasons (1947–63) Berra played for them the Yankees won 14 pennants and ten World Series. He was an all star 15 times from 1948 to 1962.

Berra excelled offensively and defensively. A career .285 hitter, he hit 358 homeruns, 313 as a catcher. He was the career leader in homers by a catcher until Johnny Bench passed him. "I knew the record would stand until it was broken," Berra congratulated Bench.[2] From 1949 to 1958 he hit more than 20 homers each year. He knocked in more than 100 runs five times and led the mighty Yankees in that category from 1948 to 1955. He often swung at bad pitches but rarely struck out. He was particularly dangerous in later innings when the game was on the line. During Berra's prime, from 1950 to 1956, he either won the American League's Most Valuable Player award (1951, 1954, 1955), finished second (1953, 1956), third (1950), or fourth (1952). Towards the end of his career, Berra returned to the outfield, playing alongside Mickey Mantle and Roger Maris during their great years in 1960 and 1961. Watching them hit back-to-back homers, he commented, "It was déjà vu all over again."[3]

As a catcher, Berra maintained an impressive .989 fielding percentage. He once caught 148 consecutive games without an error. In a span of 204 games behind the plate in 1958 and 1959, he made only two errors, leading the league with fielding percentages of 1.000 and .997 respectively. Five times he caught 140 games or more. He lead the league in put outs eight times, assists three seasons, and double plays on six occasions.

Berra excelled in post-season play. He holds records for World Series games played by a catcher, hits, at bats, and doubles, ranks second in runs batted in and third in homeruns and walks. He hit the first pinch hit homerun in series history and caught its only perfect game. "It's never happened in World Series history, and it hasn't happened since," he said of Don Larsen's 1952 masterpiece.[4] No player has won more Series championships.

II. Berra, The Manager

The Yankees named him manager in 1964. Asked how he had prepared for his new responsibility, he replied, "You can observe a lot by watching."[5] The Yankees struggled for much of the year. The turning point came after Berra chastised utility infielder Phil Linz for playing "Mary Had A Little Lamb" on the harmonica on a bus ride after the team lost four straight games to the Chicago White Sox in an August slump. The Yankees rallied, finishing with 99 wins (most in either league), and won the pennant by one game. The aging Yankees extended the 1964 World Series to seven games before losing to a historic Cardinals team which included future Hall of Famers Bob Gibson and Lou Brock. Yankees' shortstop Tony Kubek missed the series with a sprained wrist; Yankee ace pitcher, Whitey Ford, was unavailable after the first game. Berra expected to be rewarded with a two year contract. Instead, he was unceremoniously fired. The Yankees plummeted the following season. They did not win another pennant for 12 years.

Berra joined Casey Stengel as a coach of the New York Mets in 1965. He became the Mets' manager in 1972 following Gil Hodges' sudden death. That same year he was elected to Baseball's Hall of Fame (in his second year of eligibility) and the Yankees retired his number 8. In 1973 he managed the "You Gotta Believe" Mets from the National League cellar to first place in the season's final month. "It ain't over till it's over," he told his unlikely pennant winning team.[6] The Mets beat the Cincinnati Reds in a five game playoff before losing to a powerful Oakland Athletics squad in seven games. After being relieved by the Mets in 1975, he returned to the Yankees as a coach. From 1976 to 1983, he worked under Billy Martin (three times), Bob Lemon (twice), Dick Howser, Gene Michael (twice), and Clyde King on teams that won four pennants and three World Series. He became the Yankees' manager in 1984 but George Steinbrenner fired him 16 games into the 1985 season. Berra coached for the Houston Astros from 1986 to 1992. A fourteen year estrangement from the Yankees ended in 1999 when he and Steinbrenner met at the Yogi Berra Museum in Montclair, New Jersey to settle their differences.

By any measure, Berra experienced great success as a ballplayer. Even as a manager, he won pennants in two of his five full seasons and, in each case, took an over-matched team to the seventh game of the World Series. During his 45 years in baseball, he also developed a reputation for the pearls of wisdom that rolled off his tongue.

III. Law and Yogi: The Early Years

Lawyers made little use of Berra's comments during his playing career. The first reference to Berra in legal literature probably came in 1949. Professor Richard Wicks of the University of Southern California School of Law, reviewing a book on contract law, pointed out that most first year law students mistakenly believe that finding the "right" answer to legal problems is more important than understanding the process of legal analysis. The conventional law student approach reminded Professor Wicks of a question "Yogi Berra, catcher extraordinary," asked his teammate Bobby Brown, a medical student, when Brown closed his medical text at the same time Berra finished a comic book. "How did it come out?,"[7] Berra asked. Just as Berra mistakenly assumed that Brown's book contained a plot with a conclusion, beginning law students mistakenly elevate result over analysis, Professor Wicks observed.

During the next 35 years, relatively few J.D.s looked to Berra to help explain legal concepts. My research reveals no reported case and few scholarly articles quoting Berra while he was still playing.

Professor (later Dean) Hardy C. Dillard of the University of Virginia Law School was among the pioneers of the law and Berra movement. As acting President of the American Society of International Law, Professor Dillard invoked Berra's Bill Dickey comment at the organization's 1961 and 1963 Annual Dinners to pay tribute to different associates.[8] In 1970 the Virginia Law Review published tributes to Professor Dillard after he was named to the International Court of Justice; in one, his colleague, Professor T. Munford Boyd, recalled that "in support of his thesis or his theory" Dillard is "likely to quote" legal titan Roscoe Pound, Samuel Williston, or Oliver Wendell Holmes, the Greek philosopher Plato, Ann Landers or Yogi Berra.[9]

In 1970, while Berra was hitting fungoes to Mets fielders, Katherine Parkes, then Librarian for the Institute of Judicial Administration, used a Berraism in a review of a book comparing the American and British legal systems. The book authors had observed that too few people used the courts and that the courts were congested. This analysis was reminiscent, the reviewer thought, of Berra's classic comment about a restaurant "Nobody goes there...it's too crowded."[10]

Berra next appeared in legal literature in 1979 when Professor Robert M. Cover of Yale Law School published his inspired New York Times Op-ed column, "Your Law-Baseball Quiz."[11] Professor Cover's questions each mentioned a Supreme Court justice followed by four baseball figures. Readers were asked to identify the ballplayer who "bears the same relationship to baseball as the Justice bears to law." The first question was "Earl Warren;" the correct answer, "Yogi Berra," beating fellow Hall of Famers Roberto Clemente, Tris Speaker and Willie Mays.

Those astute readers who grasp the connection between the controversial Chief Justice and the beloved Yankee catcher can skip this, and the next, paragraph. Others may appreciate Professor Cover's explanation that both Warren and Berra "were enormously effective performers on teams with many stars." Teammates like Mantle, Maris, Frankfurter, Douglas and Black may have presented "a more eloquent swing or style" but Berra and Warren were "the truly most valuable players" in part because "[b]oth saw through excessive thought to the true essence of their game."

Professor Cover's "Law-Baseball Quiz" was, of course, not a scholarly article or judicial opinion. Moreover, Professor Cover's list included such forgettables as Wayne Terwilliger, Cleon Jones (whose antics contributed to Berra's demise with the Mets), and Clyde Vollmer, although as wrong answers. But Professor Cover did identify Berra's penchant for aphorism. Professor Cover contrasted a lengthy Warren quote, which suggested the intuitive nature of a sense of justice, with Berra's more entertaining statement, "How can you think and hit at the same time?" Whereas the earlier uses savored Berra's malapropisms, Professor Cover seemed to credit Berra with a profound insight.

Finally, in 1983 Justice Frank K. Richardson of the California Supreme Court told law students at California Western, that "You can observe a lot by just watching."[12]

IV. From the Diamond to the Courts

Berra's glory years in baseball ended in 1985 with his dismissal as Yankees manager. Ironically the law and Berra movement gained momentum at roughly the same time. By the mid 1980s judges and law professors perhaps thought it time to give John Marshall, Oliver Wendell Holmes, and Benjamin Cardozo a rest and quote someone a little more colorful. Yogi was their man.

Since 1984, judges have cited Berra in at least 74 cases. Federal and state judges have found Berra's words more relevant to their decisions than those of any other sports figure. Berra has not written any of the world's classic works of literature (at least not yet) but his quotes appear in judicial opinions more often than those of Henry David Thoreau, Confucius, William Faulkner, Nathaniel Hawthorne, Jane Austen, and many other luminaries. Berra is equally popular with federal judges (who have life tenure and accordingly will not risk their job by relying on a baseball player) and state judges (who generally are elected and accordingly may covet the Berra vote). Some 40 federal cases and 34 state cases cite Berraisms. While the Supreme Court has not yet quoted Yogi, the United States Courts of Appeals of the First, Fourth, Fifth, Sixth, Seventh, Eighth, Ninth, Eleventh and District of Columbia Circuits have. It is perhaps not surprising that the Tenth Circuit has managed to dispense justice without Berra's wisdom; it covers western states where little major league baseball is played. The neglect of the Second and Third Circuits is more perplexing. The Second covers Yankee and Shea Stadiums, the sites of Berra's playing and managerial careers; the Third Circuit includes New Jersey, his home. Berra has been quoted in federal district courts sitting in 15 states (including New York) and in state courts in 15 states and the District of Columbia.

At least one court has cited Berra in a case every year from 1984 to 2002. Berra averaged 3.33 court cites/year from 1984 to 1998. From 1999 to 2001, his numbers jumped to 8, 7, and 8.

A. It Ain't Over till It's Over

Berra made his debut in judicial opinions in 1984 in Keasler v. United States,[13] which involved a petition for attorneys' fees under the Equal Access to Justice Act in the Eastern District of Arkansas. Having prevailed in an action seeking a refund of excise taxes, plaintiffs sought to recover expenses including attorneys' fees. The government objected in part that the fee petition was not timely since plaintiffs had filed it after prevailing at the appellate level, not after the trial ended. Judge Eisele thought the judgment of an appealed case became "final" only once the trial court entered judgment pursuant to the appellate court's mandate. Accordingly, plaintiffs' fee petition was timely. The judge relied on Berra's "immortal words" that the "game isn't over until it's over."[14]

The Court of Appeals for the Fifth Circuit used that teaching to work through some bankruptcy cases. In In re Moody,[15] the appellate court considered whether a bankruptcy court's order compelling an individual to deliver property in his possession to the trustee was a final, thus appealable, order. Several courts had held that it was. Still, Judge Alvin Rubin, a distinguished jurist, thought it prudent to invoke even higher authority. He wrote, "For the purpose of Yogi Berra's celebrated maxim, 'The game isn't over till it's over,' a bankruptcy proceeding is over when an order has been entered that ends a discrete judicial unit in the larger case."[16]

Six months later, the same Berraism helped different judges of the Fifth Circuit resolve a related issue. Judge Irving Goldberg began by juxtaposing Berra's "It isn't over till it's over" with Ecclesiastes' "To every thing there is a season."[17] Having stated these two authoritative maxims, only one of which The Turtles turned into a hit song, Judge Goldberg developed an analogy between appellate jurisdiction and baseball. Paradoxically, the "season" of appellate jurisdiction begins only once the "game has ended." In baseball, he observed, " it is easy to tell when the game is over." (Anyone who has read this far knows, of course, that it's not over until it's over.) For reasons that remain a mystery, Judge Goldberg inexplicably elected instead to footnote a bright-line, but less memorable, rule that "[a] baseball game ends at the end of the first inning, after the eighth, that does not end in a tie."[18] After several pages in which he presented "The Lineup," "The Pitch," "Ground Rules," umpires, and after drawing upon an analysis by then Judge Steve (now Justice Stephen) Breyer, he finally brought out the heavy lumber—Judge Rubin's paragraph from In re Moody relying on Judge Berra.[19]

Judge Rubin was not only an outstanding judge but an avid Berra fan. Professor David W. Robertson, a foremost legal scholar, reported that Judge Rubin "treasured Yogi Berra's insight that 'predictions are very uncertain especially when they relate to the future'" and "more than once" borrowed Berra's "best zen line" (i.e., "déjà vu all over again").[20]

No doubt due to Judge Rubin's influence, the Court of Appeals for the Fifth Circuit used Berra's assessment of when it is over in other contexts, too. In a suit for breach of contract, the decisive question was whether a contractor was employed for a definite term. In describing objectively determinable finales, Judge Rubin wrote: "As Yogi Berra has reminded us, operas 'ain't over until the fat lady sings,' and ball games don't end until the last player is put out."[21]

Berra's "it's not over until it's over" statement was invoked to help a court work through a difficult constitutional law question. Plaintiffs challenged Ohio's motto ("With God, All Things Are Possible") as an establishment of religion in violation of the First Amendment. Under prevailing doctrine, that issue turned in part on whether the motto had a secular (instead of a purely religious) purpose. At trial, an expert witness testified that the "near tautological nature" of Ohio's motto "in both religious and non-religious contexts suggests the motto is meant to inspire rather than proclaim or define." To illustrate the point, he called upon Berra to pinch hit. The expert continued:

> [Ohio's motto] is typologically similar to Yogi Berra's tautological aphorism, 'It's never [sic] over until it's over.' The function of that statement was to urge his players to keep their sights on victory even though it didn't seem to them possible at the time. He was not making an assertion that would be new to them, nor one with which some could logically disagree. Rather, he was boosting their morale, instilling confidence and optimism, exhorting them not to give up and to continue to strive.[22]

Having quoted this testimony the Court then returned to it in holding that Ohio had not violated the First Amendment because its motto had a secular purpose. The Court reasoned:

> The record of the instant case supports the conclusion that Ohio's statement of a secular purpose is not a sham; like Yogi Berra's aphorism about its not being over until it's over, as the record indicates, the Ohio motto legitimately serves a secular purpose in boosting morale, instilling confidence and optimism, and exhorting the listener or reader not to give up and to continue to strive.[23]

The Court quoted James Madison, Abraham Lincoln and Justice Sandra Day O'Connor but, when the motto was on the line, it was Berra who delivered in the clutch.

The Eleventh Circuit Court of Appeals invoked Berra's "ain't over till it's over" comment to explain why attorneys in a class action were entitled to a fee award for work performed after the court entered a consent order. The case "ain't over" until all benefits were in hand,[24] it reasoned. Another judge, in dismissing a claim "without prejudice," explained that it was a "technical legal term which means about the same as Yogi Berra meant when he said, 'The game[']s not over until it's over!'"[25]

As these cases suggest, certain legal consequences often attach to a determination that some relevant event has occurred, that some experience has ended. Berra's insight captures and conveys the law's reliance on such triggers in the cases cited above and in many other contingencies.

B. Déjà Vu All Over Again

Just as Berra was not a one hit wonder in baseball, his "it ain't over" line does not exhaust his contributions to American jurisprudence. In fact, Berra's "déjà vu all over again" line is his most-quoted judicial saying, having been cited approximately 30 times in opinions. The statement captures the essence of the legal principle of precedent or stare decisis. Precedent is the practice of treating judicial decisions as authority for similar situations later arising. Stare decisis embraces the law's commitment to reapply the rules of decided cases to similar new cases. In other words, if some fact pattern is déjà vu and it happens all over again, the law applies the initial rule to the repeat episode. Déjà vu all over again.

For instance, Judge Bruce Selya began his opinion for the Court of Appeals for the First Circuit in Williams v. Ashland Engineering Co.,[26] with the "déjà vu" line. The case considered whether the Employee Retirement Income Security Act (ERISA) preempted a Massachusetts law requiring certain general contractors to furnish bonds. The Court had previously held that ERISA preempted a similar Massachusetts law in McCoy v. Massachusetts Institute of Technology.[27] In Williams, the Court concluded that McCoy was "clearly correct," i.e., "the real McCoy,"[28] and accordingly applied the doctrine of stare decisis, i.e., the case was "déjà vu all over again."

Courts have also used the line as a shorthand for the related doctrine of *res judicata*. The following explanation by one court illustrates Yogi's utility to clarify an obscure area of the law.

> The doctrine of res judicata provides that a final judgment rendered by a court of competent jurisdiction on the merits is conclusive as to the rights of the parties, and constitutes an absolute bar on subsequent action involving the same claim, demand, or cause of action. *Black's Law Dictionary* 1305 (6th ed. 1990). In more simple terms, to paraphrase Yogi Berra, *res judicata* prevents a court from being subjected to "*déjà vu* all over again."[29]

Generations of law students and lawyers have relied on Black's Law Dictionary. But who needs Black's if you've got The Yogi Book?

Courts have also used "déjà vu all over again" in discussing the doctrine of law of the case, the idea that once an appellate court resolves an issue, its decision binds later proceedings in the same case.[30] Long before Kenneth Starr was listening to President Clinton consider what the meaning of "is is," he was, as a judge on the Court of Appeals for the District of Columbia Circuit, applying "déjà vu" in an opinion to explain why the National Rifle Association could not again raise an issue which a prior proceeding decided against it.[31]

One court opened with "déjà vu" in a case dealing with whether Iowa could deny medical benefits for sex reassignment surgery since the Court of Appeals for the Eighth Circuit had previously addressed that issue.[32] Appropriately enough, in a case challenging baseball's exemption from antitrust laws, the line was invoked as a virtual synonym for stare decisis.[33] Courts have used "déjà vu all over again" to note the "frequency with which issues relating to the currency reporting statutes get litigated these days,"[34] or to emphasize how often they had encountered the federal racketeering statute (RICO)[35] or Providence, Rhode Island's regulations of adult entertainment.[36] Chief Judge Edenfield, perhaps with some irritation, used the "déjà vu" line to open an opinion in which he denied, for the second time, a defendant's motion for summary judgment.[37] Not surprisingly, "the déjà vu" line has been used to note recurring fact patterns;[38] the Court of Appeals for the Sixth Circuit found it useful in a criminal case involving firearms offenses. The unlucky defendant had been arrested for the second time for packing a firearm, at a brother's request, to investigate a break-in at the family liquor store.[39]

Berra's quotes have so permeated the legal culture that, at times, parties and courts communicate in exchanges of Berraisms. In Textron, Inc. v. Aetna Casualty and Surety Co., the insurer's attorney argued that its case was similar to another pending before the Rhode Island Supreme Court where the insurer had prevailed in the trial court below; this case was, the attorney contended, "déjà Yogi all over again." The Court concluded that the case was not even "déjà vu all over again." A more appropriate Yogi adage, the Rhode Island Supreme Court suggested, was that it "ain't over 'til it's over!"[40] The insurer lost (it had apparently made "too many wrong mistakes"[41]).

The Textron case suggests that citing a Berraism does not guarantee a litigant will prevail. One party learned that lesson when he appealed a decision of the Wyoming State Board of Outfitters and Professional Guides revoking his license. The appellant cited only one case; "[t]he only other reference to authority within appellant's argument [being] the quote attributed to Yogi Berra stating: 'This is déjà vu all over again.'" One can hardly fault the appellant for relying so heavily on a Berraism which had been a winner on so many occasions in court. Still, the Wyoming Supreme Court was neither persuaded nor amused. It turned the "déjà vu" quote around, observing that Berra's "quotation finds utility in this opinion" because for 35 years the Wyoming Supreme Court had summarily affirmed cases where appellant failed to file a sufficient brief.[42] It was a lawyer's worst nightmare—citing authority which the court uses to decide the case for the other side!

C. Other Yogisms in the Cases

Although "déjà vu" and "it ain't over" are the judiciary's favorite Berra teachings, other quotes also receive play. In a case considering whether a public housing plan impermissibly discriminated based on race, the court heard evidence of the white community's need for public housing. The problem of getting the white community to identify and act upon this need called to mind Berra's comment that "[i]f the people don't want to come out to the ballpark, nobody's going to stop them."[43]

In another case, a tavern owner sought to increase the size of his establishment to combat an eroding clientele. The proprietor attributed his problem to inadequate seating. The court found that argument reminiscent of the "legendary" Berra comment that "[s]ome restaurants are so crowded that no one goes there anymore."[44]

Some judges go out of their way to demonstrate their credentials as devotees of the law and Berra movement. In a 1999 opinion, Justice Janice Rogers-Brown of the California Supreme Court wrote, "As Yogi Berra once—or more than once said, 'You've got to be very careful if you don't know where you are going, because you might not get there.'" She then cited an opinion she wrote earlier that year in which she used "déjà vu."[45]

Berra's influence on the judiciary is even more evident when judges' scholarly articles are considered. Judge Frank H. Easterbrook of the United States Court of Appeals for the Seventh Circuit relied on Berra's comment that "[p]redictions are hard, especially about the future."[46] Judge Paul J. Kelly, Jr. of the Tenth Circuit used the same basic quote in discussing professionalism.[47] Chief Judge Judith S. Kaye of New York's Court of Appeals is perhaps the leading member of the law and Berra movement in the state judicial system. She cited Yogi for the proposition that the "future is not as great as it used to be,"[48] but also thinks "you can observe a lot by watching."[49] More recently, Judge Kaye wrote:

As we stand at the crossroad of the centuries—a fork in the road—I am reminded of the words of that great philosopher Yogi Berra: "When you reach a
fork in the road, take it." As with much of Yogi's wisdom, I'm not exactly sure
what his precise words mean, but I sure do feel the spirit of them.[50]

Judge Robert R. Merhige, Jr. agrees with Berra that "one may see a lot just from observing";[51] Judge Diarmuid F. O'Scannlain relied on "the learned wisdom of one last oft-
quoted commentator from the academy, Professor Yogi Berra."[52] Some of the most
prominent jurists of recent times rely on Yogi. For instance, when Judge Kenneth Starr
quoted Berra he was joined by Judge (and former New York Senator) James L. Buckley
and Judge (and former Reagan Supreme Court nominee) Douglas H. Ginsburg.[53] Judge
Alex Kozinski,[54] Judge Easterbrook, Judge Rubin, Judge Goldberg, Judge Kaye, and
other Berra devotees are among the most prestigious recent judges.

V. Yogi in the Law Schools

At about the same time Yogi entered the case reporters in 1984, law professors began
to borrow his wisdom more often. Beginning around 1985, his words began to appear
in law journals with increasing regularity. Mark G. Yudof, then dean of the University of
Texas Law School, began his "Introduction to Education Symposium" quoting Alexander Meiklejohn, the distinguished scholar of the First Amendment. He closed by invoking "the immortal" Berra who said "You've got to be very careful if you don't know
where you are going, because you might not get there."[55] Within a few years, a veritable
who's who of the American Legal Academy was invoking Berra. In 1985 Columbia Law
School Professor Louis Lowenstein quoted Berra in an article in Columbia Law Review[56]
for the proposition that "you can observe a lot just by watching." The following year,
Sterling Professor of Law Geoffrey Hazard of Yale Law School cited Berra for saying
"there is only one chance to make a first impression," an aphorism Professor Hazard applied to the Supreme Court and its missed opportunity to decide based on the intent of
the framers of the Constitution.[57] Shortly thereafter Professor Lowenstein went two for
two, citing Berra in the Columbia Business Law Review.[58] Soon Hazard's colleague, Professor Harold Hongju Koh, turned to Berra to help him explain "Why the President (Almost) Always Wins in Foreign Affairs: Lessons of the Iran-Contra Affair."[59] Professor
Koh cited Berra, in his seminal Yale Law Journal article and in his award-winning book,
The National Security Constitution, for the proposition that "[w]e could eliminate all
those close plays at first base if only we moved the bag one foot further from home
plate."[60] Professor Koh's work dealt with the proper roles of the President, Congress and
Courts in foreign affairs decision-making. He argued that the proper solution was not
simply to change the laws i.e., move the base, but to change the decision-making
process "to *reinvolve the first baseman* [Congress] *and the umpire* [courts] *in the game.*"[61]

Professor Koh acknowledged that he heard this Berraism from Professor Burt
Neuborne of the New York University School of Law, a leading scholar of the federal judiciary. Professor Neuborne used that teaching in an article discussing how judges
should interpret statutes. "I'm afraid that Yogi's approach is often used in federal statutory areas as well. We move the bases around and pretend that what we are doing is
avoiding the close plays," Professor Neuborne wrote.[62] Although Professors Koh and
Neuborne do not share Berra's faith in the efficacy of new rules to solve all problems, it
is significant that both used his words to articulate a relatively common perspective.

Leading law professors use Berraisms to illustrate concepts across the curriculum. Take Professor Hazard, a leading scholar of legal ethics. He invoked Berra in an essay comparing everyday ethics with legal ethics. In discussing the relationship between thought and action in ethical dilemmas, Hazard observed "[t]here is a way in which the plea, 'I didn't know what I was doing' is true of every ethically crucial choice. This may have been what Yogi Berra meant when he said, 'You can't think and hit at the same time.'"[63] Professor Michael E. Solimine has juxtaposed Berra's "the game isn't over till it's over" with a quotation from Justice Scalia that the Court's "finality jurisprudence is sorely in need of further limiting principles."[64] In a 1991 article regarding whether male soldiers would accept women on the front lines, Professor Kenneth Karst thought "you can observe a lot just by watching."[65] That same year, Professor Albert W. Alschuler of the University of Chicago Law School thought we "could observe a lot by just watching" whether guidelines had produced greater sentencing equality.[66] Professor Mark Tushnet of Georgetown found Yogi's prediction of the future line useful in assessing the Supreme Court's recent decisions.[67] The United States Army seems incapable of discussing legal issues without quoting Yogi. Yogi's followers have apparently taken over the Army's Judge Advocate School.[68]

So pervasive is Berra's influence that he often is invoked by both sides of a debate. Stanford Professor Pamela D. Karlan is not only a distinguished scholar of constitutional law but an avid member of the law and Yogi school. She began a discussion of the Supreme Court's race and redistricting jurisprudence in voting rights cases by citing Walt Whitman once and Berra twice ("It ain't over 'til it's over" and "How can you think and hit at the same time?").[69] In reply, Professor James F. Blumstein, who thought the Court's cases clearer than did Professor Karlan, argued that "[y]ou can see a lot just by looking."[70] It is a tribute to Berra's relative influence that while Professor Blumstein could match Karlan's two Berraisms with another Berraism of his own, he had to counter her Walt Whitman with one from country music singer Pam Tillis.

Harvard Law Professor Martha Minow began an essay in Case Western Reserve Law Review by quoting, count them, three sayings of "[o]ne of my favorite philosophers." She left two (fork in road, observe by watching) hanging. The third ("If people don't want to come out to the ball park, nobody's going to stop them.") provided her theme. This phrase, she observed, "you really have to think about." It meant that "[n]obody's going to stop the apathy." Professor Minow hoped that concerned people would act "to stop the apathy surrounding" domestic violence and violence between different groups. Seventeen pages later, Professor Minow closed with two more "Berraisms." She conceded to "taking out of context" his rhetorical question "How can you think and hit at the same time?" She pointed out that this comment is "often imported into academic circles to chide those of us who do a lot of thinking and not so much doing." But she also saw in it a "pretty nifty reminder of mindfulness as a potential guard against the brutal kind of hitting." She then reminded her readers that their work against violence "ain't over till it's over."[71]

Scholars have not hesitated to balance Berra's wisdom against that of other historical figures much as Judge Goldberg juxtaposed Berra's "ain't over" teaching with Ecclesiastes. One author argued that physician-assisted suicide ran counter to traditional western thought as expressed in 1733 by Alexander Pope ("Hope springs eternal in the human breast.") and more recently by Berra "in equally timeless fashions" ("It ain't over 'til it's over.").[72] Another used Berra to balance Karl Marx. "As Marx commented, history repeats itself, 'the first time as tragedy, the second as farce.' Or to echo Yogi Berra's sage observation: it's déjà vu all over again."[73]

Berra's influence on the law is such that in 1997 Emory Law Journal published a 92 page, 494 footnote essay entitled The Jurisprudence of Yogi Berra[74] (thereby taking the title I would have used; to avoid a claim that this essay is "déjà vu all over again" I have chosen a different title). Some 39 authors collaborated to apply Berra's classic quotes to 14 areas of law and to medicine and physics. Some 27 members of the faculty of Loyola Law School, Los Angeles, contributed, placing that institution at the head of the law and Berra league. The essay examined "Yogi's wisdom and demonstrate[d] the parallels between judges' and legislators' comments and what Yogi said; only Yogi said it better."[75]

Some of Berra's quotes are so well known that speakers at law schools often assume familiarity without reciting them. Dean Gene Nichol, now of University of North Carolina School of Law, summarized Justice Anthony Kennedy's general position on federalism and then remarked, "My word, that sounds new and inviting. Have we been here before? Where's Yogi Berra when you need him?"[76] Quite a comment when a sophisticated speaker assumes a law school audience needs to be reminded of Justice Kennedy's views on federalism but will have Berra's (déjà vu all over again) comment committed to memory!

Readers may recall that Judge Kenneth Starr is a card carrying member of the law and Berra movement, having used Berra's "déjà vu" line in an opinion. Accordingly, it must have been particularly painful for him, an unpleasant form of "déjà vu," to have a Berraism used to criticize his own conduct as independent counsel. One writer used Berra's "fork in the road" quote to analyze Starr's prosecutorial tactics regarding President Clinton. Judge Starr had two alternatives "to pry the truth from a shy, reluctant witness named Monica Lewinsky"—"dogging her with a phalanx of detectives" or "grilling her mother" before the grand jury. When Judge Starr reached this "tactical fork in the road" he "took it" electing to pursue both strategies.[77]

Berra's popularity in legal circles bridges traditional ideological divides. Edwin Meese, III, President Reagan's close associate and second Attorney General, used the "déjà vu" line of "that eminent philosopher"[78] as did President George H. W. Bush's Attorney General, Richard Thornburgh.[79] Their embrace does not render Berra's saying right wing code; some to the left, such as ACLU President Nadine Strossen, use the same phrase. Not often do all of these people find a common legal guru. The reliance Meese, Thornburgh and Kenneth Starr place on Berra may identify Berra with the Republican Party, but Senator Joseph Lieberman also invoked Berra in a law review.[80] Whereas Professor Cover compared Berra to Chief Justice Earl Warren, another scholar associated him with Justice Antonin Scalia.[81]

Law professors are not simply pulling out their Bartlett's Familiar Quotations in the privacy of their offices to toss in a Berraism to spruce up an otherwise turgid article the way they would if quoting, say, Immanuel Kant or Chief Justice William Rehnquist. On the contrary, Berra's wisdom has so permeated legal culture that some law professors can extemporaneously drop in a Berraism whenever the situation calls for it (or even when it doesn't) much as they can dazzle an audience by tossing around concepts like nunc pro tunc, expressio unius, or penumbras. (Alternatively, it may be that many law professors, invited to appear at public gatherings, do not leave home without their American Express card, a roll of tums, and a copy of The Yogi Book, and memorize the latter before stepping up to the microphone.)

Take the case of the famous Arthur R. Miller, Bruce Bromley Professor at Harvard Law School and television star. Professor Miller participated at Boston College of Law with other thoughtful jurists and scholars at a Symposium on Discovery Reform some years ago. The participants engaged in a lively discussion of managing discovery, the process by which litigants in federal cases learn information about the case from the other side and independent witnesses. After Judge Patrick Higginbotham (who signed one of the Fifth Circuit opinions relying on Berra) commented on whether cases could be tracked depending on the parties' discovery needs, the moderator invited Professor Miller to comment. He began "As Yogi Berra said, it's déjà vu all over again. And I think that's what Judge Higginbotham just said in effect."[82]

At a symposium on "The Future of the Federal Courts," Professor Charles W. Nihan, following several distinguished jurists including Chief Justice William Rehnquist to the microphone, began by drawing upon "the considerable wisdom expressed by the great legal philosopher Yogi Berra" that "'[p]redictions are risky, especially if they're about the future.'"[83]

Law professors often rely on a snappy title to help win acceptance from law review editors and attract the attention of their readers. Many have borrowed Berra's language to add pizzazz to their titles. "Déjà Vu All Over Again: Reflections on Fifty Years of Clinical Education"[84] appeared in the Tennessee Law Review in 1997, a dozen years after that journal published "The Authority of Precedent in Tax Planning: 'It Ain't Settled' Till It's Settled" in which the author acknowledged his paraphrase of Berra's line.[85] "'It's Déjà Vu All Over Again': The Covenant Marriage Act in Cultural Perception and Legal Reality" appeared in Tulane Law Review.[86] "'Déjà Vu All Over Again': The Securities and Exchange Commission Once More Attempts to Regulate the Accounting Profession Through Rule 102(e) of Its Rules of Practice" graced the Utah Law Review the following year.[87] And "'It's Like Déjà Vu All Over Again!' Yet Another Look at the Opening Statement" appeared in the June 2000 edition of Army Lawyer.[88] That same year the Cincinnati Law Review ran "Déjà Vu: The Status of School Funding in Ohio After Derolph II."[89] Prediction is, of course, uncertain about the future. Still, titles using "Déjà Vu" may soon disappear. Nobody will go there any more. It's too crowded. But other Yogisms will no doubt appear in titles as scholars try to curry favor with law review editors.

VI. Future Forks to Take

Courts and scholars have effectively exploited many of Yogi's teachings to explain various legal concepts. Still, Berra's quotes offer opportunities for legal discourse as yet untapped.

Interpreting language remains an important topic in law. Judges debate how to understand language in the Constitution, statutes and contracts. Words may have multiple meanings which may make intent and context important. Berra's play on words in a conversation with Mary Lindsay, wife of New York City Mayor John V. Lindsay, illustrates the point. Seeing Berra in a summer suit one hot day, she remarked, "You look nice and cool, Yogi." Berra replied: "You don't look so hot yourself."[90] Berra's comment, taken alone, might suggest he had insulted the City's former first lady. Restoring the context, i.e., Mrs. Lindsay's comment and our knowledge that Yogi would not insult a lady, makes clear that Berra was complimenting her on coping with the weather with style. Similarly, interpreting legal language often requires some understanding of context and purpose.

Berra's instruction "when you come to a fork in the road, take it" might also receive more play. Presumably, he means that, at the fork, either road will lead to the desired destination. Indeed, alternative paths of reasoning often will produce the same result. Yet even if both roads lead to the same destination, the path travelled may have consequence. In travelling, the journey taken is different. In law, since judicial opinions have precedential or "déjà vu all over again" effect, the rationale followed may affect later cases. Judge T. G. Nelson of the Court of Appeals for the Ninth Circuit used Berra's "fork in the road" quote to make this point. In construing the federal sentencing guidelines, Judge Nelson concurred with the majority's result affirming a sentencing enhancement although he thought it had travelled the wrong path to get there.[91] The majority thought a sentence could be enhanced for distribution of pornography if the government proved the distribution was for pecuniary gain; Judge Nelson would not impose that limitation. Although the case before the court would end the same way (since the court found pecuniary reasons for the distribution) other cases might turn upon the rule chosen.

Knowledge, of varying types, plays an important role in law. Most witnesses can testify only if they have personal knowledge of pertinent facts. Criminal responsibility is often predicated on mens rea, a guilty mind or criminal intent. Similarly, responsibility for torts often turns on whether the actor knew or should have known that his/her acts would pose certain unreasonable risks. Objective or subjective knowledge enters into contract law, too; was there mutual assent to a deal? Finally, some believe constitutional or statutory interpretation should turn on the intent of the framers. These diverse concepts carry their own analytical complications the consideration of which is for a different, and less reader friendly, book. Suffice it to say that considering many of them could draw upon Berra's conversation with a school teacher who, upon reviewing Berra's submission, asked "Mr. Berra, don't you know anything?" Berra replied: "I don't even suspect anything."[92]

Berra also offers an opportunity to explore basic issues in property law. When asked what he would do if he found one million dollars, Berra replied, "I'd see if I could find the guy that lost it, and, if he was poor, I'd give it back."[93] Berra's statement goes far beyond the familiar childhood chorus, "finders keepers, losers weepers" in its sensitivity for destitute millionaires. Does it mesh with property law? Of course, the finder's title in property is good against all but the true owner. If the true owner knows that Berra has found his one million dollars, he is generally entitled to have it returned, whether he is a poor millionaire or George Steinbrenner. But can Berra limit his altruism to the poor millionaire or does he also have a duty to return it to a rich millionaire if he can identify her, even if she does not know Yogi has found her money? Two property law scholars suggest that at common law a finder has some duty to discover the true owner if he is reasonably able to do so. In any event, some states have imposed statutory duties to deposit the find with local authorities for some period of time.[94]

Berra's line about the uncertainty of predicting the future might also help in evaluating a prominent theory which equates law with predicting. Oliver Wendell Holmes stated in his famous address, The Path of the Law, that "a legal duty so called is nothing but a prediction that if a man does or omits certain things he will be made to suffer in this or that way by judgment of the court."[95] Some years later, Justice William O. Douglas made much the same point. "Even for the experts law is only a prediction of what judges will do under given set of facts," he said.[96] If, however, predictions are difficult about the future, how reliable is Holmes' theory? What implications are there for the type of guidance the law should provide?

Contract law allows certain agreements to be excused based on the doctrine of mistake. The concept does not excuse miscalculations of risk; if it did every agreement would be in jeopardy. Rather, it addresses contracts a) based on a belief inconsistent with the facts as they existed at the time the contract was made b) which belief goes to a basic assumption of the agreement and c) has a material effect on it. Moreover, the law is much more likely to excuse a mutual mistake than one involving only one party.[97] What this suggests is that the law recognizes different categories of mistake. Yogi said that the Yankees lost the 1960 World Series because "we made too many wrong mistakes."[98] Contract law, like baseball, only excuses the right mistakes.

Some of Berra's sayings help illustrate cases. Earle v. Angell[99] is a favorite contracts case used to teach consideration, the doctrine that a promise becomes legally binding if given in exchange for a return promise or performance. In it, Mary Dewitt, an elderly woman, promised to give her nephew, Benjamin Earle, $500 if he agreed to attend her funeral. Ben attended Aunt Mary's funeral but Ms. Dewitt's executor raised some technical objections when Ben claimed the $500. The great Judge Oliver Wendell Holmes, for the Massachusetts Supreme Judicial Court, upheld the contract. In teaching the case, I find a little Berra ("Always go to other people's funerals, otherwise they won't go to yours."[100]) helps Holmes make his points.

Others can no doubt imagine additional ways in which Yogi's sayings can communicate legal concepts. This suggests that the law and Berra movement may only have just begun.

VII. Did Yogi Say Everything He Said?

Some wonder whether Berra actually said everything attributed to him. Sportswriter Phil Pepe considered whether in some instances "others came along and put words and stories in Berra's mouth" but seemed to conclude that most of the gems are authentic.[101] Berra himself raised the issue in 1961 ("The trouble with getting a reputation as an unconscious comedian is not only that you can't live it down but also that people don't think anything about inventing more stories to add on to it.")[102] and devoted a chapter to addressing the topic in Yogi: It Ain't Over. He denied saying "déjà vu all over again" and "always go to other people's funerals; otherwise, they won't go to yours" but acknowledged many others.[103] And, the subtitle of his next book was "I Really Didn't Say Everything I Said!" (in which he acknowledged "déjà vu" and "funerals").[104]

Judges and law professors have joined the debate over whether Berra said everything he said. Judge Selya noted that Berra, "a man as famous for mangling the English language as for belting baseballs" commonly, but improperly, gets credit for coining "déjà vu all over again."[105] Although Berra did deny uttering that line in his 1989 book, Yogi: It Ain't Over...,[106] by 1998, when he wrote The Yogi Book, his memory had improved and he placed the quote after watching Mantle and Maris "hit back-to-back homeruns for the umpteenth time."[107] In his most recent book, When You Come to the Fork in the Road, Take It, Berra explained that he had "mangled" "the French term meaning 'already seen'" into "déjà vu all over again."[108]

Scholars use lines and then debate whether Berra or some other luminary deserves credit. Eugene Volokh, a constitutional law professor at UCLA Law School, used the quote "I never make predictions...especially about the future" in a review in the Stanford Law Review.[109] His footnote sought to attribute credit to the person who originated the comment. He began "[t]hat someone might have been Yogi Berra." Or perhaps Casey Stengel, Samuel Goldwyn, Leo Durocher, Mark Twain, "or, for the snobs among us, Niels Bohr."[110] Professor Volokh cited authority for each attribution. Five years later, Stanford Law Review published another work citing the same quotation but reporting a discussion on National Public Radio on April 7, 2000 regarding whether Berra, Bohr or someone else deserved credit.[111] Three scholars attributed the predictions are difficult about the future quote to Niels Bohr but observed that he "sound[ed] more like Yogi Berra than a scientist." [112] Another hedged by attributing the comment to "a wise man—apparently either Niels Bohr or Yogi Berra."[113]

Judge Rubin attributed the "fat lady sings" quote to Berra although Berra's books do not claim credit for it; perhaps he never said it or has yielded to political correctness. Not all courts have been so circumspect. The Kansas Court of Appeals recently claimed that an outcome "validates the sage advice once given by Yogi Berra to the effect that "it ain't over 'til it's over" as well as the "famous [fat lady sings] saying" which it did not attribute to Berra.[114]

The Rhode Island Supreme Court began an opinion by noting "the inevitable attribution" to Berra of Samuel Goldwyn's quote that a "verbal contract isn't worth the paper it's written on."[115] Several years later the United States Court of Appeals for the Seventh Circuit did credit Berra with that quote.[116]

It is a tribute to Yogi that when people hear a quote they like they either assume he must have said it or they use him as the standard to assess it. President Calvin Coolidge's comment ("I have noticed that nothing I never said ever did me any harm.") can stand on its own but one article complimented it as a remark that "would make Yogi Berra proud."[117] High praise for a President.

Yet the tendency to credit Berra with every saying that any judge or law professor wants to attribute carries risk. Imagine the opinions and articles of the future. "As Berra wrote in McCulloch v. Maryland, 'we must never forget, that it is a constitution we are expounding.'[118] (Until now, Chief Justice John Marshall is credited with that line written in 1819). Will future discussions of the First Amendment recall Berra's exception regarding "falsely shouting fire in a theatre and causing a panic?"[119] Holmes has gotten credit for this example; Berra's claim would seem impeached by the fact that the words appeared before he was born.

Of course, the real danger to Berra's future standing is not that he will be credited with the words of Marshall or Holmes—worse things could happen—but rather that his reputation will suffer as he is cited for the pedestrian words of lesser mortals. For instance, one state judge observed, "[a]s Yogi Berra might have put it, the bottom line is, after all, the bottom line."[120] One article credited him with saying "If you want to change something, you have to change something."[121] The court reporters and journals are beginning to fill with comments attributed to Yogi that he never would have said. Berra's influence could dissipate if his admirers, in their enthusiasm for the words he did say, attribute to him less perceptive words of others.

VIII. Exceeding Expectations

It is clear that Berra's words and wisdom are finding their way into the literature of law and that their influence has steadily increased since 1984. There is no clear explanation as to why Berra apparently received very modest treatment in legal literature before the mid 1980s yet his play has increased exponentially since then. Berra's words first appeared in Bartlett's Familiar Quotations in the 15th edition published in 1980. He rated one entry in that volume, for "[t]he game isn't over till it's over."[122] Twelve years later, the 16th edition included eight entries, adding déjà vu, think-hit, observe by watching, fork in the road, and nobody's going to stop them, among others.[123] Although Pepe's The Wit and Wisdom of Yogi Berra appeared in 1974, Berra's three autobiographies laden with his teachings came out in 1989, 1998, and 2001. The rise of the internet during the 1990s made Berraisms accessible on several websites.[124] The appearance of the autobiographies and websites may explain why Yogisms appear more now, but not why they did not appear earlier, say after Pepe's book. It is not surprising that as judges and law professors heard Berra used in legal contexts they would imitate or expand those uses. But why did the law make little use of Berra before 1984? Moreover, why do judges and law professors find Yogi so attractive?

It is tempting to relate Berra's popularity to the hold baseball has on the public, particularly on lawyers. Baseball is governed by bright line rules in a way that law aspires to be but, for a variety of reasons, cannot be. Yet if baseball's popularity explained Berra's influence on the law we would expect courts and academics to quote other leading ballplayers. That has not happened. Berra's name appears in cases five times as often as Casey Stengel, seven times as often as Leo Durocher, 12 times as often as Satchel Paige, and 74 times as often as former teammate Phil Rizzuto. Only Babe Ruth rivals Berra in case citations, but most references to the Bambino refer to places named after him or to his own legal problems. Courts have yet to rely on the wisdom of Willie Mays or Barry Bonds; Hank Aaron has been quoted once. Berra outpaces these other ballplayers in law reviews by large margins.

Perhaps Berra's popularity traces to his wit. Like most people, judges and law professors like to make people laugh. Yet if lawyers were simply looking for a laugh they would also quote Bob Hope, Bill Cosby, Johnny Carson, Jay Leno, Eddie Murphy, Phyllis Diller, Lucille Ball, David Letterman, George Carlin, Leslie Nielsen, Richard Pryor, Jerry Seinfeld, and Dave Barry. These comedians' one-liners rarely make their way into the case reporters. A few cases cite Woody Allen; although millions saw his films, relatively few cases cite his jokes.

In large part, Berra's appeal relates to what he says and how he says it. The "what" is not only funny but usually wise. Phil Pepe made the point well when he wrote:

> He never went beyond the eighth grade in school, yet he has a native intelligence, an innate wisdom and a wonderfully simple way of cutting through all the folderol and getting to the heart of a matter. When he says something that seems funny, it really isn't funny at all, it is wise. He expresses himself simply and naturally.[125]

The pearls of wisdom come packaged in unpretentious and penetrating tautologies that are snappy and easy to remember. They may be innocent but they are full of insight. As Judge Selya put it, "malapropisms, despite their semantic shortcomings, often describe the human condition with unerring accuracy."[126] How can anyone improve on déjà vu, ain't over, or fork in the road?

The reliance on Berra responds also to a powerful urge to demystify the law, to make it comprehensible not simply to the elites who write legal opinions and articles about them, but to the people who must live within the terms of the law. Law has a democratic character. By definition, law reflects a commitment to equal and fair treatment. The jury system represents society's commitment to the wisdom of the community and its value as a check on legal elites. Yet a tolerable system based on the rule of law must also preserve the people's understanding of, and commitment to, the law.

Often, law is really pretty simple, reflecting as it usually does, common sense approaches to recurring problems. The basic simplicity is, however, camouflaged by vocabulary that is not easily accessible and categories that are not very inviting. During the 1970s and 1980s, some suggested that law paid a price by being too esoteric. Law could be meaningful and profound without being remote. This critical insight has caused many to seek vehicles to communicate legal concepts more clearly and simply, and with a bit of a common touch.

What better way than through Yogi! He shows that wisdom can be conveyed in simple language that all can understand and remember. Ultimately, lawyers include Yogisms in part to communicate effectively legal concepts. We also include them because we like the face they put on the law and the voice they give it. Yogi's teachings are good-natured, not cynical, essentially optimistic, not defeatist. They are uttered by a seemingly common man who achieved greatness in his profession and success in his entrepreneurial pursuits, a living embodiment of the American dream. Like the law itself, Yogi may have occasionally tripped over a word or concept but the essential core is rich and wise and true. The law and Berra movement reminds us that the brooding bearded man in robes is not the law's only face and his words are not from its only voice. The law is also in Yogi's image and is spoken, too, in his inimitable fashion. Asked whether Don Mattingly had exceeded expectations, Yogi replied, "I'd say he's done more than that."[127] In a modest way, Yogi's teachings help law reach, perhaps exceed, our expectations for it.

IX. The Future Ain't What It Used to Be?

What does the future hold for Berra's influence on the law? A new generation of law students has grown up hearing its professors indoctrinate it in Berraisms. Just as schools of legal realists, legal process thinkers, and law and economics scholars of earlier days sent disciples into the academy who perpetuated their ways of thinking, today's law and Berra faculties are likely to have even greater influence through their proteges. Recent student works, somewhat tentatively perhaps, are beginning to imitate their mentors in citing Berra.[128] Today's students, born after Berra was already in the Hall of Fame, associate the great Yankee teams with the Joe Torre era. Their view of baseball may be blurred but their image of law is clear. They see the law as did Berra. They use his words in legal argument rather than those of Holmes, Cardozo, or even Judge Richard Posner. Accordingly it seems likely, to paraphrase Yogi, that his influence on the law will continue until it stops.

X. Conclusion (i.e., "It's Over")

Yogi's teachings have provided lawyers a new and rich tool to help convey legal concepts. There is every reason to believe that the movement is just beginning. Yogi may have said, regarding left field, that "it gets late early out there"[129]; there is every reason to believe that the law and Berra movement is still in its early phases. That is good news for the law and for those of us who write about it or reflect upon it. Its future, in part due to Yogi, is better than it used to be!

Mickey Mantle

by Timothy S. Hall*

In 1995, Mickey Mantle entered Baylor University Medical Center in Dallas, Texas, for a liver transplant. Mantle's liver had been ravaged by years of alcohol abuse both during his seasons with the Yankees and during his successful post-baseball career. Mantle had reason to be optimistic, however. In the years leading up to 1995, many members of his family had found help and effective treatment for alcoholism and drug dependency, and Mantle himself had been successfully treated at the Betty Ford Center. The liver transplant was a success. Unfortunately, after the operation, doctors discovered that Mantle's liver cancer had spread to his other organs, and he died only four months after his transplant.

Of course, the New York Yankees have had their share of careers cut short by tragic illnesses. Lou Gehrig died in 1941 at the age of 37 from Amyotrophic Lateral Sclerosis ("ALS"), the disease which now bears his name. Catfish Hunter also died of ALS, at the age of 53. Babe Ruth died of throat cancer at the age of 53, and Roger Maris died at 51 from lymphatic cancer. More recently, manager Joe Torre and pitching coach Mel Stottlemyre have had highly publicized health problems.

Around the same time as Mantle received his liver transplant, there was what seemed to be a flurry of successful, powerful men undergoing liver transplants. These included Mickey Mantle, Larry Hagman, Robert Casey and David Crosby. Hagman was the television star of such hits as *Dallas* and *I Dream of Jeanie*, Casey was Governor of Pennsylvania, and Crosby was a member of the influential rock groups The Byrds and Crosby, Stills and Nash. Three of the four men (Mantle, Hagman and Crosby) were also admitted alcoholics. This was unusual, and commanded national attention, because in a country where many people die every year because of a shortage of transplantable organs, all four of these men received livers far more quickly than the national average. On average, a liver transplant candidate in the US must wait for years before a suitable organ becomes available for transplant,[1] yet Hagman and Crosby received livers within six weeks;[2] Casey received a double heart-liver transplant within hours,[3] and Mantle received a new liver within 48 hours.[4] These cases resulted in a storm of criticism in the popular press, claiming that these men had been allowed to jump in front of the thousands of ordinary citizens waiting for transplants, and had received special treatment because of their celebrity and achievements. Even today, it is not difficult to find people who believe that Mickey Mantle got a new liver because he was Mickey Mantle, not because of objectively applied medical criteria.[5]

Mickey Mantle's liver transplant allows us to explore important ethical and legal issues of organ transplantation policy. First, to what extent should transplantation authorities consider individual characteristics of recipients when allocating scarce organs? Should Mantle's status as a celebrity and an American icon give him priority on the waiting list; or should he have been disqualified or moved down the list because his lifetime of alcoholism contributed to his need for a transplant?[6] Mantle's 48-hour wait after being placed on the liver transplant list raised questions as to whether he had been given priority because of his celebrity, and despite his alcoholism.[7]

Second, how should the limited supply of organs be distributed across the nation? Mantle received his organ so quickly in part because he was lucky to be at the right place at the right time. Although organ allocation policy is in part shaped by medical necessity,[8] there is room for policy debate as to whether organs should be allocated locally, regionally or nationally. Transplant policymakers must consider how to minimize the opportunities for rich or well-connected transplant candidates to manipulate the rules of organ transplantation programs without actually breaking the rules (often referred to as "gaming the system"). Critics of Mantle's transplant argued that his wealth enabled him to jump to the front of the organ allocation queue.

Finally, Mantle's organ transplant is notable in part because of his and his family's response to it. After receiving a new liver, Mantle established the Mickey Mantle Foundation to promote organ and tissue donation.[9] Increasing the supply of donated organs is the ideal way to increase the benefit to society from organ transplant technology; yet attempts to improve the rate of donation of organs have met with very limited success.

I. The Mantle Legacy

Mickey Charles Mantle was born on October 20, 1931 in Spavinaw, Oklahoma, and spent his formative years in nearby Commerce.[10] From Mickey's earliest childhood, his father Mutt (a former semi-pro baseball player) groomed Mickey for a career as a major league ballplayer.

In 1949, straight out of high school, Mickey joined the New York Yankees organization, playing for minor league teams in Independence, Kansas and Joplin, Missouri before joining the Yankees in 1951. From the beginning of his major league career, Mantle was hailed as the successor to Joe DiMaggio. Mantle lived up to that expectation, leading the team to 12 World Series appearances, and seven World Series pennants, during his first 14 seasons. Indeed, the presence of the Yankees in the World Series during Mantle's early years was so commonplace that his wife Merlyn expressed surprise when she realized that a World Series bonus was not part of his regular pay.

Mantle's mastery of the game is reflected in the numbers he compiled. He led the American League in home runs four times (1955, 1956, 1958 and 1960),[11] and still holds more World Series records than any other player, including those for walks (43), home runs (18), RBIs (40), runs scored (42), total bases (123) and, characteristically, strikeouts (54).[12]

Despite his success, Mantle was plagued by injuries throughout his career, leading many to wonder what he might have achieved if he had been able to stay healthy.[13] In fact, Mantle almost did not have a career at all. During his high school years, he was accidentally kicked in the shin and developed a bone infection. Although doctors considered amputation of Mantle's leg, the leg was saved from this by the new 'wonder drug' penicillin. Mantle was thus a medical pioneer both at the beginning and the end of his career.

After retiring from the Yankees in 1968, Mantle's drinking problem intensified, and his health began to decline. In 1994, following the example of two of his sons, Mantle entered the Betty Ford Clinic for treatment of alcoholism. His treatment was a great success; however, the damage to his liver was done. In 1995, a combination of cirrhosis of the liver, hepatitis C and liver cancer made a liver transplant necessary.[14] Mantle was hospitalized at Baylor University Medical Center and placed on the liver transplant waiting list on June 6, 1995. Mantle received a liver transplant on June 8, 1995. At first, the transplant appeared to give Mantle "another time at bat;"[15] however, within weeks following the operation, his liver cancer spread extensively throughout his body. Mickey Mantle died from metastatic liver cancer on August 13, 1995.

II. Mantle's Transplant: Legal and Ethical Issues

A. The American Organ Transplant System

Organ transplantation is a relatively new science, and the law finds it difficult to keep pace with rapid scientific advances. The first successful human organ transplant was a kidney transplant, in 1954.[16] The first successful liver transplant occurred in 1967,[17] and today, both procedures are common.[18] Unfortunately, however, organ donations have not kept pace with demand. In 2001, 24,090 transplant operations were performed,[19] but the number of patients on waiting lists for organs exceeded 78,500.[20] A new patient was placed on a waiting list every thirteen minutes,[21] and although new technologies permit patients awaiting transplantation to live longer, 6,238 patients died awaiting transplants.[22]

Until the late 1960s, organ transplantation was regulated by a mixture of inconsistent statutes and judicial decisions. In 1968, in an attempt to bring some uniformity to organ donation procedures, the National Conference on Uniform State Laws promulgated the Uniform Anatomical Gift Act (the "1968 UAGA"),[23] which was quickly adopted as law in all 50 states. The 1968 UAGA had the benefits of harmonizing previously divergent state laws, liberalizing the provisions for donation of organs and clarifying the procedures for making or revoking a legally valid gift of an organ. For all its benefits, however, the 1968 statute still left open several important questions. For example, the 1968 UAGA does not answer the question whether a donee may compensate a donor for a donated organ; nor does it address the question of allocating scarce organs among the many patients waiting for transplants.

After the the 1968 UAGA was promulgated and adopted, organ transplantation became much more common, and in 1987, the 1968 UAGA was revised in an attempt to increase the supply of donor organs.[24] The 1987 UAGA eliminated some of the remaining formalities associated with donation, such as the requirement that a donor card be witnessed by two persons, and the requirement that next of kin consent to the donation even if the donor signed a valid donor card. The 1987 UAGA also added mechanisms designed to foster organ donation, such as the requirement that all patients, upon admission to a hospital, must be asked whether the patient is an organ or tissue donor. The 1987 UAGA also provided explicitly that "[a] person may not knowingly, for valuable consideration, purchase or sell a [human organ]...."[25]

Unfortunately, the 1987 UAGA has not been adopted with the same uniformity as was the 1968 UAGA. As of 2002, only 22 states have adopted the 1987 UAGA, diluting the effect of its liberalizations of the rules surrounding organ donation.[26] However, it is doubtful whether even unanimous adoption of the 1987 UAGA would solve the shortage.

Since 1986, the number of individuals waiting for donor organs has risen dramatically. Clearly, more is required to bring the supply of donor organs in line with demand.[27]

In 1984, in part to answer some of the remaining questions surrounding the ethics of organ transplantation, Congress passed the National Organ Transplantation Act[28] ("NOTA"), 42 U.S.C. §§ 273-274e, which established local Organ Procurement Organizations ("OPOs") to oversee the distribution of donor organs and tissues. This is the system which was in place at the time of Mantle's liver transplant in 1995.

Under the OPO system as it existed in 1995, organs were distributed according to both need and location, but location predominated. Thus, a donor organ would be offered first within the local area in which it became available. Within that local area, the sickest patient who was an otherwise appropriate medical match would be given the organ.

For purposes of establishing priority for organ donation, patients were categorized depending on the severity of their illnesses.[29] Status 1 patients were patients sick enough to be in the intensive care unit; Status 2 patients were hospitalized but not sick enough to be confined to the ICU; Status 3 patients were not hospitalized, but were confined to their homes by their illnesses; and Status 4 patients were well enough to go about their daily lives. Within a local organ distribution area, organs would be allocated to the sickest individuals first. However, only if there were no appropriate medical matches, no matter their status, within the local area, would the organ then be offered regionally or nationally, and the organ would again be offered to the sickest patients first.

Because of geographic differences in the numbers of donors and patients, this policy led to vastly divergent waiting times in different OPO areas. This policy thus potentially led to the preference of relatively healthier local patients over sicker, but more remote, patients, even though most medical authorities support the proposition that, all things being equal, donated organs should go to the sickest patients first.[30]

The local-preference system led to controversy over Mantle's operation. When Mantle was placed on the waiting list on Tuesday, June 6, 1995, there were 141 people in the Dallas area on the list, and the average waiting time was 130 days.[31] Seen in this light, Mantle's 48-hour wait seems out of line with the experience of "ordinary" transplant patients, and concern about favoritism or line-jumping is understandable. However, Mantle was the only Status 2 patient on the list, and there were no Status 1 patients in the Dallas region.[32] These factors automatically gave Mantle preference for any matching organ that became available within the Dallas region. In fact, the average waiting time for a Status 2 patient on the same list was only three days.[33] Thus, Mantle's two-day wait until an organ was found does not seem so controversial.[34]

Even though Mantle's liver transplant was performed according to then-existing allocation rules, the local-preference system of organ allocation itself was subject to increasing criticism on the grounds that it failed to allocate organs to the patients most in need of them. In 1998, partially in response to the criticism of Mantle's rapid transplant, the federal government began attempts to reform the system of organ allocation in order to minimize the perceptions of unfairness. The Department of Health and Human Services proposed creation of a national registry and organ distribution system.[35] This proposal set off a new firestorm of debate, pitting the federal government's preference for a national system against state governments, which preferred to keep local organs for the benefit of local recipients.[36]

In the end, a compromise solution prevailed. Rather than a national registry, organ-sharing regions have been expanded to enhance the role of medical necessity in the allocation process. The Institutes of Medicine have recommended that livers be allocated within regions of at least nine million people, to minimize regional variations in waiting times and ensure that the available organs go to the sickest waiting patients.[37]

B. Should Alcoholics Get Livers?

Even if all interested parties agreed on a system for distribution of available organs, thorny ethical questions would still remain in the transplant arena. Of these, one persistent issue is whether to consider a patient's history of alcoholism in determining candidacy for organ transplantation. There is in fact substantial support in the medical and bioethics communities for taking alcoholism into account in making organ allocation decisions.[38] One stated reason is to prevent "waste" of scarce organs, which may occur if an organ is given to a patient who proceeds, through neglect or abuse, to inflict further damage on the new, healthy organ.[39]

Another, perhaps more controversial, justification for taking alcoholism into account arises out of the ethical principle of justice. According to this view, to place a person whose need for a transplant was at least in part self-inflicted on an equal standing with patients whose medical need arose purely by chance does an injustice to those who, through no fault of their own, will die or be caused further suffering and waiting time for lack of the organ given to the alcoholic.[40]

A patient's status as an alcoholic or drug addict may have an impact on other issues relevant to his suitability for a transplant. Transplant surgery requires substantial followup care and a lifelong treatment regimen to minimize the danger of rejection and other complications. A patient must be able to follow directions and to comply with a complex treatment protocol in order to stay healthy after a transplant. If a potential patient is impaired by chemical dependency, he or she may be less likely to comply with doctors' orders, and less likely to maintain good health.[41]

Mickey Mantle was given a new liver despite his decades-long history of alcoholism. In Mantle's case, as in every real-life case, however, there were multiple factors to consider. First, it is not clear that Mantle's alcoholism was the sole cause of his liver failure. Many alcoholics develop cirrhosis of the liver, and Mantle clearly suffered from this condition, but he also developed liver cancer, which was not necessarily a result of his years of drinking. Even if we accept that an individual's responsibility for his own choices requires us to take lifestyle factors such as alcoholism into account when allocating scarce organs, that result is surely strongest when the disease causing the need for transplantation is unequivocally the result of the voluntary behavior. It is not clear what impact a patient's years of self-destructive behavior should have on the allocation decision when the cause of the disease or injury is not certain. Moreover, at the time of his liver transplant, Mantle was successful in his recovery from alcoholism. Between 1993 and 1995, several members of Mantle's family, as well as Mantle himself, were treated at the Betty Ford Center.[42] Since Mantle was no longer drinking, and especially since members of his family had also completed treatment and were able to provide support for post-operative therapy and treatment, the decision to give Mantle a new liver does not, in hindsight, seem subject to serious criticism on the grounds of his alcoholism. [43]

C. Organ Allocation: Gaming the System?

There are a number of ways in which individuals or their physicians may favorably affect a patient's position in the organ allocation system and reduce the patient's waiting time.

Many aspects of patient listing for organ allocation are at the discretion of individual physicians. For example, survival rates for liver cancer patients after transplant are much lower than for other patients, because of the risk that the cancer will have spread to other organs prior to transplant, and will thus continue growing despite the new liver. Baylor University Medical Center, where Mantle's transplant was performed, had the highest success rate for liver cancer cases at the time, but some other surgeons do not perform them at all due to the decreased chances for survival. There is currently no national regulation governing the appropriateness of liver transplant in cancer cases; the availability of the surgery depends largely on the discretion of one's individual physician.[44] Thus, affluent patients who are able to shop around for a physician or transplant center with more liberal policies on transplantation in cases of liver cancer have an advantage over other patients who are unable to engage in such forum shopping. Such a patient might well make a conscious choice to travel to a clinic where transplant policies are known to be favorable to that patient's particular diagnosis, in order to gain a place on the waiting list. Although Mantle certainly was wealthy enough to seek multiple opinions as to treatment, there is no indication that he did so.

In addition to doctor-shopping, some patients choose to be wait-listed at multiple transplant centers in order to maximize the chances of finding an organ.[45] So long as transplant allocation policy continues to favor local patients over sicker, more distant patients, patients will have an incentive to sign up for waiting lists in as many OPO regions as possible. While the organ transplant system could theoretically ban such a practice by agreement or regulation, no such ban has been adopted. Again, however, there is nothing to suggest that Mantle was listed on multiple waiting lists.

Ultimately, any system of allocating scarce resources will create incentives to maximize one's own benefit from those resources, and organ allocation is no different. A better approach to solving the organ allocation crisis would be to eliminate the need for allocation in the first place; that is, to increase the supply of transplantable organs so that all patients who can benefit from transplant have the opportunity to do so.

D. Making the Pie Bigger: Increasing the Supply of Organs

The central paradox of organ transplantation in the United States is that the public professes overwhelming support for organ donation, yet very few individuals actually donate their organs for transplantation.[46] This section will explore some of the likely reasons for this chronic shortfall in availability of donor organs, and Mantle's potential impact on organ donation.

1. Autonomy and Altruism: Limits on Organ Supply

The principle of autonomy is a fundamental precept of bioethics. The principle of autonomy gives rise to the legal doctrine of informed consent, summarized in the famous statement by Supreme Court Justice Benjamin Cardozo that "[e]very human being of adult years and sound mind has a right to decide what shall be done with his own body."[47] In the context of organ donation, this means that the individual has a right to either consent or refuse to consent to the use of his organs for transplant purposes. Specific consent by an individual or his family is needed to donate organs for transplant. Unfortunately, few individuals sign organ donor cards; and in 1995, fewer than half of the family members asked to donate organs of a recently deceased relative consented to the donation.[48] Organ donation is treated as a gift by the donor, motivated by altruism, not as a resource to which others, or society in general, have rights in the absence of consent to donation. As a result of these principles, many usable organs are unavailable for transplant, costing many lives annually.

2. Reasons for Low Donation Rates
a. Religious Objections

Some individuals may refuse to donate their own or a deceased relative's organs out of a sense of religious duty. Although it is certainly possible that individuals could have doctrinal religious objections to donation,[49] all major religions of the world allow the donation of transplantable organs.[50] Some of the reluctance on religious grounds may be a result of misunderstanding of the tenets of one's own religion,[51] and if that is the case, then perhaps education is the best approach to alleviate this aspect of reluctance to donate.

b. Ignorance of Need/Ability to Donate

Many Americans simply are not aware of the vast undersupply of donated organs, or the magnitude of the waiting lists for organ transplants. Congress mandated increased educational activity in 1984 through NOTA, and this activity may have had some impact. Between 1985 and 1992, the number of Americans who had signed an organ donor card, expressing their willingness to donate at least some organs upon their death, increased from 16% to 33%.[52] However, the majority of Americans still had not chosen to indicate their willingness to donate, which suggests that further educational efforts are needed.

c. Distrust of System

Further reluctance to donate one's organs may arise because of distrust of the organ donation or health care system. Individuals may fear that if it is known to their physicians that they have given consent to organ donation, they may be regarded as less of a patient and more of a donor, and may not be provided appropriate treatment, or given as much chance of recovery, before organ harvesting takes place.[53] Media coverage of cases such as Mantle's, Hagman's, Casey's, Crosby's, and those of other well-known individuals who have received organs that the public feel were either undeserved or obtained through preferential treatment, may also diminish trust in the organ transplant system and willingness to participate as a donor.[54]

Finally, cultural attitudes and beliefs may drive unwillingness to donate. Commentators have noted that African-Americans, in particular, have a distrust of institutions and systems that may seem to be part of the racist majority American culture, including the health care system.[55] This distrust may extend to a reluctance to participate in the organ transplantation system by becoming donors, in spite of the fact that the need for donated organs in the African-American community is greater than that in society as a whole.[56]

d. Disinclination to Consider Death

The decision to become an organ donor requires that one seriously contemplate one's own mortality, as well as the unsettling facts about the disposition of one's body after death. Part of the undersupply of donor organs may be due to a reluctance to face mortality.[57]

e. Lack of Compensation

Traditionally in American health law, payment or other compensation for organ donors has been strictly prohibited.[58] Although ethically grounded in a desire to avoid coercion in the decision-making process, and to avoid the appearance of trafficking in body parts, this strict prohibition has been criticized on several grounds,[59] and is beginning to relax. Although there is no sign as yet of a free market in human organs, commentators and pilot programs have begun to explore the ethically permissible limitations of financial incentives for organ donation.

3. Proposals to Increase Donation
a. Education

Education about the need for donated organs has been shown to increase the frequency with which study respondents express a willingness to donate their own organs or those of a deceased relative.[60] Educational efforts to date have proven insufficient to significantly increase the supply of donated organs, however.

b. Reduction in Burden to Donor

Many states have experimented with programs to make it easier to express one's wish to become an organ donor. In many states, it is now routine to express such a preference on one's driver's license or on a card obtained at the same time one obtains a driver's license.[61] These and other programs designed to make it easier to express a willingness to donate have made some progress in increasing the supply of organs, but by no means have they materially reduced the shortage of available organs for transplant. Clearly, while such programs are valuable, more aggressive policies and programs are needed to further increase the supply.

c. Presumed Consent/Mandated Choice

Many European countries have implemented presumed consent laws in an attempt to increase the supply of transplantable organs.[62] Under a presumed consent system, explicit consent to organ donation is no longer required before organs can be transplanted. Although these laws have resulted in higher rates of organ donation than in the United States, the supply of organs still lags behind demand. In part, this lag may be due to the fact that physicians in some countries with presumed consent laws still seek consent of the family of a deceased patient, either because such consent is required by law, as in France, or as a matter of custom, as in Belgium.[63]

Despite having demonstrated some success in improving donation rates where it has been implemented, there is not widespread support for presumed consent in the United States. American values of individualism and autonomy, combined with criticism that a presumed consent rule may have the effect of forcing unwilling individuals to become organ donors, limit the political appeal of such a system. In addition, the Ethics Committee of UNOS has considered and rejected the implementation of presumed consent in the United States.[64]

A less radical alternative to presumed consent is mandated choice, sometimes called Required Response.[65] Under this system, individuals would be required to choose whether to consent to organ donation or not. This choice would be legally binding, and posthumous consent of family members would not be necessary, unless an individual chose to delegate the decision to his family to be made after his death. However, at least one commentator notes that anecdotal evidence suggests that a system of mandated choice may be ineffective, citing a report that 80% of those asked to choose chose not to become organ donors.[66]

d. Compensation

Compensation to an individual organ donor or his family has traditionally been prohibited in the American transplant community. Indeed, the federal law governing organ procurement specifically prohibits any "valuable consideration" being given in exchange for a human organ.[67] Recently, however, several commentators and a few legislators have proposed limited financial incentives for organ donors or their families, and it seems likely that the trend toward limited financial incentives will continue. In a sign of the newfound respectability of financial incentives, the American Medical Association has recommended that further study of such incentives for organ donation be conducted, with a view to increasing the supply of transplantable organs.[68]

Some commentators have proposed various market-driven initiatives to provide incentives for organ donation. These vary from a competitive, future delivery market for organs[69] to a quasi-insurance scheme of pooled risk-sharing[70] to a system of tax credits for organ donors,[71] among other proposals. At least one commentator has suggested that incentives may be a better way to increase organ donation in the African-American community, based on survey data.[72]

Pennsylvania has recently passed a law providing that the state may contribute to organ donors' burial expenses.[73] The state contribution is minimal (the law provides for a maximum of $3000, but the practice has been contributions of approximately $300)[74] and is paid directly to the funeral home rather than to the family of the deceased, to minimize problems of unjust enrichment or coercion. Nonetheless, this payment has been subject to criticism. Although the concept of partial reimbursement of organ donors' expenses was recently approved by a committee of the American Society of Transplant Surgeons, several members of that committee disagreed with the proposal, arguing that even this indirect compensation violated the "spirit of pure altruism" that is the hallmark of American organ donation.[75]

e. Technology

Medical technology, which created the possibility of organ transplantation in the first place, may eventually help to solve the problem of undersupply of organs. Current research on stem cell lines and therapeutic cloning techniques is revealing the theoreti-cal possibility of artificially-grown organs to replace damaged or diseased organs.[76]

Another technological advance which may increase the number of organs available for transplant is the increasing use of live-donor transplant procedures. While live-donor procedures are most common in kidney transplants, because healthy adults can live with one kidney with minimal or no health consequences, techniques for live-donor liver transplants have made it possible to perform partial liver transplants.[77] In 2001, ten percent of all liver transplants performed were live-donor transplants.[78] To the extent that partial-liver transplants can be made more common, this technique seems to have the potential for greatly improving the availability of transplant organs. However, the procedures are not without risk for the donor, and some ethicists have concerns about whether family members might feel undue pressure to donate organs under such circumstances.[79]

High-tech techniques for increasing the organ supply hold much potential, but unfortunately no immediate promise of remedying the undersupply of organs. If such techniques can be made safe and cost-effective, they may someday significantly supplement or replace the need for human donors.[80] While such an outcome is desir-able, it is unfortunately not imminent. Much more basic research and experimenta-tion is needed before such organs become clinically viable, and thus for the foresee-able future, legal and policy development must, while supporting research, focus primarily on increasing the pool of human donors as the best mechanism to alleviate the shortage.

4. The Mantle Foundation

After his liver transplant, but before his death mere months later, Mickey Mantle established the Mantle Foundation to increase public awareness of the need for donor organs and tissue, and to increase the supply of such organs to match demand lev-els.[81] The Mantle Foundation espouses the philosophy that the main barriers to in-creased organ donation are lack of knowledge of the undersupply of donor organs and the difficulty of the decision-making process. As stated on the Foundation's web site, "we believe that the American public will embrace organ and tissue donation if the decision-making opportunity and the information is made more readily available. Accessability [sic] and education are the keys."[82] In order to further the goals of edu-cating the public on the need for organ donation and to give people an opportunity to make the decision to become an organ donor, the Foundation engages in "continu-ous public distribution of information relevant to organ and tissue donation," and distribution of donor cards which indicate the bearer's desire to become an organ donor upon his death.

It is unclear exactly what impact the Mantle Foundation has had on the prevalence of organ donation since its establishment in 1995. However, it is clear that the association of a famous name with a disease can raise the profile of that disease, put a human face on the suffering it causes, and help educate the public about its impact. Many Ameri-cans infected with the HIV virus were marginalized and forgotten until basketball hero Magic Johnson became infected and had the courage to share his story.[83] Mantle's fellow Yankee Lou Gehrig gave a human face and a name to Amyotrophic Lateral Sclerosis ("ALS"), the disease popularly known as "Lou Gehrig's Disease."[84] Perhaps Mantle will perform the same consciousness-raising function for organ and tissue donation, inspir-ing millions to "join Mickey's Team."[85]

III. Conclusion

Mickey Mantle's impact on the American organ donation system was substantial for many reasons. His brilliant career with the Yankees gave his case substantial media coverage and instant name recognition that would not have existed for many other transplant recipients, and this media attention focused public debate in several ways. Public debate about the justice of vastly differential waiting list times for organ transplants has led to reforms in the organ transplant system. Public debate about the appropriate consideration of individual characteristics of transplant candidates is an ongoing ethical discussion. The Mantle Foundation is a strong voice advocating for increased organ donation, potentially leading to better outcomes for many transplant candidates.

It is doubtful whether any other transplant case could have had quite the impact of Mickey Mantle's. His celebrity and recognizability as a public figure gave his case public interest and exposure. Because of the iconic status of The Mick, bioethical debates over liver allocation have been extended from academic conferences to countless ballfields, dinner tables and sports pages throughout the country, raising public awareness of a serious public health issue. Finally, Mickey's response to the transplant and the surrounding controversy, the establishment of the Mantle Foundation, allows the impact of his celebrity to continue to influence the organ transplant system and to raise the profile of organ and tissue donation programs. If the supply of donor organs can be increased, such a change will almost certainly have a direct impact on the length of transplant waiting lists and the quality of life for countless transplant candidates. Although the problem of low donation rates is recognized as one of the more difficult problems in organ transplantation, it is also the area in which change could have the greatest impact, and it is here that the greatest legacy of Mickey Mantle is, even after his death, still being written.

George Steinbrenner, Mickey Mantle, and Richard Nixon at Billy Martin's funeral. Both Steinbrenner and Nixon received presidential pardons for Watergate-related activities. Photo © Bettmann/CORBIS.

George Steinbrenner

by Robert N. Strassfeld*

> "I won't be active in the day-to-day operations of the club at all. I can't spread myself too thin. I've got enough headaches with the shipping company."
>
> George Steinbrenner, January 3, 1973 at news conference
> announcing purchase of the New York Yankees

Before the Bronx Bombers, there were boats. I am not referring here to the "Yankee Clipper," Joe DiMaggio, though as a son of a fisherman born in a small fishing community on the Northern California coast, boats figured large in his life, even before he acquired the nickname. Fortunately for baseball history, Joltin' Joe, who confessed to a tendency toward seasickness, preferred dry land and baseball to the life on the waters that his father had planned for him, as did his brothers Vincent and Dominic.[1] Nor am I referring to the second "Yankee Clipper," George Steinbrenner, though this chapter is about him.[2] Steinbrenner, of course, earned the sobriquet not through his prowess with bat and glove or his dignity on the field, but due to his periodic fixation with Yankee players' hair length. Outfielder Oscar Gamble hung the nickname on him after Manager Billy Martin sent him off to be shorn of his prodigious Afro.[3] The boats that concern us are Great Lakes freighters and ore-boats. For, like other baseball owners, George Steinbrenner had a career before baseball ownership. It was there, dealing with the "headaches with the shipping company," that he amassed the resources to purchase a controlling, and ultimately majority, share of the Yankees and that he developed his management style. It was also there that he had the first of his many experiences with law and litigation.

This chapter explores some of those early encounters with law. Baseball, for good and for bad, has always involved more than players, coaches, and managers. Owners have had an indelible impact on the fates of their teams and on baseball history. Those owners inevitably have had interests and experiences outside baseball that shaped their behavior as team owners. Sometimes, the impact of those outside interests has been direct and obvious. Perhaps most notoriously, Boston Red Sox owner Harry Frazee's bad investments in Broadway musicals led to the 1920 sale of Babe Ruth to the Yankees that changed the destinies of both teams.[4] But outside interests have influenced owner behavior in less infamous ways. For instance, Yankee owner Colonel Jacob Ruppert, brewer of Ruppert Knickerbocker beer, sought unsuccessfully to change the team's name to the Knickerbockers.[5] Fortunately, editorial opposition to the name change spared us such barbarities as *Pride of the Knickerbockers*. And who is to say that the Columbia Broadcasting System's mediocrity during its decade of Yankee ownership did not somehow infect the team?[6] Judging by the Yankee record during this period, it certainly did not help.

Perhaps, then, there is something to be learned from George Steinbrenner's experiences in the shipping industry that might shed light on his performance as a Yankees owner. If nothing else, there may be a good story or two to tell.

I. Early Years: From Bay Village to Kinsman

A. Childhood and Family Tradition[7]

George Steinbrenner, III was born on July 4, 1930, in Rocky River, Ohio, now a western suburb of Cleveland. Raised in the nearby town of Bay Village, Steinbrenner may hold the distinction of being that community's most famous resident. He has serious competition for that title, however, in Dr. Sam Sheppard, whose trials and eventual acquittal for the murder of his wife, Marilyn, made Supreme Court history and launched the career of F. Lee Bailey.[8] Sheppard's claim is a strong one. Steinbrenner, after all, only figured as a bit character, always portrayed from the rear, in the *Seinfeld* television show, while the Sheppard case inspired its own television series, *The Fugitive*. However ranked, he certainly has cast a giant shadow in Northeast Ohio and beyond.

Steinbrenner was born to the shipping industry. His Great-Great-Grandfather, Philip Minch, had found his way upon arrival in the United States from Germany to Vermillion, Ohio along the shores of Lake Erie. There he founded Minch Transit Company and operated freighters on the Great Lakes. The company, eventually renamed the Kinsman Marine Transit Company and its headquarters moved east to Cleveland, remained a family legacy, with the presidency of the company passing down through the generations of Steinbrenner's ancestors. In turn, Steinbrenner's father, Henry G. Steinbrenner, became company President, and in time, his son's employer.

Henry Steinbrenner was, by all accounts, stern, demanding, and hard, or perhaps impossible, to please. He was also somewhat larger than life and therefore a hard act to follow. The figure of Henry Steinbrenner has certainly loomed in the background throughout George's life. By George Steinbrenner's own accounts, his father instilled in him qualities of toughness and competitiveness. He encouraged entrepreneurship by giving George chickens rather than an allowance. It was up to George to turn those chickens into spending money by going into the egg business.

The family sent George off to Culver Military Academy in Indiana when he reached the age of fourteen. At Culver, he was for much of the time a more serious athlete than scholar, though he did manage to salvage his academic record in his senior year. Steinbrenner, seemingly forever running in his father's footsteps, ran track. Henry Steinbrenner, running track at that athletic powerhouse MIT, had been a national champion in the 220-yard low hurdles.[9] George also played basketball and football.

B. A Coaching Career Cut Short

Graduation from Culver in 1948 was followed by Williams College in Western Massachusetts. At Williams, Steinbrenner continued to run track and, in his senior year, played football. A stint in the Air Force followed graduation from Williams. There, Steinbrenner got his first taste of coaching, as coach of the Lockbourne Air Force Base basketball and baseball teams. Steinbrenner enjoyed coaching and, upon, completion of his enlistment, he enrolled in the masters in physical education program at Ohio State University.

The following year, 1955, the great football coach Lou Saban hired him as an assistant coach for the Northwestern University football team. At Northwestern, Steinbrenner had his first taste of the firing of coaches. After a winless season, Northwestern fired Saban and the entire coaching staff, including Steinbrenner. Steinbrenner landed on his feet as the backfield coach for the Purdue Boilermakers, coaching Len Dawson in his senior year.

II. Kinsman: Laying Waste to the City of Buffalo[10]

While Steinbrenner enjoyed coaching, he could not escape the family legacy. The small, independent Great Lakes shipping companies were struggling during the 1950s in the face of competition from the steel companies' own fleets. Bending to family pressure, Steinbrenner returned to Cleveland in 1957 to become Treasurer and Vice-President of Kinsman. American torts professors are glad that he did.

A. *Petitions of Kinsman Transit*: A Torts Student's Nightmare

In 1964 Judge Henry Friendly of the United States Court of Appeals for the Second Circuit concluded that George Steinbrenner, Treasurer and Vice-President of Kinsman Marine Transit, did not know a whole lot about boats.[11] While, for reasons discussed below, Kinsman actually welcomed this ruling, one might also see Judge Friendly as just an early critic of George Steinbrenner.

Critics there have been aplenty. Columnist George Will, for example, wrote a Newsweek column describing Steinbrenner under the title, "A One-Man Error Machine."[12] The normally mild-mannered dean of sportswriters Red Smith called him "the fuehrer of the Yankees." Not to be outdone, sportswriter Thom Green has called him "a tyrant, heartless and cold," and suggested that he deserved a public flogging.[13] As early as 1962, the Cleveland Press, admittedly not one of Steinbrenner's favorite newspapers, declared him "congenitally unsuited to be in the sporting world."[14] Recently, fellow owner Larry Dolan identified him as "a large part of [baseball's] problem."[15] Yankee fans have sometimes shared this hostility. When former Yankee star Reggie Jackson, whom Steinbrenner had let slip away through free-agency, homered upon his return to Yankee Stadium in a California Angels' uniform, the fans showed their disdain by chanting "Steinbrenner sucks."[16] Perhaps most famously, Billy Martin, shortly before his first firing as the Yankee manager (four more firings would follow), in describing Jackson and Steinbrenner in order opined, "One's a born liar and the other's convicted."[17] Hostility to Steinbrenner has supported a small publishing industry, producing such works as Bill Madden's and Moss Klein's *Damned Yankees*,[18] and Brandon Toropov's *101 Reasons to Hate George Steinbrenner*.[19]

Those of us who teach torts, the course on accident law, hold a dissenting view. We are grateful to Steinbrenner for his part in the *Kinsman Transit* case ("*Kinsman*"), now a classic part of the proximate cause canon. Before *Kinsman*, the best torts teachers could do when reaching for the bizarre with which to teach proximate cause principles was the flaming rat case, *United Novelty Co. v. Daniels.*[20] While a classic in its own right, *United Novelty* pales before *Kinsman* as an adventure in the Rube Goldbergesque world of proximate cause.

B. A Short Torts Primer Viewed through Bill Buckner's Legs

A brief overview of a negligence claim will help to explain why *Kinsman* is so marvelous a case. While courts and torts scholars have offered various configurations of a plaintiff's prima facie negligence case, or, in other words, what a plaintiff must show in order to prevail in a negligence claim, a serviceable version goes as follows: A plaintiff must show that a defendant acted unreasonably, thereby causing plaintiff's injury under circumstances where the defendant had an obligation to behave reasonably toward the plaintiff. As this description suggests, part of plaintiff's case involves showing causation. To the delight of torts teachers, and the agony of our students, tort law speaks of two aspects of causation: factual cause and proximate cause.

Proximate cause is arguably the most confusing area of tort law, although in the hands of a skillful torts teacher all areas can be made maddeningly confusing. To begin with, the name is misleading. Proximity only sometimes plays a role, and the doctrine of proximate cause is not really about causation at all, but about responsibility. As one wag has put it, "Factual causation asks 'who dunnit?' Proximate cause asks 'who cares?' "[21] In other words, are there reasons that this defendant should not be held legally accountable for harms that she clearly caused? Such reasons may include remoteness in time or space between the negligent act and the injury; the intervening acts of other persons or fortuitous natural events; or the unforseeability or downright bizarre character of the accident. In the old parable, "for want of a nail a kingdom was lost," proximate cause poses the question whether we should hold the blacksmith legally responsible.

A baseball example might help to clarify the concept. As any Bostonian and most other baseball fans know, owner Harry Frazee unleashed the Curse of the Bambino on the Boston Red Sox when he sold Babe Ruth to the Yankees, causing a world-championship famine for the Sox ever since. True Red Sox fans have no doubt that Frazee and this curse caused the Sox to lose the 1986 World Series when Mookie Wilson's easy groundball went between Bill Buckner's legs costing the Sox the critical game six and, ultimately, the Series.

The question remains: was Frazee not only the factual cause, but also the proximate cause? Should he be held responsible? After all, a variety of other intervening causes contributed to the loss. Bob Stanley's wild pitch put the winning run at third, Manager John McNamara chose to keep the badly hobbled Buckner at first in the bottom of the tenth instead of bringing in Dave Stapleton as a defensive substitute, and Buckner did let the ball go between his legs.

Any New Englander would respond: "Ask me a hard [pronounced hahd] one." Of course Frazee is responsible for every disaster that the Red Sox, and the City of Boston for that matter, have suffered ever since. Indeed, were you to visit the bars or coffeehouses near Harvard (pronounced Hahved) Square, you would doubtless encounter some postmodernist Sox fan, who, unshackled from ordinary chronological notions of causation would also blame the Boston Massacre on Frazee. I am, of course, referring to the First Boston Massacre, the one in March 1770 when a group of harassed British soldiers opened fire on the crowd killing Crispus Attucks and four other Bostonians, leading ultimately to the "shot heard round the world," the first shot of the Revolutionary War on the Lexington Green. Obviously, the Second Boston Massacre, which took place in the fall of 1978 culminating at Fenway Park on October 2, in Bucky Dent's "shot heard round the American League," was Frazee's fault.

C. Buffalo 1959

Kinsman Transit's importance does not lie in any rule of law that emerged from that case. While courts and scholars sometimes cite the court's ruling for the proposition that in order for a plaintiff to recover for a tortious harm the extent of her harm need not be foreseeable so long as the kind of harm is, the distinction drawn by the court between extent and kind of harm is murky and hard to implement. *Kinsman's* proximate cause analysis of its own facts is borderline incomprehensible, in part because of the court's rather forced analysis of forseeability, and it is not easily reconciled with a second case that emerged from the same events, also named *Petitions of Kinsman Transit Co.* (*Kinsman II*).[22] Rather, torts teachers have embraced it for its magnificent and near-impossible facts. It is the sort of story that one could not make up.

The setting for the events that produced *Kinsman* is the Buffalo River, which zigs and zags tortuously past grain elevators, factories, and docks as it makes it way to Lake Erie. During the winter months, when Great Lakes shipping comes to a halt, freighters tie up on the Buffalo River, often warehousing cargo in their holds. There, they wait out the winter without power and with only a solitary shipkeeper aboard. During the winter of 1958–59, a number of Kinsman boats were in Buffalo, including the MacGilvray Shiras. On January 21, 1959, the Shiras was docked at the Concrete Elevator, which was operated by the Continental Grain Company on the river's south bank approximately four miles upstream from the mouth of the river.

During the week before January 21, 1959, Buffalo experienced brutal weather. On Friday, January 16, snow began to fall, and it did not let up until Sunday night. By Friday afternoon, six inches had fallen, but the storm grew in intensity over the weekend.[23] The following day, the *Buffalo Evening News* reported that "A white fury of wind-blown snow squalls swept over Western New York today as a vicious storm neared the end of its first 24 hours. More of the same is due the rest of the weekend."[24] A heavy blanket of snow forced major thoroughfares to close. Buffalo's Sunday night respite was brief. An additional two to five inches fell on Monday, and the snow continued through Tuesday.

When the weather changed on Wednesday, it did not improve matters. A sudden thaw, coupled with heavy rains, melted much of the accumulated snow and swelled Buffalo's rivers, while gale-force winds battered the city. That day, the sports pages announced that baseball salaries in 1959 would reach "staggering proportions." Baseball's total payroll, sportswriter John Kuenster predicted, would reach the unheard of sum of $8,000,000, an amount that would be the rough equivalent of $47,000,000 in 2001 dollars (an amount that is less than most individual teams' payrolls in 2002).[25] Despite anticipated pay cuts for Whitey Ford and Yogi Berra because of their off years in 1958, the Yankees' payroll was expected to come in at $800,000, twice the amount Colonel Ruppert had paid to buy the team in 1915.[26] However ominous the news for baseball, the immediate threat to Buffalo was palpable. Portions of South Buffalo were already under water Wednesday afternoon, and the weatherman predicted worsening flash-floods. As if the gods were mocking the city, moviemaker Cecil B. DeMille died that day, leaving no one to part the floodwaters.[27]

During the evening of January 21, the current on the Buffalo River increased as ice jams on the river and its tributary, Cazenovia Creek, broke up. The rushing water, carrying large ice floes, beat against those portions of the Shiras that extended beyond the dock. For approximately forty minutes, as the ice and debris accumulated, the shipkeeper did nothing to ready the anchors in case the Shiras broke lose from the dock. Finally, around 10:40 P.M. precisely that happened. The lines gave way, and a "deadman," driven into the ground to hold the number one mooring cable, pulled out of the ground. The shipkeeper's belated efforts to lower the anchors were ineffectual and the Shiras began its voyage, pilotless, stern-first, and without power down the Buffalo River. A trial judge would later find that timely release of the anchors would probably have stopped the boat, or at least slowed it sufficiently to have avoided the mayhem that followed.

Even without the anchors, there was every chance that the Shiras, a 425 foot long boat, would not get very far down the narrow river before it swung around enough to get caught on one of the river's hairpin turns. The river, after all, was in many places less than 200 feet wide. Shipmasters generally agree that the Buffalo River is one of the trickiest stretches of navigable water in the Great Lakes area. Typically, traveling the river requires the assistance of two tugboats, one in front and one in back, along with a skillful Captain and a full and alert crew. Had the Shiras gotten caught on the riverbeds, it would have dammed the river at that point causing upstream flooding. But had it done so, Kinsman would have been, at best, an obscure admiralty case, and you would not be reading this story.

Instead, the miraculous, and to the mind of torts teachers the truly wonderful, occurred. The Shiras raced backwards and unguided down the twisty river, cleanly navigating the 90-degree turn just below the Concrete Elevator. It negotiated two more 90-degree turns without difficulty. Then it came to the docks of the Lake and Rail Elevator. There, silently awaiting its fate, was another boat, the newer and bigger (it was 525 feet long) Michael K. Tewksbury, owned by the Midland Steamship Line. Around 11:00 P.M. the 6,700-ton Shiras collided with the Tewksbury. The force of the collision caused the Tewksbury's lines to give way. No one would drop anchor on the Tewksbury either, since its shipkeeper had left his post earlier that day to watch television at his girlfriend's house.

One or both boats ricocheted into the Steamer Drucken-Miller, which was moored across river from the Tewksbury. Though damaged by the collision, that boat did not join the Shiras and the Tewksbury in their voyage downstream. Downriver several obstacles awaited. In addition to a number of boats docked along the river, the Michigan Avenue lift bridge stood three miles downriver from the Concrete Elevator. Both boats were now headed its way stern-first. With the current moving rapidly this would not be "a three hour tour."[28] The race was on.

Within minutes of the Shiras' coming adrift, a Continental Elevator employee notified the Coast Guard. They in turn called the Buffalo River fire station that housed its fireboat under the shadow of the Michigan Avenue Bridge. By 10:48, the fire station crew had alerted the bridge tenders that trouble might be headed their way. Within a few minutes of the Shiras' collision with the Tewksbury, a watchman at the Lake and Rail Elevator made a call to the bridge crew to alert them that now two derelict boats were headed toward them. The bridge could be raised to full elevation in a mere two minutes and ten seconds, clearing the path downriver for the two "ghost ships." Inexplicably, almost half an hour passed before the bridge crew, consisting of an operator and two tenders began to raise the bridge. The original newspaper accounts portrayed the bridge crew in heroic terms. Judge Friendly's opinion in *Kinsman* strongly suggests a different possibility. Acknowledging conflicting testimony, Judge Friendly nevertheless found that the inference was strong that the bridge operator whose shift was slated to end at 11:00 had missed the first call because he was at a bar drinking rather than at his post. Apparently, he had no girlfriend to watch television with. The shift-change at eleven complicated matters further, and the opinion suggests that the late-shift operator may have arrived a few minutes late.

Upstream, the boats still faced the Ohio Street Bend, described as "the most hazardous [bend] ship captains anywhere on the Lakes are called on to make."[29] Surely, here the boats would ground themselves and end their voyage. Yet, in a "feat of navigation that is the envy of veteran skippers," the two boats danced through the bend.[30] As if waved on by the third base coach, they were headed home, and the only remaining question was whether or not the catcher would be blocking the plate. Like Willie Randolph in the 1980 American League Championship Series against the Royals, they should have stopped at third.

Shortly before 11:17 P.M. the crew finally started lifting the bridge as they peered into the darkness knowing that two heavy freighters were headed their way. The bridge had risen perhaps twenty feet when the lead boat, the 10,000-ton Tewksbury came into view out of the blackness of that miserable night. The instinct for self-preservation overcame any for heroism, and the crew ran from the bridge as the Tewksbury ploughed into it at 11:17. Like Pete Rose crashing into Ray Fosse to end the 1970 All-Star game, nothing good was going to come of this collision.[31] Witnesses from the firehouse described an enormous crash. Charles Halloran, assistant engineer for the fireboat, Edward M. Cotter, which was moored by the bridge, compared the noise to "an auto accident magnified a million times."[32] And witnesses said that the pyrotechnics from metal scraping against metal reminded them of the Fourth of July.[33]

The middle span of the bridge collapsed immediately, trapping the Tewksberry under steel cables and twisted metal girders. Within minutes, the 180-foot-tall south tower of the bridge came crashing down. At 7:45 the next morning, the weakened north tower was toppled by gale-force winds, completing the destruction of the bridge. When it came down, the north tower crushed the roof of Connelly Brothers ship chandlers shop and damaged the fire station. The north tower, the boats, and ice initially trapped the fireboat. Eventually freed, the fireboat was stuck downstream of the bridge until the river could be made navigable. City officials estimated that replacing the bridge, which was one of only two access routes from Buffalo to the industrial facilities and homes in South Buffalo, would cost $5 million.

In addition to the destruction of the bridge, the damage to the boats and their cargoes, and the harm to the buildings that broke the north tower's fall, further mayhem ensued. Two members of the bridge crew were hurt and required hospitalization. A large cable pulley, thrown nearly 100 feet when the bridge collapsed, crushed a car. The bridge's collapse broke a water main cutting off water to some of the factories that lined the river, including General Mills' flour and cereal plant, the largest of its kind in the world, which was forced to shut down operations until a by-pass line could be established. If no water was a problem for some facilities, too much water plagued others. The Tewksberry's progress ended under the bridge. Its bow rested against Cargo Carriers' boat, the Merton E. Farr. The two boats, together with the Shiras and the debris from the bridge, dammed the river nearly completely, causing flooding and ice floes all the way upriver to the Concrete Elevator. Republic Steel was forced to shut down its South Buffalo steel mill, and other elevators and factories similarly suffered because of the flooding and water main break. Access to South Buffalo was made more difficult because of the elimination of the bridge route. Eventually, even the Buffalo Transit Company would join the litigation frenzy, asserting that loss of the bridge adversely affected their bus routes. The Transit Company lost.

Others would sue, as well. Cargill Company's boat, the Donald B. Gillies, was stuck downstream of the bridge with a cargo of wheat that it was under contract to deliver upriver. It sued for the cost of purchasing replacement wheat to fulfill the contract. The S.S. Merton, which had been pulled away from the dock when the Tewksberry ran into it, was only partially unloaded when the accident occurred. An ice jam filled the area between the Merton and the dock. Because the fireboat and the tugs usually used to break ice jams were on the Lake side of the bridge, unable to come upstream past the wreckage, Cargo Carriers had to rent special equipment to unload the boat.

Clearing the wreckage proved to be harder than initially hoped. Workers did not free the Tewksberry until January 31. The river was not navigable until March 13, nearly two months after the accident. Needless to say, the lawyers fared well.

The cases themselves are somewhat anticlimactic. As described above, the legal analysis is far less interesting than the facts. Essentially, Kinsman and the Continental Grain Company were found to be negligent for letting the Shiras loose on the river. The city was negligent for failing to raise the bridge in time. In *Kinsman I* the court held that there was proximate cause between the negligent acts and the harms suffered by the various plaintiffs before it. In *Kinsman II* the court refused to extend proximate cause to the economic harms suffered by Cargill for its undelivered grain downstream of the bridge. It also denied recovery to Cargo Carriers for the economic harms it suffered when it incurred extra costs to unload its boat (as promised the facts are more interesting than the law).

The proximate cause issues in the case obviously arose because of the highly unlikely chain of events that were necessary to produce the disaster that occurred that January night. Even with hindsight, it seems quite extraordinary that the two derelict boats could have navigated the river and done the damage that they did. Yet, remarkably, this was not the first time that a derelict boat had somehow managed to beat the odds and make its way downstream. While old Buffalo shipmasters could not quite remember when it had occurred (it was, in fact, 1916), they retold the story of another freighter that had come loose on the river, long ago. That boat also navigated the difficult twists and turns of the river. Because that time the bridge crews raised the bridges (at the time there was a second bridge at Ohio Avenue) in plenty of time for the renegade boat to pass harmlessly under, the boat made its way to the river's mouth without ravaging the city. But beyond the Michigan Avenue Bridge, it liberated (and damaged) a couple of other boats, which then joined it in its journey to the river's mouth. The derelict boat on that occasion, the Anna C. Minch—yes, named for George Steinbrenner's grandmother—was, of course, also a Kinsman boat.[34] Thus, in January 1959, Steinbrenner once again followed in the footsteps of his ancestors. This time, however, he outdid them all.

So far, lost in my account is the reason that Judge Friendly denigrated George Steinbrenner's knowledge of boats, thereby enshrining him in tort law and lore. Again, the legal issues are less interesting than the facts. The finding was necessitated by a particular admiralty law doctrine that sometimes limits the liability of ship owners for the negligent acts of their agents and by the role that Steinbrenner played in bringing the Shiras and the Tewksberry together. The Limitation Act says that where a ship does damage without the "privity or knowledge" of her owner, the owner's liability will be limited to the value of the ship and its cargo after the accident.[35] An owner generally cannot, in other words, be liable on the basis of its employee's negligence beyond that limit. Whether or not there is privity or knowledge depends, in turn, on whether or not someone high enough in the hierarchy of the company either knew of the negligent handling of the ship or boat, or was negligent in his own right.

On December 8–12, 1958, George Steinbrenner was in Buffalo working out plans for the Shiras to be moored at the Continental Elevator to be unloaded and reloaded. He or his father delegated to Captain Davies, who had been the boat's master that season, the task of dealing with the boat's mooring and loading problems. Certainly, as Vice-President and Treasurer of the company, Steinbrenner was sufficiently high up in the hierarchy to defeat the statute's limitation of liability if he either had knowledge of Captain Davies' negligence in handling the mooring operation, or if he was himself negligent in turning that task over to Davies. The court, however, emphasized Steinbrenner's lack of knowledge about boats generally, and about the specifics of the mooring operation—he left for vacation in Florida after December 12, and did not return to Buffalo until after the accident. The court emphasized his relative youth and that he was "without maritime studies or experience."[36] The court further found that Steinbrenner did not know any of the specifics of the mooring operation. Finally, though it pointedly described Captain Davies as the "*former* master" of the Shiras, it also concluded that it was appropriate for Steinbrenner to delegate supervision of mooring to Davies, who was "more competent to oversee it than [Steinbrenner] was."[37] Notwithstanding the court's not altogether justified devaluing of his knowledge, Steinbrenner must have thought the finding was a welcome one, since it saved Kinsman much money.

George Steinbrenner's generosity to his friends and to a wide range of charities is well known. Most recently, Jason Giambi has been the beneficiary of his largesse. Torts teachers, if not the city of Buffalo, are also lucky for the great gift that Steinbrenner has bestowed upon us.

III. American Ship: Learning Size (and Money) Matters and "Creeping" toward Watergate Woes

A. Conquering the Great Lakes

In 1967 Steinbrenner participated in the takeover of the American Ship Building Company, then a small operation headquartered in Lorain, Ohio on the shores of Lake Erie. In addition to its shipbuilding and ship repair business, the company maintained a small Great Lakes fleet. As a result of the takeover, Steinbrenner would become CEO of American Ship. Eventually, Kinsman would be merged into American Ship as a subsidiary.

American Ship has a history with important implications for baseball fans that predates this takeover. In the fall of 1961, the company decided to lock out its shipyard employees after negotiations for a new collective bargaining agreement had stalled. The company hoped to bring pressure on the employees and their unions in order to soften up their position at the bargaining table. It also feared the prospects of a strike during its busy winter season and wished to control the timing of any work stoppage. Previously, the United States Supreme Court had held that certain "defensive" lockouts were permissible under the National Labor Relations Act. In *American Ship Building v. NLRB*,[38] the Court overturned the National Labor Relations Board's decision that American Ship had committed an unfair labor practice when it engaged in an "offensive," or "bargaining," lockout, thereby adding the lockout to an employer's arsenal of weapons in collective bargaining. The history of collective bargaining and work stoppages in baseball over the last thirty years is a product of American Ship's approval of the bargaining lockout.

Under Steinbrenner's direction, American Ship grew considerably. One important contributing factor was Steinbrenner's successful lobbying efforts to get Congress to extend subsidies that were then available to other portions of the shipbuilding industry to Great Lakes shipping. Another reason for American Ship's prosperity was Steinbrenner's aggressive campaign to expand through acquisition of the company's rivals and their boats. Under his guidance American Ship acquired the Great Lakes Towing Company, the largest tugboat operator on the Lakes. It then turned its sights on the Wilson Marine Transit Company, a competitor Great Lakes fleet. Steinbrenner sought to purchase it and a shipyard from Litton Industries. From 1971 to 1972 American Ship's share of Great Lakes grain shipments grew from 28.5% to 78.9%. Steinbrenner believed that the addition of Wilson's fleet would expand American Ship's market share to somewhere between 85 and 88%.[39]

B. Herbert Kalmbach's Shakedown Cruise

Unfortunately for Steinbrenner and American Ship, it was entering choppy legal waters. It was locked into legal battles with the federal government on a number of fronts. First, American Ship had failed to meet its budget or its deadlines for an oceanographic survey ship that it had built for the government. The Commerce Department had proven to be unfriendly to the company's claims in negotiations regarding the overrun. Also, the Justice Department was investigating the antitrust implications of the acquisition of Great Lakes Towing. Further, the new Occupational Safety and Health Administration was investigating safety standards at the company after an ore-boat fire killed four American Ship employees.

Steinbrenner, a Democrat, who had raised substantial funds for Democratic congressional candidates; had supported the election bid of Cleveland's first black mayor, Carl Stokes; and was close friends with Senator Ted Kennedy, believed that political vindictiveness was at least partly responsible for his legal problems with the Nixon administration—an utterly believable proposition.

In March of 1972, Steinbrenner met with Nixon lawyer and fundraiser, and future convicted felon, Herbert Kalmbach. Kalmbach never directly promised that a significant campaign contribution would make American Ship's legal problems go away, but he did suggest that the Nixon campaign was looking for a gift from Steinbrenner of at least $100,000. There was certainly some suggestion that bad things might happen were he not to "get with the right people."[40] Steinbrenner would later tell a friend, "You didn't have to draw a map for me to let me know what was going on... It was a shakedown."[41]

Kalmbach further instructed Steinbrenner to make a series of contributions in amounts of $3,000 or less to various committees that had been created by the Committee to Re-elect the President ("CREEP"). The $3,000 amount was not arbitrary, but rather a means of avoiding having to report the source of the contributions, at least if the money was received prior to April 7, 1972, when a new campaign finance law would take effect. On April 6, an American Ship vice-president delivered the contributions to Kalmbach. Steinbrenner contributed $75,000 of his own money. He made up the difference by funneling American Ship money through 8 employees who were paid bonuses to convert into campaign contributions. This latter scheme was illegal, and it would prove to be costly.

Over the years Steinbrenner has made some good and some bad deals. The acquisition of Catfish Hunter, Reggie Jackson, Dave Righetti, and Roger Clemens for the Yankees obviously belong in the first category. The Jay Buhner for Ken Phelps trade and the Fred McGriff for Dale Murray and Tom Dodd trade still make Yankee fans shudder. Perhaps no Steinbrenner deal produced so little net return as did the illegal contributions to the Nixon campaign. If Steinbrenner thought that it would buy him peace with the Nixon administration, he was to be sorely disappointed. The Commerce Department disallowed the cost overruns on the research ship and imposed late delivery penalties. OSHA imposed what was then its largest penalty to date for the ore-boat deaths. When American Ship and Litton announced the sale of Wilson Marine Transit, the Justice Department immediately ran into federal district court to enjoin the sale. Eventually, the company and the government would reach a settlement that permitted the sale only if American Ship resold or scrapped a portion of Wilson's fleet. While some would see the acquisition of Wilson as very favorable to American Ship notwithstanding the Justice Department's conditions, Steinbrenner would characterize the settlement as a terrible outcome for American Ship.

The worst was obviously yet to come. As the Watergate scandal began to unravel, Kalmbach's and CREEP's fundraising machinations came into the limelight. In the race to raise money prior to the April 7 effective date of the new reporting requirements, Kalmbach, along with Nixon campaign fundraisers (and future convicted felons) John Mitchell and Maurice Stans, raised over twenty million dollars from corporations, always demanding a minimum $100,000 contribution. Some of this money would then be directed to the campaign's "dirty tricks" operations against the Democratic Party. Over a score of executives and corporations would eventually admit to making illegal campaign contributions.

Steinbrenner initially would not admit to wrongdoing. According to Steinbrenner, on the advice of counsel and against his better judgment, he stonewalled. This decision proved to be costly and led to his prosecution for campaign finance violations. Other executives who admitted to making illegal campaign contributions were not prosecuted. On opening day of the 1974 baseball season, at the behest of the Watergate Special Prosecutor Leon Jaworski, a Cleveland grand jury indicted Steinbrenner on multiple counts of illegal campaign contributions, conspiracy, obstruction of a criminal investigation, and obstruction of justice. In all, the indictment included fourteen counts. While initially inclined to go to trial, Steinbrenner eventually pleaded guilty to two of the counts of the indictment. The judge gave him no jail time and imposed only a minimal fine. Ronald Reagan would eventually wipe the slate clean with a presidential pardon. The conviction would soon prompt baseball Commissioner Bowie Kuhn to action. On November 27, 1974, he suspended Steinbrenner from baseball.

IV. Law Beyond Boats

George Steinbrenner's encounters with law and the courts have not been limited to his experiences with Kinsman and American Ship. As owner of the Yankees he has been involved in a variety of legal disputes, many of which are described in other chapters of this book. Notable litigation that has involved Steinbrenner in his role as Yankees owner has included a libel action brought against Steinbrenner for criticism of an umpire;[42] an antitrust action brought by Steinbrenner against major league baseball regarding its control of licensing agreements with sportswear manufacturers;[43] and an ongoing dispute between the Yankees Entertainment and Sports Network and Cablevision regarding the terms under which Cablevision subscribers will be able to watch Yankees games.[44] Of course, Steinbrenner's battles with the Baseball Commissioner's Office involved a different tribunal than a federal or state court, but certainly those battles are properly viewed as legal battles, also. Indeed, the battle over Steinbrenner's second suspension spawned its own ancillary litigation between Steinbrenner and the company that produced transcripts connected to those proceedings before the Commissioner.[45]

Also notable are two cases that were not brought to court. During the 1981 World Series, Steinbrenner assembled reporters to tell them that he had encountered two Dodgers fans in an otherwise empty hotel elevator. The two men, apparently in their twenties, insulted New Yorkers and the Yankees, and then one of them took a swing at Steinbrenner with a beer bottle. Steinbrenner reported that he decked them both, and that "one of them isn't smiling too well." When the elevator door opened, they ran off. The phantom attackers never materialized. Skeptics suggested that Steinbrenner had made the story up in an effort to grandstand and manipulate the media. They noted that like Sherlock Holmes' dog that did not bark in the night, the potential plaintiffs in a battery action did not come forward and sue. Fellow owner, and former Steinbrenner lawyer, Edward Bennett Williams noted wryly, "this is the first time a millionaire has ever hit someone and not been sued."[46]

The other lawsuit that wasn't also is World Series related. In the wake of the Yankees' loss to the Arizona Diamondbacks in the 2001 World Series, a satirical website posted a page asserting that Steinbrenner had sued Satan for breach of contract.[47] The website reported that Steinbrenner had stated, "I have pledged my eternal soul and servitude to him....The least he can do is give me the four consecutive World Series titles he promised." It further reported that Satan had turned to Johnnie Cochran to represent him. Obviously, the story is pure fantasy. Everyone knows that it is Yankee opponents who purchase world championships from Satan.[48]

V. Conclusion

What might we learn from this story? The glib answer is that *Kinsman* prefigures a pattern familiar to Yankee fans: when George Steinbrenner shows up, mayhem occurs and people lose their jobs.[49] After all, the court referred to Captain Davies as the Shiras' former Shipmaster, and certainly the Tewksberry's missing shipkeeper (and perhaps some members of the Michigan Avenue Bridge crew) must have also lost their jobs.

On a more serious level, Steinbrenner's early experiences in the Great Lakes shipping business must have demonstrated to him clearly the value of wise acquisitions. At his best moments, Steinbrenner has implemented this practice of aggressive acquisition with enormous success.

Perhaps most important, these early experiences may explain why Steinbrenner has been a hands-on owner despite his pledge to concentrate on the shipping business. Both Kinsman and the campaign finance mess demonstrated the perils of delegation. In Buffalo, Kinsman Transit's agent set into motion the whole disastrous set of events. Had Steinbrenner contributed the full $100,000 himself to the various CREEP front organizations, rather than funneling a portion of it through the bonus scheme, he would not have gotten into trouble. One can only wonder how the history of the Yankees might have changed, but for the impact of these events on George Steinbrenner's management style. "For want of a nail...."

II. Notable Incidents

Yankee pitcher Carl Mays, who threw the pitch that killed Ray Chapman. Luckily, most of the incidents involving the Yankees and an errant baseball have not ended so tragically. Photo © Underwood & Underwood/CORBIS.

A Most Dangerous Ball

by Thomas C. Galligan, Jr.[*]

I. Introduction

Risk turning into personal injury may seem like nothing out of the ordinary for the personal injury lawyer. That same personal injury may be tragic to the victim.[1] Parents lose a young child in an automobile accident; their lives are changed forever. A person building a cabinet loses some fingers because a saw behaves in some unanticipated manner. A practical joke involving a light punch results in serious injury because of the peculiar susceptibilities of the victim. To the personal injury lawyer, these events may seem like lazy fly balls but it is inevitable that anyone who considers the facts of these cases, even as he or she settles under that fly ball, will empathize with the victim, whether the victim recovers or not.

The New York Yankees have been involved in cases where injury gave rise to tort litigation and in incidents where a player's injury might have led to personal injury litigation but did not. This essay will deal with those cases and with those might-have-been cases.

When one thinks about a baseball-related injury, the paradigm case is the fan hit by the foul ball. Indeed, a fan hit by a foul ball has sued the Yankees and I will discuss that case later. Then, I will turn my attention to the sad case of Elliot Maddox's knee injury and the resulting law suit. From Maddox we will move to a might-have-been case that never was, involving the greatest Yankee might-have-been (who also was), Mickey Mantle, and his knee injury in the 1951 World Series. From Mantle we will move to Yankee Gil McDougald and the line drive he hit in 1957 that severely injured Indian Herb Score and arguably changed Score's pitching career forever. From Yankee Gil McDougald and Indian Herb Score, we will go back in time to Yankee Carl Mays and his fatal beaning of Indian Ray Chapman. From there we will move away from the human victim and briefly discuss Dave Winfield's warmup throw in Toronto that killed a seagull. The warmup to this sports essay is a memoir of my early life as a New York Yankee fan. That memoir is not entirely unrelated to my life as a torts teacher and the subject of this essay.

II. Risk and My Life As a New York Yankee Fan

The torts teacher learns early on that the subject of risk is at the core of what he or she teaches and writes about. Sometimes a risk may mature into an injury; sometimes it may not. Why, for instance, did I avoid injuring someone when I ran that red light last week? Why does exposure to a toxic substance, which produces a risk of developing some terrible disease, lead to the disease in Joan but not in Bill? How much care should one take to avoid a risk? When is the risk foreseeable? While we torts teachers write at length about such questions, we recognize that there is a somewhat arbitrary nature about it all.

As a young Yankee fan, I experienced the risk of bad timing. The experience got me ready for teaching torts. I was born in 1955, shortly before the Brooklyn Dodgers beat the New York Yankees four games to three in the World Series and won the first and only Series in Brooklyn Dodger history. I was barely a year old when Don Larsen threw his perfect game and can neither remember it nor say I was there; however, I do know that Sal Maglie pitched a brilliant game for the Dodgers (yes, the Barber was pitching for the Dodgers then) and that Mickey Mantle hit a homerun in the game. I was two when Aaron, Matthews, Spahn, and Burdette beat the Yankees in the World Series and I was three in 1958 when the Yankees returned the favor. I was five when Bill Mazeroski hit the homerun that ended one of the most dramatic World Series ever.[2] I grew up in the town in which Yogi Berra lived and played sandlot football with his son, Dale. But, my awareness that Yogi Berra was my neighbor came after Yogi turned his back on Mazeroski's homerun. Thus, on that autumn afternoon in 1960 I was neither aware of Mazeroski's blast nor of my neighbor's obvious despondency.

In 1961, I was at home in Montclair, New Jersey, for most of the summer as Mantle and Maris waged their homerun war. But, I confess I did not follow it. In '62 when Bobby Richardson grabbed Willie McCovey's line drive out of the air I was barely seven and beginning to learn the real joys of reading in Mrs. Anderson's second grade class. In later years that joy would lead me to baseball book after baseball book, but in 1962 I am sure that I heard the Yankees won the World Series and I am sure that I was glad of that fact but it didn't mean much more to me than that. I was eight when Koufax and Drysdale led the (now) Los Angeles Dodgers to a sweep of the Yankees. I barely remember it, except what I have read about it since.[3]

But, then came 1964. I was in the barber shop waiting to get my hair cut. How many people over the years learned about baseball in the barber shop? The conversation turned to the World Series between the St. Louis Cardinals and the New York Yankees. The back of The New York Daily News proclaimed that Mantle had just hit his 18th World Series homerun; he was the most prodigious homerun hitter in World Series history. I listened as the customers and the father and son barber team at the Watchung Plaza Barber Shop debated the respective merits of Bob Gibson and Whitey Ford. They argued about the relative merits of the various players involved: Howard, Tresh, Mc-Carver, Maris, Boyer, and Boyer! I was interested. My enthusiasm was somewhat dulled when the Yankees lost the series four games to three. But somehow or other my own interest in baseball and some unexplained loyalty to the New York Yankees had been born.

I sought information on the Yankees in print and by word of mouth. My mother told me that when my grandfather had taken her to her first baseball game at Yankee Stadium, Babe Ruth had hit a homerun. Over and over she told me this story. Several years later when I actually asked my grandfather, Carl Reuterskiöld, about that game he told me that the day my mother went to her first game Babe Ruth did not even play; however, Lou Gehrig had hit a homerun. How ironic it was in retrospect that my mother did not realize that it was Gehrig, rather than Ruth, who had hit the homerun. Gehrig, like she, the child of an immigrant, and Gehrig, like she, who died too soon.

Back to 1964, as I read more and more, from the sports page to books on the Baseball Hall of Fame to Tom Meany's History of the New York Yankees,[4] I became a devout

Yankee fan. I seriously began following box scores in the summer of 1965. But, like a risk manifesting itself as a personal injury case, failure began to manifest itself when the Yankees took the field in 1965. The 1965 Yankees were not a great team. They ended up finishing fifth.

What I could not have known at the time, as a new fan, was that several of the Yankee stars were aging. Mantle was succumbing to the long list of injuries that had plagued his career. Ford was no longer the chairman of a meaningful board. And, Maris had spent way too much of his reservoir of energy hitting 61 homeruns in the summer of 1961. Maris would never come close to 1961 (or 1960) again, but he would be an inspirational and critical member of the 1967 and 1968 Cardinals.

Looking back, I wonder why I stuck with the Yankees when they were about to enter a period of futility. The following year, 1966, they would finish last and they would not reach levels of greatness again until the mid to late 70s. When I began to root for the Yankees I did not know that for years before I came along New York had really been a National League town. I did not understand that in the 50s many in America viewed the Yankees as a symbol of the growing strength of corporate America which could achieve whatever it wanted whenever it wanted. I did not understand when I began rooting for the Yankees that my favorite team had been painfully slow in breaking the color line. I knew Elston Howard was the first African-American Yankee but I did not know how long he and the rest of us had waited for the Yankees to have an African-American in pinstripes. I did know that my father and I were listening on the radio when Elston Howard hit a homerun in the bottom of the ninth inning (I think it was a grandslam) to beat the Chicago White Sox. We hugged each other and yelled out loud. Howard had done it; the Yankees had come from behind to beat the White Sox. Unfortunately, the game was played in the mid 60s and was meaningless to few, except my father, me, and, presumably, Elston Howard.

I grew up as a Yankee fan wondering who would be the next great Yankee. Who would be the next Ruth, DiMaggio, or Mantle? I adopted Steve Whitaker as my candidate for stardom. He did not achieve it. Maybe the next great Yankee would be Jerry Kenney. Once again, it was not to be. I was used to Horace Clarke leading off, not Phil Rizzuto. I remember one season when Roy White led the league in hitting through the early part of the season, only to fade. Gladly, White would become a part of subsequent great Yankee teams. In my first game at Yankee Stadium, Curt Blefary hit a homerun against Henry Talbot and the Orioles beat the Yankees 3-0. These Yankees were not great teams but I continued to root for them.

As I rooted for them I learned several things. I learned that time had caught up with the New York Yankees; it was not on their side. The risk of failure, the risk that the system would not always produce stars, had matured. It had manifested itself in a lousy team. I had chosen that team as my own and I was stuck with it.

I also learned to deal with uncertainty. In reading baseball history, it seemed that the only certainty there was from 1921 through 1964 was that the Yankees would be in the World Series and most of the time they would win it. As I became a serious fan the uncertainty involved whether the Yankees would ever win another game.

I empathized with those failing Yankees and rooted for them with a tragic sort of voraciousness. Perhaps, like the personal injury victim who files suit because it is the only thing he or she can do, I felt that the harder I rooted maybe somehow or other the Yankees would succeed again. I realize that Yankee success in recent years had little to do with me rooting for them. It had to do with incredible investments in talent, good fortune, and great baseball. It is with these personal reflections in mind that I turn to the intersection of my favorite team and what I do for a living—studying and teaching torts.

III. Torts and the Yankees

A. Foul Ball Cases

The first thing that comes to mind when someone says "torts and baseball" is the fan in the stands who is hit by the foul ball. All of us who have been through law school will no doubt shout out immediately: "the plaintiff can't recover. She assumed the risk."

For the lay reader the phrase "assumption of the risk" may have some common sense appeal to it. The idea behind "assumption of the risk" is that one may assume certain risks when undertaking an activity; if she does so then she cannot later complain of the damage caused by those assumed risks. Underlying the "rule" are notions of free choice, personal autonomy, and the morality of accountability. One area where assumption of the risk might be important is the sports case. What risks did a spectator, or competitor, assume by attending or participating in a sport? Predictably, the assumed risk issue can get a little more complex. For instance, are there certain risks we will not, as a matter of public policy, allow a person to assume?

Related to the idea of assumption of the risk is the doctrine of consent. The law has taken the position that one may consent to certain intentional wrongs; that consent will let the defendant off the liability hook. In the intentional tort arena the law says the plaintiff consented to the risk. In the law of negligence, as noted, if the plaintiff assumed the risk the rule developed that there would be no recovery. That rule developed at a time when a plaintiff who was even the slightest bit negligent could not recover at all from the defendant. This was the harsh common law rule that the plaintiff's contributory negligence barred recovery. Now, in most jurisdictions the plaintiff's negligence may only reduce recovery by the percentage of fault attributed to the plaintiff. This is called comparative fault. Comparative fault states have wrestled with the continued viability of the assumption of the risk defense. This wrestling has made even more apparent what was always true: courts sometimes used the phrase "assumption of the risk" to mean that the plaintiff could not recover from a *negligent* defendant because she had assumed a risk. But courts also used the phrase "assumption of the risk" to mean that the risk which injured the plaintiff was so well-known and common that the defendant was not negligent at all in regards to that risk; i.e., the plaintiff could not establish that the defendant was at fault at all. Put differently, the defendant either had no duty to guard against the particular risk or did not breach any duty it owed to the plaintiff. With that brief background on "assumption of the risk," let us turn to the foul ball case.

When a plaintiff's contributory negligence or assumption of the risk barred recovery in a negligence action, it made little difference in most foul ball cases whether the court justified its conclusion by saying that the plaintiff had assumed the risk or by saying that the defendant simply had not breached its duty to exercise reasonable care towards the plaintiff. The Restatement (Second) of Torts § 493C provided the following illustration regarding assumption of risk:

A, the owner of a baseball park, is under a duty to the entering public to provide a reasonably sufficient number of screened seats to protect those who desire it against the risk of being hit by batted balls. A fails to do so. B, a customer
entering the park, is unable to find a screened seat, and although fully aware of
the risk, sits in an unscreened seat. B is struck and injured by a batted ball. Although A has violated his duty to B, B may be barred from recovery by his assumption of the risk.[5]

Of course, in the Restatement (Second)'s example the stadium owner did in fact
breach its duty to provide a sufficient number of screened seats. Despite defendant's
breach, the plaintiff would not recover because the plaintiff was fully aware of the risk
when she sat in the unscreened seat. Illustration 5 of the same section provided that if
the plaintiff was a Swede (like my grandfather) who did not understand the dangers of
baseball, A would be liable to B.[6] The Restatement illustrations turn upon the subjective
awareness of the particular plaintiff.

But, what if the stadium owner had provided an adequate number of screened seats?
Would assumption of the risk then be relevant at all? Technically, not as a defense to
negligence because the defendant was *not* negligent. The plaintiff would *not* recover because either the defendant, A, did not breach its duty to exercise reasonable care to provide an adequate number of screened seats or A had no duty to provide additional
screened seats. If the phrase assumption of the risk is used in the no-breach or no-duty
context it is not being used to describe a traditional affirmative defense on which defendant would bear the burden of proof. Rather, it is being used in a manner which implies
that the plaintiff has failed to establish its prima facie case. In this context, assumption
of the risk has often been referred to as primary assumption of the risk. It might be better to not use the phrase "assumption of risk" at all in this context.

Interestingly, the Restatement (3d) of Torts: Apportionment of Liability rejects all
notions of primary assumption of the risk. Does that mean that the result in the baseball cases would change? Not at all! If the defendant provided an adequate number of
screened seats, then there would be no recovery because the defendant either had no
duty to provide additional seats or had not breached its duty to exercise reasonable
care.[7] Merely deleting the confusing phrase "primary assumption of the risk" does not
change the result.

Okay, you say, interesting bit of law but what about the Yankees? Have the Yankees
ever been sued by a spectator injured by a foul ball? Indeed, they have. In Baker v. Topping,[8] a fan, Baker, sued Dan Topping and Del Webb, who, as partners, did business as
the New York Yankees. The fan also sued the corporation supplying ushers to Yankee
Stadium. Baker, who had been at Yankee Stadium approximately six times before, was
struck by a baseball hit into the stands as an usher led him through an aisle to his reserved seat in an unscreened section on the first-base line. The court, anticipating much
post-comparative fault jurisprudence on the subject stated, in part:

> Whether or not the basis predicative of an assumption of risk, in a factual situ-
> ation such as that before us, can more accurately be said to establish the ab-
> sence of any duty on the part of the defendant which might give rise to negli-
> gence—so that the term "assumption of risk" may have become "simply a
> left-handed way of describing a lack of duty" (2 Harper & James, op. cit., pp.
> 1162, 1190–1192...) seems not greatly material, as respects this case at least.
> The lack of duty concept would, however, render unnecessary the pleading of
> assumption of risk as an affirmative defense....[9]

Anticipating that merely pleading negligence in not providing more seats behind the screen would not be successful, the plaintiff had adeptly argued that his case was different than the run of the mill (easy fly ball) case because he was not in his seat. He alleged that the actionable negligence was the alleged negligence of the usher who conducted Baker to his seat when it was dangerous to do so and without warning of the danger from batted balls. The court rejected this argument stating:

> Thus, while first conceding the general principle that a spectator assumes the risk of the known and usual dangers inherent in the game, plaintiff then, by asserting defendant's duty to warn him of a particular and, indeed the best known danger, disputes or at least overlooks, the very basis of the rule. The recognition of plaintiff's theory would seem to necessitate the obviously impractical, if not impossible requirement that there be no movement within the stands and upon the field at the same time. If plaintiff is chargeable with knowledge of the risk of injury from a batted ball while he was in his unprotected seat, there would seem no logical basis for considering that he may reasonably be less aware of the same danger in the aisle by which he approaches his seat.[10]

Baker is in accord with most modern jurisprudence on the subject.[11] Injured fans generally do not recover when hit by foul balls.

Before leaving the subject of the Yankees and foul ball liability, it is instructive to take a short trip to Boston. The relationship between the Yankees and the Red Sox is complex. Like most complex relationships there is much irony involved. For instance, the Red Sox arguably dealt the greatest player of all time, Babe Ruth, to the Yankees. The Red Sox have not won a World Series since two years before that 1920 deal. It was the presence of the regal DiMaggio who kept Boston's Splendid Splinter, the late Ted Williams, from winning at least two additional MVP awards. DiMaggio froze him out. Moreover, it was the Yankees who, in 1978, overcame a huge Boston lead to tie the Red Sox and force a playoff that was won, in large part, by Bucky Dent's homerun off former Yankee Mike Torrez.[12]

In any event (and ironically), before the decision in Baker v. Topping the Red Sox had faced a foul ball claim by one Lillian Shaw. Like the Yankees in 1961 the Red Sox in 1950 won the case, Shaw v. Boston American League Baseball Co.[13] The court, in an opinion by the aptly named Justice Spalding,[14] concluded that Ms. Shaw had assumed risks inherent in the game, including being hit by a foul ball. Ironically, the team that the Red Sox were playing the day Ms. Shaw was hit by the foul ball was the subject of this book—The New York Yankees.

Returning to New York, not only were Topping and Webb sued in a foul ball case but they were also sued by Olga Shtekla for injuries allegedly incurred when a fight broke out between several spectators at a game. In Shtekla v. Topping[15] the applicable court reversed the judgment in plaintiff's favor because she had not established through credible evidence that there were insufficient guards who arrived too late to stop the melee in which she was allegedly injured.

In summary then, the jurisprudence involving the New York Yankees and spectator injuries is in line with national jurisprudence on the subject.[16] The Yankees were not held liable when a fan was hit by a foul ball at Yankee Stadium. In this regard, baseball's greatest team has not separated itself from most other ball clubs. However, in a case involving a player's injuries the Yankees have had a more notable presence. It is to that case which I now turn.

B. Player Injuries: The Sad Case of Elliott Maddox—Visiting Shea Can Be Dangerous to Your Health

As I indicated when I disclosed my own background as a New York Yankee fan, I was weaned on lousy Yankee teams. However, as I approached the end of my high school experience, the Yankees began to improve. The main reason for their improvement was a pretty good pitching staff still led by Mel Stottlemyre (the now Yankee pitching coach who resembles the late Gary Cooper more than Lou Gehrig resembled Cooper) and including former Rookie of the Year, Stan Bahnsen. (I used a Stan Bahnsen model glove throughout high school although I mostly watched from the bench). Additionally, a rising Yankee star had come upon the scene in the form of Bobby Murcer, a centerfielder who in 1973 (the year I graduated from high school) hit .304 with 22 homeruns and 95 RBI. In 1974, Murcer would move from center to right field to make room for a new player acquired from Texas in an off-season trade. The Yankees' new centerfielder would be East Orange, New Jersey, native, Elliott Maddox.[17] But, Maddox's debut as a Yankee and Murcer's move to right field would not occur in the house that Ruth built. Rather, like the pre-1923 Yankees, the 1974 and 1975 Yankees would play in their National League counterpart's ballpark. While Yankee Stadium was undergoing renovation, the '74 and '75 Yankees moved into Shea Stadium and shared it with the Mets. Maddox's first year in New York and in Shea was impressive. He had 466 at-bats and hit .303, including 56 doubles. Among 1974 on-base percentage leaders, Maddox was tenth behind six Hall of Famers.[18] Indeed, the Yankees finished second in the American League East in 1974. Then that winter, Bobby Murcer was traded to the San Francisco Giants for Bobby Bonds (the father). 1975 opened with great promise for the Yankees and for Elliott Maddox. Sadly, the year would not be better for the Yankees. And, while Elliott Maddox would hit .307, his success would be marred by serious injury.

On the night of June 13, 1975, before the advent of comparative fault in New York, Elliott Maddox was patrolling centerfield for the New York Yankees in a game against the Chicago White Sox. The previous day's scheduled game had been cancelled because of the weather and poor field conditions. On the night of June 13th Maddox had observed that centerfield was "awfully wet" with "some mud" and standing water. Maddox claimed to have told a grounds crew member about the poor field conditions; the game went on as scheduled. In the ninth inning as Maddox was fielding a fly ball hit to right center (right center, just like Mantle, see below), Maddox ran to his left. As Maddox sought to plant his foot to stop running, his left foot hit a wet spot and slid; however, his right foot stuck in a mud puddle and his right knee buckled. The injured knee required three separate surgical procedures and, Maddox alleged, ultimately forced him to retire from professional baseball, although not for several years.

In 1976 and 1977 Maddox sued a number of defendants, including the City of New York, as the owner of Shea Stadium; the Metropolitan Baseball Club, Inc., as lessee of Shea; and the architect and consulting engineer on the Shea Stadium project. Maddox sought $10 million in damages.[19]

Various defendants filed motions for summary judgment. The trial judge denied the motions.[20] In denying the motions the court distinguished earlier cases that had refused recovery to plaintiffs injured while participating in sporting events because those cases involved a plaintiff's voluntary participation in a sport.[21] The court noted that Maddox "was injured while performing his job as a professional baseball player."[22] The court indicated that one could generally not assume a risk which would bar recovery when the choice was between abandoning one's work and facing the risk. Additionally, the court concluded that it could be inferred that Maddox, in playing on the wet field, "was acting within the confines of his superior's instructions."[23] The trial court continued: "Thus, assuming the plaintiff knew and fully appreciated that a dangerous condition existed and that he nevertheless continued working pursuant to the expressed or implied directions of his superior, it is a question of fact whether it was reasonable under all of the circumstances for him to have continued."[24]

On appeal, the appellate division reversed.[25] The court pointed to the long-standing policy in New York that "participants in athletic events assume the risk of injury normally associated with the sport."[26] The court stated that Maddox had admitted knowing that centerfield and right centerfield were wet and that he continued to play despite his knowledge.[27] As to Maddox's argument that his superior (the manager) had directed him to proceed under dangerous circumstances, the court held that Maddox had not proven his case. Maddox had merely contended that "he informed an unidentified grounds crew member (or members) of the condition, and that he had previously commented to the team manager 'a couple of times…that the field was wet.'"[28] Maddox's assumption of the risk was not excused.

The case then went up to the New York Court of Appeals.[29] The Court of Appeals affirmed the intermediate appellate court. Reiterating the fact that Maddox's case was a pre-comparative fault case in New York, the court held that the case involved assumption of the risk implied from "plaintiff's continued participation in the game with the knowledge and appreciation of the risk which his deposition testimony spelled out and which established implied assumption as a matter of law."[30] The risks which Maddox had assumed included those risks inherent in the construction of the field and its drainage. The court noted that assumption of the risk required not only knowledge of the injury-causing defect but also appreciation and awareness of the risk.

But how were those determinations of appreciation and awareness to be gauged when the plaintiff was a professional baseball player, like Maddox? The court stated:

> It is rather to be assessed against the background of the skill and experience of the particular plaintiff…and in that assessment a higher degree of awareness will be imputed to a professional than to one with less than professional experience in the particular sport.…In that context plaintiff's effort to separate the wetness of the field, which he testified was above the grass line, from the mud beneath it in which his foot became lodged must be rejected for not only was he aware that there was "some mud" in the centerfield area, but also it is a matter of common experience that water of sufficient depth to cover grass may result in the earth being turned to mud.[31]

It was not necessary that Maddox foresaw the exact way in which he would be injured as long as he was aware of the potential for injury in the mechanism from which the injury resulted. Elliott Maddox had lost his case.

Although the case was not decided until after Maddox's playing career ended, as noted above, the injury in question did not immediately end his career. He continued to play for the New York Yankees in 1976, New York's first American League pennant since 1964, and then for Baltimore and the New York Mets until 1980. Maddox's career batting average was .261.[32] In the post-season, Maddox appeared with the 1976 Yankees in both the ALCS playoff against Kansas City and in the World Series. In the 1976 ALCS against Kansas City, Maddox batted .222, going to the plate nine times with two hits in three games. Recall that it was Chris Chambliss' dramatic ninth inning homerun which ended that ALCS and sent the Yankees to the World Series against the Reds. In that Series (the first for the Yankees since 1964), the Yankees were swept in four games by one of baseball's greatest all-time teams, the Big Red Machine. Maddox appeared in two Series games and batted five times, collecting one hit for a .200 batting average.[33]

After his baseball career ended, Maddox was involved in an effort to bring baseball to eastern Europe.[34] Subsequently, Maddox was charged with workers' comp fraud arising from his filing of a workers' compensation claim in Florida.[35]

How does Maddox's failure to recover from the knee injury fit within mainstream national law on the subject and how would the case be resolved under New York's Comparative Fault regime, adopted shortly after Maddox was injured? First, would the result in the Maddox case have been different under a comparative fault analysis? The court in dicta seemed to have answered that question in Turcotte v. Fel.[36] Turcotte, a famous Triple Crown winning jockey, suffered serious injuries in a horse racing accident, which rendered him a paraplegic. The tragic events occurred during the eighth race at Belmont Park on July 13, 1978 (the same year the Yankees beat the Red Sox in the "Bucky Dent" playoff game). Turcotte alleged that a fellow jockey had engaged in foul riding and that the New York Racing Association was negligent because it had failed to exercise reasonable care in maintaining the track. In denying recovery the Court of Appeals noted that, after the adoption of New York's Comparative Fault regime, what had formerly been assumption of the risk was best analyzed as a question of duty (or the lack thereof). Recall the court's prescient analysis in Baker v. Topping. In analyzing duty in a case involving a participant in a professional sporting event, the *Turcotte* court noted that what commentators had called primary assumption of risk involved:

> [r]isks...incidental to a relationship of free association between the defendant and the plaintiff in the sense that either party is perfectly free to engage in the activity or not as he wishes. Defendant's duty under such circumstances is a duty to exercise care to make the conditions as safe as they appear to be. If the risks of the activity are fully comprehended or perfectly obvious, plaintiff has consented to them and defendant has performed its duty.[37]

Continuing, the court stated: "As a general rule, participants properly may be held to have consented by their participation, to those injury-causing events which are known, apparent or reasonably foreseeable consequences of the participation."[38] As support for this proposition the court cited *Maddox*. Continuing, the *Turcotte* court said that the "no recovery" rule was qualified to the extent that participants in athletic contests do not consent to acts which are reckless or intentional. The court, in reliance upon those general principles, held that Turcotte could not recover from his fellow jockey.

Turning to the claim against the New York Racing Association, which it also rejected, the court said:

> Although the circumstances in the present case are similar to those in Maddox v. City of New York, [citation omitted], Maddox was decided under the laws that existed before enactment of the comparative negligence statute. The case involved a professional baseball player voluntarily playing on a field he knew was wet and soft. His claim for damages for injury resulting when he stepped on a soft spot in the outfield was denied because the City was allowed to assert assumption of risk as a complete defense. Had that cause of action arisen

under the present law, it could appropriately have been decided on the basis of duty under the same rules formulated here and with the same result.[39]

Thus, even though the last quoted sentence was dicta it would seem that *Maddox* probably would be decided the same way under New York's comparative fault scheme. Strengthening that supposition is the New York Court of Appeals' more recent decision in Morgan v. Beck,[40] involving four sports participant personal injury cases. In *Morgan*, the court reiterated that participants in athletic events assume the inherent risks of their activities as appropriate under the pertinent facts.[41] The *Morgan* court cited *Maddox*. Noting *Maddox* was a pre-comparative fault case, the *Morgan* court pointed out that the *Turcotte* court had properly indicated that assumption of the risk was a measure of the defendant's duty of care after the adoption of comparative fault.[42] The *Morgan* court ruled that liability would not be imposed on the owner or operator of a sporting venue "for inherent risks of engaging in a sport...when a consenting participant is aware of the risks; has an appreciation of the nature of the risks; and voluntarily assumes the risk...."[43] Critically, the court indicated that an "important counterweight to an undue interposition of the assumption of risk doctrine is that the participants will not be deemed to have assumed the risks of reckless or intentional conduct...or of concealed or unreasonably increased risks...."[44]

Arguably, because Maddox had been aware of the risks of being injured on the wet field, appreciated the risks he might have encountered and continued to play, he would still be barred from recovery under the *Morgan* test. However, if Maddox could have established that one of the defendants had acted recklessly or intentionally or perhaps had concealed a risk he might have been able to at least get to trial. Moreover, if Maddox had been able to assert that the defendants had unreasonably increased the risks he might have been able to recover. This last possibility is intriguing because, in part, Maddox's claim was that the defendant's failure to exercise reasonable care had in fact increased the risks of his injury. Alas, that claim would arguably fall on deaf ears.[45] In fact, one court in a case with remarkably similar facts to *Maddox* has denied recovery to a college baseball player who was injured when he stepped in a divot in a university baseball field.[46]

In New York, after *Morgan* and *Turcotte*, a participant's recovery in a sports torts suit against the facility, and probably against a co-participant, requires the plaintiff to establish that the defendant committed an intentional tort or behaved recklessly, *or* negligently concealed or increased a risk.[47] But, the increased risk category apparently is not broad, as noted by the *Maddox* discussion above. Perhaps because of a concern that under a general negligence standard juries would not adequately weigh the plaintiff's knowledge, the recklessness/intentional tort requirement holds sway in participant injury cases. And, most of these cases result in no recovery.

C. Hot Stove League Claims

For baseball fans, the off-season once meant cold weather conversation about the upcoming year and what ifs around the hot stove. Another great subject of conversation was comparing talent across generations. Who was better? Ruth? DiMaggio? Mantle? These were "hot stove" league conversations. The bulk of the rest of this essay will deal with "Hot Stove" law suits—personal injury lawsuits that might have been, involving the New York Yankees.

1. Mantle v. . . .

Ruth and DiMaggio never played side by side. But for one year, 1951, Mickey Mantle patrolled right field while DiMaggio held down center.[48] In that 1951 season the Yankees won the American League pennant while the Giants stormed from 13 games back to force a playoff with the Dodgers for the National League pennant. The Giants won that playoff in three games thanks to Bobby Thomson's ninth inning "shot heard 'round the world." The Giants took their momentum in to the first game of the World Series and beat the Yankees 5-1. Let Richard Ben Cramer pick it up from there with his description of the most significant event of game two from his book "Joe DiMaggio: The Hero's Life"[49]:

> In the second game, Steady Eddy Lopat hypnotized the Giants with junk. And though the Yanks couldn't do much (DiMaggio took another oh-fer), they squeaked out a 3-1 win that brought the series even. But still, that game brought more woe upon the Bombers. Disaster struck in inning five, when the Giants' phenom, Willie Mays, lifted a pop fly to short right center. Mantle came racing across from right field-in full jet-car mode. As Mantle described it to his co-writer Mickey Hershkovitz for the memoir *All My Octobers:*

> "I knew there was no way DiMaggio could get to it so I hauled ass. Just as I arrived, I heard Joe say, 'I got it.' I looked over and he was *camped under the ball....*"

> Mantle would tell friends, he thought — "Oh, s...! I'm going to hit DiMaggio. I'll put him in the hospital. They'll never let me play again!"

> *"I put on the brakes and the spikes of my right shoe caught the rubber cover of a sprinkler head. There was a sound like a tire blowing out and my right knee collapsed. I fell to the ground and stayed there, motionless. A bone was sticking out of the side of my leg."*

> It was a terrible price, to learn at last: *You watch the Dago-play offa him...* and to hear DiMaggio speak to him for the first time.

> "DiMaggio leaned over me and said, 'Don't move. They're bringing a stretcher.' I guess that was about as close as Joe and I had come to a conversation. I don't know what impressed me more, the injury or the sight of an aging DiMaggio still able to make a difficult catch look easy."

> (It was Mantle on his way to the hospital. But his knee — them fine young legs — would never be the same. Mantle would never again have that Bonneville speed. In later years, among friends, the Mick was neither so stoic nor impressed by the Clipper. The way Mantle figured, DiMaggio wouldn't call that ball until he was damn sure he could make it look easy. Joe had to look good... but Mickey would never play another game without pain.)[50]

Could Mantle have recovered from the Yankees? Let's ignore the fact that as an employee of the Yankees Mantle probably was barred by the exclusive remedy provision of the workers' compensation law from suing the team for negligence. Assuming away the employer's immunity, could Mantle have recovered from the Yankees or would he be deemed to have assumed the risk? Under comparative fault principles, would the Yankees be deemed to have no duty to Mantle to exercise reasonable care absent intentional or reckless conduct? Did Mantle know about the sprinkler head? If he knew that sprinkler heads were in the outfield then wouldn't he, like Maddox, have assumed an inherent risk of the sport?

Could Mantle have sued DiMaggio? As a co-employee, DiMaggio would probably be immune from the suit under most workers' compensation schemes, but workers' comp aside, did DiMaggio exercise reasonable care in not calling for the ball earlier? If Mantle's quoted hypothesis was true and DiMaggio delayed calling for the ball in order to assure that he looked good while making the catch, then perhaps in some super ballplayers' definition of reasonable care DiMaggio failed to exercise it. Was the Yankee Clipper reckless? Blasphemy! But, even though this is a hot stove lawsuit question, be serious. How could anyone sue DiMaggio? It would be simpler to sue the President, the Pope, or Apollo than to consider another Yankee suing DiMaggio. Consequently, whether Mantle might have sued the Yankees or DiMaggio, he had the good sense not to try. But what if Mantle had not injured himself on that sprinkler head? Then, who would be the greatest player in Yankee history?

2. Score v. . . .

As noted, in 1951 Mickey Mantle joined the New York Yankees; however, Mantle was not the American League Rookie of the Year that year. That honor went to another Yankee, infielder Gil McDougald, who batted .306. That same year McDougald became the first rookie to ever hit a World Series grand slam as he led the Yankees with seven RBIs in the Series victory against the Giants.[51] During his career, McDougald would play on some of the greatest Yankee teams of all time. He is still tied for tenth on the all time World Series homerun leaders list.[52] McDougald's twenty-four World Series RBIs are tied for 8th on the all time list.[53] McDougald was critical in preserving Don Larsen's 1956 perfect game against the Dodgers in the series. As the great Shirley Povich described it:

> Robinson murdered the ball so hard that Third Baseman Andy Carey barely had time to fling his glove upward in a desperate attempt to get the ball. He could only deflect it. But, luckily, Shortstop Gil McDougald was backing up, and able to grab the ball on one bounce. By a half step, McDougald got Robinson at first base, and Larsen tonight can be grateful that it was not the younger, fleeter Robinson of a few years back but a heavy-legged, forty-year-old Jackie.[54]

McDougald is remembered for these and other feats as a Yankee. However, McDougald also played a tragic role in one of baseball's most storied injuries. Maddox and Mantle were injured while chasing fly balls. Baker was injured when a player hit him with a foul ball. But, slightly higher on the list of fearsome injuries is the injury suffered when a player is hit by a batted ball. While third base is known as the hot corner, no one is at greater risk of injury from a batted ball than the pitcher. After releasing the ball the pitcher faces home plate, often off balance, in a vulnerable position, and closer to the batter than any other player on the field. One of the most horrific injuries any pitcher has ever suffered occurred on May 7, 1957 when Herb Score was hit in the right eye by a line drive off the bat of Gil McDougald. The injury occurred in the first inning and resulted in a broken nose and a seriously damaged eye for Score.[55]

Indians pitcher Herb Score had followed '51 winner Gil McDougald as the AL Rookie of the Year winner, taking the award in 1955.[56] Score led the league in strikeouts in his rookie year of 1955 with 245 Ks and again in 1956 with 263 Ks.[57] He is one of only 20 multiple leaders in American League history. In 1955, Score won 16 games, setting the stage for an outstanding 1956 season in which he won 20 games, led the league with five shutouts, and held opposition batters to a .186 average.[58] Score was one of three Indians on that 1956 team who won 20 games, teaming with Early Wynn (20-9) and Bob Lemon (20-14). Like Wynn, Score won 20 and lost nine.[59] Score remains the Indians' all-time leader in fewest hits allowed per nine innings, and in most strikeouts per nine innings. He is second in Indians' history for fewest hits allowed per nine innings in a season.[60]

But the injuries he suffered from being hit in the face by the McDougald line drive ended Herb Score's 1957 season. Although Score returned to action in 1958 he was never again the same. Score's career numbers are not so impressive, given his meteoric start. He finished with 55 wins, 46 loses, and 3.36 ERA.[61] As Bob Feller has written:

> Herb was destined for greatness, and everyone knew it. He had all the pitches, a big strong body and the kind of attitude that breeds success. He was, as they say, "coachable." He proved the book on him was right too....
>
> It all ended in a flash in May of 1957, however, on that night when Gil Mc-Dougald's line drive struck him in the face. Herb has been one of the Indians' broadcasters since then, but if it hadn't been for that line drive, he wouldn't just be in the broadcast booth. He'd be in Cooperstown, too.[62]

Lawrence Ritter and Donald Honig rank Score as one of the one hundred greatest players of all time—a might-have-been.[63]

What if Score had sued McDougald and/or the Yankees? It seems highly unlikely that he could have recovered. Sadly, one of the inherent risks of pitching is that the pitcher may be hit by a batted ball, including a line drive. Likewise, there is certainly no indication that McDougald had behaved recklessly or intended to harm or contact Score. In fact, McDougald was despondent over the episode and, like Score, McDougald may have never been the same afterwards. As he explained to Dom Forker:

> Yes, '57 was a turning point for me, and, yes, Casey did say I didn't become the player I could have been because of Herb Score. But you would have had to live through that in order to understand. That night Herb was really firing, as he always was, and I would say he was the fastest pitcher I ever saw. Faster than Sandy Koufax. He had to be throwing at least a hundred miles an hour. That was all I remember about the game. I just flicked my bat at the ball. The ball shot back at him. Herb didn't have time to get into his follow-through, because the ball hit him on the wrong eye. I saw the blood spurt. I didn't know whether to run to first or run to the mound. After the game I made a statement to the press, "If anything happens to Herb, I don't want to play anymore." The press blew it up. But that's the way I felt. It couldn't have happened to a nicer guy. He's such a beautiful person. C. I. Thomas, his doctor, called me in every town that I traveled to, to let me know Herb's condition. His mother called me the next day and said, "Gil, you had no control over what happened. Don't ever think of quitting." When people are that nice to you, you say, "Hell!" But it took the starch out of me.[64]

In fact, shortly thereafter McDougald hit Frank Lary in the knee with a batted ball and almost hit Baltimore's Skinny Brown.[65] Then, McDougald started pulling everything and his batting average plummeted.

As noted, under the mainstream participant law discussed above Score would likely have had no hot stove legal redress against either McDougald or the Yankees. Of course, if Score could have established that the lighting was inadequate then recovery against the stadium management for increasing the risk of injury would have been somewhat more likely.[66] But if Score knew of the lighting, would it be like Maddox knowing about the wet, muddy field?

Interestingly, the Score injury is not the only pitcher eye injury inflicted by a line drive off the bat of a Yankee. In 2000, Red Sox pitcher Bryce Flory suffered serious eye damage when he was hit by a line drive off the bat of Yankee Ryan Thompson in the ninth inning of a game won by the Yankees 4-0 in Fenway Park.[67] Other pitchers injured by batted balls include Houston's Billy Wagner, Detroit's Willie Blair, Baltimore's Norm Charlton,[68] then-Baltimore's Mike Mussina, and St. Louis' Bob Gibson, who was injured by a line drive off the bat of Roberto Clemente which hit him and broke his leg.

While Score pitched until 1962, Feller tells us Herb Score's baseball career was not as great as it could have been if Gil McDougald had not hit that line drive back to the box in the first inning of that 1957 game in Cleveland. As Feller also said, Score went on to have a memorable career as a broadcaster with the Cleveland Indians. Score broadcast Indian games for 34 years. Sadly, Score's personal experience with debilitating injury was not limited to the McDougald line drive. In 1998 he suffered serious injuries in an automobile accident in New Philadelphia, Ohio.[69]

3. *Chapman v. Mays*

The pitcher's greatest fear may be the hot liner back to the box. However, the batter's greatest fear is undoubtedly being hit by a pitched ball. A beaning can cause serious injury and shorten careers. Red Sox star Tony Conigliaro was never the same after he was hit in the eye by a pitch in 1967. However, the most tragic beaning of all time involved the New York Yankees. I rely extensively upon Mike Sowell's excellent book, "The Pitch That Killed," for the Ray Chapman/Carl Mays story.[70]

In 1920, the Yankees were embroiled in their first real pennant race since the early part of the century when they were the Highlanders and forty game winner Jack Chesbro's wild pitch cost the team a pennant. One of the Yankees' pitching aces in 1920 was Carl Mays, who had been obtained from the Boston Red Sox in 1919. The hitting star of the 1920 Yankees was Babe Ruth who was in his first year with the Yankees. The Yankees' main competitors in the 1920 pennant race were the Chicago White Sox and the Cleveland Indians. By the end of the season those White Sox would be forever known as the Black Sox when the story broke that several of them had taken bribes in order to influence the outcome of the 1919 World Series. The Cleveland Indians, coincidentally, were managed by a former Red Sox, centerfielder and player/manager, Tris Speaker.

Among the Indian stars and one of their most popular players was shortstop Ray Chapman. Chapman had come from humble origins to become part of Cleveland society and one of the Indians' most liked players. In the previous off-season, Chapman had married Kathleen Daley, the daughter of a Cleveland industrial magnate. Chapman was looking forward to moving from the baseball field to the corporate conference room. Indeed, he had already accepted a position as Secretary-Treasurer of the Pioneer Alloys Company. Bill James has called Chapman the best bunter of his era and opined that he may have been headed for Cooperstown until fate stepped in.[71]

Carl Mays came from "a rigid Midwestern background."[72] Mays, unlike Chapman, was a sullen fellow who Mike Sowell has described as generally unpopular among both his own teammates and opposing players. Mays had a reputation for coming inside. In fact, he owned the inside part of the plate.

As Sowell ably described in his book, Mays joined the Red Sox at the same time as Babe Ruth in 1914. After several spectacular and championship seasons, the Red Sox began to falter during the 1919 season and Mays left the team. It was only after he walked out on the team without permission that the Yankees dealt for him, setting off a controversy between the owners of the Yankees, Colonels Huston and Ruppert, and the Commissioner of the American League, Ban Johnson.

Despite his controversial introduction to Yankee baseball, Mays was having a brilliant 1920 season. At the same time, Chapman was batting over .300 for the rival Cleveland Indians. When Cleveland pulled into New York for a series at the Polo Grounds in August, Chicago was four percentage points ahead of Cleveland and one-half game (and ten percentage points) ahead of New York. During the first game of the series, Mays was pitching and Chapman came to the plate to lead off the fifth inning. Mays prepared to throw his first pitch. Let Mike Sowell take it from here:

> Chapman carried two bats with him to the plate, swinging them loosely over his shoulder. He tossed one toward the Indians' dugout, then stepped into the batter's box and pulled his cap down as he took his stance. Speaker kneeled in the on-deck area, idly waiting his turn at bat. Connolly gave the signal for play to begin, then leaned into position behind Ruel.

> On the mound, Mays stared in toward the plate, covered the ball in his gloved hand, and began his windup for his first pitch of the inning. He brought the ball chest high, raised his hands high over his head, and swung his right arm back as he stepped forward. His arm was at the farthest point of his backswing when he detected a slight shift in the batter's back foot as if Chapman was preparing to push a bunt down the first-base line. In that split second, Mays made the decision to switch to a high-and-tight pitch. The knuckles on his right hand almost scraped the ground as he whipped his arm forward and shot the ball toward home.

> Squatting behind the plate, catcher Muddy Ruel followed the path of the ball. Ruel always had difficulty handling Mays's pitches, as the pitcher's underhand motion caused the ball to take unexpected twists and turns. That was especially so on days such as this when Mays was throwing with greater speed than usual. But this pitch did not fool Ruel. It was a fastball and it took a noticeable although not extraordinary shoot as it approached the inside part of the plate. The catcher raised his glove in anticipation of catching the ball. From his vantage point, the pitch was in the strike zone.

> The ball sailed directly toward Chapman's head, but he made no effort to move. He remained poised in his crouch, apparently transfixed as the ball flew in and crashed against his left temple with a resounding crack that was audible throughout the ballpark.

> Mays heard the noise, then saw the ball bouncing toward him. Thinking it had struck the bat handle, he grabbed it and threw to first base. He watched as Wally Pipp made the catch and turned to toss the ball around the infield. It was a routine Mays had seen thousands of times before. But suddenly, Pipp froze, his arm still cocked behind his ear. Mays wondered what was happening, then he saw Pipp staring toward home plate with a look of shock on his face. Only then did the pitcher realize something was wrong.

> At the plate, Chapman, who had stood motionless for a brief moment after being struck, was sinking slowly to the ground, his face twisted in agony. Ruel stepped forward to grab him, but he slumped to his knees, never uttering a sound.

Umpire Connolly took one look at the stricken ballplayer, blood rushing from his left ear, and immediately pulled off his mask and sprinted toward the grandstands.

"We need a doctor!" he shouted to the crowd. "Is there a doctor in the house?"

Seeing Chapman fall, Speaker raced over from the on-deck area. He arrived just as Chapman was struggling to a sitting position, dazed but still conscious. As he knelt and reached for his friend, it appeared to Speaker that Chapman was trying to get up to charge at Mays.

The other Cleveland players, led by Graney, rushed from the dugout to lend their assistance. So did several of the Yankees, and as the ballplayers crowded around, Speaker ordered them to move back and give Chapman some air.

Among the Indians, only Larry Gardner stayed behind. He had been mopping his face with a sponge and had his back turned to the plate when Chapman was struck. It was a moment he would never forget.

"I heard that sound when the ball crushed his skull, and I saw him fall," Gardner later recalled. "I didn't want any closer view than that."

Cleveland Coach Jack MacCallister ran to the injured player fearing the worst. MacCallister had heard what he described as an "explosive sound" when the ball struck Chapman, and he had the awful conviction Ray would be dead within seconds.

As the players gathered around him, Chapman tried to speak. His lips moved but no words came out. A moment later, Dr. Stewart, the club physician of the Yankees, and Dr. Joseph Cascio of St. Lawrence Hospital rushed to the scene in answer to Connolly's pleas for medical assistance. They called for some ice to be applied to the injured player.

After several minutes, Chapman was revived sufficiently to be helped to his feet. When he stood, there was an outburst of applause from the relieved fans.

Chapman shrugged off all efforts at assistance and began to walk across the infield toward the clubhouse in center field. He was flanked by Graney on one side and another Cleveland player on the other. As Chapman approached second base, his knees began to buckle and the two players quickly grabbed him. They draped his arms around their shoulders and carried him the remainder of the distance to the clubhouse.[73]

Tragically, Chapman died from his injuries the following morning. The Indians were in shock. The City of Cleveland mourned the loss of one of its favorite players. However, the Indians recovered from the loss and went on to win their first pennant and the World Series. Notably, Chapman was initially replaced by Harry Lunte, a light hitting infielder, who played remarkably well until he too suffered injury.[74] Then, Cleveland took the radical step of calling up a young player from the minor leagues, a former collegian for the University of Alabama named Joe Sewell.[75] Sewell played brilliantly over the course of the season and eventually became a Hall of Famer. Sewell is most remembered for striking out less frequently than any Hall of Famer in the history of major league baseball. Ironically, Sewell finished his career not with the Cleveland Indians but with the New York Yankees.

Switching back to law, could Ray Chapman's spouse have recovered in a wrongful death claim from Mays? Recall that under the *Turcotte* and *Morgan* cases, a player is generally held to assume risks inherent in the sport. Thus, in an action against a fellow player there would generally be no recovery unless the fellow player acted recklessly or intentionally. The crux of the matter in Chapman's widow's "might-have-been" lawsuit would have been whether Mays pitched recklessly or intentionally. But, you wonder, isn't coming inside a part of the game? It is, but is an intentional beaning part of the game? And, an intentional beaning is a battery, not simply negligence. There is some jurisprudence involving intentional acts in the context of professional sports. There have been several prosecutions of hockey players for engaging in outrageous fights. Moreover, in Hackbart v. Cincinnati Bengals,[76] a Cincinnati Bengal, Boobie Clark, elbowed Denver Bronco Dale Hackbart in the head from behind as play went in the other direction. The court allowed the claim to go forward. When Laker Kermit Washington ran across the court and punched Rocket Rudy Tomjonavich in the face causing serious injury which required reconstructive surgery and ended Tomjonavich's playing career, Tomjonavich filed suit and received a trial court judgment of $3.1 million.[77]

But, does a batter consent to being beaned? Does a batter understand that one of the inherent risks of the game is that a pitcher may hit him with a pitch, even intentionally? All of us who watch Baseball Tonight on ESPN hear former players, especially pitchers, preach that current pitchers must learn to come inside. Moreover, we hear that pitchers must protect their teammates. But, is a beaning so far beyond the context of the sport that it ought to be actionable?

Odds are that merely pitching inside, whether negligently or intentionally, would certainly not be actionable if the result was a hit batter. However, what if the pitcher intentionally threw at the batter's head meaning to hit him? Would that claim be actionable?

Chapman's widow might also have filed suit against the league and umpire Tommy Connolly. As Bill James tells it:

> Chapman was killed by a dirty gray ball that he probably did not pick up as quickly as he could have. News reporters ferreted out the information that American League president Ban Johnson, some weeks earlier, had issued a directive to the league's umpires to conserve baseballs, throwing them out of play only when they were "dangerous." Carl Mays claimed that the umpire (Tommy Connolly) had permitted a ball to remain in play that was dangerous, a ball with a rough spot on it that caused it to sail. This provoked two other American League umpires, Billy Evans and Bill Dinneen, to issue a statement that "No pitcher in the American League has resorted to more trickery than Carl Mays in attempting to get a break on the ball which would make it more difficult to hit."[78]

Arguably, the risk of dirty balls was inherent in the pre-Chapman tragedy game. Inherent or not, the death was a tragedy of great, even Greek, proportions. As Bill Wambsganss, Chapman's double play partner, who pulled off an unassisted triple play in the 1920 Series, told Lawrence Ritter:

> That was a terrible thing to happen. Chappie was probably the most popular man on the team. As a matter of fact, he'd talked of retiring after that season. His wife was pregnant at the time and his father-in-law, a millionaire, was going to set him up in business. It was an awful tragedy. Such a sweet guy.[79]

The baby, Rae Marie,[80] was born that off-season. But both she and her mother would die too young; the mother at 34 and the child at 8.[81]

Carl Mays, with career numbers of 208-126 and a 2.92 ERA,[82] has not been elected to baseball's Hall of Fame although some of his teammates with similar numbers have.

Mays blamed his failure to be elected to the Hall on the Chapman incident. As Bill
James noted:

> Carl Mays was of Hall of Fame quality. He was left out of the Hall of Fame
> because of a series of unpleasant incidents with which he was associated, in-
> cluding the death of Ray Chapman. He was a better pitcher than many of his
> contemporaries who are in the Hall of Fame including, Coveleski [Indian],
> Marquard, Haines, Hoyt [Yankee], and Pennock [Yankee], and was also a life-
> time .268 hitter.[83]

The 1921 World Series may well have been another of those "unpleasant incidents"
which has kept Mays out of the Hall. In the 1921 World Series, which the Yankees lost to
the Giants, Mays gave up key hits at key times in all the games he pitched. Rumors
abounded that Mays' untimely pitching was no accident. The rumors provided that
maybe Mays was not just being paid by the New York Yankees. Miller Huggins identified
Mays as one of only two former players (the other being Joe Bush, another pitcher on
the 1921 Yankees) whom he would not help out if they were in need.[84]

As the catcher throws the ball back to the pitcher, let's throw the subject back to law.
Remarkably, there are very few bean-ball cases that have reached the appellate level. In
one, Balfezor v. Little League Baseball, Inc.,[85] the court refused to allow a player and his
mother to recover for injuries the child suffered when he was struck by a pitch during a
little league game. The court held that the risk was inherent in the game and that there
was no indication that the defendant little league baseball organization had somehow
increased the risk of being beaned. The court held that: diminished lighting had not increased the player's risk of being hit by a ball; there was no negligence in failing to remove a wild pitcher from the game; and little league baseball was not negligent in failing to provide the players helmets with faceguards. Nor was there any indication that
the pitcher had intentionally hit the batter.[86]

Current bean-ball wars involving the New York Yankees, particularly Roger Clemens
and his rivalry with Met Mike Piazza, thankfully have not resulted in anything close to
the Chapman tragedy.

IV. The Yankees and the Birds

If Ray Chapman's widow had sued Carl Mays it would have been incumbent upon
her to prove that Mays had recklessly or intentionally beaned her late husband. In 1983
that is exactly what the City of Toronto alleged Dave Winfield did to one of its inhabitants—intentionally hit it with a baseball. You see, the Yankees have not only been involved in injuries to fans and players, they have also been involved in injuries to birds.
As Winfield completed his warmups during the fifth inning (once again the fatal fifth
inning) of a game with the Blue Jays (irony abounds), Winfield turned and threw the
ball towards the ball boy. On the way, the ball hit a seagull who had been sitting on the
turf. The seagull did not survive the collision.

While the Yankees won the game 3-1, Winfield's thrill of victory was short-lived. He
was arrested in the dressing room and charged with "willfully causing unnecessary cruelty to animals."[87] Winfield faced a possible fine of up to $500 or 6 months in jail. Only
later did the Toronto police drop the charges.[88]

Winfield himself described the incident as follows in his May 18, 2002 commencement speech at the Thomas Jefferson School of Law:

> In 1983 while playing for the NY Yankees against the Toronto Blue Jays in Toronto, I accidentally hit a seagull with a practice throw before an inning that was resting on the baseball diamond. The throw killed a seagull; the fans railed and then filed a complaint, cruelty to animals. I had to make bail before the Yankees could leave the country. By this time already I had extensive experience with tax attorneys, corporate attorneys, civil litigators, but until then I never had the need for a criminal defense attorney or Barrister. Fortunately, charges were dropped and apologies for their actions were in order.[89]

Winfield is not the only athlete, let alone the only baseball player, to have had a run in with birds. During spring training in 2001, Randy Johnson hit and killed a dove which flew into the path of one of his pitches.[90] Golfer Tom Kite hit and killed a purple martin which resulted in a double bogey but not in criminal charges.[91] While the Winfield saga established that indeed a baseball is a most dangerous thing, it is somewhat outside the scope of this essay because it involves a criminal charge and not a tort case. Of course, the scholar may wonder why tort law provides no redress to the seagull. Perhaps, the state could file a tort suit as parens patriae. While the issues raised in the animal rights context are serious, I feel I have spent enough time on the birds in this piece—after all, this is not a book about the Blue Jays, Cardinals, or Orioles.

V. Conclusion

As can be seen, the New York Yankees' storied past includes several tort cases and several might-have-been tort cases. The tort cases include a foul ball case, Baker v. Topping, and a flyball case, Maddox v. City of New York. Those real cases have provided sound vehicles for discussion of "assumption of the risk" in the sports context and of the doctrinal niceties associated with that phrase. To the baseball fan, the Yankees' might-have-been cases may be more thought-provoking than their actual cases: Mantle v. New York Yankees, Score v. McDougald, and Chapman v. Mays. The animal rights advocate may be intrigued by the case of Dave Winfield and the seagull.

Personally, this exercise has been entertaining and rewarding. As I reflect on my own experience as a Yankee fan and a torts teacher, I realize that the seeds for some of my empathy for plaintiffs in personal injury cases were planted while empathizing with Yankee teams in the late 60s and early 70s, Yankee teams that simply weren't like the Yankee teams that had come before and that have come since. The fact that I came of age as the Yankees became less competitive taught me lessons about risk and uncertainty that have served me well as a torts teacher. Life is uncertain; baseball is uncertain; and, even life as a New York Yankee fan can be uncertain. What we learn is, "who knows?" We can try to deal with risk and uncertainty as a baseball fan and as a society but we can never quite eliminate it. Maybe that's why Horace Clarke always wore that batting helmet.

Jim Bouton, working out in an empty Yankee Stadium, was baseball's most famous out-sider after publication of *Ball Four*. Photo © Bettmann/CORBIS.

The Tell-All Hurler

by Mitchell J. Nathanson*

I. Introduction (or an Overly Long, Inappropriately Melodramatic, Patti Labelle-Like Rendition of Our National Anthem)

Jim Bouton deserved better than this. Oh, the room was appropriately austere, that was for sure: musty, oak paneled, smelling of moldy books and powdering glue; late afternoon sunlight streaming in through the stained glass windows and spilling all over the threadbare oriental rug. All of the necessary university speaking-engagement accoutrements. No, that was as it should be for a talk given by one of the most significant people in the history of sports. It was everything else that was the problem.

I had arrived early in order to guarantee a seat up front, where I would be certain to hear him (I have been to enough of these things to know that when it comes to student-run audio-visual departments, you typically got what you paid for). Also, I wanted to beat the crush. For I naively assumed that the appearance of a notable such as Jim Bouton would be, much like a Stones concert, a standing-room-only event. Little did I know that, at least initially, it would be more akin to a Foghat reunion show, with plenty of good seats available.

I chose my seat and placed my knapsack under my chair. For the first time since I'd left my car I was separated from my mace. I was fairly certain that I wouldn't need it now that I was inside, within the confines of the two-inch-thick steel doors that closed like a prison's behind me when I entered the building. There was a guard at the door as well. True, he appeared to be otherwise well into his retirement and dozing in his chair, but who was I to say that he didn't have things under control? He was probably a sharpshooter, able to jump to action at a moment's notice, licensed to kill, all of that good stuff. At least that was what I was telling myself as I hurried into the most brightly lit room I could find in order to gather myself and plot my next move.

These people are students, I kept repeating silently as I took in the mass of humanity passing by on both sides, they are not going to hurt me. Even that guy with the pantyhose cap and muscle shirt? Yes, even that guy. I was pretty sure that that thing in his left hand was a book. Who bludgeons someone to death with a macroeconomics text? Regardless, I wrapped my foot around the knapsack. If need be, I could kick it up to chest level, pull the zipper and grab my mace in seconds. But only if need be.

As I waited for the room to fill and the talk to begin, I wondered how Bouton had wrangled himself into this situation. Surely, he had better offers. Offers from places which regularly graduated future Supreme Court Justices, acclaimed physicians, noted thinkers. Or at least places which, when mentioned, elicited a nonchalant shrug rather than a surprised, "I didn't even know that was a college". But here he was, at New Jersey City University; the academic equivalent of Class D ball. Where you washed your own jock and spent your free time dreaming of all the places in the world you'd rather be.

The room filled slowly, as classes let out or, as I suspected, the shelters closed down for the afternoon. For as it soon became apparent, it was going to be a Statue of Liberty kind of crowd (your wretched, your tired, your huddled masses, etc.). A woman in a thick, brown jacket, worn most likely in unknowing defiance of the surprising late Fall warmth, stared deeply into the recycling bin at the back of the room. She looked around, up and down and then made her way down the aisle. Although there was plenty of available seating, she chose the seat directly in front of me. A moment later, I was engulfed in the caustic aroma of what can best be described as month-old egg salad wafting in my direction. A large sack of dough in stained sweatpants chose the seat to my left, clutching a shopping bag stuffed taut with items for Bouton to sign. He was sweating profusely under his grimy Yankees cap, his graying curls matted down against his slick, beefy neck. He seemed to me to be the type of person you saw at every baseball game; the guy who showed up alone, transistor radio glued to one ear, keeping score religiously; the guy who brought a large shopping bag of food to the game and finished everything off by the fourth inning; the guy who hummed to himself when not talking back to the radio. That guy.

Then there were the others: older people mostly, who arrived in groups of two or three and who seemed to know everyone else there over the age of 65. They filled the room with their conversation: about their morning, their afternoon or what they were planning on doing that evening. But not about Bouton. Nobody spoke about Bouton. Did they know who he was? Did it even matter to them? Or was this just an excuse to get out of the house, to "do something" as their doctors most likely exhorted them to do on a regular basis? The longer they chatted the more I realized that this crowd would've shown up to just about anything that didn't require an admission fee.

Eventually, they found their seats, interspersed between the few clearly identifiable students and those who appeared to have wandered in off the street merely looking for a place to sit. This was Bouton's audience. These, for better or worse, were his "people". This, I thought to myself, wasn't right.

Not right for the man whose 1970 publication, "Ball Four", was recently selected by the New York Public Library as one of the "Books of the Century", along with the likes of "The Great Gatsby" and "In Cold Blood".[1] Whose account of his 1969 season with the then Seattle Pilots and later, Houston Astros, provided much of the fuel for the slowly building players association movement that finally rebelled against the long-cursed Reserve Clause which tied players to an organization from the day they were drafted to the day they died, and forced its overthrow. Who drew back the curtains on the reality of life as a major league baseball player for all the world to see; a world where players were resigned to meekly signing whatever contract was placed before them because they had no other options.[2] Who created an atmosphere where someone like Curt Flood could finally stand up to management and refuse a trade from St. Louis to Philadelphia because, goddammit, he'd worked long enough and hard enough to be entitled to have some say as to where he played his final years. Who set in motion the procedural wheels which culminated in the 1975 Andy Messersmith arbitration (during which sections of "Ball Four" were read into the record as evidence of ownership mistreatment of their players) which broke the shackles once and forever, granting free agency for the first time to professional athletes in any major American sport. Who laid the first brick on the path up the mountain. Who in 1996 was featured in "The Sports 100: The One Hundred Most Important People in American Sports History".[3] No, this was not right at all.

The crowd continued to chat or, depending on the individual, hum amongst themselves even after Bouton made his appearance in the back of the room. Although I am too young to recall his days with the Yankees (where, in 1963 he won 21 games and made the All-Star team, and in 1964 won 18 and twice defeated the eventual world champion Cardinals in the World Series), I couldn't help but identify him immediately even though surrounded as he was by various academic types waiting to usher him to the podium up front. Despite the fact that he was 23 years removed from his last appearance on the Major League scene (in a surprising comeback with the then sad-sack Atlanta Braves), he still looked like an athlete, although shorter than I had expected. He waited, as if in the bullpen anticipating the call from the mound, neatly dressed in a crisp gray suit accented with a Ferrari red tie. Recalling the pictures I'd seen from his Yankee days, I noticed that he had reprised his crew cut. As such, he should have been instantly recognizable to these denizens gathering just across the river from where he first made his name. But either he wasn't or they just had more pressing topics on their minds. So they continued on, happily I supposed, until they were so rudely interrupted by the procession which finally made its way down the aisle. The Nerve, many of them probably muttered under their breath.

His introduction was handled by a member of the faculty who appeared to not just have met him moments earlier, but to have heard of him as well. It was awkward, listening to this professor fumble through the litany of statistics that so often define everything but tell nothing when it comes to baseball. It was clear from the professor's introduction that he had come up angrily short in his attempt to secure today's speaking slot for his candidate; a poet no doubt, given the numerous poetry references contained within his introductory remarks. This failure obviously still smarted, as he repeated more than once that Bouton was not an academic and as such, not the sort who usually spoke at these things. A smile crossed his face every time. Those few in the audience paying attention laughed politely. The other members on the dais squirmed in their seats, his arrow obviously having found its mark. After a few minutes, a final forced analogy between baseball and poetry was attempted without success and then mercifully, the introduction, much like America's involvement in Vietnam, came to an end.

An uncomfortable moment passed as Bouton stepped up to the podium. The chatter, which dimmed only in minute degrees during the introduction, revved up again. The humming once again became audible. Snack wrappers roared as several of the elderly women roamed through their massive purses in search of "just a little something" as the woman behind me announced to the rest of her row. Poor Jim Bouton, I thought. He was heading into a buzz-saw. There was no way the journeyman pitcher would be able to compete with everything else that occupied the minds and hands of the disinterested masses gathered ostensibly in his honor this unfortunate afternoon.

However, right away, I realized that much like many who stepped up to the plate against him during his playing days, I had sorely underestimated him. Because his first pitch was an off-the-cuff comment that caught the black of the plate. The crowd laughed. Bouton laughed. I laughed. Immediately thereafter, he zinged another one over for a strike and we laughed again. And again after that. Soon I noticed that he was speaking without notes. But even without paper, the journeyman pitcher had material. A warehouse full of it. Nearly 60 years worth, ranging from when he was a boy chasing after Willie Mays at the Polo Grounds to his predictions on the future of baseball. It didn't take long for me to see that without our even realizing it, we were his. We were hanging on his every word. We wanted more.

He went on, first with some stories about his high school days, where he was known as "Warm Up Bouton" because, not trusted to actually pitch in a real live game, that was all he ever did. Next he recounted his minor league days, leading up to spring training 1962 where he unexpectedly entered an extra-inning game only because there was no one left in the bullpen and pitched shutout ball for several innings, causing management's eyebrows to raise and leading to an eventual spot on the Yankees. This segued into stories about Yogi Berra, Mickey Mantle, heavy drinking and serious womanizing. I looked around the room. The crowd was enthralled. The chatter was gone, the humming nonexistent. Everybody was hanging on Bouton's next word.

By now the musty room was filled to capacity, the overflow packed into the hallway, straining their necks in the doorway in an effort to catch a glimpse of the man who changed the afternoon plans of the several who apparently passed by the room on their way to other appointments only to stop and be drawn in by the wit, ease and charm of the journeyman pitcher. And that's when it finally hit me. That's when I understood just what it was about Jim Bouton and "Ball Four" that so thoroughly scared the hell out of Major League Baseball ("MLB")[4] more than thirty years ago.

Because here he was: at an institution that, for the most part, didn't seem to want him, speaking to a crowd that, for the most part, didn't want to listen to him, and he grabbed them, snap! like that. For the remainder of the afternoon they were his, laughing, nodding in agreement, searching for something, anything for him to sign afterwards at the reception. I now understood that as much as you try, you can't *not* listen to Jim Bouton. Armed with such allure, anything that came out of his mouth carried the potential for danger. Anyone could have written a "Ball Four". Nobody other than Bouton could've written it such that millions of people would read it.

Major League baseball in 1969 (the year chronicled in "Ball Four") was not as most folks believed it to be. Back then, before the explosion of the NFL, it was still our national pastime and its players still larger than life; heroes even. Basketball fans may have known who Lew Alcindor was but *everybody* knew Mickey Mantle. Was there anything better than life as a major league baseball player? Surprisingly, as documented in "Ball Four", the answer was a resounding "Yes". The minimum salary was $7,000;[5] raises were at the sole discretion of management. You didn't like it, you went back home to Iowa. Even if you did like it, you worked construction in the off-season just to make ends meet, despite the fact that the game itself, due to expansion, burgeoning television contracts and sheer dominance of the sporting and entertainment market, was bringing in exponentially more revenue from one year to the next. Baseball, the proverbial goose that laid the golden egg, was growing more plump and fertile by the year. So it was with good reason that ownership was growing increasingly worried that one day, their egg was going to crack.

And crack it did. Spilling messily all over the national consciousness with the publication of "Ball Four" in 1970. Which showed the American public for the first time that life as a major league baseball player wasn't all Wheaties Box covers and movie-star wives. It was work. Hard work. Hard work without adequate compensation in many cases; with lies and deception from management thrown in to boot. Told in a style that drew the rapt interest of even the most casual of baseball fans. Was it any wonder that ownership saw the book as a direct threat to its way of life? As Bouton mentioned during his speech that afternoon, it wasn't the boozing or womanizing in the book that so scared management. No, it was everything else; everything that changed the national mindset when it came to major league baseball. Everything which caused a nation of baseball fans to become sympathetic to their heroes; to make them actually *feel sorry* for them. "Ball Four" altered the mood of the country toward its national game. After its publication, the goose would never be so fertile again.

So it was no wonder that commissioner Bowie Kuhn ("The Ayatollah", as Bouton referred to him more than once that afternoon) tried to force him to renounce every single word after "Ball Four"'s publication.[6] Tried to muscle him into signing a statement which effectively said that he had made the whole thing up. After all, Kuhn and his cohorts didn't become millionaires by accident. They knew where all this was headed. Towards Curt Flood; towards Andy Messersmith; towards Alex Rodriguez and the creation of the $25 million dollar-a-year player. Oh, maybe not the next day, or the day after that. But eventually. So they pulled out all the stops in an effort to prevent their goose from running free.

Or did they?

Because in the end, the arm-twisting that occurred in the commissioner's office that day back in 1970 was the extent of MLB's attempt to stanch the bleeding which would eventually divert much of the sport's economic lifeblood from the owners' veins to the players'. The release of "Ball Four" started the trickle and, in retrospect, the owners have been on the defensive ever since; losing battle after battle until practically everything was lost. While it is impossible to reconstruct events exactly as they occurred over 30 years ago, it's safe to assume that, given the astronomical rise in player salaries and the overwhelming power of today's players union, the legal course chosen by the owners over the past quarter century hasn't provided optimum results, at least from their perspective.

This chapter will attempt to "un-ring the bell" so to speak, and travel back to the time of the release of "Ball Four" in order to determine if there was a better response to the book, one which would have stemmed the tide right then and there. Although there was most likely no weapon available to the owners which would have frozen the economic landscape such that the balance of power would foreverafter remain as it was in 1970, perhaps there was some other approach which would have left more money in the owners' pockets than is presently the case. Given the current economic state of the game, there had to be.

In fact, there is support in the law for the proposition that the stories and anecdotes revealed by Bouton in "Ball Four" constituted legally protected confidential information. After all, there can be no question that the locker room tales told within its pages (tales of pill-popping, salary disputes and a hung-over Mickey Mantle) were exactly the ones that ownership took great pains to keep from the public in its ongoing efforts to maintain the image of the virtuous, happy, "Wheaties Box" player which drew generation after generation of admiring and envious fans to the ballpark.

However, whether the divulgence of this information constituted grounds for relief depends greatly on the categorization of this information. For as the following will show, while these "secrets" fail to meet the requirements typically imposed upon information classified under the highest and most fiercely protected type of commercial information: that rising to the level of a legally protected trade secret, they may nevertheless have served as the basis for a cause of action grounded in a breach of the fiduciary duty of loyalty.

II. Strike One: The Publication of "Ball Four" As a Divulgence of a Protected Trade Secret

"What you say here, what you see here, what you do here and what you hear here, let it stay here", read a sign hanging in the locker room of the Milwaukee Brewers clubhouse in 1969, a sign similar to the ones hanging in locker rooms across the Major Leagues at the time.[7] Communication with the outside world (particularly with reporters—the conduits to the public) on matters other than the happenings on the diamond was frowned upon.[8] The rule was clear: baseball players were to talk about baseball; management was to discuss everything else, and on its terms. This, for example, allowed ownership to publicly announce Mickey Mantle's $100,000 salary with great fanfare while keeping the droves of $9,000–12,000 salaries secret.[9]

Before becoming a player himself and discovering the truth, Bouton notes in "Ball Four" that the public perception of player salaries at the time was that if stars like Ted Williams were making $125,000, then the average players must be making at least $60,000.[10] The public discovery of the gross absence of any such middle-ground at the time would go a long way to discrediting management's very public posture that the players were well paid and fairly treated.[11]

The divulgence of this type of information, first by Bouton and later in the Curt Flood and Andy Messersmith cases, would eventually lead to the reshaping of the economic landscape. Therefore, it is not an understatement to say that the fortunes of ownership depended heavily on the maintenance of this deeply imbedded cloak of secrecy. However, although the ultimate purpose of trade secret law is to protect the sanctity of internal corporate communications and workings like those mentioned above, the absence of a competitive environment of rival baseball leagues ultimately renders the relief offered through trade secret law inaccessible to Major League Baseball.

There is little question that the type of information divulged by Bouton otherwise meets the tests commonly applied to the determination of misappropriation of a trade secret (1: the existence of a trade secret; 2: breach of a confidential relationship or improper discovery of a trade secret; 3: use of the trade secret; and 4: damages).[12] Regardless, courts have repeatedly refused to find in favor of misappropriation if the information disclosed was not intended to be used competitively for advantage against the employer.[13] Since baseball enjoyed (as it does today) the benefits of a judicially protected antitrust exemption which prevents exactly this type of competition, there is not much likelihood that it could find relief under the trade secret rubric.

Simply stated, Major League Baseball's secretly guarded "11 herbs and spices" would receive no legal protection because the Supreme Court, back in 1922[14] effectively prohibited the creation of the baseball equivalent of McDonald's, Burger King and Wendy's. And without such competitors, it is likely that a court would find no harm in the public disclosure of baseball's secret recipe. After all, what could possibly be done with such information to harm the competitive advantage of a corporation that has been granted an enforceable and absolute monopoly? Ironically, it is the very element created to protect the supremacy of Major League Baseball in the sports marketplace that ultimately rendered it impotent to defend itself (at least under the trade secret rubric) when its supremacy was finally and fatally challenged through the publication of "Ball Four." Most assuredly, Kenesaw Mountain Landis[15] never foresaw the likes of Jim Bouton during the golden era of baseball. But then again, it is the rare emperor who recognizes the over-throw of his dynasty before his head is actually on the guillotine.

III. Strike Two: "Ball Four" and Prior Restraint

Moreover, even if the information contained within "Ball Four" did rise to the level of legally protected trade secrets, it is highly unlikely that the remedy MLB would most likely have sought (a permanent injunction barring the publication of the book) would have been granted. Therefore, in any event, the cat would have been let out of the bag, the bell would have been rung, and strained metaphors and similes would have ex-ploded like game-ending homerun fireworks. Because the doctrine of "prior restraint" would have permitted eventual publication in any event.

The Supreme Court has held:

[A]lthough the prohibition against prior restraint is by no means absolute, the gagging of publication has been considered acceptable only in 'exceptional cases'. Even where questions of allegedly urgent national security, or competing constitutional interests, are concerned, we have imposed this 'most extraordi-nary remedy' only where the evil that would result from the reportage is both great and certain and cannot be militated by less intrusive measures.[16]

Although the last phrase appears to give hope to the owners' plight (for it is difficult to imagine an alternative remedy which would have protected the owners' interests as fully), even the most cursory review of prior restraint law indicates that a permanent injunction against publication would be near-impossible to achieve.

As the Sixth Circuit determined (in an opinion representative of the overall approach to the prior restraint doctrine): "the private parties' interest in protecting their vanity or their commercial self-interest does not qualify as grounds for imposing prior re-straint."[17] Only in instances where the overthrow of the government, publication of ob-scene material or publication of troop movements during wartime is at issue has the Court favorably considered the notion of prior restraint.[18] Indeed, the most well-noted prior restraint case of all, the Pentagon Papers case,[19] resulted in a holding quashing the government's attempt to enjoin the New York Times and Washington Post from pub-lishing a classified study on U.S. policy-making in Vietnam.[20] Although occurring dur-ing a time of war and despite the government's plea of protection of the national inter-est, the Court found an insufficient basis to uphold the injunction. By contrast, MLB's interest in protection of their judicially-created empire would hardly merit the Court's attention, let alone favorably.

So where does this leave MLB? Simply, facing the cold reality that the information contained within "Ball Four" would likely not rise to the level of a legally-protectable trade secret and that even if it did, an injunction prohibiting the publication of the book would most likely fail to withstand legal scrutiny. However, while all appears to be lost and although it seems as if, regardless of MLB's tactics, the slippery slope started by Bouton would have led to Flood and Messersmith anyway, giving rise to the $25 million ballplayer of today, this may not in fact have been inevitable. Because there was an av-enue available to the owners which may have at least entitled them to money damages as a result of the publication of Bouton's book, damages which might have taken some of the steam away from the hard-charging players union and made it somewhat more open to compromise and negotiation and less willing to take the Messersmith arbitration to verdict. By focusing on a lesser (but still legally protected) class of confidential information, the owners might have saved a few more slices of the metaphorically-challenged baseball pie for themselves.

IV. Strike Three? "Ball Four" As a Breach of the Duty of Loyalty Resulting in Unjust Enrichment for Bouton and the Players Association: Appeal to the First Base Umpire

Various jurisdictions have held that certain confidential information may in fact be legally protected even if it does not rise to the level of a "trade secret". This type of information receives its protection due to the violation of a confidential relationship which results from its divulgence. Thus, it is the violation of a fiduciary trust (a breach of loyalty), as opposed to the dissemination of information considered confidential regardless of who divulges it, which forms the basis of this cause of action.

As stated by the 11th Circuit: "A confidential relationship is distinguished by the expectations of the parties involved, while a trade secret is identified through rigorous examination of the information sought to be protected."[21] While the locker room secrets fail the trade secrets test due to baseball's anti-competitive antitrust exemption, they may nevertheless be legally protected given the clear and explicit intention on behalf of ownership (and repeated on the wall of every clubhouse in the Major Leagues) to keep precisely the type of information revealed by Bouton within the four walls of the locker room.

Indeed, MLB could have made a plausible argument that given the players' status as high-level employees of the game, they owed their employers (as well as corporate parent MLB) a fiduciary duty of loyalty. Concurrent with this responsibility is the prohibition from doing exactly what Bouton did—using or disclosing information for his own advantage.[22] Moreover, the divulgence of this information not only benefited Bouton personally through the receipt of royalties of his best-seller, it detrimentally affected his employers, as can be clearly shown through the downward spiral of events which quickly followed its publication. Courts throughout the country have found employees liable for exactly this type of conduct despite the absence of a legally protectable trade secret.[23]

Although, as stated above, efforts to obtain an injunction prohibiting the release of "Ball Four" would most likely have failed due to overriding First Amendment concerns, substantial money damages may have been available to the owners should they have won on liability. Under the doctrine of unjust enrichment (if such enrichment could be proven), Bouton (and by extension, the Players Association) would have been required to forfeit the full amount of all improperly-obtained benefits.[24]

But was Bouton's enrichment unjust?[25] After all, he may have breached a confidentiality which would entitle MLB to some measure of damages, but the information contained within "Ball Four" comes to the reader first-hand. Bouton was present for all of the conversations and incidents reported in the book, there was no serious contention (other than in his private conversation with Bowie Kuhn in 1970—a conversation that Kuhn demanded be kept from the public)[26] that any of the information within the book was anything but truthful. So why wasn't Bouton entitled to repeat and print what he himself heard? Surprisingly, here is one area where baseball's antitrust exemption actually would have helped MLB prove sole ownership of every piece of locker room gossip and negative opinion held by each and all of its players. As such, the unauthorized release of any of this information for profit (or benefit to the players to the detriment of MLB) would be tortious.

The rationale is as follows: since the antitrust exemption prevented competition by rival professional baseball leagues, it follows that the economic benefits derived from the professional baseball "pie" were exclusively reserved to those within the Major League Baseball corporate structure. Moreover, the prohibition of outside competition necessarily created, as a byproduct, an internal competition between the players and owners within MLB for these judicially-created scarce resources.

However, the antitrust exemption provides a strong indication that the Supreme Court also ruled that the vast majority of the "pie" rightfully belonged to the owners and not the players. After all, without outside competition, players were prevented from going elsewhere to sell their services. This necessarily diminished the value of their unique and valuable skills—skills that otherwise would most likely have fetched a high price in a free and competitive marketplace.

The antitrust exemption, coupled with the Reserve Clause which bound a player for life to the team that drafted him, reduced the galaxy of potential bidders on these skills to a universe of one. It was this, judicially-approved, system that restricted quality veteran players like Bouton to a salary of $22,000[27] in a marketplace where the top salaries (of the very few and very well-known) were in excess of $120,000;[28] that permitted owners to set league minimum salaries ($7000 in 1969)[29] in a vacuum—a vacuum so air-tight and free from market forces and player input that players openly laughed and chided Bouton when he suggested that the players take steps to raise the minimum;[30] that created an atmosphere whereby players were powerless to negotiate their yearly salary and had little choice but to meekly sign whatever contract was mailed to them that season.[31]

While all of the above might be described by the academic as "socially undesirable" or by the layman as "really lousy", it's important to remember that this system was *judicially approved*. The Supreme Court had spoken, and so it was done. Each and every inequality was absolutely legal, proper, and, what's more, mandated by the highest court of the United States. The judiciary was not about to readdress these issues, settled half a century earlier, in the absence of a compelling reason. And the only weapon in the players' arsenal powerful enough to convince the courts to visit the issues again was public opinion. If they could somehow rouse public sentiment against the owners, there was the possibility that MLB would be forced to share at least a little of what was otherwise legally theirs.

As stated earlier, this weapon was not unknown to the owners, however. And in an ongoing effort to keep the public's nose out of their empire, they repeatedly took the offensive to prevent the release of unofficial information. Hence the ubiquitous clubhouse signs, as well as confidential reprimands of players who spoke, in the eyes of ownership, a bit too freely about issues outside of the white lines of the playing field.[32] Moreover, each spring, Commissioner Bowie Kuhn made the rounds of each training camp and issued a speech best described by Bouton in his book:

The Commissioner said that baseball is a tremendous, stupendous game and that it didn't need any drastic changes, that we simply needed to improve our methods of promotion. One of the things that none of us should do, he said, is knock the game. He said if we were selling Pontiacs we wouldn't go around saying what a bad transmission it has. In other words, don't say anything bad about baseball.[33]

By writing "Ball Four", Bouton broke the explicit code of silence, knocked the game, and stirred up public opinion which led to a groundswell of support for players who the public learned, for the first time, were badly mistreated and underpaid by management.[34] The shifting public winds paved the way for Flood, Messersmith and, eventually, Barry Bonds and Alex Rodriguez.

Of course, it would be absurd to argue that the owners aren't making millions upon millions of dollars themselves in the current economic structure. However, with the average yearly salary currently hovering in the $2 million range and with quality veterans (players of comparable stature and experience to Bouton back in 1969) making $5–7 million, there can be no question that ownership is necessarily keeping less for itself than it otherwise would have if the slippery slope created by Bouton had never been traversed at all.

Given the implicit acknowledgement of the antitrust exemption that the owners were legally entitled to set salaries as they desired, it is not unreasonable to conclude that "Ball Four", which altered this monopolisitic system in direct violation of the purpose of the exemption, led to unjust enrichment not only to Bouton (who directly profited from the dissemination of confidential information) but to each and every player who indirectly benefited through the increase in salaries forced upon the owners by the events which ensued thereafter.

V. Conclusion

The information contained within "Ball Four" was: (1) confidential in that all employees and fiduciaries of MLB were repeatedly exhorted not to discuss exactly the types of activities contained with the book; (2) valuable to the owners, in that its confidentiality permitted them to enjoy the fruits of their antitrust exemption; and (3) used for the personal advantage of both Bouton and the players association. In fact, Bouton not only testified at the Messersmith arbitration which eventually resulted in the dismantling of the reserve clause, he read excerpts of "Ball Four" into the record.[35] Thus, even though the information contained within the book would not qualify as a legally protected trade secret, it appears as if it still would be protected as confidential information released in the course of a breach of Bouton's duty of loyalty to MLB, leading to unjust enrichment of Bouton and the players association as a whole.

Of course, under the prior restraint doctrine, nothing could have been done to prevent the publication of the book in any event. However, the threat of significant money damages may have given the owners some leverage in an arena where hindsight shows they had none. Perhaps they could have used the prospect of litigation as a tool to force the players association to the negotiating table in the Messersmith arbitration, thereby avoiding the eventual ruling which permanently dismantled the system that had been in place for nearly a century. Perhaps. We'll never know. All we do know is that anything would have been more effective than the defense actually used in the arbitration, a defense which resulted in a complete and total defeat for MLB.

If one were inclined to believe the owners, they still haven't recovered from this defeat, and it is the current system (the one brought on by Bouton) which is the cause of all of what ails baseball today. If this truly is the case, then it is most likely with great regret to the owners that the extent of MLB's response to the publication of "Ball Four" wasn't more than a little arm-wringing in the Commisioner's office one spring afternoon. As displayed both in print and in-person, the persuasive power of Jim Bouton's wit and wisdom required a counter-offensive utilizing the totality of baseball's arsenal and not the cap-gun employed by a commissioner cloaked in secrecy. Given MLB's meager response to the publication of "Ball Four" back in 1970, not only is it not surprising to find the balance of power shifted as radically as it has today, it is surprising that the owners have any power at all.

Until Melissa Ludtke's lawsuit, only male reporters had locker room access. Photo ©
Bettmann/CORBIS.

An Inquiring Woman

by Jan Stiglitz*

The world of professional sports has traditionally been a man's domain. Baseball is no exception. There has never been a female player on a major league roster. No woman has worked as an umpire for a regular major league game. No woman has ever been the manager of a major league team. When you see a woman on the field, the chances are pretty good that she is there to sing the national anthem or throw out the first baseball. While change has been slow, baseball has not been completely immune to the "women's movement" that swept through society in the late 60s and early 70s. Women today do represent athletes and occupy front office positions, albeit in disproportionately small numbers.

This chapter will focus on the struggle for equality that occurred in a small but important part of the baseball world: the locker room. It will begin with the story of Melissa Ludtke, a writer for Sports Illustrated, who needed access to that quintessential male bastion in order to be able to do her job.

The chapter will then show what has transpired in the time between Ludtke's suit and the present, and it will discuss the situation that exists in other sports. While progress has been made, and women do not have to fight for the same right of access as their male counterparts, this issue continues to flare up. Equal access doesn't and might never mean equal treatment.

Finally, the chapter will contrast the plight of female reporters with that of other women who want to be a part of baseball.

I. The "Inquirer": Melissa Ludtke

Melissa Ludtke was born in 1951 and was raised, primarily, in Amherst, Massachusetts.[1] She was athletic and played volley ball, basketball and tennis in high school. Her father, who was on the faculty at University of Massachusetts at Amherst, regularly took Melissa to the college's football, basketball, and baseball games. Melissa's mother was also interested in sports. She was a devoted Red Sox fan and the Sox became Melissa's team of choice.

Melissa attended Wellesley and became a member of its first interscholastic crew team. She also played basketball. Melissa did not pursue or even think about journalism in college. In fact, she'd been told early on that she wasn't very good at writing.

After graduation, Melissa initially decided to pursue an interest in elementary education. However, a chance meeting at a dinner party and a conversation with Frank Gifford resulted in a change in her career path. During the dinner, she and Gifford discussed sports in general and the tragedy that had just occurred at the Munich Olympics.

Gifford mentioned that she seemed to know a lot about sports "for a girl" and suggested that she might be interested in working for ABC Sports.

A. Getting the Job

Gifford arranged an interview for Ludtke but she was not initially hired. A few months later, she met Donna DeVerona, a former Olympic swimmer, who was doing commentary for ABC. With the help of DeVerona and an ABC production assistant named Barbara Roche, Melissa eventually landed a job with ABC as a freelance "gofer."

Because the job wasn't a full-time position and because she barely made enough money to pay expenses, Ludtke persuaded a friend at ABC to arrange an interview for her at Sports Illustrated. At the time, Melissa had no experience and no credentials. As Melissa put it, she "knew nothing about journalism... [but] was very comfortable talking about sports."

Sports Illustrated initially turned her down, but persistence eventually led to a position as a researcher, assisting writers for the magazine. Initially, her duties included just a bit of writing, but over time, her writing assignments increased.

At the time she worked for Sports Illustrated, Ludtke was not the only woman writing for the magazine and she wasn't the only woman working as a sports reporter. But women usually held second-class status: most were researchers and back-up reporters. Very few were assigned as full-time sports reporters.

There was also a disparity in the sports that women covered. Women were more likely to cover the Olympics than baseball or football, which were considered to be the "plum" assignments.

B. Getting the Stories

At some point, after another woman left, Melissa became a second string baseball reporter. In that capacity, she maintained Sports Illustrated's "log book" on baseball games and wrote an occasional free standing story or column on her own. Since she wasn't the lead baseball writer, Melissa focused on background stories and on athletes who weren't quite superstars.

One day Ludtke invited Cincinnati Reds catcher Johnny Bench to lunch. During that lunch, Bench told Ludtke about the conversations he'd had with the home plate umpire during the course of the prior night's game in an effort to get a little help for his pitcher. Melissa decided that a behind the scenes look at the conversations between catchers and umpires might make a good story.

Although Melissa had access to Yankee Stadium and could arrange to be there each time a new team came through town, she found that getting a chance to really speak with the various catchers was difficult. She'd approach each during batting practice but they'd usually tell her that they were too busy to talk. After practice, they'd disappear into the locker room where she wasn't allowed to go. Melissa would try to get players or other reporters to go into the locker and request that the catchers come out and speak with her. But more often than not, she'd wind up killing time and not getting the interview. She eventually did write the story, but it took an entire season to get it done.

C. An Immodest Proposal

During the 1977 baseball season Melissa got to know Billy Martin, the manager of the Yankees. On occasion Melissa visited with him in his office, which was attached to the locker room. From time to time Martin would even go into the locker room and bring players out so that Melissa could interview them.

The day before the 1997 World Series was about to open in the Bronx, Melissa was at Yankee Stadium and ran into Dodgers manager Tommy Lasorda. Melissa knew Lasorda from a prior story on which she had worked with sports writer Roger Kahn. Without having given it prior thought, Melissa asked Lasorda whether he might be willing to give her access to the locker room during the series if she needed it for a story. Lasorda told her it wasn't his call but introduced her to pitcher Tommy John, who was the Dodgers' player representative.

John told Ludtke that he would take a poll of the players and get back to her. The next day, he told her that he'd taken a poll and that the majority had thought it would be fine. He also told her that those players who were opposed were willing to go along with the decision. John requested that Melissa inform the Dodgers' PR person so that he wouldn't be surprised and she did.

At the time, Melissa was pleased but didn't think that she'd made history. Female sports writers had previously been allowed in locker rooms in both the NBA and the NHL. However, later that day, while Melissa was in the auxiliary press box watching the first game of the series, she was called into the main press box to meet with Bob Wirz, the Director of Information for Commissioner Bowie Kuhn's office. At the time, the Commissioner of Baseball had broad powers to investigate any action or practice deemed not to be "in the best interests of baseball" and to remedy the situation.[2]

Acting on Kuhn's behalf, Wirz told Ludtke: "This is not going to happen. You will not be getting access to the Dodgers' locker room this evening or any other evening." Wirz gave her two reasons for the decision. He said that no one had consulted the players' wives. He also told her that the league was concerned that players' children would be ridiculed. Melissa argued her position but to no avail.

Ludtke did not tell her editor about the incident or pursue the matter, but a friend who was a reporter called Ludtke's editor and told him what had happened. Sports Illustrated and Time, Inc. (its parent company) wanted to pursue the issue and had Ludtke write a letter to Kuhn, outlining both what had occurred to that point and why she felt that she needed equal access to the locker room.

Negotiations ensued and when the series got back to New York, the Commissioner's office offered to provide Ludtke with an escort who would go into the locker room and attempt to bring players out to speak with her. The arrangement didn't work. The last game in the series was the game in which Reggie Jackson hit three home runs to win the game and become the series MVP. Of course, Melissa wanted to speak with Jackson. She relayed her request to see Jackson to her escort and then waited for two hours. When Reggie finally came out, he said "Melissa, I'm just too tired. I'm on my way home."

II. Ludtke v. Kuhn

A. The Suit

Negotiations continued even after the end of the baseball season, but the parties were unable to arrive at a mutually acceptable solution. On December 29, 1977, the case of Ludtke v. Kuhn was filed in federal district court in New York.[3] Ludtke and Time, Inc. were named as plaintiffs. Bowie Kuhn, as Commissioner of Baseball, and Lee MacPhail, as President of the American League, were the primary defendants. Because the City of New York owned Yankee Stadium, and because Ludtke was being denied access to city owned property, the plaintiffs also joined the Mayor, the Commissioner of Parks and Recreation and the Director of Economic Development as defendants. However, shortly after the commencement of the suit, the parties agreed that the city officials were not "necessary," and they were dropped from the case.

The complaint asserted three claims. First, Ludtke claimed that she was denied her right to "due process" and "equal protection" as guaranteed by the Fourteenth Amendment to the United States Constitution. Second, both Ludtke and Time claimed that their First Amendment right to freedom of the press was being abridged. Finally, Ludtke made a claim that the defendants had violated New York's equal accommodation statute.

B. The Judge

In federal court, judges are randomly assigned by a lottery system. Although it might not have mattered, the plaintiffs hit the jackpot when the case was assigned to Judge Constance Baker Motley. At the time, she was the only woman on the federal bench in New York. Motley is also African American. Prior to being appointed to the bench, Motley had a long and distinguished career as a civil rights attorney. She had worked for the NAACP Legal Defense Fund and had represented Martin Luther King.[4] As a result, she well knew what it was like to be a pioneer and to be subject to discrimination.

C. The Facts

Each side submitted a number of affidavits in support of its position. Because these affidavits revealed that there was no real dispute regarding the underlying facts and that the only questions were legal ones, the case was decided by Judge Motley on a motion for summary judgment.

The facts revealed by the affidavits showed that the prohibition against women in the locker room had been part of Major League Baseball's official policy since at least April of 1975. In 1975, the National Hockey League All-Star teams decided to allow female reporters into their locker rooms for the All-Star game. As a result of this decision, Commissioner Kuhn initiated some discussion within baseball about the issue. Some teams' public relations directors had been asked for comment but no comments were solicited from the players. In April, Kuhn sent a letter to all major league baseball teams instructing them to maintain a "unified stand" against women in major league clubhouses.

In 1976, Wirz had contacted the public relations directors of all major league teams to remind them of the policy against allowing female reporters into the locker room and had asked whether any reporters had sought access. Interestingly, the Yankees' public relations director told Wirz that the players had voted to allow women into the locker room if they conducted themselves professionally. Wirz told the public relations director that if the Yankees allowed access it would be a "definite threat to breaking down the overall barrier." The Yankees' management then overruled the players. The Yankees also allowed one or more female reporters into the locker room during spring training in 1978 (after the suit had been filed) and, once again, the Commissioner's office stepped in and ordered the Yankees to bar women from entering the locker room.

The declarations and documents presented to Judge Motley also suggested that the Commissioner's policy on women was actually in conflict with baseball's general policy regarding locker room access. An Annual Notice is issued by the Commissioner's officer to all teams regarding the press. Since 1974, that notice stated that access to clubhouses "should" be granted to *all* accredited members of the media.

The current and former presidents of the Baseball Writers Association of America submitted affidavits which indicated that locker room interviews were an essential part of a baseball writer's job. They also indicated that being barred from the clubhouse put women at a competitive disadvantage in their ability to report.

The record before Judge Motley also indicated that female reporters had been allowed in men's locker rooms in both the NBA and the NHL since 1975. At the time Ludtke v. Kuhn was pending, female reporters were allowed locker room access by 14 of the 18 NHL teams (including the New York Rangers) and 22 of the 24 NBA teams (including the New York Knicks).

Physically, the clubhouse at Yankee Stadium consisted of nine separate rooms. There was a central locker room area with cubicles for each player. Judge Motley noted that these were large enough so that screens could be put up if a player wanted privacy for dressing. The central locker room was separated from the shower, toilet, sauna and trainer's room so that players using those facilities were completely hidden or, with the installation of doors, could be completely hidden from view.

D. The Legal Issues

1. *The Requirement of "State Action"*

The Fourteenth Amendment to the United States Constitution provides citizens with protection against discriminatory actions taken by states or those acting on behalf of states (including local governments and government officials). Since the Commissioner of Baseball is not a governmental official, Ludtke's first challenge was somehow to show that Kuhn was a "state actor" and that his decision constituted "state action." Without such a showing, she would lose on her due process, equal protection and free speech claims.

In a case called *Burton v. Wilmington Parking Authority,*[5] the United States Supreme Court had determined that a private entity which perpetrated an alleged discriminatory act could be deemed a state actor if the relationship between the private entity and the state was sufficiently "intertwined" so that the action of the private individual could be deemed to be the action of the state. In *Burton*, a restaurant in a parking garage had refused to serve a customer solely because he was black. The garage had been built by and was owned and operated by the Wilmington Parking Authority, an agent of the State of Delaware. The restaurant leased space from the Authority.

The Supreme Court ruled that if a state leases property for public use, it cannot abdicate its constitutional obligations to the public. The Court noted that the state could have negotiated a lease which required the restaurant not to discriminate yet it chose not to. If a state chooses to have a private individual act on its behalf, it can be liable when that "private actor" perpetrates discrimination.

Judge Motley applied that doctrine and found that Kuhn was a state actor. The City of New York had acquired Yankee Stadium through its power of eminent domain upon a showing that it was required for "public use." The City was then authorized to lease the Stadium to the Yankees (and not to the highest bidder) under a statute which declared that "Yankee Stadium is important to the cultural, recreational, and economic vitality of the state and city."

There was also a continuing financial relationship between the City and the Yankees as a result of the lease between them. The City of New York had spent $ 50,000,000 to renovate the Stadium prior to the 1976 baseball season. The City also provided police for sporting events held at the stadium. In return, the City received a substantial amount of rent. In 1977 and 1978, rent payments from the Yankees to the City amounted to around $ 1,000,000 a year.

The New York Yankees were connected to the Commissioner's office through a series of agreements. The team was a member of the American League of Professional Baseball Clubs. The American and National Leagues are parties to the Major League Agreement which created the Officer of the Commissioner and which gave the Commissioner of Baseball the power to decide who was allowed into the clubhouse at Yankee Stadium.

Judge Motley concluded that the lease arrangement between the City and the Yankees, like the lease in *Burton*, made the actions of the private entity (here, the Commissioner) state action. Yankee Stadium was a "unique" and "highly valuable" public resource. The City, as the lessor, had some power to regulate the use of the Stadium. To the extent that Kuhn was making decisions regarding right of access to Yankee Stadium, he was a government actor.

2. The Discrimination Claims

After ruling that Kuhn was a state actor, Judge Motley turned to the question of whether Ludtke's right to equal protection and right to due process of law were violated.

The Fourteenth Amendment to the United States Constitution provides that no state shall "deny to any person within its jurisdiction the equal protection of its law." "Equal protection" is generally interpreted to require "equal treatment." With regard to the equal protection claim, the parties did not seriously dispute that Ludtke was treated differently because of her sex. Instead, the focus was on whether the discrimination could be justified (i.e., found lawful) by showing that the gender discrimination "serve[d] important governmental objectives" and was "substantially related to achievement of those objectives."[6] On that question, the Commissioner contended that the protection of player privacy justified the ban against female reporters.

Citing *Roe v. Wade*,[7] Judge Motley recognized that there was a "constitutional dimension" to the right of privacy. However, she was unwilling to find a substantial relationship between the privacy needs of the players and the complete exclusion of all female reporters from the clubhouse. Judge Motley noted that the "roving eye" of the camera was routinely allowed into the locker room to broadcast the World Series victory celebrations to millions, including women and children. This suggested to her that the real purpose of the Commissioner's rule was to maintain the locker room as an "all male preserve."

During argument before Judge Motley, counsel for defendants conceded that curtains, doors and towels could take care of privacy issues but argued that it was not what players were "accustomed to." In her decision, Judge Motley ruled that "mere custom" cannot provide an adequate defense to a charge of sex discrimination.

The Fourteenth Amendment to the United States Constitution also provides that no state shall "deprive any person of life, liberty, or property, without due process of law." Ludtke had argued that she had a liberty interest in pursuing her profession and argued that the locker room ban was depriving her of the ability to pursue and protect that interest. Judge Motley agreed.

Judge Motley found that the right to pursue one's profession was a fundamental liberty within the meaning of the due process clause of the Fourteenth Amendment. At the time she decided the case it was well established that governments could not stifle fundamental liberties to achieve legitimate ends if those ends could be achieved without interference. Such action could only be permitted where supported by "important state interests" and where government's actions were "closely tailored to effectuate only those interests."

As with the discrimination claim, Judge Motley ruled that the privacy interests of the baseball players could be fully served by less sweeping means. Judge Motley also dismissed two other interests asserted by baseball: maintaining its status as a "family sport" and "conforming to traditional notions of decency and privacy." Judge Motley found both to be "too insubstantial to merit serious consideration."

3. *The Other Claims*

Because Judge Motley ruled in favor of Ludtke on the constitutional issue, she did not make a decision based on state public accommodation law. It is not clear that Ludtke would have been successful in that regard.

In 1972, New York's Human Rights Law had been used to invalidate "Ladies' Days." Ladies' Day was a long standing tradition in baseball. On Ladies' Day, women who wanted to attend a baseball game were admitted at a reduced price. This discount was designed to encourage women to attend ballgames. The disparity between male and female attendance at that time was dramatic. On the last Ladies' Day in New York, only 350 women attended the game at Yankee Stadium.

Ladies' Days ended as a result of a suit brought in 1972. In that case, New York's Human Rights Appeals Board ruled that this gender-based discriminatory practice violated state law. However, the decision apparently indicated that discrimination would be allowed "in portions of the facilities where patrons customarily disrobed."[8] It is certainly possible that a similar result might have been reached regarding Ludtke's claimed statutory right of access to areas where players disrobed.

III. The Aftermath

A. Baseball's Response

Baseball did not appeal Judge Motley's decision which came down right before the 1978 World Series. Instead, it first tried to limit all reporters' access in order to give players a chance to shower and dress. This angered the Baseball Writers of America, a reporters' group with significant clout. (The members of this organization vote on who gets into the baseball's Hall of Fame.) By the end of the World Series, the situation was back to normal—except that women had equal access to the locker rooms.

Because baseball changed its policy in light of the Ludtke decision, the legal battle did not have to be fought on a team by team or city by city basis. This is fortunate. Since the decision in Ludtke v. Kuhn was based on the fact that Yankee Stadium was government owned, the decision would not have had any precedential value with regard to Dodger Stadium or any other privately owned ballpark. In addition, the *Burton v. Wilmington* guidelines for finding state action were significantly changed in a series of 1982 Supreme Court decisions.[9] As a result, baseball might have tried to limit the decision to Yankee Stadium and might have been successful.

B. The Players' Response

Ironically, Ludtke was not the first female reporter who entered the Yankees' locker room after the decision.[10] Perhaps it was just as well. The first female reporters who came in were greeted with a cake in the shape of a penis, paid for by a member of the Yankees.

While baseball officially agreed to allow equal access, the players had their own opinions. Ludtke maintains that she did not suffer any retaliation as a result of her suit. However, other female reporters suffered from abuse and inappropriate behavior.

Dale Murphy, who played for the Atlanta Braves and who was a devout Mormon, objected to women in the locker room on religious grounds: "It goes against what I feel is right and proper....It's the men's locker room and there shouldn't be any women in there." Jack Morris, who pitched for the Detroit Tigers, was quoted as saying that he wouldn't talk to any women while he was naked "unless they are on top of me or I am on top of them."

Sometimes, these opinions were followed by acts of harassment. In 1992, Dave Kingman, while playing for the Oakland A's, refused to talk to Susan Fornoff, the beat reporter for the Sacramento Bee. He said: "A lady should be a lady." He later sent Fornoff a package containing a rat with a tag around its neck which said "My name is Sue." Kingman, who refused to apologize, was fined $3,500 and told that he would be released if there were any similar incidents. Sadly, but not surprisingly, the fan reaction to that incident was pro-Kingman.

IV. Other Sports

This pattern of official league acceptance followed by isolated and sometimes serious player unhappiness has been mirrored in other sports.

A. Football

Since the time when Pete Rozelle was commissioner, the NFL has been a model of top down organization. Maverick owners like Al Davis are the exception. Pete Rozelle started out as a public relations executive so problems involving relations with the media were dealt with quickly and with a firm hand. As a result, it is ironic that the NFL was the last of the major professional leagues to allow female reporters to have access to locker rooms.

In 1979, the Fort Myers New-Press fought for access to the Tampa Bay Buccaneers' locker room for a reporter named Michelle Himmelberg. One solution to her challenge was to have all reporters conduct interviews in a separate area. Bucs' management built a wall—dubbed "the Himmelberg Wall"—to separate the interview area from the locker area. However, male reporters objected and blamed Himmelberg rather than management.

Even after the league officially allowed open access, there were two well publicized incidents of protest.

The first occurred in 1990 and concerned a reporter named Lisa Olson, who covered the New England Patriots for the Boston Herald. Some players apparently thought that Olson stared at players while they were naked and referred to her as a "looker." One day, a few players decided to teach Olson a lesson. A group of them (including Zeke Mowatt, Michael Timpson, and Robert Perryman) surrounded Olson, while they were naked, and made obscene comments and made lewd gestures with their genitals. A few days later, Victor Kiam, the owner of the Patriots, was quoted as saying: "What a classic bitch. No wonder none of the players like her."

The NFL investigated the players' actions and Kiam's statements. The Patriots conducted their own investigation into the actions of the players. Olson also filed suit against the team and the players. The suit settled for an undisclosed but reportedly substantial amount of money: sources placed the settlement in the neighborhood of $500,000.

The case received a great deal of publicity. Lisa was featured on the cover of Time magazine. Interestingly, George Steinbrenner, the owner of the Yankees, joked about her when he hosted Saturday Night Live.

However, the incident also engendered ugly and violent fan reaction. Olson's apartment was burglarized and "leave Boston or die" was spray painted on her walls. Her car tires were slashed by someone who also left a note saying: "Next time it will be your throat." One fan in Chicago actually punched her.

Shortly after, Sam Wyche, then coach of the Cincinnati Bengals, tried to defy the league's open locker room policy. He argued: "Men and women don't conduct business in the nude in the real world. Why should a locker room be any different?" The NFL reacted by fining Wyche one game's pay, which amounted to approximately $30,000.

After these incidents, Gene Upshaw, the Executive Director of the NFL Players Association suggested that all members of the media be barred from the locker rooms. But that suggestion was never pursued. The NFL policy continues to be equal access.

The standard player contract in the NFL has a clause which requires players to cooperate with the news media. The league notifies players that there is an open locker room policy but that the shower area of all locker rooms will be screened from view and that they will be provided with wraparound towels or other clothing.

B. Basketball

As indicated earlier, the NBA allowed women into the locker room even before Major League Baseball. As with the other leagues, some players were upset. In 1978, a rookie named Toby Knight objected to the presence of female reporters, saying "We're not a nudist colony putting on an exhibition."

C. What's Good for the Goose...?

Arguably, if female reporters are allowed into men's locker rooms, men should be allowed into women's locker rooms. However, that issue has received much less attention.

In team sports like the WNBA, reporters (both men and women) are allowed in immediately after the game, before the women shower and change clothes. For the most part, women's team sports need the publicity and they'd rather women postpone their showers than lose the possibility of being covered and written about.

With individual sports, like golf and tennis, the situation is quite different. Anna Kournikova is not starved for attention. Press interest doesn't have to be generated. The solution reached by the LPGA and the Women's Professional Tennis Association is that players meet with all members of the press in a post game interview room outside of the locker rooms.

V. The Issue That Just Won't Die

Reporter Amy Sohn recently reported about her experience in the locker room at Yankee stadium.[11] Sohn found herself "thinking more about decorating than nudity." The only flesh she saw was the torso of a player who was shaving far in the distance. Sohn spoke with Derek Jeter about whether he thought having women there was a problem. Jeter didn't think so.

Similarly, Lisa Olson recently said "I looked around the Yankees' clubhouse after a game the other day, and there were 12 women in there, holding camera and microphones and writing stories....It's just so refreshing."

However, the issue continues to flare up and will probably never die. In 1999, former all pro football player Reggie White, who is an ordained Christian minister, wrote an article in the Wall Street Journal in which he advocated that athletes and their wives go to court to close men's locker rooms to women.[12] White said: "I can't see any legitimate reason for forcing male athletes to walk around naked in front of women who aren't their wives." Charlie Ward, a Knicks player who is also a devout Christian, agreed with White and passed out copies of White's article to players in the locker room. Ward feels uncomfortable with women in the locker room and believes it violates "the sacredness of his marriage."

Fortunately, the situation is now handled properly. Jonette Howard, a reporter for Newsday said that in the early days, female reporters could not count on the support of the teams and the leagues. After the Olson situation, the message is that bad behavior on the part of team members won't be tolerated. Evidence of that can be found in the Knicks' quick reaction to Charlie Ward's attempt to get players to fight against the presence of women. Dave Checketts, President and CEO of Madison Square Garden, put an end to it saying: "I believe in freedom of speech but he may not use our locker room as his pulpit."

Similarly, in 2001, Chris Gatling of the Cleveland Cavaliers was fined $ 10,000 by the NBA for his remarks to a member of the team's PR staff who was gathering quotes in the locker room after a game. Gatling had said: "I don't know why they let women in the locker room. All they want is to peek." Gatling apologized and said that he was just trying to liven things up after the team had suffered an overtime loss.

That the issue hasn't completely gone away makes sense given the combination of forces at work.

First, the issue involves sex and nudity. These are aspects of life that generate more heat than light. People frequently have fixed beliefs, some based on religion, that won't change.

Second the issue involves athletes. Some athletes are spoiled, misogynistic, egocentric individuals. Their world is more physical than mental and they may not always be sensitive to the needs of others.

Third, the issue involves confrontations with athletes in situations of great stress and emotion. Athletes who are not performing well or whose team has just lost an important game are likely to lash out at the easiest target. In this regard, female reporters are not the only targets of abuse. There is a classic Tommy Lasorda expletive-filled tirade directed at a male member of the media that demonstrates that anger can be quite gender blind.

Perhaps the most important reason why players and fans will continue to react is that baseball is a man's world. Women have faced an uphill battle in gaining admission to that world.

VI. Other Women in Baseball

Women have made some inroads in areas of baseball but in very small numbers and in limited roles.

For example, there are some women in the front office. Wendy Selig-Preib is the President and CEO of the Milwaukee Brewers. That she is also Commissioner Bud Selig's daughter is not a coincidence. Katie Feeney is Vice President of Club Relations for Major League Baseball. The fact that she is the daughter of Chub Feeney, former President of the Giants and Padres, is also no coincidence. There are some women in other positions who have gotten their jobs without baseball lineage, but not in great numbers. For example, Major League Baseball's lobbyist is a woman named Lucy Calautti.

However, the closer you get to the game itself, the more difficult it is to succeed. Out of the approximately 300 agents certified by the Major League Baseball Players' Association, there are fewer than five women. Kimarie Stratos, a former agent, identified a number of problems. First, athletes want their agents to understand both the game and what they as athletes go through. Many ballplayers don't believe that women can really understand. Second, players fear that those with whom their agents negotiate will not respect a female agent. As a result, they fear that a woman might not be able to get them the best deals possible. Finally, players' wives and girlfriends often feel threatened by the presence of another women with close ties to and influence over the players.

On the field itself, the barriers against women appear to be insurmountable. Witness the saga of Pam Postema.[13]

Pam Postema spent thirteen years as an umpire in the minor leagues. She spent seven years working at the AAA level. In 1989, she worked as an umpiring crew chief. But Postema hit the glass ceiling when it came to the major leagues and was eventually fired. The Triple A Baseball League has a rule which limits the number of years that an umpire can work. If an umpire is not deemed good enough to be offered a position by the National or American Leagues, the umpire is let go so that another person can work their way up the ranks.

Postema filed suit against the National League, the American League, and the Triple A Alliance under Title VII of the Civil Rights Act of 1964 claiming that she was a victim of sex discrimination. Postema had no trouble demonstrating that she was the victim of discriminatory treatment by many of the people she dealt with.

At one stage in the proceeding, the trial court made the following findings of fact:

* On numerous occasions, players and managers addressed her with a four-letter word beginning with the letter "c" that refers to female genitalia.

* Players and managers repeatedly told Plaintiff that her proper role was cooking, cleaning, keeping house, or some other form of "women's work," rather than umpiring.

* Bob Knepper, a pitcher with the Houston Astros, told the press that although Plaintiff was a good umpire, to have her as a major league umpire would be an affront to God and contrary to the teachings of the Bible.

* During arguments with players and managers, Plaintiff was spat upon and was subjected to verbal and physical abuse to a greater degree than male umpires.

* In 1987, the manager of the Nashville Hounds kissed Plaintiff on the lips when he handed her his lineup card.

* At a major league spring training game in 1988, Chuck Tanner, then the manager of the Pittsburgh Pirates, asked Plaintiff if she would like a kiss when he gave her his lineup card.

* Although Plaintiff was well known throughout baseball as an excellent ball and strike umpire, she was directed and required by Ed Vargo, the Supervisor of Umpiring for the National League, to change her stance and technique to resemble those used by him during his career. No such requirement was placed on male umpires.

* Plaintiff continually took action against such conduct through warnings, ejections, and reports. Although the existence of such conduct was well known throughout baseball, no one in a position of authority, including Defendants, took action to correct, stop, or prevent such conduct.[14]

However, in order to succeed, she had to show that her prospective employers (and not just the players) engaged in discrimination with regard to hiring. That was difficult in light of the very low rate of turnover among umpires in Major League Baseball and the fact that decisions about who is the best candidate are inherently subjective. Postema eventually settled out of court.

It doesn't appear that much has changed since Postema's struggle. In August of 2002, George Steinbrenner was upset about the way Ria Cortesio, a Class A Florida League umpire, called a game in which Roger Clemens pitched as part of a rehab assignment. Steinbrenner was quoted as saying: "And then you had a female umpire. Nothing against females, but...."

VII. Conclusion

The issue of female reporters in the locker room is important because it symbolizes the fact that sports are not just about and for men. However, the reality is that we don't have and might never have acceptance of the right to equal treatment without regard to gender. When you compare the results of Ludtke's struggle with Postema's, the conclusion seems to be that while women can get into the clubhouse, they are still not allowed to "join the club."

Yankees pay tribute to their teammate, Thurman Munson, the day after his tragic death in a plane crash. Munson's widow had urged the Yankees to go ahead with the scheduled game. Photo © Bettmann/CORBIS.

The Catcher Who Fell to Earth

by Ettie Ward*

"Lovers of air travel find it exhilarating to hang poised between the illusion of immortality and the fact of death."[1]

Thurman Lee Munson played his entire professional career with the Yankees. Munson was born in Ohio, grew up in Ohio, kept his family in Ohio during his baseball years, and ultimately died prematurely at age 32 in a plane crash in Ohio. Fittingly, the inevitable lawsuits, against the airplane manufacturer and the company which provided his flight training, were filed and settled in Ohio.

Just as Munson's baseball legacy and his role as Yankee team leader were greater than the mere recitation of his career statistics, so, too, the lawsuits brought after the crash reverberated beyond the final settlement by suggesting a novel theory of tort liability in aviation cases. Munson's death while piloting his own jet plane also raised questions about how baseball clubs might protect themselves from similar events by limiting off-the-field activities or insuring players.

I. Growing Up in Baseball

A. Movement up the Leagues

Munson was born on June 7, 1947 in Akron, Ohio, the fourth of four children. His family moved to a farm in Randolph, out in the country, when he was four. Munson's mother was a housewife and his father a truck driver. His father had difficulty supporting the family and, although they had money for food and clothing, there was very little to spare. By all accounts, his father was an unemotional, severe man. Though his father left home for good when Munson was a teenager, Munson credited his early introduction to baseball and his competitive drive to his father. Similarly, his devotion to his wife and three children and his need to be present at home may well have been a reaction to his own childhood experiences and family life.

Munson met Diana Dominick, who later became his wife, when they were both 12; neither had ever dated anyone else. Munson played basketball, baseball, and football in high school and, although he received a lot of interest from college football programs, he had decided that baseball would be his focus. He chose to attend Kent State University because it offered him a full scholarship and was close to home.

In 1968, at Kent State, Munson was an All-American catcher. While at Kent State, he was scouted by the Yankees and, in June 1968, was the team's No. 1 pick in the amateur

Free Agent Draft. Munson received a $75,000 signing bonus. That fall, he married Diana Dominick, his grade school sweetheart.

He spent one full season in the minors and during his second year was called up to play with the Bronx Bombers. The following year he was a full-time Yankee from the beginning of the season.

B. The Scorebox

In 1970, his first year in the majors, Munson was named American League Rookie of the Year. He was the first catcher to win that honor, going on to win Gold Gloves in 1973, 1974, and 1975.

1976 was to be a banner year for Munson. During spring training, Yankees' owner George Steinbrenner decided that Munson should be named team captain—the first to hold that position since Lou Gehrig's death in 1941. When Steinbrenner was reminded that Yankees' manager Joe McCarthy, upon Gehrig's death, had decreed that no one would ever again assume the title of team captain of the Yankees, Steinbrenner responded that if "Joe McCarthy had known Munson, he would have approved."[2] That year he batted .302 (one of five seasons in which he batted over .300) and drove in 105 runs. The Yankees won their first pennant in 12 years and Munson was named American League MVP. Indeed, Munson was the only Yankee to have won both the Rookie of the Year and MVP awards.

Munson played on three Yankee pennant-winning teams and two World Series championship teams. His statistics in post-season games were even more impressive than his consistent performance during the season. In American League playoff series, he hit .339; and, in World Series play, he hit .373. He played on seven All-Star teams.

However, by the 1979 season Munson's productivity as a player had begun to diminish. Injuries, particularly to his knees, took a great toll. In February 1979, he had shoulder surgery, which affected his throwing. He had considered retiring in 1977 and 1978 and was considering it again in 1979. Even if he did not retire, it had become apparent that he could not continue to play as a full-time catcher. He had already considered trying out other positions, rather than quitting, at least in part for his son, Mike:

> He's only four, and he's just beginning to understand what I do. I want to play a few more years, long enough for him to understand and appreciate what I have accomplished. If I have three or four more good years, I might have the kind of statistics that could get me in the Hall of Fame. I'd like that for Mike.[3]

Munson worked hard to insure his family's financial security. He had extensive business interests in Ohio involving real estate, shopping malls and other ventures. He was considered a sound and careful businessman. As the 1979 season started, he had put his baseball career in perspective:

> I'm feeling more mellow. Although I'm best known as a baseball player, I have become conscious that baseball represents at best one-third of my interests. My family comes first....Once I became a family man, baseball became the means toward securing their welfare, so that we can have a long and happy life together....

My business interests are as important to me as baseball is. I get tremendous satisfaction out of the buying and selling of real estate. I'd rather be working on figures, stocks, real estate, houses, commercial ground, shopping centers, banks and restaurants than watching television.[4]

C. "I'm little, I'm pudgy, I don't look good doing things, but nobody plays harder than I do."[5]

Politicians and sports figures leave public "legacies." Sometimes the picture we are left with is a single, consistent view—great looks, great disposition and character, and superb performances. Some athletes, such as Jackie Robinson or Arthur Ashe, fit that category. Others, like Munson, leave us with a more fragmented picture.

No one doubted Munson's skills as a catcher and hitter or the competitive edge he brought to his playing. Yet, discussions of his physique and disposition tend to be framed with qualifiers. At 5'11", 190 pounds, Munson was often described as lumpy, pear-shaped, or "chubby." His teammates often teased him, calling him, among other names, "Squatty Body"—he simply didn't look athletic or fast, but he was. In describing his personality, even his friends described two Munsons—the irascible, scowling curmudgeon who refused to talk to the press or give autographs, and the fun-loving, compassionate, marshmallow of a family man his close friends and family knew.

Munson demanded respect for his playing. His rivalry with Boston Red Sox catcher Carlton Fisk was fueled, in part, by his belief that the press and public favored Fisk because Fisk looked more like a baseball star and was perceived as more personable. Munson was quoted as saying, "My build works against me. I'm a short, chunky guy. I'm not the athletic hero type. Fisk is tall, lean and more attractive.... He got all the publicity and most of the All-Star votes...but he's never been as good a catcher as I am."[6] Although Munson complained about lack of recognition, he often avoided contact with the press. Munson simply did not see a need to reveal himself to the press.

It was repeatedly said that although he was tremendously confident, he craved recognition (especially in salary), but was never really comfortable with celebrity.[7]

His feud with Steinbrenner received a lot of attention from the press. When he signed a four-year contract in the spring of 1976, his agreement with Steinbrenner was that he would be the highest paid Yankee player other than Catfish Hunter. When Reggie Jackson was signed by the Yankees in 1977 to a more lucrative contract, Munson sought to renegotiate his contract and was publicly unhappy about what he viewed as a betrayal of trust. Munson's contract was finally renegotiated at the end of spring training in 1978, but the process left some ill-will. Part of the negotiations concerned Munson being permitted to fly home between games.[8]

The ambiguity with which Munson was viewed was captured in a comment by Steinbrenner:

One thing that saddens me about Thurman is that he spent too much of his little time growling at people....Personally, I'm sorry about Munson's untimely death, but I can't be hypocritical about his character. I can't choke up over guys who go through life saying, "I should be making more money than anybody else."[9]

II. Flying High

A. License to Fly

Munson took his first flying lesson during spring training in February 1978 in a basic civilian training plane known as a Cessna 150. He continued to take lessons, flying light single-engine airplanes, and went on to acquire his private pilot's license in June 1978. At about the same time he acquired a rating to fly multi-engine planes, as he had purchased his first plane, a Beechcraft Duke twin-piston engine aircraft. In February 1979, he also bought, and began flying, a Beechcraft King Air Model E-90, a twin-engine turbo-prop aircraft.[10]

By the summer and fall of 1978, Munson had become interested in acquiring a jet aircraft and, ultimately, he purchased the Cessna Citation I he later crashed. He had taken delivery of the Cessna Citation less than a month before the crash.

Munson took up flying so that he could spend more time in Canton with his wife and three children. In his autobiography, written in 1978, he described his feelings about flying:

> I have a new love to make things somewhat more pleasant for me this year — airplanes. I studied for my pilot's license and received it during the winter. Now…it's possible to fly from New York to Canton in about an hour and I frequently go home even during home stands.[11]

Munson had made sure that the Yankees and Steinbrenner knew that he was flying his own plane home during the season and that his contract did not preclude it. Munson had repeatedly asked to be traded to the Cleveland Indians so that he could be closer to his family, but Steinbrenner had refused to make a trade. Although Steinbrenner was not happy that Munson was regularly flying his own plane home, it seemed like an easy way to keep his star catcher content.[12]

Munson's contract guaranteed him just over $400,000 a year through 1981. The Yankees, therefore, were obligated to pay his widow, Diana Munson, $1 million over the remaining term of the contract. Munson's contract "did not include the usual clause that frees a team from payments in the event of death while flying a private plane."[13]

During the 1979 season, Munson flew home between games so often that he did not even maintain a part-time residence in the New York area. After a game, Munson would often fly home to Canton, returning the next day if there was a game scheduled. Occasionally he would stay in New York with a teammate.[14]

Although flying got Munson home more often, he found that he enjoyed the solitude as well:

> I really love flying. You get up there and nobody asks you any questions. You really enjoy yourself, although you have to stay on your toes. Flying enables you to spend a lot more time by yourself, and I need that. It also lets me spend a lot more time at home, and I need that, too.[15]

B. Too Quick a Study?

Although Munson took flying seriously and worked to improve his skills, he still lacked extensive experience. His friends were concerned about his flying, but could not dissuade him nor keep him from "upgrading" to more sophisticated planes. The $1,250,000 twin-engine Cessna jet he crashed had been delivered only a month earlier. Munson registered the Cessna under the call sign N15NY, a reference to the number on his Yankee uniform.

Although Yankees' owner Steinbrenner tried to convince Munson not to fly, the Yankees did not prohibit his flying. Teammates also had some concerns, as did Munson's wife.

Indeed, after the accident, Steinbrenner was upset at the suggestion that he might have prevented Munson's death:

> Can you imagine Dock Ellis [a former Yankee pitcher] saying that I'm responsible for Thurman Munson's death because I let him fly that plane. I didn't want him to fly that plane. Back in spring training, he told me he had ordered that Cessna Citation and I told him, "You don't need it, don't get it."
>
> Later on he told me he could lease it to somebody for $100,000 and I told him to do it because flying a jet is not like flying a prop plane. I told him that he was jumping too fast from a prop plane to a jet, that a Cessna Citation is harder to fly than a Lear, that flying a jet is a fulltime job. And his wife was dead against it too. But you know Thurman.[16]

Even a National Transportation Safety Board (NTSB)[17] spokesman described the Citation jet that Munson flew as a "hairy little aircraft" that required more than average skill to fly.[18] Experts were surprised at the speed with which Munson obtained his certification, ratings, and licenses—unusually fast for a part-time pilot.

Ironically, just a few days before the crash Steinbrenner had finally agreed to try to work out a deal to send Munson to the Cleveland Indians. Steinbrenner had contacted Cleveland Indians' president Gabe Paul, formerly the Yankees' president; Paul was interested in such a deal. After Munson's death, Paul said "I coveted him as a player. That goes without saying. I just keep thinking to myself how much he wanted to play here and how close he would have been to home."[19]

C. Crash Landing

On the afternoon of August 2, 1979 the weather was clear and beautiful, and, at 4:02 p.m., while Munson was practicing touch-and-go-landings at Akron-Canton Regional Airport, the Cessna Citation I twin-engine jet plane he was piloting crashed 870 feet short of the runway. Two friends, David Hall, a flight instructor who was in the co-pilot's seat, and Jerry D. Anderson, who was also a pilot, had joined Munson as passengers on the eight-seater plane. Neither Hall nor Anderson was F.A.A.-rated to fly a jet.

After the plane hit the ground, it ran through a wooded area, struck a large tree stump and began to burn.

Anderson and Hall attempted to pull Munson from the plane, but were unable to do so in the few minutes before the plane erupted in flames. Anderson and Hall were unable to open the main cabin entry door and, as smoke filled the cabin, escaped through an emergency hatch.

Munson had been wearing his safety belt, but not his shoulder harness, and his head struck the instrument panel during the crash. The impact dislocated the cervical vertebrae, leaving Munson conscious, but paralyzed from the neck down. As Munson had no control over his body below the neck, he was unable to help to free himself. The paralysis helped explain why Anderson and Hall were unable to remove Munson from the wrecked plane. According to the Coroner's report, Munson was "conscious and fully aware of his circumstances from the onset of the crash."[20]

The Summit County Coroner ruled that Munson died of asphyxiation from inhaling superheated air and toxic substances and the acute swelling of the voice box. According to the Coroner's report, "[h]ad Mr. Munson survived, it is highly probable he would have been a quadriplegic."[21]

D. Post-Mortem

Initial reports did not identify the cause of the crash. In fact, the two friends who had accompanied Munson and survived the crash had slightly differing accounts of the seconds prior to the crash. Hall, a licensed flight instructor who had been in the co-pilot's seat, told federal investigators that pilot error during the landing approach may have caused the crash. Hall recalled that he had noticed that Munson had not lowered his landing gear as they made their landing approach. Hall said he told Munson, who then lowered the landing gear when the plane had already slowed too much and was too close to the ground.

Anderson, on the other hand, who was kneeling between Munson and Hall during the approach, told investigators that the plane lost power just before the crash and had begun to roll. He stated that one engine had not responded when Munson tried to pull the plane up.

Both Hall and Anderson estimated that the plane's speed was at 94 knots (or approximately 108 miles per hour). The NTSB air-safety investigator assigned to the investigation, Edward P. McAvoy, noted that a safe speed for the approach should have been 104 knots (or approximately 120 miles per hour).[22]

Shortly after the crash, McAvoy indicated that the crash might have been caused by a loss of engine power. That conclusion was only tentative as the plane's engines had not yet been examined by aircraft engine specialists.

Within a few weeks after the crash, the federal investigators had ruled out mechanical failure as a cause of the crash that killed Munson, but did not then have proof of pilot error. On August 21, 1979, McAvoy announced that a final report would be forthcoming, noting "About 1 percent of our investigations end with the cause undetermined. Unless we find something more positive, I will have to make that determination in this case."[23]

When the field report by McAvoy was filed the following month, however, a cause *had* been determined—"startling mistakes" by Munson as the pilot.[24] McAvoy concluded that the "probable cause of the crash was 'improper use of throttles and flight controls'"[25] by Munson. McAvoy cited four gross errors that caused Munson to "undershoot" the airport:

(1) He made a low approach to the 6,400 foot runway and failed to correct for it, even though there were runway slope indicator lights.

(2) He neglected to keep close watch on the jet's airspeed, letting it drop 10 knots below safe speed.

(3) He forgot to lower the jet's landing gear, and when he did lower it, he failed to compensate with enough power to overcome the added drag.

(4) He was either unfamiliar with or forgot the proper engine procedure for recovery from a low approach.

In addition, he was not using the plane's flaps, which would have added lift to the plane.[26]

The NTSB Aircraft Accident Report identified a series of mistakes, omissions, and misjudgments that led the NTSB to its determination that:

> [T]he probable cause of the accident was the pilot's failure to recognize the need for, and to take action to maintain, sufficient airspeed to prevent a stall into the ground during an attempted landing. The pilot also failed to recognize the need for timely and sufficient power application to prevent the stall during the approach conducted inadvertently without flaps extended. Contributing to the pilot's inability to recognize the problem and to take proper action was his failure to use the appropriate checklist and his nonstandard pattern procedures which resulted in an abnormal approach profile.[27]

The NTSB's conclusion, set forth in its Report, was blunt and unequivocal:

> In summary, the Safety Board concludes that the pilot's conduct of the flight set the stage for oversight and confusion. His disregard for standard practices, procedures and regulations created an atmosphere in which he could not recognize a worsening situation. Perhaps a more experienced pilot would have recognized the dangerous situation more readily and may have taken proper and timely action.... Therefore, the Safety Board concludes that the manner in which the pilot conducted his flight was the primary factor which precipitated the accident sequence, not his training and experience.[28]

McAvoy, the NTSB investigator, in statements to the press, expressed surprise at the apparent ease with which Munson had obtained advanced F.A.A. flight ratings and "strongly suggested that the F.A.A. was a party to the fatal accident through lax licensing procedures."[29]

The record showed that Munson had received a single-engine pilot's license and three advanced ratings within months—multi-engine pilot, instrument pilot, and jet pilot. Munson got his private pilot's license on June 11, 1978, after 91 hours of air time—66 with an instructor and 25 solo. Four days later, Munson received the F.A.A. multi-engine rating.[30] Within six months, on December 22, 1978, Munson had obtained an instrument rating. At that point he had logged 299.3 total flying hours. On July 17 (11 days after taking delivery of the Citation jet from Cessna in Wichita), Munson received a Cessna Citation type-rating which permitted him to act as pilot-in-command of a Cessna Citation jet.[31]

McAvoy suggested that "such rapid progress is unusual for a part-time flier" and criticized the entire F.A.A. system of licensing and rating pilots by routinely delegating responsibilities to examiners employed by private companies that first teach people to fly, and then test and license them, creating a possibility for conflicts of interest.[32] Thus, one employee of A-Flite, an Akron, Ohio company, taught Munson instrument flying and another, the operator of the flight center, was the designated F.A.A. examiner. Similarly, one employee of FlightSafety International, Inc. (FlightSafety) in Wichita, Kansas, taught Munson to fly his new Citation jet, and another employee tested him and gave him an F.A.A. jet rating.

Cessna had a contract with FlightSafety to provide flight training to purchasers of Citation jets and Munson received the flight lessons as part of a purchase package. Although most purchasers were required to get their instruction at FlightSafety's Wichita site and divide their time, on a prescribed basis, between simulator training time and actual flying, much of Munson's instruction in flying his new jet took place while traveling to and from baseball games on the West Coast and the All-Star game in Seattle. At the time of the crash, Munson had had just 41 hours of flying time in the Cessna Citation, and only six hours as pilot-in-command.[33] In what was perhaps an understatement, the NTSB investigator, McAvoy, stated, "This opens the door to Munson's being a novice pilot."[34]

A Cessna spokesman said that Munson's plane was the first Citation in the country to be involved in an accident.[35]

E. Tribute to a Fallen Star

The day after the crash, August 3, 1979, the Yankees were scheduled to play the Baltimore Orioles in Yankee Stadium. Although there was strong sentiment to forfeit or postpone the game, the game was played at the behest of Munson's widow, Diana, who sent the message that Thurman would have wanted the Yankees to play. The Yankees came on the field wearing black arm bands and took their positions, but the catcher's position behind home plate was intentionally left vacant.

Cardinal Cooke offered a memorial prayer and delivered a brief eulogy, and Robert Merrill sang "America the Beautiful." A moment of silence in Munson's memory was requested. Instead, the capacity crowd of 51,151 cheered and chanted "Thurman" for at least 8–10 minutes.

Prior to the game, the Yankees announced that Munson's uniform number, 15, would be retired and that his clubhouse locker would never again be used. A plaque bearing Munson's name and likeness would be placed in centerfield's Monument Park.

The entire Yankees team and many of their wives were among the more than 500 people who attended Munson's funeral in Canton, Ohio. The funeral service was delayed by 30 minutes to await the arrival of the Yankees' charter plane from New York. The mourners in attendance included many former teammates and others in Major League Baseball. About 1,000 other people waited outside to pay their last respects and hundreds lined the route to the cemetery where Munson was to be buried.

Two of Munson's teammates, Lou Piniella and Bobby Murcer, were among those who delivered eulogies at the funeral.

Immediately after the funeral, the Yankees returned to New York to play their scheduled game against the Baltimore Orioles. Steinbrenner had been willing to forfeit the game if the team did not return on time. Again, Diana Munson had told the Yankees that Munson would have wanted the team to play.

The Yankees came from behind to win 5-4 as Murcer, one of the two Yankees who had eulogized Munson earlier in the day, drove in all five runs. Murcer hit a three-run homerun, his first Yankee Stadium homerun in six years, to bring the score to 4-3. Later, in the bottom of the ninth inning, Murcer drove two runs in with a single to left field. As Murcer later stated, "I think we were playing in the spirit of Thurman. I think that's what carried us through the game. It did me."[36]

III. Legal Flights of Fancy

A. Lawsuit by Munson's Estate

1. Developing a Theory of the Case

Increasingly, in our society, when something goes wrong or when someone is injured or killed, our kneejerk reaction is to bring a lawsuit to make the party responsible pay. We assume that someone, other than those injured, must be responsible, but determining the responsible party is not always simple or easy.

After Munson's death, his widow, Diana, was advised to sue. Like her husband, Diana Munson stayed local and retained Eugene P. Okey, an attorney located in Canton, who had been recommended by her family lawyer, to handle the case. Mrs. Munson rejected the advice of Steinbrenner, who urged her to select one of the high-powered "big city" lawyers who had solicited the case. Okey could relate to Munson. After high school, Okey had spent two years playing minor league baseball. An amateur pilot, he first soloed in 1942, although he did not seriously take up flying again until after the Munson case.[37]

Okey's challenge was to develop a viable case in light of the NTSB findings which had squarely placed the cause of the crash on Munson's serious piloting errors. Although mechanical problems were not found to have caused the crash, there was a claim that a defective opening linkage in a door in the fuselage kept Munson's passengers and a firefighter from opening the door and possibly pulling Munson to safety.

The fact that surprised Okey, as it had surprised the NTSB investigator, was the speed with which Munson had obtained his certification to fly a jet, given his limited flight experience. Was Munson really prepared to handle the "hairy little aircraft" he had purchased shortly before the crash? As Okey noted just after the case ultimately settled in 1984:

> Initially the impression of everyone—pilots and non-pilots alike—was that it was strictly pilot error. The FAA ruled that and their investigators had said that to the media. But when I learned that Thurman Munson had taken his first flying lesson in February of 1978 and was delivered a twin-engine jet aircraft just over a year later, I thought it was incredible that a man could progress that fast.[38]

Intriguing as well were the comments of the NTSB investigator, who had criticized the certification process which permitted the same company, which had taught a pilot to fly, to certify his abilities on behalf of the F.A.A.[39]

This line of inquiry and the facts uncovered in pre-complaint investigation and subsequent pre-trial discovery suggested a novel legal theory that formed the heart of the federal lawsuit brought by Mrs. Munson against Cessna, the manufacturer of the Citation aircraft, and FlightSafety, the company which trained and certified Munson to fly the Citation. Okey, a products liability plaintiff's attorney, brought in as co-counsel, Daniel C. Cathcart, an experienced aviation attorney from Los Angeles' Magana, Cathcart & McCarthy, to work on the case.

The lawsuit was filed in federal district court in Akron, Ohio, less than a year after the crash, and sought damages of $42 million. The complaint alleged that Cessna and

FlightSafety should be strictly liable because Cessna sold Munson the jet and the training in a package deal. The claim was essentially that Cessna, knowing that Munson lacked the experience to pilot a jet aircraft, nevertheless, sold him the plane and arranged for a training program which deviated from its standard practices and those of its training affiliates to accommodate Munson's baseball schedule during the 1979 season. In other words, were it not for Munson's celebrity status, he would have been required to take a prescribed formal classroom-type training program offered by one of Cessna's training affiliates. Plaintiff contended that the unique "on the road" training given to Munson by FlightSafety was arranged by Cessna and was a departure from established training protocols. Plaintiff argued that defendants' conduct was grossly negligent and, thus, fell within the principles of strict liability, so that any contributory negligence on Munson's part would not provide a defense.[40]

A second claim was based on the defective door. This claim was that the plane was not crashworthy due to a design defect in the cabin entry door. The inability to open that door blocked a means of escape and prevented a rescue of Munson from the aircraft before it burned.

The complaint sought both compensatory and punitive damages in the amount of $42 million.

2. Defenses

The defenses raised by Cessna and FlightSafety emphasized that the type rating training Munson received was "the best possible" and "uniquely suited to his individual needs."[41] Both defendants relied heavily on the NTSB findings of pilot error and on expert testimony that Munson's ability to perform "was so degraded by fatigue, stress and complacency that an accident was virtually preordained."[42] Cessna argued that

> [Munson] crashed not because he should not have been flying a Citation, but because he should have not been flying at all on August 2, 1979. He was fatigued from a late flight in bad weather the night before, and in pain from persistent knee problems which were aggravated by an injury the night before that necessitated his removal from the game. He was overly complacent in the relatively undemanding circumstances of August 2, 1979, and was under stress from various concerns. All these things together were a prescription for the disaster that occurred.[43]

In other words, as Cessna argued, Munson's accident occurred "*despite* the quality of the aircraft and his training" and "the fault lies entirely with Mr. Munson."[44]

Cessna also argued that it violated no duty to Munson in selling him the Cessna Citation I and that the sale was not effected through any misrepresentations. Cessna claimed that the Cessna Citation was actually a less complex and less demanding aircraft to fly than the Beechcraft planes Munson already owned. Cessna further argued that the Citation I met or exceeded all applicable FAA regulations on crashworthiness and that crashworthiness had nothing to do with Munson's death.[45]

3. Discovery—Training "on the Fly"

Pretrial discovery exposed, but could not explain satisfactorily, the speed with which Munson obtained his certification to fly the Citation I jet he had purchased. When Munson took delivery of the aircraft on July 6, 1979, a FlightSafety pilot-instructor was present and, thereafter, informally instructed Munson in both ground school and flight training between day and night baseball games in Oakland and Seattle.

Munson's only attendance at FlightSafety's training facility in Wichita consisted of four hours in a flight simulator on July 17, 1979, the same day he was given his flight test by an F.A.A. flight examiner, who was also a FlightSafety employee.[46]

Yet, as the NTSB Report noted and Cessna strongly argued, Munson had received more training than the minimum specified by Federal Aviation Regulations. He had recently been certified as competent in the Cessna Citation aircraft and had demonstrated "above average" skill.[47]

In addition to developing evidence about the purchase of the Citation I and the alleged inadequacy of Munson's flight training, there was extensive discovery which focused on the following issues:

(1) The events leading up to the crash and the details of the accident scene and attempted rescue.

(2) Problems Munson had experienced with the aircraft from the date of purchase.

(3) The crashworthiness of the aircraft, especially with respect to the pilot seat and cabin entry door.

(4) Munson's ability as a baseball player and his potential for the future in baseball and business.

Several members of the Yankees organization were deposed. Some, like Yankees manager Billy Martin and teammates Graig Nettles and Reggie Jackson, were able to testify about their experiences on flights with Munson in the Citation I and various troublesome incidents that had occurred during those flights. These same witnesses, and others, including Yogi Berra and Gabe Paul, testified about Munson's ability as a baseball player, as well as his potential for a future in baseball, possibly as a manager.

Family, friends and business associates were able to testify about his family life, his professional and business interests, and his future plans and goals.[48]

It would take more than four years, and approximately $127,000 in pretrial expenses, for the case to get to trial.[49]

4. Trial and Settlement

The case finally went to trial in May, 1984, almost five years after Munson's death. Federal District Judge David D. Dowd, Jr. presided over the case. He had been unable to steer the parties toward settlement during discovery prior to trial. A four week trial was anticipated. Just before the trial began, though, FlightSafety came to a settlement agreement with plaintiff, and the trial proceeded with only a single defendant, Cessna.

After four days of trial, which included jury selection and a view of the crash site and the severely damaged aircraft, the plaintiff and Cessna agreed on a settlement. Judge Dowd sealed the settlement in the case and ordered that it be kept confidential. His July 27, 1984 order ended the case. The settlement amounts were not even revealed to the probate judge for the Munson estate. Mrs. Munson, reportedly, was very satisfied with the settlement. It is generally acknowledged that the $1.69 million settlement figure reported in the press at that time[50] was an understatement.

B. Yankees' Lost Chattel

1. The Lawsuit

Almost a year after Munson's crash, and after the release of the NTSB report on the crash, the Yankees filed a $4.5 million lawsuit charging negligence and breach of implied warranty of fitness for use by Cessna and FlightSafety.[51] The case followed (sequentially and in the essential theories raised in the complaint) the $42 million wrongful death suit filed by Munson's estate on behalf of his widow. Like Diana Munson's lawsuit, the Yankees' action claimed Cessna and FlightSafety had not adequately trained Munson to fly the Cessna Citation he crashed and that defendants were negligent in permitting or encouraging Munson to fly the aircraft when they knew that he did not have the requisite training and instruction to do so safely. In addition, the Yankees alleged that Cessna breached an implied warranty of fitness for a particular purpose by failing to supply an aircraft suitable for operation by a novice jet pilot.[52]

The main difference between the lawsuits, however, was in the theory of damages, which was also without precedent. As the lawyer retained by the Yankees for the litigation, John McCarthy of Cleveland, Ohio, stated at the time, at issue was "the value of 'chattel under contract.'"[53] The amount of the lawsuit was based on Munson's estimated fair market value in Major League Baseball. McCarthy further explained:

> There are a number of owners who would offer $4.5 million for Munson. There might be two guys in the entire population of the U.S. that can catch in the major leagues and hit the way he did later in the season....
>
> In essence, under contract, a player is like merchandise, a painting. What difference does it make?[54]

There was no coordination of the Yankees' lawsuit with the Munson lawsuit, and the Yankees' action was eventually dismissed[55] while the Munson case proceeded to trial and, ultimately, settlement.

2. Three Strikes

Although the Yankees' lawsuit raised claims similar to those raised in the Munson action, legally and factually the lawsuits were fundamentally different. The Munson suit raised a novel theory of recovery based on the sale of a jet and inadequate training due to Munson's celebrity, but importing that theory into an action brought by the owners of the Yankees made for a far less sympathetic case than one brought on behalf of Munson's widow and children. In order to succeed in their action, the Yankees would have had to overcome serious legal objections which did not apply to an action brought by Munson's estate.

The first major obstacle was the concept of "chattel"[56] upon which the Yankees' lawsuit was premised. The Yankees obviously could not substitute their interest for the interests of Munson's widow and children, who were entitled to recover as heirs to Munson's estate under Ohio law. But what exactly was the interest of the Yankees, which they were suing to protect? If an individual is killed in an automobile accident which results from a manufacturer's design defect, does her employer have an interest which would justify a lawsuit against the manufacturer to recover for the employer's damages? The employer/employee relationship does not generally give rise to a protectable interest in situations where the claim arises from activity outside the employment relationship—at least not an interest protected by an action in tort.

The interest claimed by the Yankees in their lawsuit was for "the value of 'chattel under contract.'" Under this theory, a baseball player is likened to "merchandise" or a "painting" or a "racehorse" and the team can then sue to recover the value of the destroyed chattel. The Yankees argued that the theory advanced should apply only where the deceased was "unique chattel" in terms of market value.[57] With the elimination of actual slavery by the 13th Amendment to the U.S. Constitution and "baseball slavery" with the demise of the reserve system as a result of the Curt Flood litigation,[58] it is difficult to argue convincingly that baseball players, including high-salaried stars, are articles of personal property.

Another barrier to the Yankees' claim involved the question of "duty." The Yankees cannot simply step into the shoes of Munson or those of his heirs and survivors and argue that any duty owed to them is a duty owed to the team. Rather, the question is whether Cessna or FlightSafety owed any duty to the Yankees. Are the Yankees foreseeable plaintiffs within the "zone of danger"?[59] Again, although under some circumstances one might imagine a claim based on interference with the Yankees' contract with Munson, it is a stretch to argue that breach of a tort duty to Munson also constitutes breach of a duty to the Yankees. The federal district court found that neither Cessna nor FlightSafety owed a duty of care in the selling of a jet aircraft to Munson or in the training of Munson to fly the jet aircraft. The court also concluded that the existence of a professional services contract between Munson and the Yankees did not create a duty owed by defendants to the New York Yankees.[60]

Assuming that there was a breach of duty by Cessna and FlightSafety owed to the Yankees, was that breach of duty the actual or proximate cause of the Yankees' injuries? The answer to that question may depend on what conduct, if any, is characterized as a breach and whether the consequences were foreseeable.

Finally, was the injury claimed by the Yankees too remote and speculative? Do the Yankees have a claim for the loss of the services of a valuable player?

If Munson had retired in 1979, the Yankees would have lost his services. Neither Munson nor the Yankees would have had a tort claim against anyone. If Munson had suffered a career-ending injury on August 1, 1979, in the last game in which he played, the Yankees would have lost his services. His subsequent death in a plane crash on August 2, 1979 would still have given rise to a claim against Cessna and FlightSafety by the Munson estate, but damages would have been reduced because he no longer had a future as a baseball player. In this scenario, the plane crash clearly did not cause any damage to the Yankees. If instead of a plane crash, Munson had died in a car accident on the way home from Yankee Stadium, his estate might have had a tort claim in negligence against the other driver for his personal injuries. It is hard to imagine the Yankees bringing a separate lawsuit against the driver for his negligence. As the district court found, the Yankees' loss was "merely a remote and indirect consequence" of defendants' actions.[61]

3. Alternatives

Even if a baseball team has no legal right to sue for damages to a player as "chattel," there may be other ways a team may protect against the serious financial impact which results from the loss of the services of a key player. There is no question that key players may affect the finances of a team well beyond the amount of their paychecks. A star player may draw more fans to the stadium, increasing game revenues substantially. Revenues from advertising, endorsements and media deals may be affected as well. A more effective, and surer, method of hedging against the loss of a key player than post-event litigation is to anticipate the situation and address it by contract.

A team may, by contract prohibit certain activities by players. Professional baseball has used a standard agreement since the 1870s. Although a standard agreement is incorporated into Major League Baseball's collective bargaining agreement, standard contracts can be amended and additions made based upon individual negotiations.[62]

The Uniform Player's Contract for Professional Baseball includes a provision that restricts a player's participation in certain other sports activities:

> 5(b) The Player and the Club recognize and agree that the player's participation in certain other sports may impair or destroy his ability and skill as a baseball player. Accordingly, the player agrees that he will not engage in professional boxing or wrestling; and that, except with the written consent of the club, he will not engage in skiing, auto racing, motorcycle racing, sky diving, or in any game or exhibition of football, soccer, professional league basketball, ice hockey or other sport involving a substantial risk of personal injury.[63]

Another section of the standard contract gives the club the rights to obtain injunctive or other equitable relief to prevent a contract breach.[64] Whether flying private jets is or is not a "sport involving a substantial risk of personal injury," it is not uncommon for a club to bar certain non-baseball activities it considers too risky.

Munson bargained with the Yankees for the right to fly his plane home regularly. Nevertheless, the Yankees could have protected their "investment," even while accommodating Munson's needs.

The Yankees might have purchased insurance adequate to protect them from risk or required Munson to purchase equivalent insurance for the benefit of the Yankees.

Teams may not have recognized a need for such insurance in the 1970s when the average compensation paid to players was significantly lower. The insurance vehicles may not have been as accessible. At the present time, teams routinely consider insuring players signed to big-ticket contracts. Each team evaluates its own threshold of risk. Players making more than $3 million per year are considered insurable.[65] The cost of the policy or the premium paid is determined by various factors including the percentage of the contract covered, the age of the player, the player's position, and the type of sport.[66]

A player may also take out personal insurance against career-ending injuries or death.

Insurance, however, is by no means a panacea. Just as players' salaries have skyrocketed, the insurance market has been retrenching. As a result, insurance is more difficult to obtain, contains more limiting provisions and exclusions, runs for shorter terms than the length of many sports contracts, and is substantially more expensive.[67]

Yet, with guaranteed contracts, if a player dies or is injured, a risk to the club is created.[68]

IV. Afterthoughts

Every time a celebrity dies in a plane crash, particularly a small, private plane, the media begins to tick off a list of prominent people who have died in airplane accidents.

Perhaps our fascination with such lists stems from the celebrity of those on them and the sense that primarily the wealthy and famous fly their own planes.

Among the well-known sports figures who have died in plane crashes are Notre Dame football coach Knute Rockne (1931), former heavyweight boxing champion Rocky Marciano (1969), and Pittsburgh Pirates outfielder Roberto Clemente (1972). Prominent entertainers who have died in plane crashes include cowboy humorist Will Rogers (1935), actress Carol Lombard (1942), orchestra leader Glenn Miller (1944), rock star Buddy Holly (1959), country singer Patsy Cline, soul singer Otis Redding (1967), actor Audie Murphy (1971), and singer John Denver (1997). Other prominent individuals who have died in plane crashes include House Majority Leader Hale Boggs (1972), Senator John Heinz (1991), John Kennedy, Jr. (1999),[69] and Senator Paul Wellstone (2002).[70] Only a few of these celebrities were piloting their own planes at the time of the crash.

The NTSB, the federal agency responsible for investigating airplane crashes, publishes an annual review of aircraft accident data. A review of the most recent report available shows that the total number of accidents, as well as the number of accidents resulting in fatal injuries, has declined since the 1970s when Munson crashed. Although accidents often have multiple causes and contributing factors, pilots were cited as either a cause or contributing factor in 75 percent of accidents and 78 percent of fatal accidents. In contrast, environmental conditions are rarely cited as an accident cause. The aircraft was found to be a cause or contributing factor in 31 percent of accidents, as well as 21 percent of fatal accidents.[71]

Munson's plane crash fits into the most common pattern—pilot errors were identified as the cause of the crash.

V. Conclusion

Munson has not yet made it into baseball's Hall of Fame in Cooperstown, but he has not been forgotten.[72] His locker remains empty and unused. When his name is mentioned at the annual Old-Timers' Day Game at Yankee Stadium there is always a loud ovation.[73]

The lawyers who worked on the litigation have vivid memories of the case, and lawyers in the aviation field tend to be familiar with the theories advanced in the case. The Munson litigation raised novel questions about the responsibility of aircraft manufacturers to ensure that their celebrity clients are properly trained to fly the aircraft they buy.

It is in a manufacturer's interest to sell to high-profile celebrities whose purchases and lifestyle make "news." Celebrity endorsements are regularly sought for all manner of products to boost sales. For large ticket items, such as aircraft, sales to celebrities encourage other similar sales, as friends and acquaintances of the purchaser become familiar with a product bought and used by someone they know and respect. This tactic has been referred to as "a form of 'viral' marketing, a strategy meant to ensure that a product will get into the right hands—people whose endorsement creates a demand by causing a ripple effect."[74]

Celebrity purchasers may sometimes bargain for significant discounts on such acquisitions or obtain other remuneration for explicit or implicit endorsements. A celebrity may even willingly pay list price or a premium to get the newest "toy" or status item, particularly one customized to specific needs or preferences. According to Cessna, Munson had inquired about the possibility of a discount for sponsorship or promotion and was told it was unlikely. Cessna asserted that it had no interest in seeing Munson buy the plane over other potential customers, and that no discount for the Citation was given to any purchaser, including celebrity golfers Jack Nicklaus and Arnold Palmer.[75] According to Munson's associates, Munson was pressured and enticed by Cessna to purchase the jet. The vendor-celebrity relationship is often a symbiotic, commercial relationship, which does not usually impose any legal liability or responsibility.

A sports icon who purchases a high-powered sports car is not given a driving test before the keys are turned over. Jet aircraft, however, are a qualitatively different and, perhaps, unique product. Cessna was selling jet planes, not cars. Large numbers of people drive cars and many individuals fly, but relatively few are capable of flying a jet aircraft. Accordingly, Cessna was aware that it was marketing to a fairly small population and recognized that training purchasers in the operation of the aircraft was an essential part of the "package" it was selling. Making accommodations in that training package to close a sale was arguably fraught with danger.

There appear to be no reported cases which further develop the theory of recovery advanced in the Munson case. This does not mean there have been no cases—it may be that any such cases were either not reported or were settled before any legal opinion was generated. It is, however, likely that the theory would have limited application in other cases. The Cessna Citation was the first and only business jet to receive single-pilot approval. Cessna was unlikely to sanction similar training deviations or accommodations after the sizable settlement paid out in the Munson case. Other than jet aircraft, are there other products for which manufacturers might similarly be held accountable? Perhaps, but it is not a likely scenario.

Teams have necessarily become more savvy about the risks of losing key players with outsize contracts. Insurance provides the most reliable and predictable way to hedge the risks of a business that relies on the continued health and skills of individual athletes.

The Pine Tar Incident

by Paul E. McGreal[*]

"Baseball games often end with home runs, but until yesterday the team that hit the home run always won."[1]

Baseball has a love-hate relationship with its rule book. On the one hand, there is no baseball without rules. If we simply sent nine players onto a grass field with no rules, we would have chaos. Rules tame that chaos, letting players and coaches focus their talent and energy on a single endeavor. With minor variations, the games played in school yards, little league fields, college ball parks, and major league stadiums share the beauty and majesty of our national pastime. Rules make that possible.

On the other hand, rules should not foil athletic skill and strategy. Baseball is about throwing, catching, hitting, and running. It is also about knowing when and where to throw, catch, hit, and run. Games should be won and lost by players taking these actions, and coaches and managers making these decisions. Rules that hamstring talented players, or foil mastermind coaches, rob the game of its joy, yielding the sad lament that a game was decided not on the field of play, but on a technicality.

Perhaps the pine tar incident was so bitterly contested because it pitted these conflicting views against one another. As most New York Yankees fans remember, the pine tar incident involved a home run by Kansas City Royal third-baseman George Brett. Brett was called out, and the home run nullified, because pine tar extended beyond the handle onto the hitting surface of his bat. The Yankees invoked a rule against excessive pine tar, arguing that all rules should be enforced to the letter. If the pine tar rule was not enforced, then what rule next?[2]

The Royals tagged the pine tar rule a technicality. Excessive pine tar does not help a batter hit the ball farther, so why call the batter out? Doing so allows a technical rule to change the outcome of a game. The Yankees could not beat Brett with their pitching, so they retreated to the pages of the rule book.[3] Technical rules were the last refuge of scoundrels.

To lawyers, this debate has a familiar ring.[4] Lawyers are infamous for their use and abuse of rules. After all, it is within the legal system's complex web of legal rules that lawyers ply their trade. This chapter offers a lawyer's view of the pine tar saga, highlighting parallels between the on-field and off-field antics, and the legal world.[5] Before getting to the law, though, the next section recounts that fateful game.

I. A Sticky Situation

A. "A Lovely Sunday Afternoon"

It was Sunday, July 24, 1983, just two weeks after the All-Star break, and the Yankees were hosting the Royals. With their recent playoff rivalry fresh in people's minds, any meeting between the teams heightened excitement among players, coaches, and fans.[6] As both teams were once again in the hunt for their respective division crowns, the stakes were also high.[7] Throw in that the Yankees were managed by the volatile Billy Martin, and the game was a dry tinder box needing only the slightest spark to ignite.

The spark came in the top of the ninth inning. The game was close throughout, with both teams scoring a run in the second inning, and the Royals adding a second run in the fourth inning. Both teams scored again in the sixth inning, the Royals getting one run in the top of the inning and the Yankees getting three in their half, leaving the Yankees with a 4-3 lead. After two more scoreless innings, the Royals took their last licks. Yankee reliever Dale Murray retired the first two Royals that inning, Willie Wilson and Pat Sheridan. U.L. Washington then singled, bringing up Royals' clean-up hitter George Brett.

With two outs and a runner on first, Martin pulled Murray in favor of his once-dominant closer, Goose Gossage. Gossage and Brett had some history, with Brett having homered off Gossage to give the Royals the 1980 American League pennant. As Yogi Berra might have said, it was "déjà vu all over again."[8] Brett sent a Gossage fastball over the right field fence for a home run. After rounding the bases in triumph, Brett returned to high fives in the Royals' dug out. The Royals led 5-4.

Or so they thought. Soon after Brett left the field, Billy Martin walked out to speak with home plate umpire Tim McClelland.[9] Martin argued that Brett should be called out, and his home run called back, because Brett's bat had too much pine tar on it. Martin explained that the rules prohibited pine tar farther than eighteen inches from the tip of the bat handle. Because the pine tar on Brett's bat went well beyond eighteen inches, Brett violated the rule and should be called out. Watching from the dugout, Brett knew Martin was arguing about excessive pine tar, but laughed off the effort: "They didn't have a case."[10]

After Martin made his case, McClelland conferred with his crew. They took Brett's bat and used home plate, which measures 17 inches across, to determine how far the pine tar reached onto the bat. They estimated that "heavy pine tar" extended about 19 to 20 inches onto the bat, and a lighter coating extended about 24 inches. Given clear evidence that Brett's bat violated the pine-tar rule, McClelland and his crew saw no other option than to call Brett out. McClelland then "thrust his right arm in the air, signaling that Brett was out."[11]

McClelland's call set off a firestorm on the Royals' bench. Brett roared from the visitor's dugout like a locomotive, charging full boar for McClelland. If not intercepted by umpire Joe Brinkman, Brett likely would have flattened his intended target. One writer described the scene: "Tobacco spittle flying from his mouth, Brett clearly didn't have reasoned discussion on his mind, and even after a flying tackle by umpire Joe Brinkman slowed him down, it took two umpires and a Kansas City coach to wrestle him away from McClelland."[12]

Amidst this chaos, the evidence of the crime—Brett's bat—was almost secreted away. Royals pitcher Gaylord Perry, himself somewhat of a baseball scofflaw, snatched the bat from the umpires.[13] Perry ferried the bat back to the dugout, where players formed a chain handing the bat from one player to the next. The only flaw in this plan was that the human chain ended before it reached the Royals' clubhouse, in full view of the Yankee Stadium security and the umpiring crew. Umpire Brinkman merely fetched the bat from the last Royals in line and took it into custody.[14]

The Royals' rage sprang from a basic issue of fairness. It was silly that pine tar on a bat, which no one believed made a batted ball fly farther,[15] should nullify a home run. Royals manager Dick Howser did not mince his words: "To take that kind of home run away from a guy because of some stupid technicality, that's weak, and I've already appealed it."[16] He continued, "It knocks you to your knees. I'm sick about it. I don't like it. I don't like it at all. I don't expect my players to accept it." Even the Yankees expressed sympathy on this score, albeit grudgingly. Gossage remarked, "I can sympathize with George, but not that much." And Billy Martin, as only he could, summed up the Yankee perspective: "It's a terrible rule, but if it had happened to me I would have accepted it." Then, apparently in a self-congratulatory mood, he observed, "It turned out to be a lovely Sunday afternoon."[17]

B.   The Naked Truth about Pine Tar

So, why was there pine tar on Brett's bat? The generally accepted answer is that pine tar helps a batter grip the bat. Brett did not like the feel of a batting glove: "I like the feel of raw hands on raw wood."[18] So, he turned to pine tar to get a better grip.[19] Indeed, the pine tar Brett used that day was provided by the Yankees as a courtesy to the visiting Royals.

But, that raises another important question: If Brett was using pine tar to get a better grip, why was it so far up his bat? Once again, Brett had a convincing answer:

> [Y]ou...don't want to hold the bat where pine tar is, so you put it up higher on the bat, get some on your hands when you need it, and then go back to the bottom of the bat. Where I hit that ball, it was on the meat part of the bat, about five inches from the end. There's no pine tar 29 inches from the handle. The ball wasn't even close enough to the pine tar to smell it.[20]

Brett put pine tar high on his bat for convenience. Instead of carrying a container of pine tar with him to the plate, or risking that he might not have enough pine tar to complete an at bat,[21] he simply applied extra pine tar just above his hands for later use.[22] In short, Brett did not believe he was altering the bat's ability to hit the ball, only his ability to grip the bat.

C.   "A Rule's a Rule"[23]

The on-field decision to call out Brett rested on three rules. First, Rule 6.06(a) said that "a batter is out for illegal action when he hits an illegally batted ball."[24] Second, Rule 2.00 defined an "illegally batted ball" as "one hit with a bat which does not conform to Rule 1.10." Third, Rule 1.10(b) limited application of pine tar:

> The bat handle, for not more than 18 inches from the end, may be covered or
> treated with any material (including pine tar) to improve the grip. Any such

material, including pine tar, which extends past the 18 inch limitation, in the umpire's judgment, shall cause the bat to be removed from the game. No such material shall improve the reaction or distance factor of the bat.

Under these rules, the umpire's call seems straightforward: a player is out for hitting an "illegally batted ball;" a ball is "illegally batted" if it is struck with a non-conforming bat; and a non-conforming bat includes a bat where the pine tar extends more than 18 inches above the handle. Because Brett's bat had pine tar "well over 18 inches" from the handle,[25] his bat did not conform to Rule 1.10, and his home run was an illegally batted ball. Thus, Brett was out, and the home run did not count.

While supported by the rules, the umpire's decision drew fire from many quarters. The Royals, of course, were the most vocal critics. Their main argument was that it makes no sense to call a batter out for doing something that gave him no unfair advantage. Pine tar merely gives batters a better grip (which is why the league allows pine tar for eighteen inches on the bat handle), but does not otherwise aid the hitter. If the pine tar did not help Brett hit the home run, why should it affect whether the home run counts? Brett's punishment was completely unrelated to his crime. Merely removing the bat from further play would have satisfied one interpretation of Rule 1.10(b).

The Yankees and their supporters did not necessarily disagree. They mostly conceded that Brett had gained no unfair advantage, and that calling him out served no real purpose.[26] Nonetheless, then-New York Senator Alfonse D'Amato expressed the near universal Yankees' position: "Sure it's fine print, but a rule's a rule."[27]

This all raises an important question: If pine tar does not aid a batter in hitting the ball, why do the rules limit its use? The reason turns out to be quite practical and mundane. When a foreign substance, such as pine tar, gets on a ball, the umpire is supposed to remove the ball from play and replace it with a new ball.[28] If batters routinely applied pine tar on the hitting surface of their bats, any contact with the ball, even a foul tip, might ruin the ball for further play. This would dramatically increase the number of balls needed to complete a game (as well as the time needed to complete games), and those extra balls cost money. So, to save time and money, the rules prohibit pine tar on the bat's hitting surface.[29]

D. "I Would Not Want to Be Poor Lee Living in New York City"

The Royals decided to take their case to American League President Lee MacPhail, filing a formal protest shortly after the game ended. The rules allow a protest only "when a manager claims an umpire's decision is in violation of these rules,"[30] expressly forbidding protests of "judgment decisions by the umpire."[31] The Royals claimed that McClelland's call violated the rules, arguing that the proper penalty for excessive pine tar was removal of the bat, not calling the batter out. McClelland's call should be reversed, and Brett's home run should be reinstated.

The controversy was now in MacPhail's hands, and under the rules, his decision would be final. Neither team thought there was much chance that MacPhail would overrule the umpires. Yet, as Yankee owner George Steinbrenner awaited the decision, he fired a shot across the bow of his former General Manager. Perhaps betraying a hint of concern, Steinbrenner remarked: "If the Yankees should lose the Eastern Division race on the ruling of American President Lee MacPhail, I would not want to be poor

Lee living in New York City. He better start house-hunting out in Missouri, close to Kansas City."[32]

E. Lee's Decree

The day after the pine tar game, Brett's bat completed its short trip from Yankee Stadium (in the Bronx) to the American League offices (in mid-town Manhattan). MacPhail did not rule immediately, taking time to inspect the bat and consult with officials about the meaning and application of the pine tar rules.

On July 28, MacPhail held a press conference to announce his decision. The umpires' decision, while "technically defensible," violated the "spirit of the rules." As the Royals had argued, pine tar did not aid the flight of a batted ball, and thus excessive pine tar should not be grounds for calling a batter out. Rather, the penalty should be removal of the bat, unless or until the pine tar is removed. Brett's home run stood, and the game was revived, the Royals leading 5-4 with two outs in the top of the ninth inning.

MacPhail's pine tar decision not only overturned an umpire's decision, but may have upended the Yankees' season. As they walked off the field after the pine tar game, the Yankees had won nine of their last ten games.[33] And, after the next series against the Texas Rangers, the Yankees extended the winning streak to twelve of thirteen.[34] During the streak, the Yankees had moved "from fourth place to a tie for the division lead, the first time they'd been there since April 16, 1982."[35] The team was on a roll.

Then came MacPhail's decision, handed down on the off day following the Texas series. From then on, the Yankees were a different team. Beginning with the next series in Chicago, "the Yankees lost 6 of their next 7 games and 13 of 22, sliding to fifth place."[36] (Brett also hit a slump of sorts, not hitting another home run until August 17, the day before the pine tar game was completed.)[37] So, while losing the pine tar game itself did not keep the Yankees from the playoffs (they finished seven games out of first place), Yankee fans cannot shake the feeling that MacPhail's decision killed their team's momentum.[38]

II. Ambush

While Billy Martin's pine tar argument was quite clever, his timing was perhaps more so. Immediately after the game, he bragged that he had known for two weeks about Brett's pine tar problem. While playing an earlier series in Kansas City, a Yankee player brought Brett's excessive pine tar use to Martin's attention.[39] The Yankees were familiar with the pine-tar rules because back in 1975 Thurman Munson had been called out for an excessive pine tar violation.[40] The Yankees planned to do the same to Brett if and when he got a significant hit.

It turned out that Brett did not get a big hit during the series in Kansas City. So, the Yankees kept the pine tar strategy under their collective hats until the Royals came to New York two weeks later. Their strategy seemed in jeopardy when Brett broke his bat.[41] But, as most baseball players are creatures of habit, Brett's next bat had the same pine tar problem. When Brett hit a home run with the new bat, Martin pounced: "You don't call him on it if he makes an out. After he hit the home run, I went out and said he's using an illegal bat."[42]

But, should Martin have been allowed to choose when to raise the pine tar problem? Or, should he have raised the problem before Brett completed his at bat?[43] By waiting until after Brett had hit the ball, he denied both Brett and the umpire an opportunity to fix the problem. Brett could have either wiped the pine tar off the bat or gotten a new bat. Should this have made a difference?[44]

Lawyers routinely confront issues of timing. In this section, we explore two legal rules that impose time limits on lawyers—statutes of limitations and rules of waiver—and ask how those rules apply to the pine tar incident.

A. Use It or Lose It: The Statute of Limitations

Perhaps the most common timing issue is what lawyers refer to as the "statute of limitations." A statute of limitations is a time period within which a person must file a lawsuit. For example, consider a case where John is crossing the street and is hit by a car driven by Jane. If John believes that Jane was at fault, John would have to file his lawsuit within the statute of limitations. If the statute of limitations for a car accident is two years, then John would have to file his lawsuit within two years of the day the accident happened. If John waits longer than two years, he cannot bring the lawsuit.

Statutes of limitations serve some important purposes. First, they allow people to plan their affairs by limiting how long they must worry about being sued. Without a statute of limitations, Jane would spend the rest of her life wondering whether John might someday sue her over the car accident. The statute of limitations allows Jane to forget about the accident after a certain period of time.

Second, the statute of limitations forces a person to bring a lawsuit sooner rather than later, because evidence needed to try the lawsuit may be lost over time. For example, in the John and Jane accident, if John waits many years to bring his lawsuit, witnesses may forget what they saw, the location of the accident may change, and physical evidence (such as Jane's car) may no longer be available. As this evidence deteriorates over time, so does a jury's ability to decide what happened.[45] The statute of limitations prevents this by requiring the lawsuit be brought quickly or not at all.

The purposes behind a statute of limitations do not really apply to the pine tar incident. First, consider the purpose of allowing people to get on with their lives. Because Martin raised the pine tar question immediately after Brett hit his home run, the issue was resolved before the game went any further.[46] Thus, the Royals did not have the issue hanging over their head either for the rest of that game, or for the rest of the season.

The second purpose, forcing people to raise an issue before the evidence is lost, also does not apply. In the pine tar incident, Martin's delay did not result in any loss of evidence. McClelland and his crew had immediate access to Brett's bat, and the bat had not changed. In short, the umpires could determine how much pine tar was on Brett's bat just as easily after he hit the home run as before. If Martin had waited until September to object to Brett's home run, the bat would likely have changed condition or (more likely) have been discarded. But, by raising the issue immediately after Brett's hit, Martin allowed the umpires to make their decision on the best available evidence.

B. Waive Your Rights Goodbye

While statutes of limitations do not condemn Martin's delay, the legal concept of waiver might. When a party "waives" their right to do or not do something, the party loses that right. An example of waiver that comes close to the pine tar incident involves how lawyers object to evidence at a trial. During a trial, the lawyers for each side take turns offering evidence to the judge and jury, with rules of evidence establishing what types of information lawyers may offer. For example, lawyers may question witnesses who are of sound mind and have firsthand knowledge relevant to the lawsuit.[47]

During trial, the lawyers are responsible for policing the rules of evidence. The judge plays a passive role, stepping in only if a lawyer objects to evidence offered by the other party. For example, consider our John and Jane accident case, and assume that John sues Jane for his injuries. If John's lawyer offers improper evidence, such as irrelevant witness testimony, it is up to Jane's lawyer to object to that testimony. Jane's lawyer does so by standing and telling the judge why she thinks the testimony violates the rules of evidence. If Jane's lawyer does not do so, the trial goes on and the testimony comes into evidence. In other words, by not raising an objection to John's evidence, Jane waives her objection.

Jane's lawyer is under a time limit when raising evidence objections. For example, if John's lawyer asked Jane whether she had ever had an extra-marital affair, Jane's lawyer must stand up and object immediately after the question is asked. If Jane's lawyer waits and allows Jane to answer the question, Jane's lawyer will have waived the objection.[48]

This waiver serves two main purposes. First, it allows judges to easily fix the problem. If the lawyer objects before a forbidden question is answered, the judge can stop the jury from ever hearing the forbidden testimony. In the example above, the judge can keep the jury from ever hearing whether Jane had an extra-marital affair. That way, the jury is not prejudiced by irrelevant testimony.[49] If, however, Jane's lawyer waits until the end of the trial to object, the judge has no good way to fix the problem. The judge could tell the jury to ignore the irrelevant testimony, but that would be like asking the jury to ignore a skunk in the court room — not very effective. Or, the judge could hold a new trial with a different jury. But, that would waste the time and money of the court, the witnesses, the jury, the parties, and everyone else involved in the lawsuit.

Another reason parties must object in a timely manner is to allow the judge to make a quick, well-informed decision. At trial, the judge sits in the courtroom and hears the evidence as it is presented. So, when a party timely objects to a question, the judge knows the context in which the objection is made. The judge can then rule quickly with a full understanding of the circumstances. If, however, the objection is made after trial, it may be days or weeks after the question that the judge must rule. The judge has likely forgotten the precise question as well as what was going on at the time the question was asked. Thus, delay in objecting makes the judge's job more difficult.

The purposes underlying waiver cut both ways when applied to Martin's pine tar objection. On the one hand, like an evidence objection, one could argue that Martin should have raised the pine tar objection when he first noticed it — back in Kansas City — so the umpire could fix the problem quickly. If Martin had objected before Brett had gotten a hit, the umpire could have taken the offending bat out of play, and Brett's at bat would have been legal. By waiting until Brett hit the ball, then, Martin waived his objection.

On the other hand, Martin's delay did not affect the umpire's ability to make a call. After the hit, Brett's bat was available for inspection, in the same condition as when Brett began his at bat. The umpires could—and did—easily measure the pine tar and make the correct call. Delay did not affect the umpires' decision-making.

In the end, I would favor forcing Martin to object sooner rather than later. In trials, judges often frown on unnecessary delay. This is especially true when the delay is used to gain a strategic advantage. To mix in a basketball metaphor, one judge told me that he was always suspicious of lawyers "playing away from the ball." He suspected that the lawyer had a weak case if the lawyer tried to distract the jury with irrelevant information or delaying tactics.

The same could be said for Martin. One must suspect a manager's confidence in his team if he resorts to technicalities that have little to do with the fairness of the other team's play. By waiting, Martin made it quite clear that his intention was to take advantage of a technicality, not simply to enforce a rule. The rule could have been just as easily enforced by raising the objection as Brett came to bat, allowing removal of the offending bat. Indeed, the rule would have been better enforced if Martin had done so. Recall that the reason for the pine tar rule is to prevent damage to baseballs. By waiting to raise his objection, Martin ensured that more baseballs might be damaged, defeating the rule's purpose. In the end, Martin's delay served no other purpose than to take strategic advantage of a technicality. Such conduct should not be rewarded.

III. "The Spirit of the Rules"

Speaking about the Royals' protest, Billy Martin opined: "In a court of law, he wouldn't have stood a chance."[50] Martin was only half right. He was correct that MacPhail's task resembled one performed by lawyers and judges every day—interpreting statutes and other rules of law. Whether it be a local ordinance regarding excessive noise or a federal income tax statute, lawyers are routinely asked to read and apply rules.

Martin was wrong, however, in concluding that the Royals' protest "wouldn't have stood a chance" in court. In this section, we consider both how MacPhail interpreted the baseball rules, and how lawyers interpret legal rules. For all the criticism of his decision, we will see that MacPhail's arguments resemble those used by lawyers and judges every day.

A. The Rules

Before reviewing how MacPhail interpreted the rules, let's first get the text of those rules on the table. For lawyers, this is always the first step. For, what is the point of having a rule if you do not start by looking at its words?[51]

As noted above, McClelland's pine tar call involved three rules. First, Rule 6.06 lists several actions for which a player shall be called out. The action listed in subsection (a) is most relevant to the pine tar incident:

6.06 A batter is out for illegal action when—

    (a) He hits an illegally batted ball.

      . . . .[52]

Next, we need to know the definition of an "illegally batted ball." This leads us to Rule 2.00, which defines many of the terms used in the baseball rules:

2.00 Definition of Terms

    . . . .

    An ILLEGALLY BATTED BALL is (1) one hit by the batter with one or both feet on the ground entirely outside the batter's box, or (2) one hit with a bat which does not conform to Rule 1.10.[53]

Rule 1.10, in turn, sets forth several requirements regarding the type and condition of the bat. Subsection (b) is relevant to our discussion:

    (b) The bat handle, for not more than 18 inches from the end, may be covered or treated with any material (including pine tar) to improve the grip. Any such material, including pine tar, which extends past the 18 inch limitation, in the umpire's judgment, shall cause the bat to be removed from the game. No such material shall improve the reaction or distance factor of the bat.[54]

These three rules led the umpires to conclude that Brett must be called out. Their reasoning was as follows:

    (1) Rule 6.06(a) says that a batter is out for hitting an illegally batted ball.

    (2) An illegally batted ball includes a ball hit with a bat that violates Rule 1.10.

    (3) A bat with excessive pine tar violates Rule 1.10(b).

    (4) Brett's bat violated Rule 1.10(b) because it had excessive pine tar.

    (5) Brett's home run was an illegally batted ball.

    (6) Brett is out for hitting an illegally batted ball.

To Martin and the umpires, this logic was quite straightforward, and its result—that Brett was out—unavoidable.

B. I Take My Text Plain

Judges and lawyers generally agree that they must follow the clear or plain meaning of a statute or rule.[55] The United States Supreme Court has said that "courts must presume that a legislature says in a statute what it means and means in a statute what it says there. When the words of a statute are unambiguous, then, 'judicial inquiry is complete.'"[56] For example, in the case *United States v. Locke*,[57] the Court addressed a federal statute that required people claiming certain mining rights to file required paperwork "prior to December 31." Failure to do so forfeited the claim. One family filed the required paperwork a day late, on December 31. When the government rejected their paperwork, the family argued that a filing deadline on the second-to-last day of the year made no sense. Congress probably meant to say "on or before December 31," but made a mistake in drafting the statute. The Court disagreed, deciding that the statute was clear—"prior to December 31" means "prior to December 31."[58] The filing was late.

Are the baseball rules quoted above as clear as the federal filing deadline? The umpires and Yankees thought so.[59] But, consider a possible source of ambiguity. It is true that Rule 6.06(a) says that a batter is out for hitting an illegally batted ball, and that Rule 2.00 defines illegally batted ball to include balls hit with a bat that violates Rule 1.10. Rule 1.10(b), however, could be read to create an exception to these rules. Unlike the other subsections of Rule 1.10, Rule 1.10(b) provides a specific penalty: "Any such material, including pine tar, which extends past the 18 inch limitation, in the umpire's judgment, shall cause the bat to be removed from the game." No other subsection—neither Rule 1.10(a) on bat size and composition, Rule 1.10(c) on colored bats, nor Rule 1.10(d)[60] on cupped bats—provides for removal of the bat or any other specific penalty. So, one might read Rule 1.10(b) to provide the sole, special penalty for excessive pine tar, with the Rule 6.06(a) penalty (calling the batter out) applying only to the other three subsections of Rule 1.10.

C. Canons to the Left of Us.
Canons to the Right of Us.

The preceding argument is recognizable to lawyers as one of the canons of statutory interpretation. A "canon" is a rule of thumb—a guideline that lawyers follow to help them interpret rules and statutes.[61] They are the legal profession's rough attempt to describe how people use words.[62]

For example, lawyers apply a canon that goes by the name expressio unius est exclusio alterius.[63] This is a fancy Latin phrase meaning that the express listing of some things excludes those not listed. If a local ordinance forbids the use of "motorcycles, automobiles, and mopeds on pedestrian paths in a public park," the ordinance should be read to allow the use of bicycles. By listing specific vehicles that are forbidden—"motorcycles, automobiles, and mopeds"—the ordinance is presumed to allow any vehicle not listed, such as a bicycle. The instinct behind this canon is that a writer would not go through the trouble of listing specific items unless she intended the rule apply only to those items. Otherwise, why make the effort to come up with a list? Why not simply say "no vehicles in the park"?

A different canon applies to the pine tar rules: "Specific provisions targeting a particular issue apply instead of provisions more generally covering an issue."[64] Here, the general provision is Rule 6.06(a), which provides the penalty of an out for an illegally batted ball. The rule is general, covering all instances of an illegally batted ball. Rule 1.10(b) is the more specific provision, covering only excessive pine tar, and it provides a penalty of bat removal. One can read Rule 1.10(b), which is specific to pine tar, to limit Rule 6.06(a), which does not deal specifically with that issue. Rule 1.10(b) would provide the sole penalty for excessive pine tar, and Rule 6.06(a) would cover all other illegally batted balls where the rules did not provide a more specific penalty rule.

Of course, the Rule 1.10(b) bat removal language need not be read as an exception. One could read Rule 1.10(b) as requiring that the bat be removed in addition to the batter being called out for an illegally batted ball. So, the next question is whether we have any reason to read Rule 1.10(b) as the sole penalty for excessive pine tar as opposed to an additional penalty.

Lee MacPhail made a similar argument in his pine tar ruling:

Rule 1.10 outlines several requirements affecting the legality of a bat. One of these is that "the bat handle, for not more than 18 inches from the end may be

covered or treated with any material (including pine tar) to improve the grip...,"
but that no such material shall improve the reaction or distance factor of the bat.
Rule 1.10 specifically provides that if the pine tar extends past the 18 inch limitation, the bat shall be removed from the game. If it was intended that this infrac-
tion should fall under the penalty of the batter's being called out, it does not
seem logical that the rule should specifically specify that the bat should be removed from the game.

Again, the more specific provision controls the general.

D. I've Said It Before, and I'll Say It Again...

Lawyers and judges also look to language in other, similar statutes in interpreting a
statute. The idea is that a legislature wrote all of a jurisdiction's statutes, and so other
statutes hold clues as to how the legislature uses words and phrases.[65] For example, the
Supreme Court had to interpret a federal statute that allowed the winning party at trial
to recover "a reasonable attorney's fee" from the losing party.[66] The question was
whether fees paid to expert witnesses—such as doctors, economists, and other professionals—are included in the phrase "attorney's fee." When the Supreme Court looked
at how Congress used the phrase "attorney's fee" in other federal statutes, it found that
some statutes awarded the winning party "fees for attorneys and expert witnesses."
These other statutes suggested that Congress does not use the words "attorney's fee" to
include "expert witness fees." Otherwise, Congress would not have inserted the words
"and expert witnesses" in the other statutes; simply providing for "attorney's fees"
should have done the job.[67] Thus, a statute awarding only "a reasonable attorney's fee"
does not cover expert witness fees.

We can apply a similar analysis to the pine tar rules. Recall that Rule 1.10(b) sets
forth the penalty of bat removal for excessive pine tar, and our question is whether that
penalty is in addition to or instead of the penalty in Rule 6.06(a) that the batter be
called out. Rule 6.06(d) sheds some light on this question:

6.06 A batter is out for illegal action when—

> ....

> (d) He uses or attempts to use a bat that, in the umpire's judgment, has
> been altered or tampered with in such a way to improve the distance
> factor or cause an unusual reaction on the baseball. This includes bats
> that are filled, flat-surfaced, nailed, hollowed, grooved or covered
> with a substance such as paraffin, wax etc.

> No advancement on the bases will be allowed and any out or outs
> made during a play shall stand.

> In addition to being called out, the player shall be ejected from the
> game and may be subject to additional penalties as determined by his
> League President.[68]

Recall that the first words of Rule 6.06 tell us that "the batter is out" for violating any
subsection of that Rule. The last sentence of subsection (d) goes on to provide two specific penalties for a doctored bat: ejection from the game and further penalties assessed
by the League President. Note that subsection (d) expressly provides that these two
penalties are "[i]n addition to being called out." We might infer that without the phrase

"[i]n addition to," the two penalties in the last sentence of subsection (d) would have been the sole penalties for a doctored bat, replacing the penalty that the batter be called out. Otherwise, why include the words "[i]n addition to" in subsection (d)?

Rule 6.06(d) tells us something about how the rule drafters use language. Specifically, it tells us what the drafters mean when they state a general penalty in one part of a rule, and then state a more specific penalty in another part of a rule. The more specific penalty replaces the general penalty unless the rules say otherwise. Rule 6.06(d) said otherwise by providing that its specific penalties were "in addition to" Rule 6.06's general penalty that the batter be called out.

How does this apply to the pine tar rules? The first sentence of Rule 6.06 states a general penalty for batter misconduct—the batter shall be called out. Rule 1.10(b) then states a more specific penalty for specific batter misconduct: remove a bat with excessive pine tar. From what we said in the last paragraph, we may infer that the rule drafters intended the more specific penalty in Rule 1.10(b) to replace the general Rule 6.06 penalty, unless the rules say otherwise. Unlike Rule 6.06(d), which said that ejection and other penalties are to be "[i]n addition to being called out," Rule 1.10(b) contains no language even suggesting that bat removal is in addition to being called out. Because the rule drafters omitted words like "in addition to being called out" from that subsection, we may infer that bat removal was intended as the sole penalty for excessive pine tar.

E. What Were They Thinking?

In interpreting statutes and rules, one can also consider the purpose the legislature was trying to achieve.[69] While the United States Supreme Court routinely makes such arguments, perhaps the most infamous instance is the case of *Holy Trinity Church v. United States*.[70] The case involved a 19th Century labor law that prohibited employers from paying for a foreign citizen to emigrate to the United States "to perform labor or service of any kind." Employers violating the law were subject to a penalty. When a church in New York paid for an Englishman to travel to the United States to serve as its pastor, the United States government argued that the church had violated the statute and thus owed the applicable penalty. According to the government, performing the duties of a church pastor was "labor or service of any kind" within the meaning of the statute. The government believed "labor or service" meant any work done for compensation, and the phrase "of any kind" meant that Congress had not limited the types of work included within the statute.

The Supreme Court agreed that the government's argument made sense:

> It must be conceded that [performing the duties of a pastor] is within the letter of this section, for the relation of rector to his church is one of service, and implies labor on the one side with compensation on the other. Not only are the general words labor and service, but also, as it were to guard against any narrow interpretation and emphasize a breadth of meaning, to them is added "of any kind"....[71]

The Supreme Court, however, decided to look beyond the most obvious reading of the statute, placing the statute's words within the context of their times. This required the Supreme Court to ask why Congress enacted the statute, and whether Congress' reasons shed new light on the words "to perform labor or service of any kind." In doing so, the Court claimed to apply the "spirit of the law," as opposed to the "letter of the law."[72]

Before considering how the Supreme Court used purpose and context to interpret a statute, consider a simple example where context can change the perceived meaning of words. Imagine that you see a sign with the words, "Keep off the grass!"[73] What picture just came to mind? My guess is that you saw a sign planted in a patch of grass, and that the sign was telling passers-by to not trample on the grass. But, what if the sign was hanging in a drug rehabilitation clinic? We could now read the sign as imploring patients not to use marijuana. How we read the sign, then, depends on the context within which we find the sign. In the context of a lawn, we read it to ask that we not trample the lawn; in the context of drug rehabilitation, we read it to ask for forbearance of drug use. Different contexts suggest different readings.

In *Holy Trinity*, the Supreme Court looked for clues to the context surrounding the statute. Its first clue was the title Congress gave to the statute:

> [T]he title of this act is, "An act to prohibit the importation and migration of foreigners and aliens under contract or agreement to perform labor in the United States, its Territories and the District of Columbia." Obviously the thought expressed reaches only to the work of the manual laborer, as distinguished from the professional man. No one reading such a title would suppose that Congress had in mind any purpose staying the coming into this country of ministers of the gospel, or, indeed, of any class whose toil is that of the brain.[74]

Here, the Supreme Court argues that Congress meant "labor or service of any kind" to mean manual labor, and not professional service. The statute's title serves as evidence of this intent.

The Supreme Court found further evidence of intent in the statute's historical context:

> The motives and history of the act are matters of common knowledge. It had become the practice for large capitalists in this country to contract with their agents abroad for shipment of great numbers of an ignorant and servile class of foreign laborers, under contracts, by which the employer agreed, upon the one hand, to prepay their passage, while, upon the other hand, the laborers agreed to work after their arrival for a certain time at a low rate of wages. The effect was to break down the labor market....[75]

Simply put, American employers were importing cheap foreign manual laborers, which drove down the wages paid to American manual laborers. To solve this problem, Congress prohibited the importation of manual laborers. Neither the problem nor its solution dealt with service professionals. Because applying the statute to a church pastor would not serve Congress' purpose, the Court concluded that a pastor did not "perform labor or service of any kind."[76]

Lee MacPhail looked to the purpose of the pine tar rules in deciding whether Brett should be out for using excessive pine tar. He made a similar distinction between the spirit and the letter of the law:

> It is the position of this office that the umpires' interpretation, while technically defensible, is not in accord with the intent or spirit of the rules and that the rules do not provide that a hitter be called out for excessive use of pine tar.

MacPhail went on to explain the purpose behind the pine tar rules and how it affected his decision:

> It is the conviction of the League President that the intent of the...rules is to declare a batter out and inflict discipline on him for use of an illegal bat, which has been "altered or tampered with to improve the distance factor or cause an

unusual reaction on the baseball." (It has not been seriously contended that the pine tar on Brett's bat did either.) It is not the intent of the rules to declare batters out or discipline them for improper use of pine tar. (The provisions restricting the distance pine tar can extend up the barrel of the bat was primarily intended to keep from spoiling the ball and requiring new balls to be constantly brought into the game.) Conversations with several members of the Rules Committee reinforced this belief.

The logic is straightforward: if the pine tar rule is meant to protect baseballs, the best way to protect baseballs is to remove the bat.[77] Punishing the batter after he has hit the ball, and presumably caused the damage, does not achieve that purpose.

Graig Nettles' account of the pine tar incident illustrates that calling Brett out for excessive pine tar made little sense. Martin had warned Yankee catcher Rick Cerone that Brett might use an illegal bat and to check the bat if Brett made a "big hit."[78] When Brett homered in the ninth, Cerone remembered he was to check the bat, but did not know what he was supposed to check for. So, Cerone checked for the most logical problem—whether the bat was corked.[79] When Cerone saw that Brett's bat was not corked, he tossed it aside and left the matter at that. Only then did Billy Martin approach McClelland to complain about excessive pine tar.

The Cerone anecdote speaks volumes about simple baseball common sense. Cerone knew that Brett might use an illegal bat, and that he should challenge the bat if Brett got a big hit. Without knowing more, Cerone made the logical inference that you would challenge a batted ball only if the bat had given the batter an unfair advantage. Cerone's first thought was to check for cork. After all, a corked bat gives a batter a clear advantage. Pine tar never even entered his mind, as it has no affect on the bat's ability to hit the ball. To call Brett out for something that did not unfairly help him made no sense.

F.   Custom: Actions Speak Louder Than Words

Lawyers and judges sometimes consider accepted custom or practice in interpreting a rule. This goes back to the old saying we learned from our parents: "Actions speak louder than words." For example, consider once again the city ordinance that prohibits operating a "vehicle" in a public park. Assume that for the last fifty years, the city has maintained bicycle paths throughout the park, and has even encouraged citizens to use bicycles as an environment-friendly alternative to cars. If the question comes up whether a bicycle is a "vehicle" covered by the ordinance, the answer should be a clear "no." For a long time, the city and its citizens have acted like bicycles are allowed in the park. Indeed, their actions only make sense if bicycles are allowed. Lawyers and judges should interpret laws consistent with the community's long-held traditions and customs.

MacPhail made a similar argument in his pine tar ruling. At one point, he states that removing the bat, not calling the batter out, "is the manner in which batters attempting to hit with excessive pine tar have generally been restricted." Later, he says:

> [I]t has not been the usual practice in the Major Leagues to call batters out for using a bat with excessive pine tar. The general procedure, when noticed by umpires or complained about by the opposing team, has been to require use of a new bat or require that a new bat be cleaned up.

And, Brett's personal experience was the same: "Some umpires, when they see the pine tar too high, will say, 'Hey, George, clean up your bat.' "[80] MacPhail's point is that how people act is strong evidence of what they think the rules mean. Again, actions speak louder than words.

Yet, one prior case contradicted MacPhail on this point. Recall that Thurman Munson had been called out for excessive pine tar in a 1975 game. MacPhail, however, argued that the Munson incident supported his decision. Specifically, MacPhail explained that the Munson incident was partly responsible for amending Rule 1.10(b) to add the following language: "material, including pine tar, which extends past the 18 inch limitation shall cause the bat to be removed from the game."[81] MacPhail's reasoning is that (1) Munson was called out for excessive pine tar in a 1975 game, (2) the baseball powers-that-be thought that Munson should not have been called out, and (3) they changed Rule 1.10(b) so that no future batter would be called out for excessive pine tar. And, since 1975, the rules had been applied consistent with this understanding.

G.   ...It's How You Play the Game

Lawyers and judges sometimes use what they call "substantive canons" to interpret statutes. Recall that a canon is a rule of thumb for interpreting statutes. The textual canons we looked at in section C above dealt with how people use words. Substantive canons have a different focus, encouraging lawyers and judges to interpret statutes consistent with certain values or goals that are important to our legal system, such as fairness or democracy.

An example of a substantive canon is the "rule of lenity," which directs lawyers and judges to interpret criminal laws leniently (i.e., to avoid imposing a criminal penalty) if the law is ambiguous. This plea for leniency comes from the American ideal of due process. For criminal laws, when a person's liberty is at stake, due process discourages criminal punishment unless a person had prior notice of what the law required of them. Notice means both that the laws were publicly available, and that the laws were written clearly enough that people could understand what conduct is prohibited. Without such notice, citizens are never sure what they must do (or not do) to comply with the law.

MacPhail's pine tar ruling offered what could be seen as a substantive canon of baseball: "[I]t is the strong conviction of the League that games should be won and lost on the playing field—not through technicalities of the rules—and that every reasonable effort consistent with the spirit of the rules should be made to so provide."[82] Like America's commitment to due process, Major League Baseball is committed to deciding games based on athletic ability and quality of play, not the "technicalities of the rules." When a baseball rule is ambiguous, the rule should be interpreted so that games are decided by on-field play, not strategic rule manipulation. Because the pine tar rules were ambiguous, MacPhail felt that he should interpret those rules to allow the players' on-field performance (Brett's home run), as opposed to a technical rule violation (Brett's excessive pine tar did not help him hit the home run), decide the game. The rules should be read to remove a bat with excessive pine tar, not to call the batter out. Brett's home run should stand.

H.   Did MacPhail Blow the Call?

That Yankees fans vilified MacPhail for his decision is understandable. The team was in the hunt for the AL East crown, and any loss hurt that cause. Further, fans were growing restless, as the Yankees had not won the World Series for five years, which qualifies as a drought for the Bronx Bombers. (Little did they realize that it would be another thirteen years until the World Championship would come their way again.) That the loss came at the hands of the dastardly Royals only compounded the frustration.

But, looking back twenty years later, MacPhail's ruling made much sense. The pine tar rules were confusing, leaving it unclear what to do when a ball was hit with a pine tarred bat. In deciding that Brett should not have been called out, MacPhail relied on many arguments that judges and lawyers use every day. While this fact alone may be enough for some to condemn MacPhail (after all, lawyers rank one rung below politicians and used car salesmen on the social ladder), it shows that his decision was thoughtful, and not some unarticulated knee-jerk reaction.

After the 1983 season, Major League Baseball fixed the pine tar rules, enshrining MacPhail's ruling in the Rule Book.[83] Three changes achieved this result. First, Rule 6.06 was changed by deleting the language that, "A batter is out for illegal action when— … (a) He hits an illegally batted ball."[84] Second, the term "illegally batted ball" was deleted from the list of definitions in Rule 2.00.[85] Third, the following Note was added to Rule 1.10(c):[86] "If the umpire discovers that the bat [contains excessive pine tar at] a time during or after which the bat has been used in play, it shall not be grounds for declaring the batter out, or ejected from the game."[87]

IV. Is That a Fact?

A major criticism of MacPhail's decision was that he second-guessed his umpires, thereby undermining their authority. The League President should play little or no role in reviewing on-field calls, unless the decision is clearly wrong. In short, MacPhail should have kept his nose out of the matter and let the umpires do their job.

A. Law Appeal

Most lawyers would see this criticism as misplaced. In the legal system, many trials are followed by an appeal. During an appeal, the party that lost the trial asks a group of judges—known, not surprisingly, as "appellate judges"—to determine whether the trial judge or jury made any mistakes. If the appellate judges conclude that the trial judge or jury made an incorrect decision, they will "reverse" that decision and send the case back for the trial judge to fix the mistake.

The appellate judges' role varies depending on whether they are reviewing a question of fact or a question of law. To understand the difference between these two types of questions, consider once again John and Jane's car accident case. Recall that John was a pedestrian struck by Jane's car. Assume that Jane wants to argue that the accident was John's fault because he was outside the cross-walk when she hit him. Jane's argument raises two questions, one of law and the other of fact. The legal question is whether the law allows a pedestrian hit by a car while walking outside the cross-walk to sue the car's driver. The factual question is whether John was within the cross-walk at the time Jane hit him. At trial, the trial judge will decide the legal question (Does the law allow John to sue if he was outside the cross-walk?), and the jury will decide the fact question (Was John outside the cross-walk?).[88]

Assume that the trial judge decides that John cannot sue if he was outside the cross-walk, and that the jury decides that John was outside the cross-walk.[89] Based on these decisions, the judge will conclude that John cannot win his lawsuit and will enter a judgment saying that Jane wins. As the losing party, John can then appeal, asking the appellate judges to decide whether the judge and jury were mistaken in their cross-walk decisions. In short, John will ask the appellate judges to decide that the trial judge erred in concluding he could not sue if he was outside the cross-walk; or that the jury erred in concluding that he was outside the cross-walk.

The appellate judges will treat John's legal and factual questions quite differently. First, the appellate judges will decide the legal question from scratch, giving no deference to the trial judge's decision. The appellate judges and the trial judge are all lawyers who have the same legal training and the same access to the legal materials (case law, statutes, etc.) needed to decide a question of law. There is no good reason to think that the trial judge was in a better position to decide the legal question. Thus, if the appellate judges conclude that the law should allow John to sue even if he was outside the cross-walk, they will reverse the trial judge.

Second, appellate judges will not reverse the jury's factual decision unless they believe it to be clearly wrong. Unlike legal decisions, appellate judges give great deference to factual decisions made at trial. Fact decisions get different treatment because the jury had much better access to the evidence than do appellate judges. At trial, the jury sees the witnesses in person, observing behavior such as body language, facial expressions, and tone of voice. The jury uses all this information to judge a witness' credibility.

When appellate judges get a case, however, the trial is long over and all that remains is a written transcript of what the witnesses said. The appellate judge has only the witness' words, without all the other valuable clues that were available to the jury. By comparison, the jury was in a much better position to weigh the evidence. For this reason, appellate judges rarely second-guess juries, reversing only when a jury made a clear or egregious mistake. Thus, an appellate judge will not overturn the jury's decision that John was outside the cross-walk, unless those judges believe that the jury was clearly mistaken.

B.   Baseball Appeal

The appellate distinction between questions of law and fact is remarkably similar to the questions involved in the pine tar incident. Imagine that the pine tar incident was a sort of mini-trial. Martin was bringing a lawsuit against Brett, arguing that Brett had violated the pine tar rules and thus should be called out. The umpires served as trial judges who had to decide two questions, one of fact and one of law. The factual question was whether Brett's bat had pine tar more than eighteen inches from the handle. The legal question was whether to call Brett out if his bat had too much pine tar on it? On the factual question, the umpires examined the evidence—they measured Brett's bat against home plate—and decided that Brett did have pine tar greater than eighteen inches from the handle. On the legal question, the umpires considered the rules and decided that a batter must be called out for hitting a ball with an excessively pine-tarred bat. Based on these two decisions, the umpires decided that Martin should win the mini-trial, and Brett was called out.

The Royals' protest is like an appeal of the umpires' trial decision, with American League President Lee MacPhail acting as the appellate judge. As an appellate judge, MacPhail would treat the legal question (Should excessive pine tar result in an out?) differently from the fact question (Did Brett use excessive pine tar?). On the one hand, MacPhail would decide the legal question for himself. Regardless of what the umpires thought the rules meant, MacPhail should read the rules and their history and come to his own decision. Indeed, MacPhail was actually in a better position to interpret the rules than were the umpires. MacPhail had the luxury of time to study the rules and their history, as well as how the rules had been applied in the past. By comparison, the umpires had no time to study any of this information before reaching their decision. Thus, it shows no disrespect to the umpires to say that MacPhail, with the luxury of time to think about his decision, came to a different conclusion.[90]

On the other hand, MacPhail should not overturn the umpires' factual decision unless it was clearly wrong. While MacPhail ultimately got to see the bat, he did not see it immediately after Brett's hit. Since it is possible that the bat's condition changed in transport, the umpires had the best view of the evidence. Not surprisingly, MacPhail did not challenge the umpires' factual decision.

Interestingly, the Yankees later benefitted from this fact versus law distinction in a protest filed during the 1996 American League Championship Series. In the eighth inning of game one against the Baltimore Orioles, Derek Jeter hit a fly ball to the right field fence. Baltimore right fielder Tony Torasco stretched to catch the ball, but failed, with the ball ending up in the glove of a Yankee fan.[91] The question was whether the ball had flown over the outfield fence before the Yankee fan caught it, or whether the Yankee fan had reached over the outfield fence to catch the ball just above Torasco's outstretched glove.

While the "law" in this case was clear, the facts were not. The law—the baseball rules—provided that the batter is out if the fan had reached over the fence.[92] The fact issue was much murkier. On the field, no one had a clear view of how far the fan had stretched his glove. From his vantage point, right-field umpire Rich Garcia did not believe the fan had reached onto the field, and he signaled a home run. The call gave the Yankees a crucial run in their 5-4 win.[93] When video replays showed that the fan had reached over the fence, the Orioles filed a protest.

Unlike the pine tar protest, the Oriole's protest asked the League President to overrule an umpire's factual decision, or judgment call. As we discussed above, the League President, acting as an appellate judge, ought to give great deference to umpires' on-field fact decisions. And, that is exactly what American League President Gene Budig did, upholding the call and preserving the Yankee win.[94]

C. A Different Kind of Uniform

There is one further reason that MacPhail, as the American League's appellate judge, should have the last word on what the baseball rules mean. It is only fair that the rules be applied the same way in every American League game. There is no good reason for the rules to mean one thing when the Yankees play the Royals but another when the Red Sox play the White Sox. As MacPhail put it in his written ruling, "those of us in administrative positions in baseball" ought to ensure "clear, uniform instructions to the umpires on the interpretation of the rules." When inconsistent decisions change the outcome of games, it is not fair that a team's fate depends on whomever happens to be umpiring that day. Allowing the League President to decide what the rules mean for everyone avoids this problem.

Our legal system is set up in a similar way. Typically, the trial courts decide cases in a small, local area, and the appellate courts decide cases covering a larger area that includes many trial courts. In Texas, there are trial courts in every one of the state's 254 counties, with many counties having more than one trial judge. If each of these trial judges interpreted the law differently, Texas law would mean something different in each county. To prevent this problem, there is a group of appellate courts that covers many counties. For example, the Fort Worth Court of Appeals covers 12 counties in north Texas,[95] making sure that the trial judges in those counties apply Texas law the same way. Other regional courts of appeals (e.g., Houston, Dallas, El Paso, San Antonio) do the same for their counties. At the top of the pyramid, the regional courts of appeals all answer to the state's top appellate court, the Texas Supreme Court. The Texas Supreme Court ensures that all state courts apply a uniform interpretation of Texas law. This way, Texas law is not applied one way in Dallas and quite another in Houston.

Unless MacPhail interpreted the pine tar rules once-and-for-all, different umpiring crews might make different decisions. In fact, two previous pine tar calls had come out differently.[96] As I mentioned above, a 1975 Thurman Munson home run had been taken back due to excessive pine tar.[97] But, one month before the pine tar incident, the Cleveland Indians challenged a home run by Jim Rice of the Boston Red Sox on account of excessive pine tar. The umpires refused the challenge, and the home run stood. Oddly enough, the crew chief for the Indians-Red Sox game was Joe Brinkman, who was also on the crew for the pine tar game. Without a definitive ruling on the proper penalty for excessive pine tar, inconsistent calls were possible even by the same umpires.

V. Collateral Proceedings

When all the dust had settled after MacPhail's ruling, there was still more baseball to play. The Royals were now leading 5-4 with two outs in the top of the ninth inning. The American League scheduled the game's completion for the evening of August 18, an off day for both the Yankees and Royals.[98] Still stinging from MacPhail's decision, the Yankees objected to that date because their players "need time to themselves" on the off day.[99] George Steinbrenner went so far as to suggest that his team would forfeit the game if held on that day.[100] League officials would not relent, and the game was officially scheduled.

But, the pine tar controversy would not be settled that easily. A Yankee decision regarding the game's completion set off legal maneuvering, including a lawsuit. This section describes that fateful decision.

A. One Game for the Price of Two?

As August 18 approached, the Yankees announced that tickets from the July 24 game would not be honored for the August 18 completion because the July 24 game would be treated as a suspended game.[101] When a game is suspended,[102] it must be finished immediately before the two teams' next game. The fans with tickets to the next game, then, see completion of the suspended game. So, if a Tuesday night game is suspended in the top of the ninth inning due to a power failure, the teams complete that inning before playing their next game on Wednesday. Those with tickets to the Wednesday game, not the Tuesday ticket-holders, see completion of the Tuesday game. To do otherwise would be impractical, as a team would have to seat the Tuesday ticket-holders (if any showed up to see only a few outs), complete the suspended game, get those fans out of the stadium, and then admit the Wednesday ticket-holders. The baseball rules conclude that this would be more trouble than it is worth.

On this logic, the July 24 ticket-holders had no claim to attend the completion of the suspended game; that honor fell to people who purchased tickets to the completed game. So, while the Yankees would honor season tickets, they would charge fans "$2.50 for a reserved seat or $1 for a bleacher seat" to what could be as little as four outs of baseball.[103] The ticket prices were set to cover the almost $25,000 cost of opening Yankee Stadium for the game.

This did not sit well with some New York fans. While the entire pine tar incident had stayed out of the courts, the Yankees' ticket policy spurred two lawsuits. Three days before the scheduled resumption, two parents filed lawsuits on behalf of their children, three boys ages six, seven, and fourteen. The boys and their parents had attended the July 24 pine tar game, and they sued the Yankees and Lee MacPhail for free admission to the August 18 completion.[104]

B.   The Yankees Court Their Fans

The lawsuit began when the young fans, known in the lawsuit as the plaintiffs, filed a Complaint in New York state court. A Complaint is the document that formally begins the lawsuit by telling the defendants, here the Yankees and MacPhail, why the plaintiffs are suing them and what the plaintiffs want.[105] The plaintiffs' Complaint said the following about why the young fans were suing the Yankees and MacPhail:

3.   On or about July 24, 1983, the plaintiffs purchased from the defendant New York Yankees (hereinafter "Yankees") two tickets for the July 24, 1983 games [sic] between the Yankees and Kansas City Royals, and such tickets were sold, at Yankee Stadium, at about 10:00 noon [sic] on such date, for $9.00 apiece, for section 17, Box 463C, seat # 7, and the seat adjacent thereto.

4.   Such contract, the two tickets sold by the Yankees to the plaintiffs, was for Game # 52, and for the complete game # 52, not for part of the game.

5.   Game # 52 has not been completed, but is to be played on or about August 18, 1983 at 6:00 P.M. at Yankee Stadium.

6.   Plaintiffs contend that a contract exists between plaintiffs and the defendant YANKEES, for themselves and for the total of 33,944 persons who were in attendance that date, which other persons are similarly situate [sic], and entitled to see in person, the completion of the game for which a contract was entered into with the Yankees by the purchase of a ticket.

7.   The plaintiffs have called the Yankees, on August 15, 1983, at about 1:30 P.M., and requested the right from the Ticket Manager at Yankee Stadium for admission to the game on August 18, 1983 based upon the tickets sold on July 24, 1983, and such request was refused, which refusal was arbi-

trary and inconsistent with the contract made with the defendants YANKEES to see the entire game # 52, and not just a portion thereof.[106]

While the Complaint is quite wordy and filled with legal jargon, it boils down to a few simple points. The father and son bought a ticket to the July 24 game, and that ticket formed a contract between, on the one hand, the father and son, and on the other hand, the Yankees. Under this contract, the father and son agreed to pay nine dollars for each ticket, and the Yankees agreed to let the father and son watch the entire July 24 game. While the father and son had already paid the nine dollar ticket price, the Yankees had not yet fully performed their side of the contract, as the July 24 game was not over. To complete the contract, the Yankees must allow the father and son to attend the August 18 completion without further charge. The Yankees' plan to charge for attendance breached the contract.

The young fans asked the judge to do two things. First, of course, they wanted the judge to order the Yankees to allow July 24 ticket-holders to attend the completion of the pine tar game, whenever that game was played. Second, the fans asked the court to issue an injunction to stop the Yankees from completing the pine tar game until the lawsuit was over.[107] The fans wanted an injunction because they were afraid that by the time the court heard their lawsuit, the game would already be over. To decide whether the fans' July 24 tickets entitled them to admission to the August 18 continuation, the judge would have to take evidence and hear arguments from both parties. In most lawsuits, parties are allowed a period of time — anywhere from a few weeks to many months — to gather their evidence and prepare their legal arguments before the trial is held. Because the young fans filed their lawsuits only three days before the pine tar game was scheduled to resume, the game might be played before the case could come to trial, and the lawsuit would then be moot. So, the fans asked the court to postpone the game while the parties argued about whether the Yankees must honor the July 24 tickets.

To get an injunction, the young fans had to show two things. First, they had to show that they were likely to win when the case went to trial. For, there would be no reason to postpone the pine tar game if the young fans were likely to lose their lawsuit. Second, the young fans had to show that they would be irreparably harmed if the pine tar game was completed as scheduled and their July 24 tickets were not honored. If the young fans proved these two things, the court would order the Yankees not to play the game until the lawsuit was over.

C. "Play Ball"

As if the pine tar incident hadn't taken enough twists and turns, when the Yankees finally got to court, they supported the young fans' request for an injunction. In a hearing held on August 17, the Yankees' lawyer argued: "It is totally unreasonable on the part of the league to say the one time you can play the game is on Thursday afternoon at 6 P.M. with two lawsuits pending. We don't want ill will on the part of our fans in Manhattan and the Bronx. We want a full judicial determination."[108] This was precisely the argument the young fans were making: Do not play the game until the lawsuits are over. Lest one think that the Yankees had suddenly taken a fan-friendly turn, the ploy was a rather transparent attempt to stick it to MacPhail. Recall that the Yankees, still stinging from MacPhail's decision, never wanted to play the completed game.[109] They saw the young fans' lawsuit as a chance to stop the game from going forward.[110]

At 10 A.M. on game day, the trial judge, Justice Orest Marseca, announced his decision granting the young fans' injunction. Justice Marseca ruled that the injunction was proper because, first, the young fans were likely to win their lawsuit, and second, they would be irreparably harmed if the game went forward before the lawsuit could be completed. The game was off.

With less than eight hours remaining until the scheduled start time, MacPhail and his lawyers immediately appealed the trial judge's decision to an appellate court in Manhattan. Justice Joseph Sullivan heard hurried arguments that afternoon, and ruled quickly, overturning the trial judge and ordering that the game take place. Justice Sullivan believed that the young fans would not suffer irreparable harm if the game went forward. The boys could simply purchase tickets for $2.50 apiece (surely not an exorbitant sum, even for such young fans), and if they later won their lawsuit, they could seek a refund from the Yankees.[111] Then, just two and a half hours before game time, Justice Sullivan announced his order from the bench, choosing two simple, familiar words: "Play ball."[112]

VI. Conclusion:
"Is this some special kind of game?"

With game time approaching, the Yankees finally agreed to honor tickets to the July 24 game. In a spirit befitting the ignominious ending of the pine tar incident, the Yankees chose to keep the game to themselves. As the New York Times described:

> Despite the widespread interest in the game, the Yankees elected not to promote it and, in fact, adopted a policy that bordered on secrecy. Tickets did not go on sale until 4 P.M. [the day of the game], the game was never included in the list of upcoming contests on the scoreboard, the sign above Yankee Stadium that announces the day's game was blank...and the team's public relations department was never authorized to announce the ticket plans.[113]

The Royals would later take a different tack, embracing the promotional opportunity of the incident. After the season, the team announced that the first five hundred purchasers of season tickets would receive a special Louisville Slugger modeled on Brett's pine tar bat. And, to further capitalize on the incident, the team would coat the bats with pine tar. Back in August, however, Steinbrenner had no such plans. Still close to MacPhail's ruling, he chose not "to dignify what he considered a bad decision by the American League...."[114]

So, only about 1,245 people showed up to witness the official end of the pine tar game. One estimate had the Yankees spending "about $25,000 to open the stadium and probably ma[king] less than $2,000 on admissions." Yankee General Manager Murray Cook summed up the situation: "Not a very good night, was it?"[115]

The baseball was not much better. To indicate how little regard he held for the task, Martin played pitcher Ron Guidry in centerfield, and lefthander Don Mattingly at second base.[116] Then, as a final act of protest, Martin instructed pitcher George Frazier to throw the ball to each base, appealing whether Brett had touched all the bases back on July 24. Because none of the umpires from the July 24 game were present, Martin planned to argue that the current umpiring crew could not possibly know whether Brett had touched the bases. If the umpires could not confirm that Brett had touched the bases, they could not continue the game.

Frazier threw to each base, and each time the umpire signaled safe. Next, Martin walked onto the field to argue that a different umpiring crew could not possibly know whether the runners had touched all the bases. MacPhail, however, was one step ahead of him. Anticipating such last-minute shenanigans, MacPhail had obtained a statement signed by all four of July 24th umpires.[117] The statement read:

> In answer to your request of a possible appeal play of a missed base in the George Brett home run.
> Date July 24, 1983 New York vs Kansas City
> Four umpires completing game.
> Play in question
>
>> Two outs U. L. Washington on first base. Brett hits home run to right field.
>> Both runners touched all bases legally.
>
> Respectfully,
> Crew of:
>
>> Joe Brinkman /s/
>> Nick Bremigan /s/
>> Drew Coble /s/
>> Tim McClelland /s/[118]

While one might have thought that the letter settled the issue, and Martin's bag of tricks was finally empty, one would have underestimated Martin's tenacity (and perhaps over-estimated his sportsmanship). The very next day the Yankees faxed a protest to the American League offices challenging Drew Coble's signature on the statement. The Yankees argued that Coble, the first base umpire, could not possibly have seen whether Brett touched first base because Coble was watching Brett's ball fly over the right field fence. As one might expect, MacPhail denied the protest.[119]

When they got around to playing baseball that August night, both teams were retired in order—four up, four down. In only 9 minutes and 41 seconds, the Yankees and Royals finished the inning that had started three and a half weeks before.[120] The pine tar game was over; the Royals had won, 5-4.[121] Some in the crowd were not even aware of what they had seen. A Scottish tourist, when asked about the game, replied, "We just wanted to come to a baseball game. Is this some special kind of game?"[122] And so, the inning that had begun with a bang, went into the box scores with a whimper.

III. Scandalous Behavior

Although many Yankees have had scrapes with the criminal justice system, Darryl Strawberry's substance abuse problems have been particularly public. Photo by Joe Skipper, © Reuters NewMedia, Inc./CORBIS.

Crimes and Misdemeanors

by Phyllis Coleman*

A surprising number of players, coaches, and others associated with the Yankees have engaged in an astonishing variety of illegal activities. These are their stories.

I. Murder

Dennis Stockton is the only person with ties to the Yankees to be executed for murder—a crime he insisted, right up until he was put to death by lethal injection on September 27, 1995, that he did not commit.[1] Stockton had become a fan 45 years earlier because Mickey Mantle, his favorite player, was a Yankee. Indeed, he planned to get to the majors while his hero was still playing. But Stockton turned to a life of crime early, and never got further than being scouted by the team during a stint in a North Carolina jail. Despite being so nervous he walked the first two batters, he said he "settled down and pitched a pretty strong game. We won 17-0." The southpaw explained proudly that former Yankee pitcher Tommy Byrne said he had "potential."[2]

He remained a supporter until the end. Indeed, the final in a series of newspaper columns Stockton wrote from death row, penned just hours before his sentence was carried out, lamented the season "my beloved New York Yankees" were having. "[I]t looks like they're fading in the stretch run. They could sure use me in the bullpen—a ninth-inning closer. Of course, I won't know how it all comes out."[3]

The saga of Ronald Keith Williamson, a minor league pitcher who came within five days of being executed for a gruesome rape/murder, ended somewhat better. Back in 1971, his life was progressing exactly as planned. Following graduation from high school, he was the highest draft pick in Oklahoma. He married a Miss Ada beauty pageant winner. And although his constant complaining caused the Athletics to release him, he was quickly picked up by the Yankees for their farm team. But in the mid-seventies, because he continued getting into trouble and was experiencing problems with his arm, he was again cut. At that point, his life began spiralling out of control. He divorced, was hospitalized for mental problems, and was tried and acquitted twice for rape. He was also prosecuted for other violent crimes and, in 1987, he was found guilty of sexually assaulting and killing a 21-year-old barmaid almost five years earlier.[4]

But, after 12 years in prison, DNA tests not available at his trial proved hair and semen at the scene were not his; instead they belonged to a kidnapper who had been the main witness against him. On the strength of this evidence,[5] Williamson and his co-defendant (who had received a life sentence) were released. They sued the state of Oklahoma and others involved in sending them to jail for more than $100 million claiming their convictions were the result of a law enforcement conspiracy.[6]

Babe Ruth had been separated from his first wife, Helen, for three years when she died in a fire. Members of her family insisted he had used his "connections" to have her poisoned so he could marry another woman. An investigation, which turned up no evidence of foul play, attributed the blaze to "overloading of frayed electric wires."[7]

Tibor Brown was drafted in 1992 and pitched in the Yankees farm system for two years. The lefty later moved to Sandy, a small Utah town. When financial difficulties led his partner to steal from their business causing a rift between them, David Stoedter shot the former baseball player four times in the head. He disposed of the body in a shallow hole in Brown's back yard and told an inquisitive neighbor he was burying his dog. Stoedter pled guilty to first-degree felony murder and was sentenced to five years to life.[8]

II. Death Threats

True fans take win/loss records seriously, but death threats against those who are not performing well are rare. In 1984, however, Ed Whitson—who got off to a 1-6 start after signing a guaranteed $4.4 million five-year contract—was receiving such missives at home and in the clubhouse. Labeling his time in pinstripes a "living hell," the right-handed pitcher said "[t]here wasn't a day that went by where I didn't fear for my life, or the safety of my family." While he could have tolerated the nightly boos, and maybe even overlooked the tacks and nails irate zealots left littering his driveway, he could not take those "ugly phone calls." By 1986, then-manager Lou Piniella scheduled Whitson to pitch only in relief when they were at Yankee Stadium. Even so, "[h]e just became useless....He was worrying about everything except getting batters out." Finally the club agreed to Whitson's demands and traded him back to the Padres.[9]

A decade earlier, Billy Martin was the target of the following poorly written letter: "How would your wife and kids get along after you're gone. Did you write out your will yet. Don't wait untill (sic) too late…You better hurry up Have untill Monday night June 14."[10] And, in 1960, the FBI received a letter from a man who warned he would "shoot Mickey's [Mantle] knees off." Many believe the message was related to gambling.[11]

III. Substance Abuse

A. Drugs

For many Yankees, drugs have been the source of their legal troubles. For example, talented reliever Steve Howe, who holds the "'longest disciplinary record of drug abuse offenses in the history of baseball,'"[12] was arrested in December 1991 for giving a government informant $100 to buy one gram of cocaine.[13] As a result, he received his seventh suspension from baseball—this one for life. Just a few months later, however, in a much criticized move, an arbitrator reinstated Howe based on new evidence that he had suffered from Attention Deficit Disorder as a child.[14] This controversial reversal allowed

Howe to sign a $4.2 million contract with the Yankees.[15] One interesting footnote: the attorneys who defended him in the drug case had to sue Howe to collect $31,847 in unpaid fees plus interest and costs.[16]

Howe's troubles did not end with his major league career. Three years after he was released by the Yankees in June 1996, he was suspended as a volunteer coach by his daughter's softball team "pending the outcome of a background check."[17]

If the legal system kept lifetime stats, Darryl Strawberry's career numbers, including drug arrests and suspensions, would likely exceed his on-field records.[18] In fact, even by the time he joined the Yankees in 1995, everyone knew of the gifted outfielder's substance abuse. Sadly, signing with the Bronx Bombers did not end his struggle. Strawberry—who came back from colon cancer surgery and chemotherapy to march with his teammates in the October 1998 World Series victory parade—was arrested again on charges of possession of cocaine and solicitation of a prostitute in April 1999.[19] Based on his no contest plea, he was sentenced to 18 months probation plus community service and briefly exiled from baseball. He played well when he returned to the Yankees later that year and, in the postseason, he helped the team win its second straight World Series. But he could not stay clean. Following other positive drug tests and attempts at beating his habit, as well as further surgery to remove a stomach tumor, in October 2000 Strawberry was picked up in Tampa for violating his house arrest by leaving a residential treatment center and going on a binge.

Although he considered getting a gun "and blowing my brains all over the wall," four innings into the first game of the World Series between the Yankees and Mets (two teams he had helped win championships) he called a friend to get him drugs. Then Strawberry sat in his car and smoked $200 worth of crack cocaine, went home at 3 a.m., took 10 Xanax, and passed out for two days. As a result, he spent weeks in jail awaiting sentencing for violating his probation by testing positive for illegal substances. "Handcuffed and shackled" the slugger, who once seemed headed for the baseball Hall of Fame, told the judge he had lost his will to live but could not kill himself because it would not be fair to his five children. Nevertheless, he stopped his chemotherapy and said "I figure the drugs may kill me." Instead of prison, the judge sent him back to a treatment center under house arrest.

But, in April 2001, Strawberry disappeared from that facility. Friends and family frantically searched as rumors surfaced that he had been abducted and pistol whipped by kidnappers who sought $50,000 for his safe return. It was later determined, however, that he left with another addict named Beverly, supposedly to attend an Alcoholics Anonymous meeting. She tempted him with crack cocaine, took him to a nearby motel, and, aided by five men with guns, robbed him of his jewelry. He claimed they then drove to Orlando in search of more drugs and eventually abandoned him in Central Florida.[20]

When he was finally located, the eight-time All-Star was checked into a hospital where he was evaluated and treated for substance abuse and depression. As she had the other times Strawberry had been before her, in May 2001 Judge Florence Foster ordered treatment rather than jail.

However, it appears his luck ran out the sixth time he violated his probation by smoking, having sex with another resident, and trading baseballs for cigarettes. Judge Foster was on medical leave and retired Judge Ralph Steinberg, who stepped in, said incarceration was warranted. Remarkably, Strawberry seemed pleased with the 18-month sentence.[21]

Pascual Perez also had a history of repeated drug abuse, arrests, and unsuccessful re-habilitation attempts[22] when, in November 1989, he inked a three-year, $5.7 million deal with the Yankees.[23] Like Strawberry and Howe, donning a Yankee uniform did not turn his life around. Within a year he was complaining he had made "a horrible mis-take" and felt "'locked up' within the pinstripe prison."[24]

After showing up at the 1992 Yankees training camp late and underweight, and ad-mitting he had not thrown from a mound all winter, Perez tested positive for cocaine. Neither his claims that the results were invalid because he was set up, nor his accusa-tions of racism, spared him a year's banishment and forfeiture of the $1.9 million re-maining on his contract.[25] He refused to enter another treatment program and returned to the Dominican Republic where he disappeared.[26]

Unlike Howe, Strawberry, and Perez, once Dwight "Doc" Gooden put on pinstripes, he never again used drugs.[27] Despite many years of serious substance abuse problems—he was only 18 and in high school when he first tried cocaine—he apparently shaped up following his 1994 expulsion from baseball. After briefly considering suicide, Gooden began attending Alcoholics and Narcotics Anonymous meetings. His sponsor, a former batboy for the Yankees, helped pave the way for him to make a deal with George Steinbrenner in October 1995.[28]

Ironically, even though he was the youngest player to win the NL Rookie of the Year award in 1984 and the Cy Young Award in 1985, he pitched his only no-hitter shortly after signing with the Yankees following his more than year-long suspension.[29]

Dale Berra began experimenting with drugs at a New Year's Eve party when he snorted cocaine "off the end of an ignition key" with several Pittsburgh teammates.[30] Thus began his entanglement in the drug scandal which rocked Major League Baseball in the 1980s and involved more than 30 players on several teams as well as the Pirates Parrot mascot. Along with others, Berra (who switched from the infield to shortstop in 1982) was granted immunity and called to testify against several people accused of sell-ing illegal substances to athletes.[31] Traded to the Yankees by the time of the trials,[32] Berra indicated he had used cocaine for the last time the day before he was subpoenaed to be a grand jury witness.[33]

But his 1986 resolution that drugs "are all over for me" did not last. In April 1989, Berra was among 23 people arrested in a major cocaine ring operating in five New Jersey counties. In September, he pled not guilty to possession and conspiracy charges. The following month, he was accepted into a special pretrial intervention program. In addition to a $1,000 fine, he was placed on probation for three years, agreed to submit to periodic monitoring, and said he would talk to youngsters about substance abuse.[34]

Berra was not the only player who testified in the Pittsburgh drug trials to turn up on the Yankees roster. Rod Scurry, a key figure in exposing the problem, Al Holland, and Tim Raines also wore pinstripes.

Scurry had been Pittsburgh's first pick in 1974. The gifted left-handed relief pitcher, voted the shiest in his class at Hug High School in Reno, Nevada, had a difficult time adjusting to the pressures of professional baseball. He turned to cocaine, at one point doing "6, 7, 8, 9 grams a night, anywhere from $500 to $1,000" and was actually high when he won his first big league game.

At the start of the 1984 season, after passing out and hallucinating, he was sent to a rehabilitation center for 30 days. He returned to the team, confessed his addiction, and

testified against an old friend who had been his supplier. The Yankees bought his contract in 1985. Then, early on a January 1987 morning, he was arrested for reckless and
drunk driving. Although he refused to take a blood alcohol test, police suspected liquor
rather than cocaine. The charges were later dropped, but the Yankees released him the
following month.

In December 1988, the day after the Mariners cut him, Scurry was again arrested,
this time for buying two rocks of crack cocaine for $40. He pled guilty and was given a
one-year suspended sentence in exchange for an agreement to get drug counseling. Out
of baseball, he operated a car wash in Reno, fished, hunted, and tried to make his marriage work. In October 1992, despite his efforts, his wife left him and their two small
children. He reportedly was also facing an IRS claim of nearly $500,000 in back taxes
because a Texas accounting firm had put him, and many other ballplayers, into millions
of dollars of allegedly bogus tax shelters.[35] The problems all proved to be too much.

Home alone with his kids, the troubled pitcher went on a final cocaine binge. He
ran outside in only shorts begging neighbors to help rid him of imaginary snakes he
thought were biting him. He fought police who tried to take him into custody and
stopped breathing while they were cuffing him. According to the coroner, "cocaine,
plus violent behavior, plus being restrained all contributed to his death" a week
later.[36]

In 1986, Holland signed a one-year contract with the Yankees. To be allowed to play
and escape suspension for his role in the scandal, the reliever agreed to donate five percent of his base salary (approximately $30,000) to a drug prevention center, perform 50
hours of community service, and submit to mandatory random testing.[37]

At the time of the drug trials, Raines admitted his addiction—which dated back to
his rookie year two seasons earlier—had been so severe he frequently "couldn't even
see the ball."[38] In fact, he took to sliding face first so he would not break the vial of cocaine he kept in his hip pocket[39] to use between innings in the restroom behind the
dugout.[40] But since going through a rehabilitation program in 1983, the outfielder,
who played for the Yankees from 1996 through 1998, has been drug-free. He said his
only substance luxury was "the odd cigar" when he played in New York. Diagnosed
with lupus in 1999, Raines struggled to return in 2000 but a toe injury just weeks before training camp seemed to signal the end of his career. Undaunted, the 41-year-old
Raines, who once stole an American League record 40 bases in a row without being
called out, tried for a spot on the Olympic team. Even with all the hard work, he did
not make the cut, but the Expos picked him up. Then in 2002, he signed with the
Marlins.[41]

Two years after his 1983 stay in a rehabilitation center, Claudell Washington was
stopped because police noticed his car was weaving all over the road. He was arrested
when officers discovered a quarter-gram of cocaine and five grams of marijuana.[42] Despite his troubled history, the Yankees took him in a trade in 1986.

Bill Sudakis, who signed with the Yankees in 1974, retired after the next season. A
decade later, the journeyman utility player and his roommate, Theodore Earl Turina,
were picked up for attempting to sell a pound of cocaine to an undercover officer. The
police report said the cocaine belonged to Turina; Sudakis's role was bodyguard for the
$42,000 investment. Following his release eight months later, Sudakis opened a hitting
school in Orange County.[43]

Rusty Torres, who was drafted from a Brooklyn high school in 1966 and played for
the Yankees in 1971 and 1972, was forced to retire from baseball. He had no skills and

says he only knew how to drink. In March 1985, the former outfielder and two other men sold half an ounce of cocaine for $900 to an undercover officer. Torres was arrested, charged with possession, and sentenced to 300 hours of community service.[44]

An inquisitive, conscientious Federal Express secretary who alerted DEA agents about a package containing drugs led to the 1998 arrest of Butch Hobson. The third baseman, who played for the Yankees in 1982, was on the road managing the Phillies Triple A team when DEA agents knocked at his door in the Comfort Inn and discovered Hobson with the package containing 2.6 grams of cocaine. He claimed he did not use drugs and that he was a victim of entrapment. As a first time offender, he was placed in a diversion program, the charges were dropped, and he was ordered to perform community service. The team was less forgiving. He was suspended and then fired three months later.[45]

Add Joe Pepitone to the list of Yankees who spent time in jail because of drugs. Although his antics while a member of the team—drinking, substance abuse, and chasing women—often landed him in hot water, it was not until years after he retired in 1973 that he faced serious legal trouble. He was arrested in March 1985 with two other men after police stopped their car for allegedly going through a red light in Brooklyn. A search revealed cocaine, heroin, and pills with a street value of $70,000, drug paraphernalia, and a loaded .22-caliber derringer. Despite the fact that police said they found an honorary deputy sheriff's badge with the former first baseman's name on it, along with his business card in the bag containing the contraband, he consistently maintained he was innocent and had just been in the vehicle for a ride.[46] Acquitted on the more serious charges, he was sentenced to six months in prison for criminal possession of drug paraphernalia and having 300 Quaaludes. The judge lamented:

> You were once a very special person to a lot of people; you were a Bronx Bomber. Now you stand before the court as a very ordinary person, a Brooklyn criminal....It is a particularly sad day when someone who graced New York in Yankee pinstripes will now spend time in the custody of the Department of Correction wearing their pinstripes.[47]

After Pepitone served four months in Rikers, he went back to the Yankees in public relations.

Obviously many athletes battle substance abuse; some even play under the influence of drugs. But the tale Dock Ellis (who was with the Yankees in 1976 and 1977) tells about a game in June 1970 is amazing. Because he thought he had the day off, he and his girlfriend had been "dropping acid" when she picked up the sports section and exclaimed, "Dock, it says here you're pitching tonight." He hopped a plane from Los Angeles to San Diego. He was so high on LSD he needed help finding his locker before the game, his first throw bounced on the ground about two feet in front of the plate, he walked eight, loaded the bases twice, and hit two batters. Nevertheless, at the end of nine, the righty had bagged a no-hitter.[48]

George "Doc" Medich, who studied medicine at the University of Pittsburgh part-time while pursuing his baseball career, in 1999 wrote false prescriptions in the names of patients so he could obtain painkillers for himself. The orthopedic surgeon and sports doctor—who pitched for the Yankees from 1972 through 1975—pled guilty to 12 counts of possession of a controlled substance and was sentenced to nine years probation. His lawyer said this was a "cry for help" from Medich, who had struggled with addiction for years.[49]

Of course, sometimes sports figures are falsely accused, as when law enforcement personnel stopped Mel Hall at Boston's Logan Airport in September 1991. Because he was spotted racing through the terminal without luggage after getting off a plane from South Florida, the Yankee outfielder was suspected of being a drug lord. But as soon as DEA agents discovered who he was, they apologized and even drove him to his hotel "with a sniff dog in the back seat."[50]

Although Hall was understanding, others, like Don Zimmer, were not. He had to be physically restrained when, following his vehement objection to a strike call during an interleague contest against the Marlins, the home plate umpire responded, "Are you on drugs!" The Yankees bench coach said "That really did it! I've been called a lot of things in baseball but nobody's ever accused me of taking drugs—even if some of my managing moves might have led people to think that.... [I]f I had to do it all over again I might have punched [Greg] Bonin for what he said."[51]

B. Alcohol

Babe Ruth was known for drinking to excess and Prohibition did not slow him down. Instead "Jumping Joe" Dugan, third baseman for the 1927 Yankees, explained "They said you couldn't do it, so we *did* it! Ruth had a bootlegger in every town. 'Babe here, send up a case o' scotch, case o' rye, and fill the bathtub up with beer.' Standing order. And Whitey and I would help him drink it all."[52]

Pugnacious Billy Martin had several run-ins with the law. An incident in April 1984, between his third and fourth stints managing the Yankees, is illustrative.[53] He was arrested by Newport Beach police for public drunkenness and disorderly conduct after neighbors complained he was "obviously intoxicated, screaming and hollering at a female." Martin had gotten into a fight concerning travel arrangements for a horse he and Jill Guiver (his girlfriend at the time and eventually his fourth wife) owned together. Six months later, a judge found Martin not guilty because the incident occurred in a private rather than public area.[54]

IV. Driving Violations

A. DUI

In fact, Billy Martin spent a good bit of his life drinking and died in a one-car, liquor-related accident near his upstate New York farm on Christmas Day 1989. Mystery still surrounds the crash. William Reedy, who owned a sports bar near Detroit Stadium, initially stated he, rather than the five-time Yankees manager, had been behind the wheel of the pickup truck. However, when Reedy realized Martin had been fatally injured, his story changed and he claimed he only said that to protect his friend.[55] Whatever the truth, Reedy was convicted of driving with a blood alcohol level above the state legal limit and fined $350.[56]

While Martin is the only Yankee to die in a drunk driving incident, many others have mixed alcohol and automobiles.

One was Joe Pepitone who already had an impressive arrest record in October 1995, when, apparently driving under the influence at around 4:30 in the morning, he slammed into both sides of the Midtown Tunnel and two other cars. Police found him bloodied and disoriented mumbling, "I'm Joe Pepitone." The former Yankee first baseman and outfielder — by this time working in the team's public relations department — continued to insist he did not have a drinking problem. Nevertheless, he pled guilty to driving while impaired to avoid a trial. The judge fined him $350, ordered him to enroll in a rehabilitation program, and took away his license for 90 days.[57]

As he did with Pepitone, owner George Steinbrenner has given a number of players many chances; for some, however, another arrest appeared to be the final push needed to cut them loose.

For example, the Yankees knew of Rod Scurry's addiction to cocaine when they signed him. But when he was picked up in January 1987 for drunk and reckless driving, the club released him even though the charges were later dropped.[58]

Similarly, 56-year-old Eugene Michael lost his job shortly after he was taken in for drunk driving in March 1995. A policeman stopped him because he said the Yankees general manager hit a utility pole and just kept going. The case for firing him was strengthened because Michael had trouble with the roadside sobriety exam and refused to take the breath test.[59]

But Dwight Gooden, who was also arrested for drunk driving and refused a Breathalyzer in February 2002,[60] was allowed to resume his $100,000 per year position as the Yankees Tampa-based special adviser within two months of the incident.[61] One reason might be that while police said the pitcher failed the field-sobriety test, prosecutors acknowledged he appeared to be fine in the video. Fearing a defense motion to suppress the confession due to the officer's perfunctory Miranda warning caught on tape, the State allowed Gooden to plead guilty to a reduced charge of reckless driving. The judge withheld adjudication and sentenced him to a year probation on the conditions that he complete DUI school and 21 hours of community service. Although, through his attorney, he denied being under the influence, he did admit he showed "poor judgment" driving with an open beer bottle in his possession.[62]

Years earlier, Babe Ruth and several other Yankees had been driving from Washington to New York "singing and joking, their spirits lifted by alcohol" when they skidded around a curve near Wawa, Pennsylvania, the car turned over, and "bodies flew in every direction." None were seriously hurt although Charlie O'Leary was knocked out and one newspaper reported Ruth had died in the crash. No charges were filed and the next day Ruth arrived in Manhattan at the wheel of a new car.[63]

In a bizarre case, after he joined the Yankees in 1988, left-hander John Candelaria accused Don Sutton of having set him up for the first of two drunk driving arrests in 1987 by tipping police about his condition when the Angels arrived home from a road trip. Acknowledging Sutton claimed he was acting out of concern for a teammate, Candelaria said "I think he acted out of self preservation. He was pitching terrible at the time, seemed on the brink of release and was looking for a way to get me out of the rotation." The pitcher, who had suffered emotional trauma when his infant son drowned in a swimming pool the previous year, denied he had a problem with alcohol.[64]

Such behavior may also be used to prevent an athlete from joining the squad. One illustration: despite a verbal agreement in October 1986 to purchase Mike Norris's contract from the San Jose Bees, the Yankees passed on the pitcher after his December 16 DUI arrest.[65]

B. Hit and Run

Darryl Strawberry, who was temporarily banned from baseball and the Yankees as a result of problems with illegal substances, blamed prescription drugs for a hit and run accident in September 2000. Looking gaunt in his bright orange jail jumpsuit, the out-fielder claimed he had been on his way to meet his probation officer when he passed out at the wheel because he had mixed sleeping pills and painkillers. He was stopped by an off-duty policeman when he sideswiped a street sign and then clipped another sport utility vehicle with his Ford Expedition. No one was injured but the cars sustained about $2,800 worth of damage. Strawberry, who apologized for his "mistake," was warned to follow his doctor's instructions when taking medicine. He was sentenced to house arrest for violating probation.[66]

C. Speeding

Shortly after he signed with the Yankees, Babe Ruth purchased "a custom-built ma-roon Packard with a twelve-cylinder engine," nicknamed "'The Ghost of Riverside Drive'" by his teammates. In April 1921, he was charged with speeding and fined $25. He was arrested again for exceeding the New York City limit on June 8. The same judge—who accused him of "defying the law"—threatened to revoke his license and throw him in jail for six months if there was another incident. This time, however, he fined Ruth $100 and sentenced him to a day behind bars. The slugger was finger-printed and put into a cell at 11:30 a.m. with five others convicted of the same offense. He was worried about missing a 3 p.m. game against Cleveland, which, pursuant to his contract, could have cost him $500 but was saved when he learned the city jail's of-ficial day ended at 4. He had his uniform sent over and put it on under his dove-col-ored business suit. Following his release, "he made the nine-mile trip to the Polo Grounds in eighteen minutes, reaching speeds faster than the one for which he was fined." He entered the game in the sixth inning, the crowd of 20,000 gave him a stand-ing ovation and, "[a]lthough he got no hits, everyone was sure that his presence had inspired the Yankees to rally in the final inning and win, climbing to within a half game of first place."

When Ruth was arrested in January 1924 for speeding, the judge discovered he had been driving without a state registration since 1914 when it was revoked after an acci-dent. He was fined $70.[67]

Jose Canseco, who only played with the Yankees for a brief time in 2000, is infamous for driving too fast. A couple of examples suffice: back in February 1989, he was caught driving his Jaguar 125 miles per hour in a 55 zone. Amazingly, his defense was that he was only going 120. Two years later, he was stopped in Miami for driving his Porsche 104 miles per hour on a stretch limited to 55. This time he told the officer he was testing the aviation fuel he had put in the car.[68]

D. Reckless Driving

Shortly before he was released by the Yankees, Leo Durocher turned his car and hit an off-duty policeman with his automobile. Charges were eventually dropped.[69]

E.　Leaving the Scene of an Accident

About 1:30 a.m. on a December 1992 morning, Steve Howe hit a patch of ice and slid into a light pole at an intersection in Whitefish, Montana, his off-season home. Apparently not realizing he had caused damage, he drove away. When a license plate knocked from his vehicle led police to the Yankees pitcher, he was fined $125.[70]

F.　Traffic Infractions

Like just about everyone else, baseball players get tickets.

In October 1973, Reggie Jackson was hauled off to a San Francisco jail for three hours when a police check turned up two outstanding traffic warrants from Oakland five years earlier. Jackson explained "they wanted the money for the tickets from 1968 right then. All I had on me was 31 cents."[71]

V. Sexual Misconduct

All too often, an athlete's legal troubles stem from his sexual exploits. People connected with the Yankees are no exception.

At 3:53 on an October 2001 morning, a night manager at the St. Petersburg hotel where the team was staying discovered a Yankees assistant strength and conditioning coach, Brian McNamee, 34, naked in the swimming pool. He was "in a sexual position in 3 1/2 feet of water...thrusting himself into the victim." Despite tests that established the 40-year-old woman who claimed McNamee forced her to have sex with him had ingested the so-called "date rape" drug, prosecutors refused to charge him.[72]

John Montefusco, who played for the Yankees from 1983 through 1986, was accused of sexually assaulting his ex-wife more than a decade after he retired from baseball. Because he could not afford the $1 million bond the judge imposed when he violated a restraining order, the former Yankee pitcher spent two years in jail awaiting trial. Eventually acquitted on the serious counts in the indictment, he was fined and sentenced to three years probation for criminal trespass and simple assault. Broke and without a job, the 49-year-old Montefusco said he was "hoping to get back with the Yankees...[or] some other major-league club as a pitching coach."[73] While he did not make it back to the Bronx, he did catch on with the minor-league Somerset Patriots in Bridgewater, New Jersey.[74]

On July 18, 1997, Mark Whiten—who six months earlier had signed a $1 million contract with the Yankees—was arrested after a 31-year-old female accused him of sexually assaulting her in Milwaukee's Pfister Hotel.[75] Following his initial denial, Whiten, whose wife had given birth to their second child just days before the incident, admitted to having sex with the woman but insisted she had consented. Her blood alcohol level, combined with questions about her credibility and mental health, led prosecutors to drag their feet in filing charges and, eventually, to dismiss the case. Nevertheless, a few weeks later, the team released Whiten without explanation.[76]

Ironically, in August 1989, another outfielder, Luis Polonia, acquired by the Yankees just a month prior to his arrest, was convicted of having sex with a 15-year-old at the Pfister. The girl had waited at the ballpark with several of her friends to meet him. He claimed she not only told him she was 19 but also boasted she had had relations with several other baseball players. Polonia said he did not find out she was underage until after they had been intimate and her mother called the hotel. State lawyers said they prosecuted him because, following that conversation, he had intercourse with the teenager again. He pled no contest in August and was sentenced (although the judge waited until October 3, the day after baseball season ended) to 60 days in jail and a $1,500 fine.[77] He was lucky it was not worse. Because he had failed to reapply for a visa when he was traded to the Yankees, he could have been deported back to the Dominican Republic.[78]

Polonia's legal problems shifted to the civil side when, claiming "significant physical and emotional damages," the victim filed a lawsuit seeking an unspecified amount.[79] In March 1993, the weekend before the jury trial was scheduled to begin, the parties settled for "a substantial sum," enough, her lawyer said, to "cause Polonia to think twice about using his celebrity status to prey upon underage females who tend to look up to and admire professional athletes."[80]

Even before his probation expired, the 25-year-old Polonia, who had been traded to the Angels during the 1990 season, was in trouble again. He slapped an 18-year-old A's fan who was taunting him about his conviction. Police took statements from participants and witnesses, but the Alameda County District attorney decided not to prosecute.[81]

Meanwhile, Polonia has been back on the Yankees roster twice since he was banished to Anaheim. He signed as a free agent in 1993 and played 67 games before being shipped off to the Braves in August 1995. Then, on August 3, 2000, the 35-year-old lefty was picked up again after being released by the Detroit Tigers. Polonia was thrilled. "'It's always been a dream to come home to New York,' he said. 'If anybody asked me a team I'd like to play for, I always said, with my big mouth, the New York Yankees.'"[82]

Steve Sagedahl also wanted to wear pinstripes. Following a career as a three-sport star at Washburn (Minneapolis) High School, he pitched in the minor leagues for the Yankees in the 1980s. Years later, in March 1999, Sagedahl—by this time a strength trainer for the Burnsville (Minneapolis) Hockey Club—faced charges of having sexual contact with three underage girls. He allegedly fondled the teenagers under the guise of treatment for groin and other injuries.[83]

In April 1999, Darryl Strawberry was charged with soliciting a prostitute. The outfielder, who had been working out with the Yankees minor league club in preparation for returning to the team after colon surgery, was driving around a Tampa neighborhood when he pulled over and asked a female undercover officer whether she wanted "to party." After a brief exchange, Strawberry offered her $50. They agreed to meet at a nearby hotel but, two blocks away, police arrested him. A search turned up .3 grams (approximately one hundredth of one ounce) of cocaine wrapped in a $20 bill in his wallet.[84] As a result of his plea of no contest to solicitation and possession, he was sentenced to 18 months probation in addition to being ordered to submit to drug tests twice a week and perform 100 hours of community service.[85]

Years earlier, according to an FBI report, Mickey Mantle was "entertained at [a] house of prostitution."[86] However, no charges were ever filed.

Yankee David Justice was also linked to "working girls." In November 2001, responding to Halle Berry's comments that the outfielder cheated on her with "every prostitute, strippers, (sic) every twinkie walking by with a skirt," new wife Rebecca insisted his ex-spouse was simply bitter.[87] But it is true that, back in February 1996, while he was still playing for the Braves, he was stopped by police in an area in Riviera Beach, Florida, frequented by hookers and drug dealers. Justice insisted he did nothing wrong, he was never arrested, and, at the time, the couple said the incident did not influence their decision to divorce.[88]

In October 1991, a woman he met in a bar contacted David Cone (a Yankee from 1995 through 2000) while he was on the road playing for the Mets. He invited her to his hotel room. The following morning the pitcher woke up alone to a call from the club's general manager warning him he was about to be charged with rape. Although informed he might be arrested during the game, and offered the option of skipping his turn in the rotation, he took the mound. The anticipated posse never showed up and Cone got 19 strikeouts and a 7-0 win. The case was dropped a few days later when police learned the facts.[89]

The following spring, two of his teammates—who, like Cone, later played for the Yankees—were also accused of rape. A New York woman claimed she met Doc Gooden[90] and Daryl Boston[91] in a bar the previous year. She said she went back with them to the pitcher's Port St. Lucie, Florida home where she was victimized. The case against the players was eventually dismissed.[92]

When they were both first married, Mickey Mantle and Billy Martin, who were good friends, lived in adjoining apartments. The story is that each occasionally peeked into the other's bedroom window to watch his buddy have sex with his bride.[93] In fact, Mantle, and many other unnamed Yankee Peeping Toms, took their snooping seriously. An illustration makes the point: when the team went on the road, one player allegedly packed a small drill for making holes into connecting rooms and a mirror for peering under doors.[94] Although possibly illegal, none of these incidents led to criminal prosecutions.

VI. Domestic Violence

As in the case of many famous athletes, stories of how Joe DiMaggio physically abused Marilyn Monroe were initially hushed up. Surprisingly, however, one of the main reasons was that studio officials feared, given the ex-Yankee's still-hero status, releasing the information might hurt Monroe's career.

Naturally some people knew. One episode was tied to a very famous screen image: "Marilyn Monroe, in simple summer white, standing on a subway grating, cooling herself with the wind from a train below." DiMaggio, known to be exceedingly jealous, became furious when photographers and onlookers were able to see up his wife's dress. That night, the centerfielder and the movie star had a loud fight disturbing other hotel guests. The next morning, the actress complained to her hairdresser and wardrobe mistress that her husband had beaten her up.

The problems did not end with their divorce. When a detective who had been tailing Monroe told DiMaggio that she was holed up in an apartment, he and Frank Sinatra showed up around 11:15 p.m. and broke in. Unfortunately, they got the wrong place so, while their men took pictures of the 50-year-old woman who lived there, Monroe and her friend escaped from the flat a few doors away. Police initially reported it as an attempted burglary but, after a *Confidential Magazine* expose, the California State Senate launched an investigation. Sinatra and the others involved were forced to testify but DiMaggio, who sent a message that he was unable to attend, stayed outside the jurisdiction of the committee's subpoenas.[95]

Prior to joining the Yankees, Darryl Strawberry was accused of breaking his wife's nose during the 1986 playoffs and, in another instance years later, was arrested for threatening her with her .25-caliber semiautomatic pistol during a heated argument.[96] Following the couple's divorce in September 1993, Strawberry was again taken in for domestic abuse, this time for striking his girlfriend, causing a one-inch cut above her right eye.[97]

Similarly, before his brief appearance as a Yankee in 2000, Jose Canseco was twice arrested for domestic violence. In 1992, he was charged with aggravated assault for ramming his Porsche into his first wife's new BMW when she sped off during an argument. In November 1997, he was charged with battery after he allegedly struck his second wife during a fight in a friend's automobile.[98]

And, although the Yankees expressed an interest in Wilfredo Cordero in 1998 despite his guilty plea in a domestic dispute with his second wife, they ultimately passed on the leftfielder.[99]

VII. Assault

Shortly after signing a $13.5 million contract with the Yankees, David Wells broke his pitching hand in a fight and faced the possibility of being charged with felony assault. The trouble began when Wells, who was in San Diego for his mother's funeral, left his Lincoln Town Car running outside a bar very early on a morning in January 1997. Two passersby hid the keys under the seat, but Wells thought they had stolen them. Therefore, he and his friend confronted the men. Words and punches were exchanged. Despite a two-and-a-half week inquiry, the district attorney decided not to file charges.[100]

Just a few months later, Dwight Gooden was in a fist fight which led to a misdemeanor assault complaint. Gooden—who was on the disabled list at the time—got into a taxi at a strip club[101] in Arlington, Texas, between 2 and 3 on a May morning. Ziauddin Hakim, the driver, then picked up another passenger, a topless dancer. When they arrived at the Marriott, the pitcher refused to pay the $4.20 fare. Hakim, 44, followed him to the fourth floor to attempt to get his money. He said Gooden, married and the father of five, was angry the dancer had rejected his repeated invitations to accompany him to his hotel room. Gooden admitted punching the cabbie—who suffered four ruptured discs in his back—but said he did not give him the money because he was upset Hakim had accepted another customer. Within two months, the parties reached a confidential out-of-court settlement and the charges were dismissed.[102]

Decades earlier, in May 1957, one widely reported melee involved several well-known Yankees. Mickey Mantle, Whitey Ford, Yogi Berra, Hank Bauer, and Johnny Kucks joined Billy Martin at the Copacabana for his 29th birthday celebration. A rowdy, drunken group of bowlers directed racial slurs at Sammy Davis, Jr., who was performing at the New York nightclub. Bauer, who allegedly hit one of the hecklers and knocked him out, was the only player arrested. But all six team members were fined, and Martin—targeted as the instigator and a bad influence on Mantle—was traded the next month to the Athletics.[103] The following is Mickey Mantle's description of his interchange with the district attorney at the grand jury proceeding:

"Now, Mickey, were you at the Copa the night of May fifteenth?"

"Yes, sir."

"Did you see a fight take place while you were there?"

"No, sir, I didn't."

"Well, did you see a gentleman lying unconscious on the floor near the Copa entrance?"

"Yes, I did."

"All right. Do you have an opinion as to how this could have happened?"

I thought about it and said, "I think Roy Rogers rode through the Copa on his horse and Trigger kicked that man in the head."

The grand jury was still laughing when the judge dismissed the case for insufficient evidence.[104]

Almost 16 years later, Martin, who in his 61 years had many fights,[105] was arrested in Lakeland, Florida, after an altercation with a policeman who directed racial remarks to the African-American minor leaguer Ike Blessit.[106]

Similarly, a brawl in a nightclub in January 1992 landed former Yankee Joe Pepitone in jail charged with assault. The power-hitting, flamboyant athlete—who introduced hair dryers into locker rooms—was making a promotional appearance and signing autographs at a resort in the Catskill Mountains. Five apparently intoxicated men started taunting him as "washed up" and a "has-been." Pepitone asserted the men started the fight. Although he was the only one not injured, when his companion filed a lawsuit based on common law negligence against the hotel's principal, Pepitone cross-claimed maintaining they failed to provide adequate security for him. The District Court for the Southern District of New York rejected this, and other, arguments and granted a defense motion for summary judgment.[107]

During the time he was playing for the Yankees Class AAA team, Deion Sanders faced assault charges stemming from a confrontation with two men who were saying "lewd things...to my female." The centerfielder was still in the game when he noticed Richmond fans harassing his girlfriend, Carolyn Chambers. After he was replaced by a pinch hitter in the ninth, Sanders went into the stands. Denying he was reacting to taunts directed at him, and insisting he had not touched either of the men, Sanders said "[t]he only thing I shouldn't have done is go get my girl (before the game was over)."

Witnesses confirmed Sanders had not punched anyone, but he did do more wrong than break a team rule not to leave the clubhouse while the game was in progress. This disturbance occurred less than a week before the end of his six-month probation on battery and breach of the peace charges arising from a skirmish with a store clerk and security officer in a Florida shopping mall on December 24, 1988.[108] However, although the 1989 assault violated his probation, as charges were dropped after Sanders agreed to contribute to a fund for Richmond fans with disabilities, his supervisor recommended only that he be fined and ordered to pay court costs in the Christmas Eve scuffle.[109]

Roger Clemens, who just days earlier had vowed to lessen his combative image, was arrested in January, 1991, following a skirmish in Houston at the Bayou Mama's Swamp Bar. The pitcher, who became a Yankee in 1999, allegedly jumped an off-duty policeman scuffling with his older brother.[110] In December, a jury found Clemens not guilty of misdemeanor assault.[111]

VIII. Disturbing the Peace

In April 2000, more than a decade after he retired from baseball, Hall of Famer Reggie Jackson allegedly grabbed his former partner and threw him against a wall during an argument. Jeffrey Haney pressed criminal charges. Thirteen days later, Jackson sued Haney, accusing him of embezzling money from their Seaside, California gym and using it to purchase a new pickup truck for himself.[112] In November, Jackson pled no contest to disturbing the peace and was sentenced to three years probation as well as ordered to perform 40 hours of community service.[113]

IX. Disorderly Conduct

Disorderly conduct covers many kinds of bad behavior.[114] The most common seems to be fighting, frequently in a bar.

The 1986 prosecution against Reggie Jackson stemming from a scuffle in a Milwaukee tavern is illustrative. Jackson, who had left the Yankees as a free agent in 1981, was playing for the Angels. When he refused to give Donald Weimer an autograph, the 26-year-old unemployed office worker tore up a paper plate Jackson had signed for someone else and sprinkled the pieces on the outfielder's food. Weimer suffered facial cuts and a chipped tooth in the ensuing brawl.[115] The resulting disorderly conduct charges against both men were eventually dropped and Weimer's civil suit seeking $150,000 compensatory and punitive damages was settled for an undisclosed amount.[116]

Likewise, Dave LaPoint was involved in an incident at a Glens Falls bar in December 1991. The former Yankee left-hander and his wife were leaving shortly before 4 a.m. when he tried to help defuse what Laura LaPoint described as a "volatile situation."[117] Ironically, he retired to Glen Falls where he ran a bar he named Pitches. During playoffs, he sported his Yankees uniform and entertained customers with stories of the rivalry with the Red Sox.[118] In 2002, the 42-year-old, who had become synonymous with the complaint that an organization acted like it was offering an opportunity to rookies but then acquired some hired gun ("[t]hey bring in Dave LaPoint"), got the nod to be the pitching coach for the minor league Long Island Ducks—a position he hopes may lead to an opportunity to manage someday.[119]

Under very different facts, Dion James plea-bargained marijuana charges down to disorderly conduct in May 1996. The outfielder, who played for the Yankees in 1992–93 and 1995–96, left the team only hours before his arrest because he refused to play with their Columbus farm team. He was stopped at 2 a.m. for driving his Mercedes with a broken taillight. The officer said he smelled pot in the car, and, when he searched, he found a small amount along with drug paraphernalia.[120]

Dan Pasqua faced similar charges when police found a meager stash and a pipe in his home in October 1991. His problems began when the United Parcel Service alerted law enforcement after a shoe-sized box sent to the outfielder was accidently torn on a Chicago conveyor belt revealing the illegal substance. While Pasqua, who played for the Yankees from 1985 through 1987, accepted the package, he insisted he did not smoke marijuana. He reached an agreement with the State to drop the charges in return for $545 in fines and random drug tests.[121]

X. Indecent Exposure

Several Yankees have been charged with indecent exposure. Remarkably, although in separate incidents, in May 1985, Don Mattingly and Dale Berra were arrested for urinating in public at the same posh Kansas city shopping center.

First baseman Don Mattingly was nabbed around midnight and taken to the security office where he was issued a municipal citation. Berra, a shortstop, was caught at 9:45 two nights later. Because he pushed the policeman who tried to capture him, he faced an additional assault charge.[122]

For Dick Williams, the 70-year-old special adviser to the Yankees, the arrest was especially costly. Election to the Hall of Fame as a manager (after winning more than 1,500 games, guiding the Athletics to World Series championships in 1972 and 1973, and capturing pennants with the Red Sox and the Padres) seemed virtually assured until he was charged with walking naked and masturbating outside his Ft. Myers, Florida, hotel room in January 2000. Admitting he "probably did the dumbest thing of my life" by looking out his window for a few seconds before dressing, Williams insisted he did not intend to be seen and vigorously contended he would not have pled no contest if he had known the State had accused him of masturbating. He said "[t]hat part is simply not true and I want people to know it." Nevertheless, the Yankees suggested he stay away from spring training camp that year.[123]

David Cone was still pitching for the Mets when he was accused of indecent exposure. In 1992, three women claimed he exposed himself and masturbated in the bullpen at Shea Stadium. Cone vehemently denied these allegations and the charges were eventually dismissed but not before a lurid cartoon portraying the incident had been published.[124]

XI. Criminal Trespass

One Yankee fan stunned more than 56,000 spectators in the stands and millions of television viewers when he ran shirtless onto the diamond in Yankee Stadium in the top of the sixth during the sixth game of the 1996 World Series. Twenty-four-year-old plumber Paul O'Grady, a native of the Bronx, had painted on his back "Guiliani (sic) can kiss my…" with an arrow pointing downward. O'Grady maintained it was just a harmless prank, but he was charged with criminal trespass. The Bronx district attorney's office sought 90 days incarceration at Rikers, the harshest penalty ever recommended for such a stunt.[125] The prosecution dragged on for approximately a year and a half, with more than 15 court appearances before the trial, and ultimately ended with O'Grady—by this time a San Francisco resident—being sentenced to community service.[126] Notably, after this taste of standing up for free speech, O'Grady began writing for *Blunt*, a snowboarding journal owned by *Hustler* publisher Larry Flynt, who a decade earlier won his own First Amendment case before the United States Supreme Court.[127]

XII. Stealing

A. Grand Larceny

As a pitcher, Ken Clay—who was drafted out of high school in the second round by the Yankees and was part of the winning 1977 and 1978 World Series teams—tried to stop players from stealing bases. But after he retired from the sport, Clay himself became the thief.

In 1987 he pled guilty to two counts of grand larceny for depositing $16,000 obtained from class ring sales into his personal account rather than that of the Campbell County distributor for whom he worked. He was given a four-year suspended sentence and ordered to perform 1,000 hours of community service.[128]

Then, in February 1992, he was sentenced to one year in the county jail and a $1,000 fine for stealing $551.76 from another employer. This time, Clay, who was the finance and insurance manager at an automobile dealership, took money a customer gave him to purchase a warranty.[129] When Campbell County prosecutors discovered this conviction, plus two drunk-driving arrests in nearby municipalities, Clay was sentenced to three more years for violating his probation.[130]

In November 1999, he was arrested again when he stole an ex-girlfriend's identity and ran up more than $50,000 in bills. Amazingly, despite his history, Clay was allowed to escape jail time on the charges of defrauding three credit card companies. Now 46, he received 15 years probation and agreed to repay more than $40,000. However, according to court records, his only income was his $1,200 per month pension—a portion of which went to child support—and his sole asset was a 1984 Cadillac.

Almost 50 years earlier, in April 1950, Yankees ticket manager Walter Sherwin was indicted on charges of grand larceny and forgery for looting the club's funds to buy a new home for his inlaws in Beloit, Wisconsin. But his wife, Gregg Sherwood—a showgirl and 1943 Miss Wisconsin who reportedly had had a love affair with Joe DiMaggio—denied his story that the money went to her parents and divorced him.[131]

People who deal with tickets were on the police blotter again more than four decades later. Following a 15-month investigation, 16 individuals—including eight current and former Yankee box office workers—were charged with making "ice," the term used for inside trading and scalping. While icemen operate in a variety of ways, they basically "make tickets end up in all the wrong hands for all the wrong reasons, with plenty of profit for both the inside man and the outside broker."[132] What the agents did was take tens of thousands of dollars in bribes and help scalpers sell more than $300,000 in tickets at inflated prices.[133]

Benny Kauff, who played for the New York Highlanders in 1912, was tried on charges that his dealership received stolen cars. He was acquitted in May 1921 but Kenesaw Mountain Landis refused to reverse the suspension imposed when he was indicted. The outfielder's lawsuit against the Commissioner for reinstatement was dismissed.[134]

B. Pilfering from Teammates

Stealing is bad but stealing from teammates is a crime that cannot be ignored. Interestingly, however, rather than involve the legal system, athletes and clubs tend to mete out their own punishment.

For example, Babe Ruth reportedly "beat Leo Durocher senseless" for lifting cash and personal items. Ruth became suspicious because he thought he seemed to be going through money even more quickly than usual; other players were noticing their things were disappearing too. Hoping to trap the thief, Ruth marked five $100 bills. Then, because he already distrusted his road trip roommate, when Ruth returned to the hotel at 2 a.m., he went through the rookie shortstop's bag and discovered the cash and missing pocket watch. Ruth "kicked the hell out of him so badly and he made so much noise doing it" that other guests called security who unlocked the door and saved the hapless Durocher. Predictably, Durocher denied the whole thing. "If I had wanted Babe's watch…he would have given it to me."[135] Although the tale was kept out of the newspapers, without saying why, the Yankees released the man famous for saying "nice guys finish last."[136] Banned from the American League, he played for the Reds, Cardinals, and the Dodgers, then went on to manage the Dodgers, Giants,[137] Cubs, and Astros before he died October 7, 1991.

Many believe Ruben Rivera will not be so lucky. In March 2002, the potential five-tool ("hit, hit with power, run, throw, and field") outfielder stole star shortstop Derek Jeter's favorite glove and sold it to a memorabilia dealer for $2,500. Rivera returned it after the Yankees began an investigation, but despite his apology, Joe Torre insisted on releasing him. Pleas for leniency from closer Mariano Rivera—who had saved his cousin's career in the past[138]—and Hall of Famer Reggie Jackson were rejected because, the manager said, "the clubhouse is sacred."

In the end, the glove cost Rivera $800,000 as he was forced to forfeit all but the minimum major-league salary from his one-year, $1 million contract.[139] Stating Jeter "had six or seven gloves; I didn't know he would be that mad," Rivera never seemed to grasp the gravity of his offense. Nevertheless, he admitted he feared he would never play again and was grateful when he landed a job with the AA Texas League Tulsa Drillers where the crowds in the stands number around 500 rather than 45,000.[140]

C. Robbing Banks

Sometimes, the team is associated with criminal acts even if no one affiliated with the club is actually involved. This was true in the case of Edwin "Eddie" Chambers Dodson who, according to the FBI, personally robbed more banks than anyone else in United States history. Dubbed the "Yankees Bandit" because of his habit of wearing a baseball cap with the team's logo during heists, in the early 1980s Dodson was the owner of a popular collectibles store in a trendy part of Los Angeles. At 35, he was "a personable, likeable guy, drove nice cars, dated beautiful women, hung out with Holly-wood celebrities—and developed a drug habit. To support the lifestyle, and the habit, he turned to robbing banks." In fact, in 1983 and 1984, he stole from 64 banks, a record-setting six in one day. The courteous thief would arrive "with a phony gun in a bag, politely ask the teller to empty her drawer, and then walk away with a few thousand bucks."

When he finally was caught—after stealing approximately $200,000—he was sen-tenced to 15 years and said he just wanted to do his time and rebuild his life. Paroled after a decade in prison, he quickly returned to his life of crime. This time, because he looked much older than his 50 years, was apparently back on drugs, and very sick from hepatitis, he was tagged the "Down and Out Bandit." Cornered in a motel, he rushed out of his room waving a toy pistol, apparently in an attempt to get the police to shoot him. Incarcerated again, he died in 1987.[141]

The "Baseball Cap Bandit" went even further—he had the Yankees logo tattooed on his right arm.[142] Lawrence McLendon served 57 months for a string of bank robberies in the mid 1990s and was still on parole when he was arrested in June 2002 as a suspect in 12 more jobs.[143]

D. Memorabilia Thefts

Yankee collectibles are frequently valuable and, therefore, attractive to thieves. One story has it that, back in the 1960s, Joe DiMaggio left nine World Series rings in his suite at the Hotel Lexington in New York. Someone took all but the 1936 ring from his rookie year, which was the only one he ever wore. On September 27, 1998, Joe DiMag-gio Day, Steinbrenner presented him with replica rings.[144] Then the following year, a di-amond-studded 1977 World Series ring John DeLorean claimed had been stolen from him was sold at auction for $20,373.[145]

Naturally rings are not the only targets. A vintage uniform, reportedly worn by Babe Ruth during the 1924 season and 18 years later during the filming of "The Pride of the Yankees," was stolen from a collector's car in May 1995. Interestingly, the shirt and pants had once been featured on the television show "Unsolved Mysteries" because it vanished when the victim of a Las Vegas mob-style hit was killed.[146] Also, in June 1999, the Babe Ruth Museum was robbed three times in two weeks.[147] And a bronze bust commemorat-ing Mickey Mantle's 500th home run, which had disappeared nearly 20 years before, was for sale on the Internet within 10 days of the centerfielder's death. Price tag: $25,000. An FBI undercover sting operation ended with the arrest of Robert Pagani—a security guard at Yankee Stadium from 1971 to 1979—for interstate transportation of stolen goods.[148]

XIII. Cheating

Hal Chase debuted with the New York Highlanders in 1905. Three years later, he was accused of throwing games. He left the team because of the allegations but returned in 1909. Unfortunately, the charges that he fixed games continued to follow the first base-man throughout his career. Although he was never convicted, it was later revealed that he was involved in the Black Sox scandal and many baseball historians view him as the primary source of corruption within his era.[149]

XIV. Weapons Offenses

A number of Yankees have been involved in incidents with guns.[150]

Roberto Kelly, for example, was almost killed by Panamanian soldiers. The centerfielder had arrived in Panama City two days after American troops landed but inadvertently wandered into an area still controlled by Manuel Noriega. At a checkpoint, a sentry cocked his weapon against Kelly's temple. Another guard yelled "wait" and queried, "[a]ren't you the guy who plays for the New York Yankees?" When he confirmed his identity, the soldier said, "Let him go....He's ok."[151]

Steve Howe, already infamous for repeated drug abuse,[152] was arrested at New York's John F. Kennedy International Airport in June 1996—just two days after the Yankees released him—for carrying a loaded .357 Magnum in his luggage. The agent at the first class check-in "noticed what looked like a gun." Police searched Howe's carry-on bag and took him into custody. An avid collector, the pitcher said he was just transporting the revolver back to his home in Whitefish, Montana.[153] After several postponements, and a reduction of the charges, Howe pled guilty to attempting to take a loaded pistol on an airplane. He was sentenced to three years probation, and 150 hours of community service.[154]

Billy Martin was startled when a bullet whizzed by his head in the bar at Larry Bird's Boston Connection restaurant in December 1989. Someone knocked a woman's purse off the chair, causing her .38-caliber derringer to fire. No charges were filed against the owner who had a permit.[155]

Slugger Jose Canseco was dropped from a television commercial sponsored by the California Egg Commission after he was arrested in April 1989 when a pedestrian spotted a loaded nine millimeter handgun on the floor of his Jaguar in a university parking lot.[156] The outfielder, who played with the Yankees for part of the 2000 season, signed a negotiated "no contest" plea in exchange for a suspended six-month jail term and three years probation in addition to an agreement to visit pediatric wards and a pledge that he would take 100 underprivileged children to ball games.[157]

XV. Blackmail

George Steinbrenner managed to be both perpetrator and victim in a 1990 extortion scheme. Angry about the team's contract with Dave Winfield which turned out to be worth several million dollars more than he originally thought, Steinbrenner allegedly paid a shady gambler, Howard Spira, to dig up negative information about the outfielder. Although Spira, who was involved with Winfield's Foundation, signed an agreement not to disclose the payoff, he subsequently threatened to make it public unless Steinbrenner gave him an additional $110,000 and a job at his shipbuilding company. The Yankees owner accused Spira of "extortion in its purest form."[158] The whole sordid mess led to Spira serving more than two years in federal prison,[159] Steinbrenner being banned from baseball for one month longer, and Winfield's reputation being sullied.[160]

The FBI kept a file on Mickey Mantle from the late 1950s through the early 1960s. The 28 pages, discovered through a New York radio station's Freedom of Information Act request, revealed that an informant claimed the centerfielder had been blackmailed for $15,000 to keep quiet about having been caught in a compromising position with a married woman.[161] Mantle, who proudly admitted he "'shacked up' with many girls in New York City," denied the story, stating he had never been caught.[162] Actually, neither claim is believable as many people, including his wife, were aware the Hall of Famer, whose incredible 18-year career with the Yankees gained him strong fan adoration, was a womanizer. Indeed, once, right after Merlyn and her husband dined together, she attacked him because he asked their waitress for her phone number.[163]

XVI. Fraud

A 31-year-old San Francisco man impersonated Derek Jeter and other MLB stars to obtain $3,319 worth of baseball bats without paying for them. Herbert John Derungs then claimed they were game-used and sold them on eBay. One victim traded $6,000 plus a Mark McGwire and Rogers Hornsby bat for 15 of the fakes. When Derungs was caught, he pled guilty to six counts of mail and wire fraud.[164]

John DeLorean was one of 15 people George Steinbrenner recruited to purchase the team from CBS in January 1973.[165] That same year, DeLorean started his own automobile company in Northern Ireland. Sadly, few buyers could afford the $25,000 stainless steel, gull-winged sports car and, despite help from the British government, the business soon was floundering financially.[166] As allegations that millions of dollars were missing swirled around him, DeLorean was caught on videotape trying to sell $24 million worth of cocaine to an undercover police officer. DeLorean denied the government's claim that he was attempting to get cash to save his failing company and maintained he had only cooperated because he was afraid of the participants who he believed were involved in organized crime. He was acquitted and subsequently also found not guilty on charges of racketeering, fraud, and tax evasion. Nevertheless, mounting legal bills forced him to sell many of his assets, including his 10 percent share of the Yankees.[167]

Steinbrenner's other partner who faced criminal charges was not so lucky. Marvin Warner—whose professional relationship with the owner put him in a position to purchase 10 percent of the team in 1976[168]—was found guilty of fraud and conspiracy. Warner's legal woes stemmed from the 1985 collapse of his Cincinnati-based bank which triggered the savings and loan crisis in Ohio. After serving 28 months in prison on nine securities fraud-related convictions, Warner retired to his 240-acre Florida horse farm. In April 2002, he died at age 82 on a trip to Cape Canaveral where he had gone to watch a space shuttle launch.[169]

XVII. Illegal Campaign Contributions

And, of course, the "Boss" himself is a convicted felon. George Steinbrenner's $100,000 contribution in 1972 to the Committee to Re-elect the President violated election laws. Thus, on opening day of the 1974 season, a Cleveland grand jury issued a multi-count indictment. Despite initially proclaiming his innocence and vowing to fight, a few months later he pled guilty and was fined $15,000.[170] Possibly his own brush with the legal system explains why the colorful Yankees owner has given some players and coaches who ran afoul of the law so many chances to redeem themselves.

XVIII. Criminal Nonpayment of Support

Darryl Strawberry was charged with willful nonpayment of support and contempt of court after he missed a June 24, 1996 deadline to pay his ex-wife $300,000 of the $540,000 he owed her and their two children. The All-Star outfielder avoided a trial and the possibility of two years in jail when—the day after he joined the Yankees—he agreed to use his $260,000 signing bonus to partially satisfy this obligation.[171]

XIX. Possession of a Potentially Dangerous Animal

In a case which even the state enforcement agent called "fairly unusual," Mel Hall, who played for the Yankees from 1989 to 1992, was charged with possession of a potentially dangerous animal and importing a wild animal without a permit.[172] Hall insisted the year-old male and female cougar kittens were pets who "loved me, followed me around, slept on me." The outfielder also contended he did not know it was illegal to keep them in Connecticut.[173] Nevertheless, state officials confiscated the cats in July 1990 and, several months later, Hall agreed to pay $2,000 to charity in exchange for having the misdemeanor charges dropped.[174]

XX. Cruelty to Animals

Dave Winfield had his own problems with a member of the animal kingdom. While warming up in front of 36,684 spectators before the bottom of the third at Exhibition Stadium in August 1983, the centerfielder fatally beaned the hapless fowl.[175] Based on a complaint from an outraged fan, police arrested Winfield for "wilfully caus[ing] unnecessary injury to a bird, to wit, a Gull, by using a ball, CONTRARY TO THE CRIMINAL CODE." Winfield was taken to the police station in a squad car and booked. "[I]t's near midnight, and next to me on a table is 'Exhibit A,' its feet sticking up in the air. It's stiff now, and lying on a handkerchief." Charges were dropped the next day.

That winter, speaking before a sellout crowd in Toronto, Winfield quipped, "here I am on the plane, on my way to this fund raiser—mink coat, leather pants, lizard belt, alligator briefcase—and it suddenly occurs to me, Man, the way they protect their natural resources up here, this time I'm liable to get five to ten!"[176] Ironically, in 1992, toward the end of his career, Winfield played for the Blue Jays and, in the decisive sixth game in the World Series, delivered an 11th inning two-out, two-run double to win the first championship for both him and his team.[177]

XXI. Kidnapping

Ralph Johnson hatched his plot to abduct someone and demand a $1 million ransom while in prison in the 1980s. When he was released, he began researching targets. Before finally selecting former Tampa Bay Buccaneers president Gay Culverhouse (who thwarted his 1994 attempt by unexpectedly changing her routine) he was considering kidnapping George Steinbrenner.[178]

XXII. Unpaid Taxes

In 1985, the city of Detroit issued warrants for three New York Yankees because they failed to pay the city's "jock taxes" collected from visiting players.[179] Although officials refused to identify the athletes in an effort to "bend over backwards to keep it low-key because of their fame and everything," the senior investigator said, in each case, team representatives or players' agents paid before anyone was taken into custody.[180]

Almost 60 years earlier, in April 1926, Massachusetts issued an arrest warrant when Babe Ruth failed to pay state income tax for 1923 and 1924. Ruth argued that, while his wife and child lived within its borders, he was not a resident and thus did not owe the money.[181]

And in 1995, Darryl Strawberry was convicted of federal tax evasion for failure to report more than $360,000 earned from card-signing. Despite a plea agreement that he would spend three months in jail, the judge inexplicably lightened the sentence and gave him six months of home confinement, three years probation, 100 hours of community service, and mandatory drug abuse counseling. In addition, he was fined about $350,000 in back taxes, interest, and penalties.[182]

XXIII. Bouncing Checks

After he retired from baseball, Elliott Maddox, who played for the Yankees from 1974 to 1976, was charged with bouncing a check. The complaint was dropped when the former centerfielder paid $1,141 to cover advertising expenses incurred when he hired the company to sell equipment from a bankrupt ice cream parlor he had operated.[183]

XXIV. Criminal Impersonation

Given the perquisites of celebrity, many men probably dream about being famous ballplayers. But when they act out those fantasies to defraud people, it is a crime.[184]

A man who was Dan Pasqua's high school classmate used his strong resemblance to the Yankee outfielder to get free drinks and dinners and cheat a young Haverstraw, New

Jersey woman out of $7,000. Posing as Pasqua, in July 1986, James Louis Powers told her he was going to use the money to get her a red Trans Am through his sports contacts. In furtherance of his scam, he checked the schedule and made sure to disappear during the times the team was out of town and, staying in character, even signed autographs with the 25-year-old player's name.

Powers was indicted for criminal impersonation. Remarkably, shortly after he was released on bail in December, he was arrested again for pretending to be Pasqua and swindling $1,000 from a 26-year-old woman at the Meadowlands Racetrack by telling her he had left his wallet at home. Pasqua was understandably upset and testified against the imposter in the grand jury hearing. Powers pled guilty to one count of criminal impersonation and two counts of grand larceny. The judge handed him a six-month jail term and five years probation.[185]

XXV. Criminal Mischief

In June 1990, a 35-year-old Miami man inexplicably attacked Pascual Perez's new BMW. The Yankee pitcher was not hurt in the incident but his vehicle sustained $5,000 worth of damage. Police, who arrested the perpetrator at 3:45 a.m. in the Jackson Heights section of Queens, said he was "some lulu who just went wild.... That kind of thing happens."[186]

XXVI. Mob Connections

There are several links—both real and fictional—between the Yankees and the Mafia.

For example, Joe DiMaggio was allegedly able to walk away from his $100,000 per year salary in 1951 because of a "trust fund" established for him by Frank Costello. Reportedly every time the "Yankee Clipper" appeared in any of the famous New York nightclubs the mobster owned, he deposited $200 in the centerfielder's account. DiMaggio was also reputed to have ties to the New Jersey mob, particularly the infamous Abner (Longy) Zwillman and Richie (The Boot) Boiardo. "Longy had three boxes of cash which he left at Joe's house for 'safekeeping,' [biographer Richard Ben] Cramer said. "But when Longy was found hanging from his chandelier in West Orange, Joe kept the cash. Boiardo gave Joe a 4 1/2-carat emerald-cut diamond for (Dimaggio's first wife) Dorothy Arnold's engagement ring."[187]

And Carlo Gambino, who rose to the top of the most powerful American "family," died of a heart attack while watching a Yankees game from his summer home in Long Island in October 1976.[188] Additionally, a gangster in the witness protection program wore a Yankees cap while testifying against his former associates in a 2001 federal racketeering conspiracy trial.[189] Another reputed Mafia figure tried to launder his loan-sharking gains by buying and selling such sports memorabilia as a Babe Ruth glove estimated to be worth more than $100,000.[190]

Fictional characters also have ties to the club. On June 1, 2002, Lou Gehrig's famous farewell speech was repeated by a variety of celebrities in 15 major league ballparks.

Actor James Gandolfini, best known for his role as a mob boss in the popular HBO series "The Sopranos," gave the address at Yankee Stadium.[191]

XXVII. Computer Hacking

On October 27, 2000, the morning after the Yankees won their third consecutive World Series, a hacker changed the Yankees.com Web address so surfers would automatically be rerouted to a Virginia Tech computer he used as a decoy. Persons who visited the site were greeted with the message "Yankees suck" and pornographic pictures.[192]

XXVIII. Negligent Endangerment

On May 19, 1929, shortly after the opening of Yankee Stadium, the game was called when a sudden storm with heavy rains and strong wind gusts hit the Bronx. Panicked by the vicious weather, fans in the right field bleachers—an area always crowded with Babe Ruth supporters—stampeded to the only exit. The *Times* headlined the incident which left two dead and dozens hurt, alleging the team failed to provide adequate facilities to treat the injured and made the situation worse by locking other departure points so as not to have to give rain checks. Within 48 hours, the district attorney cleared the Yankees of any wrongdoing, concluding the deaths were not caused by negligence but rather were attributable to a "wild rush of people down a narrow chute with no apparent reason."[193]

XXIX. Miscellaneous

The Yankees have actually become so much a part of the American landscape that the team has been associated with illegal activities in a number of movies. The 1989 film "Sea of Love" is illustrative. Al Pacino plays a law enforcement officer who lures 45 wanted crooks into police custody by tricking them into believing they had been invited to meet the Yankees.[194] Spike Lee's 1999 flick, "Summer of Sam"—released 20 years after David Berkowitz killed six people and wounded seven others allegedly on orders of a neighbor's barking dog—featured Yankee slugger Reggie Jackson as one of the many suspects.[195]

People in the United States and abroad have worn the Yankees logo on many different kinds of apparel while committing crimes.[196] One of the more horrific examples is the case of a 35-year-old former chemical engineer with a history of mental problems who bludgeoned his parents to death with an ax while wearing a Yankees baseball hat and jacket.[197]

Notably, at least one school actually prohibits students from wearing clothes with the team insignia because it might reflect gang affiliation.[198]

Ray Materson, who was serving a 15-year sentence for kidnapping and armed robbery, used threads he unwound from socks to create a series of baseball-card-sized portraits of the starting lineup of his favorite boyhood team—the 1963 Yankees. Photographs he found in books and magazines were his models for producing nine tapestries which he sold in 1994 for $15,000.[199]

XXX. Conclusion

As has been seen, Yankees and "wanna-bes" have been involved in a substantial number and wide assortment of criminal activities. You just have to look in tomorrow's sports pages to find another story.

Affairs of the Heart

by Michael T. Flannery*

Baseball will be linked forever with family. Baseball is reminiscent of fathers and sons holding hands as they enter their first ballpark together—bonding as they crack open peanuts, reach for foul balls, and cheer for their hometown heroes. While the concept of "Yankee" baseball, particularly, epitomizes these ideals, it also conjures images of sex, scandal, Hollywood stars, and tragic downfalls.

In our minds, our Yankee heroes are gods. Ultimately, however, they are just mortal men. And mortal men do not escape the randomness of life's adversities. All of our Yankee heroes have confronted the same personal issues that almost all families face—death, divorce, custody debates, estate squabbles, domestic controversies, drug addictions—the list is familiar to all of us. For Yankee players in particular, it seems, the list is all too familiar. In dealing with family issues, many of our Yankee heroes have responded poorly. Some have acted despicably—diminishing themselves and the game. Still, some have acted heroically and warrant our admiration. But in the affairs of the heart, all have acted humanly. And so Yankee baseball unites us—fathers and sons, gods and mortals—in the affairs of the heart.

Indeed, there are many accounts of domestic differences within the Yankee organization, each of which has affected not only the Yankee players, but the Yankee organization and our perception of it. These stories are just a few of the many family law-related cases of our Yankee favorites.

I. Sex and Scandal

A. Fritz Peterson and Mike Kekich[1]

The most scandalous of the Yankee "sex" stories is probably that which involved pitchers Fritz Peterson and Mike Kekich. Peterson was a rookie in 1966. Kekich joined the club in 1969 and was known for his "wild" side.

In July 1972, thirty-one-year-old Peterson (with his wife, Marilyn) and twenty-eight-year-old Kekich (with his wife, Susanne), attended a party at the home of sportswriter Maury Allen. The two women were starkly contrasted—Marilyn was thirty-one, quiet and petite; Susanne was twenty-eight, tall, athletic, and outspoken. It was at this July party that the couples began considering the idea of exchanging families. By the time the idea came to fruition, Mike Kekich moved in with Marilyn Peterson and her children—Greg and Eric, and Fritz Peterson moved out to father Kristen and Regan Leigh Kekich, who remained with their mother, Susanne.

The couples initiated the plan for several months after the 1972 season. But while the novelty of the off-season trade seemed to invigorate the new mates, appearances at parties only confused teammates and friends who were close to the couples. Rumors of the swap spread throughout the organization, and the players finally announced their scandalous arrangement to the public during spring training of 1973. The moral response by Commissioner Bowie Kuhn (who received more mail about the incident than he did about the implementation of the designated hitter rule that same spring) and other baseball strong-arms would all but ruin the reputations of the two pitchers. And the Yankee organization would not go unscathed. Although the organization had weathered the sexual storms of the carousing Babe Ruth, the popular Joe DiMaggio, and the indulgent Mickey Mantle, it was not until Peterson and Kekich that the team had to deal publicly with an internal sex scandal. It was not long into the first season after the "swap" that the team began to feel the effects of the tension between the two pitchers. Shortly into the 1973 season, the atmosphere in the clubhouse was unbearable, and Kekich was traded to the Cleveland Indians. Ironically, Peterson would be traded to the Indians a year later, but only after Kekich had already left the team to pitch for the Texas Rangers and Seattle Mariners. Kekich later retired from the game in 1977.

Susanne Kekich would later explain that her marriage to Mike had been on shaky ground long before the swap. Fritz Peterson voiced concern over how this would affect his sons if the relationship between his former wife and teammate did not last. All the while, however, Peterson vowed never to return to his former family, despite Marilyn's desperate pleas to take her back. It was only a few months after the announcement of the swap that Peterson's concerns became a reality, and the relationship between Mike Kekich and the former Marilyn Peterson fell apart. The bond between Peterson and the former Susanne Kekich, however, survived; the couple married in 1974 and have four children of their own. After retiring from baseball in 1976, Fritz Peterson went on to other things—selling insurance, broadcasting hockey games, selling bibles for a religious group, teaching school, and working as a casino-boat dealer in Illinois. Peterson's former wife, Marilyn, spent several years alone after her breakup from Mike Kekich, but later married a physician. Kekich remarried and obtained a medical degree in Albuquerque, New Mexico. He was unable to practice medicine in the United States, so he went into the paramedic business. Kekich has said that the incident ruined his career and his life.

While none of the four ever accepted book offers about their relationships, their story continues to spark interest. The story may yet be told on the silver screen—actors Matt Damon and Ben Affleck have undertaken to write the screenplay for the story, with plans to portray the two Yankee pitchers in the film.

B. Dave Winfield[2]

If Fritz Peterson and Mike Kekich do not own the most scandalous story in Yankee history, then Dave Winfield does. Winfield married Tonya Turner in February 1988. The problem was, in 1989, Sandra Renfro wanted a divorce from Winfield, claiming that she had been married to him by "common-law marriage" since 1982! Winfield disagreed, claiming that Renfro was simply the mother of his child but not his common-law wife. Renfro's divorce claim set the stage for eight reported court cases, with very different factual accounts from both parties.

The case went to trial in June 1989, on the sole issue of the existence of a common-law marriage. To have a common-law marriage, a couple must: (1) agree to be married;

(2) live together as husband and wife; and (3) represent themselves to others as married. On July 10, 1989, a jury found by a margin of 10 to 2 that there was a common-law marriage between Winfield and Renfro that occurred on or about April 11, 1982. The court also directed Winfield to pay Renfro $210,000 in attorney's fees and $10,000 per month in temporary alimony. Winfield eventually appealed the final judgment, claiming that the trial court had incorrectly omitted the words "*in Texas*" from its jury instructions. Therefore, the question on appeal was whether Winfield and Renfro had not just satisfied the elements of a common-law marriage but had satisfied the requirements *in Texas.*

Winfield and Renfro met in 1973, when Renfro was an 18 year old student at Texas Southern University and Winfield was playing for the San Diego Padres. They remained friends and, in 1975 or 1976, they established an intimate relationship, which eventually ended.

In 1979, Renfro married Ira Terrell and had a son, Sharad Terrell. Renfro remained married until 1981, when she began seeing Winfield again. In January 1982, Winfield and Renfro took a trip to South America, where she became pregnant with Winfield's daughter, Shanel. Renfro claimed that she and Winfield spoke of marriage at that time because Winfield was concerned about his reputation in baseball and with the Winfield Foundation for Children (a charity established by Winfield).

Although Winfield denied that he ever agreed to be married to Renfro, the court found that there was such an agreement. Renfro presented evidence that, after she became pregnant, Winfield and she agreed to be married informally in Dallas on April 11, 1982. Renfro claimed that she agreed to forego a ceremony because of Winfield's concerns about the effect his fathering a child before marriage would have on his endorsement contracts and on the New York Yankees. According to Renfro, on April 10, 1982, Winfield told her to get a Mercedes Benz and a nice hotel suite in Dallas under the name of Mr. & Mrs. David Winfield. They stayed in a honeymoon suite for three days and had complimentary champagne, roses and fruit delivered to their suite daily.

To dispute this claim, Winfield asserted that he never had a present intent to be married to Renfro, that he never stayed in the hotel with her when they met in Dallas, but rather always stayed with the Yankee team, that they never drank champagne to celebrate a marriage, and that neither he nor Renfro wore a wedding ring. Winfield also submitted an insurance policy signed by Renfro in December 1982 and an income tax statement, in which she indicated that she was not married. Having reviewed the evidence, however, the court found that the parties did, in fact, agree to be married.

With respect to living together as husband and wife in Texas, Renfro claimed that Winfield told her to look for a home in which they could live together. He specifically requested that she find a home with good security because of his reputation. He subsequently purchased a condominium for them in Houston in the summer of 1982. Winfield told his secretary that he was buying the condominium for himself, Renfro and his family. Renfro moved into the condominium in August 1982, and gave birth to Winfield's daughter, Shanel, in September 1982. Renfro claimed that Winfield was always with her at the condominium whenever his schedule could accommodate his being in Houston. Winfield's secretary testified that, from October 1982 to the end of 1984, Winfield spent about 100 days in the off-season in Houston. Renfro asserted that Winfield paid all medical, food, housing, and travel expenses. She claimed that he worked around the house and acted "husbandly."

To counter this, Winfield claimed that he bought the condominium for the benefit of his daughter, not to marry her mother. He further testified that he did not have a key to the home and that he sent Renfro fruit and flowers with a card that read, "For *your* new home." Despite his secretary's testimony that he stayed in Houston about 100 days in two years, Winfield claimed that he only stayed at the condominium for 14 days in 5 years. Winfield also proved that he took another woman to Africa in November 1982, and that Renfro knew about this. Despite this evidence, the court held that there was sufficient evidence to show that Winfield and Renfro had lived together as husband and wife.

Finally, Renfro claimed that she and Winfield held themselves out as husband and wife. However, Winfield claimed that, according to the law in Texas, Renfro had to prove that they held themselves out *in Texas* as husband and wife, and that Renfro failed to prove this. In fact, Winfield asserted that the court gave improper jury instructions by omitting this requirement.

To show that the parties did hold themselves out in Texas as husband and wife, Renfro offered testimony that she had reserved a suite at the Amfac Hotel at the Dallas Airport as "Mr. and Mrs. David Winfield," and that, after the trip to Dallas, she told her mother that she and Winfield were married. The only other evidence offered by Renfro that they held themselves out to the public as husband and wife was that the mailbox at the condominium said "Winfield" on it, and Winfield did not object to this.

There was other evidence that the court determined would be sufficient to show a "holding out" by the couple. For example, a local newspaper in the Bahamas, where they were vacationing, referred to them as "Mr. and Mrs. Winfield," and they were announced at a softball game as being husband and wife, and Winfield responded, "Nice to meet you, this is my wife, Sandra." Further, the couple was referred to on invitations to a party in their honor, without correction or objection, as "David and Sandra Winfield." Also, Winfield introduced himself to the teacher of Renfro's other child as "Sharad's stepfather." Winfield called Renfro's son from her first marriage his stepson, and his mother called him her grandson. Winfield even sent Renfro's son a birthday card signed, "Daddy." Renfro accompanied Winfield to many of his honors and award ceremonies, and neighbors testified that they thought the two were married. But these events, while sufficient to satisfy the element of "holding out," did not occur within the time that the court was limited to considering.

To contest the assertions raised by Renfro, Winfield pointed to the fact that Renfro did not name her daughter "Shanel Winfield;" she named her "Shanel Renfro." And when Renfro attended Yankee games, Winfield would not let her sit in the "family" section, but rather, he made her sit in the right-field grandstands. Also, Renfro filed taxes as head of household, not as married, and she spoke of future wedding ceremonies that never took place. Further, Winfield pointed to the fact that he had married Tonya Turner on February 18, 1988. Winfield began dating Turner in 1981 and, for one brief interruption, continued dating her until 1988, when he married her. Winfield told Turner that he was not married to Renfro. On one occasion in April 1983, while Winfield was traveling with Turner, Renfro called Winfield's hotel room, and Turner answered the phone. Turner testified that Renfro claimed to be Winfield's "lady," meaning his girlfriend, not his wife. Renfro, however, claimed that she told Turner that she was married to Winfield. The court stated that, at most, this only demonstrated that Renfro held herself out as married, but not Winfield.

The court found that, had the jury been instructed to determine from the testimony that Winfield and Renfro represented themselves to others that they were married at a later time—for example, in 1983, or sometime thereafter—then perhaps the jury would have been able to reach such a conclusion. But the appellate court held that there was not sufficient factual evidence to conclude that the couple had held themselves out, *in Texas*, as being husband and wife on or about April 11, 1982. Therefore, since the instructions to the jury on this element were defective, the appellate court reversed the lower court's finding of a common-law marriage and remanded the case for a new trial.

On November 6, 1995, on the eve of the retrial, Winfield and Renfro agreed to end the decade-long debate without a contest. The agreement stated, in part, that "'no marriage—ceremonial, informal, common-law or of any other variety—ever existed.'" Winfield agreed to continue paying $3,500 per month in child support payments for Shanel (then age 13), and he agreed to pay $26,000 of Renfro's legal costs. Both parties waived any future legal claims regarding the controversy.

With regard to the original weekend that Winfield and Renfro allegedly spent together in Dallas in 1982, it was subsequently researched and reported that the Yankees were forced to remain in New York that weekend for an unscheduled double-header to make up for a game that had been previously canceled because of snow. As a result, Winfield later claimed that he was never even in Texas that weekend. Additionally, all records available at the time of the retrial showed that Winfield had spent no more than ten days in Texas during the couple's alleged relationship. Renfro continued to disagree and claimed that Winfield had maintained minimal contact with his daughter, even snubbing her after he told her that he would send for her to visit him when his team (then, the Cleveland Indians) was in the World Series against the Atlanta Braves. Of course, Winfield claims to have developed a good relationship with his daughter. Ultimately, Winfield described the entire case as "a monumental waste of time, money and emotion."

C. Babe Ruth[3]

In Bob Creamer's popular biography of Babe Ruth, Creamer spoke of Ruth's gargantuan sexual appetite and asserted that Ruth's legend was undiminished by his humanity. This description accurately portrays the legal precedent involving Ruth because, despite Ruth's legendary reputation for carousing and womanizing, there was really only one paternity suit that amounted to any scandal. Despite the headlines, most historians minimize even this one account.

The paternity case arose as a breach of promise suit filed by Dolores Dixon in 1922. Dixon sued the Babe for $50,000, claiming that she was carrying his child. When Dixon pushed for an out of court settlement, Ruth told Dixon's lawyers to "Go to hell!" Dixon responded by disclosing the allegations to the press in early 1923. Ruth, however, continued to scoff at the public allegations, claiming that, having acquired his notoriety, he had been hounded by con men, gamblers, and scheming women of every sort.

Dixon responded with more details in the press, claiming that Ruth was with her four to five times a week, often took her for car rides, and once sexually assaulted her aboard a boat in Freeport Harbor, Long Island. Reporters eventually sided with Ruth after contradicting Dixon on several accounts, including her age, which she inconsistently represented as ranging from 15 to 19 years. Ruth's lawyer even claimed to have a witness who could prove that Dixon's story was just a blackmail plot. While Ruth did not officially deny that he knew Dixon, he flatly denied that he ever promised to marry her or ever acted improperly with her. Eventually, Dixon signed an agreement to withdraw the suit without cost to either party. Ruth's lawyer also claimed to have a confession to the blackmail scheme, signed by Dixon, but this was never produced. Whether it really was blackmail or whether Ruth purchased Dixon's silence has never been determined.

It was also 1923 when Ruth met his second wife, Claire Merritt Hodgson. When the two met, Ruth was already married to his first wife, Helen Woodford, who, in 1929, died in a suspicious fire at the home of Ruth's alleged friend, Doctor Edward H. Kinder. Ruth was temporarily a suspect in the case, after Helen's family alleged that Helen was denying Ruth the divorce that he wanted so that he could marry Claire. But Ruth buried his wife, and the allegations of foul play were never substantiated. Ruth eventually married Claire and legally adopted two girls: "Julia," who was Claire's daughter from a previous marriage, and Marie Harrington, who came to live with Ruth and his first wife, Helen, in 1922. Before she died, Marie (also known as Dorothy) wrote a book in 1988, proclaiming to be Ruth's illegitimate daughter.

II. Hollywood Hardships

A. Joe DiMaggio[4]

Except for Joe DiMaggio's last year with the Yankees, his batting average dropped below .300 (to .290) only once in his career—in 1946—the same year that, in Joe's words, he was "quietly going crazy" dealing with the divorce attorneys of his first wife, Dorothy Arnold, who was a Hollywood actress. But without question, the real love of Joe's life was Marilyn Monroe. Joe and Marilyn were married in 1954, for 274 days. Joe obsessed over Marilyn during their marriage and after Marilyn's death. Many say Joe's obsession for her is what doomed the marriage from the start. Although a recent biography of Joe by Richard Ben Cramer paints an unflattering picture of Joe and his relationship with Marilyn, Joe allegedly continued to leave roses on Marilyn's grave until he died in 1999.

B. Leo Durocher[5]

Leo Durocher played for the Yankees from 1925 to 1929. He was married four times, and all of his marriages ended in divorce. The marriage for which he was known, however, was his marriage to actress Laraine Day, who was known as "the first lady of baseball."

Laraine Day was first married to singer Ray Hendricks. Day and Hendricks had two adopted children. During her marriage to Hendricks, Day developed a friendship with Durocher. Hendricks, however, viewed it as more, and confronted Durocher. According to Durocher's account, Hendricks telephoned Durocher on one occasion at 3:30 am and asked Durocher if he was in love with Day. After a face-to-face confrontation, the incident culminated not in fist-a-cuffs, but in a handshake between Durocher and Hendricks and a promise of divorce between Hendricks and Day. Hendricks also promised Durocher that there would be no publicity about the exchange. However, in the headlines the next morning, Hendricks accused Durocher of breaking up the marriage. Day soon filed for divorce, and Hendricks did not contest. Two months later, Day received an interlocutory (or temporary) decree of divorce that was to be final in one year's time. However, the night after obtaining the interlocutory decree, Day and Durocher decided not to wait for the year to pass. Instead, they flew to Juarez, Mexico, which had no residency requirement for a divorce action. After obtaining a divorce in Mexico, they flew to El Paso, Texas, and immediately married. The judge who granted the interlocutory decree in California was not pleased and wanted to annul the marriage if the two lived under the same roof (as adulterers) in California.

Durocher acknowledged the invalidity of his marriage in California and explained to the judge that he was leaving for spring training in a few weeks, and that he and Day would not be living together in California until the year under the interlocutory decree had elapsed. A year later, in 1947, Durocher and Day were married in California. The marriage lasted thirteen years.

Durocher's career in baseball took a detour in 1947, immediately after his marriage, after he was suspended from baseball for one year. Some say the suspension was because of Durocher's alleged ties to the mob and its influence on gambling and sports. Others suggest that Durocher was banned for the 1947 season because of the "adulterous" relationship with Day. Allegedly, baseball Commissioner Happy Chandler suspended Durocher to quiet officials of the Catholic Church, who were threatening a boycott of major league baseball games to protest The Lip's scandalous example to youth.

C. Lefty Vernon Gomez[6]

On February 26, 1933, Lefty Gomez married singer June O'Dea. Early in Gomez's career, the couple made headlines discussing how nice it was to be married to each other and how happily the two accommodated their respective careers. But by May 1938, O'Dea filed for separation, claiming that Gomez had beaten her, had woken her up in the middle of the night to describe to her the "perfect crime" in which he would kill her by choking her to death, and had threatened to kill himself by feigning to jump from their hotel window. Reportedly, she even testified that, in 1934, Gomez influenced her to have an abortion because they were not ready to have children. She further testified that "he drank constantly and used vile language." The two were reunited, however, during the 1939 season, and had a child the next year. O'Dea told her story to Collier's Magazine in 1942, but despite her disclosures, they remained married.

D. David Justice[7]

David Justice married actress Halle Berry in January 1993. Berry filed for divorce in California in April 1996, citing "irreconcilable differences." Two weeks later, Justice filed in Atlanta, Georgia. Reportedly, each sought financial support from the other. Justice had just signed a $28 million contract extension with the Cleveland Indians, and Berry was making approximately $2.5 million per movie at the time; she also had a contract with Revlon. In the case, Justice raised a question about Berry's relationship with actors Wesley Snipes, Eddie Murphy, and others. Of the divorce, Berry said, "Why can't all men be like dogs? . . . They have unconditional love."

The divorce was a bitter one and affected both celebrities. In 1996, during the divorce, one night before reporting to spring training in Florida, police found Justice sitting in his car in an area frequented by drug dealers and prostitutes. Justice claimed that he went for a ride and had gotten lost. Berry confessed that she attempted to kill herself by sitting in her car and asphyxiating herself and her two dogs. Berry was known to verbally attack Justice in public, especially on television talk shows. Berry was quoted as saying of the marriage, "It beat me down to the lowest of lows. The gum on the bottom of David's shoes, that's what I felt like." Berry has claimed that she often had to call police for protection.

Of Berry, Justice was quoted as saying, "I've never known a girl who could throw a tantrum like she does. I just want[ed] to get away from her, but she [wouldn't] let me... unless I [gave] her a financial settlement." Their divorce became final in June 1997, but the terms of the divorce were kept confidential.

Subsequent to his divorce from Berry, Justice weathered a palimony suit, which was thrown out of Los Angeles County Superior Court. Nicole Foster's claim fell outside the jurisdiction of California courts.

III. Divorce, Property Distribution, and Support

A. Jack Satter[8]

Probably the most high-profile Yankee divorce case involved not a Yankee player but a Yankee owner—Jack Satter. The divorce between Yankee co-owner Jack Satter and his wife, Nancy Bernard, was considered Florida's version of "The War of the Roses." The two even slung mud at each other on "Dateline NBC" in November 2001.

The couple met in 1962. Nancy was 23 years old, recently divorced, and had a small child. She worked as a manicurist in a Boston barber shop, where then-41-year-old Jack went every morning at 6:00 a.m. for a shave. Although Nancy remarried another man after her first divorce, she continued seeing Jack secretly. She remained his mistress for ten years, until she finally divorced her second husband. By that time, Jack had become owner of Colonial Provisions, a Boston meat-processing company. As convenience would have it, Jack separated from his wife at the time, and so began the couple's second affair.

Jack's company developed quickly after he landed the contract for selling hotdogs at Fenway Park. After also nabbing the contract at Yankee Stadium, he became part owner of the Yankees. As his notoriety grew, his affair with Nancy became the scandal of Boston, so he divorced his wife, Pauline, and began dating Nancy publicly.

The couple lived a lavish lifestyle. They threw affluent parties for sports figures and celebrities. They had four Mercedes-Benz and several homes. Nancy spent $30,000 a year on clothes, spent thousands of dollars on country club dinners, and flew every other week from Boca Raton to Boston to have her hair styled. Nancy would even buy herself jewelry, gift-wrap it, and leave it on Jack's dinner plate; Jack would then present the jewelry to her as a gift. By the time Jack was 65 and Nancy was in her 40's—"after more than 20 years of friendship, adultery and dating"—they agreed to take their relationship a step farther and signed a prenuptial agreement (written by Jack). Nancy claimed that she did not even read the agreement because it was not important to her.

On December 27, 1986, they married. But the pre-marital affair lasted longer than the marriage. After only a few months of "honeymooning" together in Palm Beach, Florida, they began bickering over money. After five years of bitter marriage and tumultuous allegations, Jack filed for divorce in 1991, and Nancy quickly scrambled to read every line of that prenuptial agreement.

The agreement provided for Nancy, upon divorce, to receive $1 million, a Mercedes-Benz, and a house in Cape Cod, plus another $1.5 million when Jack died. But Nancy claimed that Jack undervalued his interest in the New York Yankees. Jack asserted that his interest was negative $960,000, but Nancy's attorney thought this absurd and claimed that, had Nancy known of Jack's actual value at the time, she would never have signed the agreement. If Nancy could persuade a court to invalidate the agreement, she stood to inherit up to half of Jack's hot dog fortune, which was estimated to be worth between $13 and $46 million. But in 1991, a trial court determined that the prenuptial agreement was valid.

Jack claimed that the agreement, although valid, should not be enforced against him because Nancy breached the agreement. The pre-nuptial agreement provided that "Nancy shall not be entitled to receive anything if [she] cease[d] to cohabitate with Jack." Jack claimed that Nancy deserted him when she refused to move with him to a $2 million second home that he built in Florida, at St. Andrew's Country Club. Consequently, he claimed that he did not owe her anything. Of course, Nancy claimed that Jack drove her away. Nancy described how (and how often) Jack would beat her, emotionally abuse her, and cheat on her. She explained how she would return to their home in Boston every few weeks and find clothes in the closet that were not hers. She claimed that she was forced to communicate with Jack by writing notes and asking him to circle his responses. Despite these allegations, she never charged him with criminal domestic abuse. Jack denied the allegations of abuse but admitted the affair, blaming it on Nancy's "gold digging" lifestyle. After a second trial in 1992, the court determined that Jack had violated the agreement through a "systematic series of mental abuses" and that Nancy had sustained physical abuse during the marriage.

In the ensuing litigation, the court awarded Nancy $5,200 per month in temporary support, which she received until a final judgment of divorce was granted. It also awarded Nancy prejudgment interest on the $1 million to be awarded to her pursuant to the prenuptial agreement. Despite her award, which Jack appealed, Nancy was not satisfied. She wanted half of the $4 million in joint checking accounts that had accrued during the marriage, even though she never worked a day during the marriage. Finally, in late 1993, after a third trial, the court entered a final judgment of divorce. It held that the prenuptial agreement was enforceable, and that Nancy was entitled only to what was afforded to her in the agreement. However, it also awarded her attorney's fees, which Jack contested.

Although the divorce had been granted, the two continued to fight over pots and pans, damages to a golf cart, patio furniture, dish towels, cleaning products, and even toilet paper rolls. Jack went so far as to take pictures of everything in the house. But when he returned one day, and the house had been emptied—including the light bulbs in the fixtures—he filed to have Nancy held in contempt unless she returned certain items, including brooms and mops that he claimed were his, and unless she returned to clean the barbeque that she left in a dirty condition.

As if these tactics were not enough, Jack had yet another allegation to assert—bigamy. Jack claimed that Nancy never divorced her previous husband, and so he and

Nancy were never really married or subject to the prenuptial agreement. But Nancy proved her case; the court determined that she had been legally divorced from her previous husband and, therefore, legally married to (and divorced from) Jack. But Nancy was not to be outdone. In return, after a 1993 Florida Supreme Court decision that ended a ban on spouses suing each other for civil damages, Nancy sued Jack for $10 million, claiming physical and emotional abuse during the marriage. Consequently, the couple returned to court for a fourth trial.

This time, Jack had a cast of celebrities ready to testify on his behalf—among them were Jim Rice, Maury Povich, Red Auerbach, and John Havlicek. Jack even had his attorneys secretly follow Nancy to videotape her on golf trips and dancing excursions to show that she suffered no ill effects from her marriage to Jack. A Palm Beach judge subsequently ruled that all abuse claims but one were barred by a two-year statute of limitations. Nancy was limited to asserting one documented incident of assault with a telephone by Jack. At the conclusion of the trial, an all-male jury took less than an hour to decide that Nancy was not entitled to a cent. Nancy appealed the case. Meanwhile, Jack sued Nancy for defamation, asserting that Nancy tried to ruin his reputation by falsely claiming that he was an abusive husband during the marriage.

Also pending was Jack's appeal of Nancy's award of prejudgment interest on her $1 million award under the prenuptial agreement and a requirement that the marital residence in Cape Cod be transferred to Nancy free of encumbrances. In August 1995, the appellate court reversed the decision and held that Nancy was not entitled to prejudgment interest because she was not entitled to the $1 million until the marriage was dissolved. It held, however, that, in all other respects, the prenuptial agreement was valid. Therefore, the residence in Cape Cod had to be transferred free of any liens or encumbrances, and Nancy was entitled to what she bargained for in the prenuptial agreement.

To settle the outstanding defamation case, Nancy paid Jack $20,000 and relinquished the name "Satter." The court also later found that Nancy could not show any need for an award of attorney's fees because, even though Jack was worth over $13 million, Nancy was worth $1.1 million and, therefore, she had no need for Jack to pay her fees.

B. George Stallings[9]

George Stallings (who, in 1910, managed the Yankees—then called the "Highlanders") was married to Belle White Stallings. Belle filed for divorce and claimed that "as a result of infatuation for another woman [George] had been guilty of infidelity toward her, and ha[d] abandoned her and her two children, and refuse[d] to support them."

George and Belle established their marital home in Atlanta, Georgia, and resided there for three years. But George was a large stockholder in a baseball and amusement company in Buffalo, New York, and in a baseball company in Providence, Rhode Island, so he spent much time in other cities. As a result, when Belle filed for divorce, George was outside the state, and it was impossible for Belle to obtain personal service on him.

When Belle filed for divorce, George received a salary of $4,000 as manager of the former Yankee team, and he had an additional income of $3,000 to $5,000. He also owned a farm and several bank accounts in Jones County, Georgia. Belle suspected that George would transfer the land and withdraw his accounts, so she requested that a receiver be appointed to take charge of the property, and that she be paid alimony and attorney's fees out of the proceeds of the sale of the property. A temporary receiver was appointed and a restraining order was granted against George on the property and against the banks on his accounts. The court ordered that a copy of the order be sent to George's attorney and by registered mail to George's last known address. At the hearing, at which George did not appear, Belle's attorney testified that George's attorney was served and that she received a receipt for the registered package sent to Buffalo, New York. George was also personally served by the sheriff, but not in Georgia. George moved to dismiss the claim because no proper and legal service had been made upon him in Georgia. After hearing argument, the court ordered that the receiver pay out of George's estate $150 per month to Belle and $250 to her attorney for attorney's fees. George took exception to the court's order that he pay this money.

Upon George's exception, the court held that, in order for the court to have jurisdiction to order that George pay Belle any money, there had to have been a properly filed case before the court. And in order for there to have been a properly filed case before the court, George had to have been properly served. The only way George could have been properly served would have been for him to be personally served in Georgia. The only service that was made upon George was by registered mail to his last known address in Buffalo, New York, and to his attorney. Without perfected service, there was no sufficiently commenced proceeding to authorize jurisdiction. The court said that, since George had a known residence in Jones county, he could not be served sufficiently as a non-resident (by attorney or registered mail). The court reversed the decision, therefore, holding that the lower court erred by passing the interlocutory decree that Belle requested. Although the court reversed the decision, it stated that "the wife is not wholly helpless and subject to suffer....She is still a wife, and as such, unless prevented by her own misconduct, may purchase necessaries for her support, and the husband will be liable therefore."

C. Burleigh Grimes[10]

Burleigh Grimes was first married in 1913, but his wife divorced him in 1928. He married his second wife, Laura Virginia Grimes, in March 1931. Burleigh filed for divorce in April 1938. Although the reported case dealt mostly with attorney's fees, the allegations raised by both parties in the divorce are notable. Burleigh alleged that Laura constantly quarreled with him, nagged him, and falsely accused him of illicitly associating with other women—namely, Rose Porter, who was a maid in their home. Burleigh also claimed that Laura deceived him throughout their marriage by falsely claiming that she had only been married once, when, in fact, she had been married and divorced three times. Further, Burleigh claimed that Laura told him that she had no children, when, in fact, she had two daughters from her first marriage. Throughout their marriage, Laura led Burleigh to believe that her natural daughters were really her nieces.

Laura alleged in a crossbill that, despite being occasionally abusive, Burleigh treated her with love and respect for the first two years of their marriage. Laura alleged that, after that time, Burleigh began an intimate relationship with Rose Porter, and that he also unsuccessfully attempted to force an intimate relationship upon her daughter. Laura further alleged that Burleigh left her for long periods of time to have affairs with other women, that he struck her and threatened to kill her while she was sick, and that he was cruel to a three year old child for whom the couple had once cared.

Burleigh earned a salary of $25,000 per year as a major league pitcher in 1932. He was dropped the following year, but at the time of his divorce action, he was the manager of the Montreal baseball team under a one-year, $10,000 contract. Before the divorce was granted, the parties agreed for Burleigh to pay $150 per month in alimony and $500 for suit money and attorney's fees. The lower court granted Burleigh's petition for divorce and denied Laura's crossbill. On appeal, in May 1940, the court found that Burleigh's allegations were true and that he was the injured party. Therefore, the appellate court affirmed the lower court's decision but awarded Laura an additional $500 for attorney's fees.

D. Jose Rijo[11]

Jose Rijo was born in the Dominican Republic. His father left home when Jose was four years old. At age fifteen, Jose tried out for the Yankees and eventually signed a contract in 1981 at the age of 16. He subsequently obtained resident alien status and lived in the United States. In 1984, when he was traded to the Oakland A's, he moved to the San Francisco area, where he met his wife, Alma. Alma is the daughter of Hall-of-Fame pitcher Juan Marichal, who became the father that Jose never had as a child, growing up in the Dominican Republic.

Jose and Alma were married in September 1987. Alma was also born in the Dominican Republic. Thus, they were both citizens of that country and held Dominican passports; however, both resided in the United States as resident aliens. Alma obtained this status as an infant and has lived in the United States for most of her life.

In the fall of 1987, Jose was traded to the Cincinnati Reds. He and Alma moved to Ohio at that time. In 1988, Jose and Alma purchased a $60,000 condominium in the Dominican Republic and contracted for the construction of a $198,000 house in Ohio, which was completed in 1989. They also purchased a two-bedroom house in Boca Raton, Florida. In December 1990, however, Jose filed for divorce in Ohio. At the time, Alma was pregnant with the couple's second child. Alma said that all Jose wanted to do in the off-season was to go home to the Dominican Republic and party—coming and going as he pleased.

In the divorce, Jose claimed Ohio as his domicile. He requested temporary orders of child support of $2,000 per month and for spousal support of $5,500 per month. In February 1991, while his divorce was still pending, Jose signed with the Reds to a three-year, $9 million contract. Meanwhile, Alma spent December 1990 and January 1991 in Boca Raton and began living in the Ohio house in March 1991. In June 1991, the trial court gave Alma custody of the children and granted Jose standard visitation rights. Jose was ordered to pay child support of $10,000 per month and spousal support of $16,000 per month.

Subsequently, the couple reconciled. By October 1991, Jose dismissed his complaint, and Alma joined Jose in the Dominican Republic. They purchased a 7-bedroom house in the Dominican Republic for $1.2 million. By March 1993, Jose had signed a 4-year, $22-million contract with the Reds, and Alma was four months pregnant, but Jose filed again for divorce in the Dominican Republic. He requested an order of child support of $3,000 per month and spousal support of $2,250 per month. The claim severed Jose's strong relationship with his father-in-law, Juan Marichal. Alma filed in Ohio one month later, and Jose moved to dismiss her case, claiming that Alma was not domiciled in Ohio.

Alma testified that she had intended to make the Ohio residence the family's permanent home since it was purchased in 1989. She testified that the Boca Raton and Dominican Republic houses were vacation homes. She demonstrated a pattern of travel during Jose's employment with the Reds that supported this testimony. However, Jose testified that, throughout the marriage, and particularly with the purchase of the Dominican home in 1991, he intended to make the Dominican Republic the family's permanent home.

Alma's expert said that the Immigration and Naturalization Service ("INS") classifies foreign nationals in two categories: (1) non-immigrants, who may enter the United States on a tourist or work visa; and (2) immigrants who are "resident aliens" or "green-card holders" or "aliens admitted for permanent residence." For someone to obtain a resident alien status (such as Jose had), the INS law required that you state an intent to remain permanently in the United States and prohibited a resident alien from being absent from the country for more than a year or residing permanently in a place other than in the United States. Thus, on August 16, 1993, the court overruled Jose's motion and affirmed the judgment of the trial court in Alma's favor.

E.   Lance Johnson[12]

Kenneth Lance Johnson and Sharon Brown Johnson obtained a divorce in December 1995. In the divorce judgment, the court divided their marital property based on a written agreement between them. However, in January 1996, Sharon filed a "Motion to Set Aside the Judgment," claiming that Lance misrepresented his financial status to her in causing her to sign the agreement. Sharon alleged that, when they signed the agreement: Lance did not produce full and complete documents related to his financial accounts, income and assets; Lance claimed that he had no prospects for future employment as a major league baseball player; and he claimed that he had no hope of re-signing with his former club, the White Sox, but that just days after the judgment of divorce, he signed a two-year, $5.7 million dollar contract with the New York Mets and, after the judgment, mocked her that "she did not get any of his money."

In February 1997, Lance tried to terminate the proceedings, claiming that Sharon's motion was not a request to "set aside" the judgment, but that it was a request to "amend" the judgment, which would have meant that Sharon had filed her motion too late. In March 1997, the trial court determined that, because Sharon's claims alleged misrepresentations, her motion was really a motion for relief from judgment and, therefore, her motion was timely filed. Lance petitioned the Alabama Supreme Court, which held that it was incorrect for the trial court to treat Sharon's motion as a request for relief from judgment. It said that the lower court should have looked at the essence of the motion, not at its title. Since Sharon's motion specifically requested that the divorce judgment be "set aside" or "modified," the court held that it was consistent with a request to alter, amend or vacate the judgment rather than as a motion for relief from judgment on fraud grounds. Thus, it held that Sharon's motion was really filed too late and should have been denied by operation of law. Accordingly, the court granted Lance's motion that Sharon's motion be dismissed.

F.   David Collins[13]

David Collins married his first wife, Kimberly, on May 12, 1980. David played for the Yankees in 1982 and, after a brief stint with the Toronto Blue Jays, the Oakland A's acquired David's contract with the Yankees in 1985. Pursuant to the terms of the acquisition, the A's organization was obligated to pay Collins a ten-year annuity deferred compensation of $3,827 per month, beginning in 1988.

In July 1988, Kimberly filed for divorce. By August 1989, when the divorce became final, David was earning $225,000 per year with the Reds, although David's employment with the Reds was not guaranteed for the 1990 season.

In February 1990, the court awarded permanent custody of the child to Kimberly and ordered David to pay $100 per week in child support. The court held that, if David obtained employment for the 1990 season, this amount could increase. In dividing the couple's assets, the court awarded Kimberly two annuities valued at $220,962. The court further ordered David to pay the $820 per month mortgage on the marital home until it could be sold, at which time David and Kimberly would split the $67,000 equity in the home. Additionally, the court awarded Kimberly IRA accounts totaling $2,674 and a vehicle with $4,600 equity and a $290 monthly payment. David was awarded a $12,250 IRA and a $12,500 vehicle. Although David was still married to Kimberly at the time he acquired the annuity from the Oakland A's, the court determined that the annuity was separate property and was not part of the marital assets to be divided by the parties.

David appealed the judgment of the court regarding the division of marital property, claiming that the court abused its discretion by awarding Kimberly 85 percent of the marital estate. But the appellate court held that the lower court did not abuse its discretion in making its award. The appellate court determined that David's right to receive the Oakland A's annuity—a fixed bonus guaranteed over a certain future period—was more like an asset than income since it was really payment for past services. Since David was married while "working," the right to the deferred compensation should really be marital property. But by classifying the annuity as non-divisible, non-marital property, the court effectively sheltered from the division of property $460,000 of David's compensation that otherwise would have qualified as divisible property upon divorce.

After the divorce, Kimberly became employed and earned $14,079.60 annual income. David signed with the St. Louis Cardinals and earned $225,000 for the 1990 season. David also received a $79,000 refund from the Major League Baseball's Player's Union Settlement Fund, which was the result of a strike settlement between the Players' Association and the baseball owners. In April 1990, Kimberly filed for increased child support. In October 1990, the court ordered David to increase his child support payments to $24,000 for the year. It further held that the $79,000 Player's Union refund was a non-marital asset. Thus, the entire amount was David's individual property.

David appealed the order for $24,000 in child support, and Kimberly appealed the ruling that the entire award of $79,000 was David's individual property. Regarding David's claim, the court found that David's salary was $271,000, which accounted for 95 percent of the couple's combined income. Therefore, under Ohio law, David was responsible for 95 percent of the allowable child support award, which was more than $24,000. Therefore, even with the increase, David was paying less than what the support laws actually required him to pay. Regarding Kimberly's assertion that she was entitled to an equal share of the $79,000 strike fund as a marital asset, the court held for David because, at the time of the divorce, David (and, therefore, Kimberly) had no fixed right to receive any money from the strike fund. His right to collect the $79,000 came after the divorce because an agreement was reached between the baseball owners and the players that the owners would pay the players their refund from money acquired from a cable contract in May 1990, which was after the parties' divorce.

David soon remarried to Sherry L. Collins, and they divorced in 1994. At the time of this divorce, David was to receive approximately $103,000 in licensing fees from the Major League Baseball Players Association for 1991, 1992, and 1993. As part of the parties' property settlement, the court awarded Sherry $36,080.47 of this sum. Before Sherry could receive the award, however, the IRS seized the total amount as payment for taxes, interest, and penalties already owed to the government. Consequently, David could not pay Sherry her share of the award, and Sherry filed to hold David in contempt of court. Because the monies were no longer available to be divided, the court held that Sherry was no longer entitled to the award, finding that David should not have to pay Sherry half of a marital asset which, in effect, never existed. However, the court awarded Sherry $17,255 to compensate for a mistake made by David's attorney in distributing the marital assets.

Another issue in the case regarded the marital home. In the parties' divorce decree, David received the marital real estate. Upon the sale or refinancing of the home after divorce, David was to pay Sherry $11,150, which was her share of the equity in the real estate. Upon receipt of that amount from David, Sherry was to "quit claim" her interest in the property to David. However, David never paid Sherry her share of the equity, and Sherry filed for contempt. Although the court held that David mismanaged the sale of the property and, thereby, delayed the sale, which led to his non-payment of Sherry's equitable share, the court used the doctrine of "clean hands" to conclude that David should not be held in contempt. It reasoned that, since Sherry was equally at fault in mismanaging the sale of the property, the doctrine of clean hands prohibited her from the remedy of contempt.

Finally, Sherry asserted that David should be held in contempt for allowing the children's medical insurance to lapse and for failing to pay three marital debts ordered in the divorce decree. The court denied these assertions as well, finding that Sherry failed to meet her burden of proving by clear and convincing evidence that these failures were contemptuous behavior on the part of David. Instead, the court found that these failures were due to the actions and negotiations of the parties' attorneys.

G. Joe Pepitone[14]

Joe Pepitone was the first baseman for the Yankees from 1962 to 1969. Tired of his night-life antics, the Yankees traded him to the Houston Astros in 1970. He was twice married and divorced.

Pepitone divorced his wife, Diane, on September 19, 1973. After the divorce, Pepitone amassed significant arrears in alimony and child support. Judgment was entered against him for $35,000 in alimony arrears and $7,000 in child support arrears.

Pepitone was a member of the Major League Baseball Players Benefit Plan ("the Plan"). Under the Plan, Pepitone was eligible to elect early retirement and, therefore, receive benefits at any point between his 45th and his 60th birthday, which would have been his normal retirement date. If he chose early retirement, however, his benefits would be significantly reduced.

Diane sought to sequester Pepitone's pension benefits when he was 40 years old; this was five years before the earliest date at which vested benefits would have been payable. She wanted to sequester the benefits then so that, when Joe turned 45, she could force him to take early retirement and recoup what was owed to her in arrears. The court held that sequestration of assets was appropriate because judgment for arrears had been rendered and Pepitone failed to obey it. But the question was whether the pension benefits were, then, assets that should be included in sequestration. The trustee of the Plan argued that, by releasing funds for Pepitone's family support obligations, it would affect the Plan's tax-exempt status. But since Diane was not seeking immediate payment, concern about the effect on the tax-exempt status was unwarranted. The court was more concerned about the application of federal law, which prohibited the assignment, garnishment or alienation of any benefits in the Plan to any creditor of the member. The Plan expressly stated that, upon any attachment, garnishment or proceeding that vested the benefits in any person other than the member, payment of the benefits would cease. To address this provision, the court held that ERISA (the "Employee Retirement Income Security Act") did not immunize pension payments from family support obligations.

Having resolved the application of federal law, the court determined whether there were any state law prohibitions to sequestration of pension benefits that were not distributable at the time. Without any precedent to guide it, the court reasoned that, because the vested interest in the Plan was inaccessible to Joe for several years, the remedy of sequestration for Diane offered her no real benefit or protection; there was no further threat to the fund because Joe had no right to affect his benefits adversely. Thus, Diane's request for sequestration was denied as premature. However, the court said that Diane could again request sequestration at the proper time, provided she could show that Joe failed to pay his arrears and that she was not otherwise protected.

Diane argued that she ought to be able to sequester the funds when Joe reached age 45, thereby forcing him to take early retirement. Joe argued to reserve that decision until that time arrived. But the court felt that, to leave Diane in limbo for five years would be unfair. So, the court held that, when Joe reached age 45, notwithstanding that the benefits would be considerably reduced, Diane should compel him to take early retirement and then sequester the funds.

H. Enos Slaughter[15]

Mary K. Slaughter obtained a divorce from Enos Slaughter in November 1951. Mary was granted custody of their son, Rex, who was Mary's child from a previous marriage, and their daughter, Patricia, who was Enos' natural child. The natural father of Rex was killed in World War II, and Enos adopted the child after he and Mary married.

The divorce decree ordered Enos to pay $150 per month for the support of each child. After Enos petitioned to modify the award, the support for Rex was reduced to $50 per month. In 1957, Mary appealed the reduction and petitioned for an increase in Rex's support.

When the divorce was granted in 1951, Enos was earning $25,000 per year, plus royalties and other income from commercial advertisements. In 1956, he received $5,200 for his share of World Series receipts, but his salary after 1952 was $20,000 per year. In 1957, Enos was playing with the Yankees. Although he was 41 years old, he was under contract with the Yankees for the remainder of the season at a salary of $20,000. Enos also owned a 200-acre farm in North Carolina (Mary claimed that it was 360 acres and that, during their marriage, Enos earned between $3,000 and $3,600 per year from rent on the property; however, Enos claimed that, in 1956, after expenses, he earned approximately $200 from the farm). Enos also built a new home in North Carolina that cost between $20,000 and $23,000, but he said he had a mortgage of $15,000. Also, he had an interest in an apartment house in Illinois (which he sold), a jewelry store in Illinois (which he sold for $6,500), and stocks valued at $14,000 (from which he received stock dividends of approximately $1,300 per year).

Enos remarried twice after his divorce from Mary in 1951. By 1957, he was living with his fifth wife and her daughter in a house in New Jersey that he rented for $200 per month. Mary and the children lived in Illinois with her parents. She was employed part-time and received $5,500 gross in alimony. She also earned $27.00 per month from an unknown source. Rex received $116.00 per month from the government because of the death of his natural father while in the armed service. Mary claimed that, as of September 1956, monthly expenses were $376.50, two-thirds of which was for the children, plus other personal expenses for the children of $105 per month. Rex also received $27.00 per month from an insurance policy.

Enos was not asking the court to reduce Patricia's support of $150.00 per month, but Enos argued that Rex's support should be lowered because he was adopted and because he received approximately $100.00 per month under a federal pension. The court held that Enos could not reduce his child support payments for Rex just because he was adopted or because he received benefits due to his natural father's death, particularly since Enos agreed that the $150.00 per month for Patricia was reasonable. Therefore, the appellate court held that the lower court erred by reducing Rex's support to $50.00 and by not increasing it to $150.00. The court held that, since Rex was older and the cost of living had increased after it had been reduced to $50.00, it should be increased to $150.00. The court considered the fact that Enos was 40 years old and his days in baseball were numbered, but it held that he "may be able to secure more lucrative employment by reason of the prominence he ha[d] attained as one of the great figures in the baseball world."

I. Lynn McGlothen[16]

In 1972, Lynn McGlothen was playing for the Boston Red Sox. He met his wife, Brenda, during a road trip to California. At the end of the 1972 season, Lynn returned to San Francisco and moved into Brenda's apartment. He left that winter to play ball in Puerto Rico, leaving his car and personal effects with Brenda. They planned to marry, but they postponed those plans when Brenda learned that Lynn was already married and had a child. Nevertheless, upon the opening of the 1973 season, the two moved to Boston and cohabited there until Lynn was traded to St. Louis. They eventually continued living together there.

In November 1974, Lynn obtained a divorce and he married Brenda. A year later, they had their first child. In December 1976, Lynn was traded to the San Francisco Giants, so he and Brenda moved back to San Francisco.

During spring training in 1977, Lynn assaulted Brenda, giving her a black eye. Consequently, she returned from spring training, alone, to San Francisco. When the season commenced, Lynn rejoined her in the home, where they lived together again until June 1978. At that time, Lynn was traded to the Chicago Cubs. When Brenda decided to go with Lynn to Chicago, he instructed her to live in a trailer park in Louisiana until he could find a home for her and their child in the Chicago area. Thinking that this was a temporary arrangement until a home in Chicago could be found, Brenda moved into a trailer home in Louisiana, while Lynn moved into the Beldon Stratford Hotel in Chicago. Through the summer of 1978 and 1979, Brenda visited Lynn at the hotel. Each time she visited, Lynn insisted that he was continuing his search for a house and that Brenda should remain in Louisiana. While in Louisiana, there were many incidents of violence against Brenda by Lynn. He closed their joint checking and savings accounts. Eventually, Lynn completely refused to support Brenda or their children, even though Brenda was pregnant and about to have their second son. When the child was born, Lynn told Brenda to leave. He continued to do violence to her when he was in Louisiana, and because she had no money on which to live, she fled Louisiana for California, where her parents continued to reside.

Under Lynn's contract with the Cubs, he earned a bonus of $200,000 in October 1979, and was paid a salary of $200,000 per year. According to Brenda, Lynn threatened to quit baseball before she would get a dime of his money. She claimed to be reliant on public welfare in San Francisco, which Lynn did not challenge.

In seeking a divorce, Brenda filed for child and spousal support from Lynn. Lynn claimed that he was not a resident of California and, therefore, he was not subject to the jurisdiction of California's courts. In considering whether it had jurisdiction, the court reasoned through the law that a state may assume jurisdiction if the subject causes an "effect" in the state by an act or omission which occurs elsewhere. Because Lynn's actions left Brenda and her two children destitute in Louisiana and reliant on the taxpayers of California, the court held that Lynn caused an effect in California from which he derived the financial benefit of not having to support his family. The court said that Lynn had imposed on them the insurmountable "financial burden and personal strain of litigating a spousal and child support suit in a forum thousands of miles away...."

When Lynn appealed, the court of appeals found that Lynn had derived the benefit of being relieved of the necessity of supporting his wife and children for several years because of their presence in California, where they were supported by public welfare and Diana's parents. Therefore, the court held that it was reasonable and constitutional for California to assume jurisdiction in Diana's action for support.

J. David LaPoint[17]

David LaPoint and his wife were divorced in 1989. In 1996, LaPoint was ordered to pay $100 per week in child support for his two sons. When LaPoint requested that his child support payments be reduced, the hearing examiner determined that LaPoint had willfully violated the support order. The hearing examiner denied LaPoint's application, finding he and his second wife, who testified at the hearing, to be totally incredible.

The appellate court noted that LaPoint had been involved in child support proceedings for a decade. He was also the subject of a 1990 contested child support proceeding filed by the mother of his third child, a daughter, who was born in January 1990. In that case, the court found that LaPoint had intentionally attempted to delay the proceedings and frustrate the discovery process, and had proffered a position that the court held to be "preposterous." He argued that he should not pay more than $25 per month for the child, which is the minimum amount of child support obligation for a parent whose income is below the federal poverty line (an amount intended for the "poorest parents"). He made this assertion in 1992, when, in the previous year, he had earned $900,000 as a pitcher for the Yankees.

With this background in mind, the court considered his wife's request for child support. During his ten-year professional baseball career prior to this, LaPoint earned up to $550,000 per year playing on four other teams prior to joining the Yankees. In 1995, he was the general manager of a minor league baseball team at a salary of $40,000. LaPoint was ordered to pay $100 per week in child support, and no objections were filed to this 1996 decision.

No sooner did this litigation end, LaPoint requested a downward modification of child support because his stint as general manager was to end at the end of 1996, and he requested deductions based on the support he paid for his daughter. LaPoint claimed that he was not fired from his general manager's job, but that he had a contract dispute with owners, who wanted to change his salary to $20,000 with bonuses. He claimed to be unemployed in 1997. In 1998, he was employed as the manager of Dave LaPoint's Pitchers—a sports bar wholly owned by his then-current wife, who unilaterally paid him a salary of $24,000 per year.

The hearing examiner denied LaPoint's request to lower his child support payments. Further, LaPoint was not entitled to a deduction against his income for child support for his daughter because evidence was presented that he had surrendered her for adoption. In the end, LaPoint was ordered to pay $175.00 per week. The hearing examiner also found that LaPoint was in willful violation of the 1996 order and directed him to pay $5,000 in attorney fees. The hearing examiner said that LaPoint's testimony was "a story literally of a house of cards." The court held that LaPoint and his then-current wife "fabricated" their financial picture. It found that LaPoint was "generally non-credible and purposefully evasive," assuming "untenable" and "glaringly disingenuous" positions. Despite claiming that his salary was only $24,000, evidence showed that he had a very comfortable lifestyle, including a nice home (with real estate in New York and Florida), a new vehicle (a 1990 Porsche and a 1987 Ford pick-up), a country club membership, tens of thousands of dollars in annual credit card charges, and golf vacations. Further, his then-current wife testified that, in the year in which he was essentially unemployed and incapable of paying child support, she received $200,000 in "collusion" funds from the MLB Players Association as a result of a 1991 postnuptial agreement, whereby he had divested himself of assets and assigned them to her. It was anticipated that his wife would receive a total of $575,000 in the "collusion" funds by the end of 1998 and additional future payments of at least $400,000, all of which, but for the assignment, would have gone to him. He and his wife both denied that he was in any way a beneficiary of these funds, despite their status as husband and wife. The court held that LaPoint could not avoid his family obligations by simply assigning away his assets. It held that, when a parent does this, the court may impute income where the parent receives financial support from a relative.

Lastly, the court called itself charitable in saying that his argument was "unpersuasive" when he claimed that, even though his daughter was adopted, he ought to still receive the deduction from his income for her because, when he did pay support, he paid it by obtaining cash advances on his credit card, and since he still owed interest on the card, he ought to continue to receive a deduction for it.

IV. Estate Matters

A. Billy Martin[18]

"Billy" Martin, who was born "Alfred Manuel Pesano," played for the Yankees from 1950 to 1957. He became the manager of the Yankees in 1975. He was fired in 1979 after commenting on owner George Steinbrenner's conviction for illegal contributions to the Nixon campaign of 1972. Martin managed the Yankees again from 1983–84, 1985, and 1987–88. Overall, he was hired and fired five times by Steinbrenner.

Martin first married in 1950 to Lois Berndt, with whom he had one daughter. He and Berndt divorced in 1953. In 1959, he married Gretchen Winkler, with whom he had one son. In 1980, when Martin was 52 years old, he began living with 26 year old Heather Ervolino. They married in 1982 but separated in 1985. Ervolino filed a $500,000 lawsuit against Martin, asking the court to prohibit Martin from ejecting her and her family from the home in California in which she, her family, and Martin resided. She filed for divorce in 1986, claiming that Martin never returned home after the 1985 season. Martin subsequently married his fourth wife, Jill Guiver, in 1988.

In February 1988, while a domiciliary of California, Martin executed his last will and testament. In it, he bequeathed his entire estate to the trustees of the Martin Living Trust. Martin and his wife, Jill, executed the trust on the same day, naming each other as trustees, provided certain gifts were to be made to Martin's son, Billy Joe, his daughter, Kelly Martin-Knight, and his granddaughter, Evie Sabini, in the event that Billy predeceased his wife. Billy Joe was to receive Martin's Rolex watch and gun collection; Kelly was to receive his New York Yankee pendant; and proceeds of Martin's Yankee contract, his interest in the Philmont Center Limited Partnership, the sale of Billy Martin Western Wear clothing, and any royalties from any books that he authored (except "Billy Ball") also were to be distributed equally to his wife and his two children.

Following Martin's tragic death on December 25, 1989, his two children commenced a proceeding to compel Jill to turn over the bequests. Jill claimed that the estate was insolvent and that the enumerated bequests were community property, to which she had a one-half interest. Jill sought summary judgment, while the children sought to declare the former marital residence as community property, half the value of which, accordingly, would be part of Martin's divisible estate.

The Surrogate Court found that the former marital residence was not community property. It was acquired by Martin and Jill in September 1988, while they were domiciled in California. The deed recited that they held the property as tenants by the entirety and, therefore, it was not part of Martin's estate upon his death. However, the court found that the items that Martin bequeathed were community property, to which Martin's wife had a one-half interest. Therefore, the court determined that the bequeathed items were subject to Martin's creditors and granted Jill's summary judgment motion as to the Yankee contract proceeds, Martin's interest in the Philmont Center Limited Partnership, the Rolex watch (which was stolen prior to Martin's death), and any royalties related to books. Despite this finding, the court held that these items either were no longer part of Martin's estate or had no monetary value, so the court held that the children were estopped from raising any issues regarding these items upon the final accounting of Martin's estate. Regarding the gun collection, the Yankee pendant, and proceeds from the sale of Billy Martin Western Wear clothing, the court reserved judgment until a final ac-counting of Martin's estate was conducted. The children appealed this decision.

On appeal, the court held that the lower court was correct to find that the marital residence was not community property based on the title being held as tenants by the entirety, but that the other items enumerated in Martin's will were community property because the trust plainly listed them as community property; thus, they remained sub-ject to Martin's creditors. Because Martin remained the owner of the items by reserving in the will the right to alter, amend or revoke the trust at any time, Martin could not evade his creditors by bequeathing the property to his children. Thus, the court cor-rectly awaited a final accounting to determine if Martin's creditors would satisfy his debts with the remaining assets of his estate. Because of this, however, the court deter-mined that the children should not have been prohibited from raising issues regarding the value of any of these items at Martin's final accounting.

B. George S. Halas, Sr.[19]

It may seem that a discussion of the legendary Chicago Bears owner, George S. Halas, Sr. (hereinafter, Halas, Sr.) is misplaced in a book about the New York Yankees. But Halas, Sr. played for the Yankees for 12 games in 1919. He later founded the Chicago Bears in 1922 and was the club's president until he died in October 1983. His son, George S. Halas, Jr. (hereinafter Halas, Jr.), assisted Halas, Sr. in managing the team until his death in December 1979. Since that time, there have been eight re-ported cases involving Halas, Sr. or his family and his estate, ranging from claims for attorneys' fees to the valuation of Chicago Bears stock and Halas, Sr.'s breach of fidu-ciary duties.

Halas, Jr. married his first wife, Theresa, in 1963. They had a daughter (Christine) in 1964, and a son (Stephen) in 1968. Theresa filed for divorce in 1974, and the divorce became final in 1975. The judgment for divorce incorporated a settlement agreement in which Halas, Jr. agreed to execute a will, according to which he would leave half of his net estate to his living children. Part of the agreement provided for Halas, Jr. to pay Theresa $50,000 as alimony in gross (including child support) during the first year of the divorce, and $35,000 per year for up to nine years thereafter. The alimony pay-ments were to continue after Halas Jr.'s death. The agreement also required Halas, Jr. to maintain life insurance sufficient to guarantee these alimony payments. To comply with this requirement, in 1976, Halas, Jr. amended a trust that he had established in 1972, which consisted of nine insurance policies. The amendment directed that, upon his death, the alimony payments would be paid out of the insurance proceeds as they became due, with the remaining proceeds to be paid to testamentary trusts for the chil-dren. In the amendment, Halas, Jr. reserved the right to change, modify or revoke the agreement and the trusts, except that, if any of the alimony payments remained un-paid, he could not change, modify or revoke the agreement without Theresa's written consent.

In 1978, Halas, Jr. married Patricia Navalio. At that time, he amended the trust again and directed the trustee to retain in the trust only enough insurance proceeds to cover Theresa's unpaid alimony payments. Funds in excess of that amount were to be distrib-uted to a new trust, under which the children would receive two-thirds of the remaining proceeds, and Patricia would receive one-third of the proceeds. To fund the new trust,

Halas, Jr. executed a partial revocation of the 1972 trust (as amended in 1976), directing that the trustee surrender one of the nine insurance policies used to fund the trust.

In December 1979, Halas, Jr. died. Halas, Sr. was appointed as the executor of the estate and the trustee of the trusts. In Halas, Jr.'s will, Patricia received one-third of the residuary estate. Theresa received nothing, but the balance of her alimony was to be paid out of the insurance trust. Christine and Stephen were to receive two-thirds of the residuary estate, which consisted of the balance of the insurance trust after Theresa's alimony was paid out. Halas, Jr. also left his children stock interests in the Chicago Bears via a bequest to Halas, Sr., as trustee.

The Chicago Bears stock that was involved in this bequest led to extended litigation involving the estate of Halas, Sr. and the appraisal of the stock by three appraisers. One of the appraisers—Willamette Management Associates, Inc. ("WMA")—was employed by the estate of Halas, Jr., as well as by the Chicago Bears. In the resulting case, the IRS hired WMA to testify as an expert on the value of the stock. The estate of Halas, Sr. argued that it was a conflict of interest to have WMA testify on behalf of the IRS because WMA had a fiduciary and confidential relationship with the Bears and its owners that would be violated if the IRS were allowed to employ WMA to value the stock. But the court held that, in order for WMA to violate a fiduciary duty, WMA would have to have had a relationship with the *party* that was seeking disqualification. Here, the estate of Halas, Sr. was the party seeking disqualification. In appraising the common stock of the Bears, WMA received no confidential information about the estate of Halas, Sr., and neither the estate of Halas, Jr. nor the Chicago Bears were parties to the action. Thus, there was no conflict of interest in the IRS employing WMA as an expert.

When the will of Halas, Jr. was admitted to probate in 1980, Halas, Sr. was appointed executor. As a result of Halas, Sr. acting in that capacity, the estate of Halas, Jr. sued the estate of Halas, Sr. for breach of fiduciary duty by Halas, Sr. This claim arose as a result of the 1981 reorganization of the Chicago Bears. Originally incorporated in Illinois and having had a single class of common stock, the Bears were reorganized to incorporate in Delaware and to have four classes of common stock. When the reorganization took place, Halas, Sr., as executor of the estate of Halas, Jr., exchanged the testamentary stock in the Illinois Bears for stock in the Delaware Bears. However, notice of the exchange was never given to the beneficiaries of the estate of Halas, Jr. or to the guardian ad litem of the children. In the complaint, the estate of Halas, Jr. claimed to be injured by the restrictions placed on the new stock that were not contained in the articles of incorporation of the Illinois corporation. The reason that the court determined that the interests of the estate were not protected was because the acquired stock was subject to the right of first refusal, and cumulative voting rights were eliminated, so the estate could no longer elect a director to the board. Thus, the estate's unrestricted common stock was exchanged for restricted and subordinated class C stock, and the reorganization altered the voting, dividend and liquidation rights of the new shares, statutory protections, and tax consequences, without notification to the beneficiaries, the executor, or the guardian ad litem. The trial court held that Halas, Sr. breached his fiduciary duty by failing to notify the guardian ad litem and by failing to protect the interest of the children in the reorganization. Although, on appeal, the court held that Halas, Sr. did not act in bad faith or abuse his discretion during the reorganization, it held that his failure to give notice was a breach of fiduciary duty; it did not matter that Halas, Sr. was relying on the advice of counsel. Since damages were not proven, nominal damages of $1 were awarded, and, since the court found that Halas, Sr. acted with benevolent intentions, it did not charge him with costs and attorney's fees.

C. Thurman Munson[20]

In January 1978, Thurman Munson and his wife, Diana, executed to the United National Bank a promissory note for $350,000. They delivered a real estate mortgage as security. The mortgage contained a so-called "dragnet clause," which provided that the security of the mortgage shall extend to any additional loans by the mortgagee.

In May 1978, Munson individually borrowed $75,000 and delivered to the United Bank a demand promissory note in the amount of $75,000. The note was part of a two-part form—one being a truth-in-lending disclosure statement, and the other being the form of promissory note used by the bank for its unsecured loans. Munson signed only the promissory note portion of the form and did not sign the disclosure statement. The disclosure portion that Munson did not sign provided that no security for the note was taken by the Bank, but that the note would be secured by any collateral that Munson gave to the bank previously.

When Munson died tragically in a plane crash in August 1979, both loans remained unpaid. In September 1979, the Bank filed a claim against Munson's estate for the individual $75,000 loan. Diana requested a payoff figure on the mortgage. In June 1981, Diana received from the bank a letter giving the payoff amount as $437,060.01; this amount was the total amount due on both notes.

In July 1981, Diana filed a complaint, asking for the court to determine the parties' rights. In October 1982, the court ordered that the mortgage dated January 1978, to both Munson and Diana, would act as security for the May 1978 note between Munson and the bank. It further ordered that, since Diana did not execute the May 1978 note, only Munson's undivided, one-half interest in the real estate would act as security on the May 1978 note.

Diana appealed this judgment, and the court of appeals reversed. It reasoned that, without Munson's signature on the disclosure statement, there was no evidence showing that there was any reliance on the security of the first mortgage when the loan was granted to Munson in May 1978. The bank argued that the language above the unsigned line on the disclosure statement was part of the entire document that was signed at the bottom. But the court said, "No." By not having Munson sign the disclosure portion of the form, the bank did not include its terms in the promissory note contract. Therefore, the court reversed and held that the May 1978 loan of $75,000 was not secured by the January 1978 mortgage.

D. Charles Terrell[21]

Charles ("Walt") Terrell and his wife Karen brought suit against Talent Services, Inc. ("TSI") and its officers. TSI was an Illinois corporation that represented professional athletes, providing them with investment and tax advice, as well as general business management, primarily insuring that the athletes were financially secure after their careers were over. TSI approached Walt in 1985, while Walt was playing for the Detroit Tigers. Walt entered into a Business Management Agreement with TSI in December 1985. TSI agreed to provide a comprehensive range of financial services. In return, the Terrells paid TSI an annual fee of five percent of Walt's annual income, which TSI collected by writing checks to itself on the Terrell's checkbook. Walt forwarded all of his salary and his family bills to TSI.

According to the complaint, for six years, the Terrells were lulled into a false sense of financial well-being. In reality, they had been invested in several high-risk ventures, the nature of which were misrepresented to the Terrells. For example, TSI invested the Terrells in a property located at 2134 Pine Street in Philadelphia. They told Walt that it was a limited partnership and that his sole risk was a one-time $15,000 payment, but that it would provide a large tax write-off. Walt was assigned a 55 percent share in one of six units on the property. In reality, it was set up as a general partnership, and Walt was exposed to a significantly higher risk. John Childers, an officer at TSI, also took a $31,500 commission, which he failed to tell the Terrells. TSI told the Terrells that the property was profitable and "doing fine," when, in reality, it operated poorly and required monthly cash infusions. In late 1991, the Terrells hired an accounting firm to investigate. It uncovered the unprofitability of the Philadelphia property and several other investments and tax strategies that were misrepresented to the Terrells, who eventually filed suit.

The defendants argued that all counts should be dismissed as to Karen Terrell because she was not a party to the Business Management Agreement signed by Walt, nor was she listed as an investor in any of the subject properties. Therefore, they argued that she lacked standing to maintain the action. The Terrells argued that Karen was a third-party beneficiary of the contract, and, therefore, was entitled to sue for its breach.

The court held that the contract and the circumstances surrounding its execution supported the inference that the parties intended to confer a direct benefit upon Karen. The contract, itself, provided for services such as budget advice, tax advice, payment of expenses, insurance, and estate planning, all of which would directly affect Karen as a spouse, as compared to other subject matters, such as a spouse's increased income from employment benefits, which would only affect a spouse incidentally. Additionally, the defendants repeatedly stressed that TSI would provide financial security for Walt *and Karen* and would manage *their* finances and investments. Consequently, the Terrells provided information regarding their *family* finances and budget, forwarded the *family* bills to TSI for payment, and arranged for TSI to prepare their *joint* income tax returns. The court said that, "[g]iven the personal family nature of the arrangement, as well as the alleged representations of [the defendants] it is possible that the Terrells [could] prove, as they allege[d], that TSI intended to impart direct benefits on Karen Terrell, thus making her a third-party beneficiary to the contract." Thus, the defendant's motion to dismiss all counts of the complaint as to Karen Terrell was denied.

V. The Hall of Shame

A. Jose Canseco[22]

Jose Canseco has committed many errors—the most memorable of which was in May 1993, when a fly ball bounced off his head and over the outfield wall for a home run. But he has accumulated other errors that are much more serious, including several weapons charges, fighting in a nightclub, unruly behavior in an airport, and numerous traffic citations (reportedly, he once received four traffic tickets in one day). He has also been involved in domestic violence matters. For example, he once had to be restrained after being heckled by a fan about an alleged rendezvous with pop singer "Madonna."

The affair was revealed after Canseco was photographed leaving the singer's apartment very early one morning in May 1991. In February 1992, he was arrested on aggravated assault charges after being accused of ramming his Porsche into the new BMW of his first wife, Esther. Charges were dropped after he agreed to community service and counseling. He and Esther filed for divorce in November 1992.

In November 1997, he was charged for hitting his second wife, Jessica. According to the police report, Canseco struck his wife from the back seat of a car while returning from their daughter's first birthday party. He was charged with misdemeanor battery for allegedly grabbing Jessica's hair and slapping her face and the back of her head. In the arrest report, he denied hitting her, but she had a bruise under her left eye, and the car's driver supported Jessica's story. Canseco pleaded no contest and was sentenced to one year of probation while undergoing 26 weeks of counseling.

B.   John Montefusco[23]

The story of John Montefusco and his wife of nineteen years, Dory Sample, is a sad and sordid one. John was a "Rookie of the Year" pitcher with the San Francisco Giants in 1975. He is nicknamed, "the Count"—a name given to him by Al Michaels, then Giants' broadcaster, after Alexandre Dumas' tale of Edmund Dantes, who was arrested and falsely accused of treason. After years in prison, Dantes escapes, finds treasure on the island of Monte Cristo, and uses the jewels to exact revenge on his enemies. Few would argue the appropriateness of the name for Montefusco. After a volatile marriage with Dory, John spent two years in jail before being acquitted of 20 felony counts of abuse in November 1999. "The Count" is trying to fulfill Dumas' tale by seeking his revenge in a return to baseball.

John met Dory, who was a flight attendant, in New York, when the Giants were playing the Mets. Days later, the couple moved in together in San Francisco, and they eventually married in Nevada in 1978.

John landed with the Yankees late in the 1983 season. After three seasons with the Yankees, he retired at age 36 with a debilitating hip condition. Upon his retirement, John and Dory lived together on a six-acre estate in New Jersey. John claimed to have earned $5 million during his 13-year career, but by 1996, he and Dory were bankrupt. John wandered in and out of drug dependency clinics while working in harness racing and the casino industry. He admits taking Percocet by the handful. Dory claimed that, after John developed Lyme disease, he added morphine, codeine and valium to the mix, but John denies this.

In March 1997, police were called to John's home. Dory alleged that John banged her head against the wall. John denied it, claiming that Dory simply started an argument. Dory later dropped the charges. A month later, however, Dory filed for divorce, which John did not contest. The divorce was final in August 1997.

In October 1997, John went to Dory's house, believing that she wanted to reconcile (she denied having any such feelings). Dory claimed that she allowed John to enter the house to get medicine, but then asked him to leave. She said John threw her on the bed and started strangling her, then attempted to sexually assault her. John denied it, except they both agreed that Dory stabbed him in the eye with her keys, and that, before having sex, she went to the kitchen for water. John claims the sex was consensual. Although Dory claimed that John sexually assaulted her that night, Dory never went to the police.

Despite their respective denials of what happened, on the eve of leaving for Yankee mini-camp (John was then the pitching coach for the Yankees' minor league team), John showed up the next day with flowers, believing that they were on the road to reconciliation. Hours after getting the flowers, Dory went to the house of John's former best friend, Walter Friedauer (with whom John claims Dory was having an affair), and she drank tequila all night. At 3:37 a.m., police found Dory's car in a ditch near her home. She was twice over the legal alcohol limit.

When John returned from Florida on October 16, John asked Dory to see a marriage counselor. She declined. John then lied about winning the lottery ($1,000 a week for life from a scratch-off ticket) and Dory began to express affection for John. When John finally told her that there really was no lottery ticket, she claimed to be going to the store and, instead, went to the police and filed two sexual assault charges against him.

John was arrested at a friend's house on two counts of aggravated sexual assault. John posted $60,000 bail and was released. A restraining order was issued against him, but he could not stay away. Eight days after being released on bail, John forced his way into Dory's house. Dory claimed that John threatened her with a knife, dragged her outside the house, and attempted to pull her into his car. John claimed that Dory hurt herself running away. Dory alleged that John left only when the house alarm went off and he thought the police were coming. John drove to a friend's house in Pennsylvania and stayed there for the night. He was arrested the next morning. Because John violated the restraining order and breached the conditions of his original bail by crossing state lines, his bail was raised to $1 million, which he could not produce. Consequently, John spent two years at Monmouth County Correctional Institution awaiting trial on twenty counts of federal crimes, including aggravated sexual assault and kidnaping.

John's trial lasted three weeks. In November 1999, a jury deliberated for three hours before finding that John, who faced 149 years in jail, was not guilty of the 20 felony counts brought against him. Dory admitted having tampered with the jeans that she claimed ripped during the sexual encounter. After sewing them together again, she re-ripped them before trial. John was found guilty of three lesser charges, including trespassing and simple assault. In February 2000, John was sentenced to three years on probation and was ordered to undergo a psychiatric evaluation and anger management counseling. He vowed to appeal.

After his release from prison, John moved just twenty minutes away from Dory, who claimed that she was so scared that she carried mace in the house and purchased a $6,000 attack dog. Dory claims that John remains addicted to prescription pain killers and is dangerous. John asserts that Dory is an adulterous, publicity-seeking schemer who wanted him dead. John says that the situation has affected their two daughters and claims: "Dory and I are two immature jerks."

According to the terms of their divorce, the couple still splits John's $2,900 per month baseball pension. Dory inherited $1 million from her father when he died in June 1999. She may need this money because John wants compensation for the two years he spent in jail. Dory claims that she sometimes sees John drive by her home. He denies it.

C. Darryl Strawberry[24]

Anyone who follows baseball and reads a newspaper knows that Darryl Strawberry has had more than his share of legal problems, mostly stemming from drug and alcohol addiction. However, many of his run-ins with the law have been the result of domestic disputes. For example, his wife, Lisa, filed for legal separation in January 1987, after accusing Strawberry of breaking her nose during the 1986 playoffs. They separated briefly but reconciled (after having their respective names tattooed on their skin). But when Strawberry was named in a paternity suit by Lisa Clayton in 1989 (at about the same time that his wife was pregnant with their second child), his wife finally filed for divorce. He and his wife split their assets, including 3 houses and 8 cars, and Lisa received slightly more than half the value of his $20 million contract. She petitioned the court for $50,000 per month in spousal support, claiming that she had become accustomed to spending $20,000 per month on clothes (she claimed that Strawberry made her wear a different outfit to every game), $5,000 per month on shoes, and an average of $7,000 per jewelry purchase. But after their divorce, he was ordered to pay $12,810 a month in child support and $22,420 in spousal support.

In January 1990, Strawberry was arrested for assault with a deadly weapon during an argument with Lisa. He allegedly hit her in the face and threatened her with a .25 caliber semi-automatic handgun, but the charges were later dropped.

In September 1993, he was arrested again for striking 26 year old Charisse Simons—a woman with whom he was living at the time and later married. Charisse, who was also pregnant, suffered a 1-inch cut above her eye.

In July 1995, Strawberry was charged with failure to make child support payments. In 1996, he was ordered to pay nearly $500,000 in back support to his ex-wife, Lisa, and their two children. He paid $50,000 to get his Mercedes back when his wife had it seized, but despite having earned an estimated $30 million in baseball, Strawberry claimed that he was "broke." To add to his family troubles, he was also sued by O.J. Simpson lawyer, Robert Shapiro, who claimed that Strawberry owed him more than $100,000 in unpaid legal fees.

By March 2001, after three baseball suspensions, one paternity suit, one divorce, two arrests for domestic abuse, one arrest for assault with a deadly weapon, three cocaine arrests, four unsuccessful rehabilitation center stays, one conviction for tax-evasion, one lawsuit for failing to pay legal fees, two surgeries for colon cancer, one arrest for driving under the influence of drugs, one 2-year sentence for drugs and solicitation of prostitution, and five probation violations, Strawberry found himself millions of dollars in debt, married to Charisse Simons (the same Charisse Simons that he physically abused in 1993), and still not through binging on drugs. After being diagnosed with signs of brain damage from years of cocaine use, Strawberry, again in rehabilitation, was given a "sleep-over pass," which would have allowed him, for the first time in five months, to spend a night at home to celebrate his 40th birthday with his wife and three children, who had been living nearby during his treatment. Instead, he opted to skip his weekly chemotherapy treatment to make a final, four-day, drug binge with a female partner from his rehabilitation center. After being robbed and left in Daytona Beach, Florida, Strawberry was finally taken into custody. Reportedly, he cried for the 2 -hour trip back to Tampa.

One year later, in March 2002, Strawberry was ousted from the one successful treatment program in which he was able to remain for an extended period of time. He was expelled for constant rules violations—which included having consensual sex in a closet with another resident. Strawberry commented that, while the sexual affair with the other resident would probably cost him his marriage, he was happy that he still had his sobriety. When he left the treatment center and went to prison, Strawberry complained of mistreatment and abuse at the treatment center, which the center flatly denied. Strawberry was quoted as saying, "I am not a quitter. I will never quit." No one is quite sure how to interpret that statement.

Not all reports involving Darryl Strawberry are negative and depressing. There is one uplifting story in all of this—Darryl, Jr. He is a 6-foot, 4-inch, 17 year old, high school basketball phenomenon (much like his father was as a rookie baseball player), who is still growing and is being scouted by professional teams. Although, physically, he is the spitting-image of his father, his mental attitude is completely different. Darryl, Jr., who rarely sees Darryl, Sr., is focused and dedicated, and is far removed from the lifestyle that destroyed his father. Commenting on his father's past, Darryl, Jr. simply said, "It makes me not want to be like him."

D. Bobby Cox[25]

Bobby Cox was arrested in May 1995 for simple battery after allegedly punching Pamela, his wife of seventeen years. He called her a "bitch," pulled her hair, and punched her in the face. Although Cox only admitted to pulling her hair, Police reported that she had "visible swelling and redness on the left side of her face." Cox denied calling Pamela a name and said that she had been violent toward him in the past; he claimed that he hit her in reflex to her assault on him. According to the police report, Cox was intoxicated. Pamela told police that this had occurred many times before, but that she never called the police because of possible media attention. On this Sunday evening, however, the couple had been drinking at their home with several guests when Cox spilled a drink on the carpet. Pamela made a comment about it, and, after the guests left, an argument ensued, and Cox hit her. He was arrested and released on $1,000 bond.

E. Luis Polonia[26]

Luis Polonia served 27 days of community service and 27 nights of supervision at the Milwaukee County House of Corrections after being convicted on a morals charge for being involved with a girl who, allegedly, he was warned was only 15 years old. He was 25. He served his sentence and, after early release, was sent to the Dominican Republic because his visa ran out. He returned to spring training for the Yankees the following season.

F.   Mark Whiten[27]

Mark Whiten was arrested for second-degree sexual assault in July 1997, after he picked up a 31 year old woman and took her to his room at the Pfister Hotel (the same hotel in which Luis Polonia was arrested). He was released on $10,000 bail. Whiten's wife, Sheri, had given birth to their second child just two days before his arrest. The crime carried a maximum of ten years in prison, but prosecutors never went forward with the case. Investigators began to question the woman's credibility. Reportedly, the police report said that she went to the hotel with him in the early hours of the morning, and, according to her, he forced her to have sex with him. Whiten first told police that they did not have sex, then, later, he said that the sex was consensual. Although it was determined that the woman was " 'severely' intoxicated," ultimately, there was insufficient evidence to charge him with sexual assault. Whiten eventually told police that he did have sex with the woman "when 'the opportunity presented itself' even though 'she didn't want to be there doing that.' " Investigators felt that it was not that the victim consented, but, based on the testimony that was likely to be given, "a jury would not find [the evidence] sufficient to meet the standard of proof beyond a reasonable doubt that consent was not given."

G. Hugh Thomas Casey[28]

Hugh Casey had two World Series pitching decisions over the Yankees with the Brooklyn Dodgers. In 1948, he set an all-time record of six World Series appearances. However, in 1949, after Casey was acquired by the Yankees, a brunette model named Hilda Weissman alleged that Casey had spent four nights with her in a hotel, and that a child had resulted. In the paternity suit that followed, Casey, with tears in his eyes, denied the allegations to the jury. But Casey was found guilty and was ordered to pay expenses of $102 and $20 per week thereafter. As a result, he separated from his wife, Kathleen.

In July 1951, Casey phoned his estranged wife. "So help me, God," he sobbed. "I'm innocent of that charge." A 16-gauge shotgun was propped against his head as he spoke. Kathleen was still listening on the other end of the phone when Casey pulled the trigger. Hugh Casey was said to be a drinking pal of Ernest Hemingway. Casey killed himself on July 3, 1951. On July 2, 1961, Hemingway also killed himself with a shotgun.

VI. Inspirational Studies

A. Don Larsen[29]

While there is little that is uplifting about divorce or domestic problems, many Yankee players have found it within themselves to overcome their domestic adversities and to inspire us. There is probably no greater example of overcoming personal setbacks by performing well on the field than Don Larsen, who, allegedly, was served with divorce papers on the morning of pitching the only perfect game in World Series history in 1956.

B. Bucky Dent[30]

Bucky Dent and Karen Lynn Ullrich married in 1970. Bucky filed for divorce in October 1981. They separated in the off-season after Karen complained that Bucky was spending too much time on the banquet and promotion circuit after the Yankee's World Series triumph in 1978. In their divorce, Bucky was ordered to pay support to Karen and the children in the amount of $2,365 per month, and to maintain the mortgage payments on the former marital residence, in addition to maintaining a condominium, a home in New Jersey, and a home in Georgia, which was occupied by Bucky's mother. The support amount was later increased.

Bucky Dent's family story goes beyond his divorce, however. Bucky's real name is Russell Earl O'Dey. He was born in November 1951, in Savannah, Georgia. His mother, Dennis O'Dey, was divorced from his father, who was a serviceman stationed over seas at the time of Bucky's birth. When Bucky was born, Dennis was 26 and already had a 10 year old son, Jim. Before Bucky was a week old, his mother sent him to live in Florida with his aunt and uncle, Sarah and James Earl Dent, and he assumed their surname. Bucky spent every summer with his natural mother, but until he was ten years old, he always thought she was really his aunt.

Once he learned of his mother's true relation, Bucky would not accept Dennis as his mother, and he continued calling his aunt and uncle "Mom" and "Dad." He began to ask about his real father, but Dennis would not disclose any information; she simply ignored Bucky's inquiries. Soon, he began to ask other people. By the time he entered high school, finding his natural father had become an obsession.

Bucky enrolled in college in 1969 and married Karen in 1970. They travelled to Savannah to investigate his family history, but it proved fruitless. Finally, one day before she died, Bucky's maternal grandmother told him that his father was a Cherokee Indian and that his name was "Shorty." However, Bucky signed with the Chicago White Sox in 1970 and had little time to pursue the truth. By 1975, he had all but given up hope of ever finding his natural father.

In 1976, a mysterious call to Bucky's home by someone asking for James Earl Dent triggered Bucky to search again for the father he never knew. He finally demanded of his mother that she identify his father. Dennis finally told him that his father's name was Russell Stanford, and that he was somewhere in a nursing home in Savannah. The lead was only partly true. After spending a winter's off-season visiting every nursing home in the Savannah area, Bucky finally located a man named Russell Stanford in an upholsterer's workshop. It was his father.

Bucky was pensive about how his father might react, or if he even knew that he had a son. Bucky paged the man at the workshop, and a short, gray-haired man appeared. He said, "You probably don't know me, but I'm Bucky Dent." The man replied, "You're Russell Earl." "You know," Bucky said, smiling, "I've been looking for you for fifteen years." His father replied, "And I've been living in Savannah for fifteen years." After an awkward introduction, they went to dinner and talked. A few days later, "Shorty" threw a party for Bucky, who met many relatives that he never knew existed. Bucky did not speak with his mother after that. He could not forgive her for withholding the truth and providing false information.

Few knew of Bucky's search for his natural father, but he told the story to help others who were in the same situation to be inspired. Bucky said that finding his natural father gave him a tremendous peace of mind and a true sense of identity.

C. Jim Leyritz[31]

Inspiration from Jim Leyritz comes not just from his baseball ability, but from a story about two foster brothers, Steven and Eric Cortez. In June 1996, Steven told a reporter that he and his brother promised to behave if they could have a mother. The only other things they wanted were Yankee tickets. Jim Leyritz heard the story, and the next day, Leyritz and his wife, Karri, brought the boys Yankee tickets, autographed shirts, caps, balls, gloves, and friendship. More than a year passed, and Leyritz had been traded from the Yankees to several different teams. In November 1997, however, Leyritz flew from his home in Florida to the Bronx to be present at an adoption ceremony for the two boys. Steven announced at the ceremony that he wished to change his name to Jimmy Leyritz Cortez.

D. A Baseball Backdrop[32]

Most of these Yankee stories are filed away in our minds, overshadowed in any given season, on any given day, by a vision of a homerun blast by "the Babe" or a leaping play in the field by Derek Jeter. Although we all have our favorite Yankee player and our favorite Yankee memory, we, as Yankee fans, typically find ourselves most collectively moved by the memories for which baseball is merely the backdrop—those moments that take us beyond baseball, to the soul. For example, there is probably no more universally touching memory in Yankee history than Lou Gehrig's "farewell speech." But even more recently, for example, while our baseball juices flowed with the excitement of the 1999 World Series, our tears flowed even more as we offered a final standing ovation to Paul O'Neill, whose father, Charles, died just hours before Game 4. As Paul tipped his hat in gratitude and wiped the tears from his own eyes, we, as fans, were touched not just by his skill on the field, but by the familial bond that we shared with him. It is this type of memory that makes Yankee baseball so commonly human. So, too, that season, with Chuck Knoblauch, whose father had Alzheimer's disease, and who went through a very public divorce during his "throwing" problems; and Andy Pettitte, whose father suffered with poor health during his struggles on the mound; and Scott Brosius, who left the team during the pennant race to be in Oregon with his dying father; and Luis Sojo, whose father, Ambrosio, also passed away. These are simply one season's example of how, for a century, we have continually looked beyond just baseball to unite with our beloved New York Yankees and to reconcile our affairs of the heart.

And so, with every memory filed away of Yankee players who step to the plate, roam the outfield, and round the bases, let us continue to cherish our favorite Yankee players, not just as baseball heroes, but as human examples—good and bad—set in a baseball backdrop, to remind us of our affairs of the heart.

Kennesaw Mountain Landis, the first Commissioner of Baseball, with Yankee owner Colonel Jacob Ruppert at Yankee Stadium for the 1923 World Series. Photo © CORBIS.

Unlucky Numbers: Betting On, Against, and With the Yankee$

by Ronald J. Rychlak[*]

The evidence is anecdotal and conjectural, but the New York Yankees, the most hallowed name in all of professional sports, has probably had more money wagered on the outcome of its games than any other team in any sport in history. (Pete Rose reportedly won more money betting on the Yankees than on any other team.[1]) Although few people today may be aware of it, the team itself has a long history of association with gamblers and gambling.

The first owners of the Yankees were notorious gamblers; the team's first captain was indicted in the 1919 "Black Sox" scandal; two years after that World Series, a Yankees pitcher was suspected of having thrown another Series game; one owner had ties to underworld figures in Las Vegas; another was suspended for his dealings with a known gambler; and one of the most beloved Yankees of all time was barred from baseball due to his association with a casino. It has even been suggested that the Yankees' threat of moving to New Jersey is linked to New York State authorizing gambling![2] This relationship between the Yankees and gambling, which continues today, began even before the first Yankee players took the field.

I. Early Innings: Gambling on a New League

In the 1800s, people thought of baseball the way people today might think of horse racing or jai alai. Gambling was simply part of the sport. Brooklyn's Union Grounds was considered the finest ballpark of the 1870s. One reason was because it had a special facility inside the stadium for the use of bookmakers, and a section of the grandstands was reserved for betting spectators. As one author wrote: "Few nineteenth-century sports fans would have thought it possible to separate sports from gambling, even if it had occurred to them that it might be a good idea to do so."[3]

Early baseball leagues were so loosely structured that there was little control over players who took bribes from gamblers. As stories of bribery, drunken players, and thrown games spread to the public, confidence in the game's integrity plummeted. In 1876, Chicago businessman William A. Hulbert (who had been very influential in rebuilding that city following the Great Fire of 1871) decided that it was time to create a new league, the National League of Professional Baseball Clubs or simply the National League ("NL"). He announced three objectives: "first—to encourage, foster and elevate the game of baseball; second—to enact and enforce proper rules for the exhibition and conduct of the game; and third—to make Base Ball playing respectable and honorable."[4]

In 1877, the new league's tolerance for gambling scandals was severely tested. Word spread that gamblers from New York were paying Louisville players to throw the pennant. When four players confessed, the league held firm. All four were banned from the NL. That did not, however, mean that they were finished with baseball. The St. Louis team signed the guilty players, dropped out of the NL, and (along with teams from Louisville and Hartford) joined the old American Association. The loose rules in that league caused some writers of the day to nickname it the "Beer and Whisky league."[5]

The NL continued to work on its image. It banned open gambling and the sale of alcohol at all of its parks. It also expelled the Cincinnati team in 1881 for violating league rules. Nevertheless, with numerous leagues and lax enforcement, baseball did not have the wholesome image that it would later cultivate. Open drinking, gambling, and rumors of thrown games persisted throughout the late 1800s.

In 1900, Ban Johnson renamed his minor league organization (the Western League) as the American League ("AL"), and in 1901 he claimed major league status for it. One of his announced purposes was to clean up baseball's image. Among other things, he wanted to rid the sport of gambling. He prohibited betting in all AL ballparks.

Johnson had difficulty getting the AL off the ground, primarily because he was unable to place a team in New York City. In deciding to make the AL a major league, Johnson ignored the reserve clause in NL contracts, and he offered higher salaries to attract star players. This touched off a war between the AL and the NL. The owner of the NL's New York franchise (the Giants), Andrew Freedman, used his connections with the city leaders in Tammany Hall to block Johnson from getting a site for his stadium. Thus, while Johnson was able to place AL teams in other NL venues—including Boston, Chicago, Philadelphia, and St. Louis—Freedman kept him out of New York in the AL's first two seasons. As both men knew, without a New York team the AL would never be considered a true major league.

By 1903, Johnson was determined to get into the Big Apple. One of his old friends, sportswriter Joe Vila, put him in touch with two men with sufficient clout at Tammany Hall to overcome Freedman's blockade. They also had enough cash to give the New York AL team a good chance of survival. With qualifications like that and two years of waiting under his belt, Johnson, "the sworn foe of every kind of baseball crooks and gambling on baseball,"[6] modified his standards. He entrusted the New York franchise (relocated from Baltimore) to a notorious duo, Frank J. Farrell and William S. ("Big Bill") Devery.

Then like now, New York was the nexus of the worlds of finance, art, journalism, and politics. Gambling, it was said, "flourished, unimpeded, in every quarter of the city."[7] Highrollers, hustlers, pikers, con men, gangsters, and tycoons mingled in the city's illegal casinos. During the summer, those same gamblers could be found at Saratoga, betting on horses and playing cards, dice, or pool. Given this background, it is no surprise that the first owners of the Yankees were gamblers. It is, however, quite amazing that crusader Johnson turned his most important team over to two characters so notoriously involved with illegal gambling.

Farrell was a big-time racketeer and the owner of a racing stable. His luxurious "House with the Bronze Door" at 33 West Thirty-Third Street was one of Manhattan's best-known gambling establishments. It was famous for its class and quiet decorum. Patrons were served fine cigars, French wines, aged liquors, and an elaborate dinner buffet. No money was accepted for any of the refreshments, though much was wagered at the gaming tables.

Farrell's establishment was largely immune from police raids thanks to his friendship with Big Bill Devery, the former New York chief of police. Devery was widely regarded as the most corrupt public official in a city known for corruption. Before being named police chief, he was repeatedly castigated for taking bribes from gambling operators. His standard reply to investigative questioning was: "Touchin' on and appertainin' to that matter, I disremember."[8]

Devery's tenure as chief of police was so bad that the state legislature decided to abolish his position and replace it with a commission system. Tammany Hall, however, thwarted the legislature by having Devery take control of the new commission. After that, Devery unsuccessfully ran for mayor of New York City. His campaign speeches were known not for their anti-vice themes, but for the free beer that was usually served to those in attendance.

Perhaps most important to Yankee fans today, however, is that Devery is the reason their team has the most recognizable symbol in sports. The now-famous interlocking "NY" insignia was designed in 1877 by Louis B. Tiffany for a medal to be given to Officer John McDowell, the first NYC policeman shot in the line of duty. Because co-owner Devery was a former NYC police chief, the team adopted the design for its uniform and caps in 1909.[9]

It has been suggested that Farrell and Devery were able to outmaneuver Freedman only because they were even more corrupt than he was. Johnson sold them the Baltimore franchise, shifted it to New York, and announced that the president of the club was Joseph W. Gordon, a respectable coal merchant and Tammany stalwart. Gordon, however, was just a figurehead. After the 1903 season, he disappeared from the organization and Farrell became the president in title as well as in fact.

Farrell and Devery built a stadium for their new team and named it Hilltop Park. Because it was located on the highest point of land in northern Manhattan, the team became known as the Highlanders (sometimes they also were called the Hilltoppers). Newspapers, however, found the name too long for headlines and began calling them the Yanks or the Yankees, which the team formally adopted in 1913.

In 1903, the Highlanders finished in fourth place, 17 games behind Boston. In 1904, they improved to second place, only 1 games behind Boston, but Farrell and Devery were not satisfied. They wanted a star attraction who could help them get past Boston and attract fans away from their in-town rivals, the New York Giants. They found their man in a smooth-fielding first baseman who was an above-average hitter and an incorrigible gambler.

II. Prince Hal: A Royal Gambler

Farrell and Devery's first star player was Harold "Prince Hal" Chase. He served as the first ever team captain for the Yankees, and he even managed the team for a while. His career numbers show him to be a Hall of Fame-caliber performer, but gambling-related scandals attached to his name have kept him out of the Hall. As his biography is aptly subtitled, Prince Hal probably was "baseball's biggest crook."[10]

Chase was born on February 13, 1883, in Los Gatos, California. He began his baseball career while attending Santa Clara University, where he played for Coach Joe Corbett (brother of the famous boxer, "Gentleman" Jim Corbett). Chase supplemented his college experience by playing semi-pro ball in the summers. During a game in early

1904, Chase caught the attention of Jim Morley, president and owner of the Los Angeles club in the Pacific Coast League. That month Chase left Santa Clara and signed a contract with the Los Angeles club. By March 30, the *Los Angeles Times* wrote, "Chase has a future before him that any ball player might look forward to. He plays first base as well as anyone would care to see."

Chase was young, handsome, a good hitter, and some still consider him to be the best-fielding first baseman ever. He routinely fielded bunts on the third base side of the pitcher's mound, and it was said that he could field a squeeze bunt and tag out both the batter and the runner from third. He once even caught a throw from the shortstop with his shoe! The Highlanders signed him away from L.A. following the 1904 season. Morley, the L.A. owner, claimed that Chase's signing with New York was illegal and took the matter to court, but he could not prevent Chase from leaving.

Before Chase made it to the big leagues, first basemen played on the bag. He was the first to move off it in order to cover more ground. He also developed the now-common practices of charging bunts and moving into the outfield to retrieve cutoff throws. His first year in the big leagues (1905), he set the record for most fielding chances in a double header with 38. His final season (1919), he set the NL record with 35.

From the very beginning, Chase's performance with the glove dazzled all who saw him. He did not, however, hit that well in his first year, and the team came in sixth place in the league (71-78). He turned that around in his second year, 1906, finishing third in the American League batting race with a .323 average and helping the team to a solid second place finish (90-61).[11] That performance solidified Chase's position as a star, and the following January, *Sport Life* called him "perhaps the biggest drawing card in baseball."

To the baseball fans of the era, Chase was one of the most exciting players in the league. Babe Ruth named Chase as his "all-time" first baseman; Ty Cobb thought so too. Clark Griffith called him the "most graceful" player he had ever seen, and Grantland Rice put him on his team of all time "smart players." The tenth edition of The Baseball Encyclopedia (1996) still lists him among the top ten first basemen of all time in chances per game (reflecting the great range for which he was known) and the top 15 first basemen in putouts per game. Unfortunately it seems indisputable that he gambled on baseball and was not reluctant to throw games to help win a bet. As talented as he was, Chase led AL first basemen in errors year after year.

On the team, Chase earned a reputation as a petty crook, a card-shark, and a cheat. (He also had a habit of chewing on bats, and one time a doctor had to be called to the ballpark to remove a splinter from his tongue.) He was said to be "addicted" to stealing cigars and other small items. Former Yankee teammate Ray Fisher gave this description of him during poker games among the players: "if he wasn't playing, he'd sit right down next to you and see what you needed and he'd be trying to hand you the cards so you would cheat. Good fellow, but just wanted to do things that weren't right."[12]

While teammates seemed to enjoy playing cards with Chase, one bet caused some tension between him and his teammates early in his career. In 1906, team owner Frank Farrell had a racehorse named after the New York manager, Clark Griffith. The horse was entered in the Withers Stakes at Belmont, and Chase was sure he would win. Prince Hal convinced a number of his teammates to bet their spare money on the horse. It finished third, several lengths back. He made few friends that day.

In 1908, Kid Elberfeld replaced Griffith as manger. This did not please Chase, who wanted the job for himself. Rumors soon circulated that Chase was not playing up to the best of his ability, perhaps to sabotage Elberfeld's position with the team. If that was his intent, it only partially worked. Elberfeld was fired in 1909, but Chase did not get the job.

Elberfeld was replaced by George Stallings, a strict disciplinarian. The club improved under his leadership, moving from last place in 1908 to second place in 1910, but Chase was not happy. In March 1910, Stallings named Chase as the first captain in the history of the Yankees. By late September, however, things had fallen apart. Stallings publicly charged Chase with throwing games.

Club president Frank Farrell, who had no aversion to taking or placing bets, met with Stallings so that the manager could explain the charges against the team's star player. After the meeting, Farrell (supported by AL President Ban Johnson) exonerated Chase, saying: "Stallings has utterly failed in his accusations against Chase."[13] A few days later, Stallings was fired and Chase was named as his replacement.

Chase got off to a good start as manager of the Yankees, winning 10 of the season's final 14 games in 1910. In 1911, however, Chase's only full year as skipper, he took the Highlanders from second place (88-63) to sixth place (76-76). Chase was replaced by Harry Wolverton at the end of the season. He kept playing, but Chase never again managed; his lifetime managerial record was a respectable 86-80.

Having found ways to throw games, and having gotten away with it, Chase began turning his talent into profitable ventures. Rumors continued that Chase was "not playing up to his abilities" during the 1912 season and into 1913, when future Hall of Famer and legendary manager Frank Chance (of "Tinkers to Evers to Chance" fame) replaced Wolverton as manager of the Yankees.

The situation came to a head in 1913, when Chance went public with his suspicions. In a conversation with reporters, Chance stated, "I want to tell you fellows what's going on. Did you notice some of the balls that got away from Chase today? They weren't wild throws; they were only made to look that way. He has been doing that right along. He is throwing games on me!"[14] Two days later, on May 13, 1913, Chase was traded to the Chicago White Sox for infielder Rollie Zieder and first baseman Babe Borton.

In Chicago, Chase seems to have tried to play it straight for a while. Unfortunately, this did not last. His lackadaisical play became so blatant that fans and players alike would taunt him, shouting: "What's the odds?" before ball games.[15] Nevertheless, he was still such a talent that a newly formed league, the Federal League ("FL"), sought him out to help establish it as a true major league. On June 20, 1914, Chase gave the White Sox ten days' notice on his contract and jumped to Buffalo of the FL.

Chicago owner Charles Comiskey unsuccessfully sued to enjoin Chase from playing in the FL. After the legal proceedings, Chase joined the Buffalo club, hitting .347 during the remainder of the year and .291 in 1915. He also knocked a league-leading 17 home runs in 1915. When the FL folded after the 1915 season, the White Sox expressed no interest in Chase, and he was declared a free agent. Despite his talent, there was no bidding contest for his services. Finally Cincinnati offered him a contract, and he signed.

In 1916, while playing for the Reds, Chase led the NL in hits with 184 and in batting average with a career-high .329. He had the second highest slugging percentage in the league (.459), second most RBIs (82), and third most total bases (249). When rumors circulated that manager Buck Herzog was about to be let go, many in the press speculated that Chase was the heir apparent. Unfortunately for him, Christy Mathewson got the job.

Mathewson pitched for the New York Giants from 1900 until 1916 (he also threw one complete game victory for the Reds in 1916), and was one of the most respected players of his era. He regularly led the league in several pitching categories, including ERA, wins, and fewest walks. He also had the reputation as an honest man and solid citizen.

Mathewson and Chase seem to have gotten along well enough in 1916 and 1917. Chase led the league in at-bats in 1917 (602), was second in RBIs (86), and was in the top 10 in numerous other categories. By 1918, however, the relationship soured. Chase's offensive production dropped way off, and in August, Mathewson (who once won $600 betting that he could throw 20 consecutive pitches to the same spot), suspended Chase without pay for "indifferent playing." His error totals were not significantly up in 1918, nor was his fielding percentage significantly different from previous years, but Mathewson was now the third manager to accuse Chase of throwing games.

The play that raised Mathewson's suspicions was when Chase fielded a ground ball and tossed it to the pitcher covering first base. Mathewson had been a pitcher all his life, and he knew exactly how this play should be executed. Chase was an excellent fielder, but Mathewson noticed that he often made the throw just wild enough so the batter would be safe. To all appearances, when this play went wrong it was the pitcher's fault, but Mathewson knew better. He compiled a strong case against Chase and said that the Reds would have had a chance at the pennant if not for him. As it was, they finished in third place, 15 games back.

A hearing on Mathewson's charges took place before NL President John Heydler in January 1919. Chase's chief accusers were Mathewson (who was then in France in the armed services, but who provided an affidavit), Giants pitcher William "Pol" Perritt, and Reds pitcher Jimmy Ring (who said that Chase tried to bribe him to throw a game). Also testifying were Giants manager John McGraw and Reds players "Greasy" Neal and Mike Regan. The hearing was held behind closed doors and lasted for five hours.

At the conclusion of the hearing, NL President Heydler announced his findings:

> In substance the player was charged with making wagers against his club on games in which he participated. In justice to Chase, I feel bound to state that both the evidence and the records of the games to which reference was made, fully refute this accusation. In one game in which it was intimated that Chase bet against his club, the records show that in the sixth inning, with two men on bases and the score two to nothing against his team, Chase hit a home run, putting Cincinnati one run ahead.

> All available evidence has been carefully taken and considered. If the charge were proved, it would follow as matter of course that the player would forever be disqualified from participating in National League games. Under such circumstances I would not hesitate to so decide, as the interests of the public and of the game of baseball are far more important than the fate of any individual. These interests it is my clear duty to protect, no matter what the effect may be on players or clubs.

> Any player who during my term as President of the National League is shown to have any interest in a wager on any game played in the League, whether he bets on his club or against it, or whether he takes part in the game

or not, will be promptly expelled from the National League. Betting by players will not be tolerated.

My conclusion and finding, after full consideration of the evidence, is that it is nowhere established that the accused was interested in any pool or wager that caused any game of ball to result otherwise than on its merits, and that player Hal H. Chase is not guilty of the charges brought against him.[16]

The NL lifted the team-imposed suspension, but the Reds did not want Chase back, regardless of the outcome. In fact, Heydler later confided that he knew Chase was guilty but let him off because he did not have proof that would stand up in a court of law.[17] The proceedings have been called "the greatest whitewash in the history of baseball."[18]

Giants manager John McGraw signed Chase for the 1919 season when no other team wanted him. Ironically, on the same day that Chase signed his contract for 1919, Christy Mathewson, Chase's main accuser, joined the Giants as assistant manger and coach.

Chase played regularly for the Giants through August, but then he sprained his wrist. His appearances after that were limited to occasional pinch-hitting roles. In September, he allegedly offered pitcher Benny Kauff $500 to throw a game in St. Louis. At the end of the season the team announced that Chase and third baseman Heinie Zimmerman (who would later become a partner of the infamous Dutch Schultz in a speakeasy) had retired from baseball. It was later learned that the two players, along with Chicago infielder Lee Magee, another friend of Chase, were run out of the game for their crooked play. McGraw explained: "I got rid of Chase and Zimmerman, even though I knew it would seriously injure my team, because I didn't want such men on the club."[19]

This was the backdrop against which the 1919 World Series took place. It was played between two of Hal Chase's former teams, the Reds and the White Sox. Because Chicago threw the series to the Reds, the 1919 team is still known as the Black Sox. Early efforts to reconstruct the scheme gave Chase an important role.

According to the story as it broke in the *Chicago Tribune* on September 25, 1920, Chase approached a former featherweight boxer, Abe Attell, a few weeks before the end of the 1919 season and asked whether he could find backers willing to put up $100,000 to fix the World Series. Attell was one of Arnold Rothstein's lieutenants. Rothstein ran a casino on West Forty-Sixth Street in New York. Among those who worked for Rothstein were Charles (Lucky) Luciano, Meyer Lansky, Frank Costello, Legs Diamond, Waxey Gordon, and Dutch Schultz, all of whom went on to notable careers in organized crime. Chase then met with two members of the White Sox, most likely Chick Gandil and Swede Risberg, to confirm the scheme. Having set it all up, Chase then cashed in on it by betting against the White Sox.

New York Giants pitcher Rube Benton testified to a grand jury that Chase had received advance information about the fix and that "The Prince" had won over $40,000 betting on Cincinnati. He also testified that Chase had offered him $800 to throw a game to the Cubs in September. Anna Chase, who was in the process of divorcing Hal, testified that she had asked him about the Black Sox fix, and he had told her, "I knew of it, and I did what I could to help it along."[20] On April 25, 1922 Chase was arrested as he left a theater in San Jose. The authorities announced that extradition papers would be prepared immediately.

Although he was indicted by two separate grand juries, Chase did not stand trial for the criminal charges, nor was he made one of the notorious "eight men out." Judge Kenesaw Mountain Landis officially took office as the sole commissioner of baseball in

November 1921, and won a reputation for his fierce and automatic determination to rid the game of the taint of scandal. That Landis never publicly took action against Chase, as he did against Shoeless Joe Jackson and others, is curious, but it may simply indicate that Chase's career in the major leagues was already at an end.[21] Some writers have speculated that Landis let Chase slide to bolster public confidence in baseball by pretending that the Black Sox were the only criminal element in a sport that was otherwise clean.

Chase's good friend Joe Gedeon, second baseman for the St. Louis Browns and a one-time Yankee, was not so lucky. He was expelled by Landis for his "guilty knowledge" of the Black Sox fix. Gedeon blamed the lax treatment of Prince Hal in his earlier encounters with the league: "If Chase had been punished, it would have put the fear of God into me. I would have realized what I was doing."[22]

Following the Black Sox scandal, Chase continued to find work in the minors and the semi-pro leagues, primarily in California, Arizona, and Mexico. He played baseball into his fifties, though some leagues barred him. From his deathbed, Chase admitted knowing about the 1919 Black Sox scandal in advance but denied making any money on it. He expressed regret at the way his career turned out. "You will note that I am not in the Hall of Fame," he said. "I am an outcast and I haven't a good name. I'm the loser, just like all gamblers are....I'd give anything to start over."[23] He died in Colusa, California on May 18th, 1947 at the age of 64.

Perhaps the most fitting epitaph for Chase was provided by *The Sporting News* in an editorial after his death: "Let us try to forget about Hal's absence from Cooperstown and remember that he was a king in his time, and in the bright annals of diamond technique, still is a monarch sans reproach."

III. Carl Mays: The Betting, Not the Beaning

Yankee owners Farrell and Devery sold the team in 1915 to "the two colonels"— Colonel Jacob Ruppert and Colonel Tillinghast Huston. These owners did not have open ties to gambling, but one of their pitchers, Carl Mays, may have missed his opportunity for the Hall of Fame due to a gambling-related scandal.

Mays was born in 1891 in Liberty, Kentucky. He broke into the major leagues as a pitcher with Boston, teaming with Babe Ruth, Ernie Shore, and Dutch Leonard to form one of the best staffs in the AL. The Red Sox won the World Series in 1912, 1915, 1916, and 1918. Mays played a big part in the club's success between 1916 and 1918, averaging more than 20 wins per year during that stretch. His best year was in 1917, when he turned in a record of 22 wins and seven losses with a 1.74 earned-run average. In 1918 he led the American League in complete games with 30 and also recorded a league-high eight shutouts, but he was temperamental. At the beginning of the 1919 season, he (along with future Yankee teammate Babe Ruth) held out for a bigger contract.

Both Mays and Ruth eventually signed, but many of the other star players from the championship teams were sold off to other teams. As such, the Red Sox's play was not nearly as good as it had been in previous seasons. In one game in Chicago on July 13, 1919, Mays lost patience with the sloppy play of his teammates. He stormed off the field after two innings. Mays told his manager, future Hall of Famer Ed Barrow, "I'm through with this ball club; I'll never pitch another game for the Red Sox."[24] At first it was thought that Mays would calm down and come back to the team, but that didn't happen. Mays was suspended by AL President Ban Johnson

While Mays was still under suspension, Red Sox owner Harry Frazee, the man who would soon sell Babe Ruth to the Yankees, sold Mays to the New York club. AL President Johnson refused to approve the deal, but the Yankees took the matter to court. The Yankees were successful, and Mays was allowed to join the club on August 2, 1919.

In 1920, Mays was on his way to a fine season with the Yankees when tragedy struck. On August 16, 1920, the Cleveland Indians were visiting New York in a battle for first place. Cleveland shortstop Ray Chapman led off the fifth inning. He had a habit of crowding the plate and laying down bunts for base hits. As Mays delivered his first pitch with his unique "submarine" motion, Chapman leaned in. The pitch struck him on the head, and Chapman collapsed. He was immediately taken to a New York hospital, where he died that night. Chapman was the first and only player to be killed in a major league baseball game.

Mays went on to win 26 games in 1920, and the following year he led the American League with 27 wins against only nine losses. Coming off this tremendous season, Mays pitched the World Series opener against the Giants, throwing a five-hit shutout to win 3-0. The Yankees also won the second game by a 3-0 score, but lost the third game 13-5. That left them with a 2-1 lead in the series. (From 1919 to 1921, the World Series was the best five out of nine rather than today's seven-game format.)

Mays again took the mound for the Yankees in game four. The Yankees led 1-0 going into the eighth inning, but Mays fell apart, giving up three runs on four hits in the eighth and another run in the ninth to hand the Giants a 4-2 victory. The key hit during the eighth inning was a triple by Emil "Irish" Meusel, which came when Mays ignored Yankee manger Miller Huggins's signal for a fastball and instead threw a slow-breaking curve. The evening after the game an actor, whose name was never revealed, approached sportswriter Fred Lieb with a story that Lieb related as follows:

> The actor's tale went something like this: At the start of the eight inning, Mrs. Mays, sitting in the grandstand, flashed a signal to Carl by wiping her face with a white handkerchief. Some persons, he said, who regarded a Giants victory in the Series as absolutely necessary for their welfare, had offered Carl a rather substantial sum of cash if in close games he would serve up enough hitable pitches to lose the game. Mrs. Mays was to be the one who, by the pre-arranged handkerchief signal, would advise her husband that the money had been handed over. Lieb brought the story to the attention of Yankee co-owner Colonel Huston and then to Commissioner Landis.[25]

Landis had Mays followed throughout the rest of the Series, but no incriminating evidence was found. Mays lost two games in the Series, but he won one, his ERA was an excellent 1.73, and he walked no batters in 26 innings. Since pitchers regularly lose effectiveness in the late innings, the charges that he had thrown game four were thought to be unfounded. A couple of years later, however, Lieb was on vacation with a number of baseball figures, including Colonel Huston and Dodger manager Wilbert Robinson. Lieb reported the following:

> Some time in the evening, after Huston had imbibed more than a little, he turned to me and said, "Freddy, I am going to tell you the damnedest story a baseball owner has ever told a reporter." Every time he repeated this remark, Uncle Robby would sh-sh-sh him and say, "No, no Colonel! Don't tell him!" But Huston would return to the subject. As the rum and Coca-Cola had its ef-

fect, some of the people in the room gradually disappeared and Robby fell asleep. Only Huston, Grayson and I were left. Grayson, still consuming Coca-Cola and rum, tried to stay awake to hear the story that Huston apparently intended to tell me, but finally he too fell asleep. So I said to Huston, "Now that we're alone, what is this story you're holding back on me?"

"I wanted to tell you that some of our pitchers threw World Series games on us in both 1921 and 1922," he mumbled.

"You mean that Mays matter of the 1921 World Series?" I asked. He said, "Yes, but there were others—other times, other pitchers." By now he was almost in a stupor and stumbled off to bed.

I suppose as a good reporter I should have stuck around the next morning and press Huston for specifics—names, dates, and all that. But I didn't. Huston hadn't appeared before [a friend] and I were scheduled to leave to play golf at Sea Island, Georgia. After our game we continued north. When I next spoke with Huston alone a year or two later, he would say that he stood by what he had told me....[26]

Miller Huggins, the Hall of Fame Yankee manager, discussing former ball players in need of a helping hand, said that he would always help any of his players if they needed it, with two exceptions: Carl Mays and Joe Bush. Lieb was fairly certain that Huggins's animosity towards Mays stemmed from the 1921 World Series.[27]

Mays won 207 games against 126 losses and had an earned-run average for his career of 2.92. His lifetime batting average of .268 made him one of the best-hitting pitchers ever. He went on to scout for the Indians, A's, and Braves. In a survey conducted by the Society for American Baseball Research in the early 1970s to determine which players not in the Hall of Fame were most deserving, Mays placed eleventh; all ten of those above him are now in the Hall. He went to his grave believing that the Chapman beaning kept him out of the Hall of Fame. Sportswriter Fred Lieb, however, a member of the Hall of Fame's Veterans Committee, said that when Mays came up for discussion, it was the 1921 World Series, not the Chapman beaning, that kept him from being named to the Hall of Fame.[28]

IV. Babe Ruth: His Bat, Not His Bet

It may well be that the most important gambling in Yankee history, actually in the history of sports, was done by the owner of a different team. Moreover, the bets themselves may have had nothing to do with baseball, but they were to change the history of the game forever.

From 1912 to 1918, the Boston Red Sox franchise was the best in the American League. In four of those seven years (1912, 1915, 1916, and 1918), the Sox won the World Series. Playing as the Boston Pilgrims, they had also won the very first World Series (1903), and they finished first in the AL in 1904, but NL champion Giants refused to play a World Series against the AL champs that year.

In 1917, theatrical producer Harry Frazee bought the Red Sox franchise. He kept the dynasty together for one more year, but then things fell apart. Despite being owner of the world champions, Farzee needed money. Over the next couple of years, he sold off

15 Red Sox players, most of them to the Yankees (including Waite Hoyt, Ernie Shore, Duffy Lewis, Dutch Leonard, and Carl Mays). Even the Red Sox's General Manager, Ed Barrow, eventually moved to the Yankees. The Red Sox finished in sixth place in 1919, and things got even worse after the season ended.

On January 3, 1920, in the most significant transaction in baseball history, Frazee sold Babe Ruth's contract to the New York Yankees. In return, the Red Sox got $125,000 and a $300,000 loan against the mortgage on Fenway Park. The oft-repeated story is that Frazee sold Ruth to finance the Broadway play "*No No Nanette*." According, however, to some accounts, the real reason Frazee sold Ruth (and the other players) was to cover his gambling debts.[29]

Ruth at that time was already a legend, but primarily for his pitching. He'd thrown 29 and 2/3 consecutive scoreless innings in the World Series from 1916 to 1918 and had broken several home run records. With the Yankees, Ruth became the greatest player ever seen, and he transformed the game. In 1920, a livelier ball was introduced to the game, and Ruth responded by hitting a record 54 home runs. The fans flocked to see him, and that season the Yankees became the first team to draw over one million customers. Soon the Yankees were the most dominant team in baseball. In 1923, they moved to Yankee Stadium, "The House That Ruth Built."

As for the Red Sox, they finished dead last in nine out of the next 11 years. They did not win another World Series in the 20th century. They were said to suffer from the "Curse of the Bambino." Perhaps, however, this all traces back to some bad bets made by the owner of the Red Sox. Ironically, when the sale was made, Frazee said the Yankees were "taking quite a gamble" by paying so much for Ruth.

Today, the Harry Frazee Award is given each year in recognition of front-office incompetence. From a monetary standpoint, however, he did not do badly. Frazee bought the World Champion Red Sox for $400,000 in 1917 and sold the last-place team for $1.5 million in 1923, after having pocketed a significant sum from the fire-sale of players while he owned the team. According to the newspapers of that time, few Red Sox fans were sorry to see him leave.

V. Del Webb: Building More Than a Dynasty

In 1922, Colonel Ruppert bought out his partner's interest in the Yankees, and he held the team until his death. In 1945, Ruppert's estate sold the team to Del Webb and his two partners, Dan Topping and Larry MacPhail. Webb was a towering figure in the modern home-building business, probably best known for the Sun City retirement communities that opened in 1960. He was also an aspiring major-leaguer who played in several semi-pro leagues. They say that he was a good pitcher and might have made it to the big leagues, but at an exhibition game at San Quentin prison in 1927 he caught typhoid fever and nearly died. Although he was more than six feet tall and normally weighed 200 pounds, his weight dropped to 99 pounds. He was unable to play baseball for a year. When he recovered, he moved to Arizona for his health and settled into the business world.

Entering the construction business in 1928, Webb's only assets were: one concrete mixer, 10 wheelbarrows, 20 shovels, and 10 picks. By 1933, his company was a $3 million operation. It only continued to grow during his lifetime. He often claimed that much of his success came from applying the rules of baseball to business.

Webb brought a certain professionalism to the construction industry. For instance, rather than relying on banged-together job-site shacks made of unfinished framing lumber that most construction companies used at their work sites, Webb had portable offices, identical in color, furniture, and furnishings. A manual outlined procedures for all projects. This uniformity was much in demand in the early days of World War II, when new military facilities and war plants had to be built quickly and affordably.

World War II made Webb rich, but he referred to the purchase of the Yankees as "the best deal I ever made." Webb and his partners acquired the Yankees, its farm teams (a total of 450 players), Yankee Stadium, and stadia in Newark and Kansas City for $2.8 million. Using Webb's real estate know-how, they promptly sold unneeded real estate for $2 million. The partnership ultimately sold the club at the end of the 1964 season for $14 million. Moreover, Webb put the team to good business use while he owned it. He often handed out tickets to clinch deals for construction contracts and to make friends with politicians who had pork barrel projects that might come his way.

About the same time that Webb bought an interest in the Yankees, he also was helping construct the first "big" Las Vegas casino hotel, *The Flamingo*. Webb reportedly had taken on the project as a favor to a friend. Before he knew it, however, he found himself bound by contract to Benjamin "Bugsy" Siegel. Webb, who claimed not to have known who Siegel was at first, supposedly tried to get out of the deal with the notorious underworld figure. He later explained, however, that he could not walk away because Siegel had "a binding contract as well as a bulge under his jacket pocket."[30]

According to Webb, Siegel once bragged that he had personally killed 12 people. When another mob figure got under his skin, he told Webb: "I'm going to kill that S.O.B. too." Webb's face must have reflected his shock, but Siegel reassured him: "Del, don't worry. We only kill each other." Later, Webb said that he never had a problem with Siegel: "Bankers, lawyers, and industrialists—never knew anyone whose word was better."[31]

When Siegel was shot and killed in Los Angeles on June 20, 1947, he owed Webb money for the recently completed casino. Webb took a part ownership in the Flamingo in lieu of direct payment. His partners in this venture included the notorious gangster Meyer Lansky and Gus Greenbaum, a Phoenix mobster who later had his throat slit.

Webb apparently enjoyed Las Vegas. He went on to build City Hall and two high schools. In the early 1960s, he built the *Sahara* and *Mint* hotels, and again he was compensated with "points" or part ownership. With Del Webb Corporation having gone public in 1960, this marked the first entry of a respected public company into Las Vegas. By the 1970s, the corporation was the largest gaming employer in Nevada, with some 7,000 employees.

Webb's entry into the Nevada casino industry was welcomed by the Nevada Gaming Commission, which hoped that his name would inspire other reputable businesses to come to Nevada. Apparently it did. Howard Hughes joined the industry, perhaps because of Webb, and the two men were instrumental in polishing the image of Las Vegas.[32]

Webb's connections with organized crime received a cursory review in the late 1940s by baseball commissioner Happy Chandler. At first the story was that Webb was not really involved with gangsters because these were construction projects for which the builder received direct payment. Later, when the long-term Las Vegas partnerships were undeniable, Webb explained that his interest was confined to the hotel and that he had no stake in the casino. In the 1970s, however, journalists reviewed government documents and concluded that in addition to active ownership with mobsters in Las Vegas hotels and casinos, Webb purchased a 3,000 acre ranch near Phoenix in 1959 at an exorbitant price from Detroit mob boss, Joseph Zerilli. Buying land at an inflated price, of course, was a common technique of settling debts that needed to be kept off the books.[33]

In fairness to Webb, no evidence suggests any criminal activity or improper motives in any of his commercial or baseball ventures. His Sun City, Arizona development helped change America's view of retirement. He took the image of "grandma and grandpa" out of rocking chairs and put them on tennis and racquetball courts, bicycles, and softball diamonds. His legacy has added immeasurably to the quality of active retirement living. He was unanimously elected to the National Housing Hall of Fame.[34]

In 1964, 15 pennants and 10 world championships after they purchased the Yankees, Webb and his partners sold the team to the CBS Television Network. That same year, Webb was named Time Magazine's "Man of the Year." A few years later Webb considered buying into the Chicago White Sox, but Baseball Commissioner Bowie Kuhn told Webb that he would not support Webb's bid unless Webb divested himself of his casino interests. Webb never got back into baseball. He died in 1974.

VI. The Mick: Nice to Meet You!

Mickey Mantle is recorded in history as not only one of the greatest Yankees of all time, but as one of the greatest baseball players ever. His talent for the game and boyish good looks made him a star from the very beginning. Although his career was shortened by a series of devastating injuries, Mantle accumulated a long list of impressive records. He won three MVP awards and a Triple Crown (1956). He contributed to 12 pennants and seven World Series titles while establishing numerous World Series records, including most home runs (18), RBIs (40), runs (42), and walks (43). He finished his 18-year career with 536 home runs and a .298 batting average.

During his playing days in New York, Mantle was known for spending late nights on the town with his teammates, Whitey Ford and Billy Martin.[35] He managed, however, to stay out of serious trouble with the commissioner's office.[36] Things became a little more difficult after he retired from baseball and needed a job.

Mantle served briefly as first base coach with the Yankees in 1970, but he didn't particularly like it, nor did it pay well. "I've been offered coaching jobs," he said. "Coaches don't make a helluva lotta money. Can you imagine me making $15,000 coaching for [Yankees manager] Billy [Martin] and him making $500,000?"[37] So he looked around for a public relations job, and he found one with a casino. Unfortunately, that position took him away from baseball.

The precedent was set when Hall of Famer Willie Mays was offered a public relations position with Bally's Park Place Hotel and Casino in Atlantic City. Mays was not directly involved in the gambling operations, but he did entertain the casino's big-spenders, usually by playing golf or dining with them. This created a difficult situation for Baseball Commissioner Bowie Kuhn. On one hand, Mays was one of the great stars of the game. On the other, Kuhn had already refused to support Del Webb's bid for the White Sox. He had also made Oakland A's owner Charles Finley and three minority owners of the Atlanta Braves divest themselves of their interest in Las Vegas casinos. Kuhn barred Mays, who was working as a coach for the Mets, from baseball.

In 1983, Mantle took a similar position, as director of sports promotions for the Claridge Hotel Casino City (which was owned by the late Del Webb's company), signing a one-year contract worth an estimated $100,000.[38] Kuhn had little choice. Lee MacPhail, the AL President, spoke with Mantle a few days before he signed with the casino and told him what was in store if he took the new job. Mantle, who had two brothers working as pit bosses in Las Vegas casinos at the time, went ahead and signed with the casino. Kuhn then banned Mantle from any official association with baseball.

"I was expecting it," Mantle said. "I called him [Kuhn], but he wasn't in. I wanted to tell him I understood what he had to do and he shouldn't feel bad about it."[39] Not being able to participate in spring training, however, was about the only real penalty Mantle faced for taking the casino job. He did fairly little work for the Yankees at the time. "If they wanted someone to strike out, they'd call me," he joked about what he did in the spring. "It really was just public relations. I was not on the payroll hardly. So I'm not gonna miss it."[40] Kuhn did not prevent Mantle or Mays from playing in old-timer games or throwing out ceremonial first pitches.

Mantle did note a certain irony in his situation. During most of his playing career, the late Del Webb was one of the Yankees' co-owners, and at the same time he owned several casinos. Moreover, the hotel and casino that Mantle had contracted to work for was part of the Webb Corporation. In fact, the owner of the Yankees at that time, George Steinbrenner, also owned racehorses and had an interest in a racetrack.

Most fans sided with Mantle and Mays. Kuhn, who was already a lame-duck commissioner when he imposed the ban on Mantle, took much public criticism, but he did not back down. Mantle and Mays were not reinstated until 1986, when Kuhn's successor, Peter Ueberroth, ruled that they could return to baseball as long as they did not appear in casino advertisements. (This caused cancellation of a billboard that was to feature Mantle promoting the casino.) Later that same year, Mantle and the casino amicably ended their affiliation.

VII. Steinbrenner: Anything to Win

Yankee owner George Steinbrenner bought the team from CBS in 1973. He had made his millions as owner and chief operating officer of the Cleveland-based American Shipbuilding Company. Before that, he was an assistant football coach at Northwestern and Purdue. (Early critics complained about his "football mentality.")[41] As owner of the Yankees, Steinbrenner's drive to win caused him to pursue free agents and new managers with vigor. Early notoriety came from hiring and firing former Yankee shortstop Billy Martin as manager five times. The two men even mocked the situation in a beer commercial. Steinbrenner also poked fun at himself on *Saturday Night Live* when he appeared in a skit criticizing bosses who fire people at will. Later, Steinbrenner was depicted as a friendly buffoon on the popular television series, *Seinfeld*. No one, however, ever doubted Steinbrenner's drive to win or his love for the team. "Owning the Yankees is like owning the Mona Lisa," he said.[42]

In 1981, Steinbrenner brought future Hall of Famer Dave Winfield to New York, with the richest contract in baseball history. The Yankees made it to the World Series that year, but Winfield had a bad post-season, and the Dodgers took the Series. Winfield went on to have several great years with the Yankees, but he and Steinbrenner butted heads over contractual matters and more. In 1984, Steinbrenner tried to trade Winfield to the Texas Rangers, but Winfield (who ended up having a great year) vetoed it. Steinbrenner never forgot that. The two men stopped talking to one another.

In the late 1980s, a dispute arose over a contractual provision that called for the Yankees to make payments to Winfield's charitable organization. Winfield said that payments had not been made, and Steinbrenner countered that the charity was corrupt. Although a subsequent investigation of the charity by the Commissioner's office was dropped due to the lack of credible evidence, the investigation revealed that Steinbrenner had paid $40,000 to a small-time gambler named Howard Spira.[43] This sparked speculation that Steinbrenner had hired Spira to spy on Winfield and to obtain information about the charity.

Commissioner Fay Vincent hired prosecutor John Dowd (who is best known as the author of the "Dowd Report"—Baseball's report on Pete Rose's gambling activities)[44] to investigate. This resulted in a disciplinary hearing. Vincent found Steinbrenner's conduct to be contrary to the best interests of baseball, fined Steinbrenner, and forced him to resign as general partner of the Yankees in 1990.[45] Steinbrenner signed a statement agreeing not to challenge Vincent's actions or the disciplinary hearing in court,[46] but in 1993 Vincent reinstated Steinbrenner. After that, Steinbrenner's Yankees reemerged as the dominant team in the major leagues, winning four world championships over the next seven years, including at one point a record 14 straight wins in World Series games.

VIII. Extra Innings: What Next?

In July 2002, Michael Franzese, a former capo in the Colombo crime family and head of their gambling operations, claimed on the HBO television program, *Real Sports with Bryant Gumbel* that some Yankee players fixed games in the 1970s and 1980s. He did, however, not say how many games or which ones, nor did he identify any crooked players.

Franzese, who called himself "a big Yankee fan," said that he and a partner in a Long Island car dealership lured pro football and baseball players with free cars, then turned them on to gambling. Some of the sports figures, including some Yankees, ran up large gambling debts with Colombo family bookies. Franzese claimed that as their debts mounted, the players' choices narrowed. "You gotta work this out, get the money, borrow the money, do what you have to do," Franzese said he told them. "And if all else fails, I got another way for you to make it up: You're gonna help us win a game." He said players were ordered to miss grounders or fly balls when the game was on the line and to "not perform at the plate." If "balls come to you and the game is on the line, you don't catch the ball."[47]

According to Franzese, players were also ordered to provide him with confidential information. "You let us know what's going on in that clubhouse," Franzese says he told the players. "You know, who's sick, who's having a fight with their wife." That information, of course, gives gamblers an edge in their betting.

There were immediate questions about Franzese's credibility. He was a mob figure, and in 1986 he had been sentenced to 10 years in prison on racketeering, conspiracy, and tax-fraud charges. Some members of his family even doubted his claims. "The reason he can't give details is because it never happened," said his brother John. "It's all lies."[48] Franzese's own mother also expressed doubt about his claims.

On the other hand, Franzese had previously worked for Major League Baseball ("MLB") in its annual rookie career development program. "He talks about organized crime and gambling," explained Kevin Hallinan, baseball's senior vice president for security and facilities. Franzese had also done freelance work for MLB's security department. Hallinan said that Franzese had been recommended to MLB by the Federal Bureau of Investigation and that he had also worked for the National Basketball Association and the NCAA. In addition, he appeared in a video produced by the four major professional leagues on gambling and other dangers players should avoid.

Despite having worked for MLB's security department, Franzese had never reported to his superiors that he had conspired with Yankees to fix games. "That's brand new," said Hallinan. "I have not heard that."[49] Franzese had, however, previously told a newspaper reporter that he once controlled seven to 10 New York area pro athletes.

Both the Yankees and individual players from teams of that era denied Franzese's allegations. "I can't imagine us fixing anything if we were winning," Chris Chambliss, a former Yankee first baseman said. "We played to win every game. We showed it by being in the World Series three years."[50] The Yankees were the AL champions in 1976, 1977, 1978, and 1981. They won their division title in 1980, and won the World Series in 1977 and 1978.

Willie Randolph, the Yankees' second baseman in those years and the team's third-base coach at the time the charges were made, said if anything funny was going on, he was not aware of it. "That's so foreign to me. I was just a young guy, really intense, just into doing my job, win or lose or go home."[51]

The Yankees issued a statement through a public relations executive who said: "The charges made by Franzese are absolutely beyond belief. He's a discredited former hoodlum, and it's an outrage that any credence would be given to him with his bad reputation as he seeks personal publicity. The Yankees know nothing about any of these claims." Yankee spokesman Rick Cerone raged: "This doesn't even merit a comment, it's so ridiculous."[52]

Mickey Rivers, an outfielder for the Yankees from 1976 to 1979, was widely known as a gambler (reportedly a bad one).[53] He liked horse tracks, poker, and legal casinos. It was even said that he sometimes did not shag balls in spring training because he was hiding a racing form in his uniform. There has, however, never been any indication of illegal betting or wagering on baseball. Moreover, the Yankees made it to the World Series all three full seasons that Rivers spent with the Yanks.

IX. Conclusion

As this book is being written, MLB has yet to announce whether it will investigate Franzese's charges about gambling in the 1970s and 80s. Certainly no baseball fan wants to think that players of a more recent vintage have reverted to the corruption that was prevalent in the early years. It may well be that the desire to remove any taint from the game will force the league to undertake an investigation. Hopefully the Yanks will come up clean. In the meantime, let's keep the focus on the field, where the New York Yankees remain a good bet day in and day out.

13

Foul Language

by Mark S. Kende[*]

> "I really didn't say everything I said."[1]
> Yogi Berra

People say provocative things about professional sports. As one of the most celebrated sports franchises, many colorful statements have been made related to the New York Yankees. This chapter centers on statements related to the Yankees that have resulted in lawsuits testing free speech limits under the U.S. Constitution.

The most well known case involves Yankee owner George Steinbrenner's criticism of an umpire. Simon & Garfunkel wrote a song regarding Joe DiMaggio's place in the American psyche that created a stir. Roger Maris' family brought a billion dollar lawsuit regarding statements Anheuser-Busch agents allegedly made about the Maris beer distributorship. In addition, pitcher Steve Howe filed a defamation lawsuit against the New York Post.

Steinbrenner also played a role in creating another legal issue examined in this chapter, namely, what right does a baseball franchise have to prohibit fans from displaying controversial signs at games? In the end, this chapter shows that freedom of expression is an integral part of the "escape" that sports provide society.

I. Steinbrenner and the Umpire

A. The Case[2]

In August 1982, the Yankees were playing poorly. After a two game series against the Toronto Blue Jays in Toronto, Steinbrenner issued a press release regarding one of the series umpires. The release alleged that:

> Judging off his last two days' performance, my people tell me that he is not a capable umpire. He is a member of one of the finest crews umpiring in the American League today, but obviously he doesn't measure up. We are making no excuse for the team's play this season, but this weekend our team has had several key injuries and for [the] umpire...to throw two of our players out of ballgames in two days on plays he misjudges is ludicrous. This man, in my opinion, has had it in for the Yankees ever since I labeled him and several of the umpires as 'scabs' because they worked the American League's games in 1979 during the umpires' strike. [This umpire] must learn that the word scab is a commonly used phrase. It is in no way meant as a personal insult. However, because he

worked during the strike for baseball management does not mean he should be protected by them and annually given a job he is not capable of handling.

Many American newspapers published excerpts from the release. The umpire filed a defamation lawsuit against Steinbrenner and the Yankees, disagreeing with the press release and requesting damages.

To prevail on a defamation claim, the plaintiff must show the defendant published a false statement that injured plaintiff's reputation. The U.S. Constitution's First Amendment, however, protects freedom of expression. Thus, courts examine the injured party's interests as well as the speaker's rights.

Steinbrenner and the Yankees asked the trial court to throw out the umpire's lawsuit asserting that Steinbrenner's opinions were absolutely protected under the First Amendment since opinions can never be objectively true or false. The trial court refused to dismiss the case, ruling that the press release did not provide adequate facts to support its assertion that the umpire misjudged plays.

The New York State Supreme Court reversed and ruled in Steinbrenner's favor. The case boiled down to whether Steinbrenner's press release expressed facts or opinions. The court looked at whether the statement was ambiguous, whether the statement could be characterized as true or false, the context in which Steinbrenner made the statement, and the "broader social context" that would likely guide people (such as baseball fans) who heard the statement. The court sought to determine how the average person would view the press release's contents.

Regarding the broader social context, the court recited a brief history of the umpire in baseball. Umpiring was an honor in the early days of the sport. Yet by the 1870s, the sport's professionalization resulted in the abuse of umpires. Albert Spalding, a leading 19th century baseball sponsor, said that fans who harassed umpires were merely opposing tyranny and exercising their freedoms. On his return to America after World War II, General Douglas MacArthur reportedly said he was proud to have protected American freedoms, like the freedom to boo the umpire. Umpires have even suffered physical abuse. In 1940, a paroled felon jumped out of the Ebbets Field stands and pummeled an umpire.

The court further illustrated this history of violence by citing to the North Carolina Supreme Court's *Toone v. Adams*[3] decision. *Toone* ruled that a team could not be held responsible for one of its fans coming onto the field and striking the umpire, even though the team had aggressively disagreed with several of the umpire's decisions during the game. The New York court quoted from the North Carolina decision:

> For present day fans, a goodly part of the sport in a baseball game is goading and denouncing the umpire when they do not concur with his decisions, and most feel that, without one or more rhubarbs, they have not received their money's worth. Ordinarily, however, an umpire garners only vituperation—not fisticuffs. Fortified by the knowledge of his infallibility in all judgment decisions, he is able to shed billingsgate like water on the proverbial duck's back.

The North Carolina court also reported on an imagined discussion among umpires:

"Balls and strikes," said one, "I call them as I see them."

"Balls and strikes," said the second, "I call them as they are."

"They are not balls and strikes until I call them," declared the third.

The New York court also relied on a Colorado case[4] where a federal judge rejected a defamation claim against a minor league baseball official who allegedly called another official in the same league a "damn fat fag," "fatso," and a "liar." The Colorado federal court adopted an enthusiastic laissez-faire attitude towards the game: "Baseball mirrors our foibles and fallibilities. The game has survived the Black Sox scandal of 1919, striking umpires, striking players, drug and alcohol problems, and even perhaps George Steinbrenner." The court quoted controversial former baseball owner, Bill Veeck, who said that, "Baseball is almost the only orderly thing in an unorderly world. If you get three strikes, even the best lawyer in the world can't get you off." The Colorado court's enthusiasm is not unique. Justice Blackmun authored a famous U.S. Supreme Court opinion, regarding baseball's antitrust exemption, that included language paying homage to the game.[5]

The New York Supreme Court concluded that Steinbrenner's remarks were the ordinary "rhetorical hyperbole" that follows displeasing umpire decisions. Indeed the court said Steinbrenner's statement was pure opinion because it was not dependent on any undisclosed facts. The court elaborated:

> Moreover, on its face, and from its tone, it is immediately evident that the statement represents the view of the owner of an embattled baseball team who is obviously chafing at "the team's [poor] play this season," which has been exacerbated by a weekend of injuries and ejections of players...

Sports Illustrated writer Steve Wulf, however, criticized the reasoning:

> The decision...left the impression that the court considered umpires to be semi-comic figures without the same rights as other people. What the judges did not seem to take into account is that Steinbrenner is no common fan, but rather a powerful owner who used his club's publicity machinery to mark a man as an incompetent. Unlike MacArthur, [this umpire] did not return — he quit umpiring after the 1982 season.[6]

Based on the New York court's reasoning, one wonders if it would have ruled for the umpire had the Yankees been playing well.

Interestingly, Steinbrenner argued earlier in the case that he was not served with process correctly. Steinbrenner listed a Tampa, Florida hotel as his residence on the Yankee partnership papers and was served by mail there.[7] Yet he later maintained he should have been served at his new Florida home. The court ruled for the umpire on this issue, one of the umpire's few successes in the case.

The Yankee owner, however, did not escape unscathed. According to sportswriter Dave Anderson, in 1983, Major League Baseball Commissioner Bowie Kuhn fined Steinbrenner $50,000 for questioning the integrity of National League umpires.[8] Moreover, Anderson reported that Richie Phillips, General Counsel for the Major League Umpires Association at the time, considered filing a defamation lawsuit against Steinbrenner on behalf of National League umpires. Apparently no suit was filed.

The New York Times also reported that Steinbrenner was concerned back in 1980 when ex-Yankee coach Billy Martin was about to publish a book titled "Number 1." Steinbrenner had fired Martin from the Yankee manager position. The Times reported that Steinbrenner's attorneys filed a brief in the New York Supreme Court seeking to prevent Delacorte Press from publishing the Martin book. The brief said that Steinbrenner would hold the publisher responsible to the extent the book contained defamatory material. Counsel for Doubleday, Delacorte's parent company, denied the defamation accusation and said publication would go forward.[9] Interestingly, Dave Anderson claimed that Steinbrenner re-hired Martin as manager in 1983 partly because Martin shared Steinbrenner's critical view of umpires.[10]

B. The Case's Legacy

Several courts have relied on the *Steinbrenner* decision, including the Wyoming Supreme Court which had to resolve a defamation case between the noted trial lawyer Gerry Spence and Larry Flynt, publisher of Hustler magazine.[11] Yet one commentator has said that a later U.S. Supreme Court decision invalidates the New York court's reasoning.[12]

In the U.S. Supreme Court case,[13] the Court said there is no "wholesale defamation exemption for anything that might be labeled 'opinion'... [since] expression of 'opinion' may often imply an assertion of objective fact." The case involved a newspaper article in which a sportswriter alleged that a high school football coach committed perjury at a disciplinary proceeding. The coach disputed the allegation. The writer argued his article was automatically protected as opinion, but the Court disagreed.

The U.S. Supreme Court case though does not mean the *Steinbrenner* result was wrong. The U.S. Supreme Court and several other courts have suggested that coaches, and other prominent sports personnel, are "public figures" in defamation law. Unlike private individuals, public figures typically must show actual malice by the defendant to win a defamation case.[14] They have to show that the statement criticizing them was not only false, but that it was made with knowledge of its falsity or with reckless disregard of its truth.

Why do public figures have this extra burden? Public figures have a significant community profile and are presumed to have entered the spotlight willingly. In a democracy, citizens get to criticize those in the spotlight. Moreover, public figures are thought to have access to the press and can respond quickly to false accusations. Consequently, even if the New York Supreme Court had said the press release consisted of inaccurate facts, the umpire would have still had to show actual malice on Steinbrenner's part. That would not have been easy.

II. Joe DiMaggio and the Song

The Yankee Clipper, Joe DiMaggio, was constantly in the public eye, whether hitting in 56 consecutive games or marrying Marilyn Monroe. Not surprisingly, he valued his image. Thus, he was not happy upon learning that Simon & Garfunkel wrote a song, "Mrs. Robinson," that referred to him. The song was a number one hit in 1967 and was part of the soundtrack for the Academy Award winning movie, "The Graduate," starring Dustin Hoffman and Anne Bancroft. Here's the relevant passage:

> Sitting on a sofa on a Sunday afternoon
> Going to the candidates' debate
> Laugh about it, shout about it
> When you've got to choose
> Every way you look at it you lose.

> Where have you gone, Joe DiMaggio?
> A nation turns its lonely eyes to you
> What's that you say Mrs. Robinson
> Joltin' Joe has left and gone away.[15]

According to Pulitzer Prize winner Richard Ben Cramer's 2000 biography of DiMaggio: "When he first heard about that, DiMaggio wanted to sue. He thought those two singin' guys were trying to make him out like a bum. 'I haven't gone anywhere,' he protested. 'I'm employed.'"[16] Paul Simon elaborates:

> A few years after "Mrs. Robinson" rose to No. 1 on the pop charts, I found myself dining at an Italian restaurant where DiMaggio was seated with a party of friends. I'd heard a rumor that he was upset with the song and had considered a lawsuit, so it was with some trepidation that I walked over and introduced myself as its composer. I needn't have worried; he was perfectly cordial and invited me to sit down, whereupon we immediately fell into conversation about the only subject we had in common. "What I don't understand," he said, "is why you ask where I've gone. I just did a Mr. Coffee commercial. I'm a spokesman for the Bowery Savings Bank and I haven't gone anywhere." I said that I didn't mean the lines literally, that I thought of him as an American hero and that genuine heroes were in short supply. He accepted the explanation and thanked me. We shook hands and said good night.[17]

A New York Daily News article said of DiMaggio that, "Word was, he wanted to sue Simon. He thought he was being made fun of, not an illogical assumption considering the hallucinogenic sensibilities of the '60s that reduced virtuous All-America types to corny characters."[18] For the reasons mentioned, however, no defamation suit was filed. According to another DiMaggio biographer, the Yankee Clipper supposedly confided to a friend that, "I've never been able to figure out what that song means."[19]

But that's not the end of the defamation issues around DiMaggio. According to an article in *Vanity Fair*, Morris Engleberg, DiMaggio's personal attorney, estate representative, and apparent close friend, was unhappy about the forthcoming Cramer biography. For one thing, DiMaggio allegedly did not grant Cramer an interview. Engleberg refused to assist Cramer as well.[20]

But Engleberg went further. Prior to the book's publication, an attorney from his law firm authored a letter to Cramer which contained this last paragraph:

> Your unsubtle threat to publish serious allegations about Mr. Engleberg's conduct will be treated as a malicious and intentional attempt to defame Mr. Engleberg which will not be tolerated. We caution you against printing any unsubstantiated allegations or comments regarding Joe DiMaggio, Yankee Clipper Enterprises, Inc., Morris Engleberg, Esquire, and/or our law firm. We will pursue all remedies available to us in connection with any false statements which may appear in your book... Govern yourself accordingly.

Engleberg thought Cramer might make allegations criticizing the way Engleberg handled DiMaggio's affairs. Indeed, the *Vanity Fair* article reports that some of DiMaggio's inner circle supposedly feel that Engleberg used his connection to DiMaggio, especially after the Yankee Clipper's death, to make a profit.[21] Despite these suspicions, no defamation or other lawsuits were apparently filed regarding Paul Simon's lyrics or Cramer's book.

III. Roger Maris and the Family Business

Roger Maris is famous for hitting 61 home runs as a Yankee in 1961, breaking Babe Ruth's record of 60. After retiring, Maris worked for the family company, Maris Distributing Company (MDC), until his 1985 death. The company distributed beer in Florida for major beer producers like Anheuser-Busch (Busch). As one report said, "Anheuser-Busch, the multi-billion dollar a year beer company, which owned the St. Louis Cardinals Baseball Club, gave Roger Maris the Gainesville, Florida and Ocala, Florida exclusive Anheuser-Busch distributing rights in 1968 as part of an agreement with the ball club. That same year, Maris led the Cardinals to the World Series."[22]

Maris was in charge of MDC's sales and public relations. Maris therefore dealt directly with customers and other businesses. His celebrity status facilitated his success.[23] The relationship between MDC and Busch, however, eventually soured and resulted in multiple legal actions. Despite the ongoing litigation, Maris family members attended the game at Busch Stadium in 1998 when St. Louis Cardinal Mark McGwire broke Maris' home run record.[24]

Regarding the legal actions, in January of 1997, MDC filed a state court lawsuit alleging that Busch employees visited MDC's customers and criticized MDC's services under the guise of assessing customer satisfaction. MDC asserted that Busch's criticisms were designed to give Busch an excuse to escape from the exclusive distributorship arrangement it granted to MDC in Florida even though MDC paid Busch substantial consideration. MDC filed an amended complaint in March of 1997 alleging additional claims including defamation.[25] The trial court eventually decided that it would resolve plaintiff's breach of contract claim first alone, and that it would stay discovery regarding the remaining claims. The trial judge reasoned that this approach could make it unnecessary to address the other issues as the breach of contract claim was central to MDC's case.

An appellate court reversed in 1998 and ruled that MDC's claims should be handled together as they were interrelated. The court further rejected Busch's assertion that the complaint was unwieldy and ordered the trial court to lift the ban on discovery. MDC sought compensatory damages of $1.3 billion in the complaint.[26] At trial they sought $300 million and Busch counterclaimed for $8.6 million.[27]

According to media reports regarding the trial, MDC provided testimony that some of its customers were puzzled at the way Busch was "evaluating" their satisfaction with MDC service. The reports say Busch responded by contending that MDC breached its contract by repackaging old Busch beer, maintaining dirty warehouses and trucks, and falsifying reports. The trial presentations included photos of MDC beer delivery trucks and debates about whether the trucks were clean or dirty. Judge R.A. "Buzzy" Green dismissed MDC's defamation claim during the trial because MDC accidentally showed a certain newspaper article to the jurors. Judge Green announced, however, that MDC could re-file the defamation claim in a later lawsuit.

The trial ultimately took three months.[28] In August 2001, MDC won a jury verdict of $139,698,500. This included $89,698,500 for lost sales and $50 million for fair market value (fmv).[29] Apparently the jury believed the evidence in support of MDC's allegations. Judge Green, however, reduced the verdict to $72.6 million. This consisted of the $50 million fmv and $22.6 million in pre-judgment interest. Judge Green said Florida law prohibited damages for lost sales. After Judge Green announced the judgment, MDC filed a $1 billion defamation lawsuit against Busch "accusing the world's largest brewer of smearing the Maris' reputation by publicly claiming the family's beer distributorship had poor business practices."[30]

In addition to the state court proceedings, MDC filed a multi-count federal antitrust case alleging that Busch' distributorship agreement with MDC and other companies unreasonably restrained competition in a part of the beer distributor market throughout the United States. In March of 2000, a federal court dismissed one of MDC's claims but left the other for trial.[31] After a seven week trial, in November of 2000, a federal jury ruled for Busch. The trial judge then denied MDC's request for a new trial and awarded various costs to Busch.[32]

IV. Steve Howe: The Burdens of Celebrity

Steve Howe was a relief pitcher for the New York Yankees between 1991 and 1996. His record with the Yankees was 18 wins and 10 losses. His lifetime major league ERA was 3.03.[33] Despite these impressive statistics, the author John Helyar suggests that Howe's criminal record of multiple drug-related convictions helped lead to his professional baseball demise.[34] During his time in the majors, he filed a defamation lawsuit against the New York Post.[35]

Specifically, Howe was arrested in Montana in 1991 for attempted possession of cocaine. After raising an entrapment defense, he pled guilty and received 3 years probation. Among the probation requirements were that he undergo regular drug testing and psychotherapy, meet with his drug counselor, never use drugs again, and never go to places where drugs are used.

In August of 1993, the following allegations appeared in a New York Post article:

> The off-Broadway smash "Tony 'n Tina's Wedding" — recently starring ex-Met Lee Mazzilli — re-creates an Italian wedding. Part of the show has the cast and audience/guests going from the somber ceremony to the raucous reception afterwards. At a recent performance, as the group made its way down Christopher Street from the church to the catering hall, one person lit up a marijuana cigarette, took a few puffs, and good-naturedly handed it to the guy behind him — who promptly went ballistic. "Get that f—ing thing away from me. You're trying to entrap me you bastard." Turns out it was Yankee hurler Steve Howe, a seven-time drug offender, on his last chance with the Bombers.

Howe maintained he never attended the play. The Post did not deny the article was false. Thus, Howe sued for defamation and intentional infliction of emotional distress.

Howe alleged several Yankees staff razzed him and made comments suggesting he was using weed. His probation officer purportedly made him do an extra urinalysis test. Howe said he required additional psychiatric assistance as the article caused him great emotional distress.

The court, however, dismissed Howe's lawsuit by ruling that the article was not defamatory since it showed him acting responsibly by turning down the marijuana cigarette. The article also did not suggest he was frequenting drug dens, nor did it make fun of his rehabilitation work.

V. Other Yankees Controversies

Several other defamation claims have related to the Yankees. In August 1998, a Tampa, Florida drug testing company's female employee alleged that Darryl Strawberry touched her inner thigh, grabbed his own groin, and said he knew she wanted to see it.[36] Strawberry called the accusations "wholly untrue and fabricated...I intend to pursue all legal avenues...[against] her defamatory charges." While Strawberry did not file any defamation charges, the drug testing company eventually fired the female employee, though it denied the firing had any connection to the alleged incident with Strawberry. Another conflict between the sexes involved a Yankees partner and his ex-wife. The ex-wife agreed to end her appeal of a $10 million spousal-abuse lawsuit, which she lost, in return for her ex-"partner" settling a defamation claim for a mere $20,000.[37]

Yankees pitcher Jim Bouton's controversial book "Ball Four" produced strong reactions given its brutally honest portrayal of major league life. Miraculously, it appears that no defamation lawsuit resulted. Bouton, however, was allegedly called on the carpet by Commissioner Bowie Kuhn for writing the book. Bouton was also not invited back for years to the Yankees' Oldtimers' Day even though as he says: "Understand *everybody* gets invited back for Oldtimers' Day no matter what kind of rotten person he was when he was playing. Muggers, drug addicts, rapists, child molesters, all are forgiven for Oldtimers' Day. Except a certain author."[38]

The Yankees were tangentially involved in a Baltimore Orioles defamation case. The Orioles fired several employees based on the belief that at least one of them stole Yankees game tickets. The Orioles supervisor met with the employees as a group and said they could not be trusted. The employees sued the Orioles for defamation but the court said that a qualified privilege generally protected communications made between an employer and employee.[39]

VI. The Banner Issue and Stadium Speech

The Yankees have been involved in several disputes over what expression should be tolerated in baseball stadiums. In 1989, after George Steinbrenner fired popular Yankees manager, Dallas Green, fans took banners to Yankee Stadium which said "George Must Go," "George, YOU are the problem" and "Fire George." Steinbrenner reportedly ordered stadium personnel to take down the banners.[40]

Moreover, during Spring 2002, the Seattle Mariners' management banned fans from wearing T-shirts which said "Yankees suck."[41] One of the most interesting justifications for Seattle banning the shirts came from Paul Brians, an English professor at Washington State University, who said "It is anti-gay male terminology. It is used without thought."[42]

But teams are apparently split on whether shirts hostile to the visiting team should be permitted. The Yankees, Orioles, and Red Sox all say yes. Perhaps it's a Northeastern custom. By contrast, in Minnesota and Arizona, officials will give fans a new shirt to wear over a "Yankees suck" T-shirt. Matt Hoy, Twins Vice-President in charge of ballpark operations says, "It's the Minnesota nice thing. We might have a little different attitude if our ballpark was full every night."

Not all cases though involved the Yankees. A minister has successfully litigated two cases against the Cincinnati Reds because the Reds suppressed the minister's religious speech at their stadium on separate occasions.[43] The minister for example held up a sign at a World Series game advocating the biblical passage "John 3:16." Reds security personnel confiscated the banner. But what right do baseball teams have to suppress offending speech at their stadiums consistent with the First Amendment? The answer is complicated.

The first question is whether baseball teams that suppress speech are considered "state actors" or whether they are simply private entities like a corporation. The U.S. Constitution typically only restricts state action. Thus, if the baseball teams are private non-governmental entities, the Constitution does not outlaw their speech restrictions.

The answer to this question depends on the particular stadium and team involved. Certainly if the stadium is owned by the city, and the team is also owned by the city, then state action is present and the U.S. Constitution applies. Yet though Yankee Stadium is city-owned, the franchise is technically private. At least one federal court and one commentator have concluded that actions by the Yankees can be attributed to the state.[44] The U.S. Supreme Court has also ruled that a private restaurant operating in a government building, with a parking garage, is so inextricably entangled with the government that the restaurant is a state actor.[45] Perhaps the Yankees have such a symbiotic relationship with their stadium and New York City.

But another court has ruled that a basketball league whose games are played in a state-owned forum is not a state actor.[46] Moreover, a U.S. Supreme Court decision has held that a private entity's actions may not be attributed to the state unless the state caused or coerced the private entity into its decision.[47] It does not seem that New York City could get George Steinbrenner to do anything he did not want to do. Thus, the state action issue is unclear though several courts simply assume state action is present.

The next issue is whether a stadium is considered a public forum or a non-public forum. Traditional public forums are government owned properties that have customarily been used for public expression. The classic examples are the state capitol steps or a public park. Government may impose reasonable time, place, and manner restrictions regarding access. But the government may not generally restrict speech in public forums based on hostility to the speech's content. Courts subject content-based restrictions to strict scrutiny and require the government to show the restriction is narrowly tailored to promote a compelling government interest.

The government can also open up other property for public expression. Such places are designated or limited public forums. Free speech advocates say that stadiums are limited public forums. Many courts and commentators agree.[48] The court in *Stewart v. District of Columbia Armory Board*[49] said that Washington D.C.'s RFK Stadium was a public forum.

Other courts disagree. In *Krishna Consciousness v. New Jersey Sports & Exposition Authority*,[50] the U.S. Court of Appeals for the Third Circuit ruled that Giants Stadium was not a public forum, at least for its patrons. The U.S. Supreme Court has said that government can impose reasonable restrictions on speech in non-public forums as long as the restrictions are consistent with the forum's mission and are not based on hostility to the viewpoints being expressed. Thus, it's much easier for government to restrict banner speech if stadiums are non-public forums.

A case that supports *Krishna* is *Lehman v. City of Shaker Heights*[51] where the U.S. Supreme Court said that a bus was not a public forum because the transit system's goal

was to be financially solvent. That goal might require barring speech that could antago-
nize potential riders. Similarly, professional teams and stadiums must remain cognizant
of finances and of not antagonizing spectators. Moreover, Chief Justice Rehnquist is not
inclined to expand the category of public forums.[52]

Perhaps the most accurate statement one can make is that whether a stadium is a
public forum depends on the precise facts of each case. The U.S. Court of Appeals for
the Second Circuit ruled one government-owned stadium was a public forum, but a
different stadium was not.[53]

Speech restrictions also cannot be vague or overbroad. Vagueness gives carte blanche
to stadium officials to suppress whatever speech they want and this heightens the risk of
content discrimination. The Cincinnati Reds lost the second case brought by the minister when they tried to enforce a rule that said all banners must "pertain to baseball." The
court said the restriction was subjective and vague.

Considering these principles, and assuming state action was present, Steinbrenner's
reported order, to take down banners criticizing him, probably unconstitutionally discriminated against the viewpoints being expressed. The actions of the Seattle Mariners
also seem questionable as the Mariners prohibited the "Yankees suck" T-shirts on the
grounds that they were not in good taste. Such a justification shows content bias and is
based on a vague standard. In *Cohen v. California*,[54] the U.S. Supreme Court said the
First Amendment generally protects offensive speech because "one man's vulgarity is
another's lyric." The Court in *Cohen* therefore ruled it was unconstitutional to prosecute
someone during the Vietnam War for wearing a motorcycle jacket into a courthouse
that said "Fuck the draft" on the back. If such a jacket is protected speech, so is a "Yankees suck" T-shirt.

In sum, it's difficult for teams to write speech restrictions that are not either content-
based or vague. Perhaps the most obvious constitutional restriction a team can impose
is to prohibit all banners. Such a rule would be clear and not content-based. It would
also show the stadium is not a public forum.[55] Yet such a rule is un-American since the
display of a colorful banner at a game is one of the most entertaining parts about such
events. As a lesser alternative, the team could ban obscene speech and fighting words—
two categories of expression that the U.S. Supreme Court has said are generally unpro-
tected. But such a prohibition would not cover expressions like "Yankees suck" or "Fire
George."

VII. Conclusion

During its history, the New York Yankees organization has been involved in controversies regarding what statements are permitted about our national past-time. Yet free
speech has won out in virtually all of the cases, even against powerful defamation
claims. This result is a healthy expression of the fact that baseball is a celebration of
freedom. It is adults playing a kid's game. The expansive green baseball field reflects our
country's open pastoral legacy. Free speech restrictions do not fit such an environment.
Moreover, given the passions that baseball generates, despite snail-paced games and an
interminably lengthy regular season, attempts at restricting baseball speech are bound
to be ineffective in the long run.[56]

The Czar's Court: The Commissioner of Baseball and the New York Yankees

by Charles A. Palmer*

I. The Intimidator, Judge Kenesaw Mountain Landis

In the beginning there was the Judge. Judge Kenesaw Mountain Landis was not the first leader of baseball, but he defined the role of the commissioner.

The modern structure of professional baseball began in 1903 with the merger of the National and American Leagues. This new league was to be governed by a three person commission made up of the president of the National League, the president of the American League, and a third member, chosen by the two presidents, to be the chairman. Unfortunately "the commission" was ineffective in dealing with the infiltration of gambling and organized crime into baseball in turn of the century America. This became apparent when the players from the best team in the game, the Chicago White Sox, were charged with "fixing" the 1919 World Series.[1] The infamous "Black Sox" and the World Series they played in were a stain on the integrity of professional baseball. Baseball needed change and improvement and the owners needed a strong leader to restore the integrity of the sport.

Kenesaw Mountain Landis was an unlikely commissioner of baseball. He was the sixth of seven children of Abraham Landis, a doctor who walked with a limp as a result of a stray bullet that hit his leg during the Civil War battle of Kennesaw Mountain. Although Judge Landis was named after the battle of Kennesaw Mountain, his name, Kenesaw, was a misspelling of the mountain and battle. Landis' name was spelled Kenesaw on his birth certificate and he never bothered to change it.[2] Judge Landis never graduated from high school but did make it through law school in Chicago in 1891. "His career" according to Heywood Brown, "typifies the heights to which dramatic talent may carry a man in America if only he has the foresight not to go on the stage.[3]" Landis was named to the federal bench in 1905 by the trustbuster, Theodore Roosevelt. He quickly gained notoriety by summoning John D. Rockefeller to Chicago to testify and by fining Rockefeller's Standard Oil Company $29 million. (The decision was overturned a year later by the Circuit Court of Appeals but the Judge's reputation had been established.). The owners voted to offer the new position of commissioner of baseball to Judge Landis at their meeting in Chicago in 1920. They knew of Judge Landis because he had presided over the antitrust case brought against them by the recently established, Federal League. The 14 owners decided to personally offer Judge Landis the job. The Judge was presiding over an income tax case when they filed into the courtroom. He greeted them saying, "unless that noise ceases I shall have to clear the courtroom." There was no doubt about who would be in charge.

Judge Landis demanded absolute control over major league baseball. The newly drafted Major League Agreement (a contract between the owners) gave the commissioner authority over "any act, transaction, or practice...suspected to be detrimental to the best interests of the national game of baseball." Landis, the lawyer and judge, wanted even more power. He wanted to be free of second guessing by the courts. There would be no appeal of the commissioner's decisions in court. The owners desperately needed a strong leader to restore the integrity of the game and the Judge wasn't going to be reversed by higher authority. He thought he had already been reversed enough.

The new commissioner acted promptly by placing the eight accused Black Sox players on the "ineligible list." When they were subsequently acquitted by a local Chicago jury, after evidence had been mysteriously lost, the commissioner continued their "ineligibility." Even though they were not judged guilty by the judicial system, they had sufficiently embarrassed baseball in the eyes of the commissioner to be banned from baseball. But the Judge would soon face a public relations challenge of a far more formidable nature.

A. The King of Swat Is Suspended

A year before the owners filed into Judge Landis' courtroom , the Boston Red Sox continued their sale of star players by selling pitcher, George Herman Ruth, to the New York Yankees. Ruth quickly became a famous slugger, hitting 54 home runs in 1920 and 59 in 1921. America fell in love with the chubby, round-faced Yankee. But the flamboyant Ruth was headed for a run-in with the new commissioner.

Major league baseball players were increasingly playing post-season games in small towns' makeshift teams after the season was over, a practice known as barnstorming. World Series players were banned from playing in these post-season exhibitions, though Ruth and several of his teammates from the world champion Red Sox illegally played in a post-season exhibition game in New Haven, Connecticut in 1916. Each was fined $100, a paltry sum in relation to the money that could be earned barnstorming.

Ruth signed another barnstorming deal in 1921 with a vaudeville promoter to play after the season for $1,000 per game and then perform on the vaudeville circuit for $3,000 a week. On the last day of that season, as the Yankees were leading the American League and well on their way to the World Series, Ruth told the new commissioner "I'm notifying you that I am going to violate the rule and I don't care what you do about it." Suspending the infamous Black Sox was one thing but confronting the most flamboyant player in the game was a greater challenge. The Judge said nothing.

Ruth's injuries in the 1921 World Series made the situation worse. The slugger injured his elbow in game two and aggravated the injury in the next game. As a result, he did not play in the final games of the Series which the Yankees lost to the Giants. Three days after the Series was over, Ruth, saying "I always heal quick," played in a barnstorming exhibition game. Yankee management was, understandably, alarmed. Yankee owners Jacob Ruppert, and T.L. Huston offered to pay Ruth not to play in the exhibition season but the Babe refused.

The commissioner responded to Ruth's violations of the rules by ordering all major league clubs to bar Ruth's barnstorming games from their ballparks. The pressure was mounting against the barnstorming tour. Major league owners met and resolved to support the new commissioner. Attendance at the barnstorming games began to dwindle. After an initial crowd of 15,000 at Buffalo's Velodrome Park (the tour was barred from Buffalo's International League Park by the Judge's orders), only 1,500 showed up at the next stop in Elmira, New York.

The Yankee owners finally persuaded Babe to end the tour by buying out his contract and the contract of his tour owner. The tour was over. But it was still up to the commissioner to decide what, if any, penalty would be imposed. Although the commissioner didn't think the rule was essential to the game, violation of a baseball rule must have its consequences. Babe Ruth was fined $3,302.26, his World Series money, and suspended for 40 games at the beginning of the next season. Ruth took the news well in his hotel suite in Washington. He told the room service waiter to "bring lotsa potatoes with the steak."

The next season, the owners amended the rules to allow World Series players to petition the commissioner to play post-season exhibition games. The Yankees won the pennant again the next year and the Babe barnstormed legally. The stature of the new commissioner was intact.

B.   A World Series Game Called for Charity

The 1922 World Series between the Yankees and the Giants thrust the now powerful commissioner into a controversy that was not of his own making. The Judge was entertaining Lord Louis Mountbatten, great-grandson of Queen Victoria, in his box at the Polo Grounds for game 2 of the Series. Tied at 3-3, the game went into extra innings. Late in the afternoon, the umpires conferred and decided to call the game. There were no lights in major league ball parks. The umpires did not believe that another complete inning, could be fairly completed before darkness would halt play. The crowd was angry. They began to boo and show their displeasure.

The Judge backed the umpires but the crowd thought the game was being called to force another World Series game to generate more revenue. Displeasure with the commissioner, became intense. A police escort was necessary to remove him and Lord Mountbatten from the ballpark. Landis, who had become accustomed to public favor, was disturbed by the public disapproval. Without consulting any of the owners, the commissioner issued a written statement saying that the $20,554 receipts for the day, would be donated to the disabled soldiers charities of New York.

Three years later, a rainstorm turned Pittsburgh's Forbes Field into a soggy mess but game seven of the World Series started anyway. The rain returned in the seventh inning with the score tied 7-7. Landis refused to allow a rainout. Wheelbarrows full of sawdust were brought in to provide footing. The game, which probably should have been called, was finally won by Pittsburgh. The Judge wasn't going to be part of calling another World Series game.

C. Too Strenuous for Women

Judge Landis' reputation as the decision maker of baseball caused problems. A woman wanted to play in the Indiana American Legion's 1928 tournament. No one in the League wanted to decide whether she should be allowed to play. League officials asked the Judge to rule. Even though he had no official authority in the matter because it was not a professional baseball game, the Judge nonetheless agreed to act. He ruled that the player, Margaret Gisolo, could play. The next year, the America Legion barred all females from playing in its tournaments.

Four years later, a barnstorming team with Babe Ruth and Lou Gehrig faced a female pitcher in Chattanooga. She struck out both stars. Team owners announced that the female pitcher would appear in Southern minor league games. The Judge barred her from professional baseball saying the sport was "too strenuous" for women. Ruth and Gehrig were safe from the female fastballer from Chattanooga. Luckily, the game was "too strenuous" for her.

D. Suspension of a Bigot

Although Judge Landis has always been subject to questions concerning his regulation of interracial play, he did not hesitate to deal with the open racism of one Yankee player. Jake Powell had a checkered history in the major leagues. He once ran into Hank Greenberg, breaking the first baseman's wrist. He never said he was sorry. Many believed he had anti-semitic motives in the collision.

Before a Yankee game in 1938, Powell was interviewed by the White Sox radio announcer and asked what he did during the off-season. Powell said "I'm a cop in southern Illinois and I get a lot of pleasure beating up" black people (not Powell's words) "and throwing them in jail." The interview was terminated and the station disclaimed responsibility. Landis immediately summoned Powell to his office as baseball fans from around the country filed their protests with his office. Powell denied making the racial remarks, but too many people had heard him. Landis suspended Powell for ten days. Amazingly, Powell seemed contrite. Protests against him continued in Washington and New York. In New York, despite numerous threats, Powell went from bar to bar in Harlem buying drinks and asking for forgiveness. The sanctions imposed by the commissioner were effective

E. The Commissioner May Not Be Appealed

Judge Landis did not like baseball's growing "farm system." He thought the clubs were stockpiling good players on the farm clubs depriving those players of an opportunity to play in the big leagues. One of those players was Fred Bennett, a promising pitcher in the St. Louis Browns' system. Bennett was signed by Tulsa but then assigned to Wichita Falls, Milwaukee, and the St. Louis Browns. Many of these moves were done without having to offer Bennett to other competing clubs on waivers since Bennett had spent less than two years at each of the teams. The commissioner then discovered that the St. Louis, Tulsa, and Wichita Falls clubs were each owned by Phil Ball while Ball also owned a one-half interest in the Milwaukee franchise. Thus, Ball was able to move Bennett from one of his clubs to another every two years and avoid placing Bennett on waivers. Landis, who didn't like the farm system anyway, and knew that the St. Louis owner was one of his principal detractors, decided to act. He ordered that Bennett be assigned to the major league St. Louis Browns for at least one year or be traded to a club not owned by Ball or be released. Ball challenged the commissioner in federal court but the courts were not a hospitable place for a challenge to the commissioner's authority.

Judge Walter C. Lindley ruled that the commissioner had broad authority to rule in the game of baseball.[4] He believed that the commissioner was like an umpire presiding over every aspect of baseball, capable of ruling on "any conduct destructive" to the game. Ball's lawsuit was dismissed. The commissioner would not be overruled by the court.

F.   The Sale of the Yankees

Col. Jacob Ruppert, New York brewer, bachelor, and owner of the New York Yankees, died in 1939. Col. Ruppert divided his estate into two trusts, the Yankee trust and the residual trust of all other property. The Yankee trust owned the baseball club, the stadium and the minor league teams. It quickly became apparent that neither trust was sufficient to pay Col. Ruppert's considerable debts and federal and state estate taxes. The brewery was sold but that wasn't enough. The Yankees would also have to be sold. Major league baseball teams are rarely sold so the New York Yankees sale attracted the sporting world's attention.

Many investors expressed an interest in the Yankees but a group headed by Col. Larry MacPhail had the money to close the deal. MacPhail was a natural born promoter but also loud and often belligerent. He had been the general manager of the Cincinnati Reds where he installed lights for the major league's first night game. He was also one of the first general managers to understand the advantages of broadcasting games on the radio, hiring the legendary Red Barber to be his announcer. When he moved to the Brooklyn Dodgers he took Barber with him. In Brooklyn, he made the team's shortstop, Leo Durocher, the manager of the team, a decision he would ultimately regret.

One of the principal investors in MacPhail's group was John Hertz, the owner of a fleet of Chicago taxicabs and a string of thoroughbred racehorses. Judge Landis was not going to allow a racehorse owner to buy a major league baseball club. Without Hertz, MacPhail did not have enough money to complete the deal.

MacPhail did not have time to continue to work on the Yankee offer. He, like most other American men at the time, was in the Army. D-Day was the order of the day, not buying baseball teams. But the trustee of the Ruppert Estate still desperately needed to sell. They contacted MacPhail in Paris and asked him to continue to work on an offer. He did and, with the financial support of Dan Topping, heir to a tin plate fortune, and Del Webb, a self-made contractor from Phoenix, MacPhail's group became the owner of the Yankees.[5]

II. After the Legend — A Statesman

The major league owners put the approval of the Yankee sale on their February 1945 agenda. But there was an even more important matter to discuss at that meeting. Judge

Kenesaw Mountain Landis had died at the age of 77. Baseball needed a new commissioner. Larry MacPhail, the new owner of the Yankees, was to play an important role in that decision.

Prior to voting on a new commissioner, the owners acted to rescind some of the broad authority enjoyed by Commissioner Landis. The section of the Major League Agreement (the written contract between the individual owners regarding the governance of baseball) waiving the owners' right to challenge the commissioner's decisions in court was removed. Although the owners had supported the commissioner in his argument with St. Louis owner, Phil Ball, they didn't want the commissioner to have unquestionable authority over them. The owners also limited the commissioner's authority to void rules made by the owners. The commissioner could no longer nullify such a rule because it was not "in the best interest of baseball." The commissioner would continue to be an arbitrator but he would no longer also be the supreme court. The owners did not want another commissioner with the power of Judge Landis. [6]

A committee had been appointed to nominate a new commissioner. Ford Frick, the president of the National League, was the favorite of six committee nominees. Several votes were taken without a winner. MacPhail was frustrated by the delay and tried to leave for New York. There were no flights and MacPhail stayed on at the meeting where he nominated Albert B. "Happy" Chandler for the commissioner's job. Chandler had been the governor of Kentucky and was then serving as a United States Senator. He knew how to get his way in Washington. He was also an avid Cincinnati Reds fan. The owners found him to be an acceptable compromise and he was elected as the second commissioner of baseball after two more ballots.

A. Suspension of Durocher

The new commissioner inherited a festering problem. Dodger manager, Leo Durocher, was embarrassing the game. Judge Landis had talked to Durocher before the 1941 World Series about associating with gamblers. Durocher had provided four box tickets to his friend, actor George Raft. Landis had evidence that Raft had wagered on baseball games and he instructed Durocher to retrieve the tickets from Raft. Yet Durocher continued to be seen with gamblers after Chandler became the commissioner. The newspapers reported that Durocher was associating with gamblers and other organized crime figures. Durocher moved in with Raft after the 1946 season. Chandler even arranged a clandestine meeting with Durocher on one of the fairways of the Claremont Golf Course in Berkeley, California and gave him a list of undesirables for Durocher to avoid.

Durocher did not endear himself with postwar fans when he announced, while he was married to his second wife, that he intended to divorce her and marry a woman 15 years younger than him. His conduct was becoming a liability for baseball. Justice Frank Murphy of the United States Supreme Court called Commissioner Chandler to express his concern about Durocher. According to the Commissioner, Murphy said that if nothing was done about Durocher that he would advise the National Catholic Youth Organization (a large organization of Catholic children) to boycott major league baseball. The pressure to "do something" about Durocher was building. [7]

Two incidents brought the pressure to a head, both involving Yankee owner, Larry MacPhail. First, the Brooklyn Eagle newspaper carried a column entitled "Durocher says." The column was written by sportswriter, Harold Parrott. Parrott was the traveling secretary of the Dodgers and sought to reflect Durocher's thinking in his column. The Yankees and Dodgers were playing spring training games in South America and Cuba. The Yankees won the first game in Venezuela and were headed to Cuba for round two when the "Durocher Says" column, stated:

> This is a declaration of war I want to beat the Yankees as badly as I do any team in the National League....MacPhail tried to drive a wedge between myself and all those things I hold dear. When he found I couldn't be induced to manage the Yankees, he resolved to knock me and make life as hard as possible for me.[8]

This "declaration of war" had its intended effect. Many fans and sportswriters showed up for the games in Havana. When Durocher took the field, he was shocked to see two gamblers, Memphis Engelberg, who was on Chandler's list of undesirables, and Connie Immerman, the manager of the Havana casino, sitting next to MacPhail. Durocher thought they were sitting in the same box with MacPhail but they were actually separated by a rail. Durocher was surprised by MacPhail's open association with known gamblers. He commented to the press "if I go near them, I'm dead. Where does MacPhail come off flaunting his company with gamblers right into players' faces?" MacPhail was insulted and asked for a hearing.

MacPhail explained in the hearings held by the commissioner that he didn't have anything to do with the seating in the ballpark in Havana. Durocher offered to apologize. He and MacPhail shook hands. But that didn't end of the matter as far as the Commissioner was concerned. After Durocher testified about the MacPhail allegations, the Commissioner asked Durocher if there was any gambling in the Dodger clubhouse. Durocher admitted there was and even said that he participated once in a while. Durocher had excuses but they would not be good enough for a commissioner with an agenda.

Two weeks after the hearing, the Commissioner announced that "As a result of the accumulation of unpleasant incidents in which he has been involved which the Commissioner construes as detrimental to baseball, he (Durocher) is hereby suspended from participating in professional baseball for the 1947 season." The baseball world was shocked. Durocher and his new-found friend, MacPhail, protested loudly even though the Commissioner had issued a gag order. Nonetheless, the suspension was enforced. Baseball once again had another strong commissioner.

B. The "Race Question"

A statement was released at the Brooklyn-Montreal exhibition game at Ebbets Field on the day after Durocher was suspended. It said "the Brooklyn Dodgers today purchased the contract of Jackie Roosevelt Robinson from their Montreal farm club. He will report immediately." The Dodgers had several good African-American players on their farm clubs. Branch Rickey, the Dodgers' owner was going to play his best players. Baseball would be integrated.

Larry MacPhail of the Yankees had written a report on the "Race Question." He generally opposed the integration of baseball saying "There are many factors in this problem and many difficulties which must be solved before any generally satisfactory solution can be worked out." The report had been approved by a 15-1 vote of the baseball owners at their winter meeting. Regardless of his bosses' wishes, Chandler pledged his support to the Dodgers in bringing Robinson to the majors. The manager of the Phillies threatened to make trouble for Robinson, but Chandler immediately responded with threats of retaliation by the commissioner's office if the Phillies created problems.[9] The world champion St. Louis Cardinals threatened to strike but a commissioner guided by principle calmed the situation. The commissioner was a looming presence, ready to act against those who would oppose or make trouble for a player because of his race. Jackie Robinson played baseball for the Dodgers and Commissioner Chandler, the politician from Kentucky, received far too little credit for his courageous support.

C. The End of the Reign of Happy Chandler

Chandler signed a seven year contract to serve as the commissioner of baseball in April 1945. In 1950 he requested a renewal. If the owners weren't going to reelect him, he wanted to make other plans for the rest of his career. According to the Major League Agreement, the commissioner needed the affirmative vote of three-quarters of the owners in order to renew his contract. Chandler asked for a vote.

The Commissioner had made enemies. The Durocher suspension, his support of baseball's first African-American player, and channeling the new television revenues to the players' pension funds rather than the owners' pockets—all alienated various factions within the ownership. Chandler was also convinced that Del Webb of the Yankees was plotting against him. The original vote was 9-7, three votes short of the number of votes needed to retain the commissioner. Clark Griffith of the Washington Senators and a Chandler supporter, missed the meeting. Griffith asked Chandler to "hang tight" while Griffith campaigned for another, more favorable vote. But the March 1951 vote was the same. Even though he had another year to run on his contract, Chandler thought that he could no longer be effective. He negotiated a termination of his contract.

III. A Commissioner without Controversy: Ford Frick

After years of domination by Judge Landis and the surprising assertiveness of Happy Chandler, the owners wanted a leader who could be controlled. Ford Frick was president of the National League and had been the favorite for the Commissioner's job when Chandler had been previously elected. In September 1951 he was selected as the third commissioner of baseball. Frick presided for 14 years over a relatively controversy-free administration. The Braves moved from Milwaukee to Atlanta but Frick said little. His most controversial decision was to put an asterisk behind Roger Maris' home run record of 61 since Maris broke the record of Babe Ruth in a season that was 8 games longer.[10] (In 1991 an eight person committee including then-Commissioner Fay Vincent voted to remove the asterisk from Maris' record.)

IV. A General Becomes the Commissioner

Baseball owners have long disagreed about the authority of the commissioner. The owners have always wanted to personally run the game of baseball just as they ran their individual teams. Others believed there was a need for centralized management of baseball rather than a committee of owners. Somebody had to be in charge of the integrity of the sport. Judge Landis was given almost total power because the game required a strong commissioner when its integrity was being questioned. The integrity of the game was restored during the Landis and Chandler administration so the owners had the opportunity to take back power.

Owners can take power from the commissioner in two ways. They can take away parts of the formal, written authority of the office of the commissioner. The rule changes at the beginning of the Chandler administration were instances of the owners taking formal power away from the commissioner. The owners can also take power by electing a person who is less likely to assert the power of the office. The owners adopted that strategy in selecting the fourth commissioner of baseball.

Passing over such prominent candidates as Lee MacPhail of the Baltimore Orioles and Joe Cronin, the American League president, the owners elected General William D. Eckert as commissioner of baseball. Eckert had no baseball experience and little inclination to exercise the power of the office. Baseball was expanding but Commissioner Eckert had little to say or do in these affairs. He left office after only three seasons as commissioner

V. A Surprisingly Assertive Lawyer: Bowie Kuhn

The owners were deadlocked over a successor for Commissioner Eckert. The American League was in favor of Yankee President, Michael Burke, while the National League favored one of their own, Giant Vice President, Chub Feeney. The owners compromised, picking their legal counsel, Bowie Kuhn. He was their guy and had worked for them. But Kuhn quickly asserted his independence by steering the players and owners into a new, collective bargaining agreement. But a fundamental legal challenge to the commissioner's authority would soon confront the new commissioner.

A. The Vida Blue Case

The case of *Finley vs Kuhn*[11] was a "perfect storm" of litigation. Three explosive personalities, Vida Blue, Charles Finley and Bowie Kuhn, along with the end of the reserve clause in baseball and a talent-laden Oakland A's baseball club all combined for one of baseball's most colorful courtroom battles.

Vida Blue had burst into baseball with considerable fanfare. Blue was called to the major leagues late in 1970. He soon pitched a no-hit ball game and became baseball's MVP and the Cy Young award winner the next year with a 24-8 record and an earned run average of 1.82. That year the A's won their first Western-Division Championship. But after those first, brilliant years, Blue's pitching prowess began to wane. In 1972 his record was a disappointing, 6-10.

Charles O. Finley was the irascible owner of the world champion Oakland A's. The A's were an excellent baseball team that won the World Series in 1972, 1973, and 1974. Finley had a long history of petty fights with Commissioner Kuhn. They disagreed about whether the mayor of San Francisco should throw out the first ball in the Oakland World Series, the appropriateness of the Commissioner's intervention in his salary negotiations with Vida Blue, and the decision to place A's second baseman, Mike Andrews, on the disabled list. Finley even had the temerity to unsuccessfully oppose the reelection of Kuhn to the office of the commissioner in 1975. Kuhn's enmity for Finley was unmistakable.

Bowie Kuhn was an American blue blood.[12] He was a graduate of Princeton and the University of Virginia Law School. After law school, he joined the prestigious Wall Street law firm of Wilkie, Farr & Gallagher where he represented the National League and the owners' Player Relations Committee. He was a student of the game who studied the history of the office of the commissioner of baseball. That history was important to him and he would not permit either the game or his office to be disparaged.

Marvin Miller, the head of the Major League Players Association, had an idea. The players' standard contract had a clause (commonly called the reserve clause) which stated "if...the player and the Club have not agreed upon terms...the Club shall have the right...to renew the contract for the period of one year on the same terms." The owners had always interpreted this clause to mean that a one year extension could be renewed on a continuing basis. Miller disagreed, arguing that after one year the contract was satisfied and the player was free to contract with another club. Andy Messersmith of the Dodgers and Dave McNally of the Expos were willing to call the question. The dispute would be resolved under the standard player contract by a three person panel of arbitrators. One arbitrator was Miller who could be counted on to vote for the players and another arbitrator, appointed by the owners, would most certainly support the owners. The decision fell to a neutral and he voted for the players. The reserve clause, as a means to perpetually binding a player to a contract with one club no longer existed. The economics of baseball would never be the same.

The advent of free agency came as a blow to Charlie Finley. His Oakland A's had many of the best players in baseball and Finley was, according to the Commissioner, "a bully and cheapskate by nature." As the trading deadline for 1976 approached, Finley started unloading players who would be expected to eventually leave the A's in the free agency market. He sold Rollie Fingers and Joe Rudi to the Boston Red Sox for $2 million and Vida Blue to the Yankees for $1.5 million. When Kuhn asked Finley for an explanation of these transactions, Finley said:

> Commissioner, I can't sign these guys. They don't want to play for ol' Charlie. They want to chase those big bucks in New York. If I sell them now, I can at least get something back. If I can't, they walk out on me at the end of the season and I've got nothing, nothing at all. Now, if I get the money for them, I can sign amateurs and build the team again, just the way I did to create three straight World Series winners. I know how to do it. You know I do. You've seen me do it. And you shouldn't be thinking about getting into this.

Kuhn was thinking about "getting into" the matter. He held a hearing to consider Finley's arguments but the result was preordained. Kuhn didn't approve of Finley or his actions. Commissioner Kuhn ruled that the sale of the three players was "not in the best interests of baseball." The assignments of the player's contracts was "disallowed." Finley responded by calling the commissioner the "village idiot" and filing suit in Federal District Court in Chicago.

Finley's challenge to the commissioner's authority was significant. The owner of the A's had not engaged in any immoral acts, nor had he violated any Major League rule.

Players had been sold before. One of the greatest players of the game, Babe Ruth, had been sold by the Red Sox to the Yankees because the Red Sox owner needed money. Could the commissioner "disallow" an otherwise legitimate sale simply because he personally thought it was not "in the best interest of baseball"?

The trial lasted 15 days, with most of the major league owners testifying. Jim Campbell, the general manager of the Detroit Tigers, testified that the Tigers had made a deal with Oakland to buy Blue's contract for a million dollars but Finley, going against his word, had sold Blue's contract for more money to the Yankees. Judge Frank J. McGarr ruled in favor of the Commissioner and dismissed the lawsuit. According to the Commissioner, "Nothing so strengthened my hand during my sixteen years as commissioner as this decision." Finley immediately appealed.

The Seventh Circuit Court of Appeals in a lengthy and erudite opinion affirmed the dismissal of the lawsuit. After tracing the history of the office of the commissioner, the Court of Appeals observed:

> baseball cannot be analogized to any other business or even to any other sport or entertainment.... Baseball's management through a commissioner is equally an exception, anomaly and aberration.... In no other sport or business is there quite the same system, created for the same reasons and with quite the same underlying policies.
>
> ....
>
> The Commissioner was vested with broad authority and that authority was not to be limited in its exercise to situations where Major League Rules or moral turpitude was involved.[13]

The Commissioner's authority was complete.

While the Commissioner's power was clear, the actions of Finley were not. Finley traded Blue to Cincinnati for a minor leaguer, Dave Revering, and $1.75 million. Cincinnati had won the World Series in 1975 and 1976 but lost to the Dodgers in 1977. The Blue acquisition could possibly return them to the top. Once again, the Commissioner would not approve the trade. Finally, on March 15, 1978 Finley traded Vida Blue to the Giants for seven players and $390,000. The Commissioner took no action.

B. Steinbrenner Purchases the Yankees and Is Suspended

On January 3, 1973, a limited partnership led by George Steinbrenner III bought the Yankees from CBS. CBS had purchased the Yankees from the MacPhail interests in 1964. But it didn't take long for the new Yankee leader to get the Commissioner's attention. In 1974, Steinbrenner pled guilty to a felony for causing his company, the American Shipbuilding Company, to reimburse employees who made financial contributions to the re-election campaign of President Richard Nixon. Commissioner Kuhn suspended Steinbrenner for two years, later reduced to 16 months, for actions that were "not in the best interests of baseball." Steinbrenner opposed the suspension on the basis that his criminal conviction was completely unrelated to baseball. The Commissioner did not agree. Subsequently, President Reagan pardoned the Yankee owner but he had already served his term of suspension from baseball.

C. Ladies in the Locker Room

The National Hockey League decided to allow female reporters into their locker rooms after their All Star Game in 1975. Fourteen of the eighteen National Hockey League teams followed suit. Most of the National Basketball Association teams had already allowed female reporters into their locker rooms. But, without consulting the players, Commissioner Kuhn wrote the major league clubs asking them to take a "unified stand" against female reporters in their clubhouses. The Yankee players were "overwhelmingly" in favor of allowing female sportswriters into their clubhouse but the Yankee organization followed the Commissioner's directive.

Melissa Ludtke was a female baseball writer for Sports Illustrated. She was to cover the 1977 World Series between the Yankees and the Dodgers. Although the players were encouraged to come out of the clubhouse and into the tunnel for interviews, she was barred from the Yankee clubhouse pursuant to the Commissioner's directive. Ludtke and Time sued. The Federal District Court ruled that the "commissioner's policy was not substantially related to the privacy of the players." (Ludtke did not want access to the shower or toilet facilities. She wanted access to the same areas the male reporters are allowed to enter, the central locker room and the manager's office.[14]) The court ruled that the Commissioner's policy unreasonably interfered with Ludtke's civil rights. Even the powerful Commissioner would not win them all.

D. Another One Bites the Dust

There is an inherent conflict in the authority and responsibility of the baseball commissioner. The commissioner is the prosecutor, judge, and jury in discipline and other major league matters but he works for and needs the support of the owners, who he sometimes sanctions. Prosecutors and judges do not gain the favor of those they prosecute or discipline. Charlie Finley was not going to support Commissioner Kuhn's reelection. Yet the commissioner needed a favorable vote of three-quarters of the major league baseball owners in order to be reelected. Bowie Kuhn was in trouble.

The owners wanted to restructure the commissioner's office creating a new position. They proposed that the commissioner continue to address discipline and politics and a CEO would handle the financial complexities of the game. Bowie Kuhn disagreed. His reelection was doomed. Finley's American League voted 11-3 in favor of reelection but the National League only voted 7-5 in favor, well short of the necessary vote to reelect. Another strong commissioner had overstepped his bounds and a change would be forthcoming.

VI. The Olympian Becomes the Commissioner

The owners chose Peter Ueberroth, the former president of the successful Los Angeles Olympic Games, as the next commissioner. Ueberroth knew the owners had often failed to reelect the commissioner, so he refused to take the job, like Judge Landis, unless the Major League Agreement was amended. At Ueberroth's insistence, the Major League Agreement was amended to increase the maximum fine to $250,000, to have the League presidents report to the commissioner, and, most importantly, to provide that the commissioner could be reelected by a majority vote of the major league owners.

Ueberroth was an effective commissioner who intervened in the owners' labor negotiations with the umpires and into the dispute involving cable superstations WGN in Chicago and TBS in Atlanta. He also pushed the owners to adopt stricter drug testing rules and hire more minorities in front office positions. His actions were not well received by the owners. He resigned as commissioner following the 1988 season.

VII. Bart Giamatti and the Suspension of Pete Rose

The next commissioner of baseball, A. Bartlett Giamatti, faced the greatest public relations challenge since Landis suspended Babe Ruth. Pete Rose, one of the best baseball players of all time, was an alleged gambler. Witnesses alleged that he had bet on his own games. There is little doubt that Judge Landis would have summarily thrown him out of baseball. But the erudite new commissioner proceeded with caution. Giamatti asked his chief investigator, John Dowd, to look into the allegations. Dowd filed an eight volume report concluding that Rose did indeed bet on major league baseball games including those of the Cincinnati Reds while he was the manager. Giamatti informed Rose that he was going to hold a hearing on the matter. Rose obtained a preliminary injunction against holding the hearing from a local Cincinnati judge. The parties continued to fight in court but on August 23, 1989 Rose and the Commissioner agreed that Rose would be banned from baseball. Rose was permitted to apply for reinstatement after a year and there was no finding, and no mention, of Rose betting on baseball in the Commissioner's findings.

The Pete Rose affair was a significant change in the judicial view of the commissioner's authority. Far from the unfettered discretion of Judge Landis and Bowie Kuhn, the commissioner was restrained in the Rose case because he had "prejudged" Rose. Although this was the opinion of a local, state judge who may have favored the hometown hero, there was now hope for those who sought to restrain the commissioner's authority.

After the Rose affair, Bart Giamatti went back to his Massachusetts vacation home and, in less than a week, died of a massive heart attack.

VIII. The Deputy Commissioner Takes the Job

Giamatti had hired Francis Fay Vincent from Coca-Cola to be his deputy commissioner. Vincent was hired to be that business manager of baseball that had been proposed by the owners during the Bowie Kuhn administration. When Giamatti died, George Steinbrenner, the head of the Yankees, pushed for Vincent's promotion. The owners agreed. But Fay Vincent soon had to face his benefactor in a confrontation that would define his administration.

A. Commissioner Vincent Bans the Yankee Owner

Fay Vincent's confrontation with George Steinbrenner began with the signing of free agent, Dave Winfield. Steinbrenner evidently miscalculated the compounded cost of living allowance in the outfielder's ten year contract. Winfield had also not performed up to expectations. A series of confrontations between the two men followed which prompted Steinbrenner to place Winfield on the trading block. Unfortunately for Steinbrenner, Winfield couldn't be traded. Winfield was a 10 and 5 player (10 years in the major leagues with the last 5 with the same team). As such he could not be traded without his permission, which he refused to give.

In March of 1990, Howard Spira, a private investigator and Bronx resident, told the New York Daily News that Steinbrenner had paid him $40,000 in return for information detrimental to Winfield. Spira had also, evidently, received $15,000 from Winfield. Steinbrenner said that he had given Spira the money out of compassion, then said that he had paid him to prevent him from revealing embarrassing information about the Yankees. The Commissioner was not amused. He ordered John Dowd, the same investigator who had done the Pete Rose investigation, to look into the matter.

Dowd investigated the gambling allegations and presented his report to Commissioner Vincent. The commissioner was willing to turn over all of the supporting documents and depositions to Steinbrenner but he was not willing to turn over the report itself. A date for a hearing was set. The rules for the hearing would be similar to those proposed for the Rose hearing. Steinbrenner could be represented by counsel, the hearing would be recorded by a court reporter, and the respondent would be allowed to present his evidence.

The Yankee owner testified that he made the payment to Spira because Spira had threatened him and his children. He also testified that Spira threatened to disclose sports betting information about Steinbrenner's friends in baseball. The Commissioner later said that in listening to Steinbrenner, he was "able to evaluate a pattern of behavior that borders on the bizarre."

On July 31, 1990 Vincent summoned Steinbrenner and presented him with a proposed eleven page decision. The decision found that Steinbrenner had acted in a manner that was contrary to "the best interests of baseball." The Yankee owner took the document to a separate room to review it with his lawyers. An hour later, Steinbrenner and his lawyers returned to negotiate the sanctions. The commissioner proposed to suspend Steinbrenner from baseball for two years. But the Yankee owner feared a "suspension" from the game would jeopardize his position as vice president of the United States Olympic Committee. The parties worked out an agreement that provided that Steinbrenner would avoid suspension but would be placed on the "permanent ineligible list." There would be no limit on the length of his time on the list. Steinbrenner also agreed to waive his right to challenge his penalty in court.

The agreement soon began to fall apart. Although it specifically avoided using the word "suspended," the press and others continually referred to the "suspension." The United States Olympic Committee said they would have to look into the matter. Steinbrenner had agreed to reduce his ownership in the Yankees but only if there were no "adverse tax consequences." He ultimately concluded that these tax consequences did, in fact, exist. Nevertheless, the commissioner was not going to budge, the sanction agreement was not going to be amended.

Less than two weeks after the sanction agreement was announced, two Yankee owners, Daniel McCarthy, Steinbrenner's friend and tax attorney, and Harold Bowman filed suit in Cleveland. The owners asked the court to restrain the commissioner from removing Steinbrenner. The owners said that Dowd and the commissioner were biased and unfair in the report and hearing. "George has nothing to do with this" said a spokesman for Steinbrenner.

Steinbrenner then proposed that Yankee chief operating officer, Leonard Kleinman, succeed him. But Kleinman had also been involved in the Spira case, and the Commissioner refused to allow him to take over the Yankees. Kleinman sued.

Steinbrenner also filed suit against the court reporting firm that prepared the depositions in Dowd's investigation. He argued that the court reporter had "tampered" with the transcripts that were used by the Commissioner. That suit was dismissed.[15]

With the two pending lawsuits stalled in court and the initial two year suspension nearly completed, Steinbrenner wanted to get off the "permanent ineligible list." Vincent said he would not discuss the matter as long as the McCarthy and Kleinman lawsuits were still pending. McCarthy agreed to dismiss his lawsuit and Leonard Kleinman, after some initial hesitation, also withdrew his claim. Thus, on July 24, 1992, the commissioner announced that George Steinbrenner could return to the Yankees on March 1, 1992.[16]

Vincent was always controversial as the commissioner of baseball. The owners thought his handling of the Steinbrenner affair was excessive and high-handed. He had unilaterally realigned the National League despite the League owners' dissenting votes. Subsequent court actions prevented him from proceeding. Even though Vincent was supported by then Texas Ranger owner, George W. Bush, the owners gave him a "no confidence" vote at a private meeting. Fay Vincent resigned as commissioner of baseball.

IX. The Latest "Commissioner"

Alan "Bud" Selig was unanimously (30-0) named the ninth commissioner of baseball after serving as interim commissioner for 6 years. Selig was popular among the owners because he ruled by consensus, counting owners' noses before important decisions.

The authority of the office of the commissioner has also changed. The commissioner's authority to act "in the best interest of baseball" is now limited to issues of "public confidence and integrity." All other issues, such as labor negotiations and television contracts, are reserved by the owners. Judge Landis would not have agreed.

X. "An Exception, an Anomaly, and an Aberration"[17]

The office of the baseball commissioner is unique. The commissioner's authority doesn't come from the government. It arises because the game needs a leader and, as a result, the private owners of the game confer their authority on the commissioner. But the game of baseball is more than a private business. It is the "national pastime." The office of the commissioner will always be in the limelight; challenged and criticized but badly needed.

The authority of the commissioner will ebb and flow. When the game needs a strong commissioner, as it did after the Black Sox scandal, the owners will determine that it is in their best interests to have a strong leader like Judge Landis. When the specter of gambling and corruption wanes, the need for a strong commissioner will diminish. That is its strength. The power of the commissioner comes from the needs of the game.

IV. Yankee Stadium

1904 playoff game between the American League Boston Pilgrims and the National League New York Highlanders. The Highlanders became the Yankees in 1913. © CORBIS.

Up from Baltimore

by Maura Flood*

At the end of the 19th century, when baseball was still played with a deadball and trolley cars criss-crossed city streets, the New York Yankees were but a gleam in the eye of Byron Bancroft Johnson. The Baltimore Orioles, on the other hand, were very much alive and at the top of the National League standings for several years running. By the time that century came to a close, however, the Baltimore team, bereft of most of its star players, found itself in the American League and packing for a move to New York.[1] And therein lies an interesting tale.

I. Tammany Baseball

As New York evolved into America's biggest and most powerful city, the political machine known as Tammany Hall secured control over nearly everything of importance in that city. Any enterprise that needed city permits, police protection or other governmental services needed a connection with Tammany Hall. Any enterprise capable of earning a profit was able to do so only so long as some of that profit went into the pockets of Tammany leaders and their faithful deputies. It was, therefore, inevitable that professional baseball and Tammany Hall would become familiar with one another. Their convergence at the dawn of the 20th century gave rise to a team like no other the world has ever seen—a team worthy of the most spectacular of American cities—the team we know as the New York Yankees.

Tammany Hall played an active role in New York's baseball scene from the very beginning. The political organization that got its start in downtown taverns moved out of those taverns as its power became greater and more entrenched, and established itself in social clubs centered in the various neighborhoods of New York City. These social clubs sponsored baseball teams, whose games provided not only amusement and family entertainment for the voting public, but also recruiting opportunities for the Tammany machine. Some of Tammany's ballplayers became its district leaders and ward heelers, men charged with the responsibility of getting the voters to the polls on election day.

Tammany moved into the realm of professional baseball with the Mutuals, a team that was financed and controlled primarily by none other than Boss Tweed himself.[2] William M. Tweed, the long-reigning top dog of Tammany Hall, secured tight control of all government operations in New York City, and used them to his personal benefit to such an extent that his name became synonymous with graft and political corruption. Boss Tweed was familiar to readers of Harper's Weekly as the intimidating, rotund character in the political cartoons of Thomas Nast (the same cartoonist who gave us the jolly, rotund character of Santa Claus).

Tammany members held ownership interests in several of New York's early professional baseball teams. For example, two Tammany regulars, John B. Day and his brother-in-law, Joseph Gordon, established the Metropolitans, an American Association franchise, and the Gothams, later known as the New York Giants, a National League franchise.[3] Eventually, ownership of the Giants would pass to Andrew Freedman, a Tammany official, graduate of City College's law school, and real estate broker.[4]

II. The Original Orioles

The roots of New York's Yankee organization lie, not in the neighborhoods of 1890s New York, but in the soil of a city situated south of the Mason-Dixon line — Baltimore, Maryland. While Tammany Hall was trying its hand at baseball in New York, Ned Hanlon, the manager of the Baltimore Orioles, had just become part-owner of that team and was doing his best to take it from the bottom to the top of the National League standings.

America was struggling its way through an economic depression in 1893, when Hanlon and his co-owner, Baltimore brewer Harry von der Horst, put together a deal to add several new players to the Orioles' roster. One of those players was Wee Willie Keeler, a diminutive infielder with the Brooklyn Dodgers and son of a Brooklyn trolley switchman. Hanlon put Keeler in the outfield, where he proved himself agile and swift. Thanks to the efforts and skill of Keeler and his new teammates, including Hughey Jennings, Joe Kelley and John McGraw, the Orioles' luck began to change. Under Hanlon's direction, these four players, soon to be known as The Big Four, brought the Orioles up from last to eighth place in the National League standings by the end of their first season in Baltimore.[5]

The Big Four and their teammates had only just begun. In 1894, they surprised the league and delighted Baltimore fans by winning the pennant.[6] In just two seasons, the Orioles had batted and fielded their way from last to first place in the National League. This powerhouse team took the pennant again in 1895 and 1896, despite injuries and illnesses that plagued the players at the start of both seasons. And in 1896, the Orioles' success was particularly sweet, because they won the National League's Temple Cup in post-season play, a prize that had eluded them in previous years.[7] In 1897, however, the Orioles stumbled a bit, but only a bit, coming in at second place when they lost the pennant to the Boston Beaneaters. The disappointment of that loss was tempered, though, when the Orioles defeated the Beaneaters for the prized Temple Cup.[8]

These were the glory years for the Orioles. Their winning seasons brought larger and larger crowds to view the games at Baltimore's old Union Park, making the years profitable as well as glorious for Hanlon and von der Horst. The team's success was due in large part to the stellar, coordinated play of The Big Four — Keeler, Jennings, Kelley and McGraw. These key players, aware of their value, notified Hanlon before the start of the 1898 season that it would take more than $2,400 (the maximum salary then paid to any ballplayer) to get each of them onto the field that year.[9] After a stand-off that lasted through spring training, Hanlon finally agreed on an additional $200 per player for each of them, and The Big Four suited up for another season.[10]

III. Greater New York City

Important events were unfolding in New York, too, in the months leading up to baseball's 1898 season. On the first day of January, 1898, pursuant to a recently enacted state law, Brooklyn, Queens, the Bronx, Staten Island, and the city of New York were consolidated to form a single municipality known as Greater New York City.[11] This move ensured that New York would remain the nation's largest city by a wide margin, never to be overtaken by the rapidly growing Chicago.[12] It also ensured the continued vitality of this city by facilitating the reallocation of existing debt and the issuance of new municipal bonds to fund needed improvements to the city's infrastructure. Some who had supported the consolidation effort hoped that the newly-enlarged city would prove too massive for Tammany Hall to control.[13] That hope was not to be realized.

In the years preceding consolidation, Brooklyn had been largely under the thumb of "Boss McLaughlin's Brooklyn machine," [14] a political organization that exerted the same sort of control over Brooklyn affairs as Tammany Hall did over New York City affairs. Charley Ebbets, a minority owner of the Brooklyn Dodgers, was an active member of McLaughlin's Brooklyn machine and master schemer in his own right. Ebbets managed to acquire a majority share of the Dodgers franchise just as Greater New York City came into being.[15] He also managed to get himself elected to the Greater New York City Council, a position he intended to use to enhance the Dodgers' success and profitability. Ebbets' first move as majority owner of the Brooklyn Dodgers was to name himself president of the ball club. His second move was a brilliant one: he secured rights to a parcel of land suitable for a ballpark, which just happened to be situated near two trolley lines, and then he convinced the two trolley companies to contribute to the cost of constructing a new Dodgers facility on that land.[16]

IV. The Dodger-Oriole Syndication

As the 1898 season got underway, however, Americans were paying very little attention to baseball. The nation had just entered into war with Spain, in reaction to the sinking of the U.S.S. Maine. Ballplayers and fans alike entered the armed services, and baseball took a back seat to the war. It was not the best of seasons for baseball. Nor was it the best of seasons for the Baltimore Orioles, because Keeler suffered from a leg injury for much of the summer and the remarkably effective teamwork of The Big Four began to erode.[17] Despite these problems, the team managed to finish in second place in the league. Hanlon and von der Horst realized, however, that an infusion of new blood would be needed to enable the Orioles to maintain their first-place position, and to keep the crowds of fans filling the stands.

Enter Gus Abell, part-owner of the Brooklyn Dodgers, and a man who had his own ideas about what would be best for that team. Operating independently of Ebbets, Abell began discussions with the Orioles' Ned Hanlon, hoping to convince him to move north to manage the Dodgers, and bring a few of his star players with him.[18] These discussions expanded to include von der Horst, and to address the possibility of joint ownership of the Orioles and Dodgers. Von der Horst was happy to consider such an arrangement, because the size of the Baltimore crowds had fallen off drastically in the

1898 season. New York, of course, the largest and most boisterous of markets, could offer many more thousands of paying spectators than Baltimore ever could.

The discussions Abell commenced with the owners of the Baltimore team led to an arrangement that would have a tremendous impact on Major League Baseball. The arrangement they arrived at was a syndication: Hanlon and von der Horst would own fifty percent of both the Baltimore Orioles and the Brooklyn Dodgers; and Abell, Ebbets and their co-owner William Byrne would own the other fifty percent of these teams.[19] In addition, a crucial element of this arrangement was the plan to move several of the best Orioles to New York and attire them in Dodger uniforms.

The closing of this deal was nearly prevented by Byrne, who held a one-eighth interest in the Dodgers. Byrne was the brother of the late Charley Byrne, long-time majority owner of the Dodgers. He was also, as it happened, an office-holder in the Tammany Hall hierarchy. Byrne refused to consent to the consolidation arrangement unless he was bought out, and he demanded the price of $10,000 for his share of the team.[20] Ultimately, Byrne got his $10,000, and the deal was done.

When all of the signing was over, Abell and Ebbets owned half of the pooled assets of the Dodger and Oriole teams, and Hanlon and von der Horst owned the other half. Three of The Big Four—all but McGraw—were transferred from the Orioles to the Dodgers, along with five other players.[21] This deal destroyed the championship Orioles team, and it was the first in a chain of events that would lead to the birth of the New York Yankees.

V. Andrew Freedman and His Giants

The Dodgers' and Orioles' owners were not the only National League magnates scheming for change. Change was also on the mind of Andrew Freedman, a powerful member of Tammany Hall and a favorite of Tammany's current Boss, Richard Croker. Freedman, who gained control of the New York Giants in 1894, began pushing a few years later for the league to reduce its size from twelve to eight teams. The twelve-team roster had proven cumbersome and less than ideal for the league, so Freedman's suggestion did not fall on deaf ears.

Freedman's ultimate goal was the elimination of the Brooklyn Dodgers, since that would rid him of all competition for New York's baseball fans.[22] Once Greater New York City came into being in 1898, Freedman had a viable argument for the elimination of the Dodgers. The National League's charter provided that two NL teams could not be located in the same city; but the Giants and the Dodgers found themselves located in the same city the moment the municipal consolidation occurred. Undoubtedly, Freedman was also counting on his Tammany connections and power to help him oust the Dodgers franchise from New York. With Byrne out of the picture, Tammany no longer had a direct financial interest in the continued existence of the Dodgers.

It soon became apparent that Freedman had underestimated Charley Ebbets, who met his machinations head-on. Although not a member of Tammany Hall, Ebbets had considerable power and influence of his own, as a member of the Brooklyn political machine and an elected member of the Greater New York City Council. In his favor, Ebbets could point out that the Brooklyn team was still a successful one, with revenues in excess of those of several other National League teams, so it was not an obvious choice for elimination. After all the team owners weighed in on the subject of paring down the league, and a formal vote was taken, the Brooklyn Dodgers survived. The cities that would lose their teams were Cleveland, Louisville, Washington and Baltimore.[23]

VI. Ban Johnson's American League and the Great Baseball War

As the National League reorganized itself, it gave barely a nod to Ban Johnson, who was moving into position beside it. The NL would soon pay Johnson careful attention, however, for he was hard at work changing the face and nature of American baseball. Johnson had studied law at the University of Cincinnati, but left law school before the end of his second year to take a job as a sportswriter for the Cincinnati Commercial-Gazette.[24] There he served as writer and sports editor for several years, and became friendly with baseball greats such as Connie Mack and Charles Comiskey. In 1894, the same year Freedman took the helm of the Giants' organization, Johnson became president of baseball's Western League, a top minor league circuit.[25] He revolutionized baseball on the Western circuit in two ways: by eliminating the brawling and "rowdyism" that commonly occurred on the field in the early days of professional baseball, and by giving full support to the umpires.[26] Johnson accomplished this by imposing fines and suspensions on players—and managers—who disregarded his rules.

After six years as president of the Western League, Johnson re-named it the American League and began his move to make it the equal of the National League, with major league status. When the National League dropped its teams in Cleveland, Louisville, Washington and Baltimore, it played right into Johnson's hands. The new AL immediately established teams in two of those cities—Washington and Baltimore. Johnson bought what was left of the original Orioles team, and established a new AL team under the Orioles name. That team included John McGraw, the only one of The Big Four still in Baltimore, as player-manager and also part owner.

With the promise of higher salaries, Johnson was able to lure away several of the NL's most talented players. McGraw, Connie Mack, and others were only too happy to help him do so. As a result, the upstart American League added some impressive names to its team rosters, names like Kid Gleason, Napoleon LaJoie, and Cy Young.[27] This raiding of National League teams was the first of many battles in the Great Baseball War of 1900–1903.

Johnson directly challenged the National League in late 1900 by declining to sign onto the renewal of Organized Baseball's National Agreement, which governed the ways in which players were recruited, "farmed" and traded, and which bound all signers to the onerous reserve clause included in player contracts.[28] In addition, Johnson requested recognition of the American League as a second major league. The NL refused Johnson's request for major league status, and the Great Baseball War went into full swing.

At the same time that Johnson was seeking major league status for the AL, the NL players were seeking better treatment for themselves. They created the Players Protective Association, which demanded that the NL agree to limitations on the reserve clause, as well as on the trading and farming-out of players. The NL rejected the Association's demands unequivocally, thereby sending the players right into Ban Johnson's arms.

Johnson made the most of this opportunity. The American League owners promptly voted to accept the contract terms proposed by the Players Protective Association. This motivated the Association's legal counsel, Harry Taylor, to encourage the ballplayers to negotiate contracts with the AL instead of the NL. Taylor had been a professional ballplayer himself, until he retired from the diamond in order to practice law full time.[29]

Johnson wanted more than anything to put American League teams in the major northeastern cities, particularly Philadelphia, Boston and New York. He managed to secure options on sites for ballparks in Philadelphia and Boston,[30] but New York was another matter entirely. Johnson's plan was to move the Orioles club to New York, but he had had no success in locating a suitable site in that city. The Giants' Freedman, intent on keeping competing ballclubs out of New York, owned or had options on virtually every parcel that might be large enough and level enough to house a ballpark.[31] As a real estate broker and Tammany insider, Freedman had the New York real estate market quite firmly in his grasp. And with his political influence and power, Freedman could also threaten to have a city street put through any lot that Ban Johnson might buy. Freedman and his Tammany connections stood directly in the way of Ban Johnson's plans for an American League team in New York.

Freedman began working against Johnson in another way, too, by attempting to hire John "Mac" McGraw away from the Orioles and make him the Giants' manager. The relationship between Mac and Johnson had deteriorated, since Mac still believed in rough-and-tumble baseball, and had a habit of stomping on the umpire's feet in response to calls that went against him. More than once, Johnson suspended Mac for such conduct, or for refusing to punish players who engaged in rowdy or disruptive conduct during games. When Johnson suspended him once again, Mac decided to sign on with Freedman and the Giants.

After arriving in New York, McGraw betrayed Johnson and the American League by helping Freedman buy up enough shares to gain majority control of the Orioles. Once he had that control, Freedman picked off the best of the Oriole players for his team and other NL teams, and then released most of the remaining players. The Orioles' roster was left with fewer than nine players, which triggered a clause in the AL charter requiring forfeiture of the team's ownership to the league. Johnson took charge of the team and moved players to Baltimore from other teams so that the Orioles could finish out the season.

Once again, Freedman had underestimated his opponent. Just when it seemed that Freedman and the National League had beaten Johnson soundly, Johnson announced that he would be moving the Orioles out of Baltimore and into New York, and that Willie Keeler had signed a 2-year contract to play for the American League in New York. Willie was still an able player and a favorite with the fans, and the Dodgers would miss him. Johnson then proceeded to sign several of the stars of the Pittsburgh Pirates, the current NL champions, for his New York team.

The National League could no longer deny that Ban Johnson was a force to be reckoned with; and it had to accept the fact that his American League was not going to disappear from Organized Baseball. This time, the National League went calling on Johnson, offering major league status for the AL in exchange for an end to the Great Baseball War. Johnson agreed, the AL became the equal of the NL, and the leagues signed an agreement that prohibited any further league-jumping by players but allowed Johnson to hang onto Keeler, LaJoie, and several other players who had left the NL for the AL. It was 1903, and the Great Baseball War was at an end.

VII. Finding a Home in Gotham

While the Great Baseball War was still raging, Freedman's star had begun to dim, in New York politics as well as in the National League. A reform candidate defeated Tammany's candidate for mayor of New York in 1901, and Freedman's political mentor, Boss Richard Croker, retired to England. Freedman angered his fellow team-owners in the NL by proposing a league syndication in which he would have a thirty percent share of ownership but the other owners would have no more than twelve percent or less. Not surprisingly, that proposal—for what Freedman called the Baseball Trust—was summarily rejected. Freedman still had significant political clout in New York, however, and still could make it difficult for Johnson to find property for a ballpark. In fact, Freedman had not opposed major league status for the American League because he was certain that Johnson would not find property in New York and so would never pose a real threat to the Giants.

It became evident that Johnson would need Tammany connections of his own in order to make his New York team a reality. Despite the fact that a reform candidate was now mayor of New York, Tammany still controlled much of the city. Accordingly, among the seven original shareholders of the AL's New York team were five longstanding members of Tammany Hall: Joseph Gordon, one-time owner of the old Metropolitans and Gothams teams; Frank Farrell, the purported head of New York's gambling syndicate and owner of racing stables, billiard halls and gambling houses; William Devery, the corrupt former police chief who had been removed from office following a state investigation of corruption in his department; Tom Foley, a Tammany district leader; and retired police officer Thomas McAvoy, Tammany district leader in the Washington Heights area of Manhattan.[32] Farrell and Devery, the two most notorious of these Tammany men, were the team's primary owners.

Johnson named Gordon, the least objectionable of the Tammanyites, to be president of the team. Then, with the help of his Tammany insiders, he found a piece of property in the Washington Heights section of Manhattan, and the league secured a lease on that land with just six weeks to go until the opening of the 1903 season. The property was hilly and filled with boulders, but it was large enough for a baseball diamond and viewing stands, and it was available. Johnson hired a contractor to start blasting away the boulders, and announced to the world that American League baseball would be played that season in Hilltop Park. The team would be known as the Highlanders, in light of the park's location overlooking the Hudson, and also, in a nod to the team's president, after the famed Scottish regiment known as Gordon's Highlanders.

Freedman was caught by surprise, but rallied quickly. He and John Brush, who had purchased a sizeable share of the Giants, convinced several owners of property in the vicinity of the ballpark site to sign a petition seeking the extension of two city streets through the site.

> Whereas 165th and 168th streets formed the southern and northern boundaries of the grounds, 166th and 167th streets dead-ended at Fort Washington Avenue on the eastern edge of the property. Two weeks after the lease was an-

nounced, 125 property owners presented a petition to the Washington Heights District Governing Board demanding the cutting through of 166th and 167th streets....[33]

The proposed street-cutting would have prevented the construction of the ballpark. Johnson and Gordon continued to proceed with the site preparations. They also submitted their own petition in response, also with numerous signatures, opposing the street-cutting and arguing "that baseball was highly desirable in Washington Heights and would enhance property values."[34] The Board, by a vote of 3 to 2, despite serious pressure from Freedman and his cohorts, denied the street-cutting petition.[35] Nothing could stop Johnson now.

When Hilltop Park opened, it was with great fanfare and celebration:

> The sandwich and lemonade men shouted through the horns and the whistles and the cow bells. The grandstand was still without a roof, but more than sixteen thousand spectators had squeezed into the ballpark; each had been given a little American flag at the entrance. After Bayne's Sixty-Ninth Regiment played the 'Star-Spangled Banner,' the cheers echoed across the river to the New Jersey Palisades and back.[36]

Naturally, Ban Johnson was there, beaming with pride and satisfaction as he threw out the first ball of that first game in Hilltop Park.

The Highlanders won their first home game, but their performance during the Hilltop years was usually less than spectacular. That made the Giants and John Brush (who had bought out Freedman[37]) feel more kindly toward them, and the two teams inaugurated a city series in 1910.[38] When the Polo Grounds were heavily damaged by fire the following spring, the Highlanders graciously shared Hilltop with the Giants while repairs were made to the Polo Grounds.

In 1912, as the ten-year lease on Hilltop was coming to an end, the Giants repaid their American League neighbors' hospitality by offering them the use of the Polo Grounds as their home park. The Yankees, as the team was now commonly referred to, accepted the offer, and shared the Polo Grounds with the Giants for the next ten years.

VIII. The Yankees Come into Their Own

In 1915, Farrell and Devery sold the Yankees, the team they had purchased for $18,000, to Jacob Ruppert and Tillinghast L'Hommedieu Huston for the sum of $460,000. The new owners were known as "the colonels." Ruppert was an honorary colonel in the New York National Guard. Although he had grown up wealthy and privileged, he became a member of Tammany Hall, the political machine that served the "working man", and was elected to four terms in Congress. Huston was an engineer who had led a regiment in the Spanish-American War and stayed on in Cuba to earn a fortune in public works construction. Both men had money to spend, and they set about spending it to improve the Yankees.[39]

The improvement came slowly. As America became involved in World War I, many ballplayers enlisted in the armed services and were shipped out to join the fighting. Then came 1919, and with it the "Black Sox" scandal, the breaking-away of the minor leagues from Major League Baseball, and the demise of baseball's National Commission.

In that same year, Ruppert and Huston clashed with Ban Johnson over the purchase of Red Sox pitcher Carl Mays.[40]

The Yankees needed new and better pitching in order to improve their standings, and the team's owners were intent on adding Mays to their line-up. Johnson wanted Mays punished, by suspension or other penalty, because he had walked out on the Red Sox in mid-season, but the Red Sox had done nothing. Accordingly, Johnson called for a halt to the trade talks. Ruppert and Huston ignored him, and made a deal with Boston that would bring Mays to the Yankees.

Johnson, infuriated by this disregard for his authority, tried to prevent the trade. Ruppert and Huston went to court to prevent Johnson and the AL from enjoining Mays from playing for the Yankees, and they succeeded. Mays played for the Yankees that year, 1919, and the lawsuit was ultimately decided against Johnson and in favor of Ruppert and Huston.

The baseball season of 1919 was a winning one for the Yanks, and one in which more than 600,000 fans came to watch them play ball.[41] Things were going well for the team. "Then, on December 26, 1919, the Yankees and the Red Sox completed the most momentous deal in the history of the game."[42] In exchange for $100,000 cash and a $300,000 loan secured by a mortgage on Fenway Park, Boston owner Harry Frazee sold a wild, young ballplayer named George Herbert Ruth to the New York Yankees.

Baseball needed someone who could help it rise above the disappointments of 1919, and the Babe was just the man for the job. In his first season with the Yankees, Ruth hit 54 home runs, a major league record. He made baseball fun and exciting again, sending the team's attendance records over the one million mark—another first for Major League Baseball. Now, the Yankees, with Ruth in the vanguard, were threatening to overtake the preeminent position the Giants had long occupied. Not surprisingly, the Giants decided it was time for the Yanks to find a home of their own, and soon. The Yankees would play two more seasons in the Polo Grounds, but Ruppert and Huston began immediately to search in earnest for a site for the team's own ballpark.

IX. Home at Last

In early 1921, Ruppert announced that the Yankees would make their home in the Bronx, on property purchased from the estate of William Waldorf Astor. This site was easily reachable by way of the new subway system, which made it far superior to other available properties.[43] However, the Yankees would still have to play the 1921 and 1922 seasons at the Polo Grounds, while necessary city approvals were obtained, the site was readied, and the diamond and stands were constructed. As it happened, those were championship seasons for both teams that played their home games in the Polo Grounds. The Yankees took the American League pennant in 1921 and 1922, only to be beaten by the Giants in the World Series both years.[44]

This time around, the club's ballpark property had two city streets running through it. The Yankees would have to secure the city's approval for the closing of those streets before work on the park could proceed. New York's Mayor Hylan was the person who had the final say on the street closure request, and, after some delay, he gave it his stamp of approval.[45] Hylan was a product of Tammany Hall, so it is entirely possible that Yankees owner Ruppert's position in Tammany worked to the team's advantage on this matter.

Yankee Stadium opened at the start of the 1923 season, to much larger crowds and even more fanfare than had attended the opening day of Hilltop. More than 60,000 fans crowded into the stadium, and John Philip Sousa himself conducted the Seventh Regiment Band as it played the National Anthem.[46] "The Yankees had built the first true baseball *stadium*—a structure intended to accommodate massive crowds and make a progressive and confident statement about baseball's future."[47]

The first ball of the game was thrown out by New York's governor, Al Smith. This was particularly appropriate, in light of the fact that Smith was a Tammany politician, a protégé of the late Boss, Charles Francis Murphy.[48] Tammany had played a crucial role in New York baseball since the sport was first played in the city. It had also played a role in many of the events that led, ultimately, to this day in this stadium, this place that the American League's New York team could call home. In this home, the Yankees would go on to become the beloved Bronx Bombers, and the greatest of all teams in Major League Baseball.

The House That Ruth Built

by Gregory M. Stein[*]

> First impressions—and also last impressions—are of the vastness of the arena. The stadium is big. It towers high in the air, three tiers piled one on the other. It is a skyscraper among baseball parks. Seen from the vantage point of the nearby subway structure, the mere height of the grandstand is tremendous. Baseball fans who sat in the last row of the steeply sloping third tier may well boast that they broke all altitude records short of those attained in an airplane.[1]

The *New York Times* reporter who penned those words in 1923 was among the first 74,200 of the more than 125,000,000 baseball spectators to pass through Yankee Stadium's turnstiles during its 80-year history. The reporter witnessed a spectacle from which an additional 25,000 fans had to be turned away—the number of fans actually admitted to Yankee Stadium roughly matched the total crowds at the three other American League season openers combined.[2] John Philip Sousa led the Seventh Regiment Band in a parade that culminated in the playing of "The Star-Spangled Banner" and the raising of the American flag and the American League pennant.

"That wasn't the end of it, by any means," the reporter continued. New York Governor Alfred E. Smith and Kenesaw M. Landis, High Commissioner of Baseball, headed an enormous group of dignitaries celebrating the Stadium's inaugural. The governor threw the ceremonial first pitch to Yankee catcher Wally Schang, committing "a distinct social error" by tossing the ball accurately. "After that there was nothing to do but to play the game," which began only a minute later than scheduled.[3]

And what a game it was. The first home run to leave the stadium was launched by—who else?—Babe Ruth, a three-run shot in the third inning that sealed a 4-1 Yankees victory over the Boston Red Sox. Yankee shortstop Everett Scott extended his record-breaking streak by playing in his 987th consecutive game; the streak, which ended at 1,307, remains the third-longest in baseball history. Bob Shawkey pitched a three-hitter for the Yanks and would return 53 years later to throw out the first pitch at the newly-renovated Yankee Stadium. Red Sox manager Frank Chance, who, as a Chicago Cub, had been the first-baseman in one of baseball's most famous double play combinations,[4] was unable "to lead the Red Sox out of the baseball wilderness," a task at which many have failed since. The following week, Ruth would impress President Warren Harding by homering again at the Stadium.[5]

Viewed from today's vantage point, that 1923 game seems like the beginning of an era, but it merely was one day in a century-long history of baseball—and real property law—involving the Yankees and their four New York homes. This Chapter provides a legal and historical look at some of the real estate and land use issues surrounding the house that Ruth built. The Yankees relocated to New York from Baltimore only after an unsuccessful effort by the New York Giants to corner the market on all suitable baseball sites in the city; they played their first ten years at a makeshift firetrap of a stadium that was constructed in just six weeks; and they spent their next decade as the tenants of a Giants organization that was happy to collect rent from them only so long as they failed to outdraw their landlords.

Opening Day of 1923 also did not mark the end of legal discord over real estate for the New York Yankees. Successive Yankee owners have faced an array of property law issues, as owners of the stadium and then as its tenants, and, briefly, as the other team in Flushing Meadow. Yankee Stadium itself has hosted more than just baseball, and the home of Mickey and Reggie also has been the temporary residence of Rocky, Sugar Ray, and Muhammad, of Knute and Johnny U. It has been filled by audiences arriving to see Pink Floyd and Pope John Paul, the St. Louis Cardinals and John Cardinal O'Connor, Billy Joel and Billy Graham (though never the Beatles). Delirious fans have cheered 26 World Series championship teams, and a grieving nation mourned the deaths of thousands of victims of an act of terrorism. This Chapter will trace the legal history—and the history—of the real estate development known as Yankee Stadium.

I. Little Town Blues Melt Away[6]

In 1902, Andrew Freedman, owner of the National League's New York Giants, secretly acquired 201 of the 400 outstanding shares of the competing American League's new Baltimore Orioles. The Orioles immediately released some of their star players, who were promptly signed by the Giants. American League President Ban Johnson feared that, with only seven functioning teams, his league would disintegrate, and so he quickly took control of the Orioles franchise. Within a year, Freedman had sold the Giants, the Orioles had become the New York Highlanders, and Baltimore had begun a half-century without a major league team.[7]

The American League had been pursuing a policy of locating its teams near established National League franchises, but Freedman had prevented it from cracking the nation's most populous city. Now the junior circuit had a team in New York, but the embittered Freedman continued to hold leases or options on nearly all suitable ballpark sites in the city.[8] The Highlanders' owners quickly found a location on Broadway between 165th and 168th Streets that Freedman had rejected as too rocky and leased it for ten years from the New York Institute for the Blind.

The 16,000-seat Hilltop Park opened a remarkable six weeks later, built partly on a ledge, with a rocky field and no clubhouse—players dressed for games at a nearby hotel.[9] Excavation and filling of marsh cost nearly three times as much as construction, which says as much about the park as it does about the topography.[10] The small size of the park made for close contact between players and fans, much to the annoyance of players such as Ty Cobb, who once leaped into the grandstand at Hilltop so he could beat and stomp a particularly irksome heckler. Cobb had little to fear from the fan, who had lost all of one hand and most of the other in an industrial accident. Cobb's response: "I don't care if he has no feet."[11]

A 1911 fire at the nearby Polo Grounds had an unexpected effect on the future of New York baseball. The Highlanders' willingness to allow the rival Giants to use Hilltop Park until the Polo Grounds could be rebuilt improved relations between the teams.[12]

When the Highlanders' ground lease at Hilltop Park expired in 1913, the New York Institute for the Blind concluded that it could make more money by subdividing the land for apartment buildings. The grateful Giants offered the temporary use of the Polo Grounds to the Highlanders,[13] who by then had been dubbed the "Yankees" by headline writers searching for a shorter moniker.[14] Hilltop Park was demolished in 1914, and the land currently is the site of Columbia Presbyterian Medical Center, the hospital at which Frank Torre would receive a heart transplant 82 years later.[15]

The Yankees' decade at the Polo Grounds was marked by a change in ownership, several unparalleled player acquisitions, improvements to the team that irritated the Giants, and the decline of the Red Sox. The team's 1915 sale to two Giants fans—Colonels Jacob Ruppert and Tillinghast L'Hommedieu Huston—at first led only to cosmetic upgrades, such as daily washing of uniforms.[16] The two Colonels soon established good relations with the Red Sox's new owner, Harry Frazee, a theatrical producer who constantly needed cash to keep his non-baseball shows afloat. During the next several years, Frazee sent most of his top players to the Yankees, capped by the 1919 sale of Babe Ruth, a transaction that Ruth initially rejected. Ruth telegraphed his business manager, "Will not play anywhere but Boston," but relented when he learned that the Yankees would meet his salary demands.[17] Frazee received $100,000 for Ruth, plus a $300,000 loan secured by a mortgage on Fenway Park. Angry Red Sox fans reacted by placing "For Sale" signs on Faneuil Hall, the Boston Public Library, and other historic sites.[18] The Yankees, who had never previously won the World Series, now hold 26 championships; the Red Sox, who had won the World Series in four of the previous eight years, have not won one since.[19]

The Ruth-led Yankees drew nearly 1.3 million fans in 1920, far surpassing the Giants. The competitive threat posed by the Yankees was beginning to outweigh the $65,000 annual rent they were paying the Giants, and the Giants told the Yankees during that year that they would have to seek other accommodations.[20] The eviction was put on ice for the next two seasons while the Yankees evaluated their options and acted.[21] Meanwhile, the Giants began taking whatever measures they could to match the Babe's popularity. In an attempt to attract New York's growing Jewish population, for example, the Giants brought up minor-leaguer Mose Hirsch Solomon and billed him as the "Rabbi of Swat." Solomon's career batting average of .375 might be more memorable had he played in more than just two games, late in the 1923 season.[22]

II. A Brand New Start of It in Old New York

When the Giants first announced their decision to uproot the Yankees, the *New York Times* presciently editorialized that "Mr. Fan will travel far to see his favorite team play ball, and the new orders simply mean that he will regard the eviction as partly personal and go elsewhere when it becomes necessary."[23] The Yankees already held options on several potential sites for a new ballpark, but they could not readily build and move before the next Opening Day. The league briefly feared the Yankees might have to relocate to another city, but the Giants relented temporarily. As the *Times* noted, "It isn't that the Yankees are anxious to remain at the Polo Grounds, but for a season or two it will be a matter of necessity."[24] The delay even gave Colonels Ruppert and Huston the chance to broach the possibility of a monetary contribution from the league toward the construction of their new home, a topic on which they clearly were a generation ahead of their time.[25]

The owners were keeping their list of possible sites secret. The *Times* first reported late in January, 1921, that the Yankees planned to acquire a site on 136th Street, near Broadway, from the Hebrew Orphan Asylum, to build a stadium larger than any in the nation other than the Yale Bowl. But a week later, the team announced that it would move to a considerably larger site in the Bronx and build "a huge stadium, which will surpass in seating capacity any structure hitherto built for the accommodation of lovers of baseball." Giants' manager John McGraw referred to the site as "Goatville."[26] The Yankees purchased the site from the estate of William Waldorf Astor for a price first reported at $500,000,[27] and promptly began preliminary site preparation. Ruppert and Huston had considered and rejected the same parcel six years earlier, but the construction of two subway lines had since made for more rapid access from Manhattan. Also considered and rejected was a location at West 32nd Street in Manhattan, not far from the railyards that are under consideration today as the site of a new Yankee Stadium.[28]

Objections from neighbors delayed the Yankees' receipt of all necessary approvals, with nearby residents employing the time-tested technique of trying to head off a project they oppose by persuading the mayor to build new streets through the middle of the site. Building costs had spiked in the early 1920s, so the Colonels probably did not mind the delay;[29] in fact they would not break ground for several weeks after receiving all the required permits.[30] The Yankees closed on the Bronx property on May 16, 1921,[31] but fans may have been paying more attention that spring to the Babe's increased girth. One group of fans had waited at the Shreveport train station earlier that year to get a glimpse of "the bulky Babe." As a *New York Times* reporter observed, "Ruth has taken off about ten pounds of the extra avoirdupois which he carried to Hot Springs two weeks ago, but there remain from fifteen to twenty more pounds to be shed before he will be down to normal playing weight." But not to worry, for the Babe "does not anticipate much difficulty in shedding some more flesh by strenuous work."[32]

The Yankees began soliciting bids late in 1921. Bids for steelwork were received in December, even as public hearings on street closings were continuing. Two weeks later, the team greeted the new year by inviting bids for "[e]xcavation, grading, masonry, sewers and downspouts, reinforced concrete, lathing and plastering, ornamental metal work, tile work, terrazo floors, carpentry, toilets, roofing, sheet metal, steel sash, painting and wood bleachers," with bids on "lighting, heating and elevator construction" to be announced soon afterwards.[33] Bids had to be lump-sum, and bidders could bid on any or all aspects of the work.

By the spring of 1922, the Yankees had selected White Construction Company as the contractor in charge of all building work, and White had begun to hire subcontractors. White would work with the Osborn Engineering Company of Cleveland, previously chosen to design the stadium. With grading of the site nearly complete, Osborn risked predicting that the plan to use double shifts of workers would "smash all records in the matter of speed."[34]

Meanwhile, permitting questions were dragging on. In March, 1922, Mayor John F. Hylan delayed acting on a request that the city release its interest in the bed of streets running through the site, ostensibly because the team's owners had not complied with all terms and conditions set forth in their petition. Two weeks later, with all "i's" and "t's" respectively dotted and crossed, the Mayor signed off on the new stadium. Even the Astor family, which still owned most of the nearby property, had to consent to the street closings, from England. The Yankees finally could build their new ballpark, nearly a year after they had closed on their purchase of the site and more than a year after they had announced their plans.[35]

White Construction signed its contract on May 5, 1922, and work on the "big playground" began the next day. The owners dispensed with the traditional groundbreaking ceremony in the interest of saving time. Rather, "[t]he work will be started with vim, and at some time in the future there will be fitting ceremonies to mark the beginning of the construction of the biggest ball park in the country." White, which beat out more than 40 other bidders, was contractually obligated to complete the park in eight months, but team officials guessed that construction would take less time than that. The *New York Times* modestly predicted that the new park would bear the name "Yankee Field."[36]

While the contractor could not quite keep to its optimistic timetable, it did complete Yankee Stadium in less than one year.[37] By Thanksgiving week, groundskeeper Phil Schenck, who had supervised the grounds at Hilltop Park a decade earlier, was able to place the last bit of sod on the new field. "Just as Phil, giving the grass a final pat, straightened up and remarked to spectators of the historic occasion, 'Well, that's that,' the first snowflake was wafted down." But there was no cause for concern, for now, "if Phil's new-laid grass should lie beneath a blanket of snow until it is time for the athletes to cavort thereon in mid-April, there would be no harm done."[38] In March 1923, a team spokesman declared the stadium 95 percent finished, with final work on a portion of the bleachers and installation of a few thousand seats still to be completed, and stated that construction would be finished in time for Opening Day.[39]

Yankee Stadium sported a mezzanine level, designed to use the empty space between the upper and lower decks by hanging thousands of extra seats from the support beams and reputedly making the stadium the first triple-decker in the world. The upper deck was partially cantilevered, bringing more seats closer to the field. The designers also set new standards for fan amenities, with improvements in ticket booths, entrance ramps, telephone booths, bathrooms, refreshment stands, elevators, the scoreboard, and the arrangement of the exits.[40] "Particular attention [was] given to looking after the convenience of women patrons and making them as comfortable as possible." Yankee Stadium's planners were solicitous of women so that "[t]he tribe of female fans [would] increase speedily as soon as the new park is thrown open."[41]

Authors Ray Robinson and Christopher Jennison compiled statistics reflecting the massive scale of the real estate development:

> Almost a million feet of Pacific Coast fir, transported via the Panama Canal, was needed to build the bleachers. Over 2,300 tons of structural steel, plus a million brass screws, helped to keep the game's finest showplace in one piece. Enough sod—16,000 square feet of it—was collected to convert the place into one vast farmland. There were 135,000 steel castings for the grandstand seats, and 20,000 cubic yards of concrete were added to the mix.[42]

Another pair of commentators states that the stadium actually needed 116,000 square feet of sod—a number that seems more realistic—along with 13,000 cubic yards of topsoil.[43] The finished stadium had a seating capacity "about the same as the Roman Colosseum."[44] But the Babe, inspecting the dimensions of the field, was not terribly impressed, accurately predicting, "I don't see any fences there that I can't hit over."[45]

Ruppert and Huston had not built just another big-city ballpark: Yankee Stadium was baseball's first modern, urban stadium. Constructed of steel and concrete, the stadium was largely immune to the serious fire problems that had plagued older, wooden structures—in 1894 alone, four of the twelve major league parks had suffered fire damage. By 1923, fans were demanding greater safety and comfort, and owners were willing to build more expensive edifices and pass the costs along in the form of higher ticket prices. The greater cost and reduced mobility of the sturdy structure meant that the Yankees had to be every bit as stable and settled as their new home, which probably explains the team's decision to own both the land and the stadium. The Yankees and other teams would develop more creative structures for ownership of their real estate in the coming decades.[46]

III. King of the Hill, Top of the Heap

Opening Day of 1923 was the beginning of a remarkable run for the New York Yankees and their stadium. The team won 27 pennants and 20 world championships during its first 42 seasons in Yankee Stadium. The stadium also hosted a wide range of non-baseball events during this era. Even before the park opened, its owners were hoping to attract boxing matches, football games, track-and-field exhibitions, and even dog races.[47] Opening Day was important to the Yankees for another reason. On that day, one of their scouts attended a college game at which Columbia pitcher Lou Gehrig struck out 17. Two months later, Gehrig was $1,500 richer, and the Iron Horse was a part of the Yankee farm system.

The Yankees took the 1923 pennant by 16 games and won their first World Series by beating the Giants—the team that had defeated them in the previous two Series—in six games. The first World Series home run in Yankee Stadium history was a ninth-inning, inside-the-park line drive by the notoriously slow Casey Stengel. The Giants' only other victory also came on a Stengel home run. Between second and third, Casey thumbed his nose at Yankee pitcher Sam Jones; he aimed a similar insult at the entire Yankee bench as he rounded third.[48] Judge Landis fined Stengel $50, but Stengel maintained that he was merely swatting at a bee or a fly.[49] During this Series, former Red Sox pitchers hurled 46-1/3 of 54 innings for the Yanks, and a former Red Sox catcher caught every one of those pitches.[50]

Baseball stadiums sit empty most of the time, which meant that the Yankees had some valuable real estate available for lease. The team already had some early experience as a landlord, having leased out Hilltop Park to semipro African-American teams.[51] In its new stadium, the team wasted no time on this front, with 58,000 in attendance for the first boxing match at the stadium, during the summer of 1923. By the end of the 1920s, Yankee Stadium had been the site of eight championship fights.[52] After one 1928 fight, a ticketholder from Oklahoma City sued, claiming that he and his wife arrived after the beginning of the bout and could not gain admittance because all gates had been locked. Faced with conflicting evidence, the judge denied the claim, noting, "Plaintiff should find some consolation in the pride which must be his, that it can no longer be said that he and his wife did not visit the greatest metropolis in the world, and its splendid and stupendous places of amusement."[53]

The college football series between Notre Dame and Army relocated to the stadium in 1925. In that first game, Fighting Irish coach Knute Rockne suffered the most lopsided defeat of his coaching career. The 27-0 thrashing ended a 16-game winning streak for Notre Dame. With the same two teams scoreless at halftime of their 1928 meeting, Rockne would ask his boys "to go in there with all they've got and win just one for the Gipper," and they would, 12-6.[54] The series would continue at Yankee Stadium until 1946.

Professional football was in its infancy, but the New York Yankees of the American Professional Football League thought they could fill the stadium as well. Even Red Grange could not attract pro football fans to the Bronx, however, and the football Yankees lasted only seven games at the stadium.[55]

Meanwhile, the baseball Yankees kept winning, and Yankee players kept breaking records. In 1927, Babe Ruth personally out-homered every other club in the American League, swatting his record-breaking 60th shot on the next-to-last day of the season. The Yankees already had clinched the pennant—which they won by 19 games—and only 10,000 fans were in attendance. Lou Gehrig slugged a mere 47, to go with his 175 runs batted in and his .373 batting average. The Yankees swept the Pittsburgh Pirates in the Series, Babe hit two home runs, and Herb Pennock narrowly missed pitching a perfect game, retiring the first 22 Pirates he faced in game 3. The Yankees would also sweep in their next two Series appearances, in 1928 and 1932. Ruth came in for some criticism when it was noted that he was earning more money than President Herbert Hoover, but the slugger deflected any disapproval by noting, "I had a better year than he did."[56]

The 1930s were kind to the Yankees, and the team never went four years without a trip to the World Series. Babe Ruth may have been "the first star of the newsreel era,"[57] but the less volatile Gehrig was on his way to playing in 2,130 consecutive games. One day after pinch-hitting in 1925, Gehrig replaced regular first baseman Wally Pipp, who was suffering from a headache. Gehrig would next miss a game in 1939. "'Some day off!' Pipp was to remark in later years. 'The next time I got to play first base was a year later and in another league, with Cincinnati.'"[58] While Gehrig played on, Ruth left the Yankees after the 1934 season, and rookie Joe DiMaggio arrived in 1936.

The Yankees were off to a wonderful start in their new stadium, but even times as good as these were punctuated by tragedy. On May 19, 1929, a sudden cloudburst caused the 9,000 fans in the rightfield bleachers to sprint for the exit stairway. Two people were trampled to death and 62 were injured. That same season ended with the sudden death of manager Miller Huggins.[59]

The 1930s concluded even more sadly, even though the Yankees won the World Series again in 1939. Owner Jacob Ruppert died early that year, but the team's sorrow was only beginning. Eight games into the season, an ailing Lou Gehrig benched himself for the good of the team. Within a few weeks, the Mayo Clinic had confirmed that he was suffering from amyotrophic lateral sclerosis, the disease that will forever be associated with his name. On July 4, 1939, the Yankees held Lou Gehrig Appreciation Day. Gehrig reportedly did not plan to speak, but the fans insisted, leading to one of the most memorable moments in sports history, sometimes referred to as baseball's Gettysburg Address. Gehrig began his brief remarks by stating, "[T]oday I consider myself the luckiest man on the face of the earth," and concluded by noting, "I might have had a bad break, but I have an awful lot to live for."[60] Babe Ruth, who had not spoken to Gehrig for years, embraced his former teammate, and the team retired Gehrig's number, making him the first player ever so honored.[61] Lou Gehrig died on June 2, 1941, just before his 38th birthday.

Yankee Stadium hosted one of the more politically-charged sporting events in its history on June 22, 1938, when Joe Louis knocked out German boxer Max Schmeling in just 124 seconds. Schmeling managed only two punches. Although Louis was the heavyweight champion even before the victory, he had asked not to be called the champ until he could avenge his earlier loss to the only boxer to have defeated him so far during his professional career. President Franklin Roosevelt had told Louis before the match, "Joe, we need muscles like yours to beat Germany," but a Nazi publicist traveling with Schmeling had suggested to the newspapers that a black man could not beat Schmeling and had informed the press that the German army would use Schmeling's prize money to build more tanks.[62] The Schmeling fight represented the second of Louis' seven successful title defenses at Yankee Stadium, and surely the most significant.

The 1940s began with the establishment of a baseball record that many fans believe to be the most unlikely ever to be broken. On May 15, 1941, Joe DiMaggio hit a single before a small crowd at Yankee Stadium, and by July 16, he had hit safely in 56 consecutive games. The streak was broken the next night, in Cleveland, but only after the Indians' third-baseman snared two wicked line drives. DiMaggio then hit safely in his next 16 games.[63]

Colonel Ruppert's heirs sold the Yankees to Larry MacPhail, Dan Topping, and Del Webb in 1945. MacPhail believed in profiting by leasing the stadium out for other events, and the stadium became the home of track-and-field competitions and even fashion shows. Yankee Stadium was the site of additional championship fights during the late 1940s and early 1950s, with appearances by Joe Louis, Rocky Marciano, and Sugar Ray Robinson. Robinson was 0-2 in championship fights at Yankee Stadium, but managed to obtain a split decision with the Internal Revenue Service in a dispute arising from his compensation for the second fight.[64]

Webb, an experienced real estate developer and former semipro baseball player, had other ideas about how to profit from the stadium. Late in 1953, Webb and Topping—who by then had bought out MacPhail's interest—sold Yankee Stadium. In a complex transaction, the Knights of Columbus acquired the land under the stadium and some nearby parking lots for $2.5 million. The new owners immediately leased the property to Chicago businessmen Earl and Arnold Johnson for a period of 28 years; the Knights of Columbus ultimately would collect nearly $5 million in rent.[65]

The Johnsons also purchased the stadium itself, and they leased the stadium and subleased the land to the Yankees, also for 28 years. Webb and Topping took back a purchase-money second mortgage on the building and on the Johnsons' interest in the ground lease to secure the Johnsons' obligation to pay them $2.9 million of the purchase price. The stadium soon would come to be held by John Cox, a Rice University alumnus who donated the edifice to his alma mater in 1962. Webb and Topping netted $6.5 million in the real estate deal; they and MacPhail originally had paid only $2.8 million for the team, the stadium, and the farm system.[66]

The 1953 sale of Yankee Stadium represented a new type of baseball real estate deal. If the Yankees had shown a long-term commitment to New York in 1923 by building and owning an exceptional structure, their sale of the land and building 30 years later suggested that they might be willing to sever their ties to the city for the right price. As Neil Sullivan writes:

> The Webb-Topping sale of Yankee Stadium was a textbook on how to make the stadium game work for the ball club. Exquisite financial intricacies replaced the old model of bringing people to the ballpark, charging them admission, and selling them some food. The Stadium sale and accompanying arrangements showed the major league owners that their stadiums could trigger unrealized income. Since that time, obsolescence did not have to mean cracks in the foundation. A stadium deal that did not maximize the owner's income needed to be

restructured, or the franchise needed to consider a more sympathetic community. The stakes in the stadium game had risen considerably.[67]

But these changes in the game probably were not yet evident to most fans in the 1950s. The Yankees remained baseball's premier team, and Yankee Stadium continued to be the site of significant non-baseball events throughout the decade. In 1950, the stadium hosted an eight-day convention of the Jehovah's Witnesses. As many as 120,000 visitors may have attended for at least part of the week, and the ceremonies had to be piped into a tent-city outside the stadium and a campsite in New Jersey to accommodate the overflow crowd.[68] The Yankees initially rejected the group's request that its members be allowed to use the playing field as well as the stands, but relented when the group agreed that all members would remove their shoes before walking on the turf.[69] New York City officials marveled at the convention's organization, with one health department inspector commenting, "I've never seen anything run as smoothly as this before."[70] Eight years later, an estimated 253,922 Jehovah's Witnesses would pack a conference held at both Yankee Stadium and the nearby Polo Grounds.[71]

The stadium had been put to a more somber use in 1948, when Babe Ruth died of cancer. Babe's casket was carried into Yankee Stadium, and the American flag flying from the stadium was lowered to half-staff. A long line snaked around the building, with thousands of fans waiting to take a last look at the man who probably had saved baseball in the 1920s.[72]

Elston Howard joined the team in 1955, becoming the first African-American player in Yankee history. Jackie Robinson had broken baseball's color barrier eight years earlier, but the Yankees had remained an all-white team. Yankees' general manager George Weiss claimed that the team would "bring up a Negro as soon as one that fits the high Yankee standards is found," but Robinson attributed the segregation of the Yankees to prejudice by the team's management, a view that was supported by Weiss' 1952 declaration that "I will never allow a black man to wear a Yankee uniform."[73] Another contributing factor may have been the fact that the New York Black Yankees were paying substantial rent to use Yankee Stadium: An integrated major league likely would undercut the viability of the Negro Leagues and jeopardize this additional income.[74]

Howard wanted to become a catcher even though that position was occupied by future Hall-of-Famer Yogi Berra. He persevered during spring training of 1954 in St. Petersburg and was well-accepted by his teammates. The citizens of St. Petersburg were a different story: Fans had been known to throw black cats on the field when Jackie Robinson visited and Howard could not stay at the team hotel there. Howard ended up spending the 1954 season in Toronto, while the Yankees missed the World Series after winning the previous five. On April 14, 1955, with all deliberate speed, the Yankees became the 13th of the 16 major league clubs to field an African-American player. Howard played in 97 games that year, mostly in the outfield, batting .290 and hitting a home run in his first World Series at-bat. Manager Casey Stengel insisted early in the 1955 season that Howard be allowed to stay at the team hotel on the road, even in those cities with otherwise segregated accommodations. But it would be quite a bit later in his 14-year big league career before Howard had a roommate on the road.[75]

The 1950s and early 1960s included additional notable highlights. Allie Reynolds pitched two no-hitters during the 1951 season, and Don Larsen pitched the only perfect game in World Series history five years later. The photograph caption on page one of the next morning's *New York Times* describes Brooklyn Dodgers coach Jake Pitler as "the only Dodger to reach first base."[76] That same day, Larsen's estranged wife filed a petition seeking to withhold his World Series pay, alleging that he had failed to provide her and their daughter with adequate support.[77]

In 1959, the Yankees traded Larsen for Roger Maris. Manager Stengel correctly predicted that Maris could break Ruth's single-season home run record because "he's got more power than Stalin."[78] The following season, when Stengel was forced to resign because of advancing age, he complained that he would "never make the mistake of being seventy again."[79] Mickey Mantle came closer than any major leaguer ever had to hitting a fair ball out of Yankee Stadium, when he struck the rightfield facade about a foot from the top with a home run in 1963. The pitcher who gave up the shot remarked, "Six feet over and it would have killed somebody waiting at the [subway] station."[80] Negro League star Josh Gibson may actually have cleared the stadium's leftfield roof once.[81]

This period was not just a time of individual accomplishments, and the Yankees' glory years as a team continued through the 1950s and into the early 1960s. In the 16 years beginning in 1949, the Yankees reached the World Series 14 times, winning nine of them. Cumulative statistics for the seasons from 1920 through 1964 show that the Yankees dominated the American League, leading the league in wins, hits, batting average, runs scored, and home runs. The team allowed the fewest runs, committed the fewest errors, turned the most double plays, and possessed the lowest earned run average.[82]

The 1954 season got off to an odd start, with unionized musicians picketing in front of Yankee Stadium. The musicians, who did not themselves have any connection to the team or the stadium, worked for the owner of radio station WINS, which held broadcast rights to Yankee games. The union members chose to picket in front of the stadium in the hope that some players would not cross the picket lines, leading to greater pressure on WINS and its owner. In the end, Major Francis Sutherland and the Seventh Regiment Band, all union members, honored the strike, and the band that had played at every Yankee Stadium Opening Day since 1923 did not perform. A federal court later ruled that the union had engaged in an unfair labor practice.[83]

Courts had to rule on several other unusual cases involving the Yankees, their stadium, or their name during the 1950s. In 1959, weather forced a one-day postponement in "the pugilistic encounter in the so-called heavyweight championship contest between two individuals, [Floyd] Patterson and [Ingemar] Johansson, known in legal parlance as 'boxers.'" One Harry Hochman, who could not attend "[t]he fistic engagement" on the second night, gave his tickets to a Mr. William Rosensohn, expecting Rosensohn to sell the tickets. When Rosensohn claimed he had been unable to dispose of the tickets, but also could not produce the originals, Hochman sued. The court awarded Hochman $100.[84] A United States Supreme Court case decided that same year, focusing on possible antitrust law violations by boxing promoters, noted the high percentage of boxing championships held at Yankee Stadium during the 1930s and 1940s.[85]

Yankee Stadium also surfaced in several intellectual property cases at about the same time. In one of the strangest, Arthur Morse, the author of an article that appeared in *Collier's* magazine, sued a *New York Daily Mirror* columnist named Sidney Fields, alleging copyright infringement by Fields. The court carefully compared the two authors' pieces, each of which discussed the life and exploits of Harry "Hopalong" Abramowitz, "a very colorful individual who owns a stable in the Bronx which houses a vast array of horses and every conceivable type of carriage and stagecoach, all of which are used for advertising everything from an aspiring politician's candidacy to the opening of a neighborhood delicatessen." Abramowitz apparently would rent his equipment to traveling rodeos that occasionally appeared at Yankee Stadium, and each author found the story engaging enough to merit journalistic attention. The federal judge found insufficient evidence to conclude that Fields had copied Morse's article.[86]

A trial judge in the Bronx had to decide whether to approve a certificate of incorporation for an entity that wished to use the name "New York Braves Baseball Club, Inc." The judge plainly thought that the organizer of this team for teenage boys was attempting to capitalize on the good reputation of the Yankees and the Milwaukee Braves, noting:

> I would embrace the affirmation of the religious, the philosophers and the poets, that man's crowning glory is a good name: Like wisdom, it is to be preferred to riches and it is better than precious ointment. It is not but air with buoyancy enough to float upon the sea of fame, nor a commodity to be bought or borrowed — what is not natively one's own falls off and comes to nothing. A great name without merit is like an epitaph.[87]

He did not approve the certificate.

The 1950s and 1960s also saw the continued use of the stadium for non-baseball purposes. The New York Giants of the National Football League ("NFL") began playing at Yankee Stadium in 1956. The Giants' 18-year tenure at the stadium included their sudden-death overtime defeat at the hands of the Baltimore Colts in the 1958 NFL Championship, a game often called the greatest ever played. Grambling College football and New York Cosmos professional soccer would follow later. The stadium also would host Billy Graham and New York's Francis Cardinal Spellman during 1957.[88]

The 1960s started off well for the New York Yankees, but the team would slip dramatically in the second half of that decade. In 1961, Roger Maris hit 61 home runs, breaking Babe Ruth's single-season record, with an asterisk. Maris' record actually would stand longer than Ruth's had. In the 1961 World Series, pitcher Whitey Ford completed a streak of 32 straight scoreless World Series innings, breaking the record held by... Babe Ruth. "As writer Don Honig noted, it had been a very bad year for Mr. Ruth."[89] And two changes soon would make it a very bad eleven years for the New York Yankees. The New York Mets had been formed in 1962, and the hapless new team, led by manager Casey Stengel, was outdrawing the Yankees. By 1969, the Mets would be champions of the world and residents of the new Shea Stadium, while the Yankees languished in fifth place in their six-team division, 28-1/2 games behind the Baltimore Orioles. And in 1964, the Columbia Broadcasting System ("CBS") bought the New York Yankees.

IV. Vagabond Shoes Long to Stray

A few years after CBS bought the Yankees, the team's new president, Michael Burke, began discussing important real estate issues with New York Mayor John Lindsay. Yankee Stadium was starting to show its age, while the city had just spent in excess of $25 million to build Shea. The fan base of the Yankees was becoming increasingly suburban, and these more far-flung fans had insufficient space to park their cars at a stadium that had been designed to host spectators arriving by subway. Indeed, Burke claimed that hundreds of fans had driven to Yankee Stadium for a 1970 doubleheader with the Red Sox only to turn away when they could not park.[90] The South Bronx neighborhood near Yankee Stadium was facing severe crime problems, and the team believed that fear of crime was keeping fans away. And other cities had more modern ballparks, with up-to-date features — such as luxury boxes — that increased their teams' revenues. Meanwhile,

New Jersey was courting the Yankees and the football Giants, and Lindsay must have feared that the two teams would leave, just as the Dodgers and the baseball Giants had a few years earlier. By 1970, Lindsay was offering to spend the same amount on Yankee Stadium as the city had spent on Shea.[91]

Rice University still owned the building and the Knights of Columbus still retained the underlying land, and Lindsay planned to have the city acquire both by exercising its power of eminent domain. Once the city owned the land and building, it would renovate the stadium and lease it directly to the Yankees. New York City was struggling financially and would be unable to pay its bills by 1975, but Lindsay was making an offer that ultimately would cost more than $100 million, even as other public needs went unmet. Nonetheless, Lindsay pursued the renovation plan, because "[t]o do otherwise would be to admit that the city was in an especially grim position. Lindsay would have to admit that New York could not compete with the burgeoning cities of the Sunbelt, and he could not concede that."[92]

Under the terms of the leases from Rice University and the Knights of Columbus, the Yankees were required to pay the amount of all real estate taxes as additional rent. A 1973 dispute between the team and the city over the real estate tax assessment for Yankee Stadium highlights the problems the Yankees were suffering during this period. The court focused on determining the value of the land, the building, and the various amenities, in an effort to calculate what it would cost to reproduce the stadium, minus depreciation. But the real argument was over the cause of the Yankees' misfortunes during the previous seven tax years. The team wanted to introduce evidence of income and expenses, as a means of persuading the court that the reproduction cost of the building actually overstated its value. In the team's view, if the stadium were destroyed, it would make no economic sense to rebuild it, given the deteriorating neighborhood and the inadequate parking. Thus, when viewed as a component of a struggling ongoing business, the stadium was worth considerably less than its depreciated reproduction cost.[93]

The city argued in response that lowered receipts reflected nothing more than an unattractive product—the football Giants, after all, were selling out every game. The stadium would produce more revenue if the Yankees were a better baseball team. So the real question was whether the stadium was suffering from physical obsolescence and an undesirable location, or simply from being the home of a weak, poorly run team. The outcome was a bit of a draw. The court did not clearly choose one rationale over the other, but the numbers it selected appear to favor the city's argument. Even so, the assessment was reduced somewhat from its original level.[94]

All the while, the renovation plans were proceeding. The mayor announced early in 1971 that the city would condemn the land and the building if the parties could not agree to terms. That same day, the Board of Education voted to terminate the contracts of 3,500 teachers due to a funding shortage.[95] The city briefly toyed with the idea of having the Yankees and Giants join the Mets and New York Jets at Shea Stadium, a proposal that upset Bronx residents and elected officials and proved to be politically and physically impractical.[96] The city council approved the acquisition plan in June, but the Giants left anyway, announcing in August that they would relocate to the new Meadowlands sports complex in New Jersey.[97]

The Giants had carried through on their threat to leave, but the Yankees used their leverage to obtain a good deal from the city of New York. By March 1972, the Board of Estimate had approved a 200-page lease between the city and the Yankees that required the city to renovate the stadium, even though a suit by a group of taxpayers challenging the use of city funds for these purposes was pending. Under the terms of the lease, the city would receive annual rent based on team attendance: 5 percent of admissions and concessions receipts from the first 750,000 fans, 7.5 percent from the next 750,000 fans, and 10 percent for all fans over 1.5 million. City Council President Sanford Garelik objected to the deal strenuously, accusing the Lindsay administration of "whipping up 'a soufflé of nostalgia, apple pie and motherhood that clouded the issues.'"[98] Five months later, the city condemned Yankee Stadium and became the owner of the building and the underlying land, and the team and the city signed the lease. The condemnation terminated all subleases, thereby rendering the Giants temporarily homeless. The Yankees, meanwhile, were on their way to Shea Stadium for two seasons.[99]

The renovation plans themselves were ambitious. The grandstand decks would be reinforced, removing the need for the 105 steel support columns that previously had obstructed the view of many spectators. New field lighting would be installed, and parts of the bleachers would be removed. All seats would be replaced, with the wider new seats resulting in a reduction in seating capacity to 52,000. The field would be lowered for drainage purposes, with the outfield dimensions modified. Escalators and private lounges would be added. The architect promised that the stadium would retain its character: "We're not going to change it to some cookie-cutter ballpark like Shea Stadium, in the middle of nowheresville."[100]

Mayor Lindsay drove a bulldozer at the groundbreaking at the close of the 1973 season and presented home plate to Claire Ruth and first base to Eleanor Gehrig. The bat-rack went to the Smithsonian Institution. The old chairs, with plaques reading "A chair from the House That Ruth Built," were put on sale for $20 apiece; Rice University later would claim that the seats were its property and not that of the city.[101]

The cost of the stadium renovation project would keep rising. The original cost was estimated to be roughly $21 million for the renovations, plus $3 million for the acquisition of the property. By Opening Day, 1973, the mayor had announced that the price for the renovation alone had jumped to nearly $28 million, which Lindsay described as "routine—a modest escalation." The mayor later would be quoted as saying, "[B]y the time I retire, the stadium will be gutted and the project so far down the road it will be impossible to reverse it." That November, the figure climbed to nearly $50 million. Faced with charges that the mayor had intentionally understated the costs of the project, one of his aides pointed out that much of the extra money was earmarked for improvements near the stadium, such as subway stations, parking garages, landscaping, and streetlights.[102]

By July 1975, the cost estimate was increased to $57 million, plus acquisition costs now listed as $4 million (the court still had not established the price of the condemnation). That December, the New York Times put the cost of the renovation project at about $75 million and estimated that the property acquisition costs would come to $8 million. Two months later, the Times reported that former Mayor Lindsay had known before the groundbreaking that renovation costs would likely exceed $80 million; by the time of this newspaper report, committed expenditures already had passed $100 million. When the stadium reopened in April 1976, city officials conceded that the cost would be somewhat more than $100 million, plus debt service, including between $9 and $15 million for the acquisition of the property. By then, the Times had calculated that revenues from the stadium would never cover the city's interest payments on the debt, let alone the principal. Yankee Stadium was not, the newspaper concluded, the "House That Truth Built."[103]

Surprisingly few cases arising from the renovation of Yankee Stadium reached the law reporters or the newspapers. Construction delays led to one fairly routine dispute,[104] but the press was focused on the spiraling costs of the project and the apparently mis-leading information supplied by the Lindsay administration. Perhaps construction pro-ceeded harmoniously; more likely, the city was anxious to settle any disputes quietly rather than receiving the additional negative publicity that a trial would generate. The *New York Times* reported, for example, that the city inadvertently committed the same space in the Bronx Terminal Market to a private development company and to the Yan-kees for parking. The developer relinquished the space but insisted on receiving a sub-stitute location that reportedly cost the city about $10 million.[105]

Yankee Stadium reopened on April 15, 1976, before 54,010 fans, including Mickey Mantle, Joe DiMaggio, Yogi Berra, Joe Louis, Frank Gifford, Kyle Rote, and six mem-bers of the 1923 Yankees. Long-time Yankee announcer Bob Sheppard tested the acoustics of the public-address system before the game by announcing Yankee lineups from the past. Brendan Byrne, the governor of New Jersey, turned to Eleanor Gehrig and jokingly tried to woo her, asking, "Have you seen our new stadium? Lou Gehrig would have been proud to play there." Before the game began, ticket-takers kept fans packed outside the gates for an extra 30 minutes while they presented a list of labor de-mands, and neighborhood activists picketed across the street from the stadium to pub-licize the lack of city investment in other civic improvements. The Yankees defeated the Minnesota Twins 11-4.[106]

Neil Sullivan succinctly summarizes the Yankee Stadium renovation deal as "a trans-fer of wealth of approximately $100 million for the benefit of a baseball team that was owned by one of the richest corporations in the world."[107] At the same time, the city would teeter on the brink of bankruptcy, and the South Bronx neighborhood surround-ing Yankee Stadium would become increasingly blighted. The Yankees, however, had their renovated stadium. They had a new owner as well, and the story of the Yankees since 1973 is also the story of George M. Steinbrenner III.

V. I Want to Be a Part of It

George Steinbrenner, Michael Burke, and ten other investors bought the Yankees from CBS on January 3, 1973. CBS became the only owner in Yankee history to sell the team for less than it had paid. Steinbrenner, a graduate of Williams College and a for-mer college football assistant coach, was not a baseball man—he had made his money as a shipbuilder. When he took over the team, Steinbrenner stated, "We plan absentee ownership as far as running the Yankees is concerned. We're not going to pretend we're something we aren't. I'll stick to building ships.... I won't be active in the day-to-day operations of the club at all."[108] This would turn out not to be the case.

Steinbrenner would rebuild the team by signing free agents who had established themselves elsewhere, would see the team fade again, and then would rebuild the team once more. In 1976, the Yankees' first year in their renovated home, they won the American League pennant over the Kansas City Royals on Chris Chambliss' dramatic 9th-inning home run in the final game of the league championship series. The Yankees would lose the World Series that year, but would return to win the next two.

During the 1977 Series, Reggie Jackson would hit three home runs off three different Los Angeles Dodgers pitchers on three consecutive pitches in the sixth game. In his last nine at-bats during the Series, Jackson had five homers and six hits, scoring seven times.

When someone compared Jackson to the greatest Yankee ever, Jackson responded, "Babe Ruth was great. I'm just lucky." The following year, Bucky Dent hit a three-run homer over the Green Monster in the 163rd game of the regular season, sending the Red Sox home once more, while the Yankees were on their way to another world championship. Dent was not sure the ball would clear the Fenway fence. "I was around first base when I saw the umpire giving the home run sign, and it wasn't until I was rounding second base that I realized there wasn't a sound anywhere. Not a sound." The tragic death of star catcher Thurman Munson in an airplane crash in 1979 would help bring the Yankees' latest streak to a sad halt.[109]

Real estate in and around Yankee Stadium would be the subject of a variety of controversies at about this time. Some of that real estate was in the locker room, where Melissa Ludtke successfully sued to become the first female reporter admitted to the Yankees' clubhouse. Other real estate was in the seating area. A court in the state of Washington would decide in 1979 that the tradition of "Ladies' Night," at which female spectators were admitted to games for a reduced price, violated that state's constitution; the court made note of a similar unpublished administrative decision applicable to Yankee Stadium. Real estate near the ballpark also was the subject of legal controversy. Several New York City police officers owned shares in a Yankee Stadium concessionaire that sold pretzels outside the stadium. The Police Department argued that this constituted a conflict of interest, because the off-duty officers were doing business with a city agency, but the court disagreed.[110]

The Yankees hit their driest spell ever between 1979 and 1995, reaching the World Series only in the strike-truncated split season of 1981. The team finished below .500 in each of the four seasons beginning with 1989, reaching rock-bottom in 1990, when the Yankees lost 95 games and finished with the worst record in the American League. Ten men served as manager during this period, several of them more than once, with Steinbrenner becoming the most high-profile owner in the game, and possibly the least loved.[111]

The stadium also continued to be a subject of legal controversy during this period. The Yankees were sued by an architectural firm and a construction management firm, both of which alleged that they were not paid for performing pre-construction work in 1984 in connection with the proposed expansion of a banquet room and addition of 36 luxury suites and a glass-enclosed restaurant. The Yankees responded by denying the existence of a contract, with George Steinbrenner testifying that the two firms had known all along that they were working on an "at-risk" basis and that they would not be paid unless the Yankees proceeded with actual construction. After years of litigation, the architects received nearly half a million dollars, plus interest; resolution of the construction manager's claim is not reported. The Yankees also were involved in a dispute with an advertising company over the proper division of advertising revenues for signage within the stadium; once again, the final result is not reported.[112]

New York City performed structural repairs to the stadium in late 1982 and early 1983 to correct flaws remaining from the renovation in the 1970s. The Yankees began to worry that the facility would not be ready by Opening Day and announced that they would play their first three home games in Denver, a city that desperately wanted a baseball team at the time and had been courting the Yankees. This arrangement, however, violated the terms of the lease between the city of New York and the Yankees, which required the team to play all home games at Yankee Stadium through 2002. The city sought to enjoin this temporary relocation, and the court observed, "The Yankee pin stripes belong to New York like Central Park, like the Statue of Liberty, like the Metropolitan Museum of Art, like the Metropolitan Opera, like the Stock Exchange, like the lights of Broadway, etc. Collectively they are 'The Big Apple.'" The court granted the city's motion for a preliminary injunction, concluding, "Any loss represents a diminution of the quality of life here, a blow to the City's standing at the top, however narcissistic that perception may be.... Dare one whisper the dreaded words: 'The Denver Yankees.' No money damages can measure or assuage this kind of harm."[113]

Yankee Stadium continued to be the location of choice for major non-baseball events during the Steinbrenner era. One of the most significant of these occasions was the visit by Pope John Paul II in 1979. The Pope celebrated mass in the stadium before 80,000 cheering worshipers. He became the second leader of the Catholic Church to visit Yankee Stadium—Pope Paul VI had visited 14 years earlier, becoming the first pontiff to celebrate mass on American soil. Governor Hugh Carey of New York referred to the 1979 visit as "the World Series of religion." The archdiocese of New York paid the typical fees for use of the stadium, operating expenses, and police protection, to head off the objections raised in other cities that public funds should not be used for religious activities.[114]

The stadium would host a wide range of other celebrities in the coming years. In June, 1990, Nelson Mandela led an anti-apartheid rally at Yankee Stadium just weeks after his release from prison. Echoing President John F. Kennedy, Mandela stated, "You know who I am.... I am a Yankee." The crowd responded by shouting, "Amandla," Zulu for "power." The next day, Billy Joel performed the first of two sold out concerts at the stadium that were attended by over 100,000 fans. According to some reports, it was the first rock concert ever held at Yankee Stadium. Joel would be followed in coming years by acts including U2 and Pink Floyd. And in 1994, Yankee Stadium hosted Gay Games IV, which, according to its promoters, drew more athletes than the Olympics.[115]

The real estate on the playing field itself would generate some amusing litigation during the 1990s, with fans increasingly likely to enter the field of play during games. This was nothing new, of course—during a 1969 doubleheader against the Detroit Tigers, a fan ran to rightfield, chatted briefly with Al Kaline, and then snatched the cap from his head.[116] And a Cuban national named Antonio Pruna was arrested during game 5 of the 1958 World Series for running onto the field with a banner reading, "Castro's Invasion Frees Cuba." The Immigration and Naturalization Service later attempted to block Pruna's petition for naturalization, arguing that the incident proved he had a "meaningful association" with the Communist Party and thus should not be naturalized. The court decided that Pruna was eligible for naturalization because the crime had occurred more than five years before his petition and because Pruna had believed at the time that a triumph by Castro would lead to the restoration of representative and democratic government to Cuba.[117]

But a new standard in on-field chutzpah certainly was set in the middle of game 6 of the 1996 World Series, when Paul O'Grady, age 22, ran shirtless onto the field. On his chest was written "Howard Stern for President." His back read, "Guilliani [sic] kiss my...," with an arrow pointing to his buttocks. Millions watched as the game was interrupted for more than a minute. O'Grady was charged with third degree criminal trespass.[118]

The court seemed somewhat entertained by the case. "[O]ne can envisage a Yankees fan being enraptured by exhilaration—you crave more adrenaline, you run onto the Bronx diamond, you're in the eye of the most electrifying milieu in the universe!" In the judge's view, the prank would lead to disappointment, when "the adrenaline rush comes to a crash as you are seized, arrested, brought to the station house and—here's the most harrowing part—you miss the rest of the game." O'Grady noted that another trespasser during the same game had been sentenced to seven days of community service and argued that he was being threatened with harsher punishment because of his political views. The judge's amusement apparently had its limits, however, with the court responding that the writing on O'Grady's body showed that his act was more than just a spur-of-the-moment leap onto the field. Yankee Stadium's first political prisoner received a 30-day sentence.[119]

Sometimes, the team encourages fans to express their views. After George Steinbrenner fired manager Dallas Green in 1989, some spectators needed little encouragement, bringing banners to the park reading "George Must Go," "George, YOU Are the Problem," and "Fire George." Steinbrenner instructed workers at the stadium to confiscate the derogatory banners, while allowing other messages to remain. Two weeks later, the New York Civil Liberties Union wrote to the owner, arguing that selective confiscation violated fans' First Amendment rights. Steinbrenner responded by holding a "Banner Night," at which banners—including some critical of him—were displayed at the stadium. On another occasion, stadium security officials removed a fan for magnanimously suggesting to a member of the visiting team that he should return to Cuba.[120]

The Stadium Club also was the subject of at least one reported lawsuit, when V. Whitney Joseph, an African-American woman, was denied access because she was wearing a tank-top shirt. Joseph returned to her car, changed into a T-shirt, and was admitted to the club. Although her admission pass expressly prohibited tank tops, Joseph observed non-minority patrons in the club wearing tank tops and other clothing prohibited under the club's published rules. The Yankees sought summary judgment, arguing that she could not have been the victim of discrimination if the club admitted her, but the judge allowed the claim to proceed. "Ms. Joseph was required to satisfy a condition that Caucasians allegedly did not have to meet. The fact that Ms. Joseph ultimately complied with the condition does not eliminate the harm from the initial refusal to admit her to the club." No resolution of the case has been published to date.[121]

Yankee Stadium is not immune from routine landlord-tenant disputes. The Yankees are required to pay the city a percentage of their gross receipts, less certain deductions, as part of their rent. The New York City Comptroller audited the team's books in 2002 and determined that the Yankees had underpaid $367,000 in rent during a four-year period as a result of underreporting their revenues and overstating their credits. The disagreement focused largely on the team's treatment of revenue sharing payments, rained-out and cancelled games, insurance premiums, scorecards, and yearbooks, and also clarified the future treatment of maintenance expenses. The Yankees also disputed the real property tax appraisal on the team's training complex in Tampa, and saw the appraisal on the facility reduced from $5 million to $1 million.[122]

While these legal events were progressing, the team continued to play major league baseball, and beginning in 1996, the Yankees' fortunes took a decided turn for the better. The Yankees won the World Series in 1996, then again in 1998, 1999, and 2000, and took a lead into the bottom of the ninth inning of the seventh game in 2001 before losing to the Arizona Diamondbacks. At one point during this stretch, the Yankees won 14 straight World Series games.

David Wells pitched only the second perfect game ever in Yankee Stadium, on May 17, 1998. Coincidentally, Wells attended the same San Diego high school as Don Larsen, who had pitched the first one, 42 years earlier. In the seventh inning, Yankee teammate David Cone approached Wells and "told him it was time to break out the knuckleball," helping to relieve some of the tension in the dugout. After the game, comedian Billy

Crystal walked into the clubhouse, approached Wells, and said, "I got here late, what happened?" The following year, on Yogi Berra Day, Larsen threw the ceremonial first pitch to Berra, who then handed his glove to Yankee catcher Joe Girardi. Cone proceeded to toss a perfect game of his own into that glove, throwing only 88 pitches—68 strikes and a remarkable 20 balls.[123]

Yankee Stadium also marked one of the saddest days in the nation's history on September 23, 2001, when thousands of mourners, and millions more at home, participated in interfaith religious services to remember those lost in the attacks on the World Trade Center less than two weeks earlier. A diverse crowd attended "A Prayer for America," including "nuns, imams, ministers, women holding pictures of missing firefighters, mothers cradling babies, small children waving flags, construction workers in hard hats, teenagers in American flag do-rags, Sikhs in turbans, [and] men holding roses." The Red Cross distributed flags and tissue packets. Mayor Rudolph Giuliani promised, "To those who say our city will never be the same, I say, you are right. It will be better." A few weeks later, President George W. Bush—a former co-owner of the Texas Rangers—threw out the first pitch at Game 3 of the 2001 World Series at Yankee Stadium, amid unprecedented security.[124]

VI. It's Up to You, New York

Construction work at a real estate development as large as Yankee Stadium never ends, with the 1970s renovations themselves now more than a quarter-century old. These renovations spawned some additional corrective work soon afterwards, but the renovated stadium has since begun to show its age.[125] On April 13, 1998, just hours before a game was to begin, a 500-pound concrete-and-steel beam came loose from the bottom of the upper deck and crashed into the seats below. A coach for the California Angels who witnessed the event instinctively thought it had been caused by an earthquake, but apparently it was just old age. No one was injured, and the city postponed several games so that it would have time to perform a thorough inspection of the facility. The Yankees once again found themselves playing at Shea Stadium.[126]

The incident sparked different reactions in different New Yorkers. Mayor Rudolph Giuliani, realizing just how much worse the accident could have been, remarked, "If someone were sitting there at the time that the beam came down, that person would now be dead." A journeyman infielder named Dale Sveum, whose first appearance in the starting lineup as a Yankee was delayed as a result, noted, "That's my career in a nutshell right there, baby." Sidewalk souvlaki vendor Joseph Michails complained, "I have to throw out 30 to 40 pounds of cooked meat." Yankees' personnel sardonically speculated that owner George Steinbrenner, who had been campaigning for a new stadium, had loosened the beam's bolts himself. The following week, Yankee Stadium spent its 75th birthday closed, under scaffolding.[127]

New York has had to spend other money on Yankee Stadium. The city entered into a consent decree resulting from a dispute over the accessibility of the stadium to disabled patrons. Under this decree, the city committed to a significant increase in the number of wheelchair-accessible seats at the stadium, and agreed that these seats will have companion seating available, will be located throughout the stadium, and mostly will be available at the three lowest price levels. The city also promised to modify many physical features of the stadium, including "exterior and interior routes, signs, restrooms, telephones, drinking fountains, concession areas, elevators, ticket windows, restaurants, luxury suites, and press areas," and agreed to pay a civil penalty and make charitable contributions.[128]

Falling beams are one illustration of a larger problem. Yankee Stadium is old, and another round of major renovations may be prohibitively expensive. George Steinbrenner has been critical of both the stadium and its location and has indicated that he would prefer for the team to play in a new home on Manhattan's West Side, a view that former Mayor Giuliani appeared to share. The two men perhaps can take some consolation from a study published in the *Annals of Emergency Medicine*, which concluded that "[t]he distribution of 25,000 wooden baseball bats to attendees at Yankee Stadium [on Bat Day] did not increase the incidence of bat-related trauma in the Bronx and northern Manhattan,"[129] but there can be little dispute that the Bronx is struggling. Addressing other social needs in the neighborhood surrounding Yankee Stadium and in the city as a whole will require enormous public expenditures. In an all too typical case, a woman who was raped in the stairwell of her publicly-owned apartment building sued the New York City Housing Authority for negligence in failing to secure the building adequately. Her attorney's summation highlighted "the Housing Authority's treatment of 'poor people'" and asked the jury "to contrast the cost of installing locks with the cost of building a new Yankee Stadium."[130]

Yankee Stadium is expensive to maintain and would be even more expensive to replace. Just as in the 1970s, citizens and politicians are asking whether the taxpayers of the city should be subsidizing a successful private business. Author Neil Sullivan observes, "People who milk public assistance have been disdained from the time the programs were first created, and they now face serious restructuring of many of those same programs to protect the treasury from unwarranted claims."[131] This same argument, he continues, should apply to more affluent recipients of public largesse: "At the very point that our patience is exhausted at the prospect of giving people money that they do not deserve, we continue to lavish hard-earned money on sports owners so that they can continue to disguise their hobbies as businesses and run them in thoroughly reckless ways."[132] Sullivan reaches "the inevitable conclusion...that schoolchildren subsidize professional athletes and owners by playing under substandard conditions while professional playgrounds are maintained to the highest standards."[133]

In one of his final acts as mayor, Rudolph Giuliani entered into a tentative deal with the Yankees and the Mets to build two stadiums with retractable domes, adjacent to the sites of the two existing stadiums, for a combined cost of $1.6 billion. Each team would sign a 35-year lease. Although the financial commitments required of the two teams would be the largest ever by baseball franchises, the city's contribution would be among the largest public expenditures ever made for baseball stadiums. Mayor-elect Michael Bloomberg did not attend Giuliani's press conference and indicated that stadium-building would not be one of his first priorities. The following week, the new mayor backed away from his predecessor's commitment and restated his reservations. Mayor Bloomberg noted, "At the moment, everybody understands that given the lack of housing, given the lack of school space, given the deficit in the operating budget, it is just not practical this year to go and build stadiums."[134] The disagreement between the two mayors illustrates the divided feelings many New Yorkers share about the house that Ruth built. It will be up to the people of New York to determine the future of that house.

Despite their years of success at Yankee Stadium, the Yankees have been seeking a new, more lucrative stadium. Photo by Chris Trotman, © Duomo/CORBIS.

Greener Pastures

by Rebecca M. Bratspies[*]

To make anything last, there's got to be more
than a grand slam.
There has to be a good coach
to draw the line-up and good men
already on base.[1]

The New Jersey Yankees?
That doesn't sound right.
You can't have the house that the Babe built
in Secaucus[2]

The New York Yankees are the most famous and most successful baseball franchise in history. Since 1921, the Yankees have made 41 playoff appearances, winning 38 pennants and 26 world series. To New York City, the Bronx Bombers are much more than a successful sports team—they symbolize the brash vitality of the City itself. Despite their icon status, the Yankees perennially hint that they might leave the Bronx, and New York, unless the City antes up for a new, publically-financed baseball stadium. The Yankees claim that their existing stadium, built in the early part of the 20th century, has serious inadequacies, namely its location in a 'dangerous' neighborhood, its lack of parking and transportation links, and its lack of luxury boxes.

To a city still reeling (nearly fifty years later!) from the loss of the Dodgers, the possibility that the Yankees might move—especially, heaven forbid to New Jersey—is the stuff of nightmares. While the prospect of a move remains remote, it does raise some interesting legal questions. Could New York prevent a move? Would the Yankees still be the same team if they left the Bronx? Could they be the New Jersey Bombers? Or for that matter, if the Yankees left New York, would they even be entitled to use the name Yankees, and to wear their famous pinstripes?

I. Yankees' Relocation Plans through the Decades

For the first few years of their existence, the Yankees—then called the Orioles—played in Baltimore. It was only in 1913 that the Yankees moved to the Bronx and became the Yankees we all know and love (or hate depending on your team).[3] In 1923, the Yankees moved to their present location and began playing in Yankee Stadium—the House that Ruth Built; the Cathedral of Baseball.

By the early 1970s, the Cathedral had begun to show its age. The fifty-year old stadium was decaying and outmoded, and the Yankees began hinting about a move to New Jersey. Even though the City was on the verge of bankruptcy in those years, Mayor John Lindsay arranged for New York City to purchase and refurbish Yankee stadium. The multi-year, multi-million dollar renovation modernized the stadium by removing most of its old facade, clearing view-obstructing interior columns, and adding some luxury suites.

Yankees threats to leave New York City resurfaced in the 1980s. In 1983, the Yankees attempted to play some of their home games, including the opening series, in Denver, Colorado. New York promptly sued in state court and won an injunction prohibiting the Yankees from playing any home games in Denver. Waxing poetic, Judge Richard Lane described the Yankees as 'belong[ing] to New York like Central Park, like the Statue of Liberty, like the Metropolitan Museum of Art, like the Metropolitan Opera, like the Stock Exchange, like the lights of Broadway, etc. Collectively they are "The Big Apple."'[4] More prosaically, Judge Lane noted that the Yankees' lease agreement with the City clearly required that all home games be played in Yankee Stadium through the year 2002. Building on precedent established in the mid-1970s when the Jets tried to play some of their home games in New Jersey, Judge Lane ruled that the Yankees' plan to play their opening home games in Denver would be a clear violation of their lease agreement with the City.

In *New York City v. New York Jets Football Club, Inc*, Justice Harold Baer had written a paean to professional sports as a public good 'inextricably entwined with the vital public interest....'[5] By that reasoning, Judge Baer concluded that any home games not played in the City resulted in 'injury to the welfare, recreation, prestige, prosperity and trade and commerce of the people of the City.'[6] Although he penned these powerful words about the people's interest, Justice Baer ultimately rested his Jets ruling entirely on the terms of the contracts between New York and the Jets. Similarly, Judge Lane based his Yankees ruling not on high-flying rhetoric about the essence of the 'Big Apple,' but on the language of the lease agreement between the City and the Yankees.

In 1996, after winning their 22nd World Series, the Yankees again raised the prospect of moving. This time, their putative destination was closer to home. The Yankees began exploring a move to New Jersey's Meadowlands sports complex after their Bronx lease expired in 2002. A 1998 structural accident at the Stadium helped fuel the drive for a new stadium, with New Jersey's governor contacting the Yankees about a possible move. New Jersey even went so far as to give the Yankees a proposal for a baseball-only stadium near the Meadowlands.

In response to this new threat, New York worked with Yankees owner George Steinbrenner to study four possible New York sites as a future home for the Yankees. The most promising of these sites was located on Manhattan's West Side, just south of the Javits Convention Center. The City proposed building a domed, multi-purpose stadium for the Yankees and other, unspecified professional sports teams (generally understood to be the Jets who had expressed an interest in returning to New York). Such a stadium also had the potential to serve double duty as a concert hall for rock bands, and figured prominently in plans to bring the Olympic Games to New York in 2012.

Mayor Giuliani made it clear that he would not be 'the mayor who lost the Yankees.' Keeping the Yankees in New York was therefore a priority for his administration, and he began negotiations to build the Yankees a new stadium. Giuliani strongly backed the

Manhattan stadium plan, even going so far as to block a ballot initiative that would have prohibited New York City from spending public funds to construct a new Yankees' stadium in Manhattan.[7]

Unfortunately for the Mayor, New York's response to the prospect of the Manhattan Yankees was immediate and angry. Opinion was, and still is, solidly behind keeping the Yankees in the Bronx.[8] Bronx residents were worried about the stigma and economic costs of losing the Yankees, and Manhattanites opposed anything that would further clog their traffic-snarled streets. Both groups were united, however, in opposing any move to New Jersey. Bronx Borough President Fernando Ferrer not only led the fight against the Manhattan plan but also threatened to challenge baseball's antitrust exemption if the Yankees moved across the Hudson.

The tabloid press had a field day with the Yankee Stadium question,[9] railing against the Manhattan plan as corporate welfare in its worst form. In editorial after editorial, New York papers depicted the Yankees as a vital anchor for urban renewal in the South Bronx and as a part of the local history. Political figures, from Governor Pataki to then-candidate Hillary Clinton, rushed to register their opposition to a Yankees move from the Bronx. Since Governor Pataki directs the Metropolitan Transit Authority, owner of most of the land needed for the proposed Manhattan stadium, his opposition doomed the plan. Democratic leader Geraldine Ferraro echoed a chorus of New York voices when she proclaimed that: '[t]he Stadium is not only Yankee Stadium, it is part of the Bronx. The Bronx is part of the stadium.'[10]

New York even went so far as to consider using the power of eminent domain to prevent the Yankees from leaving New York. In 1997, the New York legislature considered establishing a New York Sports Facilities Authority with the power to condemn professional sports franchises in order to keep them in the state.[11] Since that time, similar provisions have been discussed in virtually every legislative session.

Bronx backers had more than mere outrage to vent—they also had ready answers to the primary Yankee complaints. Refurbishing the existing stadium and improving the existing transportation links (which already include three subway lines) would cost much less than a new stadium. Since the taxpayers were being called on to bear the lion's share of a new stadium, cost was a primary consideration. Moreover, despite its alleged inadequacies, Yankee stadium continued to attract millions of visitors each year, putting Yankee attendance at or near the top almost every year since 1970.[12] Even without a new, state-of-the-art stadium, the Yankees have been the most profitable and most successful baseball franchise in history, with the largest payroll in Major League Baseball.

Bowing to the tide of public opinion, Mayor Giuliani and Yankees owner George Steinbrenner began negotiating for a new Yankee Stadium in the Bronx. For a brief moment, it looked as though the Yankees would finally abandon their "cathedral of baseball" for a new stadium. Giuliani clearly identified a stadium deal as one of his highest priorities in the last year of his administration. Indeed, on September 10, 2001, Giuliani announced that a stadium deal was likely by the end of the year. The terrorist attacks of September 11, 2001 changed all that. New York suddenly had far more pressing issues to attend to, and stadiums were no longer front page news.

Nevertheless, three days before he left office, Giuliani signed a non-binding agreement with the Yankees proposing an $800 million Yankee Stadium to be built by 2007. The agreement called for the new ballpark to be built on parkland adjacent to Yankee Stadium in the Bronx, with the City funding half the construction costs. Included in this agreement were some binding amendments to the Yankees' current 30 year lease on Yankee Stadium (which had been due to expire in 2002). In exchange for renewing their lease until 2007, the Yankees received lease concessions of about $25 million, and a clause allowing them to opt out of the lease on 60 days' notice if the team "reasonably determines...that [the city] does not intend to proceed with" building a new Yankee Stadium. The Mets got a similar deal.

Upon taking office, Mayor Michael Bloomberg promptly shelved the new stadium plans. To wide applause, Bloomberg indicated that New York City had bigger things to worry about, and he made it clear that the City could ill-afford to build baseball stadiums under current circumstances.

II. City Hopping by Professional Sports Teams

The Yankees are not alone in seeking (or in at least threatening to seek) greener pastures. In the past few years, a rash of professional franchise relocations has sent shock waves through communities around the nation. Los Angeles was abandoned by both its football teams when the Rams moved to St. Louis and the Raiders moved back to Oakland. The Houston Oilers similarly abandoned Houston for Nashville and became the Tennessee Titans. In the NHL, the Winnipeg Jets relocated to Phoenix and became the Coyotes, the Minnesota North Stars became the Dallas Stars, and the Quebec Nordiques moved to Colorado and won the Stanley Cup as the Colorado Avalanche.[13] And most notorious of all are the NFL machinations that ultimately resulted in Jim Irsay's Colts abandoning Baltimore for Indianapolis and Art Modell's Browns leaving Cleveland to become the Baltimore Ravens.[14]

By contrast, in the past thirty years, Major League Baseball has not permitted a single franchise to move. In fact, Major League Baseball's policy prohibits franchise movements unless a local community has demonstrated over a sustained period that it cannot or will not support a franchise.[15] Even under those circumstances, before any move can occur, the relocating team needs the approval of two-thirds of the teams in its league and half the teams in the other league. According to Major League Baseball, it is these restrictions, made possible by baseball's antitrust exemption, that have preserved baseball from the city-hopping endemic to other professional sports.[16]

While it is true that no baseball team has relocated since 1972, team after team has used the threat of a move to extract concessions from its home city. Most recently, the Houston Astros, the Milwaukee Brewers and the Pittsburgh Pirates have all threatened to move unless their cities built new stadiums.[17] The Chicago White Sox almost moved to Tampa Bay before new Comiskey Park opened.[18] Only the opposition of the League, after owner Bob Lurie had agreed to the deal, prevented the San Francisco Giants from moving to Tampa.[19] There is talk that the Montreal Expos may break the non-relocation trend by moving to Virginia for the 2003 season. The team's former limited partners have promised to mount a court challenge to such a move, and a Virginia team would also face Baltimore Orioles owner Pete Angelos' opposition.

III. Would New York Be Able to Prevent a Move?

The Yankees' lease on Yankee Stadium requires the team to play all its home games in the Bronx. In the end, however, contracts are a slender reed for cities to rely upon. As the Jets case indicates, contract language can only keep a team in place for the duration of the contract. Stymied in 1977, the Jets simply waited until 1983, when their lease with the City ended, and then moved to the Meadowlands. Using virtually identical contract-based reasoning, a Minnesota court entered an injunction prohibiting Major League Baseball from eliminating the Twins franchise during the 2002 season. The court based its decision on the Twins' lease agreement, which required the team to play in the Hubert H. Humphrey Metrodome.[20] The injunction lasted only for the year left on the team's lease. Thus, when the lease ended after the 2002 season, Minneapolis would have had no further leverage to keep the Twins. Fortunately for Minneapolis, the 2002 collective bargaining agreement guarantees that no teams will be eliminated until at least 2006, thus postponing the issue.

A. The Power of Eminent Domain

Civic institution or no, professional team after professional team has abandoned New York City for greener pastures. The Dodgers and the (baseball) Giants moved to California, the Jets, the (football) Giants and the Nets all moved to New Jersey. And, with the prospects for a new, publicly financed stadium dim, the Yankees will be free to leave New York City without violating their lease agreement. With each team move, calls resurface for New York to use its power of eminent domain to keep sports teams in place.

Eminent domain is the government's power to seize private property for public use, so long as it pays just compensation. Although eminent domain has traditionally been invoked to seize realty, it is at least theoretically possible to use this power to condemn a sports franchise like the Yankees. The contemporary understanding of what constituted 'public use' for purposes of eminent domain is a liberal one—anything that can reasonably be described as conveying a public advantage will suffice. Indeed, under the 'public use' requirement, cities have been able to justify the condemnation of private land to build sports stadiums. In light of this fact, coupled with the vision of professional sports as a public good frequently expressed in judicial opinions in New York, there is no reason to believe that a sports franchise would not satisfy this requirement.

In the mid-1990s, New York State Assemblyman Richard Brodsky, a Democrat from Westchester, proposed the Sport's Fan Protection Act, which would have created a state-owned Sport Authority to seize teams rather than see them move out of state. Fernando Ferrer and Ruth Messinger, the Bronx and Manhattan Borough Presidents respectively, along with the editorial board of the New York Daily News, enthusiastically endorsed this idea.

Were New York to succeed in exercising its powers of eminent domain to seize the Yankees, Mr. Steinbrenner would be entitled to compensation for the fair market value of the team. The team would then be owned by New York City, or more likely, sold to new owners who would commit to keeping the team in New York. The question remains, however, of whether New York could succeed in exercising its power of eminent domain under these circumstances.

B. Would Eminent Domain Work?

Unfortunately for New York City, eminent domain has not played well in the sports team arena. Several cities have attempted, without success, to use their powers of eminent domain to prevent sports teams from moving.[21] Though not many courts have considered the question, the results have been consistently unfavorable for governments. The courts have concluded that there is no public power to order the team to stay in a city, even though the move will cause the 'injury to the recreation, prestige and prosperity of the people' that so concerned Judge Baer in the Jets case. The courts have not, however, articulated a coherent theory as to why eminent domain is inappropriate. In 1980, Oakland's attempt to use its power of eminent domain to prevent the Raiders from moving to Los Angeles was thrown out on the ground that it unconstitutionally interfered with interstate commerce. In particular, the court concluded that the city's action would pervade the entire League and would disrupt the balance of economic bargaining on stadium leases throughout the nation.

In 1984, Baltimore similarly attempted to use eminent domain to condemn the Baltimore Colts. Jim Irsay signed a 20-year lease to play the Colts' home games in Indianapolis' "Hoosier Dome," and the team immediately fled the jurisdiction under cover of night. The City of Baltimore filed a Maryland state court action in a futile attempt to acquire the Colts by eminent domain.[22] After the Colts removed the case to federal court, Judge Walter Black dismissed the action on the ground that the Colts were no longer within Baltimore's jurisdiction. Therefore, Judge Black concluded that Baltimore had no eminent domain powers to exercise over the Colts. The City lost summarily, despite the fact that this move, which so outraged the citizens of Baltimore, was undertaken secretly and suddenly for the specific purpose of defeating the state's power of eminent domain.

Baltimore and Oakland should be an object lesson for New York. The moral is that although eminent domain can, in principle, apply to a sports franchise, it would be extremely difficult to successfully condemn one. Indeed, there is no reason to believe that New York would be more successful than Baltimore or Oakland if it attempted to use eminent domain powers to condemn the Yankees. That said, New York's Fan Protection Act was reintroduced in the 2001–2002 legislative session. Section 7(12) of this Act provided: 'If a sports event, facility, or franchise, currently residing in New York, takes action to move from the state, the authority shall condemn such event, facility or franchise to insure that organization's or activity's continued presence in New York.'[23] Were the Yankees to take concrete steps toward moving, this Act would undoubtably be passed by the legislature. Yankees' owner George Steinbrenner would then find himself embroiled in a lengthy and expensive court battle challenging the validity of the Act.

IV. Could Major League Baseball
Keep the Yankees in New York?

Under Major League Baseball rules, owners are free to move their franchises within their own market. The Yankees' market, which they share with the Mets, consists of the

City of New York; Nassau, Suffolk, Rockland and Westchester Counties in New York; Bergen, Hudson, Essex and Union Counties in New Jersey; and that portion of Fairfield County in Connecticut located south of Interstate 84 and west of Route 58.[24] The Meadowlands is thus within the Yankees' market, and the Yankees could move to that New Jersey venue without the permission of Major League Baseball. Even if Major League Baseball were adamantly opposed to such a move, it would have no power to prevent it.

Any attempt by the Yankees to move outside their existing market, for example a move to Colorado or Timbuktu, would require the approval of the other owners. The National League Constitution and the Rules of the National League of Professional Baseball Clubs require three-fourths approval from all fourteen National League teams and majority approval from the fourteen American League clubs before a National League team may be sold, transferred, or change its location. The American League has similar requirements. The Leagues have rejected sales and moves of teams in the past (notably the proposed sales of the Astros to a North Virginia investors group, and of the Giants to a Florida group).

While such activity in any other field of business (including other professional sports)[25] would raise antitrust questions, an unbroken line of United States Supreme Court decisions have found that federal antitrust laws do not apply to the "business of baseball".[26] As a result of these cases, baseball was for many years considered exempt from the antitrust laws. This exemption permitted the owners to take actions intended to keep the number of teams low, and thus to keep team value high; behavior that would otherwise be illegal and costly (because antitrust violations carry the penalty of trebled damages). In 1998, Congress passed the Curt Flood Act, which clarified that federal antitrust laws applied to the relationships between major league baseball owners, teams and players. The Act did not resolve the question of whether franchise relocations were similarly subject to federal antitrust laws.

Even before passage of the Flood Act, owner attempts to prevent franchise relocations had raised significant questions about whether baseball's antitrust exemption extended to actions taken to prevent team relocations. In 1993, a group of investors offered to buy the San Francisco Giants. These investors intended to move the team to Tampa Bay, Florida. Giants owner Bob Lurie signed a letter of intent with the investors, but Major League Baseball forced Lurie to turn down the offer and keep the Giants in San Francisco. The investors sued in federal court, claiming that the owners' interference with their purchase was an unlawful and anti-competitive interference with commerce in violation of the Sherman Antitrust Act.[27] Florida's Attorney General brought an identical Florida lawsuit.[28] Major League Baseball moved to dismiss both suits on the ground that baseball was exempt from the antitrust laws.

Both courts rejected this reliance on an antitrust exemption, concluding instead that the Supreme Court had limited baseball's antitrust exemption to the reserve system. As these courts viewed baseball's antitrust exemption, all other baseball conduct would be judged by the normal antitrust standards that prohibit unreasonable restraints on trade.

To be "unreasonable," a restraint on trade must have more anti-competitive effects than legitimate business justification. If the owners' decision to reject a franchise move were viewed as an attempt to control the supply of baseball teams, and to thereby increase the value of owning a team, the conduct might well be considered anti-competitive, and therefore an unreasonable restraint on trade that violated the antitrust laws.

It is important to understand what was and was not decided in the Giants' cases. In both cases, Major League Baseball's preliminary motion to dismiss the cause of action was rejected. The courts did not decide the merits of the cases but instead concluded only that if Major League owners acted in concert to increase the price of teams and to control the terms of sale, they would have engaged in anti-competitive behavior. Rather than risk losing at trial or on appeal, Major League Baseball settled both lawsuits. Tampa Bay ultimately got an expansion team, the Tampa Bay Devil Rays for the 1998 season.

These decisions adopted a narrow view of baseball's traditional antitrust exemption, bringing baseball's status more in line with other professional sports with regard to team relocation. In *Los Angeles Memorial Coliseum Comm'n v. National Football League*,[29] for example, the NFL's then-existing restrictions on franchise relocation (which were identical to those in Major League Baseball) were found to be an unreasonable restraint of trade. *Sullivan v. National Football League* reached a similar result on the question of franchise ownership.[30]

It is entirely possible that the next court will determine that Major League Baseball's restrictions on franchise relocation are an anti-competitive and illegal restraint of trade. Any court adopting this view would not look favorably on an attempt by Major League Baseball to prevent a Yankees move. However, it is equally possible that the court will reach a contrary result. Though more courts have interpreted baseball's antitrust exemption broadly than have interpreted it narrowly, there is no judicial consensus on this point.[31] That means there is no clear, agreed-upon application of federal antitrust standards to baseball team relocations. Without clear standards, it would be impossible to predict how the litigation, which would surely result from any Major League Baseball attempt to block a Yankees' move, would ultimately be resolved. In the law, uncertainty is expensive; it almost guarantees a lawsuit. Because of the burdensome cost of defending antitrust litigation, and the real possibility of losing, Major League Baseball would probably be reluctant to oppose any Yankees move.

In 2002, Minnesota's two Senators sponsored legislation to clarify that Major League Baseball's antitrust status does not differ from other professional sports leagues with regard to franchise elimination or relocation. Although not enacted into law, the bill represented a growing sentiment, and any litigation surrounding a Yankees move would undoubtably revive that or similar legislation.

V. Could They Still Be the Yankees?

If the Yankees abandoned New York City for New Jersey, the City might pressure the team to abandon the name New York Yankees as well. At the very least, New York City might try to force the Yankees to drop the 'New York' appellation. Of course both the Jets and the Giants play in New Jersey while still using the name New York. Despite some lingering bitterness from those team moves, New York has never officially tried to make the teams change their designation to New Jersey. In fact, when the Giants put the NY logo back on their helmets in 2000, for the first time in more than a decade, it was New Jerseyans who objected, not New Yorkers. If the Yankees moved across the Hudson, however, New York politicians would probably be inclined to force the issue. Indeed, Peter Vallone, former City Council Speaker, has already intimated as much.

New Jersey would likely bring similar pressure to bear. As Richard Aregood, editorial-page editor for the Newark *Star Ledger,* wryly suggested, "For Steinbrenner to even begin negotiations for a new stadium out here he'd have to agree to put New Jersey on the caps."[32] Such a requirement would be in tune with recent New Jersey events. When the NHL's Colorado Rockies moved from Denver to New Jersey, for example, New Jersey's willingness to build the team a new arena was explicitly conditioned on the Rockies changing their name to something 'more New Jersey-ish.' Thus, the Rockies became the New Jersey Devils (after the famous "New Jersey Swamp Devil"). Similarly, when the New York Nets (who had played on Long Island) moved to New Jersey, they kept the name Nets but dropped New York, becoming instead the New Jersey Nets. (The Yankees and Nets later merged to form YankeeNets and now own the Devils as well.) In much the same way New Jersey demanded that the Devils take a name evocative of New Jersey, the state would undoubtably pressure the Yankees to drop the appellation New York. So, there would be pressure from both sides to drop New York from the Yankees name.

Whatever moral suasion the City mustered might well be persuasive, and New Jersey might be able to wring a name change concession out of a stadium deal. Otherwise, the City would have no legal basis for forcing the Yankees to drop New York from their name. The Yankees have been using the name "New York Yankees" since 1921, and have registered a federal trademark in that name. Under trademark law, the name is the property of the Yankees, not of the City of New York. Thus, if the Yankees moved to New Jersey, they would be free to continue calling themselves the New York Yankees. Even if the Yankees changed their name to the New Jersey Yankees, they would still own the New York Yankees trademark and could use it as they chose. More significantly, even if the Yankees abandoned their name entirely and became the New Jersey Mutants, they would still be able to prevent any other team from using the name.

This very situation occurred in Baltimore. After his midnight flight to Indiana, Irsay renamed his team the Indianapolis Colts. Nine years later, the Canadian Football League decided to award Baltimore an expansion CFL franchise. In response to overwhelming public support, the owner James Speros named his team the Baltimore CFL Colts. Irsay sued, claiming that the use of the name Colts infringed on the Indianapolis Colts' trademark.

Ruling for the Indianapolis Colts, Judge Posner of the Sixth Circuit Court of Appeals concluded that there would be a high likelihood of confusion were the Baltimore CFL Colts permitted to adopt that name. The court concluded that the new Baltimore CFL Colts were attempting to capitalize on the resonance of the Baltimore Colts name. However, that resonance, along with the name itself was the property of the Indianapolis Colts.[33]

The Colts had fled under cover of night. Eleven years later, in a move just as shocking, Cleveland Browns owner Art Modell, who had been on record as promising never to move his Browns, announced that he had signed an agreement to move his team to Baltimore. It was hard to overlook the symmetry: Baltimore got the Browns (who became the Ravens) the same way it lost the Colts (and only after a threatened antitrust suit persuaded the league to approve the move). Before it would give Modell permission to move the Browns to Baltimore, the NFL required Modell to rename his team so that when Cleveland got an expansion team, they could be called the Browns and use Orange and Brown as their colors.

The lawsuits that grew from Art Modell's abandonment of Cleveland set off a wave of highly publicized congressional hearings.[34] The consensus among our elected representatives was that it would not be possible to prohibit team moves, but that the law could require any team that abandoned its home city to leave the team's name and colors behind. For example, the Fan Freedom and Community Protection Act, sponsored by Cleveland Rep. Martin Hoke would not have forbid a team from moving from its home city, but would have required that the team give 180 days notice, and leave its name behind. The Bill would also have all but guaranteed the jilted city a new team. Though never enacted into law, a highly publicized and acrimonious team move, as a Yankees' move from New York would certainly be, would undoubtably revive legislative attention.

Unless and until such legislation is enacted, however, were the Yankees to move to Timbuktu and play there as the Timbuktu Yankees, New York City would not be able to attract another major league team and call it the Yankees. Moreover, were the Yankees to move to New Jersey, they, along with the Mets, would have the power to block a new team from moving to the Bronx, which is 'their market' under Major League Baseball's territorial-rights rule.

This rule has also come under attack as anti-competitive. Absent baseball's antitrust exemption, the owner of an existing team could not lawfully prevent another team from being moved to a nearby city, where it might "compete in its market." If the Yankees moved and invoked this rule, the resulting howls of protest might well prompt congressional action to remove or limit baseball's antitrust exemption. New York is, after all, the city that has still not forgiven the Dodgers for leaving. Indeed, trial testimony in a 1993 trademark infringement case brought by the Los Angeles Dodgers against a New York bar called the Brooklyn Dodger, made it abundantly clear that New Yorkers were "well aware of Los Angeles' now infamous abandonment of the Borough of Brooklyn and— to the third generation since then—remain bitter about it."[35]

VI. Conclusion

What will ultimately happen to the shelved plans for a new Yankee Stadium is anybody's guess. The stadium might never be built. If the Yankees decided to relocate because New York will not build them a new stadium, there is little anyone could do to stop them. New York City's eminent domain powers are of doubtful application, and Major League Baseball is unlikely to enter the fray on behalf of the City. That said, the Yankees are unlikely to abandon New York.

There is no way the Yankees could move to New Jersey without suffering radical decreases in home game attendance. It stretches credulity to think that fans from the five boroughs, let alone Westchester, Long Island and Connecticut, would brave rush hour traffic to the Meadowlands for the 50 weeknight home games. The typical weeknight game begins at 7:05 and sometimes lasts more than three hours. The ensuing midnight traffic jams at the tunnels and bridges leading from New Jersey back to New York would be nightmarish.

Weekday games attendance would suffer even more than the night games. Each baseball season, the Yankees play 7–10 weekday home games that start around 1:00 in the afternoon. While diehard fans will sneak from their workplaces to Yankee Stadium, sneaking to the Meadowlands is a much more daunting prospect. For one thing, there are no subways or trains to the Meadowlands, and then there is the 'returning to New York during rush hour' issue. New Jersey does not have the population base to replace this legion of New York-based fans, especially without cutting into the Phillies' market.

Moreover, any move would impose other significant financial costs for the Yankees. Popular opinion in New Jersey is solidly against using any public funds to build the Yankees a new stadium.[36] If the Yankees wanted to pay for their own stadium, they could do that in New York just as easily as in New Jersey.

Moves farther afield are even less probable. The specters of the Dodgers and Giants hang over Yankees' threats to relocate, but times have changed since the 1950s. When the Dodgers moved to Los Angeles, it was a huge and growing metropolis with no baseball team. That was then, this is now. The plain truth is that today there are no comparable untapped baseball markets left for Steinbrenner's team. He would be leaving the richest television and cable market in the country for one that would produce less than half the revenues. As a result, the Yankees could not move to another market without taking a huge cut in gross revenues.

All these factors together suggest that threats to move the team are empty. While Yankee Stadium may well need refurbishing, New York City should take care of it not merely to keep the Yankees from leaving, but because Yankee Stadium is an icon of the City's history and a vibrant part of the City's present.

Cornering the Market:
The Yankees and the Interplay
of Labor and Antitrust Laws

by Ed Edmonds*

I. Introduction

The New York Yankees are, of course, the most successful single franchise in Major League Baseball history. They established this tradition in large measure because their ownership understood better than the competition how to acquire front office, managerial, and player talent. Being located in America's largest metropolitan area is significant to the Yankees' success. However, that fact alone is not enough to produce the sustained success of the franchise. For most of their history, the Yankees have been blessed with well-funded ownership that properly exploited the value of the team to increase revenue to sustain the acquisition of talent throughout the organization. The team has long exhibited a knack for outwitting and outmaneuvering other franchises. In no small measure, the Yankees have understood best how the business of baseball works and how the relationship of law to the business of baseball can be used advantageously.

The Yankees were established as an American League team in 1903 after the purchase and relocation of the Baltimore franchise to New York. For the next 50 years, the Yankees were the youngest of Major League Baseball's sixteen teams. Although the Yankees unsuccessfully struggled to reach the top during their first 18 years, the Manhattan-based team was busily establishing the foundation for their appearance in 37 World Series contests between 1921 and 2000.

The first great period of Yankee dominance began in 1921 and lasted until 1928. They played in six World Series during the Twenties and won three, causing a shift of city power across the Harlem River from John McGraw's Giants to a team housed in newly constructed Yankee Stadium. Without a doubt, the acquisition of Babe Ruth was the most significant factor in the creation of this dominance. The purchase of Ruth from the Boston Red Sox established a trend that the Yankees have used throughout their subsequent history to produce championship teams. Whenever it seemed necessary, the Yankees have been able to acquire an additional player by simply purchasing or trading with another Major League franchise.

During the seven years between 1929 and 1935, the Yankees won only the 1932 American League crown and World Series. They returned to the top in 1936 and won six pennants and World Series crowns through the 1943 season. During the span of 22 seasons between 1921 and 1943, the Yankees won 13 American League pennants and 9 World Series championships.

The second great period of Yankee dominance stretched from 1947 through 1964. During this 18-year stretch, the Yankees captured 15 pennants and 10 World Series. From 1949 until 1957, the three New York-based teams dominated Major League Baseball by garnering 15 of the 18 World Series spots. However, in 1958 the Giants and Dodgers moved to California, leaving only the Yankees in New York until the expansion Mets entered the market in 1962.

In November 1964, Columbia Broadcasting Network purchased 80% of the Yankees for $11.2 million. The Yankees struggled through this period of corporate ownership marked by the emergence of the Major League Baseball Players Association and the creation of free agency and salary arbitration. The Steinbrenner Era started in January 1973, when a limited partnership, headed by George M. Steinbrenner III as its managing general partner, purchased the Yankees from CBS for $10 million. Steinbrenner's teams appeared in four World Series between 1976 and 1981. The current period of Yankee dominance includes appearances in all but one of the World Series from 1996–2001. This current period is marked by the dramatic increase in value of the Yankees' media rights fees, allowing the team to greatly outspend the vast majority of other teams.

II. The Reserve Clause

For three-quarters of the twentieth century, the most significant factor in the labor relationship between management and players in Major League Baseball was the existence of the reserve clause. The United States Supreme Court decided a trilogy of cases[1] that created Major League Baseball's "Antitrust Exemption," and the reserve clause was central to all three decisions. The antitrust exemption perpetuated a system that provided ownership with great leverage over players who desired both more control over the team for which they would play and increased salaries.

Baseball's exemption from antitrust scrutiny was created in 1922 when the United States Supreme Court rendered its opinion in *Federal Baseball Club v. National League*.[2] Although the Yankees were not a central part of the litigation, the importance of the New York market was a significant factor. The Yankees figured prominently in the middle case, *Toolson v. New York Yankees, Inc*.[3] The Yankees were sued in *Toolson* by a career minor leaguer acquired from the Boston Red Sox. Toolson initiated his suit after the Yankees attempted to reassign him from Newark, their AAA farm team, to Binghamton in the Eastern League. The ownership of the Yankees by Columbia Broadcasting System was a factor in the early stages of the third and final case, *Flood v. Kuhn*.[4]

The reserve clause essentially bound a player to one particular Major League team and forbid that player from jumping to another team for a higher salary. National League owners, guided by Boston owner Arthur Soden, created the reserve clause on September 29, 1879.[5] Arguing that salaries were too high, the owners reached a secret agreement to protect five players from jumping to another member team for the 1880 season. The use of the reserve clause during the final twenty years of the 19th century assisted the National League in fighting off challenges from the Players League, Union

Association and the American Association to emerge near the end of the decade as the only major league.

III. The Creation of the American League

The American League was born in 1900, under the leadership of Ban Johnson, the president of the minor league Western League.[6] When the established National League refused to recognize Johnson's league, the owners declared open war on the older league by refusing to recognize the reserve clauses of National League teams and began to raid the rosters of the older established teams. The result was a number of lawsuits by teams seeking injunctive relief to prevent the players from moving to the new league for higher salaries.

Perhaps the most significant of these suits was *Philadelphia Ball Club v. Lajoie*.[7] The Philadelphia Phillies initiated a suit seeking injunctive relief against future Hall of Fame player Napoleon Lajoie. Initially, the Court of Common Pleas of Philadelphia County refused to issue an injunction holding that "to warrant the interference prayed for 'the defendant's services must be unique, extraordinary, and of such a character as to render it impossible to replace him; so that his breach of contract would result in irreparable loss to the plaintiff.' "[8] The court simply did not consider Lajoie's qualifications to measure up to this high standard.

The lower court opinion was overturned on appeal to the Supreme Court of Pennsylvania. The justices felt that requiring a showing of impossibility of replacement of the player was too extreme. Noting that Lajoie "may not be the sun in the baseball firmament, but he is certainly a bright particular star,"[9] the court ordered the issuance of the injunction. Ban Johnson reacted by shifting Lajoie to the Cleveland Indians after ten games of the 1902 season. Because no Ohio court would claim jurisdiction and enforce the injunction, Johnson's American League succeeded in keeping Lajoie. To avoid the jurisdiction of the Pennsylvania courts, Lajoie did not come to Philadelphia during the season. Instead, he received a free vacation in Atlantic City, and the American League earned the service of one of baseball's finest second baseman.[10]

In January 1903, the owners of the American and National Leagues signed a peace agreement pledging the enforcement of the reserve clause between the two leagues.[11] Later that year, the two leagues and a number of minor leagues signed the "National Agreement." The new pact established a National Commission to ensure that teams abided by the reserve clause and territorial rights. The labor stability of baseball would not be challenged again until the rise of the Federal League.

Another major event in the history of baseball took place in January 1903.[12] Ban Johnson had wanted a team in the New York market since the founding of the league. He succeeded in talking gambling house owner Frank Farrell and former chief of police Bill Devery into purchasing the Baltimore franchise for $18,000 and moving the team to Manhattan. The two owners quickly erected a stadium at 168th Street and Broadway. The team was nicknamed the Highlanders because their park was located on one of the highest points in Manhattan and also to honor Joseph Gordon, the man chosen to be team president. Gordon's Highlanders were a well-known regiment in the British Army. The New York team debuted on the road on April 22, 1903, in Washington, D.C. Despite the presence of three future Hall-of-Famers, player-manager Clark Griffith, pitcher Jack Chesbro, and outfielder Wee Willie Keeler, they lost to the Senators, 3-1. The team would be renamed the Yankees in 1913 by Jim Price, the sports editor of the *New York Press* who was looking for a shorter nickname. That same year the team left small Hilltop Park to share the Polo Grounds with the Giants.

IV. The Rise and Fall of the Federal League[13]

In 1913, after a decade of labor peace in Organized Baseball, the Federal League was organized by a number of prosperous businessmen. Before the 1914 season, Federal League President James Gilmore requested parity with the other two major leagues and the right to operate under the National Agreement. When Gilmore and his owners were rebuffed, they decided to pour money into new stadiums in their eight cities and to compete directly with the established leagues in Brooklyn, Chicago, Pittsburgh, and St. Louis. The Federal League also refused to honor the reserve clauses of the teams bound by the National Agreement. The teams in Organized Baseball had coupled their reserve clause to another clause, known as the blacklist, that declared a player ineligible for three years if he signed with a team outside of Organized Baseball. Although attendance at Federal League games in 1914 did not rival that of the American or National League, it did impact attendance in the older two leagues.

The Feds signed 81 major leaguers and 140 minor leaguers to contracts, causing an escalation of salaries. Ray "Slim" Caldwell, a pitcher for the Yankees, signed an offer from a Federal League team after making $2,400 in 1913. Caldwell had pitched in 27 games for the Yankees in 1913 and ended the season with a 9-8 record. The Yankees were forced to give Caldwell a four-year deal at $8,000 annually to resign him before the season began. Caldwell responded with a 17-win season in 1914 and 19 wins in 1915. At the end of the 1918 season, Caldwell was sent to the Red Sox with Frank Gilhooley, Slim Love, Roxy Walter, and $15,000 for veteran players Ernie Shore, Duffy Lewis, and Dutch Leonard. Trades with the Boston Red Sox over the next decade would be a significant factor in the success of the Yankees.

Many Major League franchises filed lawsuits seeking injunctive relief to prevent the Federal League from raiding their rosters. A New York court denied a request by the Chicago White Sox to prevent controversial first baseman Hal Chase from playing for the Buffalo Federals. Chase had played with the Highlanders/Yankees from 1905 until a trade to the White Sox during the 1913 season prompted by Manager Frank Chance. Chase had irritated Chance by openly ridiculing the manager in the dugout. Chase, whose gambling habits would ultimately cost him a spot on a Major League roster, had been a fan favorite during his New York career.

On January 5, 1915, the Federal League filed suit in federal court in Chicago claiming that Organized Baseball was in violation of antitrust laws.[14] The case was assigned to trustbusting judge Kenesaw Mountain Landis. The trial was completed by January 22, but Landis was in no rush to decide the case.

The 1915 season commenced with new competition for the Yankees. Oil magnate Harry Sinclair moved the champions of the 1914 season, the Indianapolis Federals, to Newark.

Sinclair, who would later gain prominence and public disgrace for his involvement in the Teapot Dome Scandal, would be a moving force in the future events of the Federal League. The 1915 season was financially ruinous for most of the Federal League franchises. Before the season was over, the Kansas City and Buffalo teams folded under the pressure.

Federal League President Gilmore convinced Sinclair and Brooklyn Federals' owner R.B. Ward to join him in a more direct attack on Organized Baseball and New York. The three purchased an option on vacant land at 143rd Street and Lenox Avenue. They contacted Corry Comstock, the vice-president of the Pittsburgh Federals and a New York City engineer to create plans for a 55,000-seat stadium on the site. Gilmore then leaked to the press the plans for the Federal League to play in New York during the upcoming 1916 season. But Gilmore and his compatriots never intended to play in New York or build a new stadium. They simply wanted to pressure Organized Baseball into offering a settlement. They hoped that their ruse would create some leverage.

On December 13, 1915, Gilmore and Sinclair went to the office of John K. Tener, National League President and former governor of Pennsylvania, to hear a proposal from Organized Baseball. They hammered out a deal that satisfied every remaining Federal League team owner except Baltimore Terrapins owner Carroll W. Rasin. First, the owners of Federal League teams were paid $600,000 to dissolve the League and drop the antitrust action. Second, each of the Federal League owners was allowed to sell their players' contracts to the highest bidder. Third, all blacklisted players from the Federal League were declared eligible to play for National League and American League teams. Fourth, the National League owners purchased the Brooklyn Federals' stadium for $400,000. The American League owners had to pay one-half of that settlement. Fifth, Chicago Federals (Whales) owner Charles E. Weeghman was allowed to purchase the Chicago Cubs for $500,000 and the National League contributed $50,000 of the purchase price. Sixth, the National League owners purchased the Pittsburgh Federals for $50,000. Seventh, Phil Ball, the owner of the St. Louis Federals (Terriers) team received the American League franchise in St. Louis. The purchase price was $525,000.

At a meeting on December 17, 1915, National Commission President and Cincinnati Reds owner August Herrmann called a meeting of representatives of Organized Baseball and the Federal League owners at New York's Waldorf-Astoria Hotel. The assembled group, particularly Chicago White Sox owner Charles Comiskey and Brooklyn owner Charles Ebbets, ridiculed the Baltimore group by asserting that Baltimore was nothing but a minor league town, and a poor one at best. The Terrapins owners left the meeting with nothing. The Baltimore group went to the United States Department of Justice claiming that Organized Baseball was violating federal antitrust laws. However, Assistant Attorney General Todd declared that he had no reason to look into the matter.

On September 20, 1917, the owners filed suit in Washington, D.C. It took over one and one-half years of legal wrangling before the case went to trial. The jury rendered a favorable verdict to the Terrapins' owners. After trebling the assessed damages of $80,000 and adding attorneys' fees, the judgment against Organized Baseball was $254,000.

Organized Baseball appealed the decision to the Court of Appeals for the District of Columbia. On December 5, 1920,[15] Chief Justice Constantine J. Smyth rendered the court's opinion reversing the lower court. Smyth's opinion went to heart of the issue framed by lawyers for Organized Baseball, that baseball was not trade or commerce within the meaning of the Sherman Antitrust Act:

> The business in which the appellants were engaged, as we have seen, was the giving of exhibitions of baseball. A game of baseball is not susceptible of being transferred. The players, it is true, travel from place to place in interstate commerce, but they are not the game. Not until they come into contact with their opponents on the baseball field and the contest opens does the game come into existence. It is local in its beginning and in its end. Nothing is transferred in the process to those who patronize it. The exertions of skill and agility which they witness may excite in them pleasurable emotions, just as might a view of a beautiful picture or a masterly performance of some drama; but the game effects no exchange of things according to the meaning of 'trade and commerce' as defined above.[16]

The case was appealed to the United States Supreme Court. Seventeen months after the Court of Appeals had ruled in favor of Organized Baseball, over five years since the case had been filed, and nearly seven years after the last Federal League game, the Supreme Court rendered its opinion authored by Justice Oliver Wendell Holmes.[17] Holmes echoed Smyth's opinion:

> The business is giving exhibitions of base ball, which are purely state affairs. It is true that, in order to attain for these exhibitions the great popularity that they have achieved, competitions must be arranged between clubs from different cities and States. But the fact that in order to give the exhibitions the Leagues must induce free persons to cross state lines and must arrange and pay for their doing so is not enough to change the character of the business. According to the distinction insisted upon in Hooper v. California, 155 U.S. 648, 655, the transport is a mere incident, not the essential thing. That to which it is incident, the exhibition, although made for money would not be called trade or commerce in the commonly accepted use of those words. As it is put by the defendants, personal effort, nor related to production, is not a subject of commerce. That which in its consummation is not commerce does not become commerce among the States because the transportation that we have mentioned takes place.[18]

Although Holmes' opinion has been criticized extensively, one should be careful not to view a 1922 decision through the lens of a later time. The regulation of trade prior to the passage of the Sherman Act supports the noted jurist's point that "personal effort" or human labor was not considered commerce in the same sense as production or manufacturing of goods. The brunt of Holmes' point in the remainder of the paragraph is that the nature of travel could not transform something that was essentially not commerce into commerce.

Furthermore, the court's decision should be placed in the larger historical context of the history of the sport. The baseball public had been rocked by rumors that the 1919 World Series between the Chicago White Sox and the Cincinnati Reds had been fixed.[19] The image of the game was severely shaken. Seven Sox players were tried in Chicago for running a confidence game. Aided by the disappearance of grand jury testimony, the group was found not guilty after a celebrated trial closely followed by a national audience. The owners felt that the damage to the integrity of the game demanded a new administrative structure. To achieve that goal, they turned over nearly complete power of the game to new commissioner Kenesaw Mountain Landis. Landis would ban a total of eight players involved in the fixing scheme despite the court's decision. Had Organized Baseball not reacted strongly to the scandal, the Supreme Court and Congress might have shown a greater interest in becoming involved with the internal workings of the game. Instead, the decision in *Federal Baseball* allowed ownership to maintain all of the leverage in its dealings with players. Against the backdrop of the defeat of the only league to seriously challenge Organized Baseball until the Mexican League targeted Major League players in post-World War II America, the Yankees were beginning to flourish under new ownership.

V. The Arrival of New Owners[20]

The relationship between the Yankees' original owners, Farrell and Devery, quickly dissolved into bitter bickering over the direction of the on-field operation. Gordon was dismissed as president, and Farrell took over the position. Attendance declined as the owners meddled with Manager Griffith's actions, causing him to depart in the middle of the 1908 season. A succession of managers failed to produce a pennant winner, and the relationship between the two owners weakened. Meanwhile, Giants manager John McGraw had introduced Jacob Ruppert, a brewer who had developed his enterprise into a multi-million dollar venture, to Tillinghast L'Hommedieu Huston, a successful engineer during the Spanish-American War. Although the duo wanted to buy the Giants, McGraw fended them off and pushed them towards buying the Yankees from Farrell and Devery. On January 11, 1915, Ruppert and Huston purchased the Yankees for $460,000. Devery and Farrell split the money and parted company, never to speak to each other again. Devery died in 1919, and Farrell passed away seven years later. Both had squandered all of their assets.

The new owners brought significant financial resources to the Yankees and a willingness to spend it to strengthen the team. Frank "Home Run" Baker, a veteran of four World Series with the Philadelphia Athletics, was persuaded to come out of retirement if the Yankees owners would purchase his release from Connie Mack's team. This was accomplished for the sum of $25,000. Baker would play for the Yankees from 1916 until 1922. The owners made one other significant deal with Mack. In July 1915, they purchased the contract of pitcher Bob Shawkey for $18,000. Shawkey hurled for 12 more seasons in New York. From 1919 through 1924, Shawkey won at least 16 games each year including three 20-win seasons. He finished his career with nearly 200 wins. Wally Pipp and Hughie High were purchased for the waiver price of $7,500 from Detroit Tigers owner Frank Navin. Pipp anchored the infield at first base from 1915 until 1925 when a young Columbia graduate named Lou Gehrig replaced him in the lineup. High contributed three seasons of 100-plus games in the outfield. The greatest Yankee success, however, was saved for two deals with the Boston Red Sox.

VI. Huston and Ruppert Tangle with
Ban Johnson over Carl Mays[21]

The 1914 Major League season was the year of the "Miracle Braves." Boston's National League entry stormed from last place in July to grab the league crown and sweep the Philadelphia Athletics in the World Series. Late in the season, Boston's other team, the Red Sox, brought up a duo of star pitchers from the International League champion Providence Grays to play the final two weeks of the season. The two joined a strong Red Sox pitching staff including Smoky Joe Wood, Dutch Leonard, Rube Foster, and Ernie Shore. Both new men would be stars for Boston and, later in their careers, the Yankees. One would earn his fame as a hitter with immense talent and charisma while the other would gain infamy as the only pitcher to ever kill a man during a Major League game with a pitched ball. George Herman "Babe" Ruth and Carl Mays had arrived in the big leagues.

Mays quickly assumed a major role on the Red Sox staff right behind Ruth. While Ruth won 18 games in 1915 and followed up with two 20-win campaigns, Mays matched the three-year feat beginning in the following year. The Red Sox won the American League pennant three times and finished second once during the four year span. But the 1919 season started differently. Red Sox owner Harry Frazee was strapped for money. In the midst of the strong run of his Broadway hit *Nothing but the Truth*, Frazee had joined a silent partner from Philadelphia to purchase the Red Sox from Joe Lannin on November 1, 1916, for a price between $400,000 and $700,000. Frazee pledged much of the purchase price in future payments. Three years later, Frazee was without a theatrical success, and he turned to his baseball team seeking financial help. Over the winter he had engineered the trade to the Yankees of Ernie Shore, Dutch Leonard, and Duffy Lewis for Ray Caldwell. Ruth was holding out for the first time in his career, and Mays refused to sign his contract. The successful Red Sox franchise was poised to enter a prolonged era of intense frustration for its rabid fans, and their demise would benefit the Yankees by adding the players they needed to establish themselves as the dominant team in the American League in the 1920s. Mays began the year pitching well, but his team failed to provide any run support. By July 13, 1919, his record was 5-11.

Mays began that day pitching against the rising stars of the American League, the Chicago White Sox. Trailing 4-0 in the second inning, Red Sox catcher Wally Schang attempted a throw to second base to get a Chisox runner. Instead, he hit Mays in the back of the head. Although the runner failed to score, Mays left the mound at the end of the inning extremely agitated. Throwing down his glove, he headed for the clubhouse exclaiming, "I'll never pitch for this ballclub again!"[22] When Red Sox manager Ed Barrow was told his pitcher had left the field, he sent pitcher Sam Jones to check on his starter. Jones found Mays undressing in the clubhouse. When Jones told Mays that Barrow wanted him back on the field, he told his teammate to simply tell their manager, "I've gone fishing."[23] When Barrow sent another player to check on the condition of Mays, he found the star hurler sitting in front of his locker weeping.

Mays took a taxi back to the Red Sox hotel, packed his bags, and checked out. Leaving a note apparently claiming that he was "despondent over some personal problems,"[24] he left for Pennsylvania. Earlier that year, Mays' new home in Mansfield, Missouri, had burned, destroying all of his mementos from his playing career. Mays was also upset with his treatment by the Red Sox concerning a fine from American League President Ban Johnson when Mays fired a ball into the stands during a Memorial Day game in Philadelphia. The Red Sox were refusing to cover the cost of the fine.

Upon learning of the Chicago incident, Frazee saw an opportunity to raise some money. He called Barrow and said, "Don't suspend this fellow. The Yankees want him and I can get a lot of money for him."[25] Chicago, Cleveland, Detroit, and Washington were also interested in Mays. White Sox owner Charles Comiskey, whose treatment of his team would provide the undercurrent for throwing the upcoming World Series, offered $25,000. League President Ban Johnson was not amused. He contacted all of his owners trying to nix any trade talk until Frazee disciplined Mays.

Over two weeks passed with Mays relaxing in Pennsylvania when the pitcher received a call in Pennsylvania from Huston. Mays told Huston if the money was right he would be happy to pitch for the Yankees. Frazee did not need to hear anything more. He traded Mays to the Yankees for $40,000 and marginal players Allan Russell and Bob McGraw.

Ban Johnson was in St. Louis with J. G. Taylor Spink, the publisher of *The Sporting News*. He was furious to open the morning newspaper and see a story proclaiming the trade. He immediately suspended Mays, the type of action he often took when affairs in the league were not to his liking. He sent a message to all league umpires:

> You are hereby notified the American League has suspended Carl W. Mays of the Boston Club by reason of his desertion of the club and the breaking of his contract. He will not be permitted to take part in any games until you receive direct notice from me.[26]

Ruppert now claimed that Mays was a Yankee. The two Yankees' owners met with Johnson at a stormy meeting that failed to resolve the matter. Comiskey, Frazee, and the two Yankees owners were aligned against Johnson and the remainder of the owners. The Yankees owners headed to the New York Supreme Court seeking an injunction against Johnson. The court responded positively, and on August 7 the umpires were served with the court order at the Polo Grounds before a Yankees-Browns doubleheader. Mays threw a six-hitter to win 8-2. The New York press responded by naming him "The Injunction Kid."

The season continued with Mays winning nine games for his new team. The Yankees edged the Tigers for third by one-half game. Because only the top three teams shared in the World Series earnings, Detroit owner Navin moved to block the distribution of the $13,000 third-place share.

On October 26, New York Supreme Court Judge Robert F. Wagner granted an injunction for the Yankees by siding unequivocally with Huston and Ruppert against Johnson. The league president was not pleased with the brazen attack upon his usually undisputed control over the league. The Yankees, however, received a player who would win 53 games while pitching almost 650 innings over the next two seasons.

Wagner's opinion proved to be a complete attack on Johnson's position. The future United States Senator began his opinion by showing his support for the Yankees: "Suspension of a player, therefore, not only interferes with his individual contract, but may also interfere with the reputation and collective ability of the club."[27]

Before delivering his legal analysis, Wagner characterized Mays in the following manner:

> In the very early stages of the contest he played concededly below the standard of skill which he usually exhibited. At this time, and for some time prior thereto, Mays had shown a disposition of discontent and nervousness which he attributed to personal difficulties and the worry incident therto. On behalf of the defendant it is claimed that his disposition was one of recalcitrancy and desire to abandon his contract.... Barrow, the manager of the Boston club, immediately sent two players to him to ascertain his condition. The latter reported to Barrow that they found Mays in a condition of great nervous tension, and indeed of practical nervous collapse.... Mays told Frazee that he was suffering from a nervous breakdown, that he could be of no service to the Boston Club by reason of his condition, that he desired to take a rest, and that he was ready to report to the Boston Club whenever directed.[28]

Wagner started his analysis by offering two interpretations of Johnson's actions. At trial, Johnson argued his actions were meant to punish both the Boston and New York teams for the decision to go forward with the trade. However, Wagner felt that Mays was the true target for punishment. If Johnson meant to punish the teams, Wagner reasoned that the act was "clearly *ultra vires*" because the constitution of the American League did not grant to the league president the power to discipline teams.[29] Only the board of directors could exercise the power to discipline under sections 6, 7, and 10. Furthermore, Wagner argued that it was not the trade but the lack of discipline by the Red Sox that prompted Johnson's suspension. Because the Yankees could not discipline Mays for an act involving his relationship with the Red Sox, Wagner saw the Yankees as "the real sufferer" because they were "obliged to pay the salary of Mays while it was deprived of his services."[30]

Wagner turned next to a consideration of Johnson's actions under the theory that the goal was to punish Mays. Johnson had conceded that the primary right of discipline belonged to Boston, yet he asserted that he enjoyed a similar power as league president. Wagner quoted sections 20 and 24 of the league constitution. He reasoned that section 20 provided Johnson with power only with respect to the "general welfare of the game." Section 24, however, was a specific grant to the teams and general grants of power should be subordinated to specific grants of power. After quoting Matthew Bacon on equity and statutory construction, Wagner looked at the similarity between the American League Constitution and the older National League Constitution. This analysis led Wagner to conclude "the construction becomes inevitable that it was the intention of the framers to give unmodified and unrestricted power to the clubs in respect to their purely internal affairs."[31]

To strengthen his argument against Johnson, Wagner next considered whether Johnson's actions were "in the performance of his duties" as required under section 20.[32] Because Wagner felt that Mays' act of desertion or breach of contract did not happen on the field, the judge characterized Johnson's suspension as unauthorized. If Johnson's suspension was based on his supervisory powers, section 36 of the constitution did not give a right beyond the ministerial duty to send complaints to the board. Wagner finished his analysis of the constitutional provisions by concluding that Johnson had no power to issue the injunction.

Wagner was not finished criticizing Johnson. Johnson argued that he had often exercised similar powers and those actions had not been questioned. Quoting Washington's Farewell Address, Wagner made it clear that Johnson could not "acquire power by continual usurpation."[33] Completing his opinion by granting the injunction, Wagner again attacked the league president for an act that was "to say the least, not fortified with that perfect appreciation of the facts which evinces a desire to do equity to all parties concerned."[34]

The Yankees' owners were ecstatic, "Our fight has not been for Mays alone, but to safeguard the vested and property rights of the individual club owner against the encroachments on club rights by the president, who has never been clothed with the powers that he has taken unto himself."[35]

With Tigers owner Frank Navin as the peacemaker, the owners gathered in Chicago on February 10, 1920, to deal with the aftermath of the trade and Wagner's decision. They emerged at 2:00 a.m. the next morning after enduring three lengthy sessions. Johnson and his owner allies were completely defeated. Mays would remain a Yankee, and he would not be penalized. The third-place finish by the Yankees was recognized, and they would be immediately granted their World Series share. To curb the president's power, Ruppert and Griffith were appointed together to a committee to consider any major suspension or fine. If the two did not agree, the tie-breaking vote would go to a

Chicago federal judge rather than Johnson. Johnson would never regain the power he had enjoyed as league president. Now, Ruppert and Huston assumed the place of power within the ownership group. However, the most important action taken by the two owners as the team entered the 1920s was the acquisition of the one Red Sox player who would have the greatest impact of any single individual on the game. That player was Babe Ruth.

Unfortunately, tragedy accompanied the reuniting of Mays and Ruth in New York. On August 16, 1920, Mays threw a pitch that struck Cleveland Indians shortstop Ray Chapman in the head. Chapman died the next day despite a one hour and fifteen minute operation to remove both a piece of skull and to deal with numerous blood clots. Ultimately, the Yankees parted company with Mays when he was sold to the Cincinnati Reds in December 1923 for cash.

VII. The Arrival of Ruth[36]

During the last week of 1919 and the first days of 1920, the Yankees returned to Boston and Red Sox owner Harry Frazee to complete a blockbuster deal. Frazee needed money to cover his Broadway debts and to pay the notes held by Lannin on the original purchase of the Red Sox. Ruth had aggravated the Sox owner by demanding a doubling of his salary for the upcoming year. The day after Christmas, Frazee called Ruppert looking for a loan. Frazee needed $500,000 for the Broadway productions that he wanted to finance. At the same time, Frazee was telling the press in Boston that he was willing to deal any player except future Hall-of-Fame outfielder Harry Hooper. When the quick negotiations were concluded, Ruth went to the Yankees for $125,000 and a $350,000 loan against the mortgage on Fenway Park. The Uniform Agreement for Transfer of a Player was dated December 26, 1919, and included the final two years of Ruth's three-year deal with the Red Sox. The Boston owner received an immediate payment of $25,000. Because Huston was leery of a loan based upon a ballpark, Ruppert made that part of the deal on his own. It was nearly one year later before Ruppert's interest in Fenway became nationally known, but such an obvious conflict of interest was not unusual for the time. In fact, Ban Johnson's interest in the Cleveland Indians had been cited as a reason for his suspension of Mays in 1919 when the White Sox, Indians, and Yankees were battling for the American League pennant. The mortgage outlasted Frazee's ownership of the Red Sox.

Although the bulk of Ruth's purchase price was a well-secured loan, the deal cost Ruppert and Huston more than they had paid to purchase the Yankees. Furthermore, it eclipsed the $55,000 that Cleveland had paid for Tris Speaker, the $50,000 price that the White Sox paid for Eddie Collins or the $32,000 and two players involved in the purchase of Joe Jackson by the White Sox. In an oft-heard refrain throughout baseball history, the *New York Times* chided both teams because a good player could demand "an imposing salary" from one of the poorer owners, only to have "somebody in New York or Chicago…buy his services."[37]

Frazee would sell another ten players to the Yankees when he needed to raise money. On December 15, 1920, the Red Sox sent Harry Harper, Waite Hoyt, Mike McNally, and Wally Schang to New York for Muddy Ruel, Del Pratt, Hank Thomahle, and Sammy Vick. Hoyt would be a mainstay through part of the 1930 season. His annual victory totals beginning in 1921, were 19, 19, 17, 18, 11, 16, 22, 23, and 10 through the

1929 season. Herb Pennock was sent to New York on January 30, 1923, for $50,000 and players Camp Skinner, Norm McMillan, and George Murray. Frazee sold the team to Bob Quinn during the 1923 season, but the fortunes of the Red Sox and Yankees remained the same. Red Ruffing was sold to the Bronx Bombers in 1930 for $50,000 and Cedric Durst.

At the end of the 1921 season, the Yankees would embark on establishing perhaps the strongest on-field record of any major sports franchise in any sport in the United States during the twentieth century by capturing their first American League pennant. The next 22 seasons would mark the first great period of Yankees domination of baseball. From 1921 until 1943, the Yankees would capture 13 American League pennants and 9 World Series championships. Ruppert's financial resources fueled the establishment of a dynasty. On May 21, 1922, Ruppert solidified his hold on the club by purchasing all of Huston's interest for $1,500,000.

VIII. DiMaggio and Ruppert[38]

Joe DiMaggio joined the Yankees from the San Francisco Seals of the Pacific Coast League in 1936. DiMaggio was a star for his hometown team, and he barely lost out on the PCL batting championship. Oscar Eckhardt's .399 average beat Joe by one percentage point. As a rookie with the Yankees, DiMaggio hit .323, with a league-leading 15 triples, 29 home runs, and 125 RBIs. In his second full year with the Yankees, he improved on his great debut by hitting .346 with 167 RBIs and 46 home runs. He felt that his season should be rewarded with a raise from $15,000 to $40,000, and he went to New York to argue his case directly to Colonel Ruppert. Because ballplayers in the post-*Federal Baseball* case era lacked any leverage, Colonel Ruppert saw no reason to meet DiMaggio's demand. Ruppert told the New York reporters that he offered $25,000, and "I don't intend to go any higher." When the Colonel held fast, DiMaggio decided not to report. Ruppert retorted "DiMaggio is an ungrateful young man, and is very unfair to his teammates, to say the least." With the New York press firmly in the Colonel's corner, DiMaggio was eventually forced to accept Ruppert's offer after the third day of the season. Even a star of DiMaggio's magnitude could not shake a system so favorable to management. Eventually, DiMaggio would become baseball's first $100,000 player, but the Yankee Clipper never forgot his losing clash with the Yankee owner.

IX. Baseball's Antitrust Exemption Comes under Judicial and Congressional Scrutiny[39]

Kennesaw Mountain Landis ruled over Organized Baseball for a quarter century until his death in 1944, and the game enjoyed its greatest period of labor peace. However, during World War II, significant numbers of active players enlisted or were drafted into the armed services. Landis sought President Franklin D. Roosevelt's advice on the continuation of playing Major League Baseball. Roosevelt strongly endorsed the continuation of playing by issuing the Green Light Letter. Teams started to search for players of reasonable major league ability to add to their rosters.

Danny Gardella was a minor league player from 1939 through 1941. By 1944, Gardella was working in a New York shipyard. He was coaxed out of his job to join the New York Giants as an outfielder in 1944 and 1945. By the beginning of the 1946 season, the veterans were returning, and Gardella went to spring training without a signed contract, and he knew that he held little chance of continuing his career with the Giants.

While Gardella considered his post-war career options, the president of the Mexican League, Don Jorge Pasquel, had decided to elevate his league to the major league level. Pasquel arrived in New York and stated boldly at a May 3, 1946, press conference that he expected Yankees shortstop Phil Rizzuto to accompany him to Mexico, and, if not Rizzuto, than surely another member of the Yankees starting lineup. The Yankees filed suit in the New York Supreme Court seeking injunctive relief against Pasquel.[40] Pasquel's attorney argued that the inequitable and monopolistic nature of the Yankees' contracts should prevent a court from enforcing them. In May and November, two separate judges considered Pasquel's claim. Neither judge found the arguments that baseball, or in particular the Yankees, were either involved in a restraint of trade or guilty of forcing players to sign illegal contracts.

Rebuffed at his attempts to lure Yankees to Mexico, Pasquel did succeed in signing eighteen major league players to contracts. One of the signees was Gardella. In response to the signings, new commissioner Happy Chandler suspended the group for five years. Gardella responded by filing suit in the Southern District Court of New York requesting treble damages under sections 1, 2, and 3 of the Sherman Act and sections two and three of the Clayton Act. Judge Henry Goodard dismissed the case by invoking the binding power of the *Federal Baseball* decision. Gardella and his attorney Frederic A. Johnson appealed the case to the Second Circuit Court of Appeals. On February 9, 1949, a three-judge panel overturned the lower court opinion.[41] Each judge issued a separate opinion.

Judge Jerome N. Frank argued that decisions rendered by the Supreme Court after *Federal Baseball* had "completely destroyed the vitality" of that ruling leaving "that case but an impotent zombi (sic)."[42] Frank together with Judge Learned Hand voted to remand the case for a trial on the merits of the antitrust claim. Chandler responded to the assault on the reserve clause by granting amnesty to all of the players. The new commissioner's strategy paid off. Before the case went to trial, Gardella agreed to settle his case. The settlement left the *Federal Baseball* ruling intact, but the Second Circuit opinion forced Congress to consider legislation that would reinvigorate baseball's historic exemption from antitrust analysis. Ultimately, no legislation was passed, but the Supreme Court would soon be asked to reconsider the exemption when three separate suits were combined and accepted on appeal.

X. Toolson v. New York Yankees[43]

Earl Toolson began his minor league career in Greensboro, North Carolina, in 1942 as a Boston Red Sox farmhand. Greensboro won the Piedmont League crown during the playoffs after finishing the year tied for first place with Portsmouth with a 78-53 record.[44] Hall of Famer Heinie Manush was the Red Sox manager. The pitching staff was deep with Joe Ostrowski (21-8, 1.69 ERA), Adam Gluchoski (15-8), Roger Wright (15-

10), and Bill Elbert (11-5). However, the franchise was a casualty of World War II.[45] Greensboro's current team, the Bats, is one of the Yankees class A affiliates and a member of the South Atlantic League. Former Greensboro players include Jim Bouton, Derek Jeter, Don Mattingly, Otis Nixon, Mariano Rivera, and Curt Schilling. The team plays in one of the oldest minor league stadiums still in use. World War Memorial Stadium was built in 1926.[46]

In 1943, Toolson began the first of four years hurling for Louisville in the AAA American Association. After winning three and losing five in twenty-four games, Earl enlisted in the Army Air Corps while on crutches because of knee surgery. Toolson served at Williams Field in Higley, Arizona, during 1944 and 1945. After returning to baseball, Toolson had his best success in 1946 and 1947 with Louisville. In sixteen games in 1946, Toolson won five while losing three with a 3.88 ERA. The following year, he hurled in thirty-three games for Louisville, winning eleven and losing six. In 1948, Toolson won four and lost ten with a 5.21 ERA in thirty-three games despite being plagued by a back injury. At the end of the year, Boston traded Toolson to the Yankees. The Yankees, having discovered his injury, assigned him from Newark, their AAA team at a comparable level with Louisville, to Binghamton. Although Earl was not unhappy about the trade to the Yankees system, he did not like the decision to demote him to Binghamton nor the general treatment that the Yankees accorded to him. He contacted a high school friend, a California lawyer, and they filed suit against the Yankees in the United States District Court for the Southern District of California alleging that the reserve clause constituted a violation of both the Sherman and Clayton Acts.

On November 6, 1951, Judge Harrison, relying upon the precedent established in *Federal Baseball*, ruled against Toolson.[47] In his opinion, Harrison recounted Toolson's basic allegation that Organized Baseball's monopoly deprived him of his livelihood. As stated in Harrison's opinion, because Toolson had refused to report to Binghamton after the assignment from Newark, Earl had been placed on the "ineligible list" and other teams had refused to allow him to play. In fact, Toolson did play baseball in 1949 and 1950 for Oakland and San Francisco of the Pacific Coast League apparently with the Yankees' consent. The 1949 Oakland Oaks finished in second place under manager Charlie Dressen who had replaced popular field boss Casey Stengel at the helm. Stengel had managed the Oaks from 1946 though 1948. Toolson's teammates on the 1949 team included Jackie Jensen, Billy Martin, Cookie Lavagetto, and Artie Wilson.

Harrison noted in his opinion that "[t]o me, the simple issue of this case is whether the game of baseball is 'trade or commerce' within the meaning of the Anti-Trust Acts, and whether the structure known as 'Organized Baseball' is engaged in such trade or commerce."[48] Harrison cited sixteen decisions that had favorably cited *Federal Baseball*, and found that only the *Gardella* case supported a finding that Organized Baseball was now "engaged in interstate commerce."[49] Relying on the binding nature of Supreme Court precedent, Harrison declined to reconsider the underlying premises of *Federal Baseball*:

> I am bound by the decision of the Supreme Court. It is not my function to disregard such a decision because it is old. If the Supreme Court was in error in its former opinion or changed conditions warrant a different approach, it should be the court to correct the error. Trial courts in my opinion should not devote their efforts to guessing what reviewing courts may do with prior holdings because of lapse of time or change of personnel in such courts. We are supposed to be living in a land of laws. Stability in law requires respect for the decisions of controlling courts or face chaos.[50]

Therefore, he dismissed the case for lack of subject matter jurisdiction. The United States Court of Appeals for the Ninth Circuit affirmed the district court in a per curiam opinion.[51]

The United States Supreme Court case was a consolidation of *Corbett v. Chandler*,[52] *Kowalski v. Chandler*,[53] and *Toolson v. New York Yankees.* The United States Supreme Court also rendered a per curiam opinion[54] affirming the three lower court decisions by noting the holding in *Federal Baseball* that "the business of providing public baseball games for profit between clubs of professional baseball players is not within the scope of the federal antitrust laws."[55] The Court noted that "Congress has had the ruling (*Federal Baseball*) under consideration but has not seen fit to bring such business under these laws by legislation having *prospective* effect."[56] The Court upheld *Federal Baseball* "so far as that decision determines that Congress had no intention of including the business of baseball within the scope of the federal antitrust laws."[57]

Justice Harold Burton wrote a dissenting opinion that was joined by Justice Stanley Reed. The two justices could no longer accept the concept that Organized Baseball was not involved in interstate commerce. They cited as supporting this claim the exhaustive treatment of the finances and nature of baseball from the 1952 hearings of the House of Representatives Subcommittee on the Study of Monopoly Power of the Committee on the Judiciary. The justices closed by noting that Congress had never granted Organized Baseball an exemption and because baseball's popularity should increase the need for compliance with the Sherman Act, the cases should be remanded for a trial on the merits. Unfortunately for Earl Toolson and the other plaintiffs, the other seven justices could not be swayed. A few Congressmen remained interested in baseball's peculiar status, but the Yankees and the rest of Organized Baseball would be spared from further United States Supreme Court review for nearly two decades.

XI. Casey Stengel Befuddles Congress[58]

Casey Stengel was manager of the Yankees for 12 years from 1949 to 1960. In 1958 Senator Estes Kefauver summoned the skipper to discuss antitrust law before the Committee on the Judiciary. Stengel had been in Baltimore to manage the American League team in the All-Star game.

Stengel had played in the major leagues for 14 years, and he compiled a career batting average of .284. His first stint in the dugout of two Major League clubs was not distinguished. He managed the Brooklyn Dodgers from 1934 until 1936. After a year's absence, Stengel was hired by the Boston Braves. In 1938, the team finished two games above .500 and in fifth place. The next four years, the Braves finished in seventh place. He was fired in 1943 after 107 games and the Braves finished in sixth place. He was destined to toil in the minor leagues until the Yankees saw something in the man nicknamed the "Old Perfessor."

Stengel took over the helm in New York in 1949. During the next five years, the Yankees won both the American League pennant and the World Series. After slipping to second place in 1954 despite 103 wins, the Yankees played in the next four World Series, winning two and losing two. After a third place finish in 1959, Stengel led them back to the World Series in 1960 against the Pirates. Casey was fired after the 1960 season, but he came back to manage the New York Mets for three years plus 96 games in 1965. Over a 10-year period with the Yankees, his team won the world championship seven times.

Stengel started his testimony by noting his nearly 50 years in the game. Although he took pains to point out the inequity of baseball's pension fund, he largely lauded the game. Kefauver remarked that perhaps he had been unclear in his original directive to Stengel about why baseball might want legislation providing baseball with an unlimited antitrust exemption. Stengel retorted that it was alright because he probably was not going to supply a perfect answer anyway. After the laughter in the committee room subsided, Stengel offered another view before Kefauver decided to allow the other senators an opportunity to glean something meaningful from the Yankees field general. During the remainder of his time in front of the senators, he launched into a rambling stream of consciousness and disjointed observations that were typical of the speech patterns dubbed Stengelese. By the time he finished, the whole room was in an uproar. Feeling that perhaps another view might clarify baseball's need for protective legislation, the chairman asked Yankees outfielder Mickey Mantle to address the committee. In a single sentence response to the same question presented to Stengel, Mantle proceeded to up-stage his manager. Mantle simply asserted, "My views are just about the same as Casey's."[59] Congress failed to seriously consider the matter any further, and the status quo remained intact into the next decade. However, the nature of baseball and the future of the Yankees as its dominant team were approaching dynamic and dramatic changes.

XII. Curt Flood Sues Major League Baseball

In 1964, the Yankees appeared in their fifth consecutive World Series. Little did they expect that their loss in game seven to Cardinals pitching ace Bob Gibson would begin an 11-year absence from the Fall Classic. The year had been tumultuous for first year manager Yogi Berra. He was fired the day after the series concluded, replaced by Johnny Keane, the manager of the Cardinals.

Although the Yankees struggled after the 1964 season, the Cardinals returned to the World Series in 1967 and 1968. A major participant in all three series was center fielder Curt Flood, the Cardinals co-captain from 1965–1969. But in 1969, the Cardinals dropped to fourth place in the newly-created East Division of the National League. Although Flood was a seven-time Gold Glove Award winner with a lifetime .293 average, Cardinals Owner Augie Busch decided to trade Flood on October 7, 1969, together with Byron Brown, Joe Hoerner, and Tim McCarver to the Philadelphia Phillies for Dick Allen, Jerry Johnson, and Cookie Rojas. Flood refused to accept the trade and decided to sue Major League Baseball for the right to strike his own deal. Six years later, Flood would lose his case before the United States Supreme Court, but Organized Baseball's perpetual reserve clause would be altered by the ruling of an arbitration panel. Players were about to receive unparalleled freedoms with the creation of free agency and the establishment of salary arbitration.

Flood initiated his lawsuit by filing a complaint in the Southern District of New York based upon five causes of action.[60] First, Flood argued that Organized Baseball's reserve clause constituted an unreasonable restraint of trade under the Sherman Act; second, that the actions of twelve specific teams violated New York and California law; third, that the actions of these same twelve teams violated the common law; fourth, that the practice of the reserve system resulted in peonage and involuntary servitude in violation of federal statutes and the Thirteenth Amendment. The fifth cause of action specifically targeted the St. Louis Cardinals and the New York Yankees.[61]

Flood's complaint alleged that the Cardinals derived substantial revenues from the sales of concessions including beer at its baseball stadium. Because only beer produced by Anheuser-Busch was available at Busch Stadium, Flood's complaint argued that this practice violated both the Sherman and Clayton Acts. Furthermore, Flood argued that "the effect of this violation has been, and will continue to be, to increase the revenues of the beer company and diminish the revenues of defendant St. Louis National Baseball Club, Inc. available for player salaries, including that of plaintiff."[62]

Flood's second claim under the fifth cause of action targeted the Yankees:

> 48. Defendant New York Yankees, Inc. are owned by the Columbia Broadcasting System, one of the three national radio and television networks which might bid on the right to broadcast professional baseball games. On information and belief, as a result of its ownership of the New York Yankees, Inc., the Columbia Broadcasting System has refrained from bidding on such broadcast rights with consequent injury to competition, in violation of §§ 1 and 2 of the Sherman Anti-Trust Act and § 7 of the Clayton Anti-Trust Act (15 U.S.C. §§ 1, 2, and 18).

> 49. The consequence of this violation has been and continues to be, to reduce the revenues of Organized Baseball from the sale of broadcast rights, in which revenues players such as plaintiff would share.[63]

In response to the claim against the Cardinals, the District Court considered the affidavit of club vice president Bing Devine. Devine asserted that beer from brewers other than Anheuser-Busch was sold at the stadium and that the Cardinals did not control or receive concession revenue anyway. The court granted St. Louis summary judgment on their motion.[64]

The court turned its attention to the claim against the Yankees. The Yankees submitted the affidavit of William MacPhail, the Vice-President for Sports for the CBS Television Network. MacPhail stated that CBS presented a bid to the Major League Baseball Televison Committeee in 1965. That bid was turned down in favor of one from NBC and the Committee had subsequently renewed the contract. Because Flood's attorney offered no evidence to rebut the affidavit, the court granted summary judgment to the Yankees on their motion.[65]

The case proceed to trial. Flood was treated rudely by Judge Cooper who seemed to question why someone offered a large amount of money to play baseball could possibly be upset with the system. Cooper decided that baseball was still exempt from antitrust scrutiny under *Federal Baseball* and *Toolson*.[66] The decision was affirmed by the United States Court of Appeals for the Second Circuit.[67] Judge Waterman did find that baseball was involved in interstate commerce, but he refused to alter the stance taken by the district court.

The United States Supreme Court affirmed the opinion of the Second Circuit on June 19, 1972.[68] Justice Harry Blackmun presented a long historical discussion of the origins of baseball including a list of great players that included Yankees notables Babe

Ruth, Lou Gehrig, Joe McCarthy, Wee Willie Keeler, Red Ruffing, Clark Griffith, Frank Chance, and Bill Dickey. Blackmun concluded that

1. Professional baseball is a business and it is engaged in interstate commerce.

2. With its reserve system enjoying exemption from the federal antitrust laws, baseball is, in a very distinct sense, an exception and an anomaly. *Federal Baseball* and *Toolson* have become an aberration confined to baseball.

3....It is an aberration that has been with us now for half a century, one heretofore deemed fully entitled to the benefit of *stare decisis*, and one that has survived the Court's expanding concept of interstate commerce....

4. Other professional sports...are not so exempt.

5. The advent of radio and television...has not occasioned an overruling of *Federal Baseball* and *Toolson.*

6....Congress as yet has had no intention to subject baseball's reserve system to the reach of the antitrust statutes....

7. The Court has expressed concern about the confusion and the retroactivity problems that would inevitably result with a judicial overturning of *Federal Baseball....*[69]

Justices William O. Douglas and William Brennan dissented noting that *Federal Baseball* "is a derelict in the stream of the law that we, its creator, should remove."[70] Justice Thurgood Marshall offered another dissent joined by Brennan that discussed the involuntary servitude issue. Marshall wanted to overrule both *Federal Baseball* and *Toolson*, but accurately predicted the future by stating that the labor exemption may not allow Flood to prevail.

Flood had lost his case, and it sent his life into a downward spiral. He later extricated himself from depression and alcoholism to become a strong community leader and a hero among the stalwarts of baseball's labor movement. Although he sacrificed his career for little gain, he had launched a revolution in relations between owners and players. CBS would decide to sell the Yankees, and the new ownership group headed by George Steinbrenner quickly grasped the meaning of the changing landscape.

XIII. Free Agency and Jim "Catfish" Hunter[71]

During the early 1970s, Charles O. Finley had created the strongest team in the American League in Oakland. The A's captured the World Series from 1972 through 1974. The ace of their pitching staff was Jim "Catfish" Hunter who won 25 games in 1974. He had posted three straight 21-win seasons before 1974. Finley's flamboyant style placed him in stark contrast to the mainline ownership in Major League Baseball. His relationship with Bowie Kuhn became increasingly tempestuous, and his actions relative to his ballplayers would be a hallmark of the changing nature of the game.

Hunter arrived in the Major Leagues at the age of eighteen, and he quickly established himself as a star. Despite his skills, Finley saw little reason to reward him economically. After hurling a perfect game in 1968, Finley raised Hunter's salary by $5,000 and loaned him $150,000 to buy a farm in Hunter's native North Carolina. Finley was a farm owner himself in northern Indiana. His logo-emblazoned barn was a landmark along the otherwise pastoral scenes offered on the sides of the Indiana Turnpike.

Finley's activities in other professional sports franchises, however, had created cash flow problems for the A's owner. He demanded that Hunter repay the loan in full. The pitcher was forced to sell all but a small parcel of the extremely fertile land that he had purchased. The owner's move proved costly for the A's and a boon to the Yankees. Hunter signed a new two-year contract with Finley before the 1974 season. For tax purposes, Hunter arranged to have one-half of his salary paid as an insurance annuity. Finley failed to make the necessary payments into the annuity account. Hunter's attorney, J. Carlton Cherry, made repeated written requests for the payments, but they still were not forthcoming. In frustration, Hunter complained to the media and his teammates. Marvin Miller and Dick Moss of the Major League Players Association had negotiated into the 1968 Collective Bargaining Agreement the right for such deferred payments. They also had forced the creation of an arbitration method in the 1970 agreement to handle grievances.

The union took the lead in filing a grievance on Hunter's behalf. Moss notified Finley that they believed that the owner's actions were a violation of section 7(a) of the Uniform Playing Contract. The clause provided a unilateral right to declare a termination of the contract within ten days after written notification of a breach. Although the union allowed more than ten days for Finley to respond, the A's owner would not budge. On October 4, 1974, in the midst of the World Series between the A's and the Los Angeles Dodgers, the union declared that the contract was terminated and that Hunter was a free agent. Finley responded by offering Hunter a $50,000 check. However, because the cash offer constituted a taxable gift that was not the equivalent of payments to a tax-free annuity fund, Hunter requested that the money be paid to his insurance company.

The matter was submitted to a panel chaired by arbitrator Peter Seitz. Marvin Miller served as the union's panel member, and John Gaherin, represented Major League Baseball. At a hearing on November 1, 1974, Finley's main argument was that Cherry had not submitted the proper paperwork to him. Seitz considered Finley's position and the nature of the contractual language, and he rendered his decision for Hunter on December 13. Although the original statement failed to declare that Hunter was indeed a free agent, Miller convinced Seitz to correct any ambiguity in his decision. Commissioner Bowie Kuhn was angered by the ruling and encouraged the owners not to negotiate with Hunter. However, Kuhn was forced to alter his position after Miller threatened to file a lawsuit claiming a violation of the Collective Bargaining Agreement. Finley's appeal to overturn the arbitration decision failed before the California Supreme Court.

Hunter's salary for 1974 was $100,000. Every team save the Giants and A's offered lucrative deals to Hunter. The teams used creative means to entice Hunter into signing. The San Diego Padres were leading the way when the managing partner of the new Yankees ownership group, George Steinbrenner, stepped forward. The Yankees offered $3.75 million in total salary, an amount that was less than the package offered by the Padres and Royals, but Steinbrenner did present a signing bonus of $1 million, a $1 million life insurance policy, $0.5 million in deferred compensation, $50,000 in annuities for Hunter's children's college expenses, and attorney's fees for Cherry. Hunter accepted the terms on the last day of the year.

Hunter won 23 games and lost 14 for the Yankees in 1975. He followed up with a 17 win campaign in 1976 as the Yankees defeated the Royals in the American League

Championship Series before losing to the Cincinnati Reds in the World Series. After 12 years of pitching in 30 or more games, Hunter's starting appearances declined to an average of 20 during his final three years with the Yanks. He retired at the end of the 1979 season with 224 career wins. He was elected to the Hall of Fame in 1987. Ironically, Hunter died in August 1999 of amyotrophic lateral sclerosis, Lou Gehrig's disease.

XIV. Salary Arbitration

By the early 1970s, the Major League Baseball Players Association began to exhibit some clout at the negotiating table. Curt Flood's case, although ultimately won by Organized Baseball, signaled growing player unrest over the continued strict enforcement of the reserve clause. Union chief Marvin Miller also had a degree of leverage created by Dodgers pitchers Don Drysdale and Sandy Koufax.[72] In 1966, Drysdale and Koufax, two of the National League's premier pitchers, decided to hold out together unless Dodgers owner Walter O'Malley agreed to pay the tandem $1,000,000 over three years.[73] Koufax's financial adviser Bill Hayes[74] approached some attorneys for advice, and they urged him to use California's personal-service contract legislation limiting such agreements to seven years. Because baseball's reserve clause was effectively perpetual, the two pitchers were ready to go to court to argue for free agency status.[75] The prospect of a lawsuit that might attack the essence of the reserve clause on grounds other than antitrust furthered negotiations.[76] Although the two players did not get quite the deal that they sought, they were able to force Dodgers General Manager Buzzy Bavasi and O'Malley to give them the most lucrative contracts of that time in order to get them both to play. Koufax received $125,000, and Drysdale signed for $110,000.

The leverage forced ownership to offer a solution to determine salaries when both the player and management reached an impasse: salary arbitration. The agreement would force all players into this process, thus avoiding a repeat of the Koufax-Drysdale double team. Miller saw the possibilities behind the proffered arrangement. The union would agree to the anti-collusion clause in the collective bargaining process only if they received a reciprocal agreement against collusion from the owners. The collusion clause would prove invaluable to the players in the 1980s just as arbitration would prove to be a great boon to players seeking to push salaries upward.

The basic system of salary arbitration in baseball is a simple one. Eligibility is based on terms of service. Under the current Collective Bargaining Agreement, a player with at least three years of Major League service but less than six years is defined as "arbitration-eligible." A player with between two and three years of service can be eligible if "he has accumulated at least 86 days of service during the immediately prior season" and "ranks in the top seventeen percent" of players in the two-year service group. This category was bitterly negotiated during the 1994 season when ownership sought to reduce the number of players eligible for arbitration. Because players who are not "arbitration-eligible" are still tied exclusively to one team, they have little ability to force ownership to provide salaries far above the league minimum. Players with six years of service have won the right to be free agents under the Collective Bargaining Agreement.

In what is styled as "single offer" or "final offer" arbitration, the player and management each submit a single number. The arbitrator or panel of arbitrators can choose only one of the two numbers. The essence of the system is to force each party to offer a defensible wage. If one side chooses a figure that is not credible, that side runs the strong risk of having the arbitrator(s) choose the other side's number. The result in the vast majority of cases is to force each side to settle before arbitration at a point between the two offered figures. If the sides cannot settle on a figure, they proceed to arbitration understanding that they will either win completely and receive the figure they have selected or lose and be forced to live with the winner's wage.

Each party is granted one hour for an initial presentation and one-half hour for rebuttal. The arbitrator or panel can grant an extension for good cause. The parties can discuss:

> [T]he quality of the Player's contribution to his Club during the past season (including but not limited to his overall performance, special qualities of leadership and public appeal), the length and consistency of his career contribution, the record of the Player's past compensation, comparative baseball salaries..., the existence of any physical or mental defects on the part of the Player, and the recent performance record of the Club including but not limited to its League standing and attendance as an indication of public acceptance....[77]

The arbitrator or panel cannot consider the following evidence:

> The financial position of the Player and the Club;...Press comments, testimonials or similar material bearing on the performance of either the Player or the Club, except that recognized annual Player awards for playing excellence shall not be excluded;...offers made by either Player or Club prior to arbitration;... The cost to the parties of their representatives, attorneys, etc.;...Salaries in other sports or occupations.[78]

The arbitrator or panel has 24 hours to select one of the two numbers and write that number into the standard player contract. Neither side can litigate or appeal the outcome of the process.

XV. The Yankees in Salary Arbitration[79]

Salary arbitration arrived on the Major League scene at the same time that George Steinbrenner purchased the New York Yankees. Steinbrenner's feelings about the process have never been positive, and his feelings about the players that have forced him into arbitration rarely have been positive. Unless you are a key player, a trip to arbitration with the Yankees usually results in a quick exit from Manhattan regardless of the outcome.

During the first year of salary arbitration, 1974, 29 cases proceeded to a hearing. The Yankees were involved in four, winning two and losing two. Future manager Gene Michael had logged 129 games in 1973 for the Yankees at shortstop hitting .255 at a salary of $55,000. He requested an increase to $65,500, but the Yankees prevailed after offering the same $55,000. Michael played only 81 games in 1974 for New York, and he spent 1975, his last year as a player, in Detroit. Catcher Duke Sims had played only four games in 1973 for the Yankees after a trade from Detroit. Sims asked for an increase from his previous salary of $50,000 to $56,000. The Yankees again countered with the previous year's salary, and they won. Sims was traded to the Texas Rangers after playing only five games in 1974 for the Yankees.

Pitcher Wayne Granger had arrived in New York in August 1973 in a trade for Ken Crosby. Granger pitched in only seven games for the Yankees and recorded one loss. Although Granger actually submitted a request for $2,500 less than his previous salary of $47,500, the Yankees thought even $45,000 was undeserved. The team countered with an offer of $42,000. Granger won his case, but he did not even pitch in New York in 1974. Bill Sudakis, a utility player for Texas in 1973, hit .255 in 82 games. The Yankees had purchased him for cash in December 1973. Sudakis sought an increase from $20,000 to $30,000. The Yankees offered $25,000, but the arbitrator ruled in favor of Sudakis. In 89 games he could muster but a .232 batting average. In December 1974, the Yankees sent Sudakis to California in exchange for Skip Lockwood. The Yankees were able to settle with two more significant players, Lou Piniella and Graig Nettles, prior to the hearings. The Yankees were able to avoid arbitration the next year, and baseball did not have the process in 1976 and 1977.

It was not until 1981 that the Yankees again entered into arbitration, this time with catcher Rick Cerone. Cerone hit .277 with 14 home runs and 85 RBIs in 147 games in 1980. Cerone requested $440,000, and the Yankees offered $350,000. Cerone won when Jesse Simons chose the backstop's figure. Both Cerone and Simons, a New York lawyer and director of the Office of Collective Bargaining, incurred Steinbrenner's wrath:

> Cerone makes $440,000 a year, this is after I rescued him from the scrap heap at Toronto, where he was making $100,000. And as soon as he comes to New York he takes me to arbitration and wins with some garment-district arbitrator who knows nothing about baseball. And if Cerone doesn't do well is he gonna return the money to me? Hell no. It's a new age, and these players are making more than some big corporate executives. So I've got a platform where the little guy doesn't, and I use it.[80]

Cerone responded to Steinbrenner's outrage and the nickname "Brutus" applied by his teammates by noting that manager Gene Michael was the last to take Steinbrenner to arbitration, "[I]f I'm disloyal, how come he's the manager?" Michael quipped, "I was in Detroit the next season."[81] Despite the Boss's outrage, Cerone's first tour of duty with the Yankees lasted through the 1984 season. He would also play for the Yankees in 1987 and 1990.

In 1982 the Yankees' consolation prize for losing the 1981 World Series to the Los Angeles Dodgers was three victories in arbitration. Outfielder Bobby Brown, who batted .226 in 31 games for the 1981 Yankees, asked for $175,000 and the Yankees countered with $90,000. Brown wanted to force the issue with the Yankees. "If I had won, I still wouldn't have gotten what I wanted. I went to salary arbitration to get traded. I want to go somewhere that I can play. The Yankees don't have any use for me. I would think that they would want to get me out of here."[82] Arbitrator Robert Stutz sided with the Yankees, the same position he would take after hearing Ron Davis's case. Brown was peddled to Seattle on April 1, 1982, with Bill Caudill and Gene Nelson for Shane Rawley.

Pitcher Ron Davis had won 4 and lost 5 with a 2.72 ERA in 43 relief appearances. Davis requested a raise from $200,000 to $575,000, but the Yankees countered with $300,000. Davis lost the case, but still received the 50% raise and a better deal than the last pre-arbitration offer of $225,000. Vice president for baseball operations Bill Bergesh noted "I just hope that now he continues with the fine attitude he's exhibited with this thing. He's shown me a lot of spirit, the way he came in early and stayed until the night before the arbitration hearing and came back right afterward."[83] Davis argued that he did not have statistics to show his value as a set-up man to Goose Gossage. Although he stated that "I have a right to be back next year and I'll be back,"[84] he never got that opportunity with the Yankees. Davis was dealt on April 10, 1982, to Minnesota with Paul Boris and Greg Gagne for Roy Smalley.

First baseman Dave Revering wanted $325,000, but the Yankees felt that he deserved only $250,000. Arbitrator Richard Bloch finished the Yankees sweep by siding with the team against Revering. Revering quipped, "I'm just going to the beach. It's all business. My time will come."[85] Noting the difficulty for players who attend the hearing, Revering pointed out, "If they say to R.D. what they said to me, he'll go over the top of the table because he can't control his temper."[86] After 14 games in the 1982 season, Revering received the same treatment as Brown and Davis when the Yankees packaged him in a deal with Oakland that included Mike Patterson and minor league pitcher Chuck Dougherty for Jim Spencer and Tom Underwood.

No one dared push the Yankees back into arbitration over the next four years. However, in 1987 the Yankees were forced into the process when their first major star, Don Mattingly, challenged the Bronx Bombers. The first baseman had led the league in hits (238), doubles (53), and slugging percentage (.538) in 1986 while batting .352 with 31 home runs, 117 runs scored, and 113 RBIs. Mattingly's 1986 salary was $1,375,000. The Yankees were willing to offer an increase to $1,700,000, but the first baseman felt that $1,975,000 was more in order. Arbitrator Arvid Anderson agreed with the Yankees star player.[87]

Steinbrenner angrily attacked both the union and his first baseman.[88] Steinbrenner felt that the union interfered with negotiations claiming that "[h]e (Mattingly) and I were very close to an agreement (reportedly a two-year, $3.85 million contract),...but both the player and his agent came back and said they were getting pressure from the union (to go through arbitration)."[89] MLBPA Executive Director Don Fehr called the assertion "patent claptrap."[90]

The Yankees owner clearly placed the onus for winning on Mattingly:

> I fully expect Don Mattingly to lead us to a championship at these figures, like Gary Carter did with the Mets. Now the monkey's on his back. He's got to deliver....The only thing that came to me—and, mind you, there was no bitterness—is that I used to think of Don Mattingly as the little kid from Evansville. That's the way he portrayed himself. The union had a fine hand in driving this kid, and he's now no longer the little Hoosier from the Indiana river. He's out for the almighty buck.[91]

Mattingly finished his 14-year career with the Yankees in 1995 with 2,153 hits and a .307 batting average. Unfortunately, his only playoff experience was in 1995 in the divisional series.

In 1988, the Yankees were able to beat third baseman Mike Pagliarulo in arbitration.[92] Pagliarulo requested an increase from $175,000 to $625,000 after slamming 32 home runs but batting only .234 in the previous campaign. The Yankees countered with an offer of $500,000, and arbitrator Lawrence Holden agreed with them. Pagliarulo played the entire 1988 season with the Yankees, but he was traded during the 1989 season to San Diego with Don Schulze for Walt Terrell and Fred Toliver. From 1989 through 1992, the Yankees were spared from arbitration.

In 1993, the Yankees defeated pitchers Jim Abbott and John Habyan and lost to Randy Velarde. Abbott sought an increase from $1,850,000 to $3,500,000 after winning 7 and losing 15 for the California Angels in 1992. The Yankees acquired Abbott on December 6, 1992, for J. T. Snow, Russ Springer, and Jerry Nielson. The Yankees felt that a $500,000 raise was sufficient and offered $2,350,000. Arbitrator Anthony Sinicropi agreed with the Yankees. Abbott responded with an 11-14 campaign with 32 starts and a 4.37 ERA. After a 9-8 season in 1994, the Yankees lost Abbott in free agency to the Chicago White Sox on April 8, 1995.

Habyan requested a raise to $830,000 after making $500,000 the previous year. The reliever appeared in 56 games in 1992, recording 5 wins against 6 losses and 7 saves. Arbitrator Theodore High adopted the Yankees' position. Habyan departed in July 1993 in a three team trade with the Kansas City Royals and the Chicago Cubs. The Yankees received pitcher Paul Assenmacher.

Velarde requested $1,050,000 after playing for $360,000 in 1992. The utility player had managed to appear in 121 games in 1992 for the Yankees, hitting .272. The Yankees offered $600,000, but arbitrator Robert Creo sided with Velarde. Velarde responded by hitting .301 in 85 games in 1993. Velarde remained with the Yankees through the 1995 season. He played in 1996 for the California Angels.

In 1994, second baseman Pat Kelly sought an increase from $160,000 to $810,000. Kelly batted .280 in 93 games. The Yankees offered $575,000. Arbitrator Pat Hardin awarded Kelly $810,000. Kevin Maas and Terry Mulholland, however, each lost their battles with the Bronx Bombers. Maas sought $490,000 after appearing in 59 games and hitting .205 in 1993. His compensation for the previous year was $255,000. The Yankees offered $425,000. Maas had become a fan favorite when he hit 21 home runs during three months of his rookie season. Arbitrator Jerome Ross agreed with the Yankees management, who released Maas near the end of spring training. Maas did not play in the majors in 1994 after signing a minor league deal with the San Diego Padres. Maas did play in 22 games for the 1995 Minnesota Twins, but he failed to regain his rookie form.

Mulholland had played for $2,600,000 in 1993 as a member of the Philadelphia Phillies. He sought an increase to $4,050,000. The Yankees offer of $3,350,000 was determined by arbitrator Jim Duff to be satisfactory. In his only year with the Yankees, he appeared in 24 games, with 19 starts, a record of 6 wins and 7 losses and a 6.49 ERA. On April 8, 1995, Mulholland signed as a free agent with the San Francisco Giants.

After skipping 1995, the Yankees entered their second arbitration hearing with a significant star player prior to the 1996 season. Bernie Williams toiled for $400,000 in 1995, his fifth year with the Yankees. He hit .307 with 18 home runs and 83 RBIs in 144 games in the outfield. He sought an increase to $3,000,000, and the Yankees offered $2,555,000. Arbitrator Ralph Berger awarded Williams his request after a hearing that left Williams less than pleased with statements made by the Yankees about his play. General Manager Bob Watson, putting aside any feelings that he had as a former player, was also displeased with the process. Highlighting a general feeling about the role of arbitrators in the process, Watson noted:

> The whole thing leaves a lot to be desired. Obviously, there has to be a better way for both sides, where one guy rules in one side's favor one time, then feels like he has to rule the other way just to keep his job. The system we have now is not fair, and ultimately it's the fans who are losers. The salary costs are passed on to them.[93]

Despite the displeasure, Williams increased his homer output to 29 with 102 RBIs while batting .305 in 1996 in 143 games. In 1998, he led the American League in hitting with a .339 average. Williams later received a significant free agent offer from the Boston Red Sox, but he decided to stay in New York.

The Yankees avoided arbitration during the next two off-seasons, only to return in 1999 to bitter victories by Derek Jeter and Mariano Rivera over new General Manager Brian Cashman. Jeter and Rivera had both received $750,000 in 1998, the year before each became salary arbitration-eligible. Jeter requested a raise to $5,000,000, and Rivera requested $4,250,000. The Yankees offered Jeter $3,200,000 and Rivera $3,000,000. The power of the process and the stark differences between the salaries of arbitration-eligible and non-arbitration-eligible players were seldom more apparent than in these two cases.

Jeter's agent, Casey Close, offered to settle with Cashman for $4.1 million just before the hearing. Cashman felt that he had the better number, but the arbitration panel of Ira Jaffe, Gil Vernon, and Nicholas Zumas decided that $5 million was more of an accurate reflection of Jeter's worth despite the Yankees' argument that he needed to show better power numbers. Published newspaper accounts of Steinbrenner's comments were positive towards Jeter, but the same stories noted his displeasure with Cashman.

Rivera also prevailed. Arbitrator James Duff chose Rivera's 4.25 million figure. Steinbrenner reacted angrily to his second loss within one week. "Only one time out of 10 has baseball won in arbitration when a world championship team is concerned. If they want to make popularity part of it, or whether you win the championship, I don't know. I've dealt with a lot of arbitrators, but I've never seen anything like this."[94] Cashman was ordered to trim the payroll to account for the two losses.

The following year, the Yankees again failed to agree with Rivera. The star closer wanted an increase to $9,250,000. The Yankees thought that a $3,000,000 increase to $7,250,000 was more appropriate. Arbitrators Howard Block, Elisabeth Neumeier, and Alan Symonette agreed with the Yankees this time.

Jeter and Rivera were joined by catcher Jorge Posada when the trio filed for arbitration in 2001. Posada settled before exchanging numbers. Deciding to avoid the annual antagonism, the Yankees worked toward long-term deals with their shortstop and closer. Jeter asked for $18,500,000, and the Yankees countered with $14,250,000. Jeter and the Yankees signed a 10-year deal worth $189 million before the hearing took place. Rivera sought $10,250,000, and the Yankees offered $9,000,000. Rivera ultimately inked a 4-year $39.9 million deal because Steinbrenner refused to offer $40 million.

The Yankees settled all of their 2002 cases prior to any hearings and settled in for negotiations over a new collective bargaining agreement. Although a strike was averted at the last possible moment, the Yankees were left with a heavy assessment for their huge salary structure. The Yankees, however, continue to use their time-honored tradition of trading or purchasing the athletes that they need to maintain their on-field success.

XVI. The Maris Family Suit against Anheuser-Busch[95]

Roger Maris joined the Yankees prior to the 1960 season after a trade with the Kansas City Athletics. The left-handed hitting outfielder quickly adjusted to Yankee Stadium's short right field dimensions, and Maris posted five strong power seasons in-

cluding the fabled 61-homer year in 1961. When Maris failed to produce similar seasons in 1965 and 1966 and the Yankees' string of five straight World Series appearances
dissolved into a last place and a next to last place finish, the Yankees decided to trade
Maris to the St. Louis Cardinals. Maris responded by helping an already strong team to
World Series appearances in 1967 and 1968. In gratitude for Maris' ten-hit performance in the 1967 Fall Classic as the Cardinals defeated the Boston Red Sox, Cardinals
owner Augie Busch Jr. thought he had a proper reward. Busch awarded Maris and his
brother Rudy the Gainesville and Ocala, Florida, Anheuser-Busch distributorship.
Maris retired after the Cardinals lost the 1968 series to the Detroit Tigers to run the
business. Under Maris's leadership, the franchise became one of the strongest in
Florida, and Maris brought his wife, son Roger Maris, Jr., and six relatives into the
business. Roger Maris died in 1985, and his older brother Rudy assumed the presidency of Maris Distributing.

Beginning in 1991, however, Anheuser-Busch sought changes in its Florida market.
During that year, the parent company lost a federal court case launching a long battle
with their Orlando distributor over that market. The Tampa distributor lost a state
court action when the parent company blocked the Tampa group's attempt to purchase
the Sarasota distributorship. In the midst of a two-year court battle concerning Anheuser-Busch's attempt to terminate their relationship with their Jacksonville distributorship, the St. Louis-based company settled the suit by purchasing those rights and
awarding it to the Tallahassee group. That transaction allowed Susan Busch Transou,
the daughter of August Busch III, and her husband Tripp Transou to assume control of
the Tallahassee market.

In July 1996, Anheuser-Busch sent a marketing team to review Maris Distributing's facilities and practices. Family members were ordered to St. Louis where the results of the team's analysis of the Marises' practices were discussed. Sensing the potential termination of their distribution relationship with the parent company, the
family submitted in August a "Notice of Intent to Sell," as outlined in the Wholesaler
Equity Agreement that formed the contractual basis of that relationship. Anheuser-
Busch made two offers to the Maris family for the business. Because the family considered the $20.4 million and $21.5 million offers to be below market value, they
continued to look for a stronger offer from the six potential buyers that came forward. In November 1996, the parent company notified Maris that without corrections to certain noted deficiencies the agreement would be terminated. Without a favorable purchase offer and facing the imminent termination of the distribution
relationship, the Maris family responded in January 1997 by filing lawsuits in both
state and federal court.

The federal court complaint charged the parent company with violating the Sherman
Act because the Wholesaler Equity Agreement's prohibition of public ownership constituted an unreasonable restraint of trade that worked against the Maris family in their
attempt to sell the business. On March 20, 1997, Anheuser-Busch terminated its agreement with Maris Distributing Company. At the time of the termination of the relationship, Maris Distributing had a 64 percent share of its market. That performance exceeded the 55 percent overall state market share for Anheuser-Busch and the national
market share of 45 percent. Anheuser-Busch filed a countersuit claiming a breach of
contract due to "merchandising and operating procedures that were seriously deficient"
including the intentional sales of out-of-date beer. Anheuser-Busch sold the Gainesville/
Ocala market to two distributors for approximately $13 million. One of the buyers was
a close friend of August Busch III.

The federal litigation and appeal involved a complex analysis of vertical, non-price restraints. A seven-week trial resulted in a verdict for Anheuser-Busch on those issues left after the parent company's victory on a number of key summary judgment motions. The appellate court affirmed the trial court's determination that Maris Distributing did not show that Anheuser-Busch possessed the requisite market power that was central to their Sherman Act claim despite a number of imaginative arguments. The district court directed a verdict in favor of Anheuser-Busch on that issue. Despite that analysis, the district court still allowed the jury to consider whether Maris had proven actual anticompetitive effects due to the public ownership restriction in the Anheuser-Busch agreement. The jury determined that Maris had not carried the burden of proof. The trial and appeal to the Eleventh Circuit Court of Appeals proved to be extremely costly. The appellate court rebuffed attempts by Maris Distributing to reduce the cost of travel for Anheuser-Busch witnesses, costs associated with expedited transcripts used by Anheuser-Busch lawyers, and the depositions of fifteen individuals, including eight Marises, that were not used at trial.

The state litigation, however, proved to be more successful for the Maris family. Maris Distributing sued Anheuser-Busch on grounds of breach of contract, tortious interference with business relations, and wrongful termination. The Maris family hired Willie E. Gary, a Florida lawyer noted for defeating large corporate clients. Gary represented six businessmen who won a $240 million verdict against Walt Disney Co. in an intellectual property claim involving the concept for the Wide World of Sports Complex. Anheuser-Busch countered with veteran Washington, D.C. attorney Peter Moll, who had successfully represented the brewery for more than 25 years. Judge R. A. "Buzz" Green was forced to issue contempt citations early in the trial against the two attorneys and some of their associates. When that action failed to correct the behavior of the lawyers, Green appointed Stephen N. Bernstein to serve as special master to investigate the activities surrounding the trial. In his 35-page report, Bernstein concluded that the actions of the lawyers were "an insult to the integrity of the legal system."

Opening arguments commenced on May 2, 2001. The jury failed to accept Anheuser-Busch's claim that the termination was for cause despite testimony about the poor condition of delivery trucks, warehouses, and grounds surrounding the company, the repackaging and sale of out-of-date beer, the lack of attention by the Marises to recommendations from St. Louis, and fraudulent marketing practices. The jury delivered its verdict on August 3, finding that the fair market value of the business taken by the St. Louis brewer was $50 million and damages for lost sales amounted to $89,698,500. The larger award was quickly nullified as unavailable under Florida law, but Green added $22.6 million in interest charges.

On August 29, Judge Green denied a request by the Maris family to reinstate the original jury verdict of $139,658,500 and to rule that Anheuser-Busch violated Florida's Deceptive and Unfair Trade Practices Act. The later ruling deprived the Maris group of attorneys' fees. Green also rejected Anheuser-Busch's request for a new trial and a ruling that Maris Distributing had violated the Deceptive and Unfair Trade Practices Act. In response to out-of-court statements about the business practices of the Maris family, they filed a $1 billion defamation suit. No final resolution has yet been reached, and the Maris family has not collected on its judgment. As the former Yankee slugger's family remains mired in its long legal struggles with a corporate giant, the Yankees reentered the antitrust arena when they chose to increase their local broadcasting revenue.

XVII. Cablevision and Yankees Entertainment & Sports Network[96]

Despite having the most lucrative local baseball television broadcasting deal, George Steinbrenner decided in the late 1990s to regain control of the rights to Yankees games from fellow-Cleveland native and Cablevision chairman Charles Dolan and Dolan's son James, the CEO of Cablevision. On June 21, 2001, the team agreed to pay Cablevision, the parent company of Madison Square Garden (MSG) Network, $30 million to regain the rights beginning with the 2002 season. The payment came two days before a deadline set in April to resolve litigation involving the rights to Yankees broadcasts. During that litigation, the 2001 rights fees owed to the Yankees by MSG were established as $52 million for 85 games. Coupled with the successful reacquisition of 65 games broadcasted on over-the-air channel 5 in New York, the Yankees could repackage the local deal by moving approximately 130 games to cable with an additional 20 to 25 games on an over-the-air channel. Industry specialists predicted that a successful deal with each of the local cable providers in the metropolitan New York area could generate nearly $100 million more than the previous package for YankeesNets, the holding company formed in 1999 to oversee ownership of the Yankees, the NHL's New Jersey Devils and the NBA's New Jersey Nets.

Yankees telecasts were acquired in 1988 by Garden president Bob Gutkowski for $487 million. By adding the Yankees to the television rights for the NBA's Knicks and the NHL's Rangers, MSG created a powerful local network. Steinbrenner, for his part, used the money to acquire top free agents that pushed the Yankees back amongst the elite franchises in Major League Baseball.

YankeesNets worked throughout the summer to find a minority partner to help infuse additional capital into the new broadcasting entry. On September 10, 2001, the Yankees Entertainment and Sports Network (YES) was officially launched under the leadership of former AT&T Broadband president Leo Hindery, Jr. Hindery was part of a group that also included Goldman Sachs & Co., Quadrangle Group LLC, and Amos Hostetter, Jr. that purchased a 40% interest in the enterprise for approximately $350 million. Hindery immediately staked out his negotiating posture by arguing that YES should be included as part of the basic cable package on a similar footing with Fox Sports New York, MSG, and ESPN. Hindery balked at the prospect of accepting a less advertising-friendly premium slot that would not provide access to the huge New York area cable subscriber base. Hindery opened with an asking price of approximately $2 per subscriber, significantly higher than the $1.25 paid in the New York area for ESPN. Cablevision, with 2.9 million subscribers in the Bronx, Brooklyn, Long Island, Westchester County, Connecticut, and New Jersey countered by arguing that YES should only be available to their subscribers as part of a premium package. Within two weeks, Quadrangle and Hostetter had pulled their $190 million out of the deal and walked away forcing Goldman Sachs to increase their contribution. Cablevision and YES were squarely at odds as the New York community was devastated by the tragedy of September 11.

In November, YES reached a three-year agreement with WCBS-TV (Channel 2) to broadcast at least 20 games over-the-air. The deal solidified the 130–135 game package that YES expected to launch on cable or pay TV in March 2002. About 12 additional Yankees games were set to appear on national ESPN or Fox broadcasts.

In early February 2002, YES reached its first distribution deal with DirecTV and followed the deal quickly by signing up RCN with its coverage of Manhattan, Queens, sections of New Jersey, and Carmel, New York. Time Warner, with 1.7 million customers, and Comcast, with 500,000 subscribers quickly agreed to YES' demand that their programming be available on expanded basic cable. Time Warner and RCN quickly announced rate increases for their customers. Hughes Electronic and AT&T Broadband (Connecticut) also accepted YES' terms. Cablevision, however, refused to accept the YES offer. On March 26, Cablevision offered YES a premium channel spot with the rights to keep all revenues generated from Cablevision subscribers. However, YES argued that it deserved the opportunity to join MSG on Cablevision's basic plan. As the new baseball season drew near, YES ran full-page ads in local New York area newspapers targeting Cablevision for being the only major cable provider in the region without Yankees games. At the same time, Cablevision saw the value of their shares drop 52% from the previous year.

On April 9, Lenard Leeds of Leeds Morelli & Brown filed a lawsuit in federal district court in Central Islip on behalf of five New York residents against YES and Cablevision seeking both unspecified damages and a court order requiring an arbitrator to end the stalemate. The five also wanted to force the two parties to televise the games while negotiations continued. District Court Judge Thomas Platt was assigned the case and told Leeds on April 22 that he saw little merit in the action but gave Leeds three days to decide if he wished to pursue a class-action suit. YES and the Yankees were dropped from the action within a month of the original filing, squarely resting the plaintiffs' sole remedy on Cablevision. On June 15, Platt dismissed the suit.

On April 30, YES filed an antitrust lawsuit against Cablevision in federal district court in Manhattan. David Boies, lead counsel for Al Gore in the contested 2000 presidential election actions in Florida and for the federal government in its antitrust lawsuit against Microsoft, argued in his complaint that Cablevision was abusing its monopoly power in the cable market by refusing to negotiate with YES. The complaint attacked Cablevision for its ownership of the Knicks, Rangers, MSG, and FSNY as a monopoly, abusing its power in the local sports broadcasting market by favoring its own sports properties in an attempt to prevent YES from establishing its business. By filing its antitrust suit, YES was employing a time-honored technique to force a resolution of a business conflict. YES holds monopsony power with respect to the broadcast rights to the Yankees. By refusing to offer its product except on its own terms of price per subscriber and its basic cable demand as opposed to a premium offering, YES appears to be on no stronger antitrust grounds than Cablevision. Although both sides have argued about the number of consumers who opted for DirecTV's alternate outlet for access to the Yankees games, an analysis of the antitrust claims must consider the impact of that outlet on Cablevision's monopoly power.

In June, Cablevision requested that District Court Judge Deborah A. Batts grant them nearly two years to prepare for the trial and dismiss almost all of the antitrust claims filed by YES. As the impasse moved into the summer, Major League Baseball and the Players Association reached a new four-year collective bargaining agreement. On September 4, Batts allowed seven of the eight claims to stand while dismissing only one state antitrust claim. YES was given 20 days to file an amended complaint. Meanwhile, Charles and James Dolan were facing criticism as Cablevision's one-year stock loss reached 77% in September and Cablevision completed a method to address a projected cash deficit of over one-half billion dollars. Both YES and Cablevision have suffered severe losses as a result of their refusal to budge in negotiations, but pursuit of antitrust litigation as a method to solve a basic business difference is unlikely to be a major contributor to the resolution of the standoff.

XVIII. Conclusion

Although the broadcasting arm of the Yankees is still fighting an antitrust action, the history of the Yankees at the intersection of antitrust and labor law has been one of great success. From their early years when the acquisition of Carl Mays and Babe Ruth created the championship teams of the 1920s and established Yankees pinstripes as a symbol of excellence through the Steinbrenner Era of salary arbitration and free-agent acquisitions, the team has exploited the legal and business landscape to create one of the greatest traditions in American sports. As the Yankees enter the twenty-first century, there appear to be few obstacles to their continued success.

V. Bigger Issues

As the first black player on the Yankees, catcher Elston Howard had to endure the racial slurs of Yankee manager Casey Stengel. Photo © Bettmann/CORBIS.

Breaking the Color Barrier

by Timothy Davis*

On July 20, 1998, Whitney Joseph, an African-American, her two sons and a white friend attended a baseball game at Yankee Stadium. Prior to the game, the four went to the Stadium Club ("Club") for dinner. The Club maintains a dress code that is posted outside its entrance. The code prohibits "tank tops," and other "abbreviated attire." Joseph's sons and her friend (allegedly wearing shorts and a tank top) were permitted to enter the Club. Joseph, who was wearing shorts and a "tank top" which she described as a sleeveless sweater knit with a small V-neck, was denied entry for failing to comport with the Club's dress code. After putting on a t-shirt, Joseph was permitted to enter the Club.

In her lawsuit against the Yankees, Joseph claimed that "non-minority women inside the Club were wearing tank tops and clothing 'skimpier' than hers, including a 'spaghetti strap top,' a 'midriff, no sleeve top,' and a 'backless, no sleeve top.'"[1] A federal district court judge denied the Yankees' motion to dismiss Joseph's racial discrimination claim. Thereafter, Joseph and the Yankees resolved their dispute through a court-ordered mediation process.

In July 1994, Richard Kraft resigned as Yankee vice-president. His resignation came in the aftermath of an article that appeared in *New York Magazine*. In the article, Kraft was quoted as directing a racial slur toward black youths who live near Yankee Stadium. Kraft reportedly said, "It's like monkeys.... Those guys can all go up and hang on the rim and crack the rim and bend the hoops. It's a continuous maintenance problem" (referring to the basketball courts in Macombs Dam Park which is located next to the stadium).[2] Kraft also reportedly remarked that "the stadium enforces rules to show these less fortunate individuals what it's like in a society where things are ordered on a basis of gentleman- and woman-hood."[3]

Representatives of several New York City organizations condemned the statements as racially insensitive and demanded an apology. Yankee officials immediately apologized for Kraft's comments. Some critics of the Yankees viewed Kraft's alleged statements as playing on stereotypes and further polarizing the team's relationship with the community. The relationship had become strained due to the Yankees' decision to explore the possibility of relocating from the Bronx.

The forgoing scenarios provide recent illustrations of instances in which the Yankee organization has tackled matters with a racial undercurrent. In its past, the organization confronted race-related matters ranging from assertions that Babe Ruth was black to the organization's opposition to integrating major league baseball. With respect to the segregation of baseball, the Yankee history (prior to the Dodgers' signing of Jackie Robinson) paralleled the experiences of other major league baseball teams. Similar to other clubs and major league baseball officials, the Yankee approach to segregation was largely to ignore it. When forced to address baseball's "race problem", Yankee statements emphasized the non-existence of any formal bar to integration.

Given the parallels between the Yankees and other teams, an interesting question emerges—why was the Yankee organization singled-out for having historically possessed greater animosity to the entry of black ballplayers into the major leagues than most other teams? According to one writer, "[a]s mediocre as baseball's record on race has been nationwide, the Yankee record has been even worse."[4] Others share this view. Is this perception of the Yankee organization accurate? If so, was this perception influenced by factors such as the preeminence of the Yankees, the team's location in New York City, and the conduct of Yankee players and officials?

Elston Howard joined the Yankees in 1955. Thus the Yankees integrated eight years after Jackie Robinson joined the Brooklyn Dodgers and six years after Jake Thompson and Monte Irvin joined the New York Giants. Was the Yankee delay a product of the racial bigotry of an organization bent on resisting change and remaining segregated for as long as possible? As suggested by one commentator, the Yankee organization through racially motivated decisions made a direct "statement that they weren't going to have an African-American ballplayer until somebody forced them."[5]

In attempting to respond to the forgoing question, this chapter examines the Yankee approach to race relations during the years before and shortly after Jackie Robinson reintegrated major league baseball. An historical overview teaches us of the complexity of race relations in America generally and baseball specifically. Indeed, the Yankee history in regard to race presents a complex story replete with racial and nonracial factors that motivated decisions and shaped attitudes toward integrating the organization. The Yankee approach to integration also demonstrates the difficulties encountered in attempting to distinguish racial, economic, and other motivations. This chapter also examines the way in which racial attitudes during baseball's segregated era contradicted the ideals on which baseball and other sports are premised. Finally, the discussion will reveal the power of conduct and statements in creating public perception. These perceptions, whether deserved or undeserved, can significantly impact an organization's long-term relationships with its immediate constituency and the larger community in which it is situated. Before addressing these matters, I briefly review the segregated world in which major league baseball operated for almost 50 years.

I. Baseball's Segregated Era

A. Segregation

Organized baseball was not segregated during its early years. It is estimated that approximately 24 blacks played in the professional leagues during the 1880s.[6] Although small in number, blacks played on predominantly white teams and performed well. Black players such as second baseman Frank Grant and pitcher George Stovey developed reputations as fine ballplayers. Blacks played, however, under the shadow of efforts by leagues and players to exclude them. For example, the governing committee of the National Association of Base Ball Players, the first organized baseball league, recommended in 1867 to exclude "any club which may be composed of one or more colored players."[7] This written policy of segregation ended when the league disbanded. In 1876, the National League attempted to impose such a ban but its lack of control over the various circuits in baseball prevented universal implementation of the written policy of segregation.

Renewed efforts were made to exclude blacks during the 1880s and 1890s.[8] In 1887, International League teams voted six to four to exclude blacks purportedly due to concerns that some of the League's best players would leave if the League continued to allow blacks to play; the four teams voting against exclusion had blacks on their rosters. The International League vote created an informal rule of exclusion and a precedent for all levels of organized baseball.[9] Increasingly, baseball signaled to black ballplayers its unwillingness to accommodate them. This unwillingness manifested in increased levels of verbal and physical abuse from fans and players, efforts by white teammates to sabotage black players, and comments by the press and others that unfairly criticized black players and purposefully devalued their accomplishments.

Jim Crow policies, which had established a foothold in the 1890s, were completely in place by 1900. At the beginning of the twentieth century, African-Americans and dark skinned Latinos were totally excluded from organized professional baseball.

The movement toward segregation in baseball mirrored initiatives undertaken to erect barriers to entry in other professions. Racial and ethnic exclusion were considered among the negative attributes that would cause a profession to be deprived of its distinctiveness. Moreover, the exclusion of blacks from baseball reflected a national mood that manifested in the Compromise of 1887 and *Plessy v. Ferguson* in 1896.[10]

Thus began the segregation of baseball pursuant to a "gentlemen's agreement" that had the force and effect of the most tightly written formal contract. This "gentlemen's agreement" was rigidly enforced by a staunch opponent of racial integration, Judge Kenesaw Landis, baseball's first commissioner. Reflecting the hypocrisy that existed in baseball, Landis repeatedly denied the existence of a formal rule of exclusion. "There is no rule, formal or informal, or any understanding—unwritten, subterranean, or sub-anything against the hiring of Negro players by the teams of organized baseball."[11] Landis' comments reveal an effort to conceal the hypocrisy that existed in baseball and in most other aspects of American society.

B. Conspiracy of Silence

Segregated baseball illustrates the way in which sport often reflects and reinforces the values and cultural norms prevalent in society. Indeed, major league baseball's leaders adopted the prevalent approach in American society during this period—whites largely ignored segregation. For the majority of whites, no "Negro problem" existed in baseball or American society at large. This attitude, which has been dubbed the "conspiracy of silence," could be easily adhered to in the case of baseball since the sport was played primarily in northern venues, removed from the areas in which Jim Crow was rigidly enforced.

The silence regarding the race problem in baseball and other institutions in American society during this period is best described by a scholar who wrote that

> [w]e approach questions of race and treat them like a family who is hiding the crazy aunt in the attic (or the crazy uncle in the basement). Everyone knows

she is there, we feel and hear her presence, but we refuse to admit that her
shouts and musings are creating a dysfunctional situation. We choose instead
to continue our charade, behaving as if her intrusions have not influenced our
behavior toward or relationships with one another.[12]

With respect to baseball, the silence created a dysfunction that contradicted the myth of
the meritocracy that is central to sport and baseball.

C. The American Sports Creed

Sport is envisioned as embodying the dominant themes of freedom and individual-
ized achievement. It comports with the belief that conceives of "meritocracy as a system
in which benefits and burdens are distributed in accord with one's deeds—presumably
the products of rational choice—rather than characteristics over which one has no apparent control."[13]

Because sport is often considered as rising above the biases that afflict other important social institutions, it has historically been viewed as the "common carrier" of
the aspirations of those seeking upward mobility.[14] Similar to the role basketball currently plays in the lives of many young black men, baseball served such a function for
the white working class and for black migrates from the South in the late nineteenth
century.

Yet, segregated baseball contradicted the idealized belief that sport, in general, and
baseball in particular constitute venues in which those who possess the requisite ability
can have free access to all of the benefits that can be derived from successful athletic
participation. As stated by one author, "[I]f baseball was truly the national pastime, it
could not exclude a tenth of the population from participation; if baseball embodied
the essence of American competition and opportunity, it could not block entry to those
who possessed the requisite skills to succeed."[15]

Moreover, segregation in baseball illustrates what some scholars refer to as rational discrimination in which cognitive beliefs are developed in an attempt to mask
otherwise impermissible motives—in this instance racial discrimination.[16] In an effort to explain the hypocrisy resulting from segregation, major league baseball's
owners fashioned rationalizations that masked their inability to admit to discrimination and often focused on the alleged shortcomings of others. Some owners argued
that blacks lacked the requisite talent, intelligence and motivation to compete successfully in the major leagues. Some also expressed concerns that integration would
lead to discord among teammates. (Despite the racist views held by Ty Cobb and
other white players, however, a poll taken in the 1930s revealed that most major leaguers did not object to integration.[17]) Owners also rationalized black ballplayer's exclusion based on concerns that integration would lead to a violation of local laws and
customs particularly in the south where minor leagues and training facilities were located.

The owner's greatest fear was that integration would hurt them economically since
white fans would desert the ballparks if blacks were allowed to play in the major leagues.
Subsequent events disproved this rationalization. Notes historian Jules Tygiel, "[w]hite
indifference, rather than fan hostility, posed the principal obstacle to integration.
Northern whites knew that the major leagues were segregated, but the issue seldom in-
truded upon their thoughts."[18]

D. The Negro Leagues

The segregation of major league baseball led black players to act as black Americans did with respect to other cultural and educational institutions—they found other outlets to play baseball and to display their talent. In most instances, black players developed their own baseball teams that would eventually become known as the Negro Leagues. Initially these loosely organized leagues were comprised of teams that barnstormed and played against anyone willing to play, including blacks, whites and Latinos. The Negro Leagues officially established in 1920, consisted initially of the Negro National League, which was joined by the Eastern Colored League in 1923. Between 1923 and 1927, the two leagues were comprised of 14 teams that played an estimated 50 to 89 games per year.[19] The configuration of the Negro Leagues changed during its existence.

For the most part, black baseball constituted a group of independent enterprises notwithstanding efforts in the 1920s and 1930s to establish leagues that paralleled major league baseball. Lacking the integrated organizational structure of major league baseball, Negro League teams continued to depend on barnstorming against black professional teams, black and white semi-professional teams, and teams comprised of white major league all-stars.[20] In the mid-twenties, Commissioner Landis prohibited major league all-star teams from competing against Negro League teams.[21] Thereafter, competition between blacks and major league baseball players occurred on more limited and informal bases such as during the pre-season and the post-season Latin American winter leagues.[22] Here again Landis intervened to limit the number of players from any given major league team that could participate in post-season barnstorming. Thus interracial competition was played regularly but on the periphery of organized baseball.

Latin America was an option available for blacks. Cuban, Mexican, Panamanian, and Puerto Rican Leagues welcomed black players who played exclusively for teams in these leagues or earned extra money by signing on with teams in these leagues in addition to playing for Negro League teams. As noted above, the Latin leagues also provided a venue in which blacks competed against white major league ballplayers during winter season.

In the United States, Latinos were exposed to a double standard. Only Latinos who were considered to have "pure Caucasian blood" were permitted to play in the major leagues.[23] Dark skinned Latinos could not play in the major leagues. Those fair skinned Latinos who were allowed to play had to endure beanballs from opposing pitchers, the dislike of teammates and stereotyping by the press.

Segregated baseball provides insight into the lack of equity wrought by the "separate but equal doctrine." In these independent baseball regimes, black ballplayers were not afforded benefits comparable to those of their white major league counterparts. With the notable exception of Satchel Paige, black ballplayers' salaries averaged less than half that of white major league ballplayers. Although they traveled considerably more than white professional ballplayers, blacks encountered inadequate transportation, and substandard segregated accommodations. Black players also worked harder for fewer financial rewards since most black teams had rosters of 17 or 18 players, unlike the 25 on major league teams. In addition, the unavailability of spring training for black players, stunted their training in the fundamentals of the game.[24]

On the other hand, adversity resulted in creativity and innovation. Black players developed unique styles of pitching, hitting and throwing because they were less likely to get training in baseball fundamentals. Overall, Negro League contests were less orthodox than major league games. This added an element of excitement that was often missing from major league contests. After the reintegration of the major leagues, the style of play developed in the Negro Leagues would enhance the appeal of major league baseball.

E.   Reintegration

Baseball would remain segregated until Jackie Robinson broke the color line by joining the Brooklyn Dodgers in 1947. In fact prior to the 1940s, there was no significant movement by major league teams to integrate the game. However, events external and internal to baseball would eventually lead to its integration. Nazi racism forced Americans to consider the hypocrisy inherent in Jim Crow policies. The war exposed to the nation and the world the contradiction between "democratic ideals" and the racism practiced against black Americans. The idea began to develop during and after the war that racism "was fundamentally at odds with the principles of American democracy."[25] The conspiracy of silence began to lose much of its resiliency in the face of the denial of equal opportunity that confronted blacks who had been sent overseas to fight racist regimes. The war created expectations for equality of treatment that underlie postwar activism by blacks advocating for the integration of various segments of American society. Given that sport was viewed as embodying the "American Creed," it was not surprising when increasingly aggressive campaigns to achieve access to opportunities for blacks in a wide range of institutions spilled over into baseball.

Various groups began actively to campaign for integrated baseball. This pressure included the formation of an "End Jim Crow in Baseball" committee formed in the early forties that included actors, lyricists, poets and politicians such as Paul Robeson, Oscar Hammerstein II, Langston Hughes, John Garfield, and Adam Clayton Powell.[26] In 1945 New York enacted the New York State "Law Against Discrimination," known as Ives-Quinn Act.[27]

The Act, the first fair employment practices statute enacted in the country, created a commission that was empowered to "eliminate discrimination in employment on the basis of race, creed, color, or national origin...."[28] The Act encouraged some New Yorkers to lobby for the prosecution of its three major league teams, the Yankees, Giants, and Dodgers, if they failed to integrate. This effort intensified when the owners of the three teams refused to sign a nondiscrimination pledge as demanded by the state panel charged with investigating discrimination under the Act.

Other activities aimed at pressuring major league baseball to integrate included the efforts of young black sportswriters who took up the challenge to integrate baseball. They along with the Communist Party and other groups became the most ardent critics of segregation in baseball and brought the issue into the public arena at a time when many simply ignored it.[29] In addition, New York City Mayor Fiorella LaGuardia created a Committee on Baseball to examine segregation in baseball. While the committee accomplished very little, it was another statement rejecting the "conspiracy of silence in baseball."

Variables internal to baseball would also set the stage for lowering its color line. The death of Commissioner Landis in 1944 removed a crucial impediment to the integration of baseball. Economic considerations were highly relevant.[30] Notes one writer, "[a]dding impetus to the drive for baseball integration was the ever-more-apparent success of the Negro Leagues," which proved the willingness of blacks to spend on baseball entertainment.[31] In 1944, the Negro League East-West Game drew 46,247 fans in comparison to the 28,589 fans who attended major league baseball's All-Star Game.[32] The shortage of a sufficient supply of quality players, a consequence of the manpower shortage resulting from the military draft also set the stage for weakening the color line in baseball. Baseball's integration became a reality as a result of Branch Rickey, who was motivated by business judgment, his sense of morality, and external persuasion. He developed a calculated strategy that would ultimately result in Jackie Robinson joining the Brooklyn Dodgers.

In summary, the integration of the game was about more than the acts of a few individuals.

> Beginning in the 1940s the Negro press, civil rights groups, the Communist Party, progressive whites, and radical politicians waged a sustained campaign to integrate baseball that involved demonstrations, boycotts, political maneuvering, and other forms of pressure that would gain greater currency the following decade. This protest movement set the stage for Rickey's 'experiment' and for Robinson's entrance into the major leagues.[33]

II. Segregation and the Yankees

By the end of 1954, integration had eradicated the color bar in twelve of the sixteen major league teams. The nation's most celebrated team, the New York Yankees was one of the four that was not yet integrated. Reports out of New York in the early 1950s "attributed the absence of blacks to an undercurrent of racism which permeated the Yankee organization."[34] As is so often the case, however, the persons who comprise an organization do not speak with one voice on matters involving race. Such is true of the Yankees. Individuals within the Yankee organization held contrasting views on integrating the major leagues. For some, racial bigotry motivated their desire to delay integration. For others a combination of factors, including economic considerations often influenced by faulty assumptions premised in part on racial stereotypes, shaped their opinions on the question of integration. As discussed below, several factors, including racial bigotry, contributed to the Yankee delay in integrating.

A confluence of events also influenced the development of the perception of the Yankee organization as bent on systematically delaying integration for as long as possible. For instance, during a 1952 television show, *Youth Wants to Know*, a teenager on the show unexpectedly asked Jackie Robinson if he thought that the Yankees were prejudiced against Negroes. Robinson responded, "I think the Yankee management is prejudiced. There isn't a single Negro on the team now and very few in the entire Yankee farm system."[35] Robinson's comments created a storm of controversy, including vehement denials from Yankee officials.

The sincerity of Yankee management's denials was seriously undermined the following year when Ruben Gomez joined the New York Giants. Gomez, who was a product of the Yankee farm system, purchased his own contract from the club, when he concluded that he had no chance of being promoted to the Yankees. For critics of the team, the Gomez matter supported Robinson's criticism of the Yankees and provided further evidence that the Yankees were not interested in promoting black players within its minor league system. However, perceptions of the Yankees as a racist organization developed prior to the 1950s. One of the more important of the events that contributed to this view involved statements made by Jake Powell.

A. The Jake Powell Incident

On July 28, 1938, an incident occurred that would fuel the perception of the Yankees as an organization comprised of racists vehemently opposed to the racial integration of baseball. Yankee outfielder Jake Powell was interviewed during Chicago radio announcer Bob Elson's pre-game show. When Elson asked Powell how he spent his off-season, Powell responded "he worked as a policeman in Dayton, Ohio, where he kept in shape by cracking 'niggers' over the head."[36] After immediately cutting Powell off the air, Elson apologized. The radio station, WGN Chicago, was inundated with telephone calls protesting Powell's slur. The station broadcast apologies throughout the evening.

The black community's reaction to Powell's comment was immediate. A group of black leaders in Chicago met at Comiskey Park. Unable to meet with an official of major league baseball, they presented a petition to an umpire demanding that Powell be sanctioned with a life-long ban from playing baseball.[37] The submission of the petition was followed by other protest activities.

Commissioner Landis, acting on behalf of major league baseball, suspended Powell for ten days. Perhaps more revealing than the ten-day suspension that was condemned as inadequate by some segments of the black press, were Landis' comments regarding Powell's statement. Landis concluded that Powell's comments "were not purposely, but rather carelessly made." Landis shifted focus from Powell's racial slur to the problems with spontaneous broadcasts that could lead to the types of embarrassment resulting from Powell's comments.

Landis' comments suggest that Jake Powell was punished not because the commissioner viewed Powell's statement as abhorrent behavior. More than likely, Landis punished Powell in an effort to placate protesters and to return to baseball's normal state of silence with respect to race. Landis also may have punished Powell because the Yankee outfielder had broken an informal ethical canon of baseball. In comparing baseball to the law, Paul Finkelman has written that "both law and baseball have canons of ethics, which can lead to disciplinary sanctions, including permanent disbarment or banishment."[38] Powell's statement broke the rule forbidding conduct detrimental to the sport. Powell's statement damaged the sport by embarrassing league and team officials bent on avoiding any discussion of baseball's race question.

The white press and Yankee officials expressed sentiments similar to those expressed by Landis. Throughout most of major league baseball's segregated era, most members of the white press had adopted the "conspiracy of silence" in refusing to acknowledge a race issue in baseball. Consistent with this stance, the white press largely ignored Powell's statement. In reporting on the incident, it tended to reject any characterization of Powell's statement as evidence of racism. Rather, his statement was viewed as a mere slip of the tongue. For example, the *Chicago Tribune* and the *New York Times* reported that Powell's remarks were "in a jocular vein." Other white newspapers emphasized that Powell meant no harm and that Powell was unaware that he had made the comments until "after he heard about the protest to the radio station."[39] *The Sporting News* reported that "one of the close friends of the Yankees was Bill 'Bojangles' Robinson who knows that Jake meant no harm by his thoughtless remarks."[40] *The Sporting News* article stated that Powell should have exercised greater care. It also apologetically stated that Powell's character as a hustling, aggressive player frequently got him into jams.

Not all members of the white press adhered to the conspiracy of silence. Breaking the conspiracy of silence in the white press, columnist Westbrook Pegler, wrote that Powell's comments crudely reflected baseball's policy of racial exclusion. He demanded the reintegration of major league baseball. Columnist Hugh Bradley, in a column appearing in the *New York Post*, criticized Landis and the owners that he represented for their hypocrisy in expressing horror at Powell's comments, while calmly retaining the color line in major league baseball.

The Yankee characterization of the incident mirrored that of league officials and the majority of the white press. Yankee manager, Joe McCarthy defended Powell saying he was certain that his player meant no harm and cast blame on the radio station for the incident.[41] A week following the incident, responding to criticisms by the black press, Yankee president, Ed Barrow defended the organization. Barrow claimed the team had taken all steps within its power. Barrow also added that "he had discussed the Powell case with several of his 'colored friends,' as well as his 'two colored servants'...and all of them seem to feel that it was just an unfortunate mistake that cannot happen again."[42] In a similar vein, Yankee owner Jacob Ruppert apologized to the superintendent of Chicago's Third Ward. His apology noted, however, that Powell was born in the south and that such things sound differently up north than in the south. Ruppert requested that Powell's thoughtless blunder be overlooked and that he be given another chance. Understandably, the Yankee response failed to placate its critics.

On August 20, in response to criticism largely by the black press, Powell issued a signed statement in which he apologized for his remarks. Powell went to *The Chicago Defender's* New York office and sought forgiveness. Unfortunately, his written plea included the comment "I have two members of your race taking care of my home while myself and wife are away and I think they are two of the finest people in the world." Powell's plea also failed to placate the black community.[43]

The black press expressed the sentiments of a black community that would be appeased by neither major league baseball's nor the Yankees' response. The black press reported extensively on Powell's remarks and activities related to it. Black newspapers such as *The Chicago Defender* and the *Amsterdam News* reported on protests around the nation in reaction to Powell's remarks. The black press also gave accounts of how the Yankees had to be escorted to the ballpark in Chicago by three squad cars of police due to a fear of violence in the aftermath of Powell's comments. The *Amsterdam News* reported that over 6,000 signatures had been gathered on a petition demanding Powell's dismissal from baseball.

The black press also played a critical role in mobilizing public opinion regarding the incident, which it used as a vehicle for attacking baseball's policy of segregation. The black press vilified baseball, Powell and the Yankee organization as racist. The black press both called for and reported on calls for Powell's banishment from baseball. Landis's ten-day suspension of Powell was condemned as inadequate and reflective of the pervasiveness of racism in major league baseball.

The black press also used the Powell incident to comment on public resentment of the Yankees. A *Philadelphia Afro-American* editorial suggested that Powell's continued presence on the team and the Yankee objection to using black ballplayers was the source of the resentment.[44] *Philadelphia Tribune* columnist W. Rollo Wilson reported that large crowds were staying away from Yankee Stadium and that an attempt to boycott Ruppert's beer was under way. Directly criticizing the Yankees, an *Amsterdam News* column stated "as long as the Yankees retained Powell, regardless of the number of pennants won, they would be 'just a bunch of mugs named 'Cracker' "[45] Powell would end his career with the National League's Philadelphia team in 1945.

The Powell incident was an important event in the development of perceptions of the Yankee attitude toward race. Powell's slur occurred at a time when opponents of segregation in baseball were becoming increasingly vocal in demanding integration. They used the incident to indict major league baseball's policy of racial exclusion. Moreover, criticism of the Yankees demonstrated that the club could no longer remain silent on "baseball's race problem" and could be compelled by public pressure to address it.

In addition, activists used the Powell incident to emphasize the Yankees' resistance to the inevitability of the integration of major league baseball. Critics cast the Yankees as a racist organization. The Powell affair also demonstrated the inherent instability in baseball's segregated world; a single remark could embroil the sport in controversy and contribute to the shaping of public perception of the racial attitudes of a team, the New York Yankees.[46]

B. Yankee Justifications

The Yankee response to increasing external pressure to integrate during the 1940s and 1950s also contributed to perceptions of the organization as racist. Prior to 1947, the Yankee approach to integration was motivated by the complex array of social and economic considerations that underlie other major league teams' resistance to integrating baseball. Like other teams and league officials, Yankee management denied the existence of a color line in baseball and proclaimed that major league clubs welcomed black players to join them. This explanation was obviously a falsehood intended to gloss over the contradiction between segregation and the sports creed.

Yankee management offered additional explanations for the club's refusal to integrate during the 1940s and early 1950s. Yankee president Larry MacPhail expressed concern that integration would harm the Negro Leagues. Responding to black demonstrators at the 1945 Yankee season opener, MacPhail stated,

> I have no hesitancy in saying that the Yankees have no intention of signing Negro players under contract or reservation to Negro clubs. . . . The solution of this problem in professional baseball must be compatible with long-established business and property rights. It is unfortunate that groups of professional political and social drumbeaters are conducting pressure campaigns in an attempt to force major-league clubs to sign Negro players.[47]

MacPhail's desire to protect the Negro Leagues was no doubt influenced by the over $100,000 a year in rental income the Yankee organization received from Negro League teams renting its facilities. Speaking to the profit motive, MacPhail is reported to have said, "baseball [is] a business. I rented my ballparks to colored clubs this year, and the rental money is the profit I am able to pay my stockholders." MacPhail also stated that "he didn't propose disturbing the Negro clubs by hiring one of their numbers; this would rob the black leagues and make it impossible for them to operate."[48]

Evidence suggests that prior to 1947, the Yankee delay in integrating the club was not solely the product of conscious racial discrimination. What remains unclear is the extent to which racially discriminatory attitudes factored into the decision-making of Yankee officials. MacPhail's behavior illustrates the difficulty in attempting to identify the true motives of those within the Yankee organization. As discussed below, MacPhail developed a system for scouting Negro League players. This move led some to believe that the integration of the Yankees was imminent. On the other hand, it was MacPhail who co-authored a report prepared on behalf of major league baseball that addressed the "Race Question."

In July 1946, after Jackie Robinson had been signed by the Dodgers but before he was brought up from the minors, major league teams established a steering committee to consider "all matters of Major League interest...."[49] MacPhail chaired the committee and co-authored its report—The Report of the Major League Steering Committee. The "Race Question" was among the issues considered by the committee. All but one copy of the document were collected and destroyed. Happy Chandler, who succeeded Judge Landis as commissioner, made his copy of the report available in the 1980s.

The report affirmatively stated that all Americans regardless of race or creed had the opportunity to play major league baseball. It rejected suggestions that Jim Crow permeated the league. The report concluded that the time was not right for the integration of the major leagues. In reaching this conclusion, the report did not focus on developing methods for bringing blacks into the major leagues. Rather it examined "methods to protect baseball from charges that it is fostering unfair discrimination against the Negro by reason of his race and color."[50] The need to devise such a strategy was seen as necessary to avoid offending blacks who were loyal baseball customers and to respond to the growing pressure to integrate.

The report contained explanations for the absence of blacks in the major leagues that would be repeated by Yankee officials during the 1940s and early 1950s. It expressed the concern that the value of major league franchises would decrease if the addition of black players resulted in a substantial increase in the number of black patrons who attended games. A related concern held by many owners of major league franchises was the "fear that if the dam were broken, a flood of Negro league players would overwhelm the major leagues."[51]

While the reasons that may have influenced MacPhail's approach to integration are difficult to categorize, the attitude of Yankee owners, Del Webb and Dan Topping, is best described as one of disinterest. Topping, who had signed the first black football player and other blacks to the All-American conference, strongly protested charges that the Yankees were racist. While he and Webb denied such charges, they also delegated day-to-day operations to George Weiss, who became Yankee general manager following MacPhail's retirement at the end of 1947.

Although Weiss also denied charges of racism, he made statements and decisions that were perceived by Yankee critics as evidencing a clear intent to systematically delay integration for as long as possible. For example, Yankee critics were aware of the Yankees' failure to exploit opportunities to sign black players. Although not a proponent of integration, Weiss's predecessor, MacPhail, nevertheless recognized the value in signing black players. This was particularly true after Jackie Robinson joined the Dodgers. Consequently, MacPhail developed a system for scouting the Negro Leagues. Using this system, MacPhail signed several talented black ballplayers to play in the Yankee farm system. The system was intact when MacPhail resigned at the end of 1947. However, any hopes of a black ballplayer joining the Yankees around this time quickly dissipated. Following MacPhail's retirement, Weiss quickly traded or sold all of the organization's black ballplayers, except for Elston Howard.[52] As stated by one writer, "the Yankees made a complete turnaround with regard to Negro players. It was not really that diffi-cult to understand. Larry MacPhail had wanted to sign the best players he could find. Weiss wanted to sign the best white players he could find."[53] Integration advocates ar-gued that the Yankees' conduct represented a deliberate course of action to prove his contention of a dearth of quality black players.

In addition to the scouting system, the Yankees failed to exploit other mechanisms for securing the best black talent and for engendering positive relations with the black community. The club's relationships with black baseball's Newark Eagles, the New York Black Yankees and Kansas City Monarchs provided the Yankees with an unmatched "viaduct" to black players. On numerous occasions, these clubs had offered their best players to the Yankees. Signing black players would have allowed the Yankees an oppor-tunity to recoup lost rental income resulting from the drastic drop in attendance at black baseball games that led to the demise of the Eagles and Black Yankees in 1948. It would have also allowed the Yankees to develop a positive relationship with the black fans of these teams that no doubt felt abandoned following their teams' demise. Instead the Yankees sought out black talent from other Negro league teams that yielded no major league prospects.[54]

The Yankee decision to follow the path of resistance to integration appears to have been dictated by Weiss. Economic considerations appear to have played a role in Weiss's attitude toward integration. From an economic perspective, Weiss perceived no need to integrate the Yankees since the organization continued to field winning teams in the years immediately following baseball's reintegration. Reflecting a combination of snob-bery, ignorance, and race based stereotyping, Weiss also feared the economic conse-quences of a loss of his white middle-class customers from the suburbs, who he believed did not want to attend games with black fans.[55] Similarly, Weiss did not believe that his white players wanted to play on the same team with blacks. As discussed above, integra-tion had already disproved both of these assumptions.

But Weiss's approach to integrating the Yankees was motivated by more than eco-nomics. Relying on commonly held stereotypes of blacks, Weiss did not believe that black players played as hard as whites or possessed the courage of white players.[56] Notes David Halberstam,

> Weiss's racism had egregiously blinded him, for he did not see what was in front of him every day: that young black players coming into the big leagues exemplified the mental and spiritual toughness now that the Yankees had once demanded. Their lives had been strewn with far more obstacles than the white players; since owners monitored how many black players they carried, there were very few black benchwarmers or backup players. Either you were a starter or you did not make it. George Weiss did not understand the rage to succeed that drove so many of these young men, the passion to make up for so many years of racism and segregation and to avenge wrongs inflicted on those who had gotten before them and who had been denied the chance....[57]

Weiss's statements and conduct contributed to the reputation of the Yankees as a racist organization. At a cocktail party, Weiss purportedly proclaimed, "I will never allow a black man to wear a Yankee uniform. Boxholders from Westchester don't want that sort of crowd. They would be offended to have to sit with niggers."[58]

Under Weiss's leadership, the Yankees resorted to a tactic used by other clubs to delay integration. The organization would sign a few black ballplayers to minor league contracts. When accused of discriminatory practices, team officials would respond that the "Yankees will bring up a Negro as soon as one that fits the high Yankee standards is found."[59] In other words, the Yankees argued that its scouts had failed to identify black players worth signing.

Yet here too, the organization's public pronouncements were contradicted by its action. For example in responding to Robinson's accusation of Yankee racism, Weiss stated that Robinson, "like any person connected with baseball, must know of the efforts we have made to find Negro players of major-league ability. Our efforts in that respect are well known.... [W]ith the exception of Jackie Robinson we have been interested in just about every Negro player who has come up to the majors."[60] The Yankees did scout a few prominent black players. Contrary to Weiss's statements, however, the organization overlooked some of the most extraordinarily talented black players available during the early 1950s, including Larry Doby, Luke Ester, Willie Mays, Minnie Minoso, Monte Irvin, Roy Campanella, Don Newcombe, Sam Jethroe, and Ernie Banks.[61]

Other statements suggested that racial bias on the part of Weiss and his subordinates greatly influenced the Yankee position on integration. Weiss is reported to have instructed the leading Yankee scout "we don't want you crawling through any back alley trying to sign some niggers."[62] Another top Yankee scout, who also served as the club's traveling secretary, in responding to chiding from a *New York Times* reporter for having overlooked Willie Mays reportedly said, "I don't care what [Mays] did today or any other day,...I got no use for him or any of them. I wouldn't want any of them on a club I was with. I wouldn't arrange a berth on the train for any of them."[63] The scout's remarks made it into print. Such statements supported accusations by integration proponents that the Yankees engaged in racial discrimination.

Another event in the early 1950s was assailed by critics as demonstrating racial bigotry within a Yankee organization that had engaged in a systemic effort to delay the inevitability of integration for a long as possible. As a first-baseman, Puerto Rican ballplayer Vic Power hit .349 to lead the International League in batting. The Yankees traded him to the Philadelphia team. To justify the trade, the team engaged in a media blitz to discredit Power. He was accused of being "stupid, hot-tempered, a showboat. There was also talk that he liked white women."[64] The Yankees stated that Power's style of play endangered their image and he was too prone to revealing his Latin pride.[65] Yankee owner Dan Topping in response to protesters marching outside of Yankee Stadium who accused the club of Jim Crowism argued that "[o]ur scouting reports rate Power a good hitter, but a poor fielder."[66] Topping's explanation (considered by some as one of the game's most inept player assessments) and vehement denials of racial discrimination by Weiss failed to satisfy critics. They were convinced that Power was traded because if he had remained in the Yankee organization, the Yankees could not have refused to bring him up to the big leagues given his excellent record. Noted a newspaper columnist in referring to allegations of Yankee racial discrimination, "If the Yankees weren't guilty as charged, they were certainly going out of their way to look for trouble."[67]

C. Pressure to Integrate

By the mid-1950s, the pressure for the Yankees to integrate was particularly intense given the team's location in New York City. Located in the nation's media center, the club had to deal with an increasingly critical press that circulated stories suggesting an undercurrent of racism permeated the organization. The Yankees also had to contend with the fact that New York's other two major league teams were the most integrated in baseball and appeared to be realizing the benefits of integration.

Moreover, New York with its liberal establishment was one of the sources from which impetus for the civil rights movement was originating.[68] The segregated Yankees poorly represented a city in which the populace viewed itself as progressive and cosmopolitan.[69] Thus, the team's location and prominence combined to expose the Yankees to more stringent scrutiny for its failure to integrate than was experienced by other clubs.[70]

Pressures peculiar to the Yankees, along with variables that influenced other clubs to integrate, forced the Yankees reluctantly to bring Elston Howard to the major leagues in 1955. Howard became the first black player to successfully navigate his way through the Yankee farm system. In Howard, the Yankees found the black ballplayer with whom the team could feel relatively comfortable. Unlike a player such as Vic Power, Howard possessed characteristics and values that placed Yankee management relatively at ease. Howard was described as follows by a columnist for *The Sporting News*:

> Howard, the first Negro to gain a place on the Bomber machine, was chosen for that situation sui generis because of his quiet demeanor, his gentlemanly habits and instincts, and his lack of aggressive attitudes on race questions. He came to the Yankees determined to achieve the position he now occupies, not as a crusader.[71]

In bringing Howard up from the minor leagues, the Yankees had acceded to the demands of its critics. Yet the team lost the opportunity to make headway in beginning to reverse the negative perceptions of the club with respect to racial issues. Howard had to endure the racial slurs of Yankee manager, Casey Stengel, and other Yankee officials. In an often-repeated remark, Stengel pronounced to the press that "when I get a nigger, I get the only one who can't run." There were also repeated occasions when Stengel would refer to Howard as "nigger" or "eight ball." Although Howard did not respond to racist comments from Yankee officials, such remarks fed the public perception of the existence of racism within the Yankee organization.

In summary, prior to the signing of Jackie Robinson, the Yankees charted a course similar to that taken by other major league teams. It relied on the same litany of justifications offered by other clubs in defending segregated baseball. Economic considerations and racial bigotry underlie the reluctance to integrate. Economic based rationales, however, appear to have been premised in part on faulty assumptions that grew out of racial stereotypes. Given this, it is difficult to determine the extent to which purportedly non-race based justifications offered by the Yankees were legitimate or merely served as convenient means of concealing racial bias.

After Jackie Robinson joined the Dodgers, the Yankees diverged from the course of action pursued by its New York counterparts, the Dodgers and Giants. Evidence suggests that racial animus against blacks played a more direct role in Yankee decision-making regarding the integration of the team. The consequence of the Yankee "delay integration for as long as possible approach" was to nurture the perceptions that had developed of an organization permeated by racism.

Sport historians identify an important consequence of the Yankee delay in taking advantage of the opportunity presented by black ballplayers. They posit that the Yankees and other American League teams were eventually placed at a competitive disadvantage in regard to National League teams that generally exhibited a greater willingness to sign black players in the years immediately following baseball's reintegration. One study revealed that from 1947–56, teams that used more black players, on average, had higher winning percentages than teams that integrated at a slower pace.[72] Other consequences of the Yankee delay in integrating are addressed below.

III. Conclusion

If we measure the Yankees' experiences with race relations by the extent to which it has spawned case law that has significantly influenced legal jurisprudence, its impact is negligible. While interesting, *Joseph* has not helped to define civil rights law. Commissioner Landis's suspension of Jake Powell is significant in that it illustrates the breadth of authority afforded baseball commissioners to determine what constitutes "the best interests of the game" and to discipline players for conduct detrimental thereto. Yet, by the time of the Powell incident, 1938, Landis had clearly established the extraordinary power that his office possessed to police a wide range of conduct. Nevertheless, perhaps something of value can be learned from the Yankee approach to segregation and integration of major league baseball.

Whatever lessons we learn from the Yankee experience will most likely be influenced by the perceptions we hold concerning the significance of the integration of baseball. Scholars have debated the influence that the integration of baseball had on race relations in the United States. Some argue that the role of baseball in promoting social change has been overstated. They note that whatever impact baseball's integration may have had on softening the resistance of whites to integration in social institutions such as education was minimal. In so arguing, they contend that whites could separate black achievement in sports from black achievement in other aspects of society. This may have been due to the ability of whites to view black baseball players differently from ordinary black people. Those who question whether the integration of baseball served as a vehicle for promoting social change emphasize that protest activities that led to historic events such as *Brown* had nothing to do with the integration of major league baseball.[73] In short, these scholars assert that baseball's integration had little impact on lowering racial barriers in other institutions in American society.

Other scholars view the "reintegration of baseball as a central event for American society." They emphasize that baseball was one of the first institutions, public or private, in American society to integrate what had been a thoroughly segregated society. Given baseball's status as the national sport, its reintegration represented a major blow to "America's culture of racism."[74] Notes one scholar, "if blacks could play in the National League on an integrated basis, they could serve in the national army on an integrated basis. If African-Americans could play in the American League, surely they could go to any American school." [75]

Adherents of this position also emphasize that the integration of baseball demonstrated that social change can be accomplished not only by courts and legislatures but by private enterprise. "Rickey developed his own affirmative action program with Jackie Robinson because he knew integration would bring new talent into his organization. It is a message that law firms and corporations might heed well, not only on issues of race but also on issues of gender."[76] In short, the reintegration of baseball was a part of the process by which America would begin to confront racial hypocrisy not only in baseball but in other segments of its society.[77]

The severe scrutiny and criticism directed toward the Yankees was a product of the Yankees' unique role in American culture. Those who advocated for the Yankees' integration may have recognized the symbolic significance of the integration of the premier team of America's national sport.

In many ways, the team was the embodiment of the American dream. With the exception of blacks, the club had attempted to be sensitive to the changes in the ethnic composition of New York. American-born Protestants, Irish and German Catholics dominated the first generation of ballplayers. As the numbers of Jews and Southern Europeans increased in New York City, its baseball teams would slowly reflect these demographic shifts. The Yankees had difficultly fielding a Jewish superstar in the 1930s and 1940s, but nevertheless attempted to appeal to its Jewish fans. With respect to Italians, the club's roster included great ballplayers of Italian descent and was representative of the growing Italian population during the 1920s, 1930s and 1940s. Italians would come to embrace the Yankees in the manner that blacks embraced the Dodgers after Jackie Robinson joined the team.[78] Thus, the Yankees can be seen as having provided an example of America's willingness to assimilate different ethnic and racial groups and the rewards that await those who assimilate.

Except for blacks, the Yankees also symbolized the American sports creed at its best—race, ethnic background and status are subordinate to talent and ability. According to this creed, sport provides a vehicle for those with the requisite skill and determination to compete on an equal basis and chart a path out of poverty.[79] The Yankees were viewed as presenting an opportunity to all those who had the talent to play up to the Yankee standard of excellence. Additionally, if baseball possesses the potential to uplift us and provide heroes and role models, no team carried as much potential as the New York Yankees.[80]

Therefore, perhaps the most important consequence of the Yankee delay in integrating was the opportunity lost to make a profound statement regarding race relations in the United States. The Dodgers and Giants made such a statement, but neither team was the most storied franchise in the history of American sports. Unfortunately, the Yankees lacked the leadership that would have led it in such a direction. If as some say, the integration of baseball represented both a symbol of imminent racial challenge and a direct agent of social change, the Yankees lost an opportunity to play a leading role in this process.[81]

The Tax Man Cometh

by Jack F. Williams[*]

I. Yankees Pay Taxes Too!

"Taxes," according to Justice Holmes, "are what we pay for civilized society."[1] From the cases discussed in this chapter, this price is extracted even from those celebrated inhabitants of the Bronx who wear pinstripes, tossing and hitting the horsehide for a living. Although one is hard pressed to deny the existence of a New York Yankees' mystique, that mystique carries little weight in the tax court, where the arms of bronze give way to feet of clay. In this chapter, the reader will be introduced to a line-up of famous and infamous cases involving taxes and the New York Yankees. These cases will range from the most basic to the most arcane tax issues, involving Yankee marquee players as well as journeymen. Their common theme is rather basic — Yankees must pay taxes, too.

The federal government has the power to tax under the United States Constitution. In particular, Article I, Section 8, the so-called Taxing Clause, provides: "The Congress shall have the Power to Lay and collect Taxes." The 24th Amendment to the United States Constitution empowers the Congress to impose a personal income tax. Additionally, the Congress has imposed taxes on certain gifts of funds or properties. Federal tax laws are generally collected at title 26 of the United States Code (the "Internal Revenue Code or IRC").[2]

II. Famous Tax Slackers

Occasionally, ballplayers fail to report income earned from outside sources like baseball card shows, often arguing that they simply did not know the tens of thousands of dollars paid, usually in cash, constituted potentially taxable income. Internal Revenue Code section 61 provides that gross income includes all income from whatever source derived. Thus, the cash that a player receives for appearing at a baseball card show to sign autographs constitutes income for federal tax purposes. However, ballplayers are notorious for failing to report card show income, and the Internal Revenue Service ("IRS") has devoted enforcement resources to identify lax players. For example, Dwight Gooden, then of the New York Yankees, was targeted by the IRS for failure to report and pay over $200,000 in federal income taxes associated with baseball card shows. Eventually, Gooden agreed to pay the back taxes, thereby avoiding the unappealing prospect of jail time.[3]

Troubled ex-Yankee Darryl Strawberry was not so lucky. Strawberry also failed to report income from card shows and avoided paying taxes on that income for a number of years. After a thorough investigation by the IRS, Strawberry ended up pleading guilty for failing to pay income taxes between 1986 and 1990. The former outfielder received a six-month sentence of home confinement. The court also ordered that Strawberry pay $350,000 in back taxes.[4]

III. States and Cities Want Their Share Too!

Under the states constitutions and tax laws, states have the power to impose a tax on both residents and nonresidents on income derived from sources within their state. Under the 14th Amendment to the United States Constitution, however, a state's power to impose a tax on a nonresident is limited by the requirements of the Due Process and Equal Protection Clauses, and must include reasonable equality of treatment between residents and nonresidents. This taxing power is also dependent upon the nonresident maintaining certain minimum contacts with the state, such as employment within the state, performance of regular and substantial work within the state, or a tax home within the state.

As to state taxes, ballplayers pose thorny issues. First, a determination must be made as to the appropriate tax home for the ballplayer. A ballplayer has some latitude in determining his tax home for state tax law purposes. For example, it may not be unusual for a New York Yankees ballplayer to reside in the off-season in Florida, where he may maintain his family, home, a mortgage, bank accounts, voter registration, driver's license, automobile registration, country club membership, and other connections with the state. Thus, for tax purposes, the ballplayer's tax home would be Florida.

In all states other than Florida, including New York where the ballplayer may maintain an apartment, the ballplayer is considered a nonresident for income tax purposes. Each state has developed its own basis of allocating nonresident income for state income tax purposes. The most common approach is known as the "Duty Days" method. Another, less common approach is known as the "Games Played" method. In 1995, New York dropped the Games Played method, opting for the Duty Days approach as the preferred means by which the State apportions a ballplayer's income for state tax purposes.

Under the Duty Days method, one calculates (i) the total number of days spent by the ballplayer within the particular state (including games, practice, meetings, etc.) and (ii) divides that number by the total income number of days the ballplayer worked in all states for the ball club. This ratio is then multiplied by the total wages earned by the athlete for the entire tax year.

Under the Games Played method, the number of games played in the state is divided by the total number of games played. That ratio is then multiplied by the total wages earned by the athlete for the entire tax year.

A simple comparison of the two methods identified shows that the Duty Days method favors the ballplayer while the Games Played method favors the state taxing authority. The Duty Days calculation favors the ballplayer because the denominator used to calculate the ratio includes required "off days," making it larger than the ratio in the Games Played method.

As previously mentioned, prior to 1995, New York employed the Games Played method, a method favoring the state taxing authority. This is the method addressed in Roy White's tax controversy with the State of New York discussed later in the chapter.

Of course, with two professional baseball teams residing in Canada, a New York Yankees ballplayer will also have international tax law concerns that must be addressed. Under the *Convention Between the United States of America and Canada with Respect to Taxes on Income and Capital*, also known as the *Canada 3-Income Tax Treaty*, both Canada and the United States have agreed to avoid double taxation, that is, taxing the same earned income twice, and to prevent fiscal invasion with respect to taxes on income. Article XVI specifically addresses the taxation of professional athletes. That Article provides that any income derived by an athlete from personal activities is taxable in the other State (US or Canada) except where the gross receipts do not exceed $15,000. The general standard is then tempered by the statement in the same Article that the general standard does not apply to the income of an athlete of a professional team that participates in a league that regularly schedules games in both the United States and Canada or a team like the New York Yankees as described in Article XVI. Thus, a non-resident New York Yankees ballplayer is generally not taxed on his income earned while playing in Canada.

The following cases have been selected because they discuss important principles in federal, state, or local tax law issues. An added bonus is that the cases often involve very popular New York Yankees, from Roger Maris to Roy White.

IV. A Record That Will Stand the Test of Time

No chapter devoted to the Yankees and taxes could start anywhere but with the beloved Roger Maris. His feat during the 1961 season of hitting 61 regular season homeruns went seriously unchallenged until the 1998 season when Mark McGwire of the St. Louis Cardinals shattered the single-season homerun record. In *Maris v. Commissioner*, the federal tax court addressed the recurring issue of how to value the common stock of a closely-held corporation that Roger Maris and his brother gifted to their children.[5] It appears that the gift to the children was part of an overall estate planning and tax savings plan, a common strategy among high-earning professionals like baseball players.

On December 23, 1974, and May 12, 1975, the Maris brothers gifted stock in shares of Maris Distributing Company ("MDC") to their children. During the time period in question, MDC operated an Anheuser-Busch distributorship in Florida.

Although Roger's brother Rudolph, a mechanical engineer, was primarily responsible for the management of MDC, the court's opinion devotes considerable ink to a discussion of Roger Maris. The court duly noted Maris's numerous achievements, including the single-season homerun record and the League MVP awards in 1960 and 1961. After carefully chronicling his career from Cleveland to Kansas City to New York to St. Louis, the opinion matter-of-factly observed that "[b]y virtue of his outstanding professional baseball career he became a national sports figure." Building on his national reputation, Maris became the spokesman for MDC, in charge of sales, customer relations, and publicity.

The sole issue before the court was the fair market value of the common stock of MDC when gifted to the Maris brothers' children in December 1974 and May 1975 as reported in their gift tax returns. The Maris' accountant valued the stock based on the following factors:

- The assets and business acquired by MDC in 1968 were purchased at book value;
- The history of MDC;
- The sales and assets of MDC;
- The minority interests involved;
- Trends and problems in the brewing industry;
- The nature of MDC's business;
- MDC's management and the personal contributions made by both Maris brothers to the enterprise;
- The absence of advertising allowances made by the brewer;
- The price increases and inventory gained by MDC;
- The potential refrigeration cost requirements proposed by the brewer;
- The restrictions under the equity agreement on the sale of MDC stock; and,
- The average earnings of MDC over the most recent five-year period.

In determining the value of the equity in the company, the Maris brothers' accountant capitalized five-years of averaged earnings at six times earnings. As calculated, the value of the equity was less than book value. The accountant then marked up his estimate of fair value by employing the higher book value rather than the calculated value.

The Maris brothers also retained a valuation expert to value the stock gifted as of both dates. After reviewing the impressive credentials of the expert, the court noted the data and methodology employed in reaching the valuation opinion, including:

- Review of the financial statements and records pertaining to operations;
- Relevant financial and economic statistics during the years in question;
- Data on security values as evidenced by leading financial journals;
- Conditions in the economy and in the relevant industry (brewing);
- Business and sales information in the area in which MDC operated;
- Personal inspection of the facility;
- Equity agreements;
- Minority interest actually gifted;
- Comparable companies; and
- Alternative investing opportunities, including US Treasury securities.

Based on the small minority interests to be valued, the expert rendered an opinion that the equity interests were worth $1,925 (12/23/1974) and $2,125 (5/12/1975), respectively. The expert used an earnings multiple of six times earnings.

The Internal Revenue Service (IRS) offered up its own expert testimony, disputing the evidence introduced by the Maris brothers on the issue of value. The IRS expert employed two techniques in determining the value of the minority interest in MDC. First, the expert employed a method dubbed the "wholesaler valuation methodology," an approach the expert found to be the common approach used in the brewing industry to value beer distributorships. Under this approach, the selling price per share of MDC was equal to the annual number of cases of beer sold per share multiplied by an appropriate dollar multiplier. The multiplier employed was within the range of multipliers reported for the brewing industry.

The IRS expert also employed a more traditional earnings approach to share valuation. Although the method employed was similar to that employed by the Maris brothers' expert, there were some significant differences worth noting. For example, the IRS expert declined to use average annual earnings over the five years preceding the gift of stock, opting instead for the actual average earnings per share for the fiscal years in which the stock of MDC was actually gifted. The IRS expert then employed a multiple of 9.2 (11.5 times discounted by 20% for lack of marketability because of the equity agreement). The IRS expert then rendered an opinion of the value of the equity interests at $7,490 and $7,466, respectively.

Ultimately, the court found the fair market value of the stock to be $5,110.97 per share and $5,149.19 per share, respectively. Interestingly, the opinion is less important for the actual values determined by the court. Rather the case itself provides an excellent tutorial on the valuation of stock in a closely-held company. The court began its analysis of stock valuation with a consideration of *macroeconomic factors*. The court observed that in 1974, the economy was in a severe recession. Among other things, industrial production had declined sharply, inflation and interest rates had increased, and price-earnings ratios had declined.

After assessing macroeconomic conditions existing at the time of the gifts, the court next considered certain *industry-specific factors* in assessing the stock value of MDC. The court noted that there was a strong covariance between the brewing industry and the economy so that, typically, as the economy would trend downward, the brewing industry would follow suit. The court's observation was supported by an analysis of public brewing company stocks, which showed a sharp decline from 1973 levels to 1974 all-time lows.

The court then turned to *firm-specific financial information,* including the financial statements and operational information of MDC. Based on regulations, the court considered the following factors in arriving at a valuation of the stock gifted:

- MDC's net worth;
- Prospective earning power;
- Dividend paying capacity;
- Goodwill of the business;
- Economic outlook of the particular industry;
- MDC's position in the market;
- MDC's management;
- The degree of control represented by the shares gifted;
- Comparable values.

The court was impressed by the methodologies and approaches offered by both experts. However, the court was largely persuaded by the IRS expert, even though it dismissed the "wholesaler methodology" as unnecessary. In particular, the court found that the appropriate approach would consider the earnings of the years in question as opposed to an average of the earnings of the four years preceding the years the stocks were gifted. The court then adjusted its valuation downward because of the nonrecurring increase in inventory experienced by MDC in 1974. Finally, the court found a thirty percent discount rate as appropriate because of the lack of marketability of the equity shares based on the equity agreement.

It appears the case of *Maris v. Commissioner* has outlived the single-season home-run record held by Maris for some thirty-five plus years. The case figures prominently in the evolution of valuation techniques, particularly where equity interests in a close corporation are being considered. Interestingly, such situations present themselves in the sports context regularly. This will be one record that will continue to stand the test of time.

V. The Quiet Man Speaks Out
for Ballplayers Everywhere

Whitey Ford called Roy White, "One of the classiest, most popular, and most unappreciated Yankees of all times." Nicknamed the "Quiet Man," Roy White played his heart out for fifteen years with the New York Yankees. The switch-hitting left fielder could run and hit with occasional power. He was noted for his quiet dedication and his fearless approach to the game he loved. That fearlessness was evident off the field, as well.

In *In re White*, Roy White took on the State of New York with the resolve he regularly showed on the baseball field.[6] The issue before the court was whether exhibition games played by nonresident professional baseball players should be included in the allocation ratio used to apportion income based on games played within and without New York.

On his state returns for tax years 1971 and 1972, Roy White and his wife allocated his contract salary based on the total number of games played within and without New York. Roy White included the Yankees' exhibition games as games outside of New York. The State disagreed, arguing that the allocation formula must be based on regular season games, thus increasing New York state taxable income.

The hearing examiner began with the obvious—Roy White was a professional baseball player for the New York Yankees. The hearing examiner then turned to the actual contract duties between Roy White and the Yankees. The contract required White to participate in spring training activities, including the participation in exhibition games. The hearing examiner further noted that White's failure to participate in spring training activities, including exhibition games, could result in a breach of contract.

Based on the foregoing, the hearing examiner concluded that White had a contractual obligation to participate in exhibition games outside of New York. Thus, according to the hearing examiner, the contract salary must represent compensation for exhibition games. Consistent with that approach, the hearing examiner found that the allocation ratio used to apportion income based on games played within and without New York must include exhibition games, thus reducing what otherwise would be New York taxable income.

As states and local taxing authorities become more and more aggressive in the identification, taxation, and collection of income, the case of *In re White* stands as a warning against over-zealousness in tax collection. Ultimately, the State of New York rejected the Games Played method, opting for the Duty Days approach. The Quiet Man does in fact speak out for all ballplayers.

VI. Just Where Do You Work When
You Work for King George?

There can be no greater swing between exuberance and fear than serving as the General Manager of the New York Yankees under owner George Steinbrenner. The last thing that the Yankees' General Manager needs is tax trouble. But, alas, there was no respite from the taxman for Clyde King. In *In re King*, the New York hearing examiner addressed the issue of the proper income allocation formula for King, the Vice President and General Manager of the New York Yankees.[7]

The precise issue was whether the time King worked in his office in North Carolina in 1984 could be considered as income generated outside of New York for income allocation purposes. The State Tax Commission ("Commission") answered in the negative.

The case provides an interesting glimpse of the role of General Manager under George Steinbrenner. Under the contract between the Yankees and King, King agreed to do the following:

- Maintaining the morale of existing personnel;
- Assisting the manager and others in trading for and maintaining improved personnel throughout the year;
- During the season, giving the manager advice on upcoming opponents and their current physical condition and current strengths and weaknesses;
- Spotting and reporting to the manager and owner personal problems and strengths;
- From November through January, negotiating trades to improve the Yankees for the upcoming season.

The contract also provided that King could perform his services to the Yankees in North Carolina, if he so chose, during the months of November through January. Important to the Commission, however, was the fact that this provision appeared as an accommodation to King and not a requirement for employment. The Commission denied any allocation attempt by King because of the finding that any services performed by King in North Carolina were done there for his own convenience and not on account of business necessity. Clyde King may have thought that he lived in North Carolina; but, when one works as a General Manager for the Yankees, one works in New York.

VII. A Yankee Has No Tax Home, Like a Rolling Stone

Most of us can only imagine the excitement of signing a professional sports contract, let alone a contract with the New York Yankees. But that excitement can be fleeting. In 1984, Jeff Pries, a resident of Newport, California, signed a contract with the Oneonta Yankees, a farm team of the New York Yankees.

In 1985, Pries signed a contract to play with the Ft. Lauderdale Yankees, another of the New York Yankees' minor league farm system. While in Ft. Lauderdale, Pries incurred $1,324 for lodging expenses and $1,260 for meals. Asserting that the expenses constituted "ordinary and necessary traveling expenses incurred while away from home in pursuit of a trade or business," Pries deducted the expenses on his income tax return. The IRS disallowed the deductions, claiming that Newport was not his tax home; thus, any expense paid in Ft. Lauderdale could not be away "from home."

In *Pries v. Commissioner*, the court agreed with the IRS.[8] The court held that the expenses did not qualify as ordinary and necessary traveling expenses incurred while away from home in pursuit of a trade or business, noting that Pries failed to carry his burden on the issue. In support of the holding, the court noted that three conditions must be satisfied. These conditions include the following:

- The expense must be reasonable and necessary;
- The taxpayer must incur the expense while away from home; and
- The expense must be incurred in pursuit of a trade or business.

The issue in the case was whether the second condition was met. The IRS argued that Pries was not away from home when the expenses were paid. Pries asserted in response that Newport, California was his tax home.

Case law requires that a taxpayer prove that he has a recognized tax home before he can claim a deduction for expenses incurred away from home. The general rule is that a taxpayer's tax home is generally his principal place of business. Absent a principal place of business, a taxpayer's permanent home will do if the taxpayer incurs "substantial continuous living expenses" at the home.

The court found that Newport could not be Pries's principal place of business. One significant factor in determining a taxpayer's principal place of business is the location where a taxpayer receives the greater amount of income. Newport failed to qualify on the facts.

The court also found that Pries failed to prove that he incurred substantial continuous living expenses in Newport. The court noted that the record was devoid of any indication that Newport was his permanent residence. In fact, the ballplayer lived at home with his folks when he was not playing baseball in Florida. There was no evidence of rent, lodging, or maintenance expenses of any kind.

Interestingly, at least for tax purposes, Pries's tax home appeared to be Florida with his teammates and not Newport with his parents. One could then say that when Pries lived with his folks in Newport, he was living at a home away from home.

VIII. It Ain't Over until It's Over

Although much of this chapter is devoted to ballplayers, the New York Yankees has had its share of tax disputes as well. The New York Yankees are owned and operated by an Ohio limited partnership with its principal place of business in New York. When partners withdraw from the New York Yankees Partnership, certain state and federal tax issues may arise. In *New York Yankees Partnership v. O'Cleireacain*, five limited partners withdrew from the partnership.[9] Pursuant to the partnership agreement, each withdrawing partner was paid by the partnership an amount equal to the fair market value of the partnership interest.

For federal income tax purposes, the partnership treated the payments to withdrawing partners as part distributive share of partnership income and part partner's share of unrealized receivables. According to the partnership treatment of the payments, the payment to a withdrawing partner attributed to the share of unrealized receivables constituted a withdrawing partner's share in player contracts that had been amortized by the partnership in prior years and the year of withdrawal. Under the federal tax code, Internal Revenue Code §§736(a)(2) and 707(c), the partnership claimed a deduction for the payments for unrealized receivables. The identical claim for purposes of the City of New

York's Unincorporated Business Income Tax was disallowed by the City of New York. The partnership then commenced a legal action to challenge the disallowance by the City. Ultimately, the New York Court of Appeals, the highest court in New York, ruled in favor of the partnership, finding that the partnership correctly claimed the deduction.

In *McCarthy v. United States*, the U.S. Court of Appeals for the Sixth Circuit addressed yet another federal tax issue posed by the New York Yankees baseball club.[10] The court held that the existing television contracts acquired by the partnership when it acquired the major league baseball franchise had limitless life because of renewals. Thus, the contracts were not amortizable under federal tax law. The court based its ruling on the fact that broadcasting contracts in existence at the time that the Ohio partnership acquired the New York Yankees were not wasting assets. The court observed that the national contract was subject to perpetual renewal and that the local contract constituted only one of what would certainly be many consecutive contracts, so that rights to contract for televising had limitless life coextensive with the life of the franchise

Additionally, the court held that professional fees incurred in organizing the partnership which acquired the existing franchise were capital expenditures to be added to the cost basis of the franchise and were not amortizable. The court based its holding on the fact that the professional fees incurred in organizing the partnership that acquired the Yankees could not be amortized because they were incurred as part of the purchase of the ongoing business and, as such, were capital expenditures to be added to the cost basis of the acquired business. Thus, any tax benefit must be deferred until a later sale of the club.

IX. Now It Is Over

Federal and state tax laws can whip up a nasty curveball, at times. Unprepared, a ballplayer could easily go down in a colorful whiff. The beloved New York Yankees are no exception. Like many of us, they, too, must prepare and file federal, state, and local tax returns, and ultimately pay their taxes. When they don't, trouble brews. Pinstripes notwithstanding, Yankees have to pay their taxes just like the rest of us.

New York Yankees general manager Brian Cashman (L) and general partner Stephan
Swindal (C) cement relationship with Japan's Yomiuri Giants President Yoshinori
Horikawa (R). Photo Kazuhiro Nogi, © AFP/Corbis.

A Global Enterprise

by Alex Glashausser[*]

"Baseball belongs to the world, not only to the United States."
Babe Ruth[1]

New York. It is a quintessentially American city, but also the capital of the world, home to the United Nations. *Yankees.* The name is tied to the United States. The word also conjures up the American way of life to the rest of the world, and indeed the team is no stranger to globalization.

As immigrants populated New York City, the Yankees, with some glaring exceptions, featured players to match. The team's earliest superstars were Babe Ruth and Lou Gehrig, of German descent. Joe DiMaggio later led a wave of Italian-American Yankees. Unfortunately, it would be long before the Yankees embraced all ethnic groups. Some have cited the Yankees' failure to welcome African-Americans and Latin-Americans as fast as other clubs as a reason for their demise in the 1960s after decades of glory on the field.[2]

By Opening Day 2002, over one-quarter of all major leaguers were from outside the 50 states. That figure included eight Yankees.[3] In recruiting and managing their foreign players, and on occasional trips abroad, the Yankees have encountered a wide range of legal issues arising under U.S. law, the laws of other countries, and the law of nations.

Many have accused the United States of resolving all international issues based on its own national interest, regardless of its obligations under the law of nations. If so, perhaps the country has merely taken a cue from its greatest baseball star. When frustrated by authorities' failure to control unruly fans, Ruth once announced a doctrine that denounced legal niceties: "I am going to be my own law from now on."[4]

I. Beating a Path to Latin America

In recent years, baseball's team to beat has beaten other teams to young talent in Latin America. Even earlier, the Yankees had ties to the area, traveling there occasionally for exhibition games.

Today, the Yankees run one of the top teenage "baseball academies" in the Dominican Republic, which gives them an advantage in signing Latin-American players.[5] Some legal commentators have argued that through their recruiting practices, major-league teams "systematically engage in violations of the human rights of children and of international labor standards designed to protect children," in part by interfering with their education.[6] A Yankee scout in the Dominican Republic has dismissed that concern: "I

361

hear people in the United States say these kids ought to be in school, but that's ridiculous. Fewer than 20 percent of the kids in this country go to school."[7]

Doing business in other countries leads to potential liability under their laws. For example, a Venezuelan court once held the Yankees liable under Venezuelan law for firing a pitching coach, Winston Acosta, without paying him the benefits he was entitled to.[8] In addition to labor disputes, keeping up the Latin beat has exposed the Yankees to legal and political issues involving defections, visas, and age misrepresentations, to name a few.

A. A Long, Strange Trip

Larry MacPhail became the Yankees' president in 1945. An eager and ambitious man, he had an international outlook. One of his claims to fame was that he had participated in an aborted plot to kidnap Kaiser Wilhelm just after World War I. He and his accomplices supposedly made it to the Kaiser's residence in exile but could not quite close the deal. He did, however, steal an ashtray from the house to prove he had been there.[9] One of MacPhail's grand plans for the Yankees was to have them tour Latin America in the off-season to get in shape while making extra money.

In 1946, the Yankees flew to Panama for nine exhibition games, many against a U.S. Army team. The trip was uneventful, and MacPhail put together a more ambitious package for the next year. Though Commissioner Happy Chandler had banned barnstorming "outside the United States," MacPhail planned a month-long tour of Puerto Rico, Venezuela, and Cuba, where the Yankees would play local teams and some games against the Brooklyn Dodgers.[10]

One might well question whether Puerto Rico is "outside the United States." A self-governing commonwealth, it was ceded by Spain to the United States in 1898 after the Spanish-American War and occupies a gray area between foreign country and full member of the United States.[11] Baseball's treatment of the commonwealth is similarly ambiguous: Puerto Ricans are subject to the amateur draft of United States residents but are regularly included when Major League Baseball boasts of its high number of players born "outside the United States."[12] At any rate, Chandler gave his blessing to the Yankees' entire trip—a decision he surely came to regret.

On the day of the team's arrival in San Juan, the trip's sponsor, a Puerto Rican distillery, delivered a case of rum to each player's room. By midnight, a rookie had attempted a dive into the hotel pool from three stories up, in front of a throng of sotted onlookers wagering on his performance. Eventually, Manager Bucky Harris put an end to the shenanigans and reminded the players that they were there to play ball.[13]

In Caracas, the Yankees played a local team and encountered an odd legal situation during one of the games. Two of the local pitchers had just signed contracts with the Dodgers for the major-league season, and Brooklyn general manager Branch Rickey had told them not to pitch anymore in Venezuela. The promoter, though, had already paid the pair to pitch against the Yankees, and he insisted that they perform.

The pitchers refused to play. In the middle of the game, the promoter called in the authorities to deal with them. The *New York Times* reported, "[S]ince they treat a breach of contract in these parts with some severity, both were hauled off to the local jail house."

Perhaps unnerved, the Yankees blew the game in the bottom of the ninth on a two-run error. All the games in Venezuela were a great success on the business front, though—so much that the promoter threatened to force the Yankees to stay an extra week. Presumably mindful of the in-game arrest, MacPhail protested, "You can't kidnap the Yankees!" When he threatened to call in General Douglas MacArthur, the promoter relented.[14]

The team fled to Havana, although immigration difficulties almost eliminated that leg of the trip. MacPhail had heard from an official of another club that had recently played there that Cuban customs officials had given his team a hard time. MacPhail warned the Cuban promoter that the Yankees would skip the Havana jaunt unless assured of "a speedy entry and exit."[15] He apparently got his wish. But the Cuban series led to trouble with the commissioner when MacPhail was caught fraternizing with a known gambler at a game in Havana. In MacPhail's defense, he hardly could have avoided that offense, since in those days, gambling was *encouraged* in Cuban ballparks.[16]

The Yankees also had a run-in with the Dodgers in Havana. After playing only two of the three scheduled games, the Brooklyn club left abruptly for Panama, leaving the Yankees to play a makeshift Cuban squad. MacPhail was furious:

> When we arranged our contract with the local promoter for three games, it was with the understanding that the Dodgers were to be our opponents in all three.... Instead, they have deliberately walked out on us after playing only two games....[17]

The Yankees took no legal action for the alleged breach; instead, they returned home and exacted justice by beating the Dodgers in the World Series later that year.

B. Cuban Chronicles

Not until after the Cuban Revolution did a Cuban play for the Yankees. In 1964, Pedro Ramos joined the team for the stretch run as a relief pitcher. His homeland was not far from his thoughts. Roommate Phil Linz recalled: "He was getting so famous saving games for the Yankees, he was afraid [Fidel] Castro would have him kidnapped and brought back to play in Cuba. He slept with a loaded gun under his pillow."[18]

The fears of Ramos notwithstanding, the Yankees have enjoyed a friendly relationship with Cuba through the years. Ties began in the pre-Castro era, when Babe Ruth circumvented an American League ban on Caribbean barnstorming by joining the New York Giants for a tour of Cuba after the 1920 season. Ruth was lured by the salary of $1,000 per game, as well as by the opportunity to drink alcohol legally.

Ruth was impressed by the local players, particularly Cristobal Torriente, "the Cuban Babe Ruth." Although the Babe saw a need to stress that Torriente was as "black as a ton and a half of coal in a dark cellar," he coveted him as a teammate: "[I]f [Torriente] could play with me in the major leagues, we would win the pennant in July, and go fishing for the rest of the season."[19]

Off the field, Ruth found time not only to drink, but also to gamble. He was swindled by hucksters claiming to have inside information at a Santiago racetrack and lost $100,000. It was more than he could pay, and he escaped to Havana with bookies on his trail. Worried that he would not be able to leave the island, he told his wife of his trouble. She wrote a check from a secret account she kept for such emergencies to satisfy the creditors and allow Ruth to exit the country peacefully.[20]

Once Castro took over, Cuba had a baseball-crazed communist dictator who hated Yankees but loved *the* Yankees. During the revolution, he had sometimes huddled with his troops to listen to the Bronx Bombers on the radio.[21] Later, he asked Joe DiMaggio to send him an autographed ball. A friend said that DiMaggio was reluctant, "[b]ut he figured, if it helps relations between Cuba and the U.S., then okay."[22]

Despite his love for the game—in his youth, he played well enough to attract the interest of big-league scouts[23]—Castro outlawed professional baseball (and other sports) in 1961. Soon after, the United States initiated a trade embargo against Cuba and a ban on travel to Cuba by U.S. citizens.[24] No American teams would go there for decades.

In 1974, Castro announced a vision for a future game: "One day, when the Yankees accept peaceful coexistence with our own country, we shall beat them at baseball, too. Then the advantages of revolutionary over capitalist sport will be shown."[25] Presumably, he used "Yankees" to mean "Americans," but in the context of international baseball, perhaps the two are intertwined.

Three years later, one could argue about whether the United States had accepted "peaceful coexistence" with Cuba, but regardless, Castro contacted a lawyer in New York to relay an invitation for the Yankees to play a series of exhibitions in Havana. It was no surprise that the Yankees were the chosen team. As Graig Nettles noted, "They didn't invite Cincinnati. I guess they have enough Reds down there."[26]

Most Yankees welcomed the prospect of a historic trip. Ellie Hendricks had played in Cuba before, as a member of the Puerto Rican team in the Caribbean Series of 1959, and longed to return. Nettles, though, wondered about the length of the trip in light of news that Castro would want to take some cuts: "We may be over there longer than we think if Fidel doesn't get a hit."[27]

Commissioner Bowie Kuhn stepped in and barred the trip, proposing instead to send a team of all-stars. The Yankees complained, but a force greater than Kuhn was at work. The U.S. State Department had already approved the idea of sending major-leaguers to Cuba in conjunction with a proposed limited lifting of the travel ban. But it turned out that it had not intended for an existing team to go. The Department was concerned that if the Yankees took advantage of the loosening of restrictions, other teams would want to follow; it preferred to have a single all-star team go. The Cubans, however, rejected that idea: a spokesperson claimed that although the national team was physically ready to play the Yankees, it would not have enough time to prepare for games against an all-star team. It was the Yankees or nothing.[28]

Soon after Kuhn's decision, the Carter administration eased the travel restrictions enough that the Yankees would not have needed State Department approval to go to Cuba.[29] Although some speculated that the Yankees might defy Kuhn and accept Castro's invitation, they did not.[30]

In 1982, the Reagan administration largely reinstated the travel ban.[31] Two years later, the Supreme Court upheld it, holding that the constitutional freedom to travel must cede to "weighty concerns of foreign policy."[32] The Yankees had lost their chance. Or had they?

In a conversation about her friendship with owner George Steinbrenner, broadcast journalist Barbara Walters once said that the Yankees went to Cuba *sub rosa*:

> I first met him in 1977, when the Yankees were secretly in Cuba. They were helping with some sort of special program with Cuban ballplayers. I went to a ballgame with Fidel Castro and there was George Steinbrenner, whom I'd

never heard of. He was so upset that I was there, he almost took the whole team away.[33]

The Yankees had another chance to go in 1999. A Cuban official invited Steinbrenner to visit, and the owner used his political connections to try to get his team to Havana, but the Baltimore Orioles had begun the negotiating process earlier and became the team to make a historic—and publicized—trip.[34]

Later, the *New York Post* reported that Steinbrenner was quietly arranging to play home and away games in 2000 with the Cuban national team, having spoken with the U.S. State Department and representatives of Castro's government. Steinbrenner denied the report. In any event, Cuban fans would still love to have the Yankees visit.[35]

During the Cold War, some Communists did not look so kindly on the Yankees. In 1954, New York acquired Enos Slaughter from the St. Louis Cardinals over the star's objection. *Soviet Sport*, the leading Russian sports magazine, singled out the trade as an example of "flesh-peddling in disregard of the player's wishes and rights." The magazine concluded that "[t]he beizbol bosses care nothing about sport or their athletes but only about profits."[36] But news of baseball's greatest rivals has long since bridged the ideological divide. When asked if he liked his chess rival Anatoly Karpov, Gary Kasparov replied, "Do the Yankees like the Red Sox?"[37]

C. Visas to America, Express

Much of the legal drama surrounding the Yankees and Latin America has involved getting players into the United States, often as quickly as possible.

1. El and High Water

Before escaping Cuba in 1997, Orlando "El Duque" Hernandez was *persona non grata* to Fidel Castro's government. He had already met with agent Joe Cubas and considered defecting. In a celebrated prosecution of the agent's cousin, Juan Ignacio, for encouraging defections, Hernandez was a key witness. One of the documents used against Ignacio was a fake Venezuelan work visa for El Duque.[38] Though the pitcher testified that Ignacio was a "comrade," the government wanted to set an example. After Ignacio was sentenced to prison for fifteen years, Castro banned Hernandez and other players from baseball for life.[39] The official statement branded the pitcher a traitor:

> The condemnable attitude of [the players] makes them unworthy of participating in organized events of Cuban sports at any level, much less serving as advocates and representatives of our revolutionary fatherland.

After the ban, Hernandez played in an informal neighborhood league, sporting a Yankees jersey. A government official from the Sports Ministry soon appeared to announce that Hernandez was an ineligible player. With nowhere to pitch, El Duque took to the high seas.[40]

He faced rough legal waters. Under the Refugee Act of 1980, the United States had undertaken not to deport or return any alien "to a country if the Attorney General determines that such alien's life or freedom would be threatened in such country on account of race, religion, nationality, membership in a particular social group, or political opinion."[41] That law was consistent with the obligation of the United States under a multilateral treaty.[42] But a 1995 agreement between Castro and the Clinton administration had eroded some of the protection for refugees. Although a Cuban arriving on the mainland—a "dry foot"—would be welcomed, the agreement prescribed a different fate for a "wet foot":

> The United States and the Republic of Cuba reaffirm their common interest in preventing unsafe departures from Cuba. Effective immediately, Cuban migrants intercepted *at sea* by the United States and attempting to enter the United States will be taken to Cuba.[43]

Unaware of the legal details but eager to hotfoot it out of Cuba, El Duque and eight others, including unrelated player Alberto Hernandez, motored 35 miles in a fishing boat to an uninhabited Bahamian island. On the island, they were to meet another boat to take them to Miami. Before that boat arrived, they saw a U.S. Coast Guard plane. Having made it to land, they were safe from repatriation. But they did not know that, so they hid.

After subsisting on Spam and sea conchs for three days, the Cubans' priorities changed. The next time a helicopter appeared, they waved. The pilot waved back, and a day later, a Coast Guard boat arrived to pick up the castaways. Somebody told an officer that El Duque was the brother of Livan Hernandez, who had just tamed Cleveland in the World Series. The officer replied, "Tell him I'm an Indians fan. He's not getting any sympathy from me."

Because their feet were not "wet," the Cubans got some sympathy from the law and did not have to return to their homeland. But nor were their feet completely "dry": since the eight emigrants had been picked up in the Bahamas, they were subject to the laws of that country. The U.S. boat brought them to Freeport, and Bahamian officials then took them to an immigration detention center.

Outside the center, Cubas, the agent, organized a press conference as part of a public relations blitz to convince Bahamian authorities not to repatriate the group under an agreement the country had with Cuba. While the authorities vacillated, the Cuban American National Foundation lobbied the Clinton administration to grant the group "humanitarian parole."[44] The United States has long offered temporary entry into the country on a case-by-case basis, for reasons such as medical emergencies.[45] The State Department approved parole, but only for the two players and El Duque's girlfriend.[46]

Freed from the detention center, the three lucky refugees met with Cubas and decided not to use the temporary visas after all. That rejection infuriated U.S. officials.[47] But it made El Duque rich. As the agent explained to the trio, Cuban players who accept asylum in the United States are subject to the amateur draft, but if they establish residency elsewhere, they are considered free agents.[48] That rule has been called a "loophole" that "gives foreign players an economic advantage."[49] The loophole may soon close; as part of the deal to avert a strike in 2002, the players and owners agreed to a worldwide draft.[50] It was wide open for El Duque, though, and Cubas led him right through it.

Cubas procured visas for the entire group of eight to Costa Rica; on seeing the visas, Bahamian authorities released the five Cubans still in detention. Cubas then took the group to Costa Rica, where scouts from several teams came to watch El Duque pitch.

The Yankees were impressed. Their scouting report read, "reported to be 28 yrs old but may be 32—body is 25."[51] They signed the pitcher for four years and $6.6 million, a figure that resulted in part from Cubas's efforts to make it seem that many other teams were interested.[52] The agent even allegedly asked a newspaper writer to write a fake story saying that another team was close to an agreement with Hernandez.

According to a Yankee official, Cubas asked for one detail to complete the transaction: he wanted $500,000 for himself, under the table, and offered the official a 10% kickback. The official refused, but Cubas closed the deal anyway.[53] Both the bribe and the kickback would have violated baseball rules.[54] Moreover, schemes of this sort are routinely struck down by courts as fraudulent. And Cubas's alleged misrepresentation of other teams' interest could have given the Yankees the right to void El Duque's contract, but they were just happy to have him on the club.[55]

Not everybody involved in El Duque's saga was happy, though. Juan Carlos Romero, who had navigated the boat from Cuba to the Bahamas, was still in Costa Rica. He sued Hernandez there for breach of an oral contract, alleging that in exchange for assistance with the defection, Hernandez had promised to help him get into the United States and find "a well-remunerated job."[56] Romero complained, "The promises and guarantees stopped when we got to Costa Rica and [Hernandez] became a free agent. Then he treated us like dogs." The suit hung over El Duque's head for much of the 1998 season and cost him tens of thousands in legal fees.[57]

In another lawsuit, Tom Cronin, an American real estate agent who apparently dabbled in encouraging Cuban ballplayers to defect, accused Cubas of breach of contract. The contract in question set out a finder's fee for snaring El Duque:

> Cronin shall recommend and refer specific members of the Cuban national baseball team to Cubas as their exclusive agent. These players will include:... Orlando Hernandez....Cubas agrees to pay to Cronin 1/3 (one-third) of all commissions...earned as a result of major-league contracts involving the above players, with Cubas as agent.[58]

Hernandez testified that Cronin had not influenced him to sign with Cubas. The jury in federal court in Florida believed him, returning a verdict for Cubas.[59]

El Duque may ultimately leave a legal legacy that helps other ballplayers in his home country. Some U.S. Representatives have sponsored a bill called the "Baseball Diplomacy Act" that would ease the embargo against Cuba by allowing Cuban players to get visas for the duration of the season. The bill would also allow players to send money earned from baseball back to Cuba.[60] The Cuban sports minister has expressed cautious support for the idea, saying that the government would consider allowing players out of the country temporarily "as long as [the United States] respects the principles of Cuban socialist sports."[61]

Meanwhile, other Cuban defectors have followed Hernandez to the Yankees, including Andy Morales, Jose Contreras, and El Duque's former Cuban teammate (but not relative) Adrian Hernandez. "El Duquecito" (baby El Duque) left Havana on a plane to Costa Rica, but how is not clear. He has denied a story that he dressed as a woman; he is mum as to whether he forged a visa.[62]

2. Springtime Customs

Players are more likely to forget visas than to forge them. The "visa problem" is a classic excuse for reporting late to spring training, and often it occurs because players simply do not remember to initiate the process until it is almost time to show up. It has happened most often, although not exclusively, with players from Latin America because that is where most Yankees who need visas have lived.

One Yankee in particular was famous for his habit of taking time to make it through customs. The reputation of Pascual Perez as "Mr. Visa Problems" preceded his stay in the Bronx. Remembered largely for getting lost on the way to his home stadium and missing a start in Atlanta, Perez also often had a hard time making it from the Dominican Republic to the United States.[63]

In 1990, after signing with the Yankees as a free agent, Perez did not receive his visa until March 22, well into spring training, because as a former drug offender, he needed a special exit visa to leave the Dominican Republic.[64] Two days later, as he was about to board a plane to the United States, Dominican airport authorities refused to let him leave because of a pending paternity suit.

The Dominican attorney general declared that Perez could not leave the country until the suit was resolved.[65] But a local judge soon agreed to let him join the Yankees because the three-month-old child in question was too young to subject to a blood test. Perez finally arrived at spring training on March 27, denying liability and chalking the suit up to extortion: "The economic situation in the Dominican is bad, so people try to put a hand in your pocket and take what they want."[66]

In 1991, the paternity suit had been settled, but Perez was late again, by ten days, citing "visa problems." The following year, he was five days late. His vanity license plate said it all: "NO VISA."[67]

Pascual's brother Melido lived up to the family name when he joined the Yankees, arriving late in 1994 and 1996. In 1994, he was only one day late; as a reporter noted, "by family standards, he was several days early." In both years, he first cited visa problems but then offered other explanations. In 1994, he said he had taken care of personal business. In 1996, he eventually admitted that he had simply wanted to stay in his new house an extra day.[68]

Luis Polonia's visa problems were of another sort. In the middle of a 1989 jail term for sex with a minor, his visa expired, and U.S. authorities sent him back to the Dominican Republic, allowing him to count community service there as time served to complete his sentence. He then had trouble getting a visa to return to the United States to have knee surgery before the 1990 season. The trouble stemmed from his lack of a contract: the Yankees had not yet tendered one due to uncertainty about whether the 1990 season would start on time.[69]

The labor situation that delayed the start of the 1995 season wreaked more havoc on Yankee visas. Once the owners began to hire replacement players for spring training games, the Players Association successfully lobbied the U.S. Department of Labor to certify the strike. Under regulations of the Immigration and Naturalization Service ("INS"), if the Secretary of Labor certifies that a strike is in progress at the place where a visa applicant is to be employed and that employment of the applicant would "adversely affect the wages and working conditions" of the striking workers, a petition for a visa "shall be denied."[70] Therefore, once the secretary certified the 1995 strike, the INS denied visas to any foreign players who might serve as replacements.[71]

That policy caused unintended problems for regular players, who had a hard time getting their visas. When the strike ended and real spring training began, the Yankees were unsure when they would see their seven foreign players: Mark Hutton (Australia); Tony Fernandez, Melido Perez, and Polonia (Dominican Republic); Mariano Rivera and Ruben Rivera (Panama); and Robert Eenhoorn (The Netherlands). Hutton, Perez, and Polonia ended up late to camp.[72]

Although many view players' visa problems as a tired refrain, a *Sports Illustrated* writer once argued that "[a] visa problem…is not, as commonly believed, an alibi for sloth."[73] Indeed, navigating U.S. immigration law can be tricky and time-consuming. Most foreign baseball players apply for either an "O-1" or a "P-1" visa, so named for subsections of the U.S. Code. O-1 visas are available to applicants of "extraordinary ability in…athletics which has been demonstrated by sustained national or international acclaim." For players of less than "extraordinary" ability, the P-1 category is available; it requires that the applicant "perform as an athlete…at an internationally recognized level of performance."[74]

Generally, teams file petitions with the INS on behalf of their players. When the INS approves a petition, it notifies both the team and the U.S. consulate in the player's country. The player must then go in person to the consulate to submit various documents. The process often takes several weeks and can be unpredictable; therefore, even a well-meaning player might report "late."[75]

That word itself can be misleading: the Basic Agreement between Major League Baseball and the Players Association provides that although teams may *invite* players up to 45 days before the season starts, no player shall be *required* to report more than 33 days early. Teams often call players "late" based on the invitation day, but as long as a player appears before the required day, he is not subject to a fine.[76]

Although most visa problems involve delayed entry into the United States, some players end up staying too long when they get in. Once a player is no longer employed by his team, his O-1 or P-1 visa is revoked, and he must leave the country within ten days.[77] In 2002, Venezuelan Luis Sojo had received a visa for the whole season, but the Yankees released him in spring training. He remained in the country, doing some odd jobs while waiting for a better opportunity, and presumably overstaying his visa. In mid-season, he landed a job as manager of the Yankees' Class AA team in Norwich.[78]

Explaining to a reporter why he had not gone home to Venezuela after being released, Sojo claimed that because of his visa, he *had* to stay in the United States for six months.[79] But that interpretation is implausible. Visas do not *require* people to stay in the United States; they *allow* them to stay.[80] Sojo, of course, was by no means the first player to invoke a visa excuse, valid or not, to explain the otherwise inexcusable.

D. Age-Old Issues

Making up a visa problem to avoid a slap on the wrist for reporting late is one thing; making up one's age to get more money in a contract is quite another. Andy Morales learned that lesson the hard way.

Morales paid some dues just getting to the Yankees from Cuba. When he first tried to defect, he became the first Cuban ballplayer to be repatriated. A U.S. official explained, "He said he came here to play baseball. That does not constitute a well-founded fear of persecution."[81] Morales later successfully defected, by reaching land rather than being intercepted in the water, and signed with the Yankees in 2001 for four years and $4.5 million.[82]

In a matter of months, the millions were gone. Morales had allegedly told the Yankees that he was born in 1974, but the Yankees discovered that he was off by three years, in the wrong direction. Based on that misrepresentation, the team voided the deal and demanded that Morales return the money he had already received.

Under basic contract law, one who justifiably relies on a material misrepresentation in accepting an offer can void the resulting contract. Thus, Morales's liability would turn mainly on whether the Yankees justifiably relied on his representation of his age — who better to know one's age than oneself? — and on whether his age was material. Morales would not have lied about his age had it not been material; teams have good reason to want to know how old players are before signing them. Therefore, the contract would seem to be voidable.

But there may be more to the picture. Some have speculated that the real reason the Yankees voided the contract was Morales's performance: he was hitting .231 in Class AA ball. The Yankees knew his actual age from the beginning, goes the suspicion, and finally decided to play their trump card. After all, the Yankees have long known Orlando Hernandez to be older than he has claimed, but his contract has not been voided.[83]

One can lose the right to void a contract by not acting on that right. If the Yankees knew all along about Morales's age but simply waited for the right time to void the contract, they might be held to have "affirmed" the contract. Likewise, regardless of the validity of the actual contract, Morales could argue that an implied contract had arisen because the Yankees had treated him as an employee even after learning his true age.[84] Thus, Morales's millions might still be up in the air.

Morales has not been the only Yankee to grow up in a hurry. In light of both the September 11 attacks and the Danny Almonte incident, in which a Dominican-born pitcher for a Little League World Series team from the Bronx turned out to be two years older than he had represented, causing his team to forfeit its victories,[85] baseball and government officials have been scrutinizing foreign birth certificates more carefully. One casualty has been Enrique Wilson's youth.

In spring training of 2002, the Yankees discovered Wilson to be 28, not 26. When he applied for his visa at the U.S. Consulate in the Dominican Republic, he had to prove his age. He asked the Yankees to vouch for his listed date of birth, but team officials said he was on his own.[86] Once he produced a birth certificate, the consulate found the discrepancy. As a result of the hang-up, Wilson was two days late to camp. General manager Brian Cashman, though, was more concerned about the two years: "Misrepresentation of any kind is something we take very seriously [and] should be avoided at all cost."

Luis Sojo took Wilson's defense. He charged that scouts often lead Latin-American recruits into misrepresentation, telling them, "[Y]ou can sign a contract if you say you are 18, instead of 20."[87]

Understandably, teams want players to be young. But they do not want them to be *too* young. The Major League Rules provide that a foreign player can be signed if he

> (i) is at least 17 years old at the time of signing, or (ii) is 16 at the time of signing, but will attain age 17 prior to either the end of the effective season for which the player has signed or September 1 of such effective season, whichever is later.[88]

Players under eighteen, of course, are minors. They can sign contracts, but they can also void them. A player cannot, however, sign as a minor, wait indefinitely after he turns eighteen, and then use his former youth to escape from a contract.[89]

Not wanting Puerto Rican Bernie Williams to escape without a contract, the Yankees engaged in some chicanery to comply with the age rule in their recruitment of him. Because foreign players are not subject to the amateur draft, scouts in Latin America often compete to sign teenagers as soon as they become eligible. (Though Puerto Ricans are now subject to the draft, they were not when Williams signed.[90]) In fact, other teams' scouts have even signed players from the Yankees' own baseball academy in the Dominican Republic.[91]

When a Yankee scout found Williams, he was three months shy of eligibility. The scout suggested to Williams's parents that he take their son from his home in Puerto Rico to a baseball academy in Connecticut. The family accepted the plan—which prevented other teams from finding Williams in the meantime. On the day he became fair game, he signed with the Yankees. The only part of the plan that went awry was that the scout did not accept Williams's plea to have his cousin join him for the sojourn. The cousin turned out to be Juan Gonzalez.[92]

While the sequestering of Williams complied with the letter of the age rule, the violation of the rule's spirit recalls a much-maligned U.S. Supreme Court decision, *United States v. Alvarez-Machain*. In that case, U.S. authorities had circumvented an extradition treaty with Mexico through the "forcible abduction" of a Mexican charged with a crime in the United States. The Supreme Court held that the abduction did not violate the treaty.[93] To be sure, the treaty did not expressly prohibit abduction, but the mere existence of an extradition treaty suggested that suspects were not meant to be kidnapped.

Likewise, the Yankees circumvented the age rule by taking Williams to another country to avoid having other scouts find him. Happily, in the Yankees' case, Williams went willingly. In contrast, the practice of some Dominican academies of hiding teenagers so that no other scouts can sign them has led parents to file charges of kidnapping.[94]

The player forever known as "Babe" would have scoffed at the recent era's obsession with age. In 1934, while applying for a new passport, Ruth got a copy of his birth certificate, which showed him to be a year and a day younger than he had thought. When asked about the discrepancy, he growled, "What the hell difference does it make?"[95]

II. Yen for and from Japan

It has been only in the past several years that Japan has emerged as a font of major-league baseball talent, but Yankee ties to the country date back to before World War II. Yankee players have toured Japan with all-star teams and joined the Japanese leagues; as a team, the Yankees have also played exhibition series there. Although some Yankees in and from Japan have not fared well, the team is interested in expanding its presence in the Japanese market.

A. Of Rice and Man

The first Yankee in Japan was Waite Hoyt. He was also the first American pitcher to lose a game there. In 1922, on one of the first Japanese tours by American players, he and Herb Pennock, who would become a Yankee the following year, helped the U.S. team win fifteen out of sixteen games. Lou Gehrig played on a team of all-stars that toured the country in 1931 and went 17-0. For the most part, though, before and during the war, American baseball in Japan had the face of a single player: Babe Ruth.

For years, fans in Japan had wanted to see the Bambino. His glory in the Bronx fading, and his ego boosted by tour posters picturing no players but him, Ruth agreed to a seventeen-game tour after the 1934 season. Yankee teammates Gehrig and Lefty Gomez, as well as other American stars, joined him.[96]

The emperor met the team's ship on arrival and escorted the players to Tokyo. At a lunch for the players, Prince Iyesato Tokugawa hailed the international development augured by the tour: "It is no longer possible for you Americans to claim baseball as a national game for America alone." He pointed out that although many Japanese children did not know who the Premier was, "it is difficult to find a boy in Japan who does not know the [name] of . . . Babe Ruth."[97]

Amid cheers of "*banzai rusu*" ("long live Ruth") wherever he played, the Babe hit .408 with fifteen homers (his last as a Yankee) as the Americans again went undefeated. Apparently without irony, Manager Connie Mack reported that the Japanese teams would have been formidable "[w]ith better pitching and hitting."[98]

Even Ruth's strikeouts were momentous. In the closest game of the series, eighteen-year-old Eiji Sawamura fanned, in succession, Ruth, Charlie Gehringer, Gehrig, and Jimmie Foxx. Gehrig eventually homered to win the game 1-0, but Sawamura became a national hero, and his feat helped spawn Japan's first professional league two years later. Sawamura was an instant star for the Yomiuri Giants, who became known as the Yankees of Japan.[99]

Off the field, Ruth showed little appreciation for the subtleties of Buddhist temples. He loved Japanese food, though. He returned to the United States overweight, offering an unlikely explanation: "[I]n Japan the different kinds of rice and stuff puff you up."[100]

Other events away from the games hinted at a darker future. Moe Berg, a player on the trip who also happened to be a lawyer and a spy, took rooftop photos of Tokyo that later helped the U.S. military plan bombing raids during the war.[101] The tour took place amid tension between Japan and the United States over Japan's military buildup in Asia and its alleged violation of a naval treaty. The publisher of the Japanese newspaper that sponsored the series was stabbed by a radical nationalist who called the invitation of Americans "unpatriotic."[102]

Still, for the time being, as the *New York Times* reported, Ruth's baseball diplomacy worked: "The Babe's big bulk . . . blotted out such unimportant things as international squabbles over oil and navies." Mack agreed that Ruth's homers helped the two countries bond. He called the trip "one of the greatest peace measures in the history of nations."[103]

But that was before Pearl Harbor. Once the United States entered the war, *The Sporting News* questioned the effect of the tour:

> No nation which has had as intimate contact with baseball as the Japanese . . . could have committed the vicious, infamous deed of the early morning of December 7, 1941, if the spirit of the game had penetrated their yellow hides.[104]

The enmity was mutual: the Japanese government outlawed the use of American baseball terms such as "strike" and "out." Japanese soldiers even took to tormenting U.S. troops with cries of "To hell with Babe Ruth!" In return, after the Yankees won the 1943 World Series, many of them sent their caps to a Marine air commander who had promised his fliers Yankee caps for shooting down Japanese planes.[105]

Through it all, Ruth remained an ambassador of peace. He spoke out in defense of the Japanese populace:

> Despite the treacherous attack the Japs made on us only seven years later, I cannot help but feel that the reception which millions of Japs gave us [on the tour] was genuine. . . . No doubt there were plenty of stinkers among them; but looking back at that visit I feel it is another example of how a crackpot government can lead a friendly people into war.[106]

As the war neared its end, Ruth almost became a peace negotiator. Under a plan considered by the U.S. government, he would have flown to Guam to ask for peace in a series of radio broadcasts to Japan. Instead of the Bambino, though, the United States decided on the bomb.[107]

Soon after V.J. Day, Japan stopped cursing Ruth; as he neared his death in 1948, the country even celebrated "Babe Ruth Day." By 1951, Japan and the United States had signed a peace treaty, and Joe DiMaggio had become the new Yankee idol in Japan, joining a postseason tour on which he hit his last career home run. In 1955, the whole Yankee team toured the country, going 15-0-1.[108]

Despite the mass adulation of Ruth in Japan over the years, his eventual home-run-king counterpart there had a different Yankee hero. When Sadaharu Oh was asked to choose a ball signed by Gehrig or one signed by Ruth, he chose the Gehrig ball based on loyalty: like Oh, Gehrig had played for only one team.[109]

B. Striking Out

With a sense of adventure, or at least a desire for yen, many Yankees have crossed the Pacific to play Japanese baseball. Unfortunately, the most famous Yankee to strike out for Japan ended up doing mostly just that.

American players in Japanese baseball have often struggled to adjust, both to the culture and to the game.[110] For example, Don Zimmer disappointed Toei Flyers fans by hitting under .200 in 1966. But none has topped Joe Pepitone. When he signed a two-year contract with the Fukuoka club in 1973, Pepitone inspired great expectations. He was, it was thought, a star — after all, for eight years, he had been a Yankee.

One season later, after seven hits in fourteen games and an unexplained month-long absence, Pepitone left in disgrace, having earned the title of "all-time No. 1 'Ugly American.' "[111] In a column he wrote for the *New York Times*, he blamed his host: "I had to carry my own bag. I never carried my own bag in the United States, and I wasn't going to start doing it in Japan." He complained of language difficulties, noting that his only foreign teammate, Art Lopez, was "Mexican and couldn't speak English."[112]

Pepitone's diatribe prompted a reply by an American executive for a different Japanese team, who pointed out that Lopez was born and raised in New York: "Lopez uses the English language better than Pepitone, and he doesn't lie." The executive reported a conversation with Don Blasingame, a former big-leaguer who managed in Japan: "Joe told him the night before [a] game that he was trying to decide that night what his 'medical' problem would be for the next day so he wouldn't have to play."[113] Indeed, Pepitone skipped games with a number of claimed ailments, some in his leg and others purportedly resulting from hitting his head on the low doorway of his apartment. Yet he was often sighted after games dancing the night away at discos.[114] Pepitone himself admitted, "My heart wasn't in this whole damn thing."

Despite the disastrous 1973 campaign, Fukuoka was willing to honor the second year of Pepitone's contract. Pepitone, though, refused: "[M]y lawyer is trying to figure how we can call the whole thing off. I won't go back to Japan."[115] Pepitone was true to his word. He was not, however, true to his roommate, former Yankee teammate Clete Boyer, sticking him with thousands of dollars in phone and grocery bills, at least some of which Fukuoka stepped in to pay.[116]

It is not clear whether Fukuoka took any legal action against Pepitone. Under American law, Pepitone could have been liable for damages for breaching his contract, depending on its terms. The team could not have forced him to play, though, because courts do not order performance of "personal service" contracts. Such orders would be hard to oversee and would resemble the "involuntary servitude" banned by the Thirteenth Amendment.[117] Under Japanese law, it is generally harder to enforce contracts than in the United States; even judgments for damages are difficult to enforce because defendants can easily hide assets.[118]

In any event, the Pepitone episode caused Japanese teams to institute "character investigations" before signing American players. The former Yankee also contributed to the Japanese vernacular. A "*Pepiton*" became slang for a worker who fouled up a job, and "*yanki*" turned into a slur referring to white people or gangsters.[119]

Some Yankees have been better ambassadors. Boyer impressed Japanese fans with his skills at the hot corner enough to earn the nickname "Dr. Baseball." He also stressed an important point in a television interview that set him apart from other Americans: "I [am] *not* in Japan for the money." In turn, he received perhaps the ultimate compliment from a manager: "Boyer-*san* is like a samurai." Roy White, one of the few American players to learn Japanese, later evoked Boyer's dignity: "I don't think that [the manager] should have to cater to me, just because I have been in the major leagues with the Yankees."[120]

Some future Yankees have worked on their resumes in Japan in an effort to earn a shot at the majors. For instance, long before his Yankee tenure, Cecil Fielder made a name for himself by hitting 38 home runs for the Hanshin Tigers as a prelude to his 51 with Detroit the following year.[121]

Indeed, the most successful Yankee import from Japan has been none other than Dominican second-baseman Alfonso Soriano. Growing up in San Pedro de Macoris, Soriano was overshadowed by his peers and did not catch the eye of American scouts. The Hiroshima Carp, though, had a Dominican baseball academy, and when Soriano was sixteen, the team invited him to live there. Two years later, he was off to Japan, where he played in the team's farm system. In 1997, he briefly made the major-league squad. After he lost a salary arbitration, though, he was stuck with a $45,000 contract and wanted out of Japan. Just before the 1998 season, his agent, Don Nomura, had Soriano "retire."

At the time, Japanese baseball contracts granted free agency to players who retired. The Carp, however, insisted that they still had the rights to Soriano. They sent a letter to all thirty major-league teams threatening litigation against anyone who tampered with their relationship with Soriano. The team sued Nomura in Hiroshima District Court for ten million yen (roughly $100,000) in damages, alleging that he had spread lies to American teams about Soriano's contractual status. Carp officials allegedly harassed Soriano, threatening that he would never play baseball again, so much that Nomura's associate moved in with the player to protect him. Three Carp representatives even visited

Soriano's mother in the Dominican Republic to warn her that if her son did not play in Japan, he would not play anywhere else.

Hiroshima's aggressive legal campaign countered the widespread notion that Japanese people are more reluctant than Americans to assert their rights. As one expert has pointed out, that stereotype is largely a myth. Japanese do use courts somewhat less often than Americans. More tellingly, though, the effectiveness of non-litigious forms of dispute resolution prevents many people from having to sue.[122]

The Carp offensive had the desired effect for a time. Big-league teams did not risk signing Soriano, and he played in an independent league in 1998. Then Major League Baseball declared him a free agent, and he signed with the Yankees; the suit against Nomura eventually settled. Soriano flourished as a Yankee, making the majors at the end of 1999 and soon becoming an all-star. Despite the legal—and possibly illegal—action of his Japanese hosts, Soriano has spread international goodwill: "I don't hold any grudges against the Carp. With all the bad things that happened, I'm still grateful to them. They gave me my first opportunity to play pro baseball."[123]

C. Cy Young? *Sayonara*

After the United States defeated Japan in World War II under General Douglas MacArthur, a momentous peace treaty was signed in San Francisco on September 8, 1951. Instead of attending the signing, though, General MacArthur took in a game at Yankee Stadium.[124] Decades later, a Japanese pitcher took the mound at the Stadium with almost as much fanfare as the treaty: Hideki Irabu.

Billed as Japan's version of Nolan Ryan, Irabu had attracted great interest stateside when he announced that he would like to try his hand in the major leagues. He wanted to be a Yankee, and owner George Steinbrenner wanted him, but things were not so simple. By the end of the 1996 season, Irabu had spent eight years with the Chiba Lotte Marines, which was still two short of the span required for free agency in Japan. Therefore, under the Japanese rules, Chiba held his rights.[125]

In January 1997, the San Diego Padres negotiated a "working agreement" with the Marines under which they received exclusive U.S. rights to acquire Chiba players; presumably, they had a particular one in mind. Steinbrenner criticized the contract as infringing on players' freedom. Sidestepping that argument, the Padres insisted that all was fair because other teams had equal opportunities to sign similar agreements.[126] Later that month, when the Marines traded the rights to Irabu to the Padres, Steinbrenner likened the deal to "slave trade."

Agreeing with the owner in spirit if not in rhetoric, the Players Association asked the Executive Council to declare Irabu a free agent. The council refused, citing baseball's "treaty" with Japan.[127] The "treaty" was actually a simple two-page document entitled "United States-Japanese Player Contract Agreement," providing as follows:

> When a U.S. Major League Club…wishes to contact and engage a Japanese professional baseball player . . . the U.S. club or the U.S. Commissioner shall first communicate with the Japanese Commissioner and determine the status and availability of the Japanese Player…and, if the Japanese Player is under contract to, reserved by or on the inactive list of a Japanese Club, the U.S. Club shall not contact or engage the Japanese Player unless approval to do so has been given by the Japanese Club and the Japanese Commissioner.[128]

The agreement protected clubs from tortious interference with their players' contracts. Under U.S. law, a company that lures away an employee under contract with another company can be liable for damages.[129] The "treaty" implemented this principle internationally. Because the reserve clause in Irabu's contract kept him within Chiba's control until the free agency period, the council decided, Chiba had the right to choose which, if any, U.S. club could negotiate with him.

Officials from Japan and San Diego applauded the council's decision.[130] Irabu, however, already in the United States, flouted the ruling by refusing to deal with San Diego. He issued a deadline by which if the Padres did not trade him to New York, he would return to Japan. The deadline came and went, and Irabu carried out his threat. His agent, Don Nomura, referred to him as a "ronin": a masterless samurai.[131]

Irabu then threatened to sit out the 1997 season, after which he would have become a "voluntarily retired" player in Japan and thus free of Chiba's reserve clause.[132] To hear Nomura describe the situation, the Padres were "holding [Irabu's] rights in an internment camp in San Diego." The agent continued, "It's just like World War II when the Japanese were held in camps in California."[133]

Nomura's confusion of freedom of contract with physical freedom was unfortunate. Beginning in 1942, under the authority of an executive order by President Roosevelt and a parallel act of Congress,[134] the U.S. military rounded up roughly one hundred thousand immigrants from Japan and their descendants and sent them to "camps," many of which were in California.[135] The camps were surrounded by barbed wire and armed guards, although the prisoners did on occasion play baseball.[136] In 1988, Congress granted internees financial reparations and offered a national apology.[137] In 1997, the public had little sympathy for Nomura's effort to lump Irabu together with the victims of the camps.

After the season was well underway, the Padres finally surrendered and traded the rights to Irabu to the Yankees. As the Yankees were on the verge of signing him, the Japanese commissioner's office filed a tampering charge, alleging that the Yankees had negotiated with Irabu without having the rights to him, in violation of the treaty. Commissioner Bud Selig investigated the charge. Reasoning that once the Padres had gotten the rights to Irabu from Chiba, they could deal those rights to another U.S. team without Japanese approval, he found no wrongdoing.[138]

To quell lingering resentment, the major leagues and Japanese baseball renegotiated the treaty.[139] The new deal bars "working agreements" such as the one San Diego had with Chiba. Now, when any American team covets a Japanese player who is not a free agent, the U.S. commissioner's office contacts the Japanese commissioner's office to ask about the player's eligibility. If Japan approves, all major-league teams can submit bids. If the player's Japanese team accepts the highest bid, the major-league team receives the exclusive right to negotiate with the player for thirty days; if no deal occurs, the bid does not get paid, and the player must wait another season before crossing the Pacific.

In other words, most players looking to leave Japan are still limited to a single American team; for that reason, Japanese players might challenge the new agreement as violating antitrust law. But players might be satisfied because now the single team is the highest bidder for their services—and of course, that team might often be the Yankees.[140]

As for Irabu, he did little to inspire any transcontinental goodwill, bumbling his way to a 7.09 earned-run average in his first year in the Bronx. The mere presence of a

Japanese pitcher, though, had an upside for the Yankees in that all his games were broadcast in Japan, which gave the team a wider audience for marketing and brought in more television fees.[141] In 2002, the Yankees strengthened their Japanese ties by televising some Yomiuri Giants games on the Yankees Entertainment and Sports Network. Moreover, later that year, they entered into an agreement with the Giants to share facilities and scouting information. Soon after that agreement, the Yankees even managed to acquire the Giants' biggest star, free-agent slugger Hideki Matsui—his first name notwithstanding.[142]

III. European Travel and Ad Venture

Unless one counts Mark Twain's 1889 fantasy, *A Connecticut Yankee in King Arthur's Court*, which pitted lineups of kings and emperors against each other in a sixth-century baseball game at Camelot,[143] the Yankees' European ties date to the early twentieth century. In 1924, a barnstorming tour traveled to Britain, where players including Casey Stengel (not yet a Yankee but later to become the legendary manager) were photographed with King George V. The distinguished bearing of the Americans impressed the Brits. One reporter wrote that "modern professional baseball players are diverted lawyers, doctors, and possibly Presidents."[144]

Still, baseball did not catch on in England. When a promoter of a stateside vaudeville tour wired George Bernard Shaw, the English author of *Man and Superman*, to ask whether he could bill Babe Ruth as "the Superman of baseball," Shaw wired right back: "SORRY. NEVER HEARD OF HER. WHOSE BABY IS RUTH?"[145]

When Ruth toured London years later, he put on a performance that was the stuff of legends—in cricket. By his own account, he chatted with a player who said that no one had ever broken a cricket bat. Curious, Babe asked for the bowler to toss a few balls to him. On the first pitch, he hit the farthest drive onlookers had ever seen. On the second pitch, he broke the bat.[146]

Although Ruth made a name for himself in England, one place where he did not travel well was France. After walking around Paris one day without receiving the adulation he was accustomed to, he returned to the hotel and explained his foul mood to his wife: "Nobody gave a damn." The next day, instead of touring monuments, he slipped away to the American Boys School to find a kid to pitch to him.[147]

Despite the Babe's efforts, baseball never quite took hold in Europe. It has remained a soccer-mad continent. Indeed, if the Yankees have a foreign equivalent in another sport, it may be British soccer's Manchester United. Both teams have not only dominated their respective leagues, but also inspired loathing in equal measure to fandom. Much as "Yankees Suck" T-shirts sell across the United States, a popular stadium chant throughout England is "Stand Up If You Hate Man U."[148]

In 2001, the Yankees sat down with Man U and united in a "strategic alliance," the first joint marketing venture of its kind. Although details about the alliance are sketchy, it will apparently allow the teams to share marketing information, sell merchandise abroad, and pursue joint sponsorship. Manchester United expects to launch a tour of the United States soon, to be promoted by the Yankees; though no plans are yet in the works for the Yankees to go to England, more of their games will be on the telly.[149]

For Manchester United, the reason for the partnership seems clear enough. Its brand name is successful throughout Europe, on babywear and other fashion products, and the alliance gives it a platform for leverage into the U.S. market. The upside for the Yankees is less evident, although they could profit by arranging exclusive broadcasts of Manchester United games in the United States.[150] As British journalists noted, "Setting aside the unlikelihood of baseball ever cracking its image as a girls' game properly called rounders in the UK, it is...hard to see how the Yankees will benefit from this deal at all."[151]

It is easy, however, to imagine legal complications arising from the venture. Most notably, Major League Baseball collectively holds the right to enter into international marketing deals. In the 1980s, owners voted to form an entity called Major League Baseball Properties ("MLBP") to control the non-local merchandising, licensing, and marketing rights for all teams, with proceeds to be shared equally.[152] Teams must get MLBP's approval before signing nationwide or global sponsorship deals. According to a source close to baseball, if the Yankees use the alliance to unilaterally market their goods in Europe, such approval is unlikely:

> The Yankees have no marketing rights beyond a 100-mile radius of New York City.... The Yankees can't do anything outside that; the rights to do deals internationally are collectively held, so unless they are bringing along the other 29 teams, no deal would be possible. They would never, ever get the permission.[153]

The Yankees have ignored MLBP before and ended up in litigation. When they signed a marketing agreement with Adidas in 1997 without the necessary approval, baseball promptly suspended owner George Steinbrenner from the Executive Council. In response, Adidas and Steinbrenner sued MLBP, calling it a "cartel" in violation of antitrust law. They argued that baseball's antitrust exemption was no defense because the team's "baseball activities" subject to the exemption were separate from the "financial activities" of MLBP. As one commentator noted, the facts were good for an attack on the exemption because the case involved "a non-baseball industry with more global reach"—i.e., Adidas—"than any other activity previously challenged."[154] The same could be said of the venture with Manchester United.

In 1998, a settlement allowed the Yankees to continue their relationship with Adidas while making the company a business partner of MLBP.[155] A similarly fortuitous resolution of a conflict over the Manchester United alliance, however, seems improbable. It is one thing for MLBP to align itself with Adidas, but with a soccer team? Much of the value of the New York-Manchester deal stems from the comparable cachet of the two teams, and it is hard to imagine what a partnership between MLBP and Manchester United would accomplish.

Another potential legal hurdle for the transatlantic deal is that the Yankees' exclusive contract with Adidas may hamper the extent to which the team can license its trademark through Manchester United. Moreover, Adidas can be none too happy about the deal because Manchester United's merchandise is marketed exclusively by archrival Nike; Nike in turn has been said to be "nervous" about the soccer-baseball alliance.[156]

Manchester United's chief executive has tried to assure skeptics that neither the Adidas nor the Nike deal will suffer. That claim seems unlikely if the alliance with the Yankees ever gets off the ground, but that might not happen any time soon. The teams do not foresee many immediate transactions; the alliance is a long-term strategy, with no money exchanging hands right away.[157] Ultimately, the payoff from the adventurous deal might be as much a fantasy as Twain's nines of potentates.

IV. Across the Borders

Though the Yankees' travels have taken them around much of the globe, some of their legal adventures have been continental affairs, involving their neighbors to the north and south.

A. Canada Vice: Bets, Booze, and Bird-Bashing

The Yankees have played official games north of the border since 1977, when the Toronto Blue Jays joined the American League. Before then, they sometimes traveled to Canada for exhibition games. During such a trip in 1925, Babe Ruth ran off to bet on horses, flagrantly violating baseball's strict anti-gambling ban. When Judge Kenesaw Landis, the commissioner, heard about the escapade, he stormed into the Yankees' club-house and warned the Babe: "If I ever hear of you bettin' another hoss, I'm gonna put you out of baseball."[158]

Though no other Yankees got caught gambling in Canada, the reverse once happened: the Yankees caught Canada gambling. As part of its financing for the 1988 Winter Olympic Games in Calgary, the Canadian government decided to take wagers on the results of major-league games. The Yankees were one of several teams to join Commissioner Bowie Kuhn in seeking an injunction in Quebec Superior Court to halt the operation. The Yankees were eventually thrown out of the suit, though, as having no standing under Quebec's civil code.[159]

Canada has inspired other vices as well. During Prohibition, when the Yankees played in Detroit, they often took the ferry to Ontario to buy whiskey, braving border battles between smugglers and federal authorities.[160] The Eighteenth Amendment barred "the manufacture, sale, or transportation of intoxicating liquors within, [or] the importation thereof into . . . the United States," but as long as the players bought and drank their whiskey across the border, they were untouchable. Some federal laws do apply extraterritorially, making Americans acting outside the United States vulnerable to prosecution by American authorities. Happily for the Yankees, however, the Supreme Court held that the liquor ban was not one of them.[161]

Once Prohibition ended with the passage of the Twenty-First Amendment in 1933, Canada became a less attractive venue. The Yankees' legal affairs there took a turn for the absurd half a century later, when Dave Winfield took on a bird, and vice-versa.

After Winfield beaned and killed a seagull with a throw in Toronto, the local police charged him with animal cruelty. The police dropped the charges the next day, but civil litigation followed. A paralegal filed a complaint against the outfielder in Toronto Small Claims Court, purporting to represent "the estate of the dead seagull":

> The plaintiff was standing in a playing field watching a baseball game when suddenly and without warning the defendant threw a spherical object which struck the plaintiff, which caused extensive and massive injuries to various parts of the plaintiff's body. As a result of injuries sustained, the plaintiff is unable to continue flying lessons.[162]

Some law professors have argued that animals deserve standing to sue in courts, but to date, courts have found that theory to be one for the birds.[163]

B. Rizzuto in Mexico? Holy *Vaca!*

South of the border, Major League Baseball found itself in a more serious predicament in 1946: it was waging a "baseball war" with the Mexican League over the raiding of big-league rosters. The Yankees fought one of the war's major battles.

Led by a new owner with a take-charge attitude, Jorge Pasquel, the Mexican League sought out Americans under contract and asked them to switch their allegiance. That did not sit well with major-league teams, who charged the Mexicans with running an "outlaw" league. Commissioner Happy Chandler instituted five-year suspensions for players signing with Mexican teams.[164] Pasquel countered with an assault on the big leagues' economic system:

> Those who manipulate the baseball monopoly in the United States are alarmed because they are paying their players slave wages. We are paying them exactly what they are worth and this is why they are coming to Mexico.[165]

Diplomats on both sides of the border intervened. An official from the Mexican Embassy wondered why the major leagues were so defensive: "Here we are with the [newly formed] United Nations meeting in New York and baseball finds in its lap this rare opportunity for a practical demonstration of spreading ideas from one country to another."[166] Within the week, a U.S. State Department official weighed in—also in favor of Mexico. Warning that Mexico was "one of our closest allies," the official complained that baseball's failure to make peace with the Mexican League was "embarrassing" to the U.S. government. Chandler, however, was not swayed: "The State Department has enough to do without meddling in baseball."[167]

Ratcheting up the border dispute, Pasquel sent his brother, Bernardo, to New York with a mission: sign some Yankees. Just after Opening Day, Bernardo offered contracts to Phil Rizzuto and Snuffy Stirnweiss. Each player told the Yankees of the overtures.[168]

Team president Larry MacPhail was willing to let players who could not agree on contracts in New York jump to Mexico:

> If, at the close of the 1946 season we fail to come to an agreement with any player on salary, he will have a right to go to Mexico or any place else if he can better himself. I don't think it's right to keep a man out of baseball because you cannot meet his terms.[169]

Mid-season interference with players' contracts, on the other hand, was another story. The Yankees sued the Pasquels, seeking an injunction to restrain them from recruiting Yankee players. The team immediately procured a temporary restraining order against the Pasquels from the New York Supreme Court (the state's trial-level court) until the defendants could be heard.

The Pasquels were heard first in the New York media. Bernardo said he had done nothing wrong: "Rizzuto asked to talk with me and I had dinner with him and his wife. I gave him my offer and he told me he wants time to study it. That is as far as we got." The brothers hired Mexico's national attorney for the United States to represent them in court, although he was purportedly to act only in a private capacity.[170]

A couple of weeks later, the court held a hearing on the Yankees' motion for a preliminary injunction. At the hearing, Bernardo did not deny that he had said, at a press conference, "[Rizzuto] will leave the Yankees and go to Mexico when I give the word" and "I will not leave New York without taking a Yankee regular of the first rank with me."[171] When later deposed by the Yankees' attorneys, Bernardo added some details about the negotiations. On the day after the dinner party, he testified, Rizzuto had called him to say that he was ready to jump if given a $15,000 bonus. Bernardo had agreed. But Rizzuto had soon called back to say he was "undecided."[172]

Rather than denying tampering, the Pasquels attacked the standard major-league player contract, calling it "monopolistic, unconscionable, illegal and against public policy." Under the reserve clause, they alleged, players were held in "peonage" as "chattels" of the owners.[173] They cited a decision involving former Yankee Hal Chase in which a New York court had suggested that baseball was a monopoly, and they argued that because U.S. player contracts were illegal, it was not illegal to interfere with them.[174]

During the legal proceedings, Babe Ruth made headlines by snubbing his old team. The day before the hearing, he had taken off for Mexico as Jorge Pasquel's guest. When he arrived, he hailed Pasquel for "unselfishly" bringing high-level baseball to Mexico, and he promoted the globalization of the game: "Baseball is a game that should be played all over the world. It keeps kids out of trouble and develops them into better citizens."[175]

After the hearing, the court found no proof that U.S. player contracts were monopolistic and held that regardless of whether they were, the Mexican League could not interfere with them. The court thus granted the Yankees a preliminary injunction.[176] On learning of the court's rejection of the monopoly defense, Ruth, from Mexico, dissented, arguing that the proof was in the contract: "All they have to do is read it."[177]

Meanwhile, Ruth was exploring the possibility of managing a Mexican League team or even becoming the league's commissioner. During his visit, the 51-year-old was asked to put on a hitting exhibition. He disappointed the fans, swatting but a single home run; talk of Ruth as a league official quickly died out.[178] But his name still carried weight. When Mexican President Miguel Alman visited New York in 1947, he pleaded for baseball peace in the name of the Bambino:

> As to baseball in Mexico, it would be very useful if better relations in that field should develop between Mexico and the United States. . . . I can assure you that the name of Babe Ruth is as well known in Mexico as it is in the United States. A true sportsman is an internationalist.[179]

Both the Yankees and the Pasquels had told the media they would never settle their dispute. But a change in the fate of the Mexican League settled it for them. Unable to meet the financial promises Jorge Pasquel had made on their behalf, the league's owners ousted him. The new president and Chandler agreed that each would not interfere with the contracts of the other.[180] By the end of the 1947 season, the international skirmish was over, and Rizzuto had helped lead the Yankees to an intracity World Series victory.

V. Taking on the World

After six demonstrations and one exhibition, baseball became an official Olympic sport in 1992.[181] The Yankees have already had their share of Olympic heroes, including Tino Martinez and Jim Abbott, teammates on the gold-medal winning U.S. team in 1988 in Seoul. They have also scouted foreign players at the Olympics, signing two Nicaraguan pitchers after their impressive performances in Atlanta in 1996.[182] One future Yankee was on a team that toppled the United States on its way to winning gold: Orlando Hernandez pitched for Cuba in Barcelona in 1992. But El Duque did not do his country proud against the United States. Amid chants of "¡Cuba si, Yanquis no!" he pitched 1/3 of an inning and gave up five runs, although Cuba came back to win the game.[183]

Yankee Olympians became more prevalent once the Olympic Charter lifted the ban on professional athletes. Today, each sport's "International Federation" decides its eligibility criteria. Each country's "national governing body" can further restrict participation but must comply with the federation's rules.[184] In 1996, the International Baseball Association voted to allow professional players beginning with the 2000 Games, and the U.S. Baseball Federation followed suit. Major League Baseball decided that players on 40-man rosters could not play in the Olympics, but other professionals were fair game.[185]

Before the 2000 season, the Yankees wanted to sign Australian Dave Nilsson, but he had committed to represent his country in the Sydney Games that summer.[186] During the Olympics, several reports stated (despite general manager Brian Cashman's denial) that Nilsson had signed a short-term contract.[187] Apparently, the Yankees thought that he would be back in time for the playoffs. When he finally came to the United States, however, he was ruled ineligible for the postseason, over the Yankees' appeal, and he ended up never joining the club.[188]

With the advent of professional Olympians, two of George Steinbrenner's roles came into conflict: Yankee owner and Olympic supporter. The United States Olympic Committee is a corporation chartered by Congress and charged with assembling top U.S. teams for competition.[189] Steinbrenner has served two terms as the corporation's vice-president and has been a member of various other related groups; he once joked that his players had voted unanimously to have him spend more time on the Olympics than on baseball.[190] He supported the movement to allow professional baseball players in the Olympics, stating how bothered he was when the United States was beaten by "countries no bigger than...Texas."[191]

Yet when faced with a choice of country versus team, Steinbrenner has been no Yankee Doodle. In 2000, he turned down a request for minor-league pitchers Randy Keisler and Jay Tessmer to join the U.S. team in Sydney; only fellow farmhand Mike Coolbaugh was allowed to represent the country. The year before, Steinbrenner nixed Nick Johnson from playing in the Pan American Games, the qualifying tournament for the Olympics.[192] Though the Olympic Charter prohibits all forms of discrimination on the grounds of race, religion, or politics, it is silent as to the whims of an owner.[193]

VI. Conclusion

The Yankees have traveled the world and conquered various legal and political problems. Some have argued that in their international imperialism, though, they have ignored their own backyard.

The relationship between the Yankees and the Bronx started to deteriorate in the 1950s, when European immigrants started to move to the suburbs and were replaced largely by African-Americans and Hispanics. Unlike the borough, the team was slow to integrate.

Before Elston Howard finally became the first black Yankee in 1955, many had advocated signing a player of color, if for no other reason than marketing.[194] Vic Power, who played in the Yankees' farm system and eventually made the big leagues elsewhere, recalled:

> Some writers told the Yankees they should bring me up as a business move, that I'd attract a lot of Puerto Rican fans to the park. [General manager] George Weiss told them that Puerto Ricans only buy cheap seats and they didn't spend anything on concessions.[195]

The Yankees still overlook their neighborhood to some extent. They sell about 85 percent of their tickets to non-New York City residents.[196] Indeed, a team official recently acknowledged, "I don't think we have done enough to market our team to Hispanics."[197] But at least on the field, the Yankees have embraced multiculturalism to match their globalization.[198]

A recent television advertisement focused on the Yankees' international ties. In the spot, filmed at Yankee Stadium, former Secretary of State Henry Kissinger appeared, racing around the diamond, touching 'em all, and sliding into the plate.[199]

The bases of the Yankees' foreign relations—and the occasional need for diplomatic intervention—will not disappear. *First*, to stay competitive, the team will want players from abroad. For every Irabu, there will be a Soriano. *Second*, the Yankees will continue to be an international symbol of America. As Reggie Jackson once said, "Wherever you go in the world—Denmark, China, Australia—they may not have heard of the Golden Gate Bridge or Mardi Gras, but they've heard of the New York Yankees."[200] *Third*, as foreign professional leagues continue to sprout, more Yankees will ply their skills abroad. But no matter how far they range, the Yankees should never forget their connection to New York. *Home.*

Endnotes

Chapter 1 Endnotes

* David Ross Hardy Professor of Trial Practice and Law, University of Missouri-Columbia School of Law. This research was made possible, in part, through the generous support of an Edgar Mayfield Faculty Research Fellowship and a Thomas J. Patten Faculty Research Fellowship at the University of Missouri-Columbia School of Law. Thanks go to both Edgar Mayfield and Tom Patten for their support of this project and legal research generally.

1. The Record, Northern New Jersey, 1999 WL 7088012 (February 3, 1999).

2. Unless otherwise noted, factual information in this section about the end of Joe DiMaggio's life comes from Richard Ben Cramer, Joe DiMaggio, A Hero's Life 501–504 (Simon & Schuster 2000).

Cramer's book was praised by former White House advisor Lynn Nofziger and by sportswriter Bob Klapisch. See Lynn Nofziger, Showing baseball hero's darker side and his life before and after Marilyn, The Washington Post, 2000 WL 4171651 (December 10, 2000); Bob Klapisch, Joe D—The Man, The Myth, The Meanie Book Shows the Greed and Grudges, The Record, Bergen County, N.J., 2001 WL 5241118 (March 4, 2001). Another reviewer acknowledged the book as "headed for best sellerdom after rave reviews." Dave Duggan, Subway Series: Biography a Jolt to Joe's Image, Newsday, 2000 WL 10039692 (October 19, 2000).

There were other sources of misinformation about DiMaggio's health. During the 1998 World Series, Mr. Engleberg apparently told the media that he watched the games with DiMaggio in his hospital room. He noted that DiMaggio showed little reaction to the Yankee victory in the first game. "'He thinks the Yankees are going to win in four.'" Engleberg reportedly indicated that watching games with DiMaggio was an educational experience. "'He really knows this game. He knows what's coming next, what pitches.'" All of this information was in support of a further Engleberg report that DiMaggio would soon leave the hospital. See Update, Sports Day, The Dallas Morning Star, 1998 WL 13111618(October 19, 1998).

3. See Dave Saltonstall, DiMaggio to Ease Up on Sked, New York Daily News, 1998 WL 14338566 (October 18, 1998).

4. Mildred Cherfils, Yankee Star DiMaggio Hospitalized, AP Online, The Associated Press, 1998 WL 21173020 (October 17, 1998).

5. The Associated Press, Report, DiMaggio Has Cancer, The Record, Northern New Jersey, 1998 WL 5825466 (November 17, 1998).

6. See Reports on DiMaggio's condition denied; Lawyer says Hall of Famer did not have heart attack; Yankee sale talks break off, The Baltimore Sun, 1998 WL 4994905 (November 25, 1998). Actually, Mr. Engleberg only denied that DiMaggio had a heart attack and was gravely ill. He did not comment on the report of lung cancer.

7. Buzz Bissinger, For Love of DiMaggio, Vanity Fair, September 2000 362, 375.

8. American Bar Association, Model Rules of Professional Conduct, Rule 4.1. The Rules of Professional Conduct are obligatory upon Florida lawyers. See Florida Rules Regulating the Florida Bar, Discipline, Rule 3-4.2; Rules of Professional Conduct, Rule 4-4.1(2002).

9. In re Wilson, 81 N.J. 451, 455, 458, 409 A.2d 1153, 1155–56 (N.J. 1979).

10. See Joseph Durso, DiMaggio, The Last American Knight 147–48 (Little Brown, 1995).

11. See Buzz Bissinger, For Love of DiMaggio, supra note 7, at 362, 367.

12. Albert Spalding, Baseball: America's National Game 169–170 (S. Coombs & Bob West eds. 1991).

13. See Joseph Durso, DiMaggio, The Last American Knight, supra note 10, at 27–29. According to a California Delta website, Collinsville is "on the lower portion of the Sacramento River across from Pittsburg, [and is] formerly a thriving fishing village of Italian immigrants. Now it is virtually a ghost town. Towns and Cities of the California Delta, available at http://www. californiadelta.org/cities.htm#Collinsville.

14. Joe DiMaggio, Lucky to be a Yankee 26–27 (Rudolph Field, 1946). DiMaggio told his father he had a weak stomach and could not help clean the boat, but his father thought he was lazy. By his own admission, DiMaggio was more interested in tennis. Id. at 28.

15. Carl Nolte, An American Icon, Baseball legend, S.F.'s own, dies at 84, The San Francisco Chronicle, 1999 WL 2681758 (March 9, 1999).

16. See Joe DiMaggio, Lucky to be a Yankee, supra note 14, at 28–32. See also Joseph Durso, DiMaggio, The Last American Knight, supra note 10, at 33. DiMaggio played in only three games in 1932 for the Seals, going 2-9, with a long triple, while playing mostly shortstop. Id. It was that debut, however, that got him invited to spring training for the following season. Lucky to be a Yankee at 33.

17. See DiMaggio Stops at 61, Mob Charges Scorer in 1 The DiMaggio Albums 25 (R. Whittingham ed. 1989)

18. See Daniel's Dope in 1 The DiMaggio Albums, supra note 17, at 44.

19. Joe DiMaggio, Lucky to be a Yankee, supra note 14, at 43.

20. Unless otherwise noted, the factual information in this and succeeding sections about DiMaggio's years in the Pacific Coast League, his initial contracts with the Yankees, the years DiMaggio held out, his 1941 56-game hitting streak and the season of 1941, and the holdouts of Ty Cobb, all come from James R. Devine, The Legacy of Albert Spalding, The Holdouts of Ty Cobb, Joe DiMaggio and Sandy Koufax/Don Drysdale, and the 1994–95 Strike: Baseball's Labor Disputes are as Linear as the Game, supra, 31 Akron L. Rev. at 4–14, 15, 16, 19–22, 26, 28–31 (and notes therein).

About Joe DiMaggio's streak, it must also be added that DiMaggio said that he hit the ball harder in the streak-ending game than he did in games that continued the streak. Joe DiMaggio, Lucky to be a Yankee, supra note 14, at 126. He also credited his then wife Dorothy Arnold with helping with the fundamentals that got the streak started. In late 1940, when he was not hitting, Dorothy, who sat in the same seat every day reportedly said to DiMaggio: "'The number on your shirt is in a different position. You're not swinging the way you used to.'" DiMaggio figured out that he had developed a hitch in his swing. See id. at 125–26.

21. See Yankees Renew Effort to Satisfy DiMaggio in 1 The DiMaggio Albums, supra note 17, at 124. The practice of offering players their prior year's contract amount had existed within the Yankee organization for some time prior to 1938.

22. Joseph Durso, DiMaggio, The Last American Knight, supra note 10, at 95, 97.

23. See Joe DiMaggio, Lucky to be a Yankee, supra note 14, at 171.

24. Joe in Fold, But Not Forgiven, in 1 The DiMaggio Albums, supra note 17, at 199.

25. See Joseph Durso, DiMaggio, The Last American Knight, supra note 10, at 97. Ultimately, DiMaggio was penalized $1,500 from his contracted-for salary. Id. Yankee manager Joe McCarthy was delegated the responsibility of determining when DiMaggio was ready to play. See Yankee Contract is Accepted by DiMaggio in 1 The DiMaggio Albums, supra note 17, at 197. DiMaggio estimated the amount at $162 a day for each day he was not playing, "darn nearly what I made a month when I broke in on the Coast League." Joe DiMaggio, Lucky to be a Yankee, supra note 14, at 171.

26. Joe DiMaggio, Lucky to be a Yankee, supra note 14, at 172.

27. Joe DiMaggio, 1914–1999 Baseball's 'Yankee Clipper' Dies at 84, Los Angeles Times, 1999 WL 2137258 (3/9/1999).

28. See Joseph Durso, DiMaggio, The Last American Knight, supra note 10, at 138. An almost

game-for-game account of the streak is contained at id. at 115–138.

29. Carl Nolte, An American Icon; Baseball legend, S.F.'s own, dies at 84, The San Francisco Chronicle, supra note 15.

30. Carl Nolte, An American Icon; Baseball legend, S.F.'s own, dies at 84, The San Francisco Chronicle, supra note 15.

31. Joe DiMaggio, 1914–1999 Baseball's 'Yankee Clipper' Dies at 84, Los Angeles Times, 1999 WL 2137258 (March 9, 1999).

32. See Joseph Durso, DiMaggio, The Last American Knight, supra note 10, at 146–47. DiMaggio apparently thought that $50,000 for the 1942 season was a rationale amount. See id. at 147. Members of the news media speculated that $80,000 would be fair for the only member of the Yankees the public really wanted to see. See On the Line with Considine, in 1 The DiMaggio Albums, supra note 17, at 367.

33. Barrow replaced prior Yankee president Jacob Ruppert upon Ruppert's death. See Frank Graham, The New York Yankees 247–48 (1947).

34. See Joseph Durso, DiMaggio, The Last American Knight, supra note 10, at 147–48.

35. See Joe DiMaggio, Lucky to be a Yankee, supra note 14, at 31; Joseph Durso, DiMaggio, The Last American Knight, supra note 10, at 33–34, 36–38. Joe's immediately older brother Vince made it acceptable for the DiMaggio brothers to play baseball, when he brought home in excess of $1,500 in bonuses and pay from his team and set it on the kitchen table in front of his father. Joseph Durso, supra note 10, at 30.

36. Roger Kahn, Joe and Marilyn, A Memory of Love 60–61 (William Morrow & Co., 1986).

37. See Legend evolved from humble beginnings, USA Today, 1999 WL 6836199 (March 9, 1999) (providing a time line of important events in DiMaggio's life and career).

38. Anecdotal DiMaggio story in and of itself; Baseball: The private man offered few glimpses of his moods and motivations, The Orange County Register, 1999 WL 4288671 (March 9, 1999)

39. All information about Cobb's input into DiMaggio rookie contract comes from Jim Murray, His Dignity and Style Add to the Legend, Los Angeles Times, 1994 WL 2183783 (July 7, 1994).

40. Jim Murray, His Dignity and Style Add to the Legend, Los Angeles Times, supra note 39.

41. Anecdotal DiMaggio story in and of itself; Baseball: The private man offered few glimpses of his moods and motivations, The Orange County Register, supra note 38.

42. Jim Murray, His Dignity and Style Add to the Legend, Los Angeles Times, supra note 39.

43. Roger Kahn Joe DiMaggio; 1914–99 Joltin' Joe Has Gone; Yankee Always a Picture of Class, Los Angeles Times, 1999 WL 2137312 (March 9, 1999).

44. See Joe Lewis and the Jews, Jewish Virtual Library, available at http://www.us-israel.org/jsource/US-Israel/louis.html.

45. Roger Kahn, Joe DiMaggio; 1914–99 Joltin' Joe Has Gone; Yankee Always a Picture of Class, supra note 43.

46. See Joseph Durso, DiMaggio, The Last American Knight, supra note 10, at 104–105.

47. Roger Kahn, Joe DiMaggio; 1914–99 Joltin' Joe Has Gone; Yankee Always a Picture of Class, supra note 43.

48. Luke Cyphers, American Classic, New York Daily News, 1999 WL 3427415 (3/9/1999).

49. Manhattan Merry-Go-Round (1937), available at http://www.rottentomatoes.com/m/ManhattanMerryGoRound-1013237/preview.php.

50. Unless otherwise noted, information about Joe and Dorothy and Joe and Marilyn relies heavily on Richard Ben Cramer, Joe DiMaggio; A Hero's Life, supra note 2, at 129–134, 136, 192, 198, 209, 214–17, 220, 320; Joseph Durso, DiMaggio, The Last American Knight, supra note 10, at 106–108, 205, 210–11, 217; and Roger Kahn, Joe and Marilyn, A Memory of Love, supra note 36, at 36, 136, 139, 190–93, 258–64. Joe and Marilyn were married 274 days.

51. See Luke Cyphers, American Classic, New York Daily News, supra note 48.

52. See Roger Kahn, Joe DiMaggio; 1914–99 Joltin' Joe Has Gone; Yankee Always a Picture of Class, supra note 43.

53. See Joseph Durso, DiMaggio, The Last American Knight, supra note 10, at 1, 10, 13, 16–21.

54. "The Toast of the Town" was the original name of the Ed Sullivan Show, which ran on CBS on Sunday nights from 1948–1971. See The Ed Sullivan Show (variety) available at http://www.classicthemes.com/50sTVThemes/themePages/edSullivan.html.

55. Joe DiMaggio, 1914–1999 Baseball's 'Yankee Clipper' Dies at 84, Los Angeles Times, 1999 WL 2137258 (3/9/1999); Richard Ben Cramer, Joe DiMaggio; A Hero's Life, supra note 2, at 175–76.

56. "Mrs. Robinson," words and music by Paul Simon, lyrics available at http://freespace.virgin.net/r.kent/lyrics/greatist.hits. When he first heard the song, DiMaggio thought artists Simon and Garfunkel were making fun of him and he threatened to sue. See Richard Ben Cramer, Joe DiMaggio; A Hero's Life, supra note 2, at 476.

57. See In Memory of Joe DiMaggio, the Yankee Clipper (House of Representatives — March 9, 1999), News from Congressman Vito Fossella, available at http://www.house.gov/fossella/dimaggio.htm.

58. Ernest Hemingway, The Old Man and the Sea 55 (Scribner Classics, 1980). Hemingway became a part of DiMaggio's regular circle of friends. When DiMaggio attended a prize fight with Hemingway, lawyer Edward Bennett Williams, and to-be governor of New York Averell Harriman, somebody asked Hemingway if he was famous too. Hemingway reportedly responded that he was DiMaggio's doctor. See Joseph Durso, DiMaggio, The Last American Knight, supra note 10, at 206.

59. Dave Kindred, When baseball mattered the most, no one mattered as much as DiMaggio, The Sporting News Archives, available at http://www.sportingnews.com/archives/dimaggio/kindred.html.

60. Eric Zicklin and Wil Shriner, Room Full of Heroes, Frasier, production code 9.06, available at http://www.geocities.com/Hollywood/Derby/3267/96.htm.

61. Larry David, The Note, Seinfeld, Episode 19, production code 301, season 3, episode 1, broadcast date: September 18, 1991, available at http://www.geocities.com/tnguym/scripts/TheNote.html. At the end of the program, Kramer, Jerry, George and Elaine again see DiMaggio, dunking his donut, at the coffee shop.

62. Richard Ben Cramer, Joe DiMaggio; A Hero's Life, supra note 2, at 429. This vote took place in 1969; DiMaggio easily defeated Ted Williams, Willie Mays, Hank Aaron, Mickey Mantle, Roberto Clemente, and Stan Musial, among others.

63. See Roger Kahn, Joe DiMaggio; 1914–99 Joltin' Joe Has Gone; Yankee Always a Picture of Class, supra note 43.

64. Factual information for DiMaggio's distrust, unless otherwise noted, comes from Buzz Bissinger, For Love of DiMaggio, Vanity Fair, supra note 7, at 370, 372; Richard Ben Cramer, Joe DiMaggio; A Hero's Life, supra note 2, at 447–49, 451–53, 464–65, 506, 513; Joseph Durso, DiMaggio, the Last American Knight, supra note 10, at 246–47.

65. Press Release, July 23, 1999, National Baseball Hall of Fame, available at: http://www.baseballhalloffame.org/whats_new/press_releases/1999/pr1999_07_023.htm.

66. Factual information about the relationship between DiMaggio and Engleberg, unless otherwise noted, comes from Buzz Bissinger, For Love of DiMaggio, Vanity Fair, supra note 7, at 367–68, 371–75; Richard Ben Cramer, DiMaggio: A Hero's Life, supra note 2, at 453, 490–95, 502, 506, 508–509, 511–14; Joseph Durso, DiMaggio, The Last American Knight, supra note 10, at 253–54.

67. Mizell suffers apparent heart attack; Ex-pitcher, congressman is upgraded to serious; DiMaggio still in hospital; Notes, The Baltimore Sun, 1998 WL 4989717 (October 18, 1998); Big leap for Hernandez, The Toronto Star, 1998 WL 30712034 (October 18, 1998). Baseball Notes; Home Field Does Matter, Dayton Daily News, 1998 WL 12811906 (October 18, 1998).

68. American Bar Association Model Rule of Professional Conduct, Rule 1.1; Florida Rules of Professional Conduct, Rule 4-1.1.

69. See Restatement of the Law (Second) of Agency § 387 (1958).

70. See The Score Board announces exclusive autograph agreement with Hall of Famer Joe DiMaggio-two year Agreement Expected to Generate Over $10 Million, Business Wire (October 24, 1991).

71. See Bates v. State Bar of Arizona, 433 U.S. 350, 368, 97 S.Ct. 2691, 2701 (1977).

72. Letter from Jerald C. Cantor to Richard Ben Cramer, republished at Richard Ben Cramer, Joe DiMaggio; A Hero's Life, supra note 2, at 516–17. Certainly there is no evidence that Mr. Engleberg ever drafted any will or trust document in which he was a beneficiary of any portion of Joe DiMaggio's fortune, an act that most would agree is impermissible. It is unethical for a lawyer to "prepare an instrument" that gives the lawyer or an immediate family member of the lawyer "any substantial gift from a client, including a testamentary gift." American Bar Association Model Rules of Professional Conduct, Rule 1.8(c); Florida Rules of Professional Conduct, Rule 4-1.8(c).

73. See Richard Wasserstrom, Lawyers as Professionals: Some Moral Issues, 5 Human Rights 1 (1975).

74. See, e.g., In re Taylor, 695 N.E.2d 526, 529 (Ind., 1998).

75. See, e.g., In re Saladino, 71 Ill.2d 263, 375 N.E.2d 102, 16 Ill Dec. 471 (1978). Today, the "appearance of impropriety" standard has been eliminated from the American Bar Association's formal rules governing lawyer conduct, largely because the term is so difficult to define. See American Bar Association Model Rules of Professional Conduct, Rule 1.10 (Comment). The change in rubric, however, does not change the basic duty of loyalty that a lawyer owes a client, a duty exemplified in this instance by the appearance of impropriety language.

76. See American Bar Association Model Rules of Professional Conduct, Rule 1.6, 1.8(b); Florida Rules of Professional Conduct, Rule 4-1.6; 4-1.8(c) and comments thereto.

77. See generally Restatement of the Law Governing Lawyers § 64 comment e (American Law Institute 2000).

78. Information about the duties of an agent to a principal come primarily from Restatement of the Law [Second] of Agency § 387 (1958). Compare American Bar Association Model Rules of Professional Conduct Rule 1.7, Florida Rules of Professional Conduct, Rule 4-1.7.

79. American Bar Association Model Rules of Professional Conduct, Rule 1.7(b), Florida Rules of Professional Conduct, Rule 4-1.7(b).

80. American Bar Association Model Rules of Professional Conduct, Rule 1.8(a), Florida Rules of Professional Conduct, Rule 4-1.8(a).

81. Baseball Legend Improves a Little, Sun-Sentinel Ft. Lauderdale, 1998 WL 23472405 (December 8, 1998).

82. Cramer argued that it was, see Richard Ben Cramer, Joe DiMaggio; A Hero's Life, supra note 2, at 503.

83. Compare American Bar Association Model Rules of Professional Conduct 1.8(b); Florida Rules of Professional Conduct, Rule 4-1.8(b).

84. Last Will and Testament of Joseph P. DiMaggio (part 2), available on-line through Court T.V. at http://www.courttv.com/people/wills/dimaggio2.html.

85. See P.M. Buzz, Rider, San Francisco Examiner 1999 WL 6874230 (June 16, 1999); Carolina man selling balls signed on Joe D.'s death bed, The Grand Rapids Press, 1999 WL 17328142 (July 5, 1999).

86. Carolina man selling balls signed on Joe D.'s death bed, The Grand Rapids Press, supra note 85.

87. For his part, Engleberg reportedly said he did not think DiMaggio would want the collection sold in pieces, just for money. "'I know Joe is watching all the moves I make,'" he was quoted as saying. See P.M. Buzz, San Francisco Examiner, supra note 85.

88. Compare American Bar Association Model Rules of Professional Conduct, Rule 1.7(b)(2); Florida Rules of Professional Conduct, Rules 1.7(b)(2); 1.7(c).

89. See Mike McCurley & Julie P. Crawford, Mansions, Mercedes and Marital Meltdowns: A Guide to Representing the Rich and Famous, 8 Matrim. Strategist 3 (September, 2001).

90. Kenneth J. Abdo & Jack P. Sahl, Counseling Clients in the Entertainment Industry 2002: Ethics, 695 PLI/Pat 447, 462–63 (2002).

91. Factual information about Engleberg and DiMaggio is from Buzz Bissinger, For Love of DiMaggio, Vanity Fair, supra note 7, at 368, 370.

92. See The Peace Encyclopedia, The Stockholm Syndrome, available at http://www.yahoodi. com/peace/stockholm.html.

93. See Michael Maslanka, The Client Quotient: The Top 10 Rules of Effective Client Communication, 57 Bench & B. Minn. 34, 39 (Oct., 2000).

94. Richard Ben Cramer, DiMaggio; A Hero's Life, supra note 2, at 502–503.

Chapter 2 Endnotes

* Associate Dean of the Faculty and Professor of Law, Saint Louis University School of Law. Thanks to Milton I. Goldstein, Tim Greaney, Maxine I. Lipeles, and Alan Weinberger for learning me all their experience in commenting on an earlier draft, to Margaret McDermott, Joshua Stegeman, Kevin Sullivan, and especially Lacey Searfoss for their valuable research assistance in finding things that, for me, were not "déjà vu all over again," to Bob Jarvis for making this chapter necessary, to Dean Jeffrey Lewis and Saint Louis University School of Law for the support which allowed me to take this fork in the road, and to Mary Dougherty for patiently retyping this article until it was finally over.

1. Phil Pepe, The Wit and Wisdom of Yogi Berra 52 (1974).

2. Yogi Berra, The Yogi Book 90–91 (1998).

3. Id. at 30.

4. Id. at 29.

5. Pepe, supra note 1, at 76.

6. Yogi Berra with Dave Kaplan, When You Come to a Fork in the Road, Take It! 88, 91 (2001).

7. Richard Wicks, Book Review of The Rational Basis of Contracts and Related Problems in Legal Analysis (by Merton Ferson) 23 S. Cal. L. Rev. 164 (1949).

8. Annual Dinner proceedings, 57 Am. Soc'y Int'l L. Proc. 294, 295 (1963), 55 Am. Soc'y Int'l L. Proc. 198,199 (1961).

9. T. Munford Boyd, Colleague Dillard—A Review, Judge Dillard—A Preview, 56 Va. L. Rev. 5 (1970).

10. Katherine Parkes, Book Review of In Search of Justice: Society and the Legal System, 59 Geo. L. J. 459, 461 (1970).

11. Robert M. Cover, Your Law—Baseball Quiz, N.Y. Times, April 5, 1979 at A.23.

12. Justice Frank K. Richardson, A Case for Moderation, 20 Cal. W. L. Rev. 1–2 (1983).

13. 585 F. Supp. 825 (E.D. Ark. 1984).

14. Id. at 837.

15. 817 F.2d 365 (5th Cir. 1987).

16. Id. at 368.

17. Matter of Greene County Hospital, 835 F.2d 589, 595 (5th Cir. 1988).

18. Id. at 589 n.1.

19. Id. at 595.

20. David W. Robertson, In Memoriam: Alvin Rubin's Last Dissent, 70 Tex. L. Rev. 7 (1991).

21. Overman v. Fluor Constructors, Inc., 797 F.2d 217, 219 (5th Cir. 1986).

22. American Civil Liberties Union of Ohio v. Capitol Square Review Advising Bd., 243 F.3d 289, 305 (6th Cir. 2001).

23. Id. at 307.

24. Norman v. Housing Authority of City of Montgomery, 836 F.2d 1292, 1305 (11th Cir. 1988).

25. King v. Burris, 588 F. Supp. 1152, 1158 n.11 (D. Colo. 1984).

26. 45 F.3d 588, 589–90 (1st Cir. 1995), overruled by Carpenters Local Union No. 26 v. United States Fidelity & Guaranty Co., 215 F.3d 136 (1st Cir. 2000).

27. 950 F.2d 13 (1st Cir. 1991), cert. denied, 504 U.S. 910 (1992).

28. Williams, 45 F.3d at 591.

29. Smith v. Beal Acceptance Corp., 244 B. R. 487, 491 (N.D. Ga. 2000).

30. Key v. Sullivan, 925 F.2d 1056, 1061 (7th Cir. 1991).

31. National Rifle Ass'n of America v. FEC, 854 F.2d 1330, 1336 (D.C. Cir. 1988).

32. Smith v. Palmer, 24 F. Supp. 2d 955, 957 (W.D. Iowa 1998).

33. McCoy v. Major League Baseball, 911 F. Supp. 454, 458 (W.D. Wash. 1995).

34. United States v. Davenport, 740 F. Supp. 1371,1372 (S.D. Ind. 1990).

35. Davis v. Coopers & Lybrand, 787 F. Supp. 787, 804 n.41 (N.D. Ill. 1992).

36. Saints and Sinners v. City of Providence, 172 F. Supp. 2d 348, 351 (D. R. I. 2001).

37. Claussen v. Aetna Cas. & Sur. Co., 754 F. Supp. 1576, 1577 (S.D. Ga. 1990).

38. Hallwood Realty Partners, L. P., v. Gotham Partners L. P., 95 F. Supp. 2d 169, 171 (S.D.N.Y. 2000).

39. United States v. Manni, 810 F.2d 80, 81 (6th Cir. 1987).

40. 723 A.2d 1138, 1139, 1140 n.5 (R.I. 1999).

41. Yogi Book, supra note 2, at 34.

42. State v. State Wyoming Board of Outfitters, 931 P.2d 958, 959 (Wyo. 1997).

43. United States v. Charlottesville Redevelopment and Housing Authority, 718 F. Supp. 461, 470 n.14 (W.D. Va. 1989).

44. Appeal of Horsham Township., 520 A.2d 1226, 1230 n.4 (Pa. Commw. Ct. 1987).

45. In re Sanders, 981 P.2d 1038, 1060(Cal. 1999). (Brown, J. dissenting).

46. Frank H. Easterbrook, Technological Innovations and Legal Tradition: Enduring Principles For Changing Times, Cyberspace Versus Property Law?, 4 Tex. Rev. L. & Pol. 103, 107 (1999).

47. A Return of Professionalism, 66 Fordham L. Rev. 2091, 2095 (1998).

48. Business Dispute Resolution-ADR and Beyond: An Opening Statement, 59 Alb. L. Rev. 835 (1996).

49. Moving Mountains: A Comment on the Glass Ceilings and Open Doors Report, 65 Fordham L. Rev. 573 (1996).

50. Family and Conciliation Courts Review Strategies and Need for Systems Change: Improving Court Practice for the Millennium, 38 Fam. & Conciliation Cts. Rev. 166, 167 (2000).

51. Legal Education: Observations and Perceptions from the Bench, 30 Wake Forest L. Rev. 369 (1995).

52. Current Trends in Judicial Review of Environmental Agency Action, 27 Envtl. L. 1, 19 (1997).

53. National Rifle Ass'n of America, 854 F.2d at 1336 (déjà vu all over again).

54. Fetterly v. Paskett, 15 F.2d 1472 (9th Cir. 1994).

55. Introduction to Education Symposium, 16 St. Mary's L. J. 777, 782 (1985).

56. Louis Lowenstein, Management Buyouts, 85 Colum. L. Rev. 730, 764 (1985).

57. Geoffrey Hazard, Rising Above Principle, 135 U. Pa. L. Rev. 153, 164 (1986).

58. Letter to the Editor, 1987 Colum. Bus. L. Rev. 177, 178 (observe by watching).

59. 97 Yale L. J. 1255 (1988).

60. Id. at 1336, 1337.

61. Harold Hongju Koh, The National Security Constitution 204 (1990) (emphasis in original).

62. Burt Neuborne, Background Norms for Federal Statutory Interpretation, 22 Conn. L. Rev. 721, 722 (1990).

63. Geoffrey C. Hazard, Jr., Dimensions of Ethical Responsibility: Relevant Others, 54 U. Pitt. L. Rev. 965, 967 (1993).

64. Michael E. Solimine, Revitalizing Interlocutory Appeals in the Federal Courts, 58 Geo. Wash. L. Rev. 1165 (1990).

65. The Pursuit of Manhood and the Desegregation of the Armed Forces, 38 UCLA L. Rev. 499, 543 (1991).

66. The Failure of Sentencing Guidelines: A Plea for Less Aggregation, 58 U. Chi. L. Rev. 901, 918 (1991).

67. Federalism and the Supreme Court: The 1999 Term: What is the Supreme Court's New Federalism, 25 Okla. City U. Law Rev. 927, 943 (2000).

68. See e.g., Major Tyler J. Harder, Military Justice Symposium Vol. I, Recent Developments in Jurisdiction: Is This the Dawn of the Year of Jurisdiction?, 2001 Army Law. 2, 6 (2001) ("ain't over"); Faculty, The Judge Advocate General's School, U.S. Army; The Art of Trial Advocacy: "It's Like Déjà Vu All Over Again!": Yet Another Look at the Opening Statement, 2000 Army Law. 34 (2000); Major David A. Wallace et al, Contract Law Developments of 1997 — The Year in Review, 1998 Army Law. 3. 122 (1998) ("ain't over"); Major Kathryn R. Sommerkamp et al, Developments of 1996 — The Year in Review, 1997 Army Law. 3, 78 (1997) (déjà vu); Major Timothy J. Pendolino et al., 1995 Contract Law Developments — The Year in Review, 1996 Army Law. Rev. 3, 59 (1996)(fork in road); Major Nathanael Causey et al, 1994 Contract Law Developments—The Year in Review, 1995 Army Law. Rev. 3, 71 (1995) ("It gets late early out here."); Major Lawrence J. Morris, Keystones of the Military Justice System: A Primer for Chiefs of Justice, 1994 Army Law. 15 (1994) (observe by watching; can't imitate, don't copy); Major E. V. Kelly, Jr., Providence Inquiry: Counsels' Continuing Responsibility to Their Clients, 1986 Army Law. 13 (1986).

69. Pamela D. Karlan, Still Hazy After All These Years: Voting Rights in the Post-Shaw Era, 26 Cumb. L. Rev. 287, 288 (1996).

70. James F. Blumstein, Shaw v. Reno and Miller v. Johnson: Where We Are and Where We Are Headed, 26 Cumb. L. Rev. 503 (1996).

71. Between Intimates and Between Nations: Can Law Stop the Violence?, 50 Case W. Res. L. Rev. 851, 868 (2000).

72. Steven B. Datlof, Beyond Washington v. Glacksberg: Oregon's Death with Dignity Act Analyzed from Medical and Constitutional Perspectives, 14 J. L. & Health 23, 24 (2000).

73. Mark M. Hager, Review Essay: Civil Compensation and Its Discontents: A Response to Huber Review of Liability: The Legal Revolution and Its Consequences by Peter W. Huber, 42 Stan. L. Rev. 539, 576 (1990).

74. 46 Emory L.J. 697 (1997).

75. Id. at 698.

76. The New and Unfortunate Face of Judicial Federalism, 23 Ohio N.U. L. Rev. 1197, 1200 (1997).

77. Jonathan D. Rowe, "It Gets Late Early Out There": Yogi Berra Tours the Law Schools, 77 Mich. B. J. 664, 666 (1998).

78. Edwin Meese, III, Speech, Current Issues in Juvenile Justice, 23 Pepp. L. Rev. 791, 792 (1996).

79. Gramm-Rudman-Hollings and the Balanced Budget Amendment: A Page of History, 25 Harv. J. on Legis 611 (1988).

80. Reflections on the Ratings Craze, 15 Card. Arts & Ent. L. J. 147, 151, 152 (1997) (no one goes there).

81. Robert A. Connor, Justice Scalia and Yogi Berra: A Matter of Interpretation, 41 Am. J. Juris. 165 (1996).

82. Transcript of the "Alumni" Panel on Discovery Reform, 39 B. C. L. Rev. 809, 827 (1998).

83. The Future of the Federal Courts, 46 Am. U. L. Rev. 263, 301 (1996).

84. Douglas A. Blaze, Déjà Vu All Over Again: Reflections on Fifty Years of Clinical Education, 64 Tenn. L. Rev. 939 (1997).

85. Durward S. Jones, The Authority of Precedent in Tax Planning: 'It Ain't Settled' Till It's Settled, 52 Tenn. L. Rev. 269 (1985).

86. D. Jeanne Louise Carriere, It's 'Déjà Vu All Over Again': The Covenant Marriage Act in Cultural Perception and Legal Reality, 72 Tul. L. Rev. 1701 (1998).

87. Norman S. Johnson & Ross A. Albert, 'Déjà Vu All Over Again': The Securities and Exchange Commission Once More Attempts to Regulate the Accounting Profession Through Rule 102(e) of Its Rules of Practice, 1999 Utah L. Rev. 553 (1999).

88. Faculty, The Judge Advocate General's School, U.S. Army, Yet Another Look at the Opening Statement, 2000 Army Law 34.

89. Suzanne Ernst, Drummond, Déjà Vu: The Status of School Funding in Ohio After Derolph II, 68 U. Cin. L. Rev. 435 (2000).

90. Yogi Berra with Tom Horton, Yogi: It Ain't Over 8 (1989).

91. U.S. v. Laney, 189 F.3d 954, 967 (9th Cir. 1999) (T.G. Nelson, J., concurring).

92. See Stephen Landsman, Symposium: Introduction, 47 DePaul L. Rev. 227 (1998).

93. Take It, supra note 6, at 128.

94. Herbert Hovenkemp and Sheldon F. Kurtz, The Law of Property: An Introductory Survey 2–3 (5th ed. 2001).

95. The Mind and Faith of Justice Holmes 72 (Max Lerner ed. 1943).

96. "Stare Decisis" in The Benjamin N. Cardozo Memorial Lectures (Vol. I) 284.

97. See generally Restatement (Second) of Contracts §§ 151–153 (1981).

98. Take it, supra note 6, at 73, 75.

99. 32 N.E. 64 (Ma. 1892).

100. Take It, supra note 6, at 163.

101. Wit and Wisdom, supra note 1, at 61.

102. Yogi Berra and Ed Fitzgerald, Yogi: The Autobiography of a Professional Baseball Player 12 (1961).

103. Yogi: It Ain't Over, supra note 90, at 29.

104. Yogi Book, supra note 2, at 30, 73.

105. Williams, 45 F.3d at 589, 590 n.1.

106. Yogi: It Ain't Over, supra note 90, at 20.

107. Yogi Book, supra note 2, at 30.

108. Take It!, supra note 6, at 69.

109. Review: Technology and the Future of Law in a Digital World, by M. Ethan Katsh, 47 Stan. L. Rev. 1375, 1403 (1995).

110. Id. at 1403 n.156.

111. Henry T. Greely, Trusted Systems and Medical Records: Lowering Expectation, 52 Stan. L. Rev. 1585, 1593 (2000).

112. Margaret Martin Berry, Jon L. Dubin, and Peter A. Joy, Clinical Education for This Millennium: The Third Wave, 7 Clinical L. Rev. 1, 75 n.2 (2000).

113. Stuart Minor Benjamin, Proactive Legislation and the First Amendment, 99 Mich. L. Rev. 281, n.269 (2000).

114. State v. Oliver, 46 P.3d 36, 37 (Kan. App. 2002).

115. Montecal v. Mandarell, 682 A.2d 918, 920 (R.I. 1996).

116. Walthal v. Rusk, 172 F.3d 481, 482 (7th Cir. 1999).

117. Michael P. Kenny and Teresa D. Thebaut, Misguided Statutory Construction to Cover the Corporate Universe: The Misappropriation Theory of Section 10(b), 59 Alb. L. Rev. 139, 142 (1995).

118. See McCulloch v. Maryland, 17 U.S. (4 Wheat) 316, 407 (1819).

119. See Schenck v. United States, 249 U.S. 47, 52 (1919).

120. City of New York v. New York State Div. of Housing and Community Renewal, 765 N. E. 2d 829, 839 (N.Y. 2001).

121. Linda A. Suydam & David K. Elder, FDAMA Update 54 Food & Drug L. J. 21, 22 (1999).

122. John Bartlett, Familiar Quotations, 903 (15th ed. 1980).

123. John Bartlett, Familiar Quotations, 754 (16th ed. 1992).

124. See, e.g., available at http://rinkworks.com/said/yogiberra.shtml; http://www. znetsports.com/yogiberra_quotes.asp

125. Wit and Wisdom, supra note 1, at 5.

126. Williams, 45 F.3d at 589.

127. Yogi Book, supra note 2, at 98.

128. See e.g., Eben Colby Comment, What Did the Doctrine of Unconscionability Do to the Walker-Thomas Furniture Company?, 34 Conn. L. Rev. 625, 626 (2002) ("déjà vu"); Missy McJunkins, Note: Constitutional Law—First Amendment and Establishment Clause—The Wall of Separation Crumbles, Agostini v. Felton, 117 S. Ct. 1997 (1997), 20 U. Ark. Little Rock L. J. 813 (1998) (not over); Suzanne Ernst Drummond, Comment, Déjà Vu: The Status of School Funding in Ohio After DeRolph II, 68 U. Cin. L. Rev. 435, 451 (2000) (déjà vu); Don Messeloff, Note: The NBA's Deal with the Devil: The Antitrust Implications of the 1999 NBA-NBPA Collective Bargaining Agreement, 10 Fordham. Intell. Prop. Media & Ent. L. J. 521, 569 (2000) (déjà vu); Adam Arms, Metaphor, Women and Law, 10 Hastings Women's. L. J. 257 (1999); Ann K. Hadrava, Note: The Amendment to Federal Rules of Civil Procedure 26(b)(1) Scope of Discovery: An Empirical Analysis of its Potential "Relevancy" to Employment Discrimination Actions, 26 Okla. City U. L. Rev. 1111, 1119 (2001) (déjà vu); Susan Carboni, New Jersey Developments: The Entire Controversy Opinions of 1995 and Attorney Malpractice: What Price Economy in New Jersey?, 48 Rutgers L. Rev. 1273, 1296 (1996) (ain't over); Laura Bradford, Note, The Counterrevolution: A Critique of Recent Proposals to Reform No-Fault Divorce Laws, 49 Stan. L. Rev. 607, 636 n.58 (1997).

129. Yogi: It Ain't Over, supra note 90, at 14.

Chapter 3 Endnotes

* Timothy S. Hall (hallt@louisville.edu) is an Assistant Professor of Law at the Louis D. Brandeis School of Law at the University of Louisville, where he teaches Contracts, Insurance law and health law courses. A Cincinnati Reds fan, Professor Hall holds a B. Mus. from the University of Louisville and a J.D. from the Cornell Law School.

1. For waiting list registrants in 1998, the median time to transplant was 817 days. For registrants who, like Mantle, entered the waiting list in 1995, the median time to transplant was 316 days. United Network for Organ Sharing ("UNOS"), 2001 Annual Report of the U.S. Scientific Registry for Transplant Recipients and the Organ Procurement and Transplantation Network— Transplant Data: 1991–2001 (Off. of Spec. Programs, Health and Human Services Administration, U.S. Dept. of Health and Human Services), Table 9.2, available at http://www.unos.org/ Data/anrpt_main.htm.

2. Bob Mims, Surgery Gives Hagman Two Gifts: A New Liver, Renewed Lease On Life, Chi. Trib., Aug. 28, 1996, at C2; David Crosby Still Critical, But Talking, Chi. Trib., Nov. 22, 1994, at 2.

3. Major W. Cox, Did Casey Cheat Death or the System, Montgomery Advertiser, Aug. 4, 1993, available at http://www.majorcox.com/columns/casey.htm.

4. Ross Newhan & Douglas P. Shuit, Gravely Ill Mantle Gets New Liver; Doctors Optimistic, L.A. Times, June 9, 1995, at A1. Celebrities and athletes do not uniformly receive livers quickly. On November 2, 1999, Walter Payton, running back for the Chicago Bears football team, died of bile duct cancer at age 45 while waiting for a liver transplant. See Don Yeager, One of a Kind, Sports Illustrated, Nov. 8, 1999.

5. See Bernie Siegel et al, The Right to Die: An End of Life Question, 2 Quinnipiac Health L. J. 167, 182 (1999) ("You do not think Mickey Mantle got a...liver ahead of somebody else...? Of course he did...You know he jumped over somebody else.").

6. Although there is considerable debate as to the extent to which alcoholism or other "lifestyle choices" should affect one's eligibility for scarce medical resources, see, e.g., C. Cohen & M. Benjamin, Alcoholics and Liver Transplantation, 265 J. Am. Med. Ass'n 1299 (1991); A.H. Moss & M. Siegler, Should Alcoholics Compete Equally for Liver Transplantation, 265 J. Am. Med. Ass'n 1295 (1991); Eike Henner-Kluge, Drawing the Ethical Line Between Organ Transplantation and Lifestyle Abuse, 150 Canadian Med. Ass'n J. 745 (1994), there is some uncertainty whether Mantle's liver cancer was directly caused by his long-term alcoholism. See Merlyn Mantle et al., A Hero All His Life 230 (1996) (hereinafter Mantle, A Hero All His Life) ("[T]he medical opinion was undecided. His cancer could have been caused by the hepatitis virus. 'That isn't lifestyle,...that is bad luck.'" (quoting Mantle's doctor, Kent Hamilton)); Gina Kolata, Transplants, Mickey and Morality, N.Y. Times, June 11, 1995 at section 4, page 5.

7. See Newhan & Shuit, supra note 4.

8. Organs can only last so long after being harvested from a donor before they become useless for transplantation. Although this "cold ischemic time" is being extended by modern techniques, it remains preferable for transplants to occur as soon as practicable after the donor organ is harvested.

9. The mission of the Mantle Foundation is "the complete elimination of the loss of life or the loss of quality of life due to the lack of organs and tissue available for transplantation." See About the Mantle Foundation, available at http://www.transweb.org/mantle.html.

10. Facts in this section are taken from Mantle, A Hero All His Life, supra note 6, and The Official Mickey Mantle Web Site, available at http://www.themick.com.

11. For summaries of Mantle's lifetime statistics, see http://www.themick.com; Mike Downey, The Best Memory of Mantle is Taken from Players' Past, L.A. Times, Aug. 14, 1995, at C1.

12. Baseball Almanac, World Series Record Book — Career Hitting Records, at http://www.baseball-almanac.com/rb_ws1.shtml. Mantle was self-deprecating about his predilection for strikeouts, stating that "During my 18 years I came to bat almost 10,000 times. I struck out about 1,700 times and walked maybe 1,800 times. You figure a ballplayer will average about 500 at-bats a season. That means I played 7 years without ever hitting the ball." Baseball Almanac, Player Stats, at http://www.baseball-almanac.com/players/ballplayer.shtml.

13. See Lewis Early, Mickey Mantle Mini-Biography, available at http://www.themick.com ("One of the questions baseball scholars ponder is the great "What if?" What would Mickey have accomplished if he had been healthy during his career?"); John T. Dabney, Mickey Mantle: An American Legend, 7 Seton Hall J. Sport L. 1 (1997).

14. Newhan & Shuit, supra note 4.

15. The Mickey Mantle Foundation, Mickey's Team, available at http://www.transweb.org/mantle.html#join.

16. UNOS, Critical Data, Milestones, at http://www.unos.org/Newsroom/Frame_news.asp?SubCat=milestones.

17. Id.

18. In 2001, there were 5,177 liver transplants and 14,152 kidney transplants in the U.S. UNOS, Critical Data, Number of Transplants Performed in 2001, at http://www.unos.org/Newsroom/critdata_main.htm#transplants.

19. Scientific Registry of Transplant Recipients, About Transplants, at http://www.ustransplant.org/facts.html [hereinafter SRTR].

20. Id.

21. UNOS, Quick-Reference Statistics Illustrate Donor Shortage, at http://www.unos.org/Newsroom/archive_newsrelease_20011220_statquote.htm.

22. SRTR, supra note 19.

23. Unif. Anatomical Gift Act (1968), 8A U.L.A. 64 (1993)(amended 1987).

24. Uniform Anatomical Gift Act of 1987, 8A U.L.A. at 19 ("1987 UAGA").

25. Id. § 10.

26. See Unif. Anatomical Gift Act (1987) Table of Jurisdictions Wherein Act has Been Adopted (Supp. 2002).

27. Ironically, improvements in other areas of health care exacerbate the shortage of organs for transplant. Decreases in traffic fatalities (a historic source of healthy organs for transplants) and advances in emergency medicine have decreased the number of available, transplantable organs. See Warren King, In Death, There Can Be Life—Donors Needed, The Seattle Times, June 26, 1995, at A1.

28. National Organ Transplant Act, P.L. 98-507 (October 19, 1984)(hereinafter "NOTA"). See also C.E. Harris & S.P. Alcorn, To Solve a Deadly Shortage: Economic Incentives for Human Organ Donation, 16 Issues L. & Med. 213, 221–22 (Spring 2001).

29. The following description is based on Robert Veatch, Transplantation Ethics 353 (2001).

30. Robert M. Veatch, A New Basis for Allocating Livers for Transplant, 10 Kennedy Inst. of Ethics J. 75 (2000).

31. Newhan & Shuit, supra note 4.

32. Veatch, supra note 30, at 76.

33. Id.

34. See Veatch, supra note 29, at 352 ("It is hard to raise the issue of Mantle's status if the organ-procurement organization...merely gave him an organ by following the same rules that would have applied to everyone else....").

35. See U.S. Dept. of Health & Human Services, Organ Procurement and Transplantation Network: Final Rule, 42 CFR 121 (1998).

36. Roderick T. Chen, Note, Organ Allocation and the States: Can the States Restrict Broader Organ Sharing?, 49 Duke L.J. 261 (1999); Dulcinea Grantham, Comment, Transforming Transplantation: The Effect of the Health and Human Services Final Rule on the Organ Allocation System, 35 U.S.F.L. Rev. 751, 752–3 (2001).

37. Grantham, supra note 36, at 760.

38. Veatch, supra note 29, at 311–24.

39. In fact, active alcoholism is considered by most transplant centers. In Mantle's case, the fact that he had undergone successful treatment for alcoholism at the Betty Ford Center in 1994 was a factor in the doctors' decision to proceed with the transplant. See Newhan & Shuit, supra note 4; Veatch, supra note 29, at 320.

40. See supra note 6.

41. For this reason, incarcerated individuals are often denied placement on organ transplant lists because of the inadequacy of post-operative care in the prison system. See Jessica Wright, Note, Medically Necessary Organ Transplants for Prisoners: Who is Responsible for Payment?, 39 B.C. L. Rev. 1251, 1258–59 (1998).

42. See generally Mantle, A Hero All His Life, supra note 6.

43. Veatch, supra note 29, at 312 (noting that as a matter of utilitarian ethics, alcoholic cirrhosis patients actually have better survival rates than those of some other liver transplant candidates). Mantle's transplant has also been criticized as wastage because his liver cancer recurred shortly after the transplant, eventually causing his death mere months after the transplant. Liver cancer patients generally have lower chances of long term survival after transplantation; however, transplantation may be the only available treatment for a patient with both liver cancer and cirrhosis of the liver, for whom removal of the cancerous tumor is unavailable. Gina Kolata, An Experimental Plan for Man-

tle, N.Y. Times, June 8, 1995, at B16.

44. David Brown, Mantle Gets Emergency Liver Transplant; Though Prognosis "Excellent," Surgery is Controversial for Cancer Patients, Wash. Post, June 9, 1995, at A1; Kolata, supra note 43.

45. Warren King, supra note 27.

46. See Sheldon F. Kurtz & Michael J. Saks, The Transplant Paradox: Overwhelming Public Support for Organ Donation vs. Under-Supply of Organs: The Iowa Organ Procurement Study, 21 Iowa J. Corp. L. 767 (1996).

47. Schloendorff v. Society of N.Y. Hosp., 105 N.E.92, 93 (N.Y. App. Div. 1914).

48. Laura A. Siminoff & Christina M. Saunders Sturm, African-American Reluctance to Donate: Beliefs and Attitudes about Organ Donation and Implications for Policy, 10 Kennedy Inst. of Ethics J. 59, 60 (2000) (citing Siminoff et al, 1995).

49. California amended the 1987 UAGA to provide that, if a decedent is known to be a member of a religious group which "has religious tenets that would be violated by the disposition of the human body" for transplantation, then no third party may give consent to donation of such an individual's body for transplantation. Cal. Health & Saf. Code §7152 (Supp. 2002). The statute does not give examples of religions to which this section would apply.

50. See Veatch, supra note 29, at 6–12 (noting that "[t]here has been in general no objection among either the secular or religious bioethical communities to the removal of organs for lifesaving purposes from human bodies [once deceased].").

51. Id. at 7 (discussing fundamentalist Protestant belief in bodily resurrection as a potential source of reluctance to donate organs).

52. UNOS Ethics Committee, An Evaluation of the Ethics of Presumed Consent and A Proposal Based On Required Response (copy on file with author).

53. Laurel R. Siegel, Re-engineering the Laws of Organ Transplantation, 49 Emory L.J. 917, 944–45 (noting that this is not likely because the transplant team and the potential donor's health care team are made up of different health care professionals); Unif. Anatomical Gift Act (1968) §7(b), 8A U.L.A. 124 (1993) (amended 1987) (mandating that the physician "who tends the donor at his death…not participate in the procedures for removing or transplanting [an organ]."); Siminoff & Sturm, supra note 48, at 65 (21.2% of white respondents, and 37.9% of African-American respondents, agreed with the statement "I worry that if doctors know that I am an organ donor, they won't do as much to save my life.").

54. Siminoff & Sturm, supra note 48, at 65.

55. Id. at 64–65.

56. Id. at 60–62 (noting that reported rates of consent to donation in the African-American community are as low as 33%).

57. Maryellen Liddy, The "New Body Snatchers": Analyzing the Effect of Presumed Consent Organ Donation Laws on Privacy, Autonomy and Liberty, 28 Fordham Urb. L. J. 815, 819 (2001).

58. Jennifer Rutherford-McClure, To Donate or Not to Donate Your Organs: Texas Can Decide for You When You Cannot Decide for Yourself, 6 Tex. Wesleyan L. Rev. 241, 245 (Spring 2000).

59. Most tellingly, critics have argued that the prohibition on profiting from the organ trade does not seem to extend to the health care professionals involved in the transplantation industry, who live handsomely on profits from the transfer of organs. See, e.g., Phyllis Coleman, Brother, Can You Spare a Liver?: Five Ways to Increase Organ Donation, 31 Val. U.L. Rev. 1, 16 (1996).

60. See, e.g., Siminoff & Sturm, supra note 48, at 67.

61. By 1993, 35 states registered an individual's organ donation preference during the driver's license application process. UNOS Ethics Committee, supra note 52.

62. Harris & Alcorn, supra note 28, at 224.

63. Id. at notes 50–51 and accompanying text.

64. UNOS Ethics Committee, supra note 52.

65. This description of mandated choice is taken from the proposal made in UNOS Ethics Committee, supra note 52.

66. Siminoff & Sturm, supra note 48, at 67 (suggesting distrust as a reason for such a high rate of refusal).

67. 42 U.S.C. § 274(e) (1994).

68. American Medical Association Council on Ethical and Judicial Affairs, Cadaveric Organ Donation: Encouraging the Study of Motivation, CEJA Report 1-A-02 (2002).

69. Richard Schwindt & Aidan Vining, Proposal for A Future Delivery Market for Transplant Organs, 11 J. Health Pol. Pol'y & L. 482 (1996).

70. Richard Schwindt & Aidan Vining, Proposal for a Mutual Insurance Pool for Transplant Organs, 23 J. Health Pol. Pol'y & L. 725 (1998).

71. Frederic R. Parker, Jr. et al, Organ Procurement and Tax Policy, 2 Hous. J. Health L. & Pol'y 101 (2001).

72. Siminoff & Sturm, supra note 48, at 67–69.

73. 20 Pa. Cons. Stat. § 8622 (1999).

74. Sheryl Gay Stolberg, Pennsylvania Set to Break Taboo on Reward for Organ Donation, NY Times, May 6, 1999 at A1.

75. Andis Robeznicks, Drive to Increase Organ Donations Yields Novel Idea, American Medical News, May 20, 2002 (available at http://www.amednews.com).

76. Siegel, supra note 53, at 924–25.

77. Deborah L. Shelton, Living Donor Transplants Raise Ethical Concerns, American Medical News, June 5, 2000 (available at http://www.amednews.com).

78. SRTR, supra note 19.

79. Shelton, supra note 77.

80. Siegel, supra note 53, at 924–27.

81. See The Mickey Mantle Foundation, supra note 9.

82. Id.

83. Laura F. Rothstein, Don't Roll in My Parade: The Impact of Sports and Entertainment Cases on Public Awareness and Understanding of the Americans with Disabilities Act, 19 Rev. Litig. 399, 410 (2000).

84. Barney Sneiderman, Picard Lecture in Health Law—1993: The Rodriguez Case: Where Do We Go From Here—A Multi-Dimensional Approach, 2 Health L.J. 1, 2 (1994).

85. The Mickey Mantle Foundation, supra note 9.

Chapter 4 Endnotes

* Professor of Law, Case Western Reserve University School of Law. My thanks to Jonathan Entin, Erik Jensen, and Bob Jarvis for comments on a draft of this chapter.

1. See Derek Gentile, The Complete New York Yankees: The Total Encyclopedia of the Team 149 (2001); Ray Robinson & Christopher Jennison, Pennants and Pinstripes: The New York Yankees 1903–2002, at 77 (2002).

2. Others who have claimed the nickname include numerous seaside inns, yachts, a ferry service to Yankee Stadium, and every mohel living within three hundred miles of New York State. For information on the ferry service, see http://www.nywaterway.com/baseball_yankee.html.

3. See Dick Schaap, Steinbrenner 162 (1982). As Karl Marx so aptly put it, "Hegel remarks somewhere that all facts and personages of great importance in world history occur, as it were, twice. He forgot to add: the first time as tragedy, the second as farce." Karl Marx, The Eighteenth Brumaire of Louis Bonaparte 15 (1852, 1963, International Publishers Co. paperback ed.). Here, and elsewhere I rely heavily on Schaap's discussion of Steinbrenner's life. Steinbrenner had some

weak precedent that he could point to. While Sal "The Barber" Maglie is rightfully thought of as a New York Giant, he spent portions of his last two seasons as a Yankee.

4. See Dan Shaughnessy, The Curse of the Bambino (1990). To Bostonians this move (along with the dumping of a number of other players such as Ernie Shore, Duffy Lewis, and Red Ruffing) have led to Mr. Frazee, of regrettable memory, being dubbed "the original Boston Strangler." To readers who notice that this seems to be something of an obsession with me, I apologize. It is.

5. Harvey Frommer, The New York Yankee Encyclopedia 8 (1997).

6. In six of the eight full television seasons that coincided with CBS's ownership of the Yankees, some other network (generally NBC, the National Broadcasting System) had the season's top-rated show. See Art McDonald, This Date in New York Yankee Hating: Going Negative on Baseball's Most Despised Team 253 (1998).

7. My account of Steinbrenner's biography relies heavily on two sources: Michael Roberts, Edward Whelan & Gary Diedrichs, George M. Steinbrenner III, A Profile, available at http://www.clevelandmagazine.com/editorial/thismonthfeatures.asp?docid=278 (originally published in Cleveland Magazine, April 1974); and Dick Schaap, Steinbrenner! (1982).

8. Rather eerily, the Sheppard murder occurred on Steinbrenner's birthday, July 4, 1954. This is not as spooky, I suppose, as John Adams and Thomas Jefferson dying within hours of each other on July 4, 1826, fifty years after the signing of the Declaration of Independence.

9. While the athletic powerhouse comment is facetious and inserted in deference to my colleague Erik Jensen, who played outfield for the MIT Engineers, Henry Steinbrenner's athletic accomplishments were real. Jensen, on the other hand, proved abler at tax law than at hitting a curve ball.

10. The only somewhat hyperbolic image of the events to be described below as laying waste to Buffalo is Grant Gilmore's and Charles Black's. Grant Gilmore & Charles Black, The Law of Admiralty 890 (2d ed. 1975).

11. Petitions of the Kinsman Transit Co., 338 F. 2d 708, 714, 715 (2d Cir. 1964), cert. denied, 380 U.S. 944 (1965).

12. George F. Will, "A One-Man Error Machine," reprinted in The Yankees Reader 247 (Miro Weinberger & Dan Riley eds. 1999).

13. Schaap, Steinbrenner, supra note 3, at 49.

14. Quoted in McDonald, This Date in New York Yankee Hating, supra note 6, at 240 (1998).

15. Mary Schmitt Boyer, "Dolan: Yankees' Steinbrenner a Big Part of Woes," Cleve. Plain Dealer, July 17, 2002, at D5. Dolan is hardly a disinterested observer. His brother, Charles, owns Cablevision, which is locked in litigation with Steinbrenner over the terms under which it will provide the Yankees Entertainment and Sports Network broadcast of Yankees' games to Cablevision subscribers. Steinbrenner responded by saying that Yankee critics were simply jealous. "Steinbrenner: Don't Blame Yankees for Baseball's Woes." S. Fla. Sun-Sentinel, July 18, 2002, at 3C.

16. Schaap, Steinbrenner, supra note 3, at 316.

17. Id. at 225.

18. Bill Madden & Moss Klein, Damned Yankees: A No-Holds-Barred Account of Life with "Boss" Steinbrenner (1990) (with cartoons by Ed Murawinski).

19. Brandon Toropov, 101 Reasons to Hate George Steinbrenner (1997).

20. I knew this would make you look. In United Novelty, 42 So. 2d 395 (Miss. 1949), the employer, United Novelty, had sent plaintiffs' son to a small room to clean coin-operated machines. A gas heater with an open flame heated the room. The job was to be done with gasoline as a solvent. Instead of the predictable accident, caused by gas fumes permeating the room and igniting, flame and gasoline were brought together through an intermediary, a startled rat. The rat, which had been nesting in the machine that the employee had started to clean, had been upset by his drenching with gasoline and darted across the room seeking shelter. Unfortunately, it headed directly for the heater. Its gasoline-impregnated coat ignited, sending the rat scurrying back to its original shelter. The inevitable explosion caused the son's fatal burns. The decision does not recount the fate of the rat, but one can only assume the worst. The court was not troubled that the accident had occurred in an unpredictable way.

21. Robert Strassfield, Causal Comparisons, 60 Fordham L. Rev. 913, 916 n. 16 (1992). This is an example of shameless, gratuitous self-citation.

22. 388 F. 2d 821 (2d Cir. 1968).

23. "Ice on Lake Erie Cuts Snowfall but More is Forecast," Buff. Evening News, Jan. 16, 1959, at 1. My account of what occurred that night and subsequently relies on the published opinions in the Kinsman cases and in newspaper accounts in the Buffalo Evening News and the Buffalo Courier-Express appearing between January 16 and February 14, 1959.

24. "Squalls Continue in Hard Hit WNY," Buff. Evening News, Jan. 17, 1959, at 1.

25. My conversion from 1959 to 2001 dollars relies on the inflation calculator at http://www.westegg.com/inflation/.

26. John Kuenster, "Baseball Payroll to Hit $8 Million," Buff. Evening News, Jan. 21, 1959, at 53; "Yanks Cut Pay of Ford, Berra for 'Bad Years'," Id.

27. "Cecil B. DeMille Dies at Age 77," Buff. Evening News, Jan. 21, 1959, at 40. DeMille directed the 1956 Biblical epic, The Ten Commandements.

28. The reference is, of course, to another famous boat accident, the stranding of the S.S. Minnow on a desert island on the television series, Gilligan's Island. For a discussion of the "legal facets" of Gilligan's Island, see Robert M. Jarvis, Legal Tales from Gilligan's Island, 39 Santa Clara L. Rev. 185 (1998).

29. Bob Watson, "'Ghost Ships' Make History with Amazing, Costly Trip," Buff. Evening News, Jan. 24, 1959, at A12.

30. Id.

31. Fosse, along with Thurman Munson and Carlton Fisk, was one of a triumverate of promising young American League catchers in the early 1970's. Rose ran over Fosse, who was blocking the plate, to score the winning run for the National League in the twelfth inning of the All-Star Game. Fosse continued to play after the incident, though x-rays would later show that he had a fractured shoulder. Sadly, he was never the same player after that game.

32. "Freighter Collapses Michigan Avenue Lift Bridge," Buff. Courier-Express, Jan. 22, 1959, at 1.

33. Eerily, there's that date again.

34. For the folkloric version of the event, see "Bridges Escaped Ship in Incident Years Ago," Buff. Courier-Express, Jan. 23, 1959, at 11. A more accurate account of events can be found in the case that it spawned. The Anna C. Minch, 271 F. 192 (2d Cir. 1921).

35. 42 U.S.C. § 183.

36. Kinsman, 338 F 2d at 714.

37. Id., at 714, 715 (emphasis added).

38. 380 U.S. 300 (1965).

39. Thomas S. Andrzejewski & John E. Depke, "AmShip Locks Up Lake Grain Trade," Cleve. Plain Dealer, Nov. 2, 1972, at 1.

40. Quoted in Schaap, Steinbrenner, supra note 3, at 120.

41. Quoted in William H. Chafe, The Unfinished Journey: America Since World War II 421 (3d ed. 1995).

42. Parks v. Steinbrenner, 131 A.D. 2d 60, 520 N.Y.S.2d 374 (N.Y. App. Div. 1987).

43. The Yankees and baseball settled this dispute without going to trial.

44. This is discussed supra at note 15.

45. Steinbrenner v. Esquire Reporting Co., Inc. 1991 WL 102540 (S.D.N.Y. 1991).

46. Schaap, Steinbrenner, supra note 3, at 290–94.

47. Leigh Gull, "Steinbrenner Sues Satan, Alleges Breach of Contract," The True Dork Times, available at http://www.truedorktimes.com/1101/Tdsteinbrenner.htm.

48. See Jerry Ross, Damn Yankees: A Musical Comedy (1957) (based on the novel by Douglass Wallop); Douglass Wallop, The Year the Yankees Lost the Pennant: A Novel (1954).

49. The oxymoronic nature of the phrase, "Steinbrenner employee with job security," is so well-known that no footnote is necessary. This was not true of fictional Steinbrenner employee George Costanza, however. In Episode 153 of Seinfeld, "The Millennium," George's efforts to get fired so he could take a job as director of scouting for the Mets repeatedly backfired.

Chapter 5 Endnotes

* Dean and Professor of Law, University of Tennessee College of Law. I am in debt to Anita Monroe for all her hard work on this project. Thanks to my colleague, Greg Stein, for his comments and insights.

1. Thomas C. Galligan, Jr., The Tragedy in Torts, 5 Cornell J. of L. & Pub. Policy, 139 (1996).

2. I confess that, as I matured as a baseball fan, the team I rooted for in the National League was the Pittsburgh Pirates. Thus, while I could not consider myself a Pirate fan in 1960, I do not look back on Mazeroski's homerun as sadly as many Yankee fans do.

3. I do take pride in the fact that I won a small bet from my friend Malcolm O'Hara after the American League's Baltimore Orioles returned the favor in 1966 by sweeping the Dodgers in the Series. I'm not sure, in retrospect, that I would have been quite so gleeful in taking his 50 cents if I had known then that Sandy Koufax's brilliant career was over.

4. Tom Meany, The Yankee Story (1960).

5. Restatement (2d) of Torts, § 496C.

6. Id., Illustration 5.

7. See, e.g., William Powers, Jr., Sports, Assumption of Risk, and the New Restatement, 38 Washburn L.J. 771 (1999). See also, Robert L. Rabin, The Duty Concept and Negligence Law: A Comment, 54 Vand. L. Rev. 787, 790–92 (2001).

8. 15 A.D. 2d 193, 222 N.Y.S. 2d 658 (1961).

9. Id. at 660–661.

10. Id. at 661. Compare: Jones v. Three Rivers Management Corp., 483 Pa. 75, 394 A. 2d 546 (1978). There, the court held that someone who was hit by a foul ball while using an interior walkway could recover. The risk was not a common, frequent and expected part of the game. Therefore, the general no-duty rule did not apply and the operator of the stadium could be held liable.

11. See, e.g., Neinstein v. Los Angeles Dodgers, Inc., 185 Cal. App. 3d 176, 229 Cal. Rptr. 612 (1986); Romero v. Pittsburgh Associates, 787 A. 2d 1027 (Pa. Sup. Court 2001). But see, Yates v. Chicago National League Ball Club, 595 N.E. 2d 570 (Ill. App. Ct. 1992). Yates was then apparently overruled by the Baseball Facility Liability Act. 745 Ill. Comp. Stat. 38/10 (West Supp. 1998). For a discussion of the Baseball Facility Liability Act see Ted J. Tierney, Heads-Up!: The Baseball Facility Liability Act, 18 N. Ill. U.L. Rev. 601 (1998). The general rule that a fan hit by a foul ball may not recover has also been applied to a fan hit by a piece of a baseball bat during a game. See, e.g. Benejan v. Detroit Tigers, Inc., 246 Mich. App. 645, 635 N.W. 2d 219 (2001).

12. Actually, after the Dent homerun, Reggie Jackson homered in a later inning and the Red Sox mounted two formidable attempts at late inning comebacks only to be thwarted in the end when Carl Yastrzemski popped up to Graig Nettles with Gossage pitching.

13. 325 Mass. 419, 90 N.E. 2d 840 (1950).

14. I am not aware of any relationship between Justice Spalding and the former pitching great and sports manufacturing magnate, A.G. Spalding. See, e.g., Peter Levine, A.G. Spalding and the Rise of Baseball (1985). I do know A.G. Spalding pitched for the Boston Red Stockings. Id. at 13–20.

15. 23 A.D. 2d 750, 258 N.Y.S. 2d 982 (1965).

16. A football fan injured in a scuffle over a football kicked into the stands has fared somewhat better than the average baseball fan. See, e.g., Hadden v. University of Notre Dame, 716 N.E. 2d 603

(Ind. Ct. App. 1999). The case is ably discussed in Stefan A. Mallen, Note: Touchdown! A Victory for Injured Fans at Sporting Events?, 66 Mo. L. Rev. 487 (2001).

17. See, Dan Castellano, Shea Has Place in Yankees Lore, http://www.greatlinks.com/yankees/stories/0415dan.html.

18. The Hall of Famers in their order of finish as 1974 on-base percentage leaders were Rod Carew, Joe Morgan, Carl Yastrzemski, Willie McCovey, Willie Stargell and Mike Schmidt. Schmidt actually finished ninth. Between Stargell and Schmidt were Jeff Burroughs and Mike Hargrove of Texas and Bob Bailey of Montreal. http://www.elverson.com/sports/baseball/obp/1974.html.

19. See, e.g., Maddox v. City of New York, 90 A.D. 2d 535, 455 N.Y.S. 2d 102 (1982)(allowing Maddox to increase his ad damnum clause from $1.5 million to $10 million based upon his allegations that his then recent development of arthritis in his knee and his worsening condition had effectively put a complete end to his athletic career).

20. Maddox v. City of New York, 121 Misc. 2d 358, 467 N.Y.S. 2d 772 (1983).

21. Id. at 360.

22. Id.

23. Id.

24. Id.

25. Maddox v. City of New York, 108 A.D. 2d 42, 487 N.Y.S. 2d 354 (1985). Actually, there is another short memorandum decision by the appellate court in Maddox's case. That opinion, Maddox v. City of New York, 104 A.D. 2d 430, 478 N.Y.S. 2d 923 (1984), denied plaintiff's motion to dismiss the city's appeal as untimely.

26. 487 N.Y.S. 2d at 356.

27. Maddox also alleged that he was excused from the defense of assumption of risk or contributory negligence because his employer had violated a statutory duty to supply him with a safe place to work. The court analyzed the applicable sections of New York labor law and concluded that Maddox was not within the class of persons whom the statutes were enacted to protect. The court stated that clearly the purpose of those provisions was to protect a worker engaged in industry and there was nothing that revealed any legislative intent to expand the class of protected individuals to include baseball players. Id. at 357–58. Even if Maddox was within the class of protected individuals he had still not established that his employer had violated a duty to exercise reasonable care to provide him with a safe workplace.

28. Id. at 358.

29. Maddox v. City of New York, 66 N.Y. 2d 270, 487 N.E. 2d 553, 496 N.Y.S. 2d 726 (1985).

30. 487 N.E. 2d at 554.

31. Id. at 557.

32. http://www.baseball-reference.com/m/maddoe101.shtml.

33. Id.

34. http://www.larrymirkinstudios.com/polbb2.html.

35. http://www.claimsmag.com/Issues/April00/Briefs/ExYankee.asp.

36. 68 N.Y. 2d 432, 502 N.E. 2d 964, 510 N.Y.S. 2d 49 (1986).

37. 502 N.E. 2d at 967.

38. Id.

39. Id. at 971.

40. 90 N.Y. 2d 471, 685 N.E. 2d 202, 662 N.Y.S. 2d 421 (1997).

41. 685 N.E. 2d at 204.

42. Id. at 207.

43. Id. at 207.

44. Id. at 208.

45. Cf. Locilento v. John A. Coleman Catholic High School, 134 A.D. 2d 39, 523 N.Y.S. 2d 198 (1987).

46. Zachardy v. Geneva College, 733 A. 2d 648 (Pa. Super. 1999), affirmed, 751 A. 2d 193 (Pa. 2000).

47. Couldn't the law adhere to the general negligence/reasonable care standard and simply use the plaintiff's knowledge of the risk as a relevant circumstance in the determination of reasonable care? Perhaps because of a concern that under a general negligence standard juries would not adequately weigh the plaintiff's knowledge, the recklessness/intentional tort requirement holds sway in participant injury cases. And, most of these cases result in no recovery. See, e.g., West v. Sundown Little League of Stockton, Inc., 96 Cal. App. 4th 351, 116 Cal. Rptr. 2d 849 (2002); Higgins v. Pfeiffer, 215 Mich. App. 423, 546 N.W. 2d 645 (Mich. App. 1996); Dillard v. Little League Baseball, Inc., 55 A.D. 2d 477, 390 N.Y.S. 2d 735 (N.Y. App. 1977) (umpire in a baseball game struck in the groin by a pitched baseball had assumed the risk of his injury); Karr v. Brant Lake Camp, Inc., 261 A.D. 2d 342, 691 N.Y.S. 2d 427 (N.Y. App. 1999); Bowser v. Hershey Baseball Association, 357 Pa. Super. 435, 516 A. 2d 61 (1986) (member of unincorporated association organizing tryout could not recover).

Of course, it also may be possible for an athlete to sue a referee or umpire for failure to exercise reasonable care or recklessness. Perhaps the most famous recent case is the case of Orlando Brown, whose football career was ended when he was hit in the eye by a penalty flag weighted with BB pellets. See, e.g., Brown v. National Football League, 2002 Westlaw 417175 (S.D.N.Y. 2002). See generally, Shlomi Feiner, The Personal Liability of Sports Officials: Don't Take The Gun Into Your Own Hands, Take Them To Court!, 4 Sports Law. J. 213 (1997).

Returning to participant player injuries, there are several cases in which player claims are either successful or at least move forward. See, e.g., Wattenbarger v. Cincinnati Reds, Inc., 28 Cal. App. 4th 746, 33 Cal. Rptr. 2d 732 (Cal. App. 1994) (defendant major league baseball team owed a duty of care to protect a participant in a tryout from aggravating an injury given defendant's superior knowledge of the game and risks of injury); Kevan v. Manesiotis, 728 A. 2d 1006 (Pa. Comm. Ct. 1999) (player was injured by a hard hit ground ball in a gymnasium practice with allegedly poor lighting); Kloes v. Eau Claire Cavalier Baseball Association, Inc., 170 Wis. 2d 77, 487 N.W. 2d 77 (1992).

Interestingly, the issue sometimes arises as to whether or not the participant is engaged in an athletic activity. See, e.g., Bush v. Parents Without Partners, 17 Cal. App. 4th 322, 21 Cal. Rptr. 2d 178 (1993) (primary assumption of risk doctrine did not apply to recreational dancing and owners or occupiers of dance facility who increased the risk of falling while dancing by adding a slippery substance to the floor). See generally, Nick Hornby, About a Boy (1999).

Commentators have also discussed the issue of participant recovery in sports cases. See, e.g., Raymond L. Yasser, Torts and Sports (1985). See also, Alexander J. Drago, Assumption of Risk: An Age-Old Defense Still Viable in Sports and Recreation Cases, 12 Cardozo Intel. Prop. Media & Ent. L.J. 583 (2002); Mark M. Rembish, Liability for Personal Injuries Sustained in Sporting Events After Jaworski v. Kiernan, 18 QLR 307 (1998); Daniel E. Wanat, Torts and Sporting Events: Spectator and Participant Injuries-Using Defendant's Duty to Limit Liability as an Alternative to the Defense of Primary Implied Assumption of the Risk, 31 U. Mem. L. Rev. 237 (2001); Barry McWhirter, How the Abolishment of the Assumption of Risk Doctrine in Tennessee Affected Common Law Doctrines Associated with Primary Implied Assumption of the Risk, 31 U. Mem. L. Rev. 461 (2001).

48. Ironically, Elliott Maddox's arrival moved Bobby Murcer from center to right field.

49. Richard Ben Cramer, Joe DiMaggio: The Hero's Life (2000).

50. Id. at 310–11.

51. http://www.baseballsavvy.com/archive/w_mcdoug.html.

52. http://www.slam.ca/BaseballPlayoffs99/ws_hr.html.

53. http://www.canoe.ca/BaseballPlayoffs99/ws_rbi.html Mantle, by the way, is at the top of both lists with eighteen homeruns and forty RBIs.

54. This Morning With Shirley Povich, Washington Post, October 9, 1956, page A1 at http://www.washingtonpost.com/wp-srv-sports/longterm/general/povich/launch/larsen.htm.

55. http://www.cbssportsline.com/u/baseball/mlbcom/history/today/0507.htm.

56. http://www.usatoday.com/sports/baseball/mlbfs50.htm.

57. http://www.hickoksports.com/history/mlbaso.shtml.

58. http://www.pubdin.net/baseballlibrary/ballplayers/S/Score_Herb.stm.

59. http://www.sportsillustrated.cnn.com/baseball/mlb/news/2001/09/27/20_teammates/.

60. http://www.baseballreference.com/teams/CLE/leaders_pitch.shtml.

61. http://www.pubden.net/baseballlibrary/ballplayers/S/Score_Herb.stm.

62. Bob Feller with Bill Gilbert, Now Pitching Bob Feller, 209 (1990). Hear also, Terry Cashman, The Ballad of Herb Score.

63. Lawrence Ritter and Donald Honig, The 100 Greatest Baseball Players of All Time, 95 (1981).

64. Dom Forker, The Men of Autumn, 162 (1989).

65. Id. at 162–63.

66. See, e.g., Kevan v. Manesiotis, 728 A. 2d 1006 (Com. Ct. Pa. 1999); Kloes v. Eau Claire Cavalier Baseball Association, Inc., 170 Wis. 2d 77, 487 N.W. 2d 77 (1992).

67. http://www.acmi.canoe.ca/Slam000909/mlb_i.html.

68. http://www.chron.com/content/chronicle/sports/bb/98/07/17/liner.2-0.html.

69. http://www.newsnet5.com/news/stories/news-981009-053216.html.

70. Mike Sowell, The Pitch That Killed (1989).

71. Bill James, The New Bill James Historical Baseball Abstract, 98 and 490 (2001).

72. Sowell, supra note 70, at 5–9.

73. Id. at 77.

74. Sowell, supra note 70, at 230–35.

75. Id.

76. 601 F. 2d 516 (10th Cir. 1979).

77. Raymond L. Yasser, Torts and Sports 26 (1985).

78. Bill James, The New Bill James Historical Baseball Abstract, 121–22 (2001).

79. Lawrence Ritter, The Glory of Their Times, 220 (1966).

80. Sowell, supra note 70, at 286.

81. Id. at 286–87.

82. Id. at 307.

83. Bill James, The Politics of Glory, 336 (1994).

84. Sowell, supra note 70, at 301–02. For law review commentary on management of intentional torts in the sports context, see Heidi C. Doerhoff, Note, Penalty Box or Jury Box? Deciding Where Professional Sports Tough Guys Should Go: McKichan v. St. Louis Hockey Club, 64 Mo. L. Rev. 739 (1999); Kevin A. Fritz, Note: Going to the Bullpen: Using Uncle Sam to Strike Out Professional Sports Violence, 20 Cardozo Arts and Ent. L.J. 189 (2002); Wyatt N. Hicks, Presenting and Punishing Player-to-Player Violence in Professional Sports: The Court System Versus League Self-Regulation, 11 J. Legal Aspects Sport 209 (2001); Steven I. Rubin, The Vicarious Liability of Professional Sports Team For On-the-Field Assaults Committed By Their Players, 1 Va. J. Sports & L. 266 (1999). See also, Michael D. Mirne, The Brawl at Wrigley: An Analysis of Tort Liability, 9 Sports L. J. 95 (2002).

85. 62 Cal. App. 4th 47, 72 Cal. Rptr. 2d 377 (1998).

86. In one reported case, Kiley v. Patterson, 763 A. 2d 583 (R.I. 2000), the court remanded for a trial in a take-out slide scenario. The court held that there were material issues of fact whether the runner was merely negligent or whether he had acted deliberately or in reckless disregard of injuring the second-baseperson. Cf. Leonard v. Behrens, 601 N.W. 2d 76 (Iowa 1999) (participant in paintball game failed to establish that fellow participants acted recklessly).

87. H-1583 Time Mag. 34, 1983 WL2001717.

88. See, id. See also, 1/17/01 Star Trib. (Minneapolis/St. Paul) 03S, 2001 WL9609727. The seag-

ulls at Toronto's Exhibition Stadium were actually a huge problem and in 1984 Toronto hired a falconer (a falconer!) to help control unwanted seagull visits. 11/23/84 Rec. N. N.J. C02, 1984 W.L.
2456150.

89. Dave Winfield Commencement Speech at Thomas Jefferson School of Law, reproduced at
http://www.tjsl.edu/index.cfm?sID_int= 60&rID_int=59&xID=42.

90. 3/27/01 Nat'l Post B15, 2001 WL 16664770. See also 4/1/01 Dallas Morning News 19B, 2001
WL 16944213.

91. 6/25/01 Boston Globe D.1, 2001 WL 3939544.

Chapter 6 Endnotes

* Professor of Legal Writing, Villanova University School of Law.

1. Jim Bouton, Jim Bouton Official Website <http://jimbouton.com/bio.html> (last accessed
Jan. 10, 2003).

2. Jim Bouton, Ball Four 261 (20th Anniversary Edition, Macmillan 1990).

3. Brad Herzog, The Sports 100: The One Hundred Most Important People in American Sports
History (Paperback, Hungry Minds Inc. 1996).

4. Hereinafter, "MLB" will refer to the corporate power-structure of major league baseball, consisting of the various team owners as well as the commissioner's office.

5. Bouton, Ball Four at 409.

6. Id. at 408.

7. Id. at 219.

8. Id. at 34.

9. Id. at x.

10. Id. at 4.

11. Id. at x.

12. See e.g., IBP, Inc. v. Klump, 2001 WL 1456173 (Tex.App-Amarillo 2001); Taco Cabana Int'l
v. Two Pesos, Inc., 932 F.2d 1113 (5th Cir. 1991).

13. Id. See also Robert Unikel, Bridging the "Trade Secret" Gap: Protecting "Confidential Information" Not Rising to the Level of Trade Secrets, 29 Loy. U. Chi. L.J. 841 (1998) (analyzing the purpose of trade secret law as a body of law intended to protect certain types of corporate information
from improper competitive tactics).

14. Federal Base Ball Club of Baltimore v. National League of Professional Base Ball Clubs, 259
U.S. 200 (1922).

15. The Commissioner of baseball at the time of the Supreme Court's 1922 antitrust ruling.

16. CBS v. Davis, 510 U.S. 1315, 1317 (1994).

17. Proctor & Gamble Co. v. Bankers Trust Co., 78 F.3d 219, 225 (6th Cir. 1996).

18. Ford v. Lane, 67 F.Supp. 2d 745, 751 (1999) (citing Near v. Minnesota, 283 U.S. 697 (1931).

19. New York Times Co. v. United States, 403 U.S. 713 (1971).

20. Id.

21. Roboserve, Ltd. v. Tom's Foods, Inc., 940 F.2d 1441, 1456 (11th Cir. 1991).

22. See Unikel, supra note 13, at 860 (discussing the parameters of a breach of loyalty or trust tort).

23. See id. at 865–66. The author cites, in footnote 110, decisions from the 4th and 5th Circuits,
as well as several state court decisions which so held.

24. See Unikel, supra note 13, at 865–66.

25. See Sikes v. McGraw-Edison Co., 665 F.2d 731 (5th Cir. 1982) The court held that a proper measure of damages in a breach of confidentiality action (in that instance, wrongful appropriation of a trade secret) may include an award consisting of both actual damages as well as the amount by which the defendant was unjustly enriched as a result of the breach. As these are two distinct theories of damages, it follows that each would require its own burden of proof. Therefore, in the hypothetical case of MLB v. Bouton, MLB would need to demonstrate not only its own damages suffered as a result of the publication of "Ball Four", but the measure of improperly gained benefits by both Bouton and the Players Association as well in order to recover on an "unjust enrichment" theory. As such, it would necessarily have to prove ownership of the information contained within the book.

26. Bouton, Ball Four at 408.

27. Id. at 345.

28. Id. at 4. Bouton notes that the salary of Ted Williams, as reported by Arthur Daley of The New York Times, was widely reported to be $125,000 at some point in the late 1950s or early 1960s.

29. Id. at 233. Bouton notes that the minimum salary was set at $7000 in 1958 and hadn't risen in the subsequent 11 years.

30. Id.

31. Id. at 261. Recalling a conversation with teammate Fred Talbot on his negotiating strategy and whether he ever considered using statistics as a bargaining tool. "Aw hell," remarked Talbot, "I don't keep statistics. Whatever they send me I just sign and send back. Of course, I call them a few names first."

32. Id. at 49–50. ("Mike Marshall was in the Tigers organization for a while and he says that, like the Yankees, they frown on players telling reporters the truth. A reporter asked Mike what he was being paid and he said he didn't feel he could say, but it was less than the minimum. The reporter printed it and asked how the hell the Tigers could be paying their No. 1 reliever less than the minimum. So Mike got called in by Jim Campbell, the general manager. Campbell wasn't angry that Mike was making less than the minimum, but that he told.")

33. Id. at 56.

34. Id. at 407. Discussing baseball's traditional "code of silence" and how, by breaking that code, he has become, in the eyes of Major League Baseball, a deviant.

35. Id. at x.

Chapter 7 Endnotes

* Jan Stiglitz is a Professor of Law at California Western School of Law. Professor Stiglitz taught Sports Law for 10 years and has published a number of articles and chapters on Sports Law topics. A lifetime Dodgers fan, Professor Stiglitz has a B.A. from the State University of New York at Buffalo, a J.D. from Albany Law School and an LL.M. from Harvard Law School.

1. Unless otherwise noted, all background information about Melissa Ludtke is taken from a series of interviews by the Washington Press Club Foundation done as part of an oral history project entitled Women in Journalism. Transcripts of these interviews can be found at http://npc.press.org/wpforal/lud.htm.

2. See Article I, § 2 of the Major League Agreement.

3. Unless otherwise noted, all information about the case that was filed and the decision is from Ludtke v. Kuhn, 461 F.Supp. 86 (S.D.N.Y. 1978).

4. Background on Judge Motley came from a review of her autobiography. Randall Kennedy, Equal Justice Under Law: An Autobiography, The American Lawyer, July–August, 1998, at 47.

5. 365 U.S. 715, 81 S. Ct. 856, 6 L. Ed. 2d 45 (1961).

6. Judge Motley quoted from the standard enunciated in Craig v. Boren, 429 U.S. 190, 197, 97 S.

Ct. 451, 457, 50 L. Ed. 2d 397 (1976).

7. 410 U.S. 113, 93 S. Ct. 705, 35 L. Ed. 2d 147 (1973).

8. Abosh v. New York Yankees, Inc. (No. CPS-25284, Appeal No. 1194 (N.Y. State Human Rights Appeal Board, July 19, 1972), reported in Barbara A. Babcock, Ann E. Freedman, Eleanor Holmes Norton, Susan C. Ross, Sex Discrimination and the Law, Causes and Remedies 1069–70 (Little, Brown and Company 1975). Claims of discriminatory pricing for women have resulted in a number of suits with mixed results. In 1981, the Supreme Court of Washington found that having a "Ladies' Night" discount for Seattle Sonics basketball game did not violate state law. (See McLean v. First Northwest Industries of America, Inc., 96 Wash. 2d 338, 635 P.2d 683 (1981). In 1985, the California Supreme Court held that discount pricing for women on Ladies' Days violated California State Law. See Koire v. Metro Car Wash, 40 Cal. 3d 24, 707 P.2d 195, 219 Cal.Rptr. 133 (1985).

9. The three decisions were Rendell-Baker v. Kohn, 457 U.S. 830, 102 S.Ct. 2764, 73 L.Ed.2d 418 (1982); Lugar v. Edmonson Oil Company, Inc., 457 U.S. 922, 102 S.Ct. 2744, 73 L.Ed.2d 482 (1982); and Blum v. Yaretsky, 457 U.S. 991, 102 S.Ct. 2777, 73 L.Ed.2d 534 (1982).

10. The locker room incidents related in this and the following sections came from a number of newspaper and journal articles, including: Donal P. Myers, The Locker Room, Newsday, June 8, 1999 (1999 WL 8175772); Jane Havsy, Women Are Sportswriters Too: The Fractured Relationship Between Reporters and Athletes at http://www.stwing.upenn.edu/~jahavsy1/reporters.html (unpublished manuscript on file with the University of Pennsylvania); Jack Armstrong, Locker Rooms Bring Out Worst in Men, Jack Armstrong. Denver Post, November 5, 2000 (2000 WL 25833427).

11. Amy Sohn, In the Yankees Clubhouse, I Want to Redecorate, Not Ogle, New York Post, Thursday, August 24, 1999 (1999 WL 22882876).

12. The Locker Room, Newsday, June 8, 1999 (1999 WL 8175772).

13. Most of the information for this section comes from two law review articles: Melissa M. Beck, Fairness on the Field: Amending Title VII to Foster Greater Female Participation in Professional Sports, 12 Cardozo Arts & Ent. L.J. 241 (1994) and Sharlene A. McEvoy, The Umpire Strikes Out: Postema v. National League: Major League Gender Discrimination, 11 U. Miami Ent. & Sports L. Rev. 1 (1993).

14. Postema v. National League of Professional Baseball Clubs, 799 F.Supp. 1475, 1478–1479 (S.D.N.Y. 1992), rev'd, 998 F.2d 60 (2d Cir. 1993).

Chapter 8 Endnotes

* Professor, St. John's University School of Law. A lifelong Yankees fan and Bronx resident, Professor Ward holds an A.B. from Barnard College and a J.D. from Columbia University. She would like to thank her research assistants, Ryan C. Goldberg, Joseph J. Bozzuti, and Eugenie Cesar-Fabian, and St. John's Law Librarians Barbara G. Traub and Arundhati Satkalmi, for their invaluable assistance; her father, Jacob B. Ward, for his editorial comments and for obtaining her first Yankees' autographs; St. John's University School of Law for providing a summer research grant; and St. John's Law School Secretarial Services for "playing ball" with me. She would also like to thank Judge David D. Dowd, Jr. (N.D., Ohio), the federal district judge who presided over the Munson case, Alton L. Stephens (attorney for Cessna), and Eugene P. Okey and Daniel C. Cathcart (attorneys for the Munson estate), who were all generous with their time and in making litigation documents available.

1. Alexander Chase, Perspectives (1966).

2. Dick Schaap, Steinbrenner! 168 (1982). For information on Munson's early life, his career, and his death, I relied on numerous contemporary articles from the New York Times and the New York Daily News.

3. Phil Pepe, Thurman is Dead! Numbed Yankees Weep, Sporting News, Aug. 18, 1979, at 21.

4. Phil Pepe, His Abilities Did the Talking, N.Y. Daily News, Aug. 5, 1979, at 9.

5. Iver Peterson, Munson's Town: City of Family, Factory and Sport, N.Y. Times, Aug. 6, 1979, at A12.

6. Ken McMillan, Tales from the Yankee Dugout 120 (2001).

7. Jerry Kirshenbaum, Scorecard, Sports Illustrated, Aug. 13, 1979, Vol. 15, at 27.

8. Murray Chass, Thurman Munson Was Proud Captain of the Yankees, N.Y. Times, Aug. 3, 1979, at 14.

9. Dick Young, Young Ideas, Sporting News, Aug. 18, 1979, at 1.

10. Plaintiff's Trial Brief 3–4, Munson v. Cessna Aircraft Co., C80-280A.

11. Thurman Lee Munson & Martin Eliot Appel, Thurman Munson, an autobiography with Martin Appel 195 (1978).

12. Christopher Devine, Thurman Munson: A Baseball Biography 173–74 (2001).

13. Munson Crash Survivors Differ, N.Y. Times, Aug. 8, 1979, at C15.

14. Devine, supra note 12.

15. Mike Lupica, Munson: The man New York never knew, N.Y. Daily News, Aug. 3, 1979, at 54 (quoting from interview with NBC reporter).

16. Dave Anderson, Face on the Scoreboard, N.Y. Times, Aug. 4, 1979, at Sports 13.

17. The National Transportation Safety Board (NTSB) is the federal agency charged by Congress with the responsibility for investigating serious and fatal aviation accidents in the United States.

18. Brian Kates, Thurm loved that plane, N.Y. Daily News, Aug. 30, 1979, at 3.

19. Jim Naughton, Yankees' Thurman Munson Killed Piloting His Own Small Jet in Ohio, N.Y. Times, Aug. 3, 1979, at A1.

20. Coroner: Paralysis Hit Munson, N.Y. Times, Sept. 8, 1979, at 15.

21. Id. Details of the crash come from various contemporaneous newspaper accounts, the NTSB report on the crash, and Stipulation of Facts filed May 29, 1984 in the lawsuit brought by Munson's wife, Diana Lynn Munson v. Cessna Aircraft Co., et. al., C 80-280A (Dowd, J.).

22. Munson Crash Survivors Differ, supra note 13.

23. Engine Trouble Excluded As Cause of Munson Crash, N.Y. Times, Aug. 22, 1979, at Sec. 2, p. 7.

24. Richard Haitch, Mistakes by Munson Blamed in Jet Crash, N.Y. Times, Sept. 17, 1979, at 1.

25. Id.

26. Id.

27. NTSB Aircraft Accident Report on NTSB Accident No. CHI-79-FA-064, at pp. 21–22.

28. Id. at p. 19.

29. Haitch, supra note 24.

30. Stipulation of Facts, Pars. 2–5, filed May 29, 1984, Diana Lynn Munson v. Cessna Aircraft Co., et. al., Case No. C80-280A (Dowd, J.). The multi-engine rating permitted Munson to act as pilot-in-command of any multi-engine propeller-powered airplane with a maximum weight of less than 12,500 pounds.

31. Id. Pars. 6, 13. An instrument rating authorizes an otherwise properly certificated pilot to operate an airplane in weather conditions that do not permit outside visual reference.

32. Haitch, supra note 24.

33. Munson Crash Survivors Differ, supra note 13.

34. Thurm Had Beef About Plane Warning Systems, N.Y. Daily News, Aug. 8, 1979, at 50.

35. Jim Naughton, Yankees' Thurman Munson Killed Piloting His Own Small Jet in Ohio, N.Y. Times, Aug. 3, 1979, at A1.

36. Murray Chass, Mercer Drives in 5 as Yanks Win, 5-4, N.Y. Times, Aug. 7, 1979, at C13.

37. Telephone interview with Eugene P. Okey (May 30, 2002).

38. John S. Riley, A 'Risk' Pays Off in Canton; From Minor Leagues to Major Wins, National Law Journal, Dec. 9, 1985 at 1.

39. See notes 29, 32–34, supra, and accompanying text.

40. Plaintiff relied on the Restatement of Torts 2d, §§402A and B and Ohio case law to support its argument based on strict liability. Plaintiff's Trial Brief 11–12, Munson v. Cessna Aircraft Co., C80-280A. The Restatement 2d §402B, Misrepresentation by Seller of Chattels to Consumer, provides:

> One engaged in the business of selling chattels who, by advertising, labels, or otherwise, makes to the public a misrepresentation of a material fact concerning the character or quality of a chattel sold by him is subject to liability for physical harm to a consumer of the chattel caused by justifiable reliance upon the misrepresentation, even though:
>
> (a)   it is not made fraudulently or negligently, and
>
> (b)   the consumer had not bought the chattel from or entered into any contractual relation with the seller.

41. Defendant Cessna Aircraft Company's Trial Brief 42.

42. Id. at 43.

43. Id. at 50.

44. Id. at 50–51.

45. Id. at 41–43.

46. Stipulation of Facts, Par. 13.

47. NTSB Aircraft Accident Report at p. 19; Defendant Cessna Aircraft Company's Trial Brief, Munson v. Cessna Aircraft Co., C80-280A.

48. Plaintiff's Trial Brief 20–22.

49. John S. Riley, supra note 38.

50. Munson Case Settled, N.Y. Times, Aug. 26, 1984, at §5, p. 7.

51. New York Yankees Partnership d/b/a New York Yankees v. Cessna Aircraft Co., et al., Civil Action C80-1370A, was filed in federal district court in the Northern District of Ohio. The Honorable Leroy J. Contie was the judge assigned to the case.

52. Order of Judge Contie, filed July 2, 1981, granting defendants' motions to dismiss the complaint, pp. 2–3.

53. The Crash That's Still Being Heard, McClean's, Aug. 18, 1980, vol. 93, at 32.

54. Id.

55. Defendant Cessna filed a motion to dismiss the complaint and defendant FlightSafety made a motion for summary judgment. As FlightSafety's summary judgment motion raised essentially the same grounds as Cessna's motion to dismiss and was not supported by matters outside the pleadings, the district court treated FlightSafety's motion as one to dismiss the complaint and decided the motions together. July 2, 1981 Order of Judge Leroy J. Contie, Jr. dismissing complaint.

56. Black's Law Dictionary 229 (7th ed. 1999) defines chattel as "movable or transferable property; esp., personal property."

57. Yankees Suit Based on Munson as "Merchandise," Aviation Convention News, Nov. 1, 1980, at 1.

58. Flood v. Kuhn, 407 U.S. 258 (1972). In rejecting the Yankees' claim, the federal district court noted widespread criticism of early common law actions permitting a master to sue for loss of services of his servant caused by a third party. Those early common law actions arose at a time "when the servant was considered the personal property of the master so that damage or injury to the servant was considered damage or injury to the property of the master." Order of Judge Contie filed July 2, 1981 granting defendants' motions to dismiss the complaint, at p. 8.

59. Palsgraf v. Long Island R.R. Co., 248 N.Y. 339, 344 (N.Y 1928).

60. Order of Judge Contie, filed July 2, 1981, granting defendants' motions to dismiss the complaint, p. 12.

61. Id. at p. 14.

62. Gary A. Uberstine, ed., Law of Professional and Amateur Sports 4–11 (West Group 2001).

63. Id. at Appendix 5A. Standard contracts for other professional sports leagues often have similar provisions. Sometimes the agreement prohibits participation in certain other sports. In other cases, the agreement is somewhat more restrictive. For example, Paragraph 17 of the NBA standard contract is a covenant by the player not to engage in "ultrahazardous activity" which might impair his ability to play skilled basketball. If a player is injured while participating in such an activity, the contract may be terminated. Id. at 7-15, 7-29.

64. Id. § 4(a) at Appendix 5A.

65. Darren Rovell, Sports Insurance 101: A Primer, March 9, 2002 at http://espn.go.com/mlb/s/2001/0307/1136588.html.

66. Id. This article notes that the NBA and the NHL have league programs that require their teams to insure a certain number of players on their roster. The NBA has had a mandatory rule since the early 1990s that requires a team's top salaried players to be insured. MLB does not have a league insurance policy.

67. Dan Aznoff, Insurance Strikes Out: Major League Players Offer Big Returns…and even bigger risks for insurance carriers, Insurance Journal, Mar. 25, 2002, at 28.

68. From 1967–2000, 18 active MLB players died. Many others have suffered injuries preventing them from playing. Pete Williams, Selig Holds the Ropes to Safety Net, Street & Smith's Sports Business Journal, Feb. 28, March 5, 2000, at 20.

69. Famous Victims of the Deadly Skies, N.Y. Post, July 18, 1999 at 24; Daniel Rapoport, The Heavy Toll of Private Plane Crashes, The Washington Post, Sept. 23, 1979, at C1.

70. Katherine Q. Seelye, Frequent Flights and Small Planes Have Made Politicians Vulnerable," Oct. 26, 2002, at A19. This article points out that Wellstone was the fourth sitting United States Senator to die in a plane crash and lists several other prominent political figures who died in airplane crashes.

71. NTSB, U.S. General Aviation, Calendar Year 1997: Annual Review of Aircraft Accident Data 1–3, 11, 47 (Sept. 2000).

72. In 1999, fragments of Munson's crashed plane were put up for auction on eBay. Bids ranging from one cent to $12.54 were received for small pieces of metal and 2-inch pieces of nylon harness. The auction was ended when Mrs. Munson complained. The owner of the fragments apologized. He had gathered debris as a 12-year old when he visited the crash site with his father. Internet Auction of Munson's Plane Wreck Debris Halted, Dayton Daily News, Nov. 11, 1999, at 5D.

73. Thurman's son, Michael, was signed by the Yankees to a minor league contract in July, 1995. He began in their Rookie League Club, but lasted only one game with one of the Yankees' Class A affiliates. Michael Thurman then played briefly with the Indians' minor league team in Canton. That team played at Thurman Munson Memorial Stadium. Devine, supra note 11, at 235.

74. See Ruth La Ferla, Front Row, N.Y. Times, Oct. 22, 2002, at B11.

75. Defendant Cessna Aircraft Company's Trial Brief 15–18.

Chapter 9 Endnotes

* Harry and Helen Hutchens Research Professor and Professor of Law, South Texas College of Law; B.A. Williams College; J.D. SMU Law School; LL.M. Yale Law School (pmcgreal@stcl.edu). I owe a large debt to Monica Ortale, who provided extraordinary research support as well as comments on a prior draft. I also owe thanks to friends, family, and colleagues who commented on prior drafts, including Bruce Burton, Chris Giglio, Marianne McGreal, Bill Wilks, Kevin Yamamoto,

and Jo Anne Ziaja. Last, my work on this chapter was supported by a summer research stipend from the South Texas College of Law.

My chapter is for Joseph Vierno, who gave me my love of baseball, and Patrick McGreal, for whom I hope to do the same.

1. Murray Chass, Brett Homer Nullified, So Yankees Win, N.Y. Times, July 25, 1983, at A1. In a trial, lawyers and judges often refer to "the record," which consists of the written transcript of witness testimony together with the documents and other material introduced at trial. After the trial is over, when someone wants to know what happened at the trial, they can look at the record. As a glance at the following notes reveals, I primarily rely on the New York Times as my "record" of the pine tar incident.

2. Jane Gross, Angry Yankees Defend the Rules and Umpires, N.Y. Times, July 29, 1983, at A13. The article offers some choice Yankee quotes about the pine tar rules:

Lou Piniella: "A rule is a rule is a rule."

George Steinbrenner: "If he [American League President Lee MacPhail] thinks the rule is no good, then get it out. But if it's in there, enforce it."

Sammy Ellis: "They might as well burn the rule book."

Yogi Berra: "Now a guy can go up and hit any way he wants."

Billy Martin: Unless Brett is called out, "nothing in the rule book will mean anything."

3. Royals' manager Dick Howser made this point nicely: "I don't want any favors from the umpires, I don't want any edge. Let's just put Gossage against Brett and see what happens. Well, you saw what happened—four hundred and fifty feet away." Geoffrey Stokes, Pinstripe Pandemonium 88 (1984).

4. Russell Baker noted that the pine tar incident involved the "deep philosophical quarrel about the difference between law and justice." Russell Baker, Bumble Humbles Yanks, N.Y. Times, August 3, 1983, at A23. And another commentator remarked, "The incident led to a tremendous popular debate about the spirit and letter of the law. The arguments constituted perhaps the most widespread popular legal debate in American history." Joseph Lukinsky, Law in Education: A Reminiscence with Some Footnotes to Robert Cover's Nomos and Narrative, 96 Yale L.J. 1836, 1855–56 (1987).

5. Two law review articles look at aspects of the pine tar incident. One article examines similarities and differences between interpreting baseball rules and interpreting legal texts. Jared Tobin Finkelstein, In re Brett: The Sticky Problem of Statutory Construction, 52 Fordham L. Rev. 430 (1983). A second article discusses procedural aspects of the incident. Christopher H. Clancy & Jonathan A. Weiss, A Pine Tar Gloss on Quasi-Legal Images, 5 Cardozo L. Rev. 411 (1984). Both articles are reprinted in Baseball and the American Legal Mind (Spencer Weber Waller, Neil B. Cohen, & Paul Finkelman eds., 1995), which also reprints other essays on various topics connecting law and baseball.

6. From 1976 through 1978, the Yankees defeated the Royals in the American League Championship Series. In 1980, the Royals got their revenge, beating the Yankees.

7. In the end, neither team won their respective division, ultimately making the game's outcome of little significance. The Yankees finished the 1983 season in third place, seven games behind the Baltimore Orioles. While the Royals finished in second place, they were a distant twenty games behind the division-winning Chicago White Sox.

8. See Yogi Berra with Dave Kaplan, When You Come to a Fork in the Road, Take It! Inspiration and Wisdom from One of Baseball's Greatest Heroes 68 (2001).

9. Martin almost missed the chance to make the pine tar argument. Though warned to check Brett's bat if he got a significant hit, Yankee catcher Rick Cerone mistakenly believed he was to check for cork. When the bat did not feel corked, he tossed it aside, and the Royals batboy fetched it. Seeing the bat leaving the playing field, Graig Nettles and Don Zimmer began yelling for Cerone to check for pine tar. Cerone then grabbed back the bat before the batboy reached the dugout. Don Zimmer explained why it was a "big thing" to keep Brett's bat from reaching the dugout: "If they get that bat back in the dugout, it's all over. They get it in the rack and there's no way you can tell what bat it was. Even if you can talk the umpires into looking at it, they could hand the umps a goddamn cane and there'd be no way to prove he hadn't used it." Stokes, supra note 3, at 89.

10. Chass, supra note 1. In using quotations that appear in newspaper articles, I make two omissions for reasons of style. First, I use only one set of quotes, even though the speaker's words are ac-

tually a quotation within a quotation. In all cases, however, I cite to the printed source of the quotation. Second, I often omit, without ellipses, narrative remarks—such as "Martin said"—that appear in the newspaper article.

11. Id.

12. Stokes, supra note 3, at 88; see also Chass, supra note 1 (Umpire Brinkman remarked, "In that situation, you know something is going to happen. It was quite traumatic. He was upset.").

13. Chass, supra note 1 (Royal manager Dick Howser described the scene: "I didn't know what was going on. I saw guys in sport coats and ties trying to intercept the bat. It was like a Brink's robbery. Who's got the gold? Our players had it, the umpires had it. I don't know who has it—the C.I.A., a think tank at the Pentagon.").

14. Id. (Brinkman explained: "The security people went after it, but I got in there and got it. Steve Renko, another Kansas City pitcher, had it. He was the last in line. He didn't have anyone to hand it to.").

15. Brinkman, the umpiring crew chief for the game, acknowledged as much immediately after the pine tar game. Id.

16. Stokes, supra note 3, at 88.

17. Chass, supra note 1.

18. Glen Waggoner, Kathleen Moloney, & Hugh Howard, Spitters, Beanballs, and the Incredible Shrinking Strike Zone 24 (2000).

19. Ira Berkow, The Gun Doesn't Smoke, N.Y. Times, July 26, 1983, at B5.

20. Chass, supra note 1.

21. The rules had recently changed to prevent a batter from delaying a game by leaving the batter's box to obtain more pine tar.

22. Graig Nettles, who also used pine tar to grip the bat, offered another innocent explanation for why pine tar might appear high on a bat: "Sometimes you touch the pine tar, and then you put your hand high on the bat, and if you do that enough times, a buildup of pine tar becomes visible." Gregg Nettles & Peter Gollenbock, Balls 151 (1984).

23. Yankees, Bats and Nicaragua, N.Y. Times, July 26, 1983, at A20 (quoting New York Senator Alfonse D'Amato).

24. Rules of Major League Baseball, Rule 6.06(a) (1983). From this point on, all references are to the 1983 rules in effect during the pine tar game, unless otherwise noted.

25. Text of League President's Ruling In Brett Bat Case, N.Y. Times, July 29, 1983, at A16. All references to MacPhail's ruling are to this version reprinted in the New York Times.

26. After MacPhail's ruling, Martin and Steinbrenner suggested that pine tar might have aided the flight of the ball. Gross, supra note 2.

Although not obviously a question for rocket scientists, some at NASA have chimed in on the effects of pine tar. When posed the question whether pine tar would aid the flight of a batted ball, the answer came back: "A ball hit with backspin can provide its own lift due to the Magnus Effect...and can travel farther than a ball without spin. Some think that pine tar can enhance the contact friction during a hit and create more backspin." July, 1999, Aeroquiz Questions and Answers, http://www-psao.grc.nasa.gov/psao.quiz/july.99.html. The authors also noted, however, that pine tar could have the opposite effect, possibly "hid[ing] 'grooving' marks on the bat" that might impart spin on a batted ball. Id. In the end, they concluded that "[b]atters who illegally coat...their bats are not likely helping themselves." Id.

27. Yankees, Bats and Nicaragua, supra note 23.

28. Rule 3.02(e)(2) ("alternate balls shall be put in play when...A ball has become discolored or unfit for further use"). And, Rule 3.02 forbids applying any foreign substance to a baseball: "No player shall intentionally discolor or damage the ball by rubbing it with soil, rosin, paraffin, licorice, sand paper, emery paper or other foreign substance." Rule 3.02 (2002). Rule 8.02(a) and (b) specifically addresses such actions by the pitcher. In a 1988 playoff game against the New York Mets, Los Angeles Dodgers' relief pitcher Jay Howell was ejected for applying pine tar in his glove to pitched balls. Murray Chass, Sticky Situation for Dodger Reliever, N.Y. Times, Oct. 9, 1988, §8, at 1.

29. See Murray Chass, Kansas City Wins Protest on Canceled Homer, N.Y. Times, July 29, 1983, at A1 (Lee MacPhail noted that the pine tar rules were formulated because "batters were putting pine tar all the way up their bats, and every time the ball was hit it became soiled and had to be removed from the game."); Richard D. Lyons, Pine Tar Popular Because It Grips, N.Y. Times, July 29, 1983, at A16 ("the only reason that the rules limit [pine tar] to the area extending 18 inches from the handle of the bat is that the rulemakers thought that a bat more fully covered with it would require an excessive number of new baseballs and thus cause innumerable delays in the game."); Sydney H. Schanberg, Something You Can Count On, N.Y. Times, July 30, 1983, § 1, at 21.

30. Rule 4.19.

31. Id.

32. George Vecsey, The Spirit of the Rules, N.Y. Times, Aug. 1, 1983, at C5. Lou Piniella made a more concrete threat: "[i]f the game does matter—if the season ends up tied, or one of us is up by less than a game—baseball's gonna be in a bad predicament. It's gonna be more than a public relations problem, too. There's gonna be lawsuits." Stokes, supra note 3, at 99.

33. Stokes, supra note 3, at 90.

34. Id.

35. Id.

36. Michael Martinez, Anger Dies; Bat Lives On, N.Y. Times, July 24, 1985, at B7.

37. Brewers, on Sweep, Take First Place, N.Y. Times, Aug. 18, 1983, at B16.

38. Of course, in MacPhail's defense, if Martin had not made the pine tar challenge, there would have been no later pine tar ruling to blame. So, the pine tar debacle was of the Yankees' own making. Further, one author notes that not making the pine tar challenge may have had an equally devastating effect on Yankee morale. Winning streaks are fragile things, and if the Yankees had lost the pine tar game on a Brett home run, they might have also lost their momentum. Stokes, supra note 3, at 90. The bottom line is nobody knows what would have happened, and each person's best guess is colored by their personal loyalties.

39. Graig Nettles claims that he told Martin about Brett's excessive pine tar use. According to Nettles, he was aware of the rule because a similar call had been made on a Thurman Munson home run back in 1975. Nettles & Golenbock, supra note 22, at 151. Martin then instructed catcher Butch Wynegar to raise the issue when Brett got a significant hit.

Don Zimmer tells a different version of the story in his autobiography. According to Zimmer, "Before the game, I happened to notice that George Brett...had excessive pine tar on his bat." Don Zimmer & Bill Madden, Zim: A Baseball Life 168 (2001). When Zimmer told Martin, Martin replied, "That's good. But don't say anything about it. We'll protest it when the time is right." Id. In this version, the Yankees only noticed Brett's pine tar on the day of the game.

While Martin did not identify who alerted him to Brett's pine tar, he supports Nettles' version that the Yankees noticed the pine tar two weeks before. In an interview immediately after the pine tar game, Martin said, "We noticed the pine tar on his bat in Kansas City." Chass, supra note 1.

40. Nettles & Golenbock, supra note 22, at 151.

41. Id.

42. Id.

43. See Rule 6.04 (2000) ("A batter has legally completed his time at bat when he is put out or becomes a runner.").

44. In a letter to the editor, one fan commented: "You challenge the culprit before he does the damage, not afterward.", Letter to the Sports Editor, from Joseph W. Leonard, N.Y. Times, August 7, 1983, § 5, at 2.

45. For this reason, some statutes of limitations are longer than others. In cases where the evidence may deteriorate quickly, such as a car accident where witnesses' fading memories are important, the statute of limitations is likely to be shorter. Conversely, in cases where much of the evidence lies in documents or business records that are preserved for long periods of time, such as a lawsuit over a contract, the statute of limitations may be longer.

46. Rule 9.02(b) identifies to whom the appeal must be made, but does not specifically address timing of the appeal: "If there is reasonable doubt that any umpire's decision may be in conflict with the rules, the manager may appeal the decision and ask that a correct ruling be made. Such appeal shall be made only to the umpire who made the protested decision." Rule 9.02(b) (2000). The Yankees' pine tar challenge would be an appeal, which is defined as "the act of a fielder in claiming violation of the rules by the offensive team." Rule 2.00. This is different from Rule 6.07(c), which addresses an appeal when a batter has batted out of order: "(c) When an improper batter becomes a runner or is put out, and a pitch is made to the next batter of either team before an appeal is made, the improper batter thereby becomes the proper batter, and the results of his time at bat become legal." The same timing rule specifically applies to several other appeals. See, e.g., Rule 7.08(d) (appeal on grounds that a runner did not properly tag a base before advancing on a caught fly ball); 7.10(d) (appeal on grounds that runner failed to touch home plate).

47. Fed. R. Evid. 401.

48. Of course, Jane may blurt out her answer before her lawyer has a chance to object. In that case, the objection is not waived as long as Jane's lawyer objects as soon as she can. Only an unreasonable delay in making an objection waives the objection.

49. In the case where the witness blurts out the answer before the lawyer has a chance to object, the judge can only instruct the jury to disregard the testimony that was objectionable.

50. Reversal on Brett Has Martin Upset, N.Y. Times, July 30, 1983, at 31.

51. See Kaiser Aluminum & Chemical Corp. v. Bonjorno, 494 U.S. 827, (1990) ("The starting point for interpretation of a statute 'is the language of the statute itself.'"); see generally Antonin Scalia, A Matter of Interpretation (1997). Lawyers largely debate what other sources in addition to text may be used to interpret a statute. See William N. Eskridge, Jr., Philip P. Frickey, & Elizabeth Garrett, Legislation and Statutory Interpretation 211–374 (2000) (discussing various theories or methods of interpreting legal texts).

52. Rule 6.06(a).

53. Rule 2.00.

54. Rule 1.10(b).

55. Of course, determining whether a statute has a plain or clear meaning is not always easy, and may require some analysis. See Eskridge, et al., supra note 51, at 251–63.

56. Connecticut National Bank v. Germain, 503 U.S. 249, 253–54 (1992).

57. 471 U.S. 84 (1985).

58. Id. at 96 ("The phrase 'prior to' may be clumsy, but its meaning is clear.").

59. As one author describes, those around Martin were not as sure:

> Prior to each of the Texas games [following the pine tar game], Martin held what amounted to lawyers' discussions in his office. The participants weren't actually attorneys but the usual parade of scouts, old friends, and baseball writers, who pored over the rule books in a typical scholarly fashion. Everyone kept coming back to the same point—the rules were ambiguous....

Stokes, supra note 3, at 91.

60. The 1983 Rule Book lists cupped bats as subsection (3) of Rule 1.10. This is likely a typographical error, as the subsection appears directly after subsection (c), and there are no subsections (1) or (2) in Rule 1.10. Further, in the 1984 Rule Book, that subsection is designated by a letter. Thus, to avoid confusion, I refer to the cupped bat provision as Rule 1.10(d), and not Rule 1.10(3).

61. Germain, 503 U.S. at 253 ("canons of construction are no more than rules of thumb that help courts determine the meaning of legislation").

62. For an comprehensive list of various canons used by judges and lawyers, see William N. Eskridge, Jr., Dynamic Statutory Interpretation 323–28 (1994).

63. As I tell my students, lawyers never use an English term when a Latin phrase is available. My guess is that it allows lawyers to charge more for their work.

64. Eskridge, supra note 62, at 324.

65. Many lawyers, however, recognize that this is largely a fiction. Different statutes may be enacted at different points in time, when different people sat in the legislature. A statute enacted in 1950 was drafted and voted on by a different group of people than a statute enacted in 2002. So, the 1950 statute probably tells us little, if anything, about how the 2002 legislature used words or phrases. Nonetheless, many lawyers believe that it is a useful fiction to pretend that the same group drafted both statutes, because doing so brings coherence and uniformity to the law.

66. The case is West Virginia University Hospital v. Casey, 499 U.S. 83 (1991).

67. Id. at 88–92. Congress later amended the statute to make clear that a party could recover its expert fees. Civil Rights Act of 1991, P.L. 102-166, § 113 (codified at 42 U.S.C.A. § 1988(c) (West 1999)).

68. Rule 6.06(a). The American League Regulations made clear that pine tar was not considered a substance that violated Rule 6.06(d).

69. A related method is to examine a statute's legislative history. Legislative history consists of the testimony, speeches, reports, and other materials created while Congress researched, drafted, debated, and voted on a statute. See Eskridge, et al., supra note 51, at 295. While some judges oppose using such materials, see Scalia, supra note 51, at 29–37; the Supreme Court routinely consults legislative history when interpreting statutes. After all, if words only have meaning within a certain context, what better evidence of a statute's meaning than the documents and other materials that memorialize the context within which a statute was created?

The baseball rules do not have an authoritative set of legislative history materials. A special committee proposes changes to the game's rules. In a correspondence with Major League Baseball, however, I learned that written records are not kept of the committee's work. Fax from Edward Alvarado to Monica Ortale, July 3, 2002. While MacPhail looked into the history of the pine tar rules, he did so by speaking to people involved in drafting the rules. We, however, do not have access to the same information, and thus I accept his word about what those sources revealed about the purpose of the pine tar rules.

70. 143 U.S. 457 (1892).

71. Id. at 458.

72. Id. at 459.

73. This example is discussed at greater length in Gerald Graff, "Keep of the Grass," "Drop Dead," and Other Indeterminacies: A Response to Sanford Levinson, 60 Tex. L. Rev. 405, 407–08 (1982).

74. Holy Trinity, 143 U.S. at 463.

75. Id.

76. Id. at 465.

77. One person consulted by MacPhail contradicted him on this point. George Sisler, a member of the Rules Committee when the pine tar rules were written, explained his view of the rules:

> "I wouldn't say that worry about replacing the ball, about slowing up the game, was primary," he said. "It was a consideration, but the real difficulty wasn't so much the need to replace a spoiled ball so much as what happened to the ball while it was still in play. If the ball's got a big smudge on one side of it, it's going to be harder for fielders to read it—particularly if you get a chipped or spinning foul. Also," he added, "there was some concern that if pine tar went too far up the barrel, a player could bury nail heads under it, or that it might disguise the gluing on a corked bat."

Stokes, supra note 3, at 96. The author also notes that MacPhail "was not persuaded" that these additional concerns motivated the rule. Id. Given that Major League Baseball has no official legislative history materials for its rules, we have no way to decide whether Sisler or MacPhail was correct about the rule's purpose. MacPhail has the last word not because he was in a better position to know the rule's purpose, but rather because, as League President, the decision fell to him. Justice Robert Jackson made a similar observation about the United States Supreme Court: "We are not final because we are infallible, but we are infallible only because we are final." Brown v. Allen, 344 U.S. 433, 539 (1953).

78. Nettles & Golenbock, supra note 22, at 151.

79. Corking a bat entails drilling a hole in the end of the bat to remove some of the wood, then replacing the wood with cork. See Waggoner, et al., supra note 18, at 21–22. Because cork is lighter than wood, the corked bat will be lighter and allow the hitter to swing faster. The increased swing speed means increased force when the ball is hit, which means the ball should fly farther. Id. at 22 ("Some say that corking adds as much as fifty feet to a long ball and gives a grounder added zip to carry it through the infield."). The rules specifically prohibit corking a bat to prevent a batter from obtaining this unfair advantage.

80. Chass, supra note 1.

81. Id.

82. Id.

83. Murray Chass, The Pine-Tar Rule Is Clarified, N.Y. Times, Dec. 10, 1983, §1, at 21.

84. Rule 6.06 (1984).

85. Rule 2.00 (1984).

86. The provision limiting pine tar to 18 inches was re-designated Rule 1.10(c) (1984).

87. Rule 1.10(c), Note (1984). The Rule Book states that the Notes "in essence have the same effect as rules when applied to particular sections for which they are intended." Official Baseball Rules 3 (1984).

88. While judges always decide questions of law, juries do not always decide questions of fact.

89. These two decisions would be made at different times. First, the judge would decide whether John could sue even if he was outside the cross-walk. Assume that the judge answers "no." Next, after the parties put on all of their evidence, the judge will ask the jury to decide whether John was in the cross-walk at the time of the accident. The jury will answer this question, as well as other questions (e.g., Was Jane driving carelessly?), in their verdict.

90. Joe Brinkman, an umpire from the pine tar game, made a similar observation about an umpire's situation: "Umpires are not afforded the luxury of a period of deliberation of several days, being allowed time to receive and evaluate advice and input from a myriad of sources before determining whether the spirit and letter of the law are in accord with each other." Joe Brinkman, How Baseball Became Unstuck by a Rules Dispute, N.Y. Times, Aug. 7, 1983, §5, at 2.

91. Murray Chass, "Magic Trick" Causes Orioles to Disappear, N.Y. Times, Oct. 10, 1996, at B17.

92. Rule 2.00 defines "spectator interference" to include "when a spectator reaches out of the stands...and touches a live ball." Rule 2.00 (2000). An approved ruling under Rule 3.16 then provides: "If spectator interference clearly prevents a fielder from catching a ball, the umpire shall declare the batter out."

93. Jeter's home run tied the score at 4-4, and the Yankees won on a home run in the bottom of the eleventh. Chass, supra note 91.

94. Murray Chass, Game 1 Protest Is Denied, N.Y. Times, Oct. 12, 1996, §1, at 33.

95. Tex. Gov't Code Ann. §22.201 (Vernon 1988).

96. No Ruling Yet on Bat, N.Y. Times, July 27, 1983, at B6.

97. That same year, the California Angels protested a home run by John Mayberry of Kansas City for excessive pine tar. League President Lee MacPhail denied the protest because pine tar did not aid the home run. Id. It is not clear why MacPhail's 1975 ruling did not settle the issue.

98. Steinbrenner originally criticized the decision to hold the completion at night, saying that the Yankees had planned to invite children from New York-area camps to attend a day event. 6 P.M. Start for Yanks-Royals, N.Y. Times, at A15, Aug. 12, 1983 ("We had already been making arrangements to have camp groups and kids from all over. We were planning to have entertainment and giveaways. It would have been a pretty darn nice day at the ballpark, but Lee MacPhail has deprived us of that."). When MacPhail tried to explain that a day game was not an option because Kansas City had a night game scheduled the preceding day, Steinbrenner reportedly replied, "F___ Kansas City, we're playing a day game." Lee MacPhail, My 9 Innings: An Autobiography of 50 Years in Baseball 179 (1989). Major league rules, however, required this scheduling. The then-existing player-owner agreement provided that "if a team must fly more than an hour and a half to the next city, it cannot play a day game there if it played the previous night." Id. Because the Royals were scheduled

to play a night game in Kansas City on August 17, and the Kansas City-to-New York flight was longer than an hour and a half, the player-owner agreement prohibited a day game on August 18.

99. Jane Gross, Appellate Justice Orders "Play Ball," N.Y. Times, Aug. 19, 1983, at A15.

100. 6 P.M. Start for Yanks-Royals, N.Y. Times, Aug. 12, 1983 ("Steinbrenner…said that if his players voted not to play, 'I'll back them. If it means forfeiting, if it means we lose the pennant, that's all right with me.'"). A forfeit would not have hurt the Yankees at that point, as they had slipped far in the standings since MacPhail's ruling: "[T]he Yankees lost 6 of their next 7 games and 13 of 22, sliding to fifth place." Michael Martinez, Anger Dies; Bat Lives On, N.Y. Times, July 24, 1985, at B7.

101. Some Fans Stuck, N.Y. Times, Aug. 13, 1983, at 18. Lee MacPhail paved the way for this argument in his decision overruling the pine tar call: "The game becomes a Suspended Game at that point.…"

102. A game may be suspended for weather, curfew, exceeding a league-established time limit, darkness, light failure, or "malfunction of a mechanical field device." Rule 4.12(a) (As an example of a "mechanical field device," the rule cites an "automatic tarpaulin or water removal equipment.")

103. Id.

104. The lawsuits were filed in separate state courts, one located in Manhattan and one in the Bronx. In both cases, the parents were lawyers and filed the lawsuits on behalf of their children. The Manhattan suit involved a fourteen year-old boy, and the Bronx lawsuit involved two boys, ages six and seven. The Manhattan lawsuit was quickly transferred to the Bronx court so the cases could be heard together. As both suits raised the same basic issues, I do not distinguish them in the text.

105. Quite sensibly, the plaintiffs not only file the complaint with the court but must also deliver copies of the complaint to the defendants. Along with the complaint, the plaintiff must also give the defendant a summons, which is a separate document that explains to the defendant where they have been sued and by what date they must respond to the lawsuit.

106. Verified Complaint, Morrison v. New York Yankees Baseball Club, Inc., at 1-2, N.Y. S. Ct., Aug. 15, 1983.

107. Id.

108. Murray Chass, Finale of Game in Doubt, N.Y. Times, Aug. 18, 1983, at B15.

109. American League Lawyer Robert Kheel made this point during one of the court hearings: "[W]hat you're really hearing here is echoes from Mr. Steinbrenner still being unhappy with Mr. MacPhail's original decision. It is a subtle and skillful way of throwing a monkey wrench into the works." Gross, supra note 99. The Yankees' lawyer, Roy Cohn, strongly disputed this charge: "I resent any statements on his part that we are responsible for this. The continuing reference to the fact that this was somehow inspired by us is an outright falsehood. We didn't bring these cases. We're being sued." Id.

110. Indeed, the Yankees' decision to support the fans against MacPhail and Major League Baseball was in large part responsible for Bowie Kuhn fining George Steinbrenner $250,000 after the 1983 season. Murray Chass, Yankees and Steinbrenner Fined $250,000 by Kuhn, N.Y. Times, Dec. 24, 1983, § 1, at 19.

111. Gross, supra note 99. While the young fans lost their lawsuit, they won an invitation from George Brett to attend the Royals' August 22 home game against the Chicago White Sox. Kevin DuPont, Yankees Triumph on 2 in 9th, N.Y. Times, Aug. 22, 1983, at C1.

112. Gross, supra note 99. The on-again-off-again see-sawing of the judges' decisions had the unfortunate effect of leaving the Royals unsure where they were supposed to go and what they were supposed to do. Steve Wulf, Pine-Tarred and Feathered, Sports Illustrated, at 48, Aug. 29, 1983.

113. Tiny Crowd After Big Dispute, N.Y. Times, Aug. 19, 1983, at A15.

114. Pine Tar Special, N.Y. Times, Nov. 25, 1983, at D6.

115. Id.

116. Murray Chass, Resumed Game Ends in 5-4 Loss to Royals, N.Y. Times, Aug. 19, 1983, at A13; Zimmer & Madden, supra note 39, at 169. Martin needed to make these substitutions because

the player at each position on July 24 was unavailable for the August 18 game. Center fielder Jerry Mumphrey had been traded to Houston, and second baseman Bert Campaneris was on the disabled list. Chass, supra.

117. MacPhail explained that his discussions with the Yankees over scheduling completion of the pine tar game led him to further gamesmanship from the Yankees. MacPhail, supra note 98. He explained that he knew something was up when "[o]ne of the Yankee officials…asked…if the same umpires would be" at the August 18 game. Id.

118. Letter from Joe Brinkman, et al., to Dick Butler, dated Aug. 11, 1983. The letter was notarized, meaning that it was signed in front of a person licensed by the state of New York to take sworn statements. Such a sworn statement is given under penalty of perjury.

119. See Murray Chass, A's Beat Yanks in 14th by 3-2, N.Y. Times, Aug. 23, 1983.

120. Murray Chass, Resumed Game Ends in 5-4 Yankee Loss to Royals, N.Y. Times, Aug. 19, 1983, at A13. Sports Illustrated writer Steve Wulf quipped: "Time of the game: three weeks, four days, four hours, and fourteen minutes." Wulf, supra note 112.

121. An unintended consequence of MacPhail's decision was that Royal reliever Dan Quisenberry received an additional save opportunity, which he seized by retiring the three Yankee batters he faced. The save added to Quisenberry's single-season save record, which was 45 by season's end. Previously, the single-season save record was held by John Hiller, who had 38 saves in 1973. The current record of 57 was set in 1990 by Bobby Thigpen, then with the Chicago White Sox.

122. Tiny Crowd after Big Dispute, supra note 113.

Chapter 10 Endnotes

* A life-long Yankees fan, Phyllis Coleman is a Professor of Law at Nova Southeastern University where she teaches Sports Law, Family Law, and Bioethics. She holds a B.S., M.Ed., and J.D. from the University of Florida.

1. For a vivid depiction of Stockton's years on death row, see Joe Jackson & William F. Burke, Jr., DEAD RUN: The Untold Story of Dennis Stockton and America's Only Mass Escape from Death Row (1999).

2. Dennis Stockton, Contemplating the Past—and the Possibilities, Va.-Pilot & Ledger Star, Sept. 3, 1995, at A10.

3. Dennis Stockton, Final Entry: Wrapping Up Life's Loose Ends; Last Words in Stockton's 12-Year Prison Journal: "Free As a Bird", Va.-Pilot & Ledger Star, Sept. 28, 1995, at A7.

Yankees fans recall their team finished second in the American League East, having lost the division series 3-2 to the Mariners. http://www.baseball-reference.com/teams/NYY/1995.shtml.

4. Williamson v. Reynolds, 904 F. Supp. 1529, 1581 (E.D. Okla. 1995) (affidavit of Gary E. Simmons), aff'd sub nom. Williamson v. Ward, 110 F.3d 1508 (10th Cir. 1997).

5. The state attorney general insisted this new information failed to establish Williamson was innocent. Instead, he contended, it is consistent with the government's theory of multiple perpetrators. Moreover, he claimed sufficient direct and circumstantial evidence exists—including Williamson's statement to the police describing a "dream" during which he killed the victim—to support the conviction. William Neikirk, Senate Panel Stuck on DNA Testing, Chi. Trib., June 14, 2000.

6. Ginnie Graham, Wrongful Conviction Spurs Suit, Tulsa (Okla.) World, Apr. 19, 2002, at 16.

7. Kal Wagenheim, Babe Ruth: His Life and Legend 185–91 (2001 ed.).

8. Kevin Cantera, Partner Is Sentenced In Murder, Salt Lake Trib., Oct. 27, 2001, at B2.

9. Bob Nightengale, Big City, Big Troubles for Padre Pitching Ace Whitson, 18 Months in New York Was a 'Living Hell', L.A. Times, July 10, 1989, at 9 (Sports).

10. FBI Snoops Between Pinstripes, N.Y. Post, Oct. 30, 1999, at 30.

11. Phil Rogers et al., Alleged Exploits Land Mantle in FBI Files Over 8-Year Period, Chi. Trib., May 5, 1998, at 1 (Sports).

12. Marty Noble, He's Back! Reinstated, Howe Seeks Yankee Deal, Newsday, Nov. 13, 1992, at 190 (quoting former Commissioner Fay Vincent).

13. Howe entered a plea which permitted him to maintain his innocence while pleading guilty because he believed he would be convicted. The idea was that he could then attempt to avoid suspension by telling Commissioner Fay Vincent he had not committed the crime. The ploy did not work and Howe was suspended before he even arrived home from the courthouse. Tim Layden, Fay Throws Curve; Responds to Howe's Plea By Suspending Him, Newsday, June 9, 1992, at 134.

14. Baseball Arbitrator Asserts Howe Victimized by Psychiatric Disorder, Portland Oregonian, Nov. 20, 1992, at E2.

15. Baseball's Slipping Standards, L.A. Daily News, Dec. 9, 1992, at N16.

16. Howe Being Sued By Attorneys, Record (N. N.J.), Jan. 20, 1993, at D6.

17. Howe Adds to Career Suspension List, Chi. Sun-Times, Apr. 2, 1999, at 109.

18. For example, Strawberry was arrested twice for domestic abuse, once for assault with a deadly weapon, three times for cocaine possession, once for driving under the influence of prescription drugs, and once for prostitution. In addition, he violated his probation six times, was convicted of tax evasion, and was sued for paternity, legal fees, and child support. Kevin Horrigan, Squandered Promise: The Superstar Who Never Grew Up, St. Louis Post-Dispatch, Nov. 12, 2000, at B3.

19. For further discussion of the solicitation charge, see infra notes 84–85 and accompanying text.

20. Robert Ingrassia, Strawberry Went On a Crack Binge; Says Addict Lured Him From AA Meeting, N.Y. Daily News, Apr. 4, 2001, at 8.

21. Ken Davidoff, Straw Heads to Jail; Gets 18 Months for Latest Violation, Newsday, Apr. 30, 2002, at A6.

22. In 1984, Perez spent time in a Dominican Republic jail after he was convicted on cocaine possession. Following another off-season incident in February 1989, Perez checked into his third rehabilitation program. Jon Heyman, Pascual's In Big Trouble; Source: He Failed Drug Test, Newsday, Mar. 6, 1992, at 182.

23. Yankees Take a Risk on Perez, S.F. Chron., Nov. 22, 1989, at D4.

24. Unhappy Perez Begs to Be Freed From Pinstripe Prison, Seattle Times, July 27, 1990, at D4.

25. Perez 'Set Up' By Yankees?, Chi. Sun-Times, Mar. 9, 1992 at 6 (Sports).

26. Joe Sexton, Pascual Perez Was Hard to Hit, But Now He's Just Hard to Find, N.Y. Times Abstracts, Jan. 25, 1993, at 2.

27. But see infra notes 60–62 and accompanying text for a discussion of Gooden's arrest for drunk driving after he retired from baseball and became a Yankees executive.

28. Bill Chastain, One Good Turn Deserves Another, Tampa Trib., May 6, 1997, at 1.

29. Gooden No-Hits Mariners; Revived 'Doc' Hurls Unlikely Gem, Chi. Sun-Times, May 15, 1996, at 132.

30. Dale Berra Testifies About His Drug Use, Hous. Chron., Sept. 10, 1985, at 3. The following story demonstrates how involved in the drug scene he became: after a rainout May 4, 1984, Berra—who had angered his girlfriend because he forgot to buy her a birthday present—got her a gram of coke for $100. Chuck Finder, Baseball's Trying Times, Pitt. Post-Gazette, June 11, 1995, at F1.

31. Baseball Disciplines 21 In Drug-Use Crackdown, S.F. Chron., Mar. 1, 1986, at 1.

32. Dale is the son of former Yankees catcher and manager Yogi Berra. He played 16 games with the team before his father was fired in the beginning of 1985. Dale Berra, BaseballLibrary.com, available at http://www.pubdim.net/baseballlibrary/ballplayers/B/Berra_Dale.stm.

33. Leonard Admits Cocaine Buys, Implicates Chili, S.F. Chron., Sept. 11, 1985, at 59.

34. Berra Enters Probation Program, Newark (N.J.) Star-Ledger, Oct. 28, 1989.

35. Steve Wilstein, Cocaine Was Opponent Scurry Couldn't Master, Las Vegas Rev.-J., Nov. 25, 1992, at 8E.

36. Ron Cook, The Biggest Victim; Rod Scurry Knew How to Throw Curves, But Never Learned How to Handle Them, Pitt. Post-Gazette, June 11, 1995, at F8.

37. Mike Kiley et al., Baseball Belts Drug Abuse; Ueberroth Suspends 11 — But Gives Them a Way Out, Chi. Trib., Mar. 1, 1986, at 1 (Sports).

38. Chronology of Baseball Drug Cases Since 1980, L.A. Times, May 12, 1985, at 6 (Sports).

39. Thomas Boswell, Higher We Put Them, Harder They Fall, Wash. Post, July 1, 1994, at C1.

40. How Cocaine is Helping Decide Baseball Games, S.F. Chron., Aug. 20, 1985, at 1 (quoting Raines admitting cocaine "certainly hurt my performance").

41. David Dorsey, Raines Wants to Finish Career with Flourish, News-Press (Ft. Myers, Fla.), Mar. 18, 2002, at 8C.

42. Claudell Reports to Braves' Camp, S.F. Chron., Mar. 1, 1985, at 79.

43. John Strege, Getting a Grip; Sudakis, Now a Hitting Teacher, Puts Past Behind Him, Orange County (Cal.) Reg., Apr. 14, 1990, at C1.

44. Ron Howell, A New Ballgame; Ex-Yankee Throws Himself Into Helping Kids, Newsday, Oct. 26, 2000, at A8.

45. Doug Fernandez, Still in the Game; Butch Hobson Played Hard, Fell Even Harder, But It Seems Nothing Can Keep Him From Baseball, Sarasota-Herald Trib., July 25, 1999, at 2C.

46. David Firestone, Testimony Begins in Pepitone Drug Trial, Newsday, Aug. 27, 1986, at 19.

47. Joe Pepitone Is Sentenced to Six Months in Jail, L.A. Times, Oct. 23, 1986, at 6 (Sports).

48. Jerry Crowe, Dock Ellis The Man Who Pitched a No-Hitter While Under the Influence of LSD Has Found a New Delivery: He Coordinates a Substance-Abuse Rehabilitation Program, L.A. Times, June 30, 1985, at 3 (Sports).

49. David Ray Papke, Athletes in Trouble with the Law: Journalistic Accounts for the Resentful Fan, 12 Marquette Sports L. Rev. 449, 457 (2001).

50. Mel Hall Mistaken for Drug Lord, Balt. Sun, Sept. 21, 1991, at 2C.

51. Don Zimmer with Bill Madden, Zim: A Baseball Life 240 (2001).

52. Kal Wagenheim, supra note 7, at 3–4.

53. Martin played second base for the Yankees between 1950–53 and 1955–57. George Steinbrenner hired, and then fired, him as manager of the team five different times: 1975–78, 1979, 1983, 1985, and 1987–88.

54. Michael Fleming et al., Inside New York, Newsday, May 13, 1988, at 6.

55. Martin Pal Changing Stories on Fatal Crash, Chi. Sun-Times, Apr. 12, 1990, at 100.

56. Hal Bock, Alcohol, Athletes, Autos Form Tragic Triple Threat, Austin Am.-Statesman, May 7, 1991.

57. Tunnel Vision, Buff. News, Feb. 27, 1996, at B2.

58. Wilstein, supra note 35, at 8E.

59. John Hughes, Yanks' GM, Lions' Blades Arrested by Same Officer, Ft. Lauderdale Sun-Sent., Apr. 1, 1995.

60. Because he would not take the test, his Florida driver's license was automatically revoked. As the refusal also covered blood and urine, no one knows if Gooden, who had been battling substance abuse for years but was apparently in recovery, was using drugs that night. Bob Klapisch, Troubled Gooden Left Without a Plan, Record (N. N.J.), Feb. 21, 2002, at S1.

61. Bob Klapisch & Howard Bryant, Boss Puts Gooden Back to Work, Record (N. N.J.), Apr. 15, 2002, at S6.

62. Christopher Goffard, Gooden Gets 1 Year Probation in Traffic Incident, St. Petersburg Times, June 5, 2002, at 3B.

63. Kal Wagenheim, supra note 7, at 69–70.

64. Candelaria Says Sutton Set Him Up for DUI Arrest, Chi. Trib., Mar. 2, 1988, at 2 (Sports).

65. Steve Kelley, Norris Starts Over in Bid to Rejoin A's, Seattle Times, May 31, 1989, at F1.

66. "He can leave his house to go to the doctor and attend support group recovery meetings. But he can't leave the state without special permission and he can't go to the movies or out to dinner." Lyda Longa, Strawberry Gets House Arrest After Accident, Tampa Trib., Sept. 13, 2000, at 1 (Metro).

67. Kal Wagenheim, supra note 7, at 88–90, 126.

68. Canseco Arrested for Ramming Wife's Car, Dallas Morning News, Feb. 14, 1992, at 3B.

69. Gerald Eskenazi, The Lip: A Biography of Leo Durocher 48 (1993).

70. Howe Fined by Montana Court, Tulsa (Okla.) World, Feb. 13, 1992, at B6.

71. Bill Pennington, Reg-gie! Newest Hall of Famer Is Already an Immortal, The Record (N. N.J.), Aug. 1, 1993, at S1.

72. Leanora Minai, Yankees Employee Queried in Sex Case, St. Petersburg Times, Oct. 24, 2001, at 3B.

73. Tom Canavan, Former Rookie of the Year Sentenced, AP Online, Feb. 2, 2000.

74. Mike Vaccaro, The Count Knows What Counts—Back in Baseball with Jail Stint in Past, Every Day is Beautiful to Montefusco, Newark (N.J.) Star-Ledger, Aug. 7, 2002, at 47 (Sports).

75. The Pfister, described as a hotel which has "retain[ed] its turn-of-the-century charm," is the place where most MLB teams stay when playing in Milwaukee. Henry Schulman, Pfister Hotel: Room for Trouble, S.F. Chron., June 2, 1998, at E2.

In 1974, the Pfister lobby was the scene of a "pretty good" brawl between Yankee catcher Rick Dempsey and infielder Bill Sudakis that expanded to involve several of their teammates. Sudakis made death threats and Dempsey received a call "from a guy with a thick New York accent, offering to break Sudakis' legs. 'No thanks,' Dempsey said." Wayne Coffey, Years Have Taken Nothing From Rick Dempsey's Spunk, St. Louis Post-Dispatch, July 20, 1997, at 4F. Although the fight did not result in legal charges, some believe it cost the Yankees a chance at the pennant. Dempsey had inadvertently stepped on, and broken, Bobby Murcer's finger so he was out for the final series. Two muffed plays to right led to a Brewers win which allowed the Orioles to clinch. Bob Wolfley, "Pfister-cuffs" Add to Hotel's Legend of Sports Incidents, Milwaukee J. & Sent., May 27, 1998, at 2.

76. Whiten's Accuser Got Into Pickup, Dayton (Ohio) Daily News, July 28, 1997, at 2C and Whiten Will Not Be Charged, Newsday, Sept. 10, 1997, at A63.

77. Polonia Given Jail Term; Yankee Outfielder Sentenced for Sex Offense, S.F. Chron., Oct. 3, 1989, at E2. He was also ordered to donate $10,000 to a sexual assault treatment center. Id.

78. Pat Calabria, Luis Could Be Denied Visa, Newsday, Oct. 5, 1989, at 161.

79. Girl Sues Polonia; Damages Sought From Outfielder, Milwaukee Hotel, L.A. Daily News, June 21, 1991, at S4. She also named the Pfister, asserting the hotel was negligent because an employee let Polonia bring her in through a locked side door. Id.

80. Michael R. Zahn, Ballplayer Settles Suit Over Sex With Girl, Milwaukee J. & Sent., Mar. 15, 1993.

81. Tim Brown, District Attorney Clears Polonia of Wrongdoing, L.A. Daily News, July 28, 1990, at S4.

82. Julian Garcia, Third Party for Polonia; Luis Hopes to Fill Yank Outfield Void, N.Y. Daily News, Aug. 4, 2000, at 91.

83. Kent Youngblood & Shela Mulrooney Eldred, Hockey Strength Trainer Faces New Charges, Star-Trib. (Minn.-St. Paul), Mar. 9, 1999.

84. Ace Atkins & Katherine Smith, Another Mess for Troubled Yankee Star; Police Officers, Baseball Fans and the Yankees React to the Arrest of Outfielder Darryl Strawberry, Tampa Trib., Apr. 16, 1999, at 1.

85. Darryl May Come Back to Baseball in Mid-July, Times Union (Alb., N.Y.), June 2, 1999, at C4.

86. See FBI Snoops Between Pinstripes, supra note 10, at 30.

87. Justice Is Served as New Wife Sounds Off, Newark (N.J.) Star-Ledger, Nov. 26, 2001, at 36. In fact, she says she trusts him so much he is hosting the behind-the-scenes video and interviewing the bikini clad models on her new calendar, "Exotic Spices." Id.

88. Robert Fachet, Justice's Marriage Hits the Skids, Wash. Post, Feb. 24, 1996, at H2.

89. Roger Angell, A Pitcher's Story: Innings with David Cone 175–76 (2001).

90. Gooden pitched for the Yankees in 1996 and 1997. For a discussion of his substance abuse problems, see supra text accompanying notes 27–29.

91. Boston played outfield with the Yankees in 1994. Vince Coleman—who was never on the Yankees roster—was also a defendant.

92. Roger Angell, supra note 89, at 176–78.

93. William B. Mead, The Official New York Yankees Hater's Handbook 22 (1983).

94. Jim Bouton, Ball Four 37–39 (1970).

95. Richard Ben Cramer, Joe DiMaggio: The Hero's Life 366–75 (2000).

96. Martin Kasindorf, Lisa: I Was Threatened; Wife Alleges That Strawberry Said He'd Shoot Her, Newsday, Feb. 1, 1990, at 135.

97. Maryann Hudson, Strawberry Is Accused of Assault; Jurisprudence: Dodger Outfielder Arrested After Allegedly Striking His Girlfriend, Opening a Cut Above Her Eye, L.A. Times, Sept. 5, 1993, at 1 (Sports).

98. Jules Crittenden, Ex-Sox Slugger Canseco Accused of Beating Wife, Boston Herald, Nov. 7, 1997, at 14.

99. Ken Davidoff, Yanks Court Cordero; 'Exploring All Aspects' of Troubled Outfielder, Record (N. N.J.), Feb. 27, 1998, at S1.

100. Jack Curry, Wells Avoids Felony Charge, Times Union (Alb., N.Y.), Jan. 29, 1997, at C1.

101. Yankees Charlie Hayes and Mark Whiten had accompanied Gooden to the bar, further angering owner George Steinbrenner. Whiten, of course, had his own problems with the law. See supra notes 75–76 and accompanying text.

102. David Lennon, Fare Deal: Doc Settles With Cabbie, Newsday, July 9, 1997, at A73. Hakim sought $500,000 but a source said the actual figure was going to be closer to $100,000. Id.

103. Tim Leonard, Some More Basebrawl Lore, Newsday, July 20, 1986, at 4.

104. Mickey Mantle with Herb Gluck, The Mick 151–52 (1985).

105. Other Martin opponents include: St. Louis Browns catcher Clint Courtney (while playing for the Yankees in July 1952); Cubs pitcher Jim Brewer (while playing for the Reds in August 1960); Twins pitcher Dave Boswell (while managing the Twins in August 1969); Baltimore Orioles fan (while managing the Tigers in April 1972); Cleveland Indians traveling secretary (while managing the Texas Rangers in May 1974); Reggie Jackson (while managing the Yankees in June 1977 the two almost came to blows); sportswriter Ray Hagar (between stints as Yankees manager in November 1978); Illinois marshmallow salesman Joseph Cooper (while managing the Yankees in October 1979); A's locker room (while managing the A's in August 1982 smashed everything in the locker room after a tough loss); California bar patron Robin Olson (while managing the Yankees in May 1983); urinal in visiting team's clubhouse at Municipal Stadium in June 1983); pitcher Ed Whitson and hotel bar patron in Baltimore (while managing the Yankees in September 1985); three men in restroom of the Lace topless bar in Arlington, Texas (while managing the Yankees in May 1988), and buffet table in Yankees clubhouse (while managing the Yankees in June 1988).

106. Tom Verducci, Just Some Brawls, Bumps and Bruises, Newsday, May 8, 1988, at 4.

107. Giovia v. Kiamesha Concord, Inc., 1993 WL 539530 (S.D.N.Y. 1993).

108. Chris Mortensen, Sanders: I Defended 'My Female'; Deion Says Altercation Was Started by Fans' Harassing of Girlfriend, Atlanta J. & Const., Aug. 8, 1989, at F1.

109. Len Pasquarelli, Probation Officer Urges Fine for Sanders in Florida Case, Atlanta J. & Const., Aug. 22, 1989, at D3.

A short time later, just as Sanders was signing a $4.5 million contract with the Atlanta Falcons, the auxiliary policeman filed a lawsuit seeking an undisclosed amount of compensatory and punitive damages. Sanders Is Sued Over Shopping Mall Fracas, Atlanta J. & Const., Sept. 8, 1989, at E7.

110. Clemens Charged in Scuffle, Dallas Morning News, Jan. 20, 1991, at 18B.

111. Names in the News, L.A. Times, Dec. 13, 1991, at 7 (Sports).

112. Reggie Jackson Pleads No Contest in Fight, Milwaukee J. & Sent., Nov. 22, 2000, at 2C.

113. Baseball: Mr. October Gets Probation in November, Nat'l Post, Nov. 22, 2000, at B10.

114. Of course, through the years, a number of Yankees fans have been accused of disorderly conduct during games. In one particularly outrageous incident, after heavily imbibing a mixture of rum and Coke, a 24-year-old Yonkers man dove 60 feet from the upper deck at Yankee Stadium. Luckily for him, two years earlier, the Yankees had decided the screen behind home plate was not high enough to protect against foul balls. Therefore, they installed a top-of-the-line net which very likely saved his life. Charged with disorderly conduct and reckless endangerment, after he was released from the hospital he spent four nights in jail awaiting trial. Gordon Edes, Fan Pulls Scary Stunt; Net Result: He's Ok, Boston Globe, May 27, 2000, at G6.

115. Gene Wojciechowski, Jackson-Incident Interviews Continuing, L.A. Times, May 8, 1986, at 6 (Sports).

116. Shortly after the suit was filed, Jackson indicated he planned to fight it and thought the whole thing was ridiculous. "'Two days before I left town, they (Weimer and his attorney) said they'd settle for $75,000,' Jackson said. 'With that, I'll loan him my girlfriend, give him my Porsche, dinner reservations and a weekend in Monte Carlo.'" John Weyler, Man Involved in Altercation With Jackson Files a $150,000 Civil Suit in Milwaukee, L.A. Times, May 15, 1986, at 1 (Sports).

117. Viola Gets OK From Red Sox's Doctor, S.F. Examiner, Dec. 25, 1991, at D3.

118. Kathleen Nelson, Looking at Who's In and Who's Out in the World of Sports, St. Louis Post-Dispatch, Nov. 1, 1999, at C2.

119. Mark Herrmann, Ducks Put In a Call for LaPoint as Pitching Coach, Newsday, Feb. 27, 2002, at A56.

120. Paul J. Toomey, Ex-Yankee Agrees to Hackensack Plea Bargain, Record (N. N.J.), May 10, 1996, at N3.

121. Joyce A. Venezia, Ex-Yank Pasqua Agrees to Testing in Deal on Marijuana Possession, Newark (N.J.) Star-Ledger, Dec. 12, 1991.

122. Sports News, UPI, May 14, 1985. Saying they were "disappointed" in the men, the Yankees fined each $1,000 which was donated to charity. Id.

123. Former Manager Says He's No Deviant, Fla. Times-Union, Mar. 12, 2000, at C3.

124. Angell, supra note 89, at 176–77.

125. Mark Kriegel, Free-Speech Streak? Bared Views on Rudy & Faces Fight with DA, N.Y. Daily News, Dec. 31, 1997, at 6.

126. Ken Garcia, Bronx Jeerer Needs S.F.'s Support; Prank Provoked Legal Wrath of N.Y. Mayor, S.F. Chron., May 16, 1998, at A15.

127. Hustler Mag. v. Falwell, 485 U.S. 46 (1988).

128. Ex-Yankee Clay Pleads Guilty, Chi. Trib., Aug. 28, 1987, at 3 (Sports).

129. Former Ballplayer Gets a Year in Jail in Employer Theft, Rich. (Va.) Times-Dispatch, Dec. 31, 1991, at 17 (Sports).

130. Clay Sentenced Again, Rich. (Va.) Times-Dispatch, Mar. 26, 1992, at D7.

131. Doug Moe, Unfinished Tale of '40s State Beauty, Capital Times (Wis.), Jan. 15, 2001, at 2A.

132. Phil Mushnick, A Good Start, But…Met, Yankee Ticket-Scam Bust Doesn't Totally Solve Problems, N.Y. Post, July 28, 2000, at 104.

133. Ticket Ring Busted; Yankees, Mets Agents Among 16 Netted in Scalping Plot, Newsday, July 25, 2000, at A5.

134. Baseball Suspensions, Chi. Sun-Times, Aug. 27, 1989, at 7 (Sports).

135. Joe Gergen, Leo Rarely Finished Last, Newsday, Oct. 8, 1991, at 125.

136. Elden Auker & Tom Keegan, Sleeper Cars and Flannel Uniforms 21–24 (2001).

Even more uncertainty surrounds the issue of whether Durocher stole Lou Gehrig's World Series ring. Although the mystery is unlikely to be solved, children of people who saw the first baseman storm into Durocher's home town looking for him still talk about it. Gerald Eskenazi, supra note 69, at 47–48.

137. Durocher continued his thieving ways during his time managing the Giants. First, while a guest at their house, he stole his best friend's wife, actress Laraine Day. Then, in the 1951 National League pennant race, in the series against the Dodgers, Durocher set up a system to steal signs. A spy in the Polo Grounds clubhouse, armed with a telescope, intercepted the catcher's movements and notified players in the dugout or bullpen who relayed the information to the batter by agreed-upon gestures. Vic Ziegel, About Time We Gave This Story a Rest, N.Y. Daily News, Feb. 1, 2001, at 78.

138. In 1995, reacting to being benched for being habitually late while playing for Triple A Columbus, Ruben Rivera packed his gear and left. The reliever called his cousin and told him to get back in uniform. Jack O'Connell, Rivera Just Doesn't Get It, Hartford Courant, Mar. 17, 2002, at E2.

139. Peter Schmuck, Glove-Snatcher Upset Torre's Belief in Team Chemistry, Balt. Sun, Mar. 17, 2002, at 7D.

140. Bill Campbell, Resurrecting a Career, Seattle Times, Apr. 19, 2002, at D7.

141. Gordon Dillow, Eddie Dodson: Gentler, Kinder Bank Robber, Orange County (Cal.) Reg., June 24, 1999, at B1.

142. Patrick Jenkins, Police Seek Ex-Convict for Info on Bank Heists, Newark (N.J.) Star-Ledger, May 25, 2002, at 22.

143. George Berkin, Police Seize Suspect in String of Bank Robberies, Newark (N.J.) Star-Ledger, June 22, 2002, at 26.

144. Richard Ben Cramer, supra note 95, at ix. Cramer disputes the story. "Joe didn't lose those rings to theft. More likely he traded them for free lodging, food, transportation, services of every kind." Id. at x.

145. Baseball Briefs, Deseret News, July 10, 1999, at D3.

146. Jinxed Jersey? Babe Ruth Uniform Has a History, St. Louis Post-Dispatch, May 28, 1995, at 1F.

147. Gunmen Rob Babe Ruth Museum-Again, Deseret News, June 13, 1999, at D8.

148. Richard Sandomir, Case of Mantle's Long-Missing Bust Going, Going, But No Longer Gone, N.Y. Times Abstracts, Nov. 1, 1995, at 11.

149. Kyle Lobner, Hal Chase: Prince Hal, Baseball Almanac, available at http://www.baseball-almanac.com/articles/halchase.shtml.

150. Interestingly, the main perpetrator in what federal officials called the country's "largest black-market weapons trafficking case" used Roger Maris—after the Yankees slugger—as his alias. Seth Rosenfeld, East Bay Gun Ring Biggest in Nation, BATF Says; Officials Say Trafficking Was Easy, and Weapons Were Used in Crimes, S.F. Examiner, May 29, 1999, at A1.

151. Tom Fitzgerald, Close Call for Yankee In Panama City, S.F. Chron., Jan. 20, 1990, at D6.

152. See supra notes 12–17 and accompanying text.

153. Still Packing Heat? Howe Faces Charges; Former Yankee Reliever Arrested on Felony Gun Count at Airport, Seattle Times, June 25, 1996, at C5.

154. Around the Majors, Wash. Post, Nov. 8, 1996, at C3.

155. Martin Truly a Gun-Shy Guy, Chi. Sun-Times, Dec. 13, 1989, at 111.

156. Neil MacCarl, The Yolk's On Him; Canseco Loses Deal, Toronto Star, Apr. 27, 1989, at B2.

157. Canseco Given Sentence for Carrying Gun, Chi. Sun-Times, Sept. 1, 1989, at 80.

158. Steinbrenner Charges 'Extortion', Wash. Post, Mar. 18, 1990, at D2.

159. When he was released from prison and could not get a job, Spira claimed Steinbrenner prevented him from obtaining work. The Anti-Boss, 31 N.Y. Mag. 18 (June 1, 1998).

160. Jeff Goldberg, No Love Lost in the Spira Affair, Hartford Courant, Aug. 3, 2001, at C6.

161. Michael Bauman, FBI's Mantle File a Waste of Money, Rocky Mtn. News, May 10, 1998, at 24C.

162. Juicy Secrets From FBI Files Going Online, Seattle Times, June 12, 1998, at A18.

163. 'The Mick' Hero at the Plate, Nightmare at Home; Mantle's Sons Describe the Dark Side of Living in Shadow of America's Favorite Baseball Player, Rocky Mtn. News, Oct. 13, 1996, at 34C.

164. Man Pleads Guilty to eBay Bat Fraud, AP Online, Apr. 3, 2002. For example, Derungs sent the following e-mail to the Original Maple Bat Company: "I will place an order for 50-60 for the 2001 season, because my contract with Louisville Slugger is up, and I am trying to get a feel of what's out there before I decide what bats to use next year. The sooner the better. Thanks[.] Derek." Id.

165. Jim Donaghy, Winning Comes First to Controversial Yankee Owner, Seattle Times, Jan. 10, 1988, at C8.

166. Bev McCarron & Jeanette Rundquist, Mystique May Be All DeLorean Can Bank On; Rumors of Riches Surround Fallen Carmaker, Newark (N.J.) Star-Ledger, Oct. 4, 1998, at 25. The company folded after producing only 8,500 vehicles. Despite its economic failure, however, the car was made famous in the movie "Back to the Future." William T. Quinn & Mark Mueller, Highflier DeLorean Hits Ground Zero-Judge Approves Sale of Prized Estate and Orders Him to Get Out, Newark (N.J.) Star-Ledger, Jan. 13, 2000, at 1.

167. Susan Bischoff, DeLorean: Ever Optimistic, He's Chock Full of Ideas, Ideals, Hous. Chron., Oct. 6, 1985 (Bus.), at 1.

168. Dan Cook et al., The Rise and Fall of Marvin Warner, 2893 Bus. Wk. 104 (May 6, 1985).

169. Barry M. Horstman, Banking Scandal's Warner, 82, Dies, Cin. Post, Apr. 12, 2002, at 1A.

170. Dick Schaap, Steinbrenner! 120–42 (1982). Fifteen years later, just two days before leaving office, President Ronald Reagan pardoned Steinbrenner. Russell Mokhiber & Garth Bray, When the Rich, Famous Steinbrenner Gets a Pardon, Justice Takes Strike 3, L.A. Times, Feb. 26, 1989, at 5.

171. Strawberry Applies Bonus to Child Support, Dayton (Ohio) Daily News, July 6, 1996, at 2D.

172. Schuerholz Quits Royals, Joins Braves, Wash. Post, Oct. 11, 1990, at B8.

173. Cops Rip Hall's Play With Cubs, Chi. Trib., Oct. 11, 1990, at 3 (Sports).

174. Yanks' Hall Off Hook By Making Donation, Record (N. N.J.), Nov. 7, 1990, at C2.

175. Case of the Fouled Fowl, 122 Time Mag. 34 (Aug. 15, 1983).

176. Dave Winfield with Tom Park, Winfield: A Player's Life 168–70 (1988).

177. Peter Finney, Winfield's Ecstacy Is Atlanta's Agony, New Orleans Times-Picayune, Oct. 26, 1992, at D1.

178. Ex-Bucs' President Foils Kidnap Plan, Tulsa (Okla.) World, Sept. 13, 1995, at S5.

179. Sam Walker, On Sports: Play Ball, Pay Tax! Cities and States Clamp Down On Taxes for Visiting Jocks; A $500,000 Tab for A-Rod, Wall St. J., June 1, 2001, at W1.

180. Benjamin Marrison, City Set to Make Its Pitch for Taxes on Visiting Players' Pay, Clev. Plain Dealer, Mar. 3, 1991.

181. Robert A. Baker, A Look Back to 1926, Post-Standard (Syracuse), Apr. 13, 1996, at B3.

182. Strawberry Gets Off Lightly for Tax Trouble, Fin. Post, Apr. 25, 1995, at 61. Ironically, Strawberry used the tax court decision and the fact that he thought he was going to jail as an excuse to return to cocaine. Thomas Stinson, Inside Baseball, Atlanta J. & Const., Feb. 12, 1995, at D2.

183. Ex-Yank Pays $1,100 Debt, Newark (N.J.) Star-Ledger, June 27, 1989.

184. A variation on the theme: in a federal narcotics smuggling case, Barry Rosen, one of the defendants, claimed he had earned the $250,000 he was going to use to purchase the drugs playing for the Yankees. United States v. All Funds in "The Anaya Trust" Account, 1997 WL 578662, at *1 (N.D. Cal. 1997). Of course there is no evidence that he ever had any connection with the team.

185. Jeff Simmons, Fake Yankee Gets 6 Months in Jail, Record (N. N.J.), Feb. 27, 1987, at C5.

186. Greg Henry, Yankees' Perez' Car Attacked in Queens, Ark. Gazette, June 25, 1990, at 6D.

187. Bill Madden, DiMaggio a Hit with the Mob; Book Details Wiseguy Links, Grim Last Years, N.Y. Daily News, Oct. 15, 2000, at 6.

188. Carlo Gambino, available at http://www.gambino.com/bio/carlogambino.htm.

189. Mob Figure Talks at Atlanta Trial, AP Online, May 24, 2001.

190. Denise Buffa, Cops Catch 'Loan Sharks' with Babe's Glove, N.Y. Post, June 13, 2002, at 7.

191. Michael Silverman, 'Sopranos' Star Recites Gehrig Speech, Boston Herald, June 2, 2002, at B18.

192. Shay Wessol, Tech Computer Involved in Yankees Hacking; From Blacksburg to the Bronx, With Loathing, Roanoke Times & World News, Nov. 9, 2000, at NRV1.

193. Dean Chadwin, Those Damn Yankees: The Secret Life of America's Greatest Franchise 77–78 (Paperback ed. 2000).

194. Tom Robbins & Robert Winnett, 'Sea of Love' Stings Net Police a Criminal Catch, Sunday Times (London), Nov. 25, 2001 at 25 (Home News).

195. Hillel Italie, "Son of Sam" an Old-Fashioned Scare Flick, Deseret News, July 2, 1999, at W6.

196. See, e.g., arobb (sic), Wanted, Aberdeen Press & J. (U.K.), Nov. 8, 2001 (man who brutally raped a 21-year-old Aberdeen woman in the harbor area's Miller Street was wearing a beige Yankees baseball cap); Eric Arroyo & Dave Hartman, U. Pittsburgh: U. Pittsburgh Student Kidnapped at Gunpoint, U-Wire, Jan. 10, 2002 (man who kidnapped 21-year-old University of Pittsburgh student at gunpoint, robbed him of $115, and forced him to drive him to several locations around Pittsburgh was wearing a black hat with a white New York Yankees logo); London Robber Linked to Kitchener Crime, Police Say, Kitchener-Waterloo Record, Mar. 7, 2002, at B6 (man who robbed London bank wore blue Yankees baseball cap); Larry Oakes, Blom Family Members Testify About Yankees Jersey, Truck; William Pince Said He Never Used or Stored His Brother's Truck, Contradicting What Blom First Told Police, Star-Trib. (Minn.-St. Paul), July 27, 2000, at 1B (man who kidnapped and killed clerk identified on store video by dark Yankees jersey with white sleeves and number 23 on the back); Amanda Ripley et al., The Case of the Dirty Bomb; How a Chicago Street Gangster Allegedly Became a Soldier for Osama bin Laden, 159 Time Mag. 28, 30 (June 24, 2002) (man who had been sent by Osama bin Laden's operation chief to attack America with a "dirty bomb"—a conventional explosive packed with radioactive waste that escapes on detonation—"was a scary, scary guy with a Yankees cap covering his eyebrows" when he was arrested years earlier for firing a gun during a road rage incident); Guy Sterling, Man Pleads Innocent to Postal Thefts, Newark (N.J.) Star-Ledger, Jan. 14, 2000, at 28 (man who held up three letter carriers in separate incidents, twice brandishing guns, arrested after inspectors retrieved his Yankees cap lost during a police chase); Theresa Vargas, New Homicide Chief on Familiar Turf, Newsday, Mar. 5, 2002, at A16 (man who pistol-whipped his estranged wife and murdered her brother was wearing a Yankees cap when police arrested him at a cricket match nine years after the crimes by tracking him through the Internet); Waterford Shooting Death Called Homicide, Hartford Courant, Apr. 14, 2002, at B7 (man who carjacked black 1999 Dodge Intrepid wore gray Yankees cap).

197. Shaun Sutner, Pepper Sentenced in Slayings; 24–26-Year Term for Killing Parents, Telegram & Gazette (Worchester, Mass.), Apr. 8, 1998, at A1.

198. D. James Romero, Pros and Cons of Zero Tolerance, L.A. Times, Nov. 8, 1996, at E1.

199. Kris Worrell, Ex-Con Turned Artist Finds Solace in Sewing with Socks, Times Union (Alb., N.Y.), Nov. 21, 1999, at I1.

Chapter 11 Endnotes

* Michael T. Flannery is a Professor of Legal Writing at Villanova University, where he also teaches Family Law. A life-long Philadelphia Phillies fan, Professor Flannery holds a B.A. from the University of Delaware and a J.D. from the Catholic University of America, Columbus School of Law.

1. For the discussion of Fritz Peterson and Mike Kekich, see Maury Allen, All Roads Lead To October, 26–32 (St. Martin's, 2001). See also Kelli Anderson, et al., Lost and Found, Sports Ill., July 31, 2000, at 142; Marty York, Wife-Swapping Yankees Go Separate Ways, Tulsa Trib., July 4, 1992, at 3B; Les Bowen, Bouton Introduced Us to Off-Field Antics, Seattle Times, July 24, 1988, at C4. For all of the players in this chapter, see generally Derek Gentile, The Complete New York Yankees (Black Dog & Leventhal 2001).

2. For the discussion of Dave Winfield, see Winfield v. Renfro, 821 S.W.2d 640 (Tex. App. 1991); Winfield v. Renfro, 792 S.W.2d 525 (Tex. App. 1990); Winfield v. Renfro, 718 F. Supp. 613 (Tex. 1989); Winfield v. Daggett, 1989 WL 97584 (Tex. App. 1989); Winfield v. Daggett, 775 S.W.2d 431 (Tex. App. 1989). See also George Flynn, Winfield's 10-Year Legal Slump Ends, Houst. Chron., Nov. 7, 1995, §A, at 13; Baseball Star Dave Winfield Says A Week In Rio With Ex-Lover Now Haunts Him, Jet, May 23, 1988, at 48.

3. For the discussion of Babe Ruth, see Kal Wagenheim, Babe Ruth: His Life and Legend, 120–21, 185–90 (2001); Robert W. Creamer, Babe: The Legend Comes To Life, 268, 281–84, 334–47 (Fireside, 1974).

4. For the discussion of Joe DiMaggio, see Richard Ben Cramer, Joe DiMaggio: The Hero's Life (Touchstone, 2001); Al Stump, Baseball's Biggest Headache-Dames!, True, May 1959, at 76.

5. For the discussion of Leo Durocher, see Bill Reel, If Same-Sex Pairs Are Blessed, Then What's Next?, Newsday, July 25, 1997, at A48; Leo Durocher (with Ed Linn), Nice Guys Finish Last 225–35 (Simon and Schuster, 1975).

6. For the discussion of Lefty Gomez, see John M. McGuire, Bound Volumes Are Bound to Catch Your Eye at the P-D, St. Louis Post-Dispatch, July 29, 2002, at D4; June O'Dea Gomez, Don't Marry A Ball Player, Collier's Aug. 29, 1942, at 14; Henry McLemore, Lefty Gomez: Fire Ball, Screw Ball, Eight Ball, Look, April 11, 1939, at 46.

7. For the discussion of David Justice, see George Rush and Joanna Molloy, Halle's Narrow Escape From Tragedy, Daily News, Mar. 21, 2002, at 36; Ex-Assistant Is Almost Litigious, L.A. Times, Aug. 21, 2001, Part 5, at 2; Leslie Doolittle, Hey, Morley, It's Better to be Safer Than Sorry, Orlando Sentinel, June 26, 1997, at A2; Jay Croft, Friends in End: Justice, Berry Get Walking Papers, Atlanta J. and Constitution, June 24, 1997, at 1C; I.J. Rosenberg, Justice: Happy Cleveland Marriage, Nasty Berry Divorce, Atlanta J. and Constitution, June 19, 1997, at 1G; Liz Robbins, New Tribe Outfielders Are A Study in Contrasts, Plain Dealer, Mar. 26, 1997, at 5D.

8. For the discussion of Jack Satter, see Satter v. Satter, 709 So.2d 617 (Fla. Dist. Ct. App. 1998); Satter v. Satter, 659 So.2d 1185 (Fla. Dist. Ct. App. 1995). See also NBC News, Dateline NBC, Nov. 16, 2001 (found at 2001 WL 24017843 & 24017844); Stephen Van Drake, Extra-Inning Fight, Broward Daily Bus. Rev., Nov. 7, 2000, at A1; Ex-Wife Settles Abuse Case, Sun-Sentinel, Jan. 16, 1997, at 1B; Mike Folks, Former Wife Strikes Out in $10 Million Lawsuit, Sun-Sentinel, June 20, 1996, at 4B; Gayle Fee and Laura Raposa, Satters Keep Slicing the Bologna, Bost. Herald, June 16, 1996, at 10; Stephanie Smith, Lawsuit Says Abuse is Worth $10 Million, Sun-Sentinel, June 13, 1996 at 3B; Gayle Fee and Laura Raposa, Ex Puts $10M Bite on Hot Dog King, Bost. Herald, Oct. 18, 1993, at 8.

9. For the discussion of George Stallings, see Stallings v. Stallings, 56 S.E. 469 (Ga. 1907).

10. For the discussion of Burleigh Grimes, see Grimes v. Grimes, 139 S.W.2d 1055 (Mo.App. 1940).

11. For the discussion of Jose Rijo, see Rijo v. Rijo, 1995 WL 35730 (Ohio App. 1995). See also Jack Brennan, Baseball Family In Tatters: Marichal Blames It On Rijo, Sporting News, Feb. 18, 1991, at 3; Jerry Crasnick, Jose Rijo, 82 Sport 21 (July 1991).

12. For the discussion of Kenneth Lance Johnson, see Johnson v. Johnson, 715 So.2d 783 (Ala. 1998); Johnson v. Johnson, 707 So.2d 251 (Ala. Civ. App. 1997).

13. For the discussion of David Collins, see Collins v. Collins, 1997 WL 232235 (Ohio App. 1997); Collins v. Collins, 1991 WL 1067 (Ohio App. 1991); Collins v. Collins, 1991 WL 202191 (Ohio App. 1991).

14. For the discussion of Joe Pepitone, see Pepitone v. Pepitone, 108 Misc.2d 12, 436 N.Y.S.2d 966 (1981). See also, George Vass, The Gals Behind the Guys in Baseball, Baseball Digest, June 1973, at 71.

15. For the discussion of Enos Slaughter, see Slaughter v. Slaughter, 313 S.W.2d 193 (Mo.App. 1958).

16. For the discussion of Lynn McGlothen, see McGlothen v. Sup. Ct. of San Fran., 121 Cal.App.3d 106, 175 Cal.Rptr. 129 (1981).

17. For the discussion of David LaPoint, see Phelps v. La Point, 725 N.Y.S.2d 461 (2001).

18. For the discussion of Billy Martin, see In re Estate of Martin, 686 N.Y.S.2d 195 (1999). See also Peter Golenbock, Wild, High and Tight: The Life and Death of Billy Martin (St. Martin's, 1994); Andrew Rosenheim, Obituary: Billy Martin, The Independent, Jan. 9, 1990, at 13; Newswire, L.A. Times, Sept. 21, 1986, Part 3, at 15, col. 3; Gossage Reinstated, Loses $25,000 in Pay, Chi. Trib., Sept. 19, 1986, at 5; Michael Goodwin, The Two Sides of Billy Martin: A Study in Contrast, N.Y. Times, May 6, 1985, §C, at 6, col. 1.

19. For the discussion of George S. Halas, Sr., see In re Estate of Halas, 209 Ill.App.3d 333, 568 N.E.2d 170 (1991); Estate of Halas, Sr. v. Commissioner of Internal Revenue, 94 T.C. 570 (1990); Estate of Halas v. Commissioner of Internal Revenue, 1989 WL 111305 (U.S. Tax Ct. 1989); In re Estate of Halas, 175 Ill.App.3d 180, 529 N.E.2d 768 (1988); In re Marriage of Halas, 173 Ill.App.3d 218, 527 N.E.2d 474 (1988); In re Estate of Halas, 159 Ill.App.3d 818, 512 N.E.2d 1276 (1987); Halas v. McCaskey, 104 Ill.2d 83, 470 N.E.2d 960 (1984); Halas v. Estate of Halas, 112 Ill.App.3d 940, 445 N.E.2d 1264 (1983).

20. For the discussion of Thurman Munson, see Munson v. United National Bank & Trust Co., 1983 WL 6410 (Ohio App. 1983).

21. For the discussion of Charles W. Terrell, see Terrell v. Childers, 1997 WL 305318 (N.D. Ill. 1997); Terrell v. Childers, 1997 WL 162889 (N.D. Ill. 1997); Terrell v. Childers, 1996 WL 509883 (N.D. Ill. 1996); Terrell v. Childers, 1996 WL 509882 (N.D. Ill. 1996); Terrell v. Childers, 920 F. Supp. 854 (N.D. Ill. 1996); Terrell v. Childers, 889 F. Supp. 311 (N.D. Ill. 1995); Terrell v. Childers, 1993 WL 433687 (N.D. Ill. 1993); Terrell v. Childers, 836 F. Supp. 468 (N.D. Ill. 1993).

22. For the discussion of Jose Canseco, see Dave Cunningham, Ray of Light, Orlando Sentinel, Feb. 21, 1999, at C1; Gordon Edes, Similar Cases, Different Outcome, Chi. Trib., Mar. 6, 1998, at 3; Michael Clarkson, Canseco Takes Heat for Past, Toronto Star, Feb. 7, 1998, at B16; Jose Can-psych-o?, USA Today Baseball Weekly, Nov. 12, 1997, at 3; Forget All-Stars, Now There's 'Team Tempera-mental', Sporting News, May 27, 1991, at 25.

23. For the discussion of John Montefusco, see Teddy Greenstein, Down For the Count, Chi. Trib., Feb. 13, 2000, at 1; Teddy Greenstein, Sordid Tale Leaves A Shattered Family, Chi. Trib., Feb. 13, 2000, at 8.

24. For the discussion of Darryl Strawberry, see J. A. Adande, Strawberry, Part II, Sun-Sentinel, July 3, 2002, at 1C; Strawberry Like A Cat Living on Borrowed Lives, Winnipeg Free Press, Mar. 15, 2002 (CP Wire); Jon Heyman, Straw: Jail Beats Phoenix, Newsday, Mar. 15, 2002, at A87; Strawberry Broke Rules While at Phoenix House, N.Y. Times, Mar. 14, 2002, §D, at 7, col. 4; Michael Sokolove, Observer Sport Monthly, The Observer, June 3, 2001, at 52; Squandered Promise: The Superstar Who Never Grew Up, St. Louis Post-Dispatch, Nov. 12, 2000, at B3; Richard Justice, Strawberry Out on Third Strike, Wash. Post, Feb. 29, 2000, at D1; Alan Hahn and Tom Rock, The Darryl Strawberry Chronology, Newsday, Oct. 2, 1998, at A102; The Ups and Downs of Strawberry, Daily News, Oct. 2, 1998, at 94; Strawberry to Pay Child Support, United Press Int'l, Apr. 22, 1996; Michelle Caruso, Strawberry Flat Broke, [Says] Lawyer, Daily News, Mar. 17, 1996, at 4; Marc Topkin, Straw's Back by George, St. Petersburg Times, June 23, 1995, at 1C; Thomas Stinson, A Day of Turmoil, Atlanta J. and Constitution, May 9, 1995, at 6D; Sheryl McCarthy, Abuse Is Abuse, Star or No Star, Newsday, Feb. 5, 1990, at 4; Around the Majors: Strawberry Divorce, Wash. Post, May 19, 1989, at B4.

25. For the discussion of Bobby Cox, see I. J. Rosenberg, Cox Accused of Punching Wife, Atlanta J. and Constitution, May 8, 1995, at 1A.

26. For the discussion of Luis Polonia, see George Vecsey, For Polonia, A New Leaf and Season, N.Y. Times, April 13, 1990, §A, at 23, col. 1.

27. For the discussion of Mark Whiten, see The Yanks Who Played Around, Daily News, Oct. 18, 1998, at 6; David Doege, DA Drops Sexual Assault Case Against Ex-New York Yankee, Milwaukee J. Sentinel, Sept. 10, 1997, at 1; Jack Curry, A Hearing for Whiten Is Delayed by Inquiry, N.Y. Times, July 23, 1997, §B, at 9, col. 5; Jack Curry, Yank's Whiten Arrested in Sexual Assault Case, N.Y. Times, July 22, 1997, §B, at 9, col. 5.

28. For the discussion of Hugh Casey, see Douglas Martin, Seeking the Soul of the City's Sum-mer, N.Y. Times, May 9, 1999, §14, at 1, col. 1; Bill Conlin, DiMaggio's Strange Life Mostly an Un-told Story, Pitt. Post-Gazette, Nov. 26, 1998, at D-11.

29. For the discussion of Don Larson, see Gerry Fraley, Singled Out, Dallas Morn. News, Oct. 23, 2000, at 12B.

30. For the discussion of Bucky Dent, see Dent v. Dent, 450 So.2d 327 (1984); Dent v. Dent, 438 So.2d 903 (Fla. 1983). See also Byron Rosen, Wash. Post, Aug. 2, 1979, at C8; Richard O'Connor, Bucky Dent's 15-Year Search for His Father, 68 SPORT 16 (Jan. 1979).

31. For the discussion of Jim Leyritz, see Catcher Finds It Better To Give Than Receive, USA Today Baseball Weekly, Nov. 26, 1997, at 3.

32. For this discussion, see Michael O'Keeffe, For Yanks, It's A Season to Believe, Daily News, Oct. 31, 1999, at 6.

Chapter 12 Endnotes

* Professor of Law and Associate Dean for Academic Affairs, University of Mississippi, School of Law.

1. Report: Standard bet $2,000, The Tulsa Tribune, June 27, 1989 ("Pete Rose won with the New York Yankees, lost a lot with Philadelphia and never bet on Montreal.").

2. Marianne T. Caulfield, Comment, Will It Take a Move by the New York Yankees for the Seneca Tribe to Obtain a Class III Gaming License?, 44 Cath. L. Rev. 279 (1994). Internet sources (most notably the home pages of the New York Yankees and the Webb Corporation) were very helpful throughout this chapter.

3. Thomas Gilbert, Superstars & Monopoly Wars: Nineteenth-Century Major League Baseball 10 (1995). Much of the information it this chapter also came from Neil Sullivan, The Diamond in the Bronx: Yankee Stadium and the Politics of New York (2001).

4. Gilbert, supra note 3, at 27.

5. Id. at 63.

6. Martin Donell Kohout, Hal Chase: The Defiant Life and Turbulent Times of Baseball's Biggest Crook 25 (2001), quoting Fred Lieb, The Baseball Story 159 (New York: G.P. Putnam's Sons, 1950).

7. Kohout, supra note 6, at 27.

8. Sullivan, supra note 3, at 16.

9. This information is set forth on the Yankees' web page <http://newyork.yankees.mlb.com/ NASApp/mlb/nyy/history/nyy_history_logo.jsp> (visited October 28, 2002).

10. See note 6.

11. The 1906 season also saw the Highlanders once win five consecutive double headers, going 10-0 over the course of five very busy days.

12. Kohout, supra note 6, at 195.

13. Daniel E. Ginsburg, The Fix Is In: A History of Baseball Gambling and Game Fixing Scandals 88 (1995).

14. Id.

15. Robert Lusetich, White Sox Scandal Blackened Baseball, The Australian, April 17, 2000 at 32.

16. Kohout, supra note 6, at 208–10.

17. Id. at 210.

18. Ginsburg, supra note 13, at 92.

19. Kohout, supra note 6, at 240.

20. Id. at 244.

21. Shoeless Joe Jackson is also on baseball's ineligible list. His career statistics, including a lifetime .356 batting average, would certainly justify placement in the Hall of Fame, but like Rose he

was barred due to his association with gamblers. Jackson played on the 1919 Chicago White Sox team that lost the World Series to the heavy underdog Cincinnati Reds.

When Judge Kenesaw Mountain Landis, the first commissioner of baseball, determined that Jackson and seven other players had accepted bribes to throw the series (despite an acquittal by a Chicago jury), they were forever barred from baseball and the 1919 team became known as the Chicago "Black Sox."

Jackson's supporters point out that he hit the only home run of the 1919 World Series, fielded flawlessly, and batted .375. See, e.g., Donald Gropman, Say It Ain't So, Joe (1988). Some also argue that being aware that the fix was in, Jackson asked to sit out prior to the first game, but White Sox owner Charles Comiskey refused. It seems likely, however, that Jackson's absence from the field of play would have suited the gamblers just fine. Moreover, Jackson's performance is not above all scrutiny.

If it is assumed that the White Sox did not attempt to "throw" the games that they won, we must eliminate from consideration games three, six and seven. In those games, Jackson was six for 11. Moreover, several accounts have it that the gamblers were slow in coming across with the money, so that by the end of the series (perhaps as early as game six; certainly by game eight) the Sox were no longer trying to throw the games. Jackson was six for 13 in the final three games. We might also exclude from consideration game two, which the Sox seem to have been attempting to win, probably to keep the action going for the gamblers. The Sox had more hits (10-4) and fewer errors (2-1) than the Reds in that game, but the Reds won 4-2. Jackson was 3 for 4 in that game.

That leaves in the first, fourth and fifth games as the ones that most likely were thrown. Jackson was only one for 12 in those three crucial games. The one hit was a double to short center field that came in the second inning of game four, with no one on base, and Jackson did not score. Although he was not charged with any errors, in both the fourth and the fifth game, Jackson made throws to the plate that failed to get a scoring runner out. Certainly these facts do not prove that Jackson attempted to lose games one, four, or five, but they tend to diminish the commonly asserted argument that Jackson's performance was completely above question.

22. Kohout, supra note 6, at 210.

23. The Mid-County Post, March 4–17, 1997.

24. Ginsberg, supra note 13, at 169.

25. Id. at 171, quoting Frederick Lieb, Baseball as I Have Known It (1977).

26. Id. at 172, quoting Frederick Lieb, Baseball as I Have Known It (1977).

27. Id.

28. Id. at 173.

29. See, e.g., Editorial: Deadline Is Near For The Giants, The San Francisco Chronicle, September 9, 1988.

30. Sullivan, supra note 3, at 81.

31. Id.

32. Hughes and Webb shared an interest in flying, and they often played golf together (along with Bing Crosby, Bob Hope, and the Goldwater brothers, Barry and Robert). Editorial: The passing of an era, Las Vegas Review-Journal, May 3, 2001. In fact, Webb was one of the few associates who continued to meet face-to-face with Hughes as the eccentric billionaire grew increasingly reclusive. Hughes reportedly would call Webb, give him directions like: "Go 10 miles to a dirt road, then go five miles to the top of a sand dune, then blink your lights twice." A.D. Hopkins, Man of the Years, Las Vegas Review-Journal, May 2, 1999. They would then get together and talk until the early morning hours. Webb never seemed to mind the eccentricities, perhaps because Webb did more than $1 billion worth of business with Hughes. Id.

33. Sullivan, supra note 3, at 82.

34. Del E. Webb unanimously elected posthumously to National Housing Hall of Fame, Business Wire, April 23, 1984.

35. Micky Mantle, All My Octobers: My Memories of Twelve World Series When the Yankees Ruled Baseball 221 (1995).

36. His carousing did, however, cause the FBI to keep a file on him. Sullivan, supra note 3, at 82 (noting that the FBI did not keep a similar file on Del Webb, despite his ties with organized crime).

37. Milton Richman, Today's Sport Parade, UPI Sports News, February 8, 1983.

38. Micky Mantle with Herb Gluek, 248 The Mick (1986); Jim Murray, An Autobiography 71–72 (1993). In addition, newspapers (primarily the *New York Times* and the *Los Angeles Times*) and magazines (primarily *Sports Illustrated* and *The Sporting News*) were very helpful in studying this matter.

39. Milton Richman, Today's Sport Parade, UPI Sports News, February 8, 1983.

40. Id.

41. E.g., Jack O'Connell, Record book could become Murph's turf this year, The Record, May 5, 1985 (On the firing of Yogi Berra for Billy Martin: "Boss George again revealed his football mentality.").

42. Ira Berkow, Sports of the Times; Yankee fans hostages to Steinbrenner's whims, The N.Y. Times, August 16, 1987.

43. See Jill Lieber & Craig Neff, Bad Job, Baseball, Sports Illustrated, Oct. 8, 1990, at 34, 34–41.

44. See Ronald J. Rychlak, Pete Rose, Bart Giamatti, and the Dowd Report, 68 Miss. L.J. 889 (1999) (introduction to the report, which is printed in full thereafter).

45. See Murray Chass, Steinbrenner's Control of Yanks Severed, N.Y. Times, July 31, 1990, at A1. See generally Jill Lieber & Craig Neff, Bad Job, Baseball, Sports Illustrated, Oct. 8, 1990, at 34; A Finding Based on 2 Key Premises, N.Y. Times, July 31, 1990, at B8.

46. See Maryann Hudson, Steinbrenner Lawyer Calls For Investigation, L.A. Times, Oct. 12, 1990, at C1.

47. Murray Chass, Baseball; Ex-mobster says he influenced Yankees, The N.Y. Times, July 24, 2002.

48. Mobster Kin: Yankees fix is just a big lie, N.Y. Post, July 28, 2002.

49. Chass, supra note 47.

50. Id.

51. Id.

52. Bill Hoffman, Yanks Rip Mob Claim of Fixed Ballgames, N.Y. Post, July 23, 2002.

53. Bob Hertzel, Any Pastime is Fair Game, The Record, July 23, 1993.

Chapter 13 Endnotes

* Professor of Law, The University of Montana School of Law. B.A. Yale University. J.D. University of Chicago Law School. I want to thank Sibylle Clark, Stacey Gordon, Edward LeClaire, Charlie Palmer, Chase Rosario, and Peggy Tonon for their assistance. Any errors in this chapter are solely the author's fault, and, surprisingly, not the fault of the Chicago Cubs, the author's favorite team.

1. William D. Araiza, et al., The Jurisprudence of Yogi Berra, 46 Emory L.J. 697 (1997). This "Foul Language" chapter discusses several defamation cases and a few other reported incidents of controversial speech. The chapter only reprints the allegedly defamatory statements to comment about the cases and reports in which they were discussed.

2. Parks v. Steinbrenner, 520 N.Y.S.2d 374 (N.Y.App. Div. 1987).

3. 137 S.E.2d 132 (N.C. 1964). In the 19th Century some umpires were even killed by irate players using bats. Ralph Berrier, Jr., There's Nothing Spit and Polish About Game's Past, Roanoke Times & World News, Sports, Oct. 6, 1996 at C5.

4. King v. Burris, 588 F.Supp. 1152 (D. Colo. 1997).

5. Flood v. Kuhn, 407 U.S. 258, 260–264 (1972).

6. Steve Wulf, The Man in Blue, Sports Illustrated, Aug. 3, 1987 at 12.

7. Parks v. Steinbrenner, 496 N.Y.S.2d 25 (N.Y. App. Div. 1985).

8. Dave Anderson, 50,000 Fine and Dandy, N.Y. Times, Sec. B, April 20, 1983 at 8.

9. Metropolitan Desk, Notes on People: Publishers Going to Bat for Billy Martin, N.Y. Times, Sec. C, July 24, 1980 at 17.

10. Supra note 8.

11. 816 P.2d 771 (Wyo. 1991), cert. denied, 503 U.S. 984 (1992).

12. Darryll M. Halcomb Lewis, Defamation of Sports Officials, 38 Washburn L.J. 781, 813–815 (1999).

13. Milkovich v. Lorain Journal, 497 U.S. 1 (1989).

14. Gertz v. Robert Welch, Inc. 418 U.S. 323 (1974). The U.S. Supreme Court in Curtis Publishing Co. v. Butts, 388 U.S. 130 (1967), ruled that the University of Georgia's athletic director was a public figure.

15. Paul Simon, The Silent Superstar, N.Y. Times, Sec. A, March 9, 1999 at 23 (Editorial reprinted in Joost Lenders, The Paul Simon Pages, <http://www.pspages/nl.news/pseditorial.htm>.).

16. Richard Ben Cramer, Joe DiMaggio: A Hero's Life 476 (Simon & Schuster 2000).

17. Supra note 15.

18. Mark Kriegel, DiMaggio was Perfect Fit for My Song, Simon Says, New York Daily News, Nov. 27, 1998 (reprinted in Christoffer Hansen, The Paul Simon Anthology, <http://home.c2i.net/chrhansen/index1.html>, "Resources" section).

19. Joseph Durso, Joe DiMaggio: The Last American Knight 236 (Little, Brown 1995).

20. Buzz Bissinger, The Final Days of Joe DiMaggio, Vanity Fair, Sep. 2000 at 365 (lengthy interview with Engelberg).

21. Id. at 374.

22. Financial News, Maris Family Files $1 Billion Defamation Suit Against Anheuser Busch, P.R. Newswire (Gainesville, Fla. Aug. 31, 2001) (on file with chapter author).

23. Maris v. Commr. of Internal Revenue, 1980 Westlaw 4270 (T.C. 1980).

24. Rob Rains, Mark McGwire: Home Run Hero 230 (St. Martin's 1999).

25. Maris Distrib. Co. v. Anheuser-Busch, Inc., 710 So.2d 1022 (Fla. Dist. Ct. App. 1st Dist. 1998).

26. Joe Coombs, Witnesses testify in favor of Marises, Gainesville Sun, June 7, 2001 (on file with chapter author). All of the information in the text's next paragraph comes from this article.

27. Lise Fischer, Maris-Busch ruling near, Gainesville Sun, Aug. 2, 2001 (on file with chapter author).

28. Id.

29. Lise Fisher, Maris, brewer motions denied, Gainesville Sun, Aug. 30, 2001 (on file with chapter author).

30. Judge enters final judgment in Maris Brewer Case, Dallas Morning News, 2001 Westlaw 27698241 (Sep. 7, 2001).

31. Maris Distrib. Co. v. Anheuser-Busch, Inc., et al., 2000 Westlaw 33403622 (M.D. Fla. 2000).

32. Maris Distrib. Co. v. Anheuser-Busch, Inc., et al., 2001 Westlaw 862642 (M.D. Fla. 2001), aff'd, 303 F.3d 1207 (11th Cir. 2002).

33. Steve Howe's statistics can be found at <http://www.baseball-reference.com/h/howest01.shtml>.

34. John Helyar, Lords of the Realm 498 (Villard 1994).

35. Howe v. New York Post, Inc., 1995 Westlaw 572884 (N.Y. Gen. Term), 23 Media L. Rep. 1955.

36. Larry Dougherty, Strawberry Accused of Groping, St. Petersburg Times, Sports, Aug. 12, 1998 at 4C.

37. Local Look, Ex-Wife Settles Abuse Case, Fort Lauderdale Sun-Sentinel, Local, Jan. 16, 1997 at 1B.

38. Jim Bouton, Ball Four Plus Ball Five xi (1981)(italics in original).

39. Stevenson v. Baltimore Baseball Club, Inc., et al., 243 A.2d 533 (Md. 1968).

40. Lawrence A. Israeloff, The Sports Fan v. The Sports Team Owner: Does a Franchise Prohibition of Spectators' Banners Violate the First Amendment, 24 Colum. J.L. & Soc. Probs. 419 (1991). Another article on this topic is by Robert Misey, Free Speech at the Ball Park, 3 Geo. Mason U. Civ. Rts. L.J. 227 (1993).

41. Craig Hill, What's in a word?; Appropriate v. vulgar: Major league teams split on whether 'suck' shirts acceptable in different ballparks, Tacoma News Tribune, Sports, 2002 Westlaw 3196996 (May 8, 2002).

42. Id.

43. Aubrey v. Cincinnati Reds, et. al., 841 F. Supp. 229 (S.D. Ohio 1993); Aubrey v. City of Cincinnati, 815 F.Supp. 1100 (S.D. Ohio 1993), remanded as moot, 65 F.3d 168 (6th Cir. 1995). An article inspired by the Aubrey litigation is: Gerhardt A. Gosnell II, Note, Banner Policies at Government-Owned Athletic Stadiums: The First Amendment Pitfalls, 55 Ohio St. L.J. 1143 (1994).

44. Ludtke v. Kuhn, 461 F. Supp. 86 (S.D.N.Y. 1978); Israeloff, supra note 40.

45. Burton v. Wilmington Parking Auth., 365 U.S. 715 (1961).

46. Ponce v. Basketball Fedn. Of Puerto Rico, 760 F.2d 375 (1st Cir. 1985).

47. Rendell-Baker v. Kohn, 457 U.S. 830 (1982).

48. Supra notes 40 and 43. See also Cinevision Corp. v. City of Burbank, 745 F.2d 560 (9th Cir. 1984), cert. denied, 471 U.S. 1054 (1985).

49. 789 F.Supp. 402 (D.D.C. 1992).

50. 691 F.2d 155 (3d Cir. 1982).

51. 418 U.S. 298 (1974).

52. Intl. Socy. For Krishna Consciousness, Inc. v. Lee, 505 U.S. 672 (1992).

53. See Calash v. City of Bridgeport, 788 F.2d 80 (2d Cir. 1986); Paulsen v. County of Nassau, 925 F.2d 65 (2d Cir. 1991).

54. 403 U.S. 15 (1971).

55. Gosnell, supra note 43.

56. Three interesting articles that deal with the subject of sports defamation are: Babcock, Mc-Cown, Sports and the Media, June 1, 1997, <http://www.jw.com/articles/details.cfm?articlenum= 78>; Andrew S. Craig, Comment, The Rise in Press Criticism of the Athlete and the Future of Libel Litigation Involving Athletes and the Press, 4 Seton Hall J. Sport L. 527 (1994); Christopher H. Hall, Defamation of Professional Athlete or Sports Figure, 54 A.L.R. 4th 869 (1987).

Chapter 14 Endnotes

* Charles Palmer is a Professor of Law at the Thomas M. Cooley Law School and a long-suffering Detroit Tiger fan. The author would like to thank Dirk Roskam, a recent graduate of the Thomas M. Cooley Law School, and John Michaud for their generous assistance in helping to research this chapter and Professors Mark Kende and Ernie Phillips for their helpful comments.

1. Harold Seymour et al,. Baseball: The Golden Age (July 1971).

2. Don Amore, The Nine Ways To Fix Baseball; As America's Game Enters Its Second Consecutive Season Without A Full-Time Commissioner, We Look For Answers From The Great Beyond, Statewide, April 1, 1994 at C12.

3. Information on Judge Landis can be found in the article, Ron Fimrite, His Own Biggest Fan ; Baseball's First Commissioner, Kenesaw Mountain Landis, Was Part Hero, All Ego, Sports Illustrated, July 19, 1993, at page 76.

4. Milwaukee American Assoc. v. Landis. 49 F2d 298 (N.D. Ill. 1931).

5. For more information on Larry MacPhail *see* Don Warfield, *The Roaring Redhead: Larry MacPhail, Baseball's Great Innovator* (1987).

6. Ted Curtis, *In the Best Interests of the Game: the Authority of the Commissioner of Major League Baseball,* 5 Seton Hall J. Sports L. 5 (1995). This article is a good source of information on the amendment of the Major League Agreement and the election of the new baseball commissioner.

7. See Jerome Holtzman, *The Commissioners: Baseball's Midlife Crisis,* Total Sports, June 1998.

8. Roger Kahn, *The Era 1947–1957, When the Yankees, the Giants, and the Dodgers Ruled the World,*(1993).

9. Albert B. Chandler and Vance Trimble, *Heroes, Plain Folks, and Skunks: The Life and Times of Happy Chandler* (1989).

10. Mike Shatzkin, *Ballplayers, Duke Maas to Dutch Zwilling: Baseball's Ultimate Biographical Reference* (1999).

11. See Charles O. Finley v. Kuhn, 569 F.2d 527 (7th Cir. 1978).

12. For information on Bowie Kuhn and his era as commissioner, *see* Bowie Kuhn, *Hardball: The Education of a Baseball Commissioner* (1987).

13. See Geoffrey C. Ward and Ken Burns, *Baseball* (1994); and Finley v. Kuhn, supra at 536.

14. Ludtke v. Kuhn, 461 F. Supp 86 (S.D.N.Y. 1978).

15. Jack Sands and Peter Gammons, *Coming Apart At The Seams* (1993).

16. Information on the Steinbrenner hearings was obtained from several articles in the The New York Times including articles on May 13, 1990; July 2, 1990; July 31, 1990; August 17, 1990; and June 4, 1991.

17. Finley v. Kuhn, 569 F.2d 527, 536 (7th Cir, 1978)

Chapter 15 Endnotes

* Associate Professor, Gonzaga University School of Law. I am grateful to my parents, my colleagues and my students for the encouragement they have given me; to the late C. Frank Harrigan, Syracuse attorney and baseball aficionado, who taught me much of what I know about the workings of local government; and to Gonzaga University for its support.

1. The sources I have relied on most heavily in preparing this chapter are: Oliver E. Allen, The Tiger: The Rise and Fall of Tammany Hall (1993); Eugene C. Murdock, Ban Johnson: Czar of Baseball (1982); Steven A. Reiss, Touching Base: Professional Baseball and American Culture in the Progressive Era (1980); Burt Solomon, Where They Ain't: The Fabled Life and Untimely Death of the Original Orioles, The Team that Gave Birth to Modern Baseball (1999); and Neil J. Sullivan, The Diamond in the Bronx: Yankee Stadium and the Politics of New York (2001).

2. Reiss, Touching Base, at 66.

3. Id.

4. Id., at 67.

5. Solomon, at 62.

6. Id., at 86.

7. Id., at 110.

8. Id., at 123.

9. Id.

10. Id., at 126. See also, Harvey Frommer, Primitive Baseball: The First Quarter-Century of the National Pastime (1988), at 110.

11. Edwin G. Burrows and Mike Wallace, Gotham: A History of New York City to 1898 (1999), at 1108–09.

12. In the days before consolidation, Brooklyn was the nation's 4th-largest industrial city. Id.

13. Burrows and Wallace, at 1230.

14. Solomon, Where They Ain't, at 139.

15. Id., at 140.

16. Id., at 141.

17. Id., at 134.

18. Id., at 145–146.

19. Id., at 147.

20. Id., at 154.

21. Id., at 154.

22. Id., at 180.

23. Id., at 187.

24. Murdock, Ban Johnson, at 18.

25. Id., at 30.

26. Id., at 31–41.

27. Id., at 44–47.

28. Id., at 46. Subsequently, in September 1901, the American League formally announced that it would not participate in the National Agreement. Id., at 53.

29. Id., at 45.

30. Id., at 47.

31. Reiss, Touching Base, at 69.

32. Id., at 71.

33. Murdock, Ban Johnson, at 64.

34. Id.

35. Id., citing Sporting News April 11, 18, 1903 and Sporting Life, April 11, 18, 1903.

36. Solomon, Where They Ain't, at 139–140.

37. Id., at 231; Reiss, Touching Base, at 69.

38. Sullivan, Diamond in the Bronx, at 17.

39. Id., at 18–19.

40. Id., at 23.

41. Id., at 24–25.

42. Id., at 25.

43. Id., at 30.

44. Id., at 31.

45. Id., at 32.

46. Id., at 2.

47. Id., at 1.

48. Allen, The Tiger, at 207. See also, Sullivan, Diamond in the Bronx, at 3. Murphy was an interesting character. He was the first Tammany Boss to use the power of his position to support the passage of beneficial social legislation. He also rid Tammany Hall of many men he deemed unsavory characters. One of those characters was William Devery, former Yankees owner, whom Murphy ousted from Tammany's executive committee. Allen, at 207.

Chapter 16 Endnotes

* Gregory M. Stein (gstein@utk.edu) is a Professor of Law at the University of Tennessee College of Law, where he teaches Property, Land Use Law, Land Finance Law, and Land Acquisition and Development. A New York Mets fan, Professor Stein holds an A.B. from Harvard University and a J.D. from Columbia University. He would like to thank Jeanette Kelleher, Tom Galligan, and Patrick Fiel for their helpful comments on an earlier draft, and the University of Tennessee College of Law for providing a summer research grant.

1. 74,200 See Yankees Open New Stadium, N.Y. Times, Apr. 19, 1923, at 1.

2. Neil J. Sullivan, The Diamond in the Bronx 10 (2001). This statement assumes that the actual attendance at the Yankee game was closer to 60,000, as the *New York Times* later conceded. Yankee Stadium Seats Only 62,000, N.Y. Times, May 17, 1923, at 15.

3. 74,200 See Yankees Open New Stadium, N.Y. Times, Apr. 19, 1923, at 1.

4. See Franklin P. Adams, Baseball's Sad Lexicon. Different sources give different citations for Adams' poem; it may have appeared first in the *New York Globe* on July 10, 1908, or the *New York Evening Mail* on July 18, 1910. The poem is known more commonly as "Tinker to Evers to Chance."

5. 74,200 See Yankees Open New Stadium, N.Y. Times, April 19, 1923, at 1; Harding Sees Ruth Drive Out Home Run, N.Y. Times, Apr. 25, 1923, at 17.

6. All Section headings are derived from John Kander & Fred Ebb, Theme from "New York, New York" (1977).

7. Burt Solomon, Where They Ain't: The Fabled Life and Untimely Death of the Original Baltimore Orioles, The Team that Gave Birth to Modern Baseball 229–31 (1999).

8. Steven A. Riess, Touching Base: Professional Baseball and American Culture in the Progressive Era 108–10 (rev. ed. 1999).

9. Derek Gentile, The Complete New York Yankees: The Total Encyclopedia of the Team 12 (2000). Another source recalls the clubhouse being located in centerfield. Curt Smith, Storied Stadiums: Baseball's History Through Its Ballparks 19 (2001).

10. Ray Robinson & Christopher Jennison, Yankee Stadium: 75 Years of Drama, Glamor, and Glory 1–2 (1998). See also Riess, supra note 8, at 108–10; Sullivan, supra note 2, at 17.

11. ESPN.com, The End of the Century: The most infamous moments (December 31, 1999), at http://espn.go.com/endofcentury/s/other/infamous.html (last visited Oct. 23, 2002); see also Robinson & Jennison, supra note 10, at 4.

12. Riess, supra note 8, at 122–23.

13. Id. at 127.

14. Solomon, supra note 7, at 249.

15. Gentile, supra note 9, at 14; Robinson & Jennison, supra note 10, at 166.

16. Gentile, supra note 9, at 15.

17. Lyle Spatz, Yankees Coming, Yankees Going: New York Yankee Player Transactions, 1903 Through 1999, at 38–39 (2000).

18. Sullivan, supra note 2, at 25. The sale was not announced until January 3, 1920. Id. Different sources furnish slightly different dollar figures for the Ruth sale. See, e.g., Robinson & Jennison, supra note 10, at 9 (noting a sale price of $115,000 and a $350,000 loan); Spatz, supra note 17, at 39 (noting a sale price of $125,000 and a $350,000 loan). See also Ed Linn, The Great Rivalry: The Yankees and the Red Sox, 1901–1990, at 84 (1991).

19. Tom Meany, The Yankee Story 29 (1960).

20. Yanks Lose Home at Polo Grounds, N.Y. Times, May 15, 1920, at 18.

21. The Giants apparently raised the annual rent to $100,000. Riess, supra note 8, at 129.

22. Sullivan, supra note 2, at 270. Solomon hit two singles and a double in eight at-bats, but his fielding left something to be desired. See Mose Solomon Statistics—Baseball Reference.com, at http://www.baseball-reference.com/s/solommo01.shtml (last visited Oct. 23, 2002).

23. Eviction of the Yankees, N.Y. Times, May 17, 1920, at 12. The article proceeded to note, "The game itself and the personnel of the team form the main attraction, with the field a secondary consideration." Id.

24. Hunt for Home Is Spared To Yanks, N.Y. Times, May 22, 1920, at 19.

25. League Says Yanks Shall Have A Park, N.Y. Times, Aug. 25, 1920, at 10 (noting that "[t]he owners of the Yankees believed that the league as a body should shoulder some of the great expense entailed in the erection of a park larger than any yet attempted in baseball").

26. Yankees Pick Site for New Ball Park, N.Y. Times, Jan. 30, 1921, at 1; Yankees To Build Stadium In Bronx, N.Y. Times, Feb. 6, 1921, at 20; Bill Pennington, For 75 Years, a Raucous Stage in the Bronx, N.Y. Times, Apr. 19, 1998, at I:1.

27. Yankees To Build Stadium In Bronx, N.Y. Times, Feb. 6, 1921, at 20. The Times later reported the price as $625,000. Work On Yankees' Park Starts Today, N.Y. Times, Feb. 7, 1921, at 13. Riess lists the price as $675,000. Riess, supra note 8, at 130.

28. Work On Yankees' Park Starts Today, N.Y. Times, Feb. 7, 1921, at 13; Bill Pennington, For 75 Years, a Raucous Stage in the Bronx, N.Y. Times, Apr. 19, 1998, at I:1.

29. Yankees Call for Bids on Stadium, N.Y. Times, Jan. 4, 1922, at 15 (noting that if bids "proved to be beyond the bounds of reason," the team's owners "would undoubtedly prefer to postpone the completion of the plans rather than to get what they considered the worst of it financially").

30. Riess, supra note 8, at 130.

31. Yankees To Take Title, N.Y. Times, May 15, 1921, at VIII:1.

32. Arrival of Ruth Stirs Shreveport, N.Y. Times, Mar. 7, 1921, at 13.

33. Yankees Ask for Bids on Steel Work at New Stadium, N.Y. Times, Dec. 5, 1921, at 23; Yankees Call for Bids on Stadium, N.Y. Times, Jan. 4, 1922, at 15.

34. Yanks Pick Firm To Build Stadium, N.Y. Times, Apr. 19, 1922, at 15; Gentile, supra note 9, at 36.

35. Action on Yankee Stadium Deferred, N.Y. Times, Mar. 18, 1922, at 11; Hylan Sanctions Yankee Stadium, N.Y. Times, Apr. 1, 1922, at 12.

36. Work Begins Today on Yankee Stadium, N.Y. Times, May 6, 1922, at 8.

37. Although one source states that the stadium was constructed in as little as 284 days, Robinson & Jennison, supra note 10, at 12, the dates of various New York Times articles describing the progress of the stadium project suggest that construction actually took closer to a year.

38. Yankee Field Is Given Final Touch, N.Y. Times, Nov. 28, 1922, at 26.

39. Yankees' New Park Almost Completed, N.Y. Times, Mar. 11, 1923, at I(Pt. 2):1.

40. See generally Riess, supra note 8, at 129–32.

41. Yankee Stadium to Seat 80,000 Fans, N.Y. Times, Dec. 18, 1921, at VIII:3.

42. Robinson & Jennison, supra note 10, at 13.

43. George Sullivan & John Powers, Yankees: An Illustrated History 29 (1982).

44. Robinson & Jennison, supra note 10, at 13.

45. Yankees' New Baseball Stadium As It Appears Today, N.Y. Times, Feb. 4, 1923, at I(Pt. 2):1.

46. Riess, supra note 8, at 113–17.

47. Yankee Ball Park Big Sports Arena, N.Y. Times, Aug. 30, 1922, at 11.

48. Meany, supra note 19, at 168.

49. Robinson & Jennison, supra note 10, at 24–25. Tom Meany's version of the story has an amused Landis refusing to discipline Casey at all, explaining that "Stengel is Stengel." Meany, supra note 19, at 168.

50. Dean Chadwin, Those Damn Yankees: The Secret Life of America's Greatest Franchise 85 (1999).

51. Riess, supra note 8, at 51.

52. Robinson & Jennison, supra note 10, at 26, 53.

53. Schafer v. Rickard, 229 N.Y.S. 471, 473 (N.Y. Mun. Ct. 1928).

54. Robinson & Jennison, supra note 10, at 32–35, 40.

55. Id. at 36.

56. Id. at 37–40, 48, 71.

57. Sullivan, supra note 2, at 58.

58. Meany, supra note 19, at 89.

59. Chadwin, supra note 50, at 77–78; Sullivan, supra note 2, at 61.

60. Robinson & Jennison, supra note 10, at 54–57.

61. A photo of Ruth embracing Gehrig is reproduced at Richard J. Tofel, A Legend in the Making: The New York Yankees in 1939, at 145 (2002).

62. Robinson & Jennison, supra note 10, at 53, 56; International Boxing Hall of Fame, Louis Destroys Schmeling in Rematch, at http://www.ibhof.com/ibhfhvy5.htm (last visited Oct. 23, 2002).

63. Robinson & Jennison, supra note 10, at 60–62.

64. Id. at 53, 68–69; Robinson v. Commissioner, 44 T.C. 20 (1965).

65. Sullivan, supra note 2, at 83–86. Webb and Topping bought out MacPhail for $2 million after the 1947 season. Id. at 79.

66. Id. at 83–90. The New York Times reports that the transfer of the land to the Knights of Columbus did not occur until 1957, when Cox sold it to them, while retaining the building. Murray Chass, Pope's Mass Outdrew Sports at Stadium, N.Y. Times, Mar. 3, 1971, at 36. See also Kathleen Corr, Sports Commentary: The House That Ruth Built, The House That Rice Owned, at http://www.rice.edu/ projects/thresher/issues/86/981016/Sports/Story01.html (last visited Oct. 23, 2002).

67. Sullivan, supra note 2, at 96.

68. 40,000 More Arrive For 'Witness' Rally, N.Y. Times, July 30, 1950, at 64; 60,000 'Witnesses' Open Week's Rally, N.Y. Times, July 31, 1950, at 19; 'Witnesses' Lead 3,300 Into Water, N.Y. Times, Aug. 4, 1950, at 36.

69. Robinson & Jennison, supra note 10, at 83.

70. Tiny 'City' Serves Stadium Visitors, N.Y. Times, July 31, 1950, at 19.

71. Jehovah's Witnesses—Who Are They? What Do They Believe? Their Modern Development and Growth, at http://www.watchtower.org/library/jt/article_02.htm (last visited Oct. 23, 2002).

72. Robinson & Jennison, supra note 10, at 72–77.

73. Arlene Howard with Ralph Wimbush, Elston and Me: The Story of the First Black Yankee 27–28 (2001) (biography by widow of Yankee star).

74. Id. at 27; James R. Devine, The Racial Re-Integration of Major League Baseball: A Business Rather than Moral Decision; Why Motive Matters, 11 Seton Hall J. Sport L. 1, 50–51 & note 343 (2001) (citing confidential 1946 internal report from major league baseball and noting that Yankees earned $100,000 in rent and concession fees from leases to Negro League teams playing at Yankee Stadium and minor league stadiums).

75. Howard & Wimbush, supra note 73, at 36–45.

76. John Drebinger, Larsen Beats Dodgers in Perfect Game; Yanks Lead, 3-2, on First Series No-Hitter, N.Y. Times, Oct. 9, 1956, at 1.

77. Larsen's Wife Petitions Court To Withhold His Series Share, N.Y. Times, Oct. 9, 1956, at 38.

78. Spatz, supra note 17, at 127–29 (discussing trade involving Larsen, Maris, and five other players); Robinson & Jennison, supra note 10, at 110.

79. Id.

80. Smith, supra note 9, at 266.

81. Id. at 143; Robinson & Jennison, supra note 10, at 123.

82. Jack Mann, The Decline and Fall of the New York Yankees 240–48 (1967). These figures do not include the statistics for the California Angels and the new Washington Senators, both of which joined the league in 1961. Earned run average statistics are not available prior to the 1930 season.

83. Douds v. Associated Musicians of Greater New York, 123 F. Supp. 798 (S.D.N.Y. 1954); Gentile, supra note 9, at 38.

84. Hochman v. Rosensohn, 196 N.Y.S.2d 55, 56 (N.Y. Mun. Ct. 1959).

85. Int'l Boxing Club of New York v. United States, 358 U.S. 242, 246–47, 254 (1959).

86. Morse v. Fields, 127 F. Supp. 63, 64 (S.D.N.Y. 1954). See also Sunbrock v. Commissioner, 48 T.C. 55 (1967) (finding that petitioner understated receipts from his rodeo show at Yankee Stadium).

87. Application for the Approval of a Certificate of Incorporation of New York Braves Baseball Club, Inc., 195 N.Y.S.2d 80, 83 (N.Y. Sup. Ct. 1959).

88. Robinson & Jennison, supra note 10, at 86.

89. Id. at 115.

90. Maurice Carroll, City Defers Action On Yankee Stadium As Giants Hold Out, N.Y. Times, Mar. 26, 1971, at 1.

91. Sullivan, supra note 2, at 117–18, 131–33. Sullivan points out that Lindsay, and not Burke, initiated these discussions.

92. Id. at 135–40; see also Harold C. Schonberg, The Year The Yankees Beat Lincoln Center, N.Y. Times, Mar. 14, 1971, at B13 (arguing that Lincoln Center is more valuable to city and thus more deserving recipient of capital expenditures).

93. New York Yankees, Inc. v. Tax Comm'n, 345 N.Y.S.2d 858 (N.Y. Sup. Ct. 1973).

94. Id.; Stadium Assessment Reduced, N.Y. Times, June 15, 1973, at 42.

95. Edward Ranzal, City to Buy Yankee Stadium In Move to Keep 2 Teams, N.Y. Times, Mar. 3, 1971, at 1; Five Things You May Not Know About Yankee Stadium, N.Y. Times, Apr. 19, 1998, at 39.

96. Maurice Carroll, Garelik Proposes Yanks and Football Giants Join Mets and Jets, N.Y. Times, Apr. 11, 1971, at 34.

97. Council Approves City's Plan To Try to Buy Yankee Stadium, N.Y. Times, June 5, 1971, at 57; Ronald Sullivan, Football Giants to Leave City For Jersey After 1974 Season, N.Y. Times, Aug. 27, 1971, at 1.

98. Yankee Stadium Lease Goes to Board of Estimate, N.Y. Times, Feb. 11, 1972, at 41; Ralph Blumenthal, Yankees To Stay 30 Years In Pact Approved By City, N.Y. Times, Mar. 24, 1972, at 1. I have found no reported cases or news articles discussing the resolution of the taxpayer challenge to the stadium funding. The stadium, of course, ultimately was renovated with taxpayer dollars.

99. City Acquires the Title To Yankee Stadium, N.Y. Times, Aug. 11, 1972, at 19; Haggling Is Expected In Stadium Acquisition, N.Y. Times, Aug. 16, 1972, at 28; Edward Ranzal, Yanks, City Sign 30-Year Stadium Lease, N.Y. Times, Aug. 17, 1972, at 43.

100. Steve Cady, Demolition Teams Take Yanks' Place at Stadium, N.Y. Times, Sept. 30, 1973, at V:2.

101. Id.; Murray Schumach, $27-Million Face-Lifting of Yankee Stadium Starts, N.Y. Times, Oct. 2, 1973, at 51.

102. Edward Ranzal, Cost of Renovation At Yankee Stadium Climbs $7 Million, N.Y. Times, Apr. 6, 1973, at 1; Murray Schumach, $27-Million Face-Lifting of Yankee Stadium Starts, N.Y. Times, Oct. 2, 1973, at 51; Edward Ranzal, Estimate For Work At Yankee Stadium Up to $49.9 Million, Nov. 15, 1973, at 1; John L. Hess, Stadium's Costs Now Seen As Loss, N.Y. Times, Apr. 15, 1976, at 1.

103. Peter Kihss, Stadium Project Put At $57-Million, N.Y. Times, July 17, 1975, at 33; Martin Waldron, Yanks Get Windfall As City Shifts Plans, N.Y. Times, Dec. 1, 1975, at 1; John L. Hess, Memo Indicates City Obscured Stadium's High Cost, N.Y. Times, Feb. 3, 1976, at 63; John L. Hess, Stadium's Costs Now Seen As Loss, N.Y. Times, Apr. 15, 1976, at 1 (emphasis added).

104. Nab-Tern Constructors v. City of New York, 507 N.Y.S.2d 146 (N.Y. App. Div.), on remand from Corinno Civetta Constr. Corp. v. City of New York, 493 N.E.2d 905 (N.Y. 1986).

105. John L. Hess, Stadium's Costs Now Seen As Loss, N.Y. Times, Apr. 15, 1976, at 1.

106. Philip Bashe, Dog Days: The New York Yankees' Fall from Grace and Return to Glory, 1964–1976, at 328 (1994); Joseph Durso, Yankee Stadium, Old and New: Remodeled Structure To Open on Thursday, N.Y. Times, Apr. 11, 1976, at V:1; Joseph Durso, Yankees Win First Game in Rebuilt Stadium, N.Y. Times, Apr. 16, 1976, at 1.

107. Sullivan, supra note 2, at 143.

108. Id. at 145–46.

109. Robinson & Jennison, supra note 10, at 134–46; Bashe, supra note 106, at 352–55; Linn, supra note 18, at 11.

110. Ludtke v. Kuhn, 461 F. Supp. 86 (S.D.N.Y. 1978); MacLean v. First Northwest Indus. of America, Inc., 600 P.2d 1027, 1031 (Wash. Ct. App. 1979); Smith v. McGuire, 429 N.Y.S.2d 870 (N.Y. App. Div. 1980). See also 1978 N.Y. Op. Atty. Gen. 25, 1978 WL 27494, at *2 (rejecting "ethnic night" promotions at racetrack).

111. The Yankees had the best record in the American League in 1994, but a strike ended the season early and pre-empted the World Series.

112. GSGSB, Inc. v. New York Yankees, 1996 WL 456044 (S.D.N.Y. 1996) (resolving claim by architect), aff'd, 122 F.3d 1056 (2d Cir. 1997) (unpublished); Lehrer McGovern Bovis, Inc. v. New York Yankees, 615 N.Y.S.2d 31 (N.Y. App. Div. 1994) (reversing trial court's granting of defendant's motion for summary judgment in claim by construction manager, without reaching merits); New York Yankees v. Adler, 553 N.Y.S.2d 327 (N.Y. App. Div. 1990) (discussing significance of procedural delay only and not addressing merits of claim concerning advertisements).

113. City of New York v. New York Yankees, 458 N.Y.S.2d 486, 490 (N.Y. Sup. Ct. 1983).

114. Church to Pay for Pope To Use City's Stadiums, N.Y. Times, Sept. 22, 1979, at 23; Alan Richman, 80,000 Gather in Yankee Stadium for Historic Papal Mass, Oct. 3, 1979, at B3.

115. Robinson & Jennison, supra note 10, at 86; Bill Pennington, For 75 Years, a Raucous Stage in the Bronx, N.Y. Times, Apr. 19, 1998, at I:1; Kevin Reuther, Queer Rights Are Human Rights: Thoughts From the Back of a Cab, 8 Harv. Hum. Rts. J. 265, 265 (1995).

116. Chadwin, supra note 50, at 78.

117. In the Matter of Petition for Naturalization of Pruna, 286 F. Supp. 861 (D.P.R. 1968).

118. People v. O'Grady, 667 N.Y.S.2d 895 (N.Y. Crim. Ct. 1997); Chadwin, supra note 50, at 81.

119. O'Grady, 667 N.Y.S.2d at 897; Chadwin, supra note 50, at 81.

120. Lawrence A. Israeloff, The Sports Fan v. The Sports Team Owner: Does A Franchise's Prohibition of Spectators' Banners Violate the First Amendment?, 24 Colum. J.L. & Soc. Probs. 419, 420–21 (1991); Karen Martin Dean, Can The NBA Punish Dennis Rodman? An Analysis of First Amendment Rights in Professional Basketball, 23 Vt. L. Rev. 157, 157–58 (1998).

121. Joseph v. New York Yankees P'ship, 2000 WL 1559015, at *4 (S.D.N.Y. 2000).

122. New York Yankees Underpaid City, 8 City L., No. 3, at 66 (May/June 2002); Turner v. Hillsborough County Aviation Auth., 739 So. 2d 175 (Fla. Ct. App. 1999), aff'd sub nom. Fuchs v. Robbins, 818 So. 2d 460 (Fla. 2002).

123. Chadwin, supra note 50, at 7; Smith, supra note 9, at 496–97; Baseball Almanac—Box Score of Perfect Game by David Wells, at http://baseball-almanac.com/boxscore/05171998.shtml (last visited Oct. 23, 2002); Baseball Almanac—Box Score of Perfect Game by David Cone, at http://baseball-almanac.com/boxscore/07181999.shtml (last visited Oct. 23, 2002).

124. Robert D. McFadden, In a Stadium of Heroes, Prayers for the Fallen and Solace for Those Left Behind, N.Y. Times, Sept. 24, 2001, at B7; Margaret Ramirez & Bobby Cuza, United in Tears, Prayer, Thousands Join Yankee Stadium Interfaith Service, Newsday, Sept. 24, 2001, at A3; Al Baker, Precautions Turn House That Ruth Built Into the Fortress That Bush Visited, N.Y. Times, Oct. 31, 2001, at B5.

125. Yankee Stadium Repairs To Be Performed by City, N.Y. Times, Mar. 9, 1979, at A22; E.J. Dionne, Estimate Board Votes An Engineering Study For Yankee Stadium, N.Y. Times, Aug. 17, 1979, at B4.

126. Randy Kennedy, Yankee Stadium Closed as Beam Falls Onto Seats, N.Y. Times, Apr. 14, 1998, at A1; Buster Olney, Yankees' Home Schedule Is Disrupted by an Accident, N.Y. Times, Apr. 14, 1998, at C1; David Rohde, Bronx Cheer Unleashed In Stadium Environs, N.Y. Times, Apr. 14, 1998, at C3; Murray Chass, Beam May Be The Leverage, N.Y. Times, Apr. 14, 1998, at C1; Bill Pennington, For 75 Years, a Raucous Stage in the Bronx, N.Y. Times, Apr. 19, 1998, at I:1.

127. Randy Kennedy, Yankee Stadium Closed as Beam Falls Onto Seats, N.Y. Times, Apr. 14, 1998, at A1; Buster Olney, Yankees' Home Schedule Is Disrupted by an Accident, N.Y. Times, Apr. 14, 1998, at C1; David Rohde, Bronx Cheer Unleashed In Stadium Environs, N.Y. Times, Apr. 14, 1998, at C3; Murray Chass, Beam May Be The Leverage, N.Y. Times, Apr. 14, 1998, at C1; Bill Pennington, For 75 Years, a Raucous Stage in the Bronx, N.Y. Times, Apr. 19, 1998, at I:1.

128. John L. Wodatch, Jr., Enforcing the ADA: Looking Back on a Decade of Progress, ALI-ABA Program on Legal Problems of Museum Administration 229, 249 (2001).

129. S.L. Bernstein et al., Impact of Yankee Stadium Bat Day on Blunt Trauma in Northern New York City, 23 Annals of Emergency Medicine 555 (1994). The study did find a correlation between daily temperature and the incidence of bat injury, suggesting, perhaps, that the event would best be held in April or September.

130. Ortiz v. New York City Hous. Auth., 22 F. Supp. 2d 15, 35 (E.D.N.Y. 1998) (rejecting defendant's request for new trial).

131. Sullivan, supra note 2, at 176–77.

132. Id. at 177.

133. Id. at 185.

134. Jennifer Steinhauer & Richard Sandomir, In Bottom of 9th, Giuliani Presents Deal on Stadiums, N.Y. Times, Dec. 29, 2001, at A1; Jennifer Steinhauer, Mayor Says There's No Money To Build 2 Baseball Stadiums, N.Y. Times, Jan. 8, 2002, at B3.

Chapter 17 Endnotes

* Rebecca M. Bratspies (rbratspi@uidaho.edu) is an Associate Professor of Law at the University of Idaho (Moscow), where she teaches Administrative Law, Environmental Law, and Property. A New York Mets fan, Professor Bratspies holds a B.A. from Wesleyan University and a J.D. from the University of Pennsylvania. She would like to thank her grandfather Ben Bratspies for taking her to her first baseball game, her father Jeffrey Bratspies for buying her a baseball mitt, and B. Allen Schulz for reminding her how much she loves the game.

1. Linda Kittel, What Baseball Tells Us About Love, in Diamond's Are a Girl's Best Friend: Women Writers on Baseball (Elinor Nauen, ed. 1993).

2. Whitey Ford, quoted in Paul Mulshine, The New Jersey Giants? We're bigger than that, The Newark Star-Ledger (April 16, 2000)

3. In 1954, when the St Louis Browns moved to Baltimore, they decided to become the Baltimore Orioles. Today, that choice would undoubtably have sparked a whole series of lawsuits à la the Indianapolis Colts.

4. City of New York v. New York Yankees, 458 N.Y.S.2d 486, 490, 117 Misc.2d 332, 336 (1983).

5. New York City v. New York Jets Football Club, Inc., 394 N.Y.S.2d 799, 90 Misc.2d 311 (1977).

6. Id.

7. The Council of the City of New York v. Giuliani, 248 A.D. 1, 3679 N.Y.S.2d 14, 15 (1998).

8. See, e.g., Karen Friefeld, Safe at Home, Newsday, April 10, 1996; Bob Kappstatter, Keep Yanks in the Bronx, New York Daily News, July 16, 1998.

9. Luke Cyphers, Boss Hog Steinbrenner Wants Stadium on His Own Terms, New York Daily News (February 28, 1999).

10. Bob Kappstatter, Keep Yanks in the Bronx, New York Daily News, July 16, 1998 (quoting Geraldine Ferraro).

11. New York State Fan Protection Act, A.B. 684, 220th Gen. Assembly, 1997–1998 Reg. Sess. (1997). In 1996, the Senate Judiciary Committee held hearings on a proposed federal Sports Fan Protection Act.

12. Statistics available at http://www.baseball-reference.com/teams/NYY/attend.shtml.

13. Andrew D. Baharlias,...YES, I THINK THE YANKEES MIGHT SUE IF WE NAMED OUR POPCORN 'YANKEES TOFFEE CRUNCH'. A COMPREHENSIVE LOOK AT TRADEMARK IN-FRINGEMENT DEFENSES IN THE CONTEXT OF THE PROFESSIONAL AND COLLEGIATE SPORTS INDUSTRY, 8 Seton Hall J. Sport L. 99, n. 124 (1998).

14. Id.

15. Baseballs Antitrust Immunity: Hearing Before the Subcomm. on Anti-Trust, Monopolies and Business Rights of the Senate Comm. on the Judiciary, 102d Cong. 110 (1992) (statement of Allan H. Selig, Owner, Milwaukee Brewers Baseball Club).

16. Hearing Before the Subcomm. on Econ. and Commercial Law of the House Comm. on the Judiciary, 103d Cong. 49 (1993) (statement of Allan H. Bud Selig, Chairman, Executive Council of Major League Baseball and President, Milwaukee Brewers Baseball Club).

17. See Mark Maske, Brewers' Possible Relocation May Aid N. Virginia Cause, Washington Post, Jun. 18, 1996, at E5.

18. See Bob Harig, Tampa Bay's Swings And Misses...Again, St. Petersburg Times, June 10, 1992, at 3A.

19. See Sen. Connie Mack, Bring Free-Market System Back...Should Congress Revoke Base-ball's Antitrust Exemption; Commentary, USA Today, December 10, 1992, at 4C.

20. Metropolitan Sports Facilities Comm'n v. Minnesota Twins Partnership, 638 N.W.2d 214, 223 (Minn.App. Jan 22, 2002).

21. Mayor and City Council of Baltimore v. Baltimore Football Club Inc., 624 F. Supp. 278 (D.Md.,1985); City of Oakland v. Oakland Raiders, 32 Cal.3d 60, 183 Cal.Rptr. 673, 646 P.2d 835 (1982)(en banc).

22. Mayor and City Council of Baltimore v. Baltimore Football Club, Inc., 624 F. Supp. 278 (1986).

23. An Act to Create the New York Sports Facilities Authority, 2001 NY A.B. 1316, 2001–2002 Regular Session, available on Westlaw.

24. Major League Baseball Rules, reprinted in Paul C. Weiler and Gary R. Roberts, Statutory and Documentary Supplement to Sports and the Law, Text, Cases and Problems, 2d Ed. (1998).

25. There are 29 NBA teams, 27 NHL teams, 30 major league baseball teams and 32 NFL franchises.

26. See, Flood v. Kuhn, 407 U.S. 258, 92 S. Ct. 2099 (1972); Toolson v. New York Yankees, Inc., 346 U.S. 356 (1953); Federal Baseball Club v. National League, 259 U.S. 200 (1922).

27. Piazza v. Major League Baseball, 831 F. Supp. 420 (E.D. Pa. 1993).

28. Butterworth v. National League of Prof'l Baseball Clubs, 644 So. 2d 1021 (Fla. 1994).

29. 726 F.2d 1381 (9th Cir.), cert. denied, 105 S. Ct. 397 (1984).

30. Sullivan v. National Football League, 34 F.3d 1091 (1994).

31. Finley v. Kuhn, 569 F.2d 527 (7th Cir.), cert. denied 436 U.S. 876 (1978); Professional Base-ball Sch. & Clubs, Inc. v. Kuhn, 693 F.2d 1085 (11th Cir. 1982).

32. Richard Aregood quoted in: Allen Barra, Yankee Stay Home, available at http://www.newyorkmetro.com/nymetro/news/sports/features/2860/index.html.

33. Indianapolis Colts v. Mayor & City Council of Baltimore, 733 F.2d 484, 741 F.2d 954 (1984), 775 F.2d 177 (7th Cir.1985).

34. See House Judiciary Committee Holds Hearing on Legislation Dealing with the Antitrust Implications of Sports Franchise Relocation, February 6, 1996, 1996 WL 56230.

35. Major League Baseball Properties, Inc. v. Sed Non Olet Denarius, Ltd., 817 F. Supp. 1103 (S.D.N.Y. 1993) (finding no likelihood of confusion and therefore no trademark infringement); vacated per settlement, 859 F. Supp. 80 (S.D.N.Y. 1994).

36. New Jerseyans Supportive of Yankees Moving Across the Bridge As Long As they Pay Their Own Toll, Star Ledger/Eagleton-Rutgers Poll, September 27, 1998 (reporting that only 15% of New Jersey residents would support a Yankees move to New Jersey if tax dollars were needed to build a new stadium).

Chapter 18 Endnotes

* Ed Edmonds, Director of the Law Library and Professor of Law, University of St. Thomas School of Law, Minneapolis, Minnesota. Professor Edmonds holds a B.A. from the University of Notre Dame, an M.L.S. from the University of Maryland, and a J.D. from the University of Toledo. Professor Edmonds acknowledges the support of research assistant Matt Frerichs and Earl Toolson's brother Bill Toolson and son Pete Toolson.

1. The cases creating baseball's Antitrust Exemption are Federal Baseball v. National League, 259 U.S. 200 (1922), Toolson v. New York Yankees, Inc., 346 U.S. 356 (1953), Flood v. Kuhn, 407 U.S. 258 (1972).

2. 259 U.S. 200 (1922).

3. 346 U.S. 356 (1953).

4. 407 U.S. 258 (1972).

5. Lee Lowenfish, The Imperfect Diamond: A History of Baseball's Labor Wars 16 (rev. ed. 1991).

6. Id. at 60. See also Robert F. Burk, Never Just a Game: Players, Owners, & American Baseball to 1920 (1994).

7. 202 Pa. 210, 51 A. 973 (1902).

8. Id. at 973.

9. Id. at 974.

10. Lowenfish, supra note 5, at 68–69.

11. Id. at 70.

12. For the early history of the Yankees, see Frank Graham, The New York Yankees: An Informal History (1943). Graham's book, one of a series of team histories issued by G.P. Putnam's Sons, was recently reissued by the Southern Illinois University Press.

13. In writing this section, I relied on Gary Hailey, *Anatomy of a Murder: The Federal League and the Courts*, The National Pastime 62 (1985).

14. Lowenfish, supra note 5, at 88–90.

15. 269 F. 681, 50 App. D.C. 165 (Ct. App. D.C. 1920).

16. 269 F. at 685, 50 App. D.C. at 168–169.

17. 259 U.S. 200 (1922).

18. Id. at 208–209.

19. For an excellent history of the 1919 series and subsequent trial, see Eliot Asinof, Eight Men Out (1963).

20. For this section, I relied primarily on Graham, supra note 12.

21. In writing this section, I relied on Mike Sowell, The Pitch That Killed: Carl Mays, Ray Chapman and the Pennant Race of 1920 (1989) and American League Baseball Club of New York v. Johnson, 109 Misc. 138, 179 N.Y.S. 498 (1919).

22. Sowell, supra note 21, at 40.

23. Id.

24. Id. at 41.

25. Id. at 45.

26. *Johnson*, 109 Misc. at 142–143, 179 N.Y.S. at 501.

27. Id. 109 Misc. at 140, 179 N.Y.S. at 499–500.

28. Id. at 141–142, 179 N.Y.S. at 500–501.

29. Id. at 143, 179 N.Y.S. at 500.

30. Id. at 144, 179 N.Y.S. at 501–502.

31. Id. at 148, 179 N.Y.S. at 504.

32. Id. at 149, 179 N.Y.S. at 504.

33. Id. at 150, 179 N.Y.S. at 505.

34. Id. at 152, 179 N.Y.S. at 506.

35. Sowell, supra note 21, at 56.

36. In writing this section, I relied upon Marshall Smelser, The Life That Ruth Built: A Biography (1975). I spent three semesters as an undergraduate in Professor Smelser's history classes at the University of Notre Dame.

37. Id. at 131.

38. In writing this section, I relied on Richard Ben Cramer, Joe DiMaggio: The Hero's Life (2000).

39. In writing this section, I primarily used the account of Danny Gardella's career and lawsuit as discussed in Lowenfish, supra note 5.

40. American League Baseball Club of New York, Inc. v. Pasquel, 187 Misc. 230, 63 N.Y.S.2d 537, and 188 Misc. 102, 66 N.Y.S.2d 743 (1946).

41. Gardella v. Chandler, 172 F.2d 402 (2d Cir. 1949).

42. 172 F.2d 408 at 408–409.

43. For my discussion of the Toolson case, I have talked with Earl Toolson's brother Bill Toolson and son Pete Toolson about his career. My interest in seeking out family members was to learn more about the case and to resolve an issue raised by the record of his career contained on his official card housed at the Baseball Hall of Fame Library. The card showed that Earl Toolson was a member of the Boston organization for a total of seven years before his trade to the Yankees. During that time, he played for five seasons in the minors and served two years in the military. Also, contrary to nearly every account of his case, he played in the Pacific Coast League for two years after he was supposedly blacklisted for his refusal to report to Binghamton.

44. For a discussion of Greensboro and all other minor league teams in North Carolina, see J. Chris Holaday, Professional Baseball in North Carolina: An Illustrated City-by-City History, 1901–1996.

45. Id. at 77.

46. See http://www.greensborobats.com/history.html.

47. 101 F. Supp. 93 (S.D. Cal. 1951).

48. Id. at 94.

49. Id.

50. Id. at 94–95.

51. 200 F.2d 198 (9th Cir. 1952).

52. 202 F.2d 428 (6th Cir. 1953).

53. 202 F.2d 413 (6th Cir. 1953).

54. Toolson v. New York Yankees, Inc., 346 U.S. 357 (1953).

55. Id. at 357.

56. Id.

57. Id.

58. For this section, I relied on Robert W. Creamer, Stengel: His Life and Times (1984). For a text of Stengel's testimony, see Spencer Weber Waller, Neil B. Cohen, and Paul Finkelman,, editors, Baseball and the American Legal Mind 103–116 (1995). An edited version is available in Miro Weinberger & Dan Riley, The Yankees Reader 141–144 (1991).

59. See also Mickey Mantle & Mickey Herskowitz, All My Octobers: My Memories of Twelve World Series When the Yankees Ruled Baseball 97 (1994).

60. Flood v. Kuhn, 309 F. Supp. 793, 796 (S.D.N.Y. 1970).

61. Flood v. Kuhn, 312 F. Supp. 404 (S.D.N.Y. 1970).

62. Id. at 408.

63. Id. at 410.

64. Id. at 411.

65. Id.

66. Flood v. Kuhn, 316 F. Supp. 271 (S.D.N.Y. 1970).

67. Flood v. Kuhn, 443 F.2d 264 (2d Cir. 1971).

68. Flood v. Kuhn, 407 U.S. 258 (1972).

69. Id. at 282–283.

70. Id. at 286.

71. For this section, I relied on Robert F. Burk's account for Much More Than a Game: Players, Owners, & American Baseball Since 1921 (2001).

72. For a discussion of events from Don Drysdale's perspective, see Don Drysdale & Bob Verdi, Once a Bum, Always a Dodger: My Life in Baseball from Brooklyn to Los Angeles (1990), pp. 123–138.

73. Roger I. Abrams, The Money Pitch: Baseball Free Agency and Salary Arbitration, (2000) pp. 28–29.

74. Drysdale, supra note 72, at 126.

75. Id. at 129–130.

76. Id. at 130.

77. Collective Bargaining Agreement, Article VI(F)(12).

78. Id.

79. For this section, I relied on numerous newspaper articles obtained from LexisNexis and Westlaw concerning specific arbitration hearings. For helpful information on the Internet consult Dave Pappas' Business of Baseball information on arbitration at http://roadsidephotos.com/baseball/data.htm.

80. Ira Berkow, Steinbrenner: I'm Like Archie Bunker, N.Y. Times, Sept. 20, 1981, § 5, at 1.

81. Id.

82. Murray Chass, Brown of Yankees Loses Pay Case, Seeks a Trade, N.Y. Times, Feb. 23, 1982, § B, at 5.

83. Davis a Loser in Arbitration, N.Y. Times., § 5, at 11.

84. Id.

85. Murray Chass, Revering Loses Arbitration Bid for Higher Pay Than $250,000, N.Y. Times, Feb. 19, 1982, § A, at 24.

86. Id.

87. See Murray Chass, Mattingly Wins 1.975 Million in Arbitration, N.Y. Times, Feb. 18, 1987, Ross Newhan, L.A. Times, Feb. 18, 1987.

88. Mattingly Wins Record Salary, Chi. Trib., Feb. 18, 1987, C1.

89. Id.

90. Id.

91. Id.

92. Marty Noble, Newsday, Feb. 1, 1988, Murray Chass, New York Times, Feb. 11, 1988, L.A. Times, Feb. 11, 1988.

93. Bob Klapisch, Howe 'Bout That: Lefty's Back Yanks' Wetteland, Williams In Fold, North. N.J. Record, Feb. 14, 1996.

94. Steinbrenner Can't Stand to Lose, Even If the Winners Are His Own Players, Milw. J. & Sentinel, Feb. 28, 1999.

95. For my discussion of the Maris family antitrust suits against Anheuser-Busch, I relied on published newspaper articles in LexisNexis and Westlaw and articles available on the Internet. The most helpful source was The Gainesville Sun. Published decisions involving the suit are Maris Distributing Co. v. Anheuser-Busch, Inc., No. 5:97CV15-C-10C, 2000 WL 33403622 & 2001 WL 862642, aff'd, 302 F.3d 1207 (11th Cir. 2002).

96. For my discussion of the Cablevision-Yankees & Entertainment Sports Network controversy, I relied on published newspaper articles in LexisNexis and Westlaw and articles available on the Internet. The most helpful sources were the N.Y. Post, N.Y. Daily News, & the N.Y. Times.

Chapter 19 Endnotes

* The John W. and Ruth H. Turnage Professor of Law at Wake Forest University School of Law. The author gratefully acknowledges the research assistance of Nancy Ladson, Jeff Lepchenske and Paul McNamara. The author also wishes to thank Dean Robert K. Walsh and Wake Forest University for providing financial support for this project.

1. Joseph v. New York Yankees Partnership, 2000 WL 1559019, S.D.N.Y.

2. David L. Lewis, Yanks Official in Hot Water, San Francisco Examiner, July 18, 1994, at C-5.

3. Id.

4. Dean Chadwin, Those Damn Yankees: The Secret Life of America's Greatest Franchise 134 (1999).

5. Paul H. Johnson, Racism in Ruth's House, The Record, April 7, 2002, at 101.

6. Jules Tygiel, Baseball's Great Experiment 13 (1983).

7. Mark Ribowsky, A Complete History of the Negro Leagues 1884 to 1955, 13 (1995); Tygiel, supra note 6, at 13.

8. Ribowsky, supra note 7, at 31.

9. Id. at 32.

10. Id. at 30.

11. Tygiel, supra note 6, at 30.

12. John O. Calmore, Close Encounters of the Racial Kind: Pedagogical Reflections and Seminar Conversations, 31 U.S. F. L. Rev. 903 (1997).

13. Barbara J. Flagg, "Was Blind, But Now I See," White Race Consciousness and the Requirement of Discriminatory Intent, 91 Mich. L. Rev. 953 (1993).

14. Ribowsky, supra note 7, at xiii.

15. Tygiel, supra note 6, at 30.

16. See John C. Calmore, Race/ism Lost and Found: The Fair Housing Act at Thirty, 52 U. Miami L. Rev. 1067, 1100 (1998).

17. Tygiel, supra note 6, at 33.

18. Id. at 34.

19. Larry Moffi & Jonathan Kronstadt, Crossing the Line: Black Major Leaguers, 1947–1959, 6 (1994).

20. Tygiel, supra note 6, at 16–17.

21. Id. at 17.

22. Id. at 25.

23. Id. at 25.

24. Id. at 21.

25. Mary L. Dudziak, Desegregation as a Cold War Imperative, 41 Stan. L. Rev. 61, 66–67 (1988).

26. Harvey Frommer, Rickey and Robinson 103 (1982).

27. J. Gordon Hylton, Essay: American Civil Rights Law and the Legacy of Jackie Robinson, 8 Marq. Sports L.J. 387, 396 (1998).

28. Morroe Berger, The New York State Law Against Discrimination: Operation and Administration, 35 Cornell Law Quarterly 747, 750 (1950).

29. Tygiel, supra note 6, at 35.

30. Hylton, supra note 27, at 393.

31. Donn Rogosin, Invisible Men, Life in Baseball's Negro Leagues 189 (1983).

32. James R. Devine, The Past As Moral Guide to the Present: The Parallel Between Martin Luther King, Jr.'s Elements of A Nonviolent Civil Rights Campaign and Jackie Robinson's Entry Onto the Brooklyn Dodgers, 3 Vill. Sports & Ent. L.J. 489, 517 n. 130 (1996).

33. Peter Dreier, Jackie Robinson's Legacy: Baseball, Race, and Politics, in Baseball and the American Dream (Elias ed. 2001).

34. Tygiel, supra note 6, at 294.

35. Id. at 295.

36. Richard Crepeau, The Jake Powell Incident and the Press: A Study in Black and White, Baseball History 32 (Summer 1986).

37. Id. at 32.

38. Paul Finkelman, Baseball and the Rule of Law, 46 Clev. St. L. Rev. 239 (1998).

39. Crepeau, supra note 36, at 36.

40. Id. at 36.

41. Id. at 37.

42. Id. at 38.

43. Rogosin, supra note 31, at 131.

44. Crepeau, supra note 36, at 43.

45. Id. at 38.

46. Rogosin, supra note 31, at 192.

47. Frommer, supra note 26, at 103–104.

48. Id. at 104.

49. Tygiel, supra note 6, at 82.

50. Id. at 83.

51. Rogosian, supra note 31, at 201.

52. John Tullius, I'd Rather Be a Yankee 277 (1986).

53. Id. at 140.

54. Tygiel, supra note 6, at 244–45.

55. Peter Golenbock, Dynasty: The New York Yankees 1949–1964, 139 (1975).

56. David Halberstam, October 1964, 231 (1994).

57. Id. at 231.

58. Golenbock, supra note 55, at 139.

59. Id. at 140

60. Arlene Howard with Ralph Wimbish, Elston and Me 28 (2001).

61. Id.

62. Id.

63. Id.

64. Golenbock, supra note 55, 141.

65. Samuel O. Regalado, Viva Baseball! Latin Major Leaguers and Their Special Hunger 74 (1998).

66. Moffi & Kronstadt, supra note 19, at 8.

67. Regalado, supra note 65, at 75.

68. Golenbock, supra note 55, at 140.

69. Chadwin, supra note 4, at 134.

70. Golenbock, supra note 55, 141.

71. Halberstam, supra note 56, at 234.

72. Lawrence M. Kahn, Discrimination in Professional Sports: A Survey of the Literature, 44 Ind. & Labor Rel. Rev. 395, 397 (1991).

73. Jonathan L. Entin, Book Review, Baseball and Civil Rights Down on the Farm, 35 Tulsa L.J. 317, 319 (2000).

74. Finkelman, supra note 38, at 251.

75. Id. at 250.

76. Id. at 253.

77. Dreier, supra note 33, at 47.

78. Chadwin, supra note 4, at 137–43.

79. See Samuel O. Regalado, Sammy Sosa Meets Horatio Alger, in Elias, supra note 33, at 71.

80. See George McGlynn, *Beyond the Dougout*, in Elias, supra note 33, at 187.

81. Tygiel, supra note 6, at 9.

Chapter 20 Endnotes

* Professor, Georgia State University College of Law, Atlanta, Georgia. Thanks to Susan Seabury and Lee Shellhouse for their help.

1. *Compania General de Tabacos de Filipinas v. Collector of Internal Revenue*, 275 U.S. 87 (1927) (Holmes, J., dissenting).

2. In this article, the Internal Revenue Code, found in Title 26 of the United States Code, is referred to as "I.R.C." Individual sections of the I.R.C. will be preceded by "I.R.C."

3. *Sports: American League Notes*, 1996 WL 11289443, Milwaukee Journal Sentinel (September 5, 1996).

4. Catherine Valenti, *Famous Tax Slackers: Some Celebrities Who Fought the Losing Battle with the Tax Man*, ABCNEWS.COM (April 15, 2002).

5. 41 T.C. Memo (CCH) 127 (1980). The remainder of the *Maris* discussion may be found throughout the cited case.

6. 1979 WL 30150 (N.Y. Dept. Tax. Fin. 1997). The remainder of the *White* discussion may be found throughout the cited case.

7. 1987 WL 60396 (NY. Dept. Tax. Fin.1987). The remainder of the King discussion may be found throughout the cited case.

8. 61 T.C. Memo (CCH) 2442 (1991). The remainder of the *Pries* discussion may be found throughout the cited case.

9. 83 N.Y.S.2d 805 (1994). The remainder of the case discussion may be found throughout the cited case.

10. 807. F2d 1306 (6th Cir. 1986). The remainder of the case discussion may be found throughout the cited case.

Chapter 21 Endnotes

* Associate Professor of Law, Washburn University School of Law. B.A. 1990, Harvard University; J.D. 1995, Duke University School of Law. Many fans shared ideas for this chapter, including most notably Lincoln Mitchell and Mike Laskawy. Most importantly, I would like to thank Jenny Orth for her magnificent research assistance.

1. Alan M. Klein, Baseball on the Border 99 (1997).

2. Bill Madden, Acceptance Was a Long Time Coming, Daily News, May 23, 1999, at 99.

3. More Than 26 Percent of Major League Players Born Outside the U.S., Bus. Wire, Apr. 4, 2002.

4. Dean Chadwin, Those Damn Yankees 73 (1999).

5. Stephen Cannella et al., Saving Baseball: And While We're at It..., Sports Illustrated, Aug. 5, 2002, at 44, 46.

6. Arturo J. Marcano & David P. Fidler, The Globalization of Baseball: Major League Baseball and the Mistreatment of Latin American Baseball Talent, 6 Ind. J. Global Legal Stud. 511, 551 (1999).

7. Michael M. Oleksak & Mary Adams Oleksak, Beisbol: Latin Americans and the Grand Old Game 186 (1991) (quoting Ramon Naranjo).

8. Angel Vargas, The Globalization of Baseball: A Latin American Perspective, 8 Ind. J. Global Legal Stud. 21, 31 n.21 (2000).

9. Ray Robinson & Christopher Jennison, Pennants and Pinstripes: The New York Yankees 1903–2002, at 84; Ron Bush, Sewanee Celebrates 1899 Feat, Chattanooga Times, Oct. 7, 1999, at D5; Patrick Reusse, It's That Old Familial Feeling, Minneapolis Star Trib., Sept. 29, 1991, at 22C.

10. Richard Ben Cramer, Joe DiMaggio: The Hero's Life 218–19, 226 (2000); Chandler Bars Major Leaguers from Playing in Cuban Circuit, N.Y. Times, Aug. 15, 1947, at 20; John Drebinger, M'Phail Reveals Big Yank Program, N.Y. Times, Jan. 8, 1946, at 19.

11. Pedro A. Malavet, Puerto Rico: Cultural Nation, American Colony, 6 Mich. J. Race & L. 1, 2–4 (2000).

12. More Than 26 Percent of Major League Players Born Outside the U.S., Bus. Wire, Apr. 4, 2002; Gordon Edes, Japanese Players Making a Major Impact, Boston Globe, Apr. 8, 2001, at D11.

13. Fred Down, 38 Years Later, Yankee Training Camp of 1947 Is Remembered, L.A. Times, Feb. 24, 1985, §3, at 11.

14. John Drebinger, Yanks Bow in Exhibition at Caracas, 4-3, N.Y. Times, Mar. 2, 1947, §5, at 1; Down, supra note 13.

15. John Drebinger, Yankees Beat Dodgers Under Lights at Caracas, N.Y. Times, Mar. 11, 1947, at 33.

16. Down, supra note 13; Steve Fainaru & Ray Sanchez, The Duke of Havana 18 (2001).

17. John Drebinger, MacPhail Aims Blast at Dodgers for "Running Out" of Third Game, N.Y. Times, Mar. 11, 1947, at 33.

18. Richard Lally, Bombers: An Oral History of the New York Yankees 178 (2002).

19. Edna Rust & Art Rust Jr., Art Rust's Illustrated History of the Black Athlete 15 (1985); Samuel O. Regalado, Viva Baseball! Latin Major Leaguers and Their Special Hunger 33 (1998); Oleksak & Oleksak, supra note 7, at 23; Cesar Brioso, Baseball Paradise Revisited, Sun-Sentinel, Mar. 26, 1999, at 1C.

20. Kal Wagenheim, Babe Ruth: His Life and Legend 80 (1974).

21. Tom Shales, The Man Who Is an Island, Wash. Post, July 18, 1996, at C1.

22. George Rush & Joanna Molloy, Yanqui Clipper Autographs Ball for Reds' El Capitan, Daily News, Apr. 1, 1998, at 14.

23. John Krich, El Beisbol 221 (1989); Susan Orlean, Rough Diamonds, New Yorker, Aug. 5, 2002, at 34, 35.

24. Cuban Assets Control Regulations, 28 Fed. Reg. 6974 (July 9, 1963).

25. Orlean, supra note 23, at 35–37.

26. Murray Chass, Yanks Upset As Kuhn Vetoes Their Cuba Trip, N.Y. Times, Mar. 9, 1977, at A17.

27. Murray Chass, Yankees Like Idea of Cuban Trip, but a Few Prefer to Duck Castro, N.Y. Times, Mar. 8, 1977, at 39; Murray Chass, Behind the Kuhn-Cuba Tangle, N.Y. Times, Mar. 12, 1977, at 17.

28. State Dept. Not Opposed to Yanks Visiting Cuba, N.Y. Times, Mar. 5, 1977, at 14; State Dept. Doesn't Object, N.Y. Times, Mar. 8, 1977, at 39; Kim Willenson, Cuba: Another Fresh Start, Newsweek, Mar. 14, 1977, at 33; Chass, supra note 26.

29. Cuban Assets Control Regulations, 42 Fed. Reg. 16621 (Mar. 29, 1977).

30. Chass, supra note 26.

31. Cuban Assets Control Regulations: Travel-Related Transactions, 47 Fed. Reg. 17,030 (Apr. 20, 1982).

32. Regan v. Wald, 468 U.S. 222, 242 (1984).

33. James Barron, Public Lives, N.Y. Times, Nov. 24, 1999, at B2.

34. Yanquis Make Cuba Pitch, N.Y. Post, Feb. 12, 1999, at 9; Buster Olney, Steinbrenner Invited to Visit Cuba, N.Y. Times, Jan. 6, 1999, at D4.

35. Peter Botte, Boss: No Cuba Trip for Yanks, N.Y. Daily News, May 7, 1999; Niles Lathem et al., Yanks May Play Beisbol, N.Y. Post, May 6, 1999, at 3; Cuba Trip Deemed a Success, Miami Herald, Mar. 30, 1999, at 10D.

36. The Ultimate Baseball Book 244 (Daniel Okrent & Harris Lewine eds., 1984) (quoting Soviet Sport).

37. Glenn Liebman, Yankee Shorts 83 (1997).

38. Fainaru & Sanchez, supra note 16, at xxiii, 93, 99–100, 142, 148.

39. Robinson & Jennison, supra note 9, at 225; Fainaru & Sanchez, supra note 16, at 149–51, 155.

40. Fainaru & Sanchez, supra note 16, at 158–59, 163–64.

41. Refugee Act of 1980, Pub. L. No. 96-212, sec. 202, 94 Stat. 102, 107 (1980).

42. Protocol Relating to the Status of Refugees, Jan. 31, 1967, 19 U.S.T. 6223, 606 U.N.T.S. 267.

43. Cuban Refugee Adjustment Act, Pub. L. No. 89-732, 80 Stat. 1161 (1966); Cuba-United States: Joint Statement on Normalization of Migration, Building on the Agreement of September 9, 1994, 35 I.L.M. 327, 328 (1996) (joint statement of May 2, 1995) (emphasis added).

44. Fainaru & Sanchez, supra note 16, at 206–16.

45. Maria E. Sartori, The Cuban Migration Dilemma: An Examination of the United States' Policy of Temporary Protection in Offshore Safe Havens, 15 Geo. Immigr. L.J. 319, 348–50 (2001).

46. Cuban Baseball Player Asylum Case Garners Headlines (1998), at http://www.visalaw.com/98feb/16feb98.html.

47. Fainaru & Sanchez, supra note 16, at 218–21.

48. Major League Rules, Rule 4.

49. Jason S. Weiss, The Changing Face of Baseball: In an Age of Globalization, Is Baseball Still As American As Apple Pie and Chevrolet?, 8 Int'l & Comp. L. Rev. 123, 140 (2000).

50. Ross Newhan, Game Became the First Priority, L.A. Times, Aug. 31, 2002, pt. 4, at 4. The parties put off solidifying details about the format and timing of the draft. Id.

51. Fainaru & Sanchez, supra note 16, at 218–21, 230.

52. Buster Olney, Defector from Cuba Will Join the Yanks, N.Y. Times, Mar. 7, 1998, at C3.

53. Fainaru & Sanchez, supra note 16, at 234–36.

54. Major League Rules, Rule 3(b)(6); Major League Baseball Players Association Regulations Governing Player Agents § 3B(2)–(3), *cited in* Diane Sudia & Rob Remis, Ethical and Statutory Limitations on Athlete Agent Income: Fees, Referrals, and Ownership Interests, 27 Fla. St. U. L. Rev. 787, 807 n.124 (2000).

55. Stubbs v. Sec. Consumer Discount Co., 426 A.2d 1014 (1981); Restatement (Second) of Contracts § 164 (1981).

56. L. Jon Wertheim & Don Yaeger, Fantastic Voyage, Sports Illustrated, Nov. 30, 1998, at 60, 61–63.

57. Fainaru & Sanchez, supra note 16, at 226, 266.

58. Id. at 84; Steve Fainaru, The Cuba Connection, Boston Globe, May 28, 2000, at D14.

59. Hernandez Testifies, N.Y. Times, Nov. 3, 2000, at D6; Williams in Hospital Intensive-Care Unit, St. Petersburg Times, Nov. 4, 2000, at 1C.

60. H.R. 26, 107th Cong. (2001); H.R. 262, 106th Cong. (1999).

61. Bill to Allow Cubans to Play Without Defecting, Buffalo News, Nov. 2, 1998, at 20S.

62. Ira Berkow, Yanks' Universe Has Two El Duques, N.Y. Times, June 16, 2000, at D5; Thomas Hill, Like Duque? Just a Little, Daily News, June 18, 2000, at 58.

63. New York Yankees, Orlando Sentinel-Trib., Mar. 5, 1991, at D6; Walt Smith, U.P.I., Aug. 20, 1982.

64. In 1984, Perez spent three months in jail in the Dominican Republic after he was convicted of cocaine possession. Court Reduces Perez Charge, N.Y. Times, Apr. 6, 1984, at A26.

65. Don Burke, Yanks Feel Long Arm of the Law, Rec., Mar. 27, 1990, at D1.

66. David E. Pitt, Perez Finally Arrives, N.Y. Times, Mar. 28, 1990, at A24; Michael Martinez, New Piece Added to Puzzle on Perez, N.Y. Times, Mar. 25, 1990, §8, at 6; Jack O'Connell, Perez Finally Finds His Way to Camp, Sporting News, Apr. 9, 1990, at 41.

67. Jon Heyman, Late, but Here, Newsday, Mar. 5, 1991, at 127; Jon Heyman, Injuries May Prompt Change, Newsday, Mar. 25, 1991, at 103; Dave Anderson, Yankees Didn't Check Time Bomb, N.Y. Times, Mar. 8, 1992, §8, at 1.

68. Jon Heyman, Melido Springs Ahead, Newsday, Feb. 19, 1994, at 89; John Giannone, Melido the Mouth, Daily News, Feb. 17, 1996, at 40; Visa Problems Keep Players from Camps, Hamilton Spectator, Feb. 18, 1994, at D6; Jack Curry, Perez May Become Odd Man Out, N.Y. Times, Feb. 17, 1996, §1, at 33.

69. Polonia's Term Over, Rec., Feb. 18, 1990, at S2; Jon Heyman, A Rebuilding Year for Luis, Newsday, Mar. 25, 1990, at 13.

70. 8 C.F.R. § 214.2(o)(14), (p)(16).

71. Jack Curry, Yanks Open the Door, and 3 Players Come In, N.Y. Times, Apr. 4, 1995, at B13; Mark Maske, Relief Is All Too Comic, Wash. Post, Feb. 26, 1995, at D11; Rod Beaton, Visa Rules Could Sideline Top Foreign Prospects, USA Today, Jan. 12, 1995, at 3C.

72. David Lennon, Baselines, Newsday, Apr. 4, 1995, at A61; David Lennon, Baselines, Newsday, Apr. 9, 1995, at 10.

73. Steve Wulf, 20 Questions, Sports Illustrated, Apr. 4, 1988, at 68.

74. 8 U.S.C. §§ 1101(a)(15)(O)(i), (P)(i), 1184(c)(4)(A); 8 C.F.R. § 214.1(a)(2).

75. 8 U.S.C. § 1201(h); 8 C.F.R. § 214.2(o)(2)(i), (o)(6)(i), (p)(2)(i), (p)(8)(i); Austin T. Fragomen, Jr. & Steven C. Bell, Immigration Fundamentals §§ 5:1.2, 5:21.2 (4th ed. 2002).

76. Basic Agreement of December 7, 1996, art. XIV(A).

77. 8 C.F.R. §214.2(o)(8), (o)(10), (p)(10), (p)(12).

78. Ken Davidoff, Sojo Manages to Dream, Newsday, June 25, 2002, at A56.

79. Anthony McCarran, Sendoff Shocks a Saddened Sojo, Daily News, Mar. 30, 2002, at 49.

80. 8 U.S.C. §1182(a)(9)(B)(I).

81. Defector Sent Home, Sports Illustrated, June 19, 2000, at 34; Christopher Marquis, United States Sends Cuban Athlete Home, N.Y. Times, June 8, 2000, at A14.

82. Charlie Nobles, Yanks Agree to Terms with Defector, N.Y. Times, Feb. 14, 2001, at D2; Anthony McCarron, Morales Showing Staying Power, Daily News, Mar. 26, 2001, at 100.

83. Buster Olney, Team Says Morales Lied About Age, N.Y. Times, July 16, 2001, at D5; Jack O'-Connell, Teams Are Hypocrites on Age-Shaving Issue, Hartford Courant, Feb. 24, 2002, at E3; Murray Chass, Changing Birthdates: An Ancient Practice, N.Y. Times, Feb. 24, 2002, §8, at 6; Restatement (Second) of Contracts §164(1) (1981).

84. Restatement (Second) of Contracts §380(2) (1981); 1 Samuel Williston, Williston on Contracts §1.5 (Richard A. Lord ed., 4th ed. 1990).

85. Ian Thomsen & Luis Fernando Losa, One for the Ages, Sports Illustrated, Sept. 3, 2001, at 62; Robert D. McFadden, Star Is 14, So Bronx Team Is Disqualified, N.Y. Times, Sept. 1, 2001, at A1.

86. Ken Davidoff, Yankees Notebook, Newsday, Feb. 17, 2002, at C16.

87. Don Amore, The Aging Process, Hartford Courant, Feb. 22, 2002, at C3; Chass, supra note 83.

88. Major League Rules, Rule 3(a)(1)(B).

89. In re Score Board, Inc., 238 B.R. 585, 593–94 (D.N.J. 1999).

90. Phil Rogers, Sphere of Influence Spreads, Chi. Trib., Mar. 30, 1998, §N, at 7.

91. Marcano & Fidler, supra note 6, at 544; Alan M. Klein, Sugarball: The American Game, the Dominican Dream 53 (1991).

92. Gordon Edes, In Signing Williams, Ex-Yank Scout 1 for 2, Sun-Sentinel, Oct. 15, 1996, at 1C; Bob Elliott, The Last Word, Toronto Sun, Oct. 7, 1999, at 110.

93. 504 U.S. 655, 663–69 (1992).

94. Klein, supra note 91, at 53–54.

95. Wagenheim, supra note 20, at 225; Notes and Quotes, at http://ultimateyankees.com/NotesandQuotes.html.

96. Robert Whiting, You Gotta Have Wa 40, 42 (1989) [hereinafter Whiting, Wa]; Robert Whiting, The Chrysanthemum and the Bat 222 (1977) [hereinafter Whiting, Chrysanthemum]; Wagenheim, supra note 20, at 225.

97. Wagenheim, supra note 20, at 226; Prince Tokugawa at Luncheon Pays Warm Tribute to Ruth and Mack, N.Y. Times, Nov. 16, 1934, at 29.

98. Connie Mack Says Ruth Played Better Ball on Tour Than He Did in Past Two Seasons, N.Y. Times, Jan. 27, 1935, at 27.

99. Geoffrey C. Ward & Ken Burns, Baseball: An Illustrated History 217 (1994); Whiting, Wa, supra note 96, at 43; Whiting, Chrysanthemum, supra note 96, at 222; Ron Fimrite, Land of the Rising Fastball, Sports Illustrated, Sept. 9 1985, at 62.

100. James P. Dawson, Return from World Tour Finds Babe Ruth Hopeful of Remaining in Baseball, N.Y. Times, Feb. 21, 1935, at 25.

101. Whiting, Wa, supra note 96, at 43; Nicholas Dawidoff, The Catcher Was a Spy (1994).

102. Wagenheim, supra note 20, at 226.

103. Tokyo Gives Ruth Royal Welcome, N.Y. Times, Nov. 3, 1934, at 9; Mack Hails Ruth As Peace Promoter, N.Y. Times, Jan. 6, 1935, §3, at 7.

104. Ward & Burns, supra note 99, at 276.

105. Franz Lidz, Yankees Go Home, Sports Illustrated, May 27, 1985, at 15; Lawrence S. Ritter & Mark Rucker, The Babe: The Game That Ruth Built 238 (1997); Robinson & Jennison, supra note 9, at 82.

106. Babe Ruth, The Babe Ruth Story 202 (1948).

107. Whiting, Wa, supra note 96, at 46; Simon Kuper, Ballgames That Can Help Bridge That Gap, Financial Times, July 6, 2002, at 24.

108. Ritter & Rucker, supra note 105, at 238–39; Whiting, Wa, supra note 96, at 332; Whiting, Chrysanthemum, supra note 96, at 223.

109. Whiting, Wa, supra note 96, at 195.

110. Whiting, Chrysanthemum, supra note 96, at 150–51.

111. Clyde Haberman, Americans Ruffle Japan's Pastime, N.Y. Times, Aug. 6, 1984, at C4.

112. Joe Pepitone, The Joe Pepitone Prayer: Don't Let Me Die in Japan, N.Y. Times, May 19, 1974, § 5, at 2.

113. Marty Kuehnert, The Pepitone Problem in Japan: Maybe the Problem Is Pepitone, N.Y. Times, Aug. 25, 1974, § 5, at 2.

114. Whiting, Chrysanthemum, supra note 96, at 173–75.

115. Pepitone, supra note 112.

116. Whiting, Chrysanthemum, supra note 96, at 173–75.

117. Am. Broad. Cos. v. Wolf, 420 N.E.2d 363, 366 (N.Y. 1981).

118. Hiroshi Oda, Japanese Law 197 (1992); Comment, Japanese Labor Relations and Legal Implications of Their Possible Use in the United States, 5 Nw. J. Int'l L. & Bus. 585, 593 (1983); John O. Haley, Sheathing the Sword of Justice in Japan: An Essay on Law Without Sanctions, 8 J. Japanese Stud. 266 (1982), in Meryll Dean, Japanese Legal System 38, 38 (1997); Minpo [Civil Code], art. 628.

119. Whiting, Chrysanthemum, supra note 96, at 173–75, 179; Todd & Erika Geers, Making Out in Japanese 64 (1988); Fruitz, at http://www.time-catcher.com/~fruitz/fbv1e4.txt (visited Aug. 10, 2002).

120. Whiting, Chrysanthemum, supra note 96, at 154, 178–80; Whiting, Wa, supra note 96, at 94, 175–76.

121. Brian Maitland, Japanese Baseball 81–82 (1991).

122. John O. Haley, The Myth of the Reluctant Litigant, 4 J. Japanese Stud. 359, 379, 389 (1978).

123. Jeff Pearlman, He's Arrived, Sports Illustrated, Aug. 26, 2002, at 40; Bob Nightengale, Oh, to Be Young and a Yankee, USA Today Baseball Weekly, May 15–21, 2002, at 8; Anthony McCarran, Star Wars: Alfonso Soriano Is Second to None, but It Took a Fight Against an Entire Country, Daily News, July 7, 2002, at 86; Carp File Suit Against Don Nomura, Daily Yomiuri, June 9, 1998, at 2.

124. In Our Pages, 50, 75 and 100 Years Ago, Int'l Herald Trib., Sept. 10, 2001, at 8.

125. Japanese Ace Says He Won't Play for Padres, Austin American-Statesman, Mar. 1, 1997, at E9.

126. Murray Chass, Padres Strike Deal with Team in Japan, N.Y. Times, Jan. 16, 1997, at B13.

127. Irabu Grateful to Join Yankees, Wants to Forget Lotte, Japan Economic Newswire, May 31, 1997.

128. United States-Japanese Player Contract Agreement between William D. Eckert, U.S. Commissioner of Baseball, and Tosiyosi Hiyasawa, Chairman, High Commission of Japan Professional Baseball, Oct. 17, 1967, ¶ 5 (on file with author).

129. Cent. Sports Army Club v. Arena Assocs., Inc., 952 F. Supp. 181 (S.D.N.Y. 1997).

130. Japanese Pitcher Must Play for Pads, Dayton Daily News, Feb. 28, 1997.

131. Irabu Claims Lotte-San Diego Deal Was "Slave Trade," Japan Economic Newswire, Mar. 20, 1997.

132. Scott Kaufman, Orient Express, Orlando Sentinel, Mar. 23, 1997, at C13.

133. Johnette Howard, Scorecard, Sports Illustrated, Mar. 17, 1997, at 15.

134. Executive Order 9066, 7 Fed. Reg. 1407 (Feb. 25, 1942); Act of Mar. 21, 1942, ch. 191, 56 Stat. 173 (1942).

135. Greg Robinson, By Order of the President: FDR and the Internment of Japanese Americans 3–4, 148 (2001).

136. Ward & Burns, supra note 99, at 276.

137. Act of Aug. 10, 1988, Pub. L. No. 100-383, sec. 2, 102 Stat. 903, 903-04.

138. Murray Chass, A Dear Is Near with Irabu, but Tampering Is Charged, N.Y. Times, May 23, 1997, at B9; Irabu Probe Slated, Chi. Tribune, May 24, 1997, at 6.

139. Tom Haudricourt, Baseball Closer to Conduct Code, Milwaukee J. Sentinel, Apr. 10, 1997, at 4.

140. William B. Gould IV, Baseball and Globalization: The Game Played and Heard and Watched 'Round the World (With Apologies to Soccer and Bobby Thomson), 8 Ind. J. Global Legal Stud. 85, 113–15, 119–20 (2000).

141. Anthony Bianco, A Grand-Slam Season, Bus. Wk., Nov. 2, 1998, at 104, 106.

142. Tyler Kepner, Matsui Agrees to 3-Year Contract with Yankees, N.Y. Times, Dec. 20, 2002, at C15.

143. Mark Twain, A Connecticut Yankee in King Arthur's Court 518–20 (1889).

144. George Vecsey, If You Collect It, They Will Come, N.Y. Times, Mar. 15, 2002, at 31, 39; Appearance Astounds Critics, N.Y. Times, Oct. 24, 1924, at 23.

145. Wagenheim, supra note 20, at 97.

146. Ruth, supra note 106, at 204.

147. Id. at 203; Ruth Tired of Paris, Wants to Come Home, N.Y. Times, Jan. 19, 1935, at 16.

148. Warren Hoge, The Spice Girl and the Soccer Idol: What a Team!, N.Y. Times, Dec. 18, 2001, at A4.

149. Herman Miller, Yankees: Why All the Fuss?, Observer, Feb. 11, 2001, at 7; Richard Sandomir, YankeeNets Makes a Deal with Manchester United, N.Y. Times, Feb. 8, 2001, at D2.

150. Sport Wakes Up to the Value of Brands, Sports Marketing, Oct. 23, 2001, at 13; Frank Dell'appa, Man United Plays Ball with the Yankees, Boston Globe, Feb. 13, 2001, at F2.

151. Jon Rees & Matthew Goodman, British Soccer Club Tries to Score in America, Sunday Bus., Feb. 11, 2001.

152. Cynthia Rigg, Baseball, Finally, Hits Licensing Home Run, Crain's N.Y. Bus., Apr. 1, 1991, at 3.

153. Nick Szczepanik, United's Union with Yankees Is Not Quite the Perfect Marriage, The Times, Feb. 8, 2001.

154. Adidas Sponsorship Could Open Expensive Can of Worms, Sun-Sentinel, Mar. 4, 1997, at 5C; Yankees, Adidas File Antitrust Suit Against Major League Baseball, Intell. Prop. Litig. Rep., May 21, 1997, at 11; Murray Chass, Steinbrenner Banned as Executive Council Member, N.Y. Times, May 14, 1997, at B11; James D. Weinberger, Baseball Trademark Licensing and the Antitrust Exemption: An Analysis of New York Yankees Partnership v. Major League Baseball Enterprises, Inc., 23 Colum.-VLA J.L. & Arts 75, 92–96 (1999).

155. Ken Davidoff, Rec., May 1, 1998.

156. Dell'appa, supra note 150; Miller, supra note 149.

157. Chris Ayres & Oliver Kay, Fans United in Opposition to Yankees Deal, The Times, Feb. 8, 2001; Jason Kerrigan & James Fletcher, Start Spreading the News, Mirror, Feb. 8, 2001, at 62.

158. Wagenheim, supra note 20, at 137.

159. Ottawa Goes to Bat for Baseball Gambling, Bus. Wk., May 21, 1984, at 41; David Purcell, Canadian Plan to Allow Betting on U.S. Sports Opposed in Both Nations, Christian Sci. Monitor, Apr. 13, 1984, at 4; Wesley Goldstein, U.P.I., Apr. 27, 1984.

160. Wagenheim, supra note 20, at 137.

161. Cunard Steamship Co. v. Mellon, 262 U.S. 100, 123 (1923).

162. U.P.I. Int'l, Nov. 13, 1987.

163. Steven M. Wise, Rattling the Cage: Toward Legal Rights for Animals 56–57 (2000); Christopher D. Stone, Should Trees Have Standing?—Toward Legal Rights for Natural Objects, 45 S. Cal. L. Rev. 450, 464–73 (1972).

164. Klein, supra note 1, at 66–70, 78, 82; Players Who Jumped Contracts Ruled Automatically Suspended, N.Y. Times, Apr. 17, 1946, at 35.

165. Mexican Is Ready to Bet $2,000,000, N.Y. Times, Apr. 4, 1946.

166. Mexican Embassy Heard, N.Y. Times, Apr. 7, 1946, §5, at 3.

167. U.S. Urges an End to Baseball Fight, N.Y. Times, Apr. 12, 1946, at 19.

168. Court Restrains Mexicans in Raid on Yankee Players, N.Y. Times, May 5, 1946, §5, at 1.

169. Klein, supra note 1, at 92.

170. Court Restrains Mexicans in Raid on Yankee Players, N.Y. Times, May 5, 1946, §5, at 1; Hearing on Yankees' Application to Restrain Pasquels Postponed, N.Y. Times, May 8, 1946, at 30.

171. Am. League Baseball Club v. Pasquel, 63 N.Y.S.2d 537, 538 (Sup. Ct. 1946).

172. Rizzuto Offer Disclosed, N.Y. Times, June 9, 1946, §3, at 2.

173. Organized Baseball a Monopoly, Mexicans Charge in Court Action, N.Y. Times, May 17, 1946.

174. Am. League Baseball Club v. Chase, 149 N.Y.S. 6 (Sup. Ct. 1914).

175. Milton Bracker, Babe Ruth Hailed by 15,000 Mexicans, N.Y. Times, May 17, 1946, at 16; Ruth Off to Mexico as Pasquel Guest, N.Y. Times, May 16, 1946, at 25; Milton Bracker, Ruth's Visit Stirs Interest of Fans, N.Y. Times, May 16, 1946, at 25.

176. Am. League Baseball Club, 63 N.Y.S.2d at 538–39; Curb on Mexicans Granted to Yanks, N.Y. Times, May 21, 1946, at 26.

177. Ruth Hits Court Decision, N.Y. Times, May 22, 1946, at 27.

178. Klein, supra note 1, at 99–100.

179. Mexico's No. 1 Ball Fan Regrets He Can't See Game, N.Y. Times, May 4, 1947, at 44.

180. Ruth Off to Mexico as Pasquel Guest, N.Y. Times, May 16, 1946, at 25; New Mexican Baseball Chief Orders End of Players Raid, N.Y. Times, Oct. 29, 1947, at 38.

181. Baseball, 1992 Olympic Rev. 498; Bob Rybarczyk, Baseball: A User's Guide, 1992 Olympic Rev. 374; Stephen Wilson, Olympic Games: Baseball Faces Fight for Survival, Indep., Aug. 30, 2002, at 24.

182. New York Yankees Team Notes, Sports Network, Aug. 9, 1996.

183. Fainaru & Sanchez, supra note 16, at 35, 38–39.

184. International Olympic Committee, Olympic Charter, rule 45 bye-law.

185. Roger Vaughan, Aussie Coach Welcomes US Pro Baseballers to Games, AAP Newsfeed, Jan. 28, 1999; Murray Chass, Summer Olympics Fever: Catch It!, N.Y. Times, Feb. 15, 1998, §8, at 3; Nikki Tugwell, Star Pair on Games Trail, The Advertiser, Feb. 21, 2000, at 55; La Velle E. Neal III, Steinbach Not Exactly Through Yet, Star Trib., Feb. 7, 2000, at 3C.

186. Bernie Pramberg, Yankee Doodle Dandy, Daily Telegraph, Sept. 8, 2000, at 128.

187. David Heuschkel & Don Amore, With 4 Starts at Most, It May Not Add Up, Hartford Courant, Sept. 10, 2000, at E9; In Brief, The Australian, Sept. 8, 2000, at 19.

188. Buster Olney, Yankees Try a New Line on Royals: 000 000 007, N.Y. Times, Sept. 8, 2000, at D4; George King, Yanks Say Ramiro on Course, N.Y. Post, Nov. 30, 2000, at 65.

189. Amateur Sports Act of 1978, Pub. L. No. 95-606, 92 Stat. 3045; Act of Aug. 12, 1998, Pub. L. No. 105-225, 112 Stat. 1253, 1465–78.

190. Sports Shorts, St. Louis Post-Dispatch, Feb. 19, 1989, at 9E.

191. US Continues Olympic "Dream Team" Fight, Agence France Presse, June 12, 1994.

192. Bob Hunter, Rumblings, Columbus Dispatch, Sept. 1, 2000, at 1D; George King & Joel Sherman, No Sydney for Yanks' Tessmer, N.Y. Post, Sept. 9, 2000, at 48; Michael Kinsley, International Strikeout?, Sporting News, Aug. 2, 1999, at 27.

193. International Olympic Committee, Olympic Charter, Fundamental Principles, no. 6, rule 3.2.

194. Bill Madden, Acceptance Was a Long Time Coming, Daily News, May 23, 1999, at 99.

195. Lally, supra note 18, at 98.

196. Matt Bai, Yankee Imperialism, New York, July 25, 1994, at 30.

197. Michael O'Keefe, Yankees, Mets Slow to Reach Out to Latin Community, Daily News, June 4, 1999.

198. Chadwin, supra note 4, at 165; Douglas Montero, City's Latinos Find Lots to Cheer About, N.Y. Post, Oct. 30, 1999, at 20.

199. Celebrities in Spoof to Promote Tourism, N.Y. Times, Nov. 9, 2001, at D2.

200. Liebman, supra note 37, at 117.

Index